HANDBOOK OF CLINICAL BEHAVIOR THERAPY

Recent titles in the
Wiley Series on Personality Processes
Irving B. Weiner, *Editor*
University of South Florida

Handbook of Clinical Behavior Therapy (Second Edition) *edited by Samuel M. Turner, Karen S. Calhoun, and Henry E. Adams*

Psychological Disturbance in Adolescence (Second Edition) *by Irving B. Weiner*

Prevention of Child Maltreatment: Development and Ecological Perspectives *edited by Diane J. Willis, E. Wayne Holden, and Mindy Rosenberg*

Interventions for Children of Divorce: Custody, Access, and Psychotherapy *by William F. Hodges*

The Play Therapy Primer: An Integration of Theories and Techniques *by Kevin John O'Connor*

Adult Psychopatholody and Diagnosis (Second Edition) *edited by Michel Hersen and Samuel L. Turner*

The Rorschach: A Comprehensive System. Volume II: Interpretation (Second Edition) *by John E. Exner, Jr.*

Play Diagnosis and Assessment *edited by Charles E. Schaefer, Karen Gitlin, and Alice Sandgrund*

Acquaintance Rape: The Hidden Crime *edited by Andrea Parrot and Laurie Bechhofer*

The Psychological Examination of the Child *by Theodore H. Blau*

Depressive Disorders: Facts, Theories, and Treatment Methods *by Benjamin B. Wolman, Editor, and George Stricker, Co-Editor*

Social Support: An Interactional View *edited by Barbara R. Sarason, Irwin G. Sarason, and Gregory R. Pierce*

Toward a New Personology: An Evolutionary Model *by Theodore Millon*

Treatment of Family Violence: A Sourcebook *edited by Robert T. Ammerman and Michel Hersen*

Handbook of Comparative Treatments for Adult Disorders *edited by Alan S. Bellack and Michel Hersen*

Managing Attention Disorders in Children: A Guide for Practitioners *by Sam Goldstein and Michael Goldstein*

Understanding and Treating Depressed Adolescents and Their Families *by Gerald D. Oster and Janice E. Caro*

The Psychosocial Worlds of the Adolescent: Public and Private *by Vivian Center Seltzer*

Handbook of Parent Training: Parents as Co-Therapists for Children's Behavior Problems *edited by Charles E. Schaefer and James M. Briesmeister*

From Ritual to Repertoire: A Cognitive-Developmental Approach with Behavior-Disordered Children *by Arnold Miller and Eileen Eller-Miller*

The Practice of Hypnotism. Volume 2: Applications of Traditional and Semi-Traditional Hypnotism: Non-Traditional Hypnotism *by Andre M. Weitzenhoffer*

The Practice of Hypnotism. Volume 1: Traditional and Semi-Traditional Techniques and Phenomenology *by Andre M. Weitzenhoffer*

Children's Social Networks and Social Supports *edited by Deborah Belle*

Advances in Art Therapy *edited by Harriet Wadeson, Jean Durkin, and Dorine Perach*

Psychosocial Aspects of Disaster *edited by Richard M. Gist and Bernard Lubin*

Handbook of Child Psychiatric Diagnosis *edited by Cynthia G. Last and Michel Hersen*

Grief: The Mourning After—Dealing with Adult Bereavement *by Catherine M. Sanders*

Problem-Solving Therapy for Depression: Theory, Research, and Clinical Guidelines *by Arthur M. Nezu, Christine M. Nezu, and Michael G. Perri*

Peer Relationships in Child Development *edited by Thomas J. Berndt and Gary W. Ladd*

The Psychology of Underachievement: Differential Diagnosis and Differential Treatment *by Harvey P. Mandel and Sander I. Marcus*

Treating Adult Children of Alcoholics: A Developmental Perspective *by Stephanie Brown*

Innovative Interventions in Child and Adolescent Therapy *edited by Charles E. Schaefer*

Delusional Beliefs: Interdisciplinary Perspectives *edited by Thomas F. Oltmanns and Brendan A. Maher*

Clinical Relaxation Strategies *by Kenneth L. Lichstein*

Fatherhood Today: Men's Changing Role in the Family *edited by Phyllis Bronstein and Carolyn Pape Cowan*

Handbook of Forensic Psychology *edited by Irving B. Weiner and Alan K. Hess*

Handbook of Infant Development (Second Edition) *edited by Joy D. Osofsky*

Handbook of Juvenile Delinquency *edited by Herbert C. Quay*

HANDBOOK OF CLINICAL BEHAVIOR THERAPY

Second Edition

Edited by

SAMUEL M. TURNER
KAREN S. CALHOUN
HENRY E. ADAMS

John Wiley & Sons, Inc.
New York • Chichester • Brisbane • Toronto • Singapore

In recognition of the importance of preserving what has been
written, it is a policy of John Wiley & Sons, Inc., to have
books of enduring value published in the United States
printed on acid-free paper, and we exert our best efforts
to that end.

Copyright © 1992 by John Wiley & Sons, Inc.

All rights reserved. Published simultaneously in Canada.

Reproduction or translation of any part of this work
beyond that permitted by section 107 or 108 of the
1976 United States Copyright Act without the permission
of the copyright owner is unlawful. Requests for
permission or further information should be addressed to
the Permission Department, John Wiley & Sons, Inc.

This publication is designed to provide accurate and
authoritative information in regard to the subject
matter covered. It is sold with the understanding that
the publisher is not engaged in rendering legal, accounting,
or other professional services. If legal advice or other
expert assistance is required, the services of a competent
professional person should be sought. *From a Declaration
of Principles jointly adopted by a Committee of the
American Bar Association and a Committee of Publishers.*

Library of Congress Cataloging-in-Publication Data:
Handbook of clinical behavior therapy / edited by Samuel M. Turner,
  Karen S. Calhoun, Henry E. Adams. — 2nd ed.
    p.   cm. — (Wiley series on personality processes)
  Includes index.
  ISBN 0-471-63563-4 (cloth : alk. paper)
  1. Behavior therapy. 2. Psychology, Pathological. I. Turner,
Samuel M., 1944–   . II. Calhoun, Karen S. III. Adams, Henry E.,
1931–   . IV. Series.
  [DNLM: 1. Behavior Therapy—handbooks. WM 34 J2355]
RC489.B4H37 1992
616.89′142—dc20
DNLM/DLC
for Library of Congress   91-44490

Printed in the United States of America

10 9 8 7 6 5 4 3

Contributors

Henry E. Adams, Ph.D.
Research Professor of Psychology
Department of Psychology
University of Georgia
Athens, GA

Frank Andrasik, Ph.D.
Professor of Psychology
Department of Psychology
University of West Florida
Pensacola, FL

Ileana Arias, Ph.D.
Assistant Professor of Psychology
Department of Psychology
University of Georgia
Athens, GA

David H. Barlow, Ph.D.
Professor of Psychology
Department of Psychology
Phobia and Anxiety Disorders Clinic
State University of New York
   at Albany
Albany, NY

J. Gayle Beck, Ph.D.
Associate Professor of Psychology
Department of Psychology
University of Houston
Houston, TX

Deborah C. Beidel, Ph.D.
Assistant Professor of Psychiatry
Department of Psychiatry
Western Psychiatric Institute and Clinic
University of Pittsburgh
School of Medicine
Pittsburgh, PA

Alan S. Bellack, Ph.D.
Professor of Psychiatry
Department of Psychiatry
The Medical College of Pennsylvania at
   EPPI
Philadelphia, PA

Janet W. Borden, Ph.D.
Assistant Professor of Psychology
Department of Psychology
University of Louisville
Louisville, KY

Marjorie H. Charlop, Ph.D.
Associate Professor of Psychology
Department of Psychology
Claremont McKenna College
Claremont, CA

W. Edward Craighead, Ph.D.
Professor of Medical Psychology
Department of Psychiatry
Duke University Medical Center
Durham, NC

Michelle G. Craske, Ph.D.
Assistant Professor of Psychology
Department of Psychology
University of California, Los Angeles
Los Angeles, CA

Barbara A. Cubic, M.A.
Department of Psychology
Louisiana State University
Baton Rouge, LA

Elizabeth Cuddy, Ph.D.
Post-Doctoral Fellow
Mayo Clinic
Rochester, MN

Karen K. Downey, M.A.
Doctoral Candidate
Department of Psychology
Wayne State University
Detroit, MI

Jean E. Dumas, Ph.D.
Associate Professor of Psychology
Department of Psychological Sciences
Purdue University
West Lafayette, IN

Donald D. Evans, Ph.D.
Associate Professor of Medical Psychology
Department of Psychiatry
Duke University Medical Center
Durham, NC

Cynthia L. Frame, Ph.D.
Associate Professor of Psychology
Department of Psychology
University of Georgia
Athens, GA

Greta Francis, Ph.D.
Assistant Professor of Psychiatry
Brown University Medical School
Bradley Hospital
East Providence, RI

Richard D. Fuller, M.A.
Department of Psychology
Louisiana State University
Baton Rouge, LA

Robert J. Gerardi, Ph.D.
Clinical Research Psychology
Albany Veterans Administration Medical Center
Albany, NY

Martha Hamilton
Doctoral Student
Department of Psychology
Louisiana State University
Baton Rouge, LA

Stephen P. Hinshaw, Ph.D.
Associate Professor of Psychology
Department of Psychology
University of California, Berkeley
Berkeley, CA

Terence M. Keane, Ph.D.
Chief of Psychology
Boston Veterans Administration Medical Center
Boston, MA

Patricia F. Kurtz, Ph.D.
Post-Doctoral Fellow
Department of Psychology
Claremont Graduate School
Claremont, CA

Brett T. Litz, Ph.D.
Psychology Service
Boston Veterans Administration Medical Center
Boston, MA

John R. Lutzker, Ph.D.
Ross Professor and Chairman
Department of Psychology
University of Judaism
Los Angeles, CA

Johnny L. Matson, Ph.D.
Professor of Psychology
Department of Psychology
Louisiana State University
Baton Rouge, LA

Richard D. McAnulty, Ph.D.
Assistant Professor of Psychology
Department of Psychology
University of North Carolina at Charlotte
Charlotte, NC

Randall L. Morrison, Ph.D.
Department of Mental Health
American Medical Association
Chicago, IL

Kim T. Mueser, Ph.D.
Associate Professor of Psychiatry
Department of Psychiatry
The Medical College of Pennsylvania at EPPI
Philadelphia, PA

Oliver Oyama, Ph.D.
Clinical Associate
Duke University Medical Center
Fayetteville Area Health Education
Fayetteville, NC

William E. Pelham, Ph.D.
Associate Professor of Child Psychiatry
Department of Psychiatry
Western Psychiatric Institute and Clinic
University of Pittsburgh
School of Medicine
Pittsburgh, PA

Stephen J. Quinn, Ph.D.
Psychology Service
Boston Veterans Administration Medical Center
Boston, MA

Ronald M. Rapee, Ph.D.
Senior Lecturer in Psychology
Department of Psychology
The University of Queensland
St. Lucia, Queensland
Australia

Clive J. Robins, Ph.D.
Assistant Professor of Medical Psychology
Department of Psychiatry
Duke University Medical Center
Durham, NC

Shirley L. Robinson, Ph.D.
Post-Doctoral Fellow
Department of Pediatric and Adolescent Medical Services
University of Oklahoma
Health Sciences Center
Children Hospital of Oklahoma
Oklahoma City, OK

Thomas E. Rudy, Ph.D.
Assistant Professor of Anesthesiology and Psychiatry
Associate Director, Pain Evaluation and Treatment Institute
Center for Preventive Medicine and Rehabilitation
University of Pittsburgh
School of Medicine
Pittsburgh, PA

Laura Schreibman, Ph.D.
Professor of Psychology
Department of Psychology
University of California, San Diego
La Jolla, CA

Bruce A. Sorkin, Ph.D.
Staff Psychologist
Pain Evaluation and Treatment Institute
Center for Preventive Medicine and Rehabilitation
University of Pittsburgh School of Medicine
Pittsburgh, PA

Melinda A. Stanley, Ph.D.
Assistant Professor of Psychiatry
Department of Psychiatry and Behavioral Sciences
The University of Texas
Health Science Center at Houston
Houston, TX

Ruth M. Townsley, M.S.
Research Associate
Department of Psychiatry
Western Psychiatric Institute and Clinic
University of Pittsburgh
School of Medicine
Pittsburgh, PA

Jalie A. Tucker, Ph.D.
Professor of Psychology
Department of Psychology
Co-Director, Clinical Training Program
Auburn University
Auburn, AL

Dennis C. Turk, Ph.D.
Professor of Psychiatry and Anesthesiology
Director, Pain Evaluation and Treatment Institute
Center for Preventive Medicine and Rehabilitation
University of Pittsburgh
School of Medicine
Pittsburgh, PA

Ira D. Turkat, Ph.D.
Chief Psychologist/Venice Hospital
Clinical Associate Professor
Department of Psychiatry
University of Florida College of Medicine
Venice, FL

Samuel M. Turner, Ph.D.
Professor of Psychiatry
Department of Psychiatry
Western Psychiatric Institute and Clinic
University of Pittsburgh
School of Medicine
Pittsburgh, PA

Vincent B. Van Hasselt, Ph.D.
Associate Professor of Psychiatry
Director, Adolescent Drug and Alcohol Program
Department of Psychiatry
Western Psychiatric Institute and Clinic
University of Pittsburgh
School of Medicine
Pittsburgh, PA

Rudy E. Vuchinich, Ph.D.
Professor of Psychology
Department of Psychology
Co-Director, Clinical Training Program
Auburn University
Auburn, AL

Donald A. Williamson, Ph.D.
Professor and Director of Psychological Services Center
Department of Psychology
Louisiana State University
Baton Rouge, LA

Series Preface

This series of books is addressed to behavioral scientists interested in the nature of human personality. Its scope should prove pertinent to personality theorists and researchers as well as to clinicians concerned with applying an understanding of personality processes to the amelioration of emotional difficulties in living. To this end, the series provides a scholarly integration of theoretical formulations, empirical data, and practical recommendations.

Six major aspects of studying and learning about human personality can be designated: personality theory, personality structure and dynamics, personality development, personality assessment, personality change, and personality adjustment. In exploring these aspects of personality, the books in the series discuss a number of distinct but related subject areas: the nature and implications of various theories of personality; personality characteristics that account for consistencies and variations in human behavior; the emergence of personality processes in children and adolescents; the use of interviewing and testing procedures to evaluate individual differences in personality; efforts to modify personality styles through psychotherapy, counseling, behavior therapy, and other methods of influence; and patterns of abnormal personality functioning that impair individual competence.

IRVING B. WEINER

University of South Florida
Tampa, Florida

Preface

Since the first edition of *Handbook of Clinical Behavior Therapy* appeared in 1981, behavioral theories and treatment strategies have continued to be refined. In addition, the applicability of behavioral treatments to a broader range of clinical problems has been demonstrated and new treatments as well as innovations of more traditional methods for various disorders have been introduced. Thus, it seemed that this was an appropriate time to reexamine the clinical application of behavioral principles.

As with the first edition of this volume, it was our intention to construct a clinically useful text; one that illustrates the use of behavioral strategies with clinical problems, as well as one that provides empirical evidence of their efficacy through a review of the latest treatment outcome studies. Because an intimate knowledge of a given condition's psychopathology is essential for the successful implementation of behavioral treatments, chapters are dedicated to specific clinical syndromes and begin with a succinct overview of the clinical state. Critical theoretical points are highlighted within the context of the discussion and case vignettes frequently are provided to further illustrate important points. It is our hope that clinicians, educators, and students alike will find this volume helpful.

Since the first edition of this text was published, there have been many changes with respect to populations for which behavioral treatments have proven effective as well as in the development of new procedures. Each of the chapters was completely rewritten. Also, this edition contains two less chapters than the first because some of the original contributions were not retained. However, there are a number of chapters that were not in the first edition. This volume does not cover exhaustively all of the areas of clinical applicability of behavioral interventions but it does survey most of the major areas. Part One (Adult Disorders) covers the major adult syndromes; Part Two (Childhood Disorders) addresses the major areas of child applicability); Part Three (Behavioral Medicine) is concerned with behavioral treatment and prevention of medical disorders; and Part Four (Special Populations) is concerned with family and marital intervention.

Many thanks are expressed to our contributors who endeavored to construct their chapters in accord with our criteria. Also the support and advice of Herb Reich, our editor at John Wiley & Sons, is gratefully acknowledged. Finally, we appreciate the secretarial and technical assistance provided by Sandra Gray, Joyce Martin, Amy Lederer, and Gregorio Febraro.

SAMUEL M. TURNER

Pittsburgh, Pennsylvania
October 1991

Contents

PART ONE	**ADULT DISORDERS**	1
1.	Behavioral Treatment of Simple Phobia *Janet W. Borden*	3
2.	Behavioral Treatment of Social Phobia *Samuel M. Turner, Deborah C. Beidel, and Ruth M. Townsley*	13
3.	Cognitive-Behavioral Treatment of Panic Disorder, Agoraphobia and Generalized Anxiety Disorder *Michelle G. Craske, Ronald M. Rapee, and David H. Barlow*	39
4.	Obsessive-Compulsive Disorder *Melinda A. Stanley*	67
5.	Behavioral Treatment of Post-Traumatic Stress Disorder *Terence M. Keane, Robert J. Gerardi, Stephen J. Quinn, and Brett T. Litz*	87
6.	Unipolar Depression *W. Edward Craighead, Donald D. Evans, and Clive J. Robins*	99
7.	Behavioral Intervention with Personality Disorders *Ira D. Turkat*	117
8.	Behavioral Interventions in Schizophrenia *Alan S. Bellack, Randall L. Morrison, and Kim T. Mueser*	135
9.	Behavioral Approaches to Sexual Dysfunction *J. Gayle Beck*	155
10	Behavior Therapy with Paraphilic Disorders *Richard D. McAnulty and Henry E. Adams*	175
11.	Substance Abuse *Jalie A. Tucker, Rudy E. Vuchinich, and Karen K. Downey*	203

PART TWO CHILDHOOD DISORDERS — 225

12. Behavioral Treatment of Childhood Anxiety Disorders — 227
    Greta Francis
13. Behavioral Treatment of Childhood Depression — 245
    Cynthia L. Frame, Shirley L. Robinson, and Elizabeth Cuddy
14. Behavioral Intervention for Attention Deficit-Hyperactivity Disorder — 259
    William E. Pelham and Stephen P. Hinshaw
15. Conduct Disorder — 285
    Jean E. Dumas
16. Mental Retardation — 317
    Martha Hamilton and Johnny L. Matson
17. Behavioral Treatment for Children with Autism — 337
    Laura Schreibman, Marjorie H. Charlop, and Patricia F. Kurtz

PART THREE BEHAVIORAL MEDICINE — 353

18. Eating Disorders — 355
    Donald A. Williamson, Barbara A. Cubic, and Richard D. Fuller
19. Chronic Pain: Behavioral Conceptualizations and Interventions — 373
    Dennis C. Turk, Thomas E. Rudy, and Bruce A. Sorkin
20. Behavioral Strategies in the Prevention of Disease — 397
    Oliver Oyama and Frank Andrasik

PART FOUR SPECIAL POPULATIONS — 415

21. Family Violence — 417
    John R. Lutzker and Vincent B. Van Hasselt
22. Behavioral Marital Therapy — 437
    Ileana Arias

AUTHOR INDEX — 457

SUBJECT INDEX — 475

PART ONE
Adult Disorders

CHAPTER 1

Behavioral Treatment of Simple Phobia

JANET W. BORDEN

Simple phobias are defined by a persistent fear of a situation or object, a compelling desire to avoid the situation or object, significant distress, and recognition by the individual that the fear is excessive. This chapter reviews the clinical syndrome of simple phobia, including formal diagnostic criteria and prevalence. This review is followed by an examination of issues related to the assessment of simple phobias. Next, the methods and outcome results of behavioral treatment approaches are discussed. Finally, future directions for investigation in the etiology and treatment of simple phobias are suggested.

CLINICAL SYNDROME

Barlow (1988) refers to simple phobia as "the most familiar and the most enigmatic of the anxiety disorders" (p. 475). Indeed, fears and aversions *are* familiar because they are quite common and are routinely found in the normal population (Agras, Sylvester, & Oliveau, 1969; Marks, 1987). For example, in an early, well-designed, epidemiological study, Agras and his colleagues reported the frequency of common fears and phobias. As an indication of the ubiquity of fears, they reported that fear of snakes was present in 390 people per 1,000 studied. Similarly, 307 per 1,000 individuals reported a fear of heights. Although these fears are common, the significant majority of individuals who experience them are not considered to be phobic.

The revised third edition of the *Diagnostic and Statistical Manual of Mental Disorders* (DSM-III-R; American Psychiatric Association, 1987) defined simple phobia as a "persistent fear of a circumscribed stimulus . . . other than fear of having a panic attack . . . or of humiliation or embarrassment in certain social situations" (p. 244). Simple phobias, then, are phobias not related to panic disorder or social phobic syndromes. Further, the diagnostic criteria specify that, at some point, exposure to the feared stimulus provokes an anxiety response and that avoidance is common. The diagnosis is made when the fear or avoidance interferes significantly with usual functioning. For example, numerous individuals report an apprehensive concern about bridges. In order to travel unimpeded, most cross the bridges despite their anxiety about doing so. A smaller portion of individuals will expend great effort to chart the course of their driving so as to avoid all bridges and, if this is not possible, may restrict their travel altogether. Based on the criteria of anxiety and interference, approximately 5% to 10% of the population has a simple phobia (Myers et al., 1984). These more recent epidemiological data generated in the Epidemiological

Catchment Area Survey replicate the earlier findings of Agras and his colleagues, who reported the prevalence rate of simple phobia to be approximately 7% of the population.

Theoretically, an individual could develop a fear of any stimulus. Yet, various models have been postulated regarding "preparedness" to develop certain fears (Seligman, 1971). Preparedness, as defined by Seligman, refers to an innate predisposition to develop fears in relation to certain stimuli because avoidance of these stimuli had survival value (e.g., snakes, heights). A discussion of the preparedness notion is beyond the scope of this chapter, but the concept of preparedness poses interesting questions about the etiology of phobias and the nature of fears. However, it has been commonly noted that simple phobias tend to cluster into general types such as animal/insect, blood/injury, dental, and claustrophobia (Agras et al., 1969; Landy & Gaupp, 1971; Ost, 1987).

In perhaps the most comprehensive study of simple phobics to date, Ost (1987) examined the age of onset and mode of acquisition of different phobic disorders. His results indicated that animal phobias develop earliest; the mean age of onset is around 7 years. Blood phobias are the next earliest to develop (mean age around 9 years); then come dental phobias (12 years). Claustrophobia develops much later (around 20 years). The clear differences in age of onset among the various types of simple phobias are most interesting and suggest the heterogeneity of the diagnostic group. A further suggestion of the group's heterogeneity is the various modes of acquisition of simple phobias. These modes include: conditioning experiences, modeling, or informational transmission. Ost (1987) reported that approximately 50% of the animal phobics in his sample described a conditioning experience, whereas approximately 25% endorsed acquisition through vicarious processes.

The second descriptive Barlow (1988) used for simple phobias was "enigmatic"—an apt term, for several reasons. Simple phobics are rarely seen in clinical practice. Agras and his colleagues (1969) reported that of the 7% of the population who have a phobic disorder, fewer than 1 in 1,000 was receiving treatment. Individuals may have several reasons for not seeking treatment for their simple phobias. They may structure their lives in a way that minimizes exposure to the feared stimulus. A phobia may seem fairly insignificant to the affected person. Alternatively, these individuals may be embarrassed and reticent about disclosing the nature of their fear. Additionally, the term "simple" phobia may promote a sense among professionals that the disorder is fairly trivial. Marks (1987), among others, has suggested use of the term "specific" or "focal" to avoid the misleading implications of mildness that "simple" connotes. Clinically, when these individuals do present for treatment, they are often suffering a significant degree of distress.

Simple phobics are interesting in how they differ from patients with other anxiety disorders: they generally do not have the concomitant generalized anxiety, depression, or dysphoria that accompanies other anxiety states (Marks, 1987). This raises the question of what prompts them to seek treatment. A life change may prevent them from continuing their avoidance of the feared stimuli. The snake phobic may move to a more wooded area; the height phobic's promotion may depend on acceptance of a move to a higher floor or to a new, taller office building; the needle phobic may require immunization before traveling overseas. All of these people experience some event that alters their ability to avoid contact with the feared stimuli and may prompt them to seek treatment. Another route to treatment may be marked by a fear that leads to life restriction. The individual may become isolated and lonely, and these feelings then become the impetus for seeking help. Perhaps more frequently, the fear and/or avoidance yields a level of distress or impairment that becomes intolerable for the individual or a significant other.

The comparatively small research literature on simple phobia is related, in part, to the infrequency with which simple phobics seek treatment. Additionally, when they do seek treatment, they are likely to have complicating disorders; rarely does a clinician see a "pure" simple phobic who seeks unsolicited treatment. Finally, simple phobics appear to be a heterogeneous group with various modes of acquisition and differing feared stimuli. Together, these factors have resulted in less attention being directed toward simple phobia than has been focused on other anxiety disorders.

ISSUES RELATED TO ASSESSMENT

Assessment of simple phobia is relatively straightforward and, for the most part, can be completed with a thorough clinical interview and a behavioral assessment of the anxiety and fear. Most phobics show an increase in heart rate upon exposure to their feared stimuli (Marks, 1987). Although psychophysiological assessments have not been evaluated extensively with simple phobics, a measure of heart rate can be a useful clinical tool for assessment as well as for monitoring the effect of treatment.

Several points about the assessment of simple phobias merit attention. First, the idiosyncratic nature of the fears makes standardized behavioral approach tasks less informative than an approach task customized to the specific fears of the patient. For example, a woman who was evaluated for a phobia of cats was only fearful of long-hair cats. The more usual short-hair cats did not elicit fear and were irrelevant stimuli to her. The idiosyncratic stimulus cues must be elicited for designing a treatment program. Most fears can be broken down readily into component parts to construct a hierarchy individualized to the phobic patient.

A second assessment issue, as discussed above, is that simple phobics rarely present with only a simple phobia when they seek treatment. Attention must be paid to their additional distress. The relative ease with which most phobias can be treated often leads clinicians to ignore other problems. At times, what appears to be a simple phobia may actually be a manifestation of another disorder, generally another anxiety disorder. In particular, claustrophobics appear quite similar to agoraphobics and indeed have similar onset to the agoraphobia syndrome (Klein, 1981; Ost, 1987). Obsessive-compulsive disorders may initially appear to be phobic in nature, but with careful assessment, should be easily differentiated. A clinician may see individuals who are highly avoidant of animals and appear initially to have a simple phobia. After more detailed examination, a subgroup of these individuals reports concerns about the animals contaminating them in some way. The anxiety regarding animals in these cases is more likely a manifestation of an obsessive-compulsive disorder and not a simple phobia.

TREATMENT

Simple phobias are somewhat of an anomaly in the clinical treatment literature because there is a consensus among individuals of varied training and from differing orientations that exposure-based treatments are the treatment of choice (Barlow, 1988; Linden, 1981; Marks, 1987).

The goal of exposure-based treatments is to intentionally bring the phobic individual into contact with the feared stimuli. Variants of exposure treatments utilize differing procedural means of effecting this contact as well as differing theoretical rationales for the mechanism of fear reduction. The three most common methods of exposure utilized in the treatment of simple phobia are flooding (either in complete or graded presentations), systematic desensitization, and participant modeling. A brief discussion of these procedures is presented below; their relative effectiveness is then evaluated.

Flooding involves exposure, through imagery or in vivo, to the feared stimuli. The therapist seeks to elicit intense levels of anxiety while preventing an avoidance response. The rationale, based on Mowrer's (1960) two-factor theory, is that avoidance reinforces phobic behavior by preventing the possibility of extinction through structured contact with the stimuli. The phobic individual is kept in contact with the fear-relevant stimuli until the level of anxiety demonstrates evidence of reduction. Flooding can be conducted with the maximal level of the stimuli or presented in a graded fashion. The important elements are elicitation of anxiety through exposure, and prevention of an avoidance response.

As an example of the flooding paradigm, a 30-year-old male acrophobic was treated with graded levels of exposure. He was taken to a 10-story building and the first step in his hierarchy was to ride the elevator to the fifth floor. The individual remained on the fifth floor until his level of anxiety diminished to baseline levels, providing evidence of within-session habituation. Trial rides to the fifth floor were repeated until there was a decrement in baseline anxiety and minimal increase in distress. The next step in the hierarchy was to look out of a sixth-story window. Each step, to the final one of standing alone atop the roof of the 10-story building, was repeated until the baseline decreased and a minimal increase in level of anxiety over baseline was reported, providing evidence of between-session habituation.

In this approach, a therapist must ensure that the building is tall enough to elicit the relevant fear cues, that the procedure is safe (that the phobic cannot, as is likely feared, fall from the building), and that the phobic remains in the situation long enough for the anxiety response to habituate. Habituation can be demonstrated most easily by the return of self-reported distress to baseline levels. Ample evidence indicates that terminating exposure before achieving habituation serves to sensitize the phobic to the fear cues (Baum, 1970; Rachman, 1969).

Another example of a graded approach to exposure was completed with a 25-year-old female who presented with a phobic avoidance of needles and injections. She had successfully managed to avoid contact with injections for several years, but sought treatment because she required immunizations for an overseas trip. This patient presented no significant pathology other than her distress regarding injections. This distress was quite significant, however, and a graded approach was deemed most likely to successfully reduce her fear while not overwhelming her. Treatment began with having the patient touch a syringe sealed in its original sterile wrapping. The syringe was then taken out of the wrapper and touched. Gradual increases in contact progressed to the patient's injecting an orange and then to her finally receiving the immunizations. Because she had little time before her travel, treatment was conducted in a massed fashion and was completed within approximately 3 weeks.

Both of these individuals were treated with graduated levels of their fear-relevant stimuli until the maximal intensity was reached. Initial presentation of the maximal intensity stimuli could also be considered as a viable treatment option. The acrophobic described above could have been presented with the maximal intensity of his fear, standing alone on the roof of the 10-story building until his level of anxiety diminished to baseline levels. This step would have been repeated several times; each repetition would usually require less time to achieve habituation and thereby provide evidence of between-session habituation. The number and length of sessions will vary by individual and by the fear presented.

There is no empirical basis for deciding whether to use a maximal or graded approach. The clinician's choice is generally made after an assessment of the nature of the fear, the strength of the patient, and the patient's ability to tolerate a maximal approach. Would it seem too threatening and lead the patient to prematurely end a flooding session (likely sensitizing the phobic further) or to drop out of treatment?

Another treatment decision involves whether to use imaginal or in vivo presentations. For simple phobics, there is no empirical evidence to suggest the superiority of one over the other. Research suggests that in vivo is superior to imaginal exposure for agoraphobics (Emmelkamp & Wessels, 1975), but whether this is true for simple phobics is not known. In vivo is generally preferred because it increases the salience of the fear cues and is especially helpful when individuals have difficulty imaging.

Imaginal flooding can be a quite useful procedure when feared stimuli cannot be readily presented in real-life form. For example, dental and flying phobias present some challenges for designing in vivo exposure programs. In vivo exposure of a dental phobic requires a large degree of cooperation from a dentist and is often difficult to structure adequately so that habituation can occur. Flying phobias can have associated practical difficulties, given the relative lack of control that the therapist has over airline travel. Further, fears of turbulence or of unusual noises and their implications for the safety of passengers may be manifest in a more catastrophic cognitive mode. These fears may be most easily recreated through imagery: the therapist's control over the cues is increased and the cues are available in a structured fashion.

Systematic desensitization also utilizes the hierarchical approach described for graded exposure. However, the rationale is quite different from that of flooding and most often derives from Wolpe's (1973) description of reciprocal inhibition. According to Wolpe, relaxation serves to inhibit anxiety because it activates the parasympathetic portion of the autonomic nervous system. Sympathetic activity, related to anxiety, is inhibited by this activation. Wolpe stated that the anxiety inhibition becomes conditioned to the steps in the hierarchy and competes with anxiety as a response. In practice, individuals are taught relaxation skills, generally deep-muscle relaxation. In imagery, the steps of their hierarchy are then presented, beginning with the least fearful item. When the phobics can imagine this item without anxiety, the next item in the hierarchy is introduced, and so on until the hierarchy has been completed.

The third common exposure method, *participant modeling,* is largely based on Bandura's work (Bandura, 1971; Bandura, Blanchard, & Ritter, 1969; Bandura, Jeffery, & Gajdos, 1975). The procedure is completed in a graduated fashion. The phobic individual observes as a model completes a series of contacts with the phobic stimuli. The client, at his or her own pace, begins graduated contacts, with the support of the therapist. The therapist may present either a mastery model (no fear is demonstrated) or a coping model (initial fear is overcome) (Kazdin, 1973).

The treatment studies on simple phobia have demonstrated no meaningful differences among the various types of exposure.

In a review of the treatment literature, Linden (1981) reported the superiority of exposure but found no differences among the variants of exposure. The following section reviews studies utilizing exposure-based treatments with phobic subjects seen in the clinical setting (as opposed to analogue designs).

Exposure-Based Treatments in Clinical Setting

Ost, Lindahl, Sterner, and Jerremalm (1984) treated blood phobics with either exposure or relaxation. Both groups improved, but the exposure treatment appeared more effective in the reduction of self-reported fear. Bourque and Ladouceur (1980) compared five exposure treatments for acrophobia and found no differences in outcome among them. Ost (1978) compared a fading group, a systematic desensitization group, and a wait-list control group in the treatment of spider and snake phobics. (Fading involves successive trials of pairing slides associated with positive affect and with the phobic stimuli, yielding a gradual increase in exposure to the phobic slides.) The fading and systematic desensitization groups were significantly more improved than the wait-list group, but the two active treatments did not differ on outcome measures. In a rather complex design, Denny, Sullivan, & Thiry (1977) examined participant modeling and self-verbalization training in the treatment of spider fears. Nine groups were formed for the analyses by including combinations of modeling, overt and covert rehearsal, and self-verbalizations. The most meaningful results indicated that participant-modeling conditions were superior to no-participant-modeling conditions and that overt and covert rehearsal did not differ.

Several other researchers have sought to examine the impact of adding cognitive strategies to exposure-based treatments for simple phobics. The results are mixed and do not clearly support an incremental efficacy of cognitive approaches. In an investigation by Marshall (1985), cognitive strategies were found to be beneficially related to outcome. Marshall treated 20 acrophobics with exposure. Half of the subjects were taught to utilize coping self-statements, and half received no additional treatment beyond exposure. After a 4-week follow-up period, results indicated that exposure plus self-statements was superior to exposure alone.

Biran and Wilson (1981) treated individuals who had height, elevator, and darkness fears. In five 50-minute sessions, subjects received either exposure in vivo or cognitive restructuring and brief imaginal exposure. One month after treatment, exposure was found to be superior to cognitive restructuring on measures of avoidance, fear, and self-efficacy.

In another comparison of exposure with and without added cognitive components, Ladouceur (1983) treated 36 dog and cat phobics in one of four groups: participant modeling alone; participant modeling and self-instructional training; participant modeling and self-verbalization; or discussion. The discussion group did not change. Posttreatment, all three participant modeling groups were improved. However, after one month, the group given participant modeling alone showed results superior to those of the other groups. The author suggested that the addition of self-instruction or self-verbalization may be a distraction to the modeling procedure.

The addition of cognitive factors to exposure has received only minimal support. It is possible that cognitive changes may accompany exposure or may be a product of the changes produced by exposure (Borkovec, 1978). Another interesting possibility is that cognitive interventions may be effective for some simple phobics and not for others. For example, flying phobics may respond to a cognitive intervention to target their catastrophic cognitions. If indeed different modalities are found to be effective with particular individuals, group data would obscure individual outcomes. Given this possibility, one approach would be to tailor treatment to the individual's modal way of responding to the feared stimuli (e.g., cognitive, behavioral, or physiological), or what has been referred to as the *response pattern* of the individual.

The work on response patterns has been completed mostly by Ost and his colleagues. For example, Jerremalm, Jansson, and Ost (1986) examined whether outcome could be predicted by varying the treatment based on individual response patterns of dental phobics. They divided subjects into cognitive and physiological reactors. *Cognitive reactors* were individuals who responded to a dental examination with catastrophic cognitions; *physiological reactors* responded with increased heart rates. Half of those in each group were assigned to self-instructional training (a cognitive treatment modality) and the rest were assigned to applied relaxation (a physiological modality). Accordingly, the self-instructional group and the applied relaxation group each had half of the cognitive reactors and half of the physiological reactors. Jerremalm et al.'s results demonstrated that both groups improved with no significant interactions occurring between type of reactor and treatment modality. Matching did not appear to have any effect on outcome in this investigation.

An earlier study by Ost, Johansson, and Jerremalm (1982) did find some support for tailoring treatment to individual response patterns. In this study, 34 claustrophobics were divided into behavioral reactors (showing avoidance primarily) and physiological reactors (showing elevated heart rate without significant avoidance). A similar procedure to the Jerremalm et al. (1986) study was utilized: half of the behavioral reactors and half of the physiological reactors were assigned to exposure, and the rest, to relaxation. The two treatment conditions were compared to a wait-list control. Both treatment groups improved. Interestingly, exposure was slightly superior to relaxation for the behavioral reactors and, conversely, relaxation was slightly superior to exposure for the physiological reactors.

More work is needed before a definitive decision can be made regarding the empirical status of tailoring treatments to response patterns. Simple phobias can be highly idiosyncratic; one idiosyncrasy is the characteristic mode the phobic individual utilizes to respond to the fear. It then makes sense clinically to tailor treatments to the individual's idiosyncratic fear cues. Based on the literature to date, however, this tailoring should be grounded as much as possible within an exposure-based treatment program because exposure has been shown most clearly to be the treatment of choice for simple phobics.

An interesting variant of an exposure procedure was described by Ost (1989), who has recently suggested a one-session treatment approach for simple phobics. His method involves a combination of exposure and modeling. To be included in this treatment, subjects must have a circumscribed fear, be motivated for treatment, and have no secondary gains from their phobia. To date, outcome data from 20 patients have been reported. The mean time of treatment across the 20 patients was 2.1 hours. Mean improvement at an average of 4 years' follow-up was 90%. Although treatment was relatively brief, continued self-exposure was urged, to expand the total amount of exposure the subjects received. Ost's one-session approach appears to be a single, intense exposure session, followed by repeated self-exposure. In actual clinical practice, the "clean" simple phobics Ost requires for his approach are generally unusual. Although phobics are traditionally seen more often than in one session, these results underscore the efficacy of exposure.

Most information about simple phobias discusses treatment as applicable across phobias. Simple phobics tend to cluster into types, as discussed above, and exposure appears beneficial regardless of the type of phobia. Blood phobia, however, merits separate attention. The response of blood phobics differs from the usual phobic reaction in that is is biphasic. When exposed to stimuli related to blood, these phobics show the initial increases in heart rate, blood pressure, and subjective distress found across phobias in general (Ost, Sterner, & Lindahl, 1984). However, this response changes rapidly to bradycardia, hypotension, and, on occasion, actual fainting. Nausea and sweating are also fairly common (Connolly, Hallam, & Marks, 1976). This vasovagal response requires some changes in treatment procedures. Marks (1987) cogently recommended that blood phobics lie down during initial stages of treatment, to minimize the dangers associated with fainting. Marks also suggested that tensing muscles may decrease the likelihood of fainting. An additional difference between blood phobics and other simple phobics is that judgments of habituation must be made with an understanding of the biphasic response. As such, increases in heart rate (after the initial increase, which will be followed by a decrease) will indicate a return to baseline. However, exposure treatments do appear to be effective for blood phobics (e.g., Ost, Lindahl, et al., 1984).

One recently developed approach for treating blood phobics involves exposure but adds a component directly targeted to decrease the likelihood of fainting (Ost & Sterner, 1987). Termed *applied tension,* this procedure teaches blood phobics to tense gross muscle groups. Once this tensing is taught, the skill is applied during exposure to blood-related stimuli. To date, the results of 10 patients have been reported. At posttreatment, all 10 were significantly improved and improvement was maintained by all after a 6-month follow-up period. It will be important to compare applied tension to exposure alone, to determine the added benefits.

SUMMARY AND FUTURE DIRECTIONS

The empirical literature is consistent in supporting the superiority of exposure-based treatments for simple phobias, but finds no systematic differences among the variants of exposure. The addition of cognitive interventions does not appear to enhance outcome. At this point, the task is one of refining treatments to improve their efficacy. An interesting area of research is that of tailoring treatment to individual response patterns. The limited research on this approach was presented. To date, it is difficult to recommend tailoring, despite some support from one study (Ost et al., 1982). Another interesting area for future research also utilizes tailoring treatment to the individual but, in this case, tailoring it to the mode of acquisition (e.g., Wolpe, 1981). For example, those individuals whose fears were acquired through a conditioning experience would be predicted to respond best to an exposure-based treatment; those who acquired fears through misinformation or vicariously, might be expected to respond best to a cognitive intervention. An area that has been relatively understudied is the relationship of simple phobias to other anxiety disorders. Recent research reports a fairly high prevalence of simple phobia among the anxiety disorders (e.g., Barlow, DiNardo, Vermilyea, Vermilyea, & Blanchard, 1986; Sanderson, Rapee, & Barlow, 1987). The relationships between etiology and treatment of simple phobias are interesting areas deserving of further systematic investigation.

REFERENCES

Agras, W. S., Sylvester, D., & Oliveau, D. (1969). The epidemiology of common fears and phobia. *Comprehensive Psychiatry, 10,* 151–156.

American Psychiatric Association. (1987). *Diagnostic and statistical manual of mental disorders* (3rd ed. rev.). Washington, DC: Author.

Bandura, A. (1971). Psychotherapy based on modeling principles. In A. E. Bergin & S. L. Garfield (Eds.), *Handbook of psychotherapy and behavior change* (pp. 653–708). New York: Wiley.

Bandura, A., Blanchard, E. B., & Ritter, R. (1969). The relative efficacy of desensitization and modeling approaches for inducing behavioral, affective, and attitudinal changes. *Journal of Personality and Social Psychology, 13,* 173–199.

Bandura, A., Jeffery, R. W., & Gajdos, E. (1975). Generalizing change through participant modeling with self-directed mastery. *Behaviour Research and Therapy, 13,* 141–152.

Barlow, D. H. (1988). *Anxiety and its disorders.* New York: Guilford.

Barlow, D. H., DiNardo, P. A., Vermilyea, B. B., Vermilyea, J. A., & Blanchard, E. B. (1986). Co-morbidity and depression among the anxiety disorders: Issues in diagnosis and classification. *Journal of Nervous and Mental Disease, 174,* 63–72.

Baum, M. (1970). Extinction of avoidance responding through response prevention (flooding). *Psychological Bulletin, 74,* 276–284.

Biran, M., & Wilson, G. T. (1981). Treatment of phobic disorders using cognitive and exposure methods: A self-efficacy analysis. *Journal of Consulting and Clinical Psychology, 49,* 886–899.

Borkovec, T. D. (1978). Self-efficacy: Cause or reflection of behavior change? *Advances in Behaviour Research and Therapy, 1,* 163–170.

Bourque, P., & Ladouceur, R. (1980). An investigation of various performance based treatments with agoraphobics. *Behaviour Research and Therapy, 15,* 161–170.

Connolly, J. C., Hallam, R. S., & Marks, I. M. (1976). Selective association of fainting with blood-injury-illness fear. *Behavior Therapy, 7,* 8–13.

Denny, D. R., Sullivan, B. J., & Thiry, M. R. (1977). Participant modeling and self-verbalization training in the reduction of spider fears. *Journal of Behavior Therapy and Experimental Psychiatry, 8,* 247–253.

Emmelkamp, P. M. G., & Wessels, H. (1975). Flooding in imagination vs. flooding in vivo: A comparison with agoraphobics. *Behaviour Research and Therapy, 13,* 7–15.

Jerremalm, A., Jansson, L., & Ost, L. G. (1986). Individual response patterns and the effects of different behavioural methods in the treatment of dental phobia. *Behaviour Research and Therapy, 24,* 587–596.

Kazdin, A. E. (1973). Covert modeling and the reduction of avoidance behavior. *Journal of Abnormal Psychology, 81,* 87–95.

Klein, D. F. (1981). Anxiety reconceptualized. In D. F. Klein & J. Rabkin (Eds.), *Anxiety: New research and changing concepts* (pp. 235–264). New York: Raven Press.

Ladouceur, R. (1983). Participant modeling with or without cognitive treatment for phobias. *Journal of Consulting and Clinical Psychology, 51,* 942–944.

Landy, F. J., & Gaupp, L. A. (1971). A factor analysis of the fear survey schedule—III. *Behaviour Research and Therapy, 9,* 89–93.

Linden, W. (1981). Exposure treatments for focal phobias. *Archives of General Psychiatry, 38,* 769–775.

Marks, I. M. (1987). *Fears, phobias, and rituals.* New York: Oxford University Press.

Marshall, W. L. (1985). The effects of variable exposure in flooding therapy. *Behavior Therapy, 16,* 117–135.

Mowrer, O. H. (1960). *Learning theory and the symbolic processes.* New York: Wiley.

Myers, J. K., Weissman, M. M., Tischler, C. E., Holzer, C. E., III, Orvaschel, H., Anthony, J. C., Boyd, J. H., Burke, J. D., Kramer, M., & Stoltsman, R. (1984). Six-month prevalence of psychiatric disorders in three communities. *Archives of General Psychiatry, 41,* 959–967.

Ost, L. G. (1978). Fading versus systematic desensitization in the treatment of snake and spider phobia. *Behaviour Research and Therapy, 16,* 379-389.

Ost, L. G. (1987). Age of onset in different phobias. *Journal of Abnormal Psychology, 96,* 223-229.

Ost, L. G. (1989). One-session treatment for specific phobias. *Behaviour Research and Therapy, 27,* 1-7.

Ost, L. G., Johansson, J., & Jerremalm, A. (1982). Individual response patterns and the effects of different behavioural methods in the treatment of claustrophobia. *Behaviour Research and Therapy, 20,* 445-460.

Ost, L. G., Lindahl, I. L., Sterner, V., & Jerremalm, A. (1984). Exposure in vivo vs. applied relaxation in the treatment of blood phobia. *Behaviour Research and Therapy, 22,* 205-216.

Ost, L. G., & Sterner, U. (1987). Applied tension: A specific behavioural method for treatment of blood phobics. *Behaviour Research and Therapy, 25,* 25-30.

Ost, L. G., Sterner, U., & Lindahl, I. L. (1984). Physiological responses in blood phobics. *Behaviour Research and Therapy, 22,* 109-117.

Rachman, S. (1969). Treatment by prolonged exposure to high intensity stimulation. *Behaviour Research and Therapy, 7,* 295-302.

Sanderson, W. C., Rapee, R. M., & Barlow, D. H. (1987, November). *The DSM-III-Revised anxiety disorders categories: Descriptions and co-morbidity.* Paper presented at the annual meeting of the Association for Advancement of Behavior Therapy, Boston.

Seligman, M. E. P. (1971). Phobias and preparedness. *Behavior Therapy, 2,* 307-320.

Wolpe, J. (1973). *The practice of behavior therapy* (2nd ed.). New York: Pergamon.

Wolpe, J. (1981). The dichotomy between classically conditioned and cognitively learned anxiety. *Journal of Behavior Therapy and Experimental Psychiatry, 12,* 35-42.

CHAPTER 2

Behavioral Treatment of Social Phobia

SAMUEL M. TURNER, DEBORAH C. BEIDEL, and RUTH M. TOWNSLEY

Social phobia, a relatively new diagnostic category, was first introduced into the diagnostic nomenclature with the publication of DSM-III (American Psychiatric Association, 1980). The diagnostic criteria were consistent with the characteristics that had been described earlier by Marks and Gelder (1966) and, in particular, Marks (1970). The DSM-III defined social phobia as a "persistent, irrational fear of, and compelling desire to avoid, situations in which the individual may be exposed to scrutiny by others" (American Psychiatric Association, 1980, p. 227). The DSM-III-R (American Psychiatric Association, 1987) essentially retained the DSM-III criteria but added provisions for a subtype. Using DSM-III-R, the generalized subtype should be specified when social fear or avoidance is present in most social situations. Although the DSM-III-R was silent regarding social fears that are relatively circumscribed, these have been referred to in the literature as comprising the specific subtype. The subtypes will be addressed within the context of the discussion of the clinical syndrome and the evaluation of treatment outcome.

The discussion of the clinical syndrome is intended to provide the reader with an overview of the clinical picture of social phobia and to introduce briefly some of the parameters that appear to have particular relevance for understanding the phenomenology and nature of the syndrome. The discussion of treatments and treatment outcome provides a synthesis of what the current literature reveals rather than a detailed critique of each study.

CLINICAL SYNDROME

Because social phobia is a relatively new disorder, there only are a few empirical studies pertaining to its phenomenology. However, extant studies clearly show that the disorder is a much more distressing and inhibitory condition than heretofore believed. Social phobics present with various degrees of avoidance behavior, types of social fears, number of feared situations, degree of distress, and features that are idiosyncratic to their particular fear. Thus, some social phobics have rigid avoidance of rather restricted situations such as public performance (e.g., giving speeches); others have more generalized patterns of fear, including social events or general social interaction. For some, the

---

Preparation of this manuscript was supported in part by NIMH grants MH41852 and MH43252.

fear may be associated with specific types of people (e.g., men, women, peers, colleagues, authority figures) and is expressed when in the presence of these individuals, regardless of the particular setting. The setting may have a more central role for those social phobics whose difficulties are restricted to meeting rooms, large lecture halls, or informal social gatherings. Table 2.1 lists situations that typically are feared and avoided by social phobics, based on a sample previously reported in (1986) and a second, much larger sample. Note that current diagnostic criteria do not require one to avoid any of the feared situations for the diagnosis of social phobia to be made. The diagnosis is appropriate if significant distress is experienced in the social situations, even in the absence of avoidance. Thus, many individuals with the disorder suffer in silence, undetected by those around them.

In an examination of the number and types of fears seen in social phobia, Turner, Beidel, Dancu, and Keys (1986) reported that there was an average of 2.4 fears in that small sample. Among the social phobics seen in our clinic to date, the average number of situations endorsed by the patients as creating at least a moderate degree of distress is 5.6 (Turner, Beidel, & Townsley, in press). The difference is most likely accounted for by the standardized interview schedule (the Anxiety Disorders Interview Schedule—Revised) that was used in the current investigation. The most common type of social fear, by far, was of formal public speaking, followed by informal public speaking (see Table 2.1). An interesting finding from the earlier study was that if one fear was present, there was a high likelihood of other social fears. Few social phobics in this sample had only one fear; hence, "specific" is likely to be a relative term. In our opinion, the diagnosis of specific social phobia may be appropriate even if two or three circumscribed performance situations are involved in the social fear. In most cases, specific fears such as eating and drinking in public appear to be secondary and result from fear that eating and drinking utensils will not be handled properly due to tremulousness, which increases the fear of embarrassment. These types of social fears normally occur within the context of other social fears. Fear of using public restrooms is included as a type of social phobia when the fear is socially based. These fears are relatively rare. In our experience, they are somewhat more difficult to treat, and individuals with these fears have many avoidant and paranoid personality features.

Because social phobics often hide their fears, it has been difficult to ascertain the level of debilitation associated with the disorder. Our clinical experience is that individuals with social phobia sometimes underestimate the impact that the condition has had on their lives. The disorder has an early onset (usually in adolescence) and the individual often develops a pattern of behavior that protects against experiencing the fear. Avoidance often is pervasive but is sometimes subtle and may not be recognized by the patient as

TABLE 2.1 Percentage of Social Phobics Distressed in Social Situations

	Turner, Beidel, Dancu, & Keys (1986) n = 21	Turner, Beidel, & Townsley (in press) n = 88
Formal speaking	81%	99%
Informal speaking/meetings	76	88
Eating	33	—
Drinking	5	—
Eating/drinking	—	39
Writing	19	31
Taking tests	10	N/A
Initiating conversations	N/A*	60%
Maintaining conversations	N/A	64
Parties	N/A	76
Restrooms	N/A	8

*Not assessed in the investigation.

avoidance because it has become part of the routine behavior pattern.

Until recently, the prevailing clinical lore was that social phobia is a relatively mild condition. In 1970, Marks noted that, on the dimension of severity, social phobia seemed to occupy an intermediate position between simple phobia and the more pervasive anxiety states. Using a psychometric assessment strategy, Turner, McCann, Beidel, and Mezzich (1986) confirmed Marks's clinical observations. On all of the instruments used, social phobics scored in the intermediate range—less than the anxiety states, but greater than simple phobics. Within the past decade, a reasonably clear picture of social phobics' emotional response has emerged. The autonomic nervous system of the majority of social phobics shows the characteristic elevated response pattern seen in phobic patients who are confronted with the phobic stimulus (Beidel, Turner, & Dancu, 1985; Turner, Beidel, & Larkin, 1986), and there typically are cognitive, somatic, and behavioral features of that response. However, Turner and Beidel (1985) found that there were subtypes of social phobics, based on their physiological reactivity to a feared stimulus. Some did not show the characteristic autonomic response pattern seen in phobic patients; rather, they showed virtually no reactivity within the context of a behavioral performance task, despite the fact that the cognitive or psychic component of distress was present. The existence of a group of social phobics who are autonomic system nonreactors was identified by other researchers as well (Jerremalm, Jansson, & Ost, 1986; Ost, Jerremalm, & Johansson, 1981). Heimberg, Hope, Dodge, and Becker (1990) reported a similar dichotomy based on an examination of specific and generalized subtypes of social phobia: the generalized social phobics exhibited less reactivity. The conclusions from that study, however, are limited by the fact that identical tasks were not used for the two groups. Differences in reactivity could possibly have been due to the specific task demands, rather than the characteristics of the patients. Although it is unclear why social phobics have different autonomic nervous system response patterns, their presence could have some ramifications for treatment outcome. This issue will be addressed again in the context of treatment selection and evaluation.

With respect to distress, Amies, Gelder, and Shaw (1983) reported that social phobics showed symptoms of depression that were sometimes associated with "parasuicidal" acts. Excessive alcohol use was common among social phobics, and both alcohol use and parasuicidal acts were more frequent in these patients than in agoraphobics. There also have been reports of considerable use of anxiolytic and beta-blocking drugs by social phobics attempting to control the discomfort associated with their social fears (Sanderson, Rapee, & Barlow, 1987; Turner, Beidel, Dancu, & Keys, 1986).

Social phobics tend to show evidence of significant general anxiety, as measured by self-report inventories and clinical rating scales. In addition, they experience numerous somatic symptoms such as tachycardia, sweating, blushing, tremors, muscle aches and pains, headache, and gastrointestinal distress. Tachycardia, tremors, blushing, and sweating—responses that are mediated by the beta-adrenergic system—are considered to be particularly characteristic of social phobia (Gorman & Gorman, 1987). Also, it is not unusual for social phobics to experience panic attacks, which primarily occur in the phobic situation. Although significant depression sometimes is seen (as noted by the Amies et al. (1983) study), depressive symptoms tend to be relatively mild in most cases. For example, in a sample of 93 social phobics assessed in our clinic, the mean Hamilton Depression Scale score was 10.1, ranging from 7 to 20 (14 often is used as the cutoff for depression). Some patients experience very high levels of anxiety as well as more significant symptoms of dysphoria. These patients tend to be of two types: those who are under acute distress and those who have other concurrent Axis I and II disorders. Acute distress often occurs when individuals are unable to continue their established avoidance pattern, which has protected them against their fear. An example is a 23-year-old male patient who sought treatment in our clinic with the primary complaint of being unable to speak before groups of people, a problem that had been present since age 16. He had been notified of a promotion to a supervisory position that would require him to make presentations and to conduct meetings on a regular basis. Avoidance strategies that had served him well in the past would no longer work. This type of scenario is frequently the impetus for social phobics to seek treatment.

The second type of social phobic, one who has a concurrent Axis I or II disorder, is likely to present a more complex clinical picture. With respect to Axis I disorders, a recent study by Turner, Beidel, Borden, Stanley, and Jacob (1991) found that generalized anxiety disorder was the most common concurrent Axis I disorder (33%), followed by simple phobia (11%). Table 2.2 lists all concurrent Axis I disorders that were found. The most common concurrent Axis II condition was avoidant personality disorder. (DSM-III-R allows the concurrent diagnosis of these disorders whereas DSM-III did not.) A more interesting finding was the fact that, when avoidant and obsessional characteristics were considered, virtually all of the social phobics had significant features of one or both of these disorders. The Axis II disorders that were found are listed in Table 2.3. The overall percentage of personality disorders in the sample was 43%, much higher than the 17% reported earlier by Klass, DiNardo, and Barlow (1989). The most obvious difference between the two studies was that Turner et al. (1991) used a semi-structured interview schedule (Structured Clinical Interview for DSM-III-R Axis II; Spitzer, Williams, Gibbon, & First, 1988) to determine personality diagnosis whereas Klass et al. did not.

TABLE TABLE 2.2 Frequency and Percent of Concurrent Axis I Disorders*

Diagnosis	Number (n)	Percent (%)
Generalized anxiety disorder	24	33.3
Simple phobia	8	11.1
Dysthymic disorder	4	5.6
Panic disorder	2	2.8
Major depressive disorder	2	2.8
Obsessive-compulsive disorder	1	1.4
Substance abuse	1	1.4

*All patients had a primary diagnosis of social phobia (n = 71).

Note. From "Social Phobia: Axis I and II Correlates" by S. M. Turner, D. C. Beidel, J. W. Borden, M. A. Stanley, & R. G. Jacob, *Journal of Abnormal Psychology*, in press. Copyright 1991 by the American Psychological Association. Reprinted by permission of the publisher.

No data addressing the impact of these concurrent Axis I and II conditions with respect to treatment outcome are available at this time; however, one would expect this to be an important factor because the presence of a concurrent Axis I disorder resulted in a more distressed clinical picture (Turner et al., 1991). Furthermore, in our clinical experience, the presence of any concurrent disorder (Axis I or II) complicates the treatment of social phobia. The role that these other anxiety and personality disorders might play in the etiology and maintenance of social phobia has yet to be elucidated.

IMPACT OF SOCIAL PHOBIA ON SOCIAL FUNCTIONING

No studies have addressed specifically how social phobia affects quality of life, but recent studies do provide some insight. For example, Turner, Beidel, Dancu, and

TABLE 2.3 Frequency and Percent of Concurrent Axis II Disorders in a Sample of Social Phobia Patients

Personality Disorder	Diagnosis		Subthreshold Diagnosis		Diagnosis or Subthreshold Diagnosis	
	n	%	n	%	n	%
Avoidant	15	22.1	36	52.9	51	75.0
Obsessive-compulsive	9	13.2	33	48.5	42	61.8
Histrionic	3	4.4	14	20.6	17	25.0
Antisocial	2	2.9	7	10.3	9	13.2
Dependent	1	1.5	10	14.7	11	16.2
Paranoid	1	1.5	15	22.1	16	23.5
Narcissistic	1	1.5	7	10.3	8	11.8
Borderline	1	1.5	3	4.4	4	5.9
Passive-aggressive	0	0.0	10	14.7	10	14.7
Self-defeating	0	0.0	2	2.9	2	2.9
Schizotypal	0	0.0	3	4.4	3	4.4
Schizoid	0	0.0	2	2.9	2	2.9

n = 68.

Note. From "Social Phobia: Axis I and II Correlates" by S. M. Turner, D. C. Beidel, J. W. Borden, M. A. Stanley, & R. G. Jacob, *Journal of Abnormal Psychology*, in press. Copyright 1991 by the American Psychological Association. Reprinted by permission of the publisher.

Keys (1986) found that the disorder was associated with a pervasive pattern of interference in social functioning. Their data showed that many social phobics experienced occupational and academic impairment as well as restricted social interaction (see Table 2.4). Similar observations were reported by Liebowitz, Gorman, Fyer, and Klein (1985). Furthermore, our clinical experience suggests that social and occupational impairment ranges from relatively mild to very severe.

AGE AND OTHER CHARACTERISTICS OF ONSET

Social phobia is the only adult anxiety disorder with initial onset occurring during adolescence, but the syndrome clearly exists in younger children as well (Beidel, 1988). Early reports indicated that the age of onset was late adolescence to young adulthood (Amies et al., 1983; Marks, 1970; Marks & Gelder, 1966); more recent studies suggest a somewhat earlier onset. Liebowitz et al. (1985) reported an average onset age of 15 to 20. Turner, Beidel, Dancu, and Keys (1986) reported a mean onset age of 16.5. In a sample of 93 social phobics assessed in our clinic during the past 3 years, the mean age of onset was 15 years, with a range of 1 to 41 years.

It is unclear why the onset of social phobia tends to occur in adolescence, but this is a time of significant social change in which social demands take on a new

TABLE 2.4 Impairment in Occupational or Social Functioning

	Percent of Sample Impaired	
Life Area	Turner, Beidel, Dancu, & Keys (1986) (n = 21)	Turner et al. (1991) (n = 99)
Academic	85%	91%
Occupational	92	96
General social relationships	67	80
Heterosocial relationships[1]	50[2]	79[3]

[1] Asked of only unmarried patients.
[2] n = 8.
[3] n = 29.

dimension and the individual is faced with establishing a new social position outside of the nuclear family. Based on nonhuman primate data, Öhman (1986) suggested that the critical period for learning social fears is likely to be adolescence or early adulthood—the period during which the individual must establish a niche within the social group. Extrapolating from this nonhuman primate research, Öhman postulated that social position usually is established through expressions of dominance. Following this line of reasoning, those who are weak and fearful (as a result of constitutional factors or prior learning history) are more likely to be candidates for lower positions within the hierarchy. Whether the dominance notion has relevance for understanding the development of social fears in humans awaits further study, but the increasing social demands of this age group do appear to be a factor in the emergence of social phobia.

Although the most common age of onset is during adolescence, it was noted that social phobia can occur among children, and that those who develop the condition at a later age often report some degree of social difficulty during childhood. This raises the question of whether social phobia is an inherited condition or whether some type of constitutional vulnerability or early learning history may play a role. Although few data are available to address this issue, those that exist are worth examining.

In a small study that examined familial patterns of social phobia in 21 patients in our clinic, 9 patients (43%) could identify at least one first-degree relative who experienced some type of social fear. In addition, Reich and Yates (1988) found the frequency of social phobia in the relatives of diagnosed social phobics to be higher than in the families of panic patients. However, the number of patients' relatives in the two groups who had the disorder was small (5 vs. 2), and the study suffered from a serious methodological shortcoming (the interviews were not blind). It remains unclear whether social phobia is familial, as are other anxiety disorders. The information from twin studies is equally limited. For example, the largest existing study of anxiety disorders patients included a comparison of twins who were assessed by interview (Torgersen, 1983). Four probands had social phobia. Of this group, none had a co-twin who was concordant for social phobia, but two co-twins did have generalized anxiety disorder. Based on available data, little can be said about the role of genetics in social phobia at this time.

Despite the paucity of information regarding familial transmission, there are some interesting data pertaining to the possible role of temperamental or "personality" factors in the etiology of social fear. In this regard, a summary of the work of Kagan and his colleagues with "behaviorally inhibited" children is relevant. Kagan and his colleagues identified a group of children (at approximately 2 years of age) who exhibited "anxiety like" behaviors, including social reticence, and these behaviors remained stable over 7 years (Kagan, Reznick, Snidman, Gibbons, & Johnson, 1988). Interestingly, the behaviors defining this syndrome were evident only under "challenge" conditions (i.e., the child was placed in a particular situation, and, although the authors have not addressed it as such, the behaviors comprising this "syndrome" primarily occurs in the context of social situations). Kagan and his colleagues argued that these enduring features are biological in origin (Kagan, Reznick, & Snidman, 1988). In our view, this conclusion is premature, but the findings are interesting. For example, these characteristics may be risk factors for social phobia or other anxiety disorders. Similar types of behavior have been observed in nonhuman primates when placed under challenge conditions. Likewise, these appear to be stable and enduring characteristics (Suomi, 1986). Determining the etiology of these behaviors and their possible role in the development of maladaptive anxiety will be an important link in efforts to understand the nature of anxiety in general and social phobia in particular.

There are no studies available that have addressed the role of prior learning history (other than discrete conditioning episodes) in social phobia. Clearly this is a viable explanation for why some individuals report early social difficulties prior to the onset of social phobia. The emergence of social phobia during adolescence could be the culmination of a series of life experiences. Recent evidence suggests that conditioning can be cumulative (Mineka, 1985). Furthermore, it is possible that individual characteristics (biological or nonbiological) combine with learning histories or environmental events to produce social phobia.

Additional data using personality assessment strategies suggest that individual characteristics might be associated with the development of social phobia. The results of the assessment of social phobics with the Eysenck Personality Inventory (EPI) showed that these patients were neurotic and introverted (Amies et al., 1983). Similarly, a large sample of social phobics in our clinic was neurotic and introverted as measured by the EPI. Whether these personality features constitute risk factors or are simply correlates of social phobia will need to be determined by future research.

In examining the onset characteristics of social phobics, Öst (1987) reported that 58% noted that the development of their condition followed some type of conditioning episode. However, this sequence was determined only by the subjects' response to one question. In a study that used an extensive interview of 71 social phobics in our own clinic, approximately 50% reported what appeared to be a conditioning experience (very close to the 58% figure reported by Öst). However, it is important to note that, even when a conditioning episode was present, a large percentage of patients reported premorbid "shyness" or "timidness." Moreover, the mere fact that one has had a traumatic conditioning experience does not eliminate the possibility that individual variables contribute to the genesis of the disorder. As noted above, it is currently unclear what role preexisting vulnerability factors might play in the development of social phobia, but, for many individuals, it seems likely that factors other than a single conditioning experience are important, and that these include both biological and nonbiological variables.

SOCIAL PHOBIA AND SHYNESS

It is important to differentiate the clinical syndrome of social phobia from the personality style described as shyness. There is no extant study comparing shy subjects with diagnosed social phobics, but the different prevalence rates for the two syndromes suggest that they are not one and the same. In a series of studies, shyness was currently present in 40% of college students (Zimbardo, Pilkonis, & Norwood, 1975); social phobia had a 2% prevalence rate in a community sample (Pollard & Henderson, 1988). Turner, Beidel, and Townsley (1990) reviewed the available literature and concluded that, although there are a number of similarities between the two syndromes (i.e., somatic and cognitive features), there also are a number of distinguishing factors other than the vastly different prevalence rates. First, the degree of social and occupational impairment in those who are diagnosed as socially phobic tends to be much greater than among those who are merely shy.

Second, shyness appears to have a much earlier onset than social phobia. Third, from the available evidence, social phobia is a chronic, unremitting condition, whereas shyness appears to be transitory for many individuals. The sometimes transitory nature of shyness is a particularly important distinguishing feature because the other parameters mainly reflect a severity dimension. Finally, avoidance tends to be associated with social phobia much more than with shyness, and the severity of the avoidance in social phobics is much greater. The fact that there are a number of differences (particularly in severity) does not eliminate the possibility that these conditions are related in some fashion. For example, both conditions may be mediated by some third variable. A number of possibilities exist, some of which include factors noted earlier. However, further discussion would be unduly speculative because research addressing this question is nonexistent at this time.

SUBTYPES OF SOCIAL PHOBIA

As noted earlier, the DSM-III-R specified that the generalized subtype should be specified when anxiety is experienced in most social situations. Patients not meeting this criterion have come to be known as the specific subtype. There was no obvious rationale for why the subtype division was made. Furthermore, no clear criteria were delineated for determining what "most" social situations means. Nevertheless, two studies have attempted to address the issue of differences and similarities between the subtypes. The first of these by Heimberg et al. (1990), retrospectively reviewed the records of 57 social phobics and assigned a subtype diagnosis. Patients with public speaking fears were assigned the specific subtype and those with fears in "most or all" social situations were given the generalized diagnosis. There were few differences between the two groups but, when differences were found, the generalized subtype was more severe.

In the second study, Turner, Beidel, and Townsley (in press) divided 89 social phobics into specific and generalized subtypes. Those with fears of general social interaction such as informal social conversations or attending social events were judged to be generalized and those with performance-oriented fears (e.g., speech phobia) were judged to be specific. The generalized subtype was more severe with respect to greater general distress, higher social anxiety, greater social difficulty, and poorer performance on a behavioral task. Thus, although the criteria for dividing the group into subtypes are vague, there is some evidence that they might be useful with respect to severity. Similarly, some preliminary data from a treatment study in our clinic indicated that the subtype distinction might have predictive utility; specific social phobics tended to respond better to both drug and behavioral treatment than the generalized subtype. Nevertheless, it appears that basically this is a severity dimension and not a qualitative distinction, because the core fear of both subtypes is the same (i.e., fear of negative evaluation).

OVERVIEW OF BEHAVIORAL INTERVENTIONS FOR THE TREATMENT OF SOCIAL PHOBIA

During the past decade, a number of studies reporting the effects of various behavioral and cognitive-behavioral treatments of social phobia have appeared in the literature. Those that have used DSM-III or DSM-III-R diagnosed patient groups will be described and summarized here. However, it might be instructive to first discuss broadly the approach that has been taken in the treatment of social phobia.

One of the earliest behavioral treatments was social skills training. This intervention is based on the rationale that social anxiety stems from inadequate or inappropriate social skills and that remediating the deficits would enable the individual to enter social situations with significantly less distress. Although recent research indicates that only a subset of social phobics possesses inadequate social skills (Emmelkamp, Mersch, Vissia, & van der Helm, 1985; Turner, Beidel, Dancu, & Keys, 1986), social skills training also can be conceptualized as a counterconditioning procedure. The behavior rehearsal and initial practice in nonthreatening settings (usually the therapist's office), followed by further practice in more anxiety-producing, in vivo settings (i.e., hierarchical approach), are consistent with a counterconditioning model. Thus, social skills training may be beneficial for those with or without skills deficits.

More recently, a broad variety of interventions has been used, including some typically considered as classical behavioral strategies and others regarded as cognitive-behavioral. Other than this dichotomy, discussion of the anxiety-reduction mechanisms involved in behavioral treatments has not been in vogue in recent years. It is not our purpose here to discuss in detail the various models of anxiety or fear reduction, but we do think this is an important issue that deserves mention when treatment is discussed. It has become fashionable to refer to many fear reduction strategies as exposure procedures, and we do so in many cases throughout this chapter. However, exposure is not a treatment per se; rather, it is a procedure. The underlying mechanisms of change in these treatments traditionally were thought of as either extinction or habituation (e.g., flooding, response prevention) or counterconditioning (e.g., systematic desensitization, various methods of graduated exposure). These methods of fear reduction have been shown to be effective with most of the anxiety disorders and, in some cases, one method is considered more effective than another. Often, individual patient characteristics dictate which strategy should be used, rather than the particular disorder. Thus, effective use of these treatments requires knowledge of their theoretical basis as well as an intimate understanding of the clinical syndrome to be treated.

The newer cognitive-behavioral strategies differ from more traditional behavioral treatments in their emphasis on cognitive phenomena and their attempt to directly alter those cognitions thought to be important in maintaining the maladaptive behavior. Because treatment studies using cognitive-behavioral strategies include a heterogeneous group of interventions, cross-study comparisons are difficult. There are more standardized cognitive-behavioral interventions, such as Beck's cognitive therapy, but research addressing their effectiveness in the treatment of social phobia has not been published to date. To further complicate attempts to evaluate these therapies, treatment studies almost always incorporate elements of exposure (e.g., practicing speaking in front of others) into the protocol. Hence, it is difficult to ascertain whether these treatments offer a new mechanism of change or are actually variants of the more traditional behavioral interventions. In critiquing the various treatment studies of social phobia, these issues will be noted and discussed as appropriate. For a more complete discussion of theoretical issues related to cognitive-behavioral and behavioral treatments, the reader is referred to Beidel and Turner (1986).

Studies that have actually examined the process of fear change in the behavioral treatment of social phobia have not been conducted. Some preliminary data from our clinic suggest that when using flooding, that within-session habituation and between-session are necessary for successful treatment outcome. Despite our limited understanding of the specific elements necessary for successful outcome, many variations in the traditional procedures have evolved. Some, such as using anxiety management strategies simultaneously with an exposure procedure (e.g., Butler, Cullington, Munby, Amies, & Gelder, 1984), are actually counterintuitive to an extinction model of change (i.e., they provide escape), but the use of these strategies does not appear to diminish the basic effectiveness of the intervention. Such augmentation in the form of either anxiety management training or cognitive restructuring, does not appear to significantly enhance its effectiveness (Butler et al., 1984; Mattick, Peters, & Clarke, 1989).

STATUS OF CURRENT TREATMENT OUTCOME LITERATURE

All of the treatment studies to be reviewed here have used traditional behavioral interventions and/or cognitive-behavioral treatments; some have provided direct comparisons, and several have included various types of control groups. Two studies attempted to match specific intervention strategies to behavioral characteristics. Following this review, the treatment issues currently facing the field will be highlighted.

Three studies have investigated the efficacy of social skills training (SST) for social phobia. Falloon, Lloyd, and Harpin (1981) treated 16 social phobics with SST in dyads. Treatment consisted of two 6-hour sessions alternated with two therapist-unassisted in vivo practice sessions. SST consisted of instruction, modeling, role play, and therapist-assisted real-life practice. Concurrent with SST, patients were randomly assigned to treatment with propranolol (a beta-blocker) or pill placebo. The results indicated significant improvement on a number of self-report instruments and patient rating scales from pre- to posttreatment. Six-month follow-up data collected on several selected instruments showed additional significant pretreatment to follow-up improvement. On a role-play task, there was no significant heart rate change, but there was significant improvement on overt anxiety and competence ratings. However, assessment of these same variables during in vivo performance revealed no change from pre- to posttreatment. The addition of the drug had no effect on treatment outcome. Despite the improvements, the posttreatment ratings were 8.9 and 8.5 respectively, on 0-to-16 and 0-to-14 scales, indicating that there was still much room for further improvement. Perhaps the greatest limitations of this investigation were the lack of a control group, the brevity of the treatment, and the failure of the skills to generalize to real-life situations. Nonetheless, the results are promising and perhaps a more extensive treatment program would be more effective, particularly if only patients who exhibited social skills deficits were included.

In a second study, Stravynski, Marks, and Yule (1982) compared social skills training (SST) with and without cognitive restructuring (CR) in 22 social phobics. All of the patients received a DSM-III diagnosis of Avoidant Personality Disorder and half reported other significant psychological problems. Patients were assigned randomly to either traditional SST (instruction, modeling, role rehearsal, feedback, self-monitoring, and homework) or SST plus CR (SST/CR; using past situations as material to analyze activating events, irrational beliefs, emotional consequences, disputation of beliefs, and plans for new actions). Target behaviors were treated in 12 90-minute sessions using a multiple baseline design. Multivariate analyses comparing untreated behaviors yoked to treated behaviors indicated that frequency of performance and associated anxiety improved more rapidly and to a greater extent for the targeted behaviors than for the untreated behaviors. However, at posttreatment or 6-month follow-up, there were no group differences on self-monitoring data or the battery of self-report inventories. All patients showed identical improvement over time, but without generalization to intimate relationships. These results suggest that SST was effective for individuals with social phobia and concomitant Avoidant Personality Disorder. Because there were no between-group differences, CR did not appear to have enhanced these effects. Given the short-term nature of the treatment, the positive results that were maintained at follow-up are quite encouraging.

As part of a larger study, Lucock and Salkovskis (1988) used cognitively based SST to treat eight social phobics. Cognitive therapy, conducted in eight weekly group sessions, consisted of thought monitoring, reality testing (behavioral experiments), activity scheduling, and role playing with emphasis on identifying and challenging thoughts. Significant improvement was reported for patients' scores on the Social Avoidance and Distress Scale (SAD), and on the total score, world view, and view of the future subscale scores on the Cognitive Style Test (CST; Beck, 1976), but not on the view of self subscale. Patients' perception of the frequency of the occurrence of negative events significantly improved. Although the patients appeared improved as a result of this treatment, the findings were limited by the small sample size, assessment of outcome based solely on self-report, lack of treatment comparison groups, and absence of follow-up. A critical issue is the hypothesized mechanism of change. Although the intention was to examine the effectiveness of modifying cognitions in order to reduce social phobia symptoms, the social skills treatment encompassed both cognitive and behavioral components, rendering it difficult to attribute change to cognitive or behavioral strategies.

In contrast to SST, other investigators have used exposure as the focus of their treatment programs. In one of the first well-controlled studies, exposure therapy (EX) was compared to exposure therapy with anxiety management (EX/AM) and to a waiting-list control group (Butler et al., 1984). Forty-five social phobics were treated in individual treatment sessions. For both groups, exposure therapy was therapist-unassisted and involved the development of a hierarchy of situations to be practiced between treatment sessions. During the therapy sessions, patients received either anxiety management training or "associative therapy." Anxiety management was designed to train patients to identify early signs of anxiety and to use relaxation, distraction, and rational self-talk to control distress. Associative therapy served as a control for therapeutic contact for patients in the EX-only group and consisted of history taking and free association. At posttreatment, both treatment groups were significantly different from the waiting-list control group on all of the following outcome measures: patient ratings of phobic severity; difficulty of phobic hierarchy items; anticipatory anxiety, and peak anxiety during a behavioral task; blind assessor ratings of phobic severity and general anxiety; the Social Avoidance and Distress Scale (SAD); the Fear of Negative Evaluation Scale (FNE); the Fear Questionnaire (FQ); the Trait Anxiety subscale of the State–Trait Anxiety Inventory (STAI); and the Beck Depression Inventory (BDI). There were no differences among the groups on assessor ratings of depression or average number of social contacts. With respect to the two treatment groups, the EX/AM group showed significantly more improvement than the EX group only on the FNE and the SAD. When the EX and EX/AM groups were compared again at 6-month follow-up, the EX/AM group was superior on patient ratings of phobic severity and several self-report inventories (SAD, FNE, several subscales of the FQ, and the STAI trait subscale). No differences were found on any of the clinical ratings, on other subscales of the FQ, or on the BDI.

The results of this study clearly showed the superiority of graduated exposure over no treatment. Although it was concluded that the EX/AM treatment was superior at posttreatment, based on the FNE and SAD scores, given the large number of measures on which there were no differences, such a conclusion seems unwarranted. However, the follow-up results indicated that the addition of the anxiety management strategies may have facilitated continued improvement after the formal treatment program had ceased. This important finding deserves further study. Several issues related to this study warrant comment. First, the use of a graduated hierarchy coupled with exposure instructions to remain in the situation for a set time period (rather than until extinction) is not entirely congruent with an extinction model. It would be interesting to see the results of this treatment if sessions were terminated when anxiety had diminished, rather than after a fixed time. Terminating treatment sessions only after extinction had been achieved may have produced a more favorable long-term treatment outcome for the EX-only group. Second, at posttreatment, groups did not differ on anticipatory and peak anxiety levels during exposure to the phobic situations, which suggests that, despite the availability of the coping strategies, both groups were still experiencing equal distress. Another consideration is that a period of time is required for the patient to become proficient with these anxiety management skills. The significantly greater improvement for the EX/AM group at follow-up might be a result of increased proficiency in the use of the coping strategies.

Even so, at follow-up, the patients differed on only one of the three measures directly related to the phobia, but differed more widely on measures of general distress. Therefore, the effect of the anxiety management package may have been to decrease general distress rather than specific aspects of social phobia.

Using 34 social phobics, Emmelkamp et al. (1985) compared the effectiveness of three treatments: in vivo exposure (EX), rational-emotive therapy (RET), and self-instructional training (SIT). Treatment consisted of six group sessions. Patients in the EX group received approximately 120 minutes of exposure per session, in situations ranging from giving speeches to participating in activities in stores, on streets, and in bars. Habituation was not reported to be a criterion for termination of the exposure session. SIT consisted of generating and practicing adaptive cognitive responses. Preparing, confronting, coping, and reinforcing self-statements were practiced during imaginal presentation of social situations. Thus, this treatment included an extensive imaginal component. RET consisted of analyzing feelings in terms of activating events and beliefs about the events, and the emotional or behavioral consequences. Emphasis was placed on disputing "discomfort and ego anxiety." No imaginal or in vivo exposure was involved in RET.

The results of the study indicated that scores on the Phobic Anxiety Scale (an assessment of anxiety in five social situations) were significantly different at posttreatment. Planned contrasts (RET versus SIT, or EX versus RET and SIT combined) revealed that the RET patients had lower scores than did the SIT patients. EX patients' scores were not significantly different from those attained in the other two treatments combined. Also, the EX group's pulse rates, before and after interaction with a blind confederate of the opposite sex, were lower than rates among the other two treatment groups combined (their rates were not significantly different). There were no significant group differences at posttreatment on any of the self-report instruments. At 1-month follow-up, planned contrasts revealed that the EX group scored significantly lower on the Phobic Anxiety Scale than did the SIT and RET groups combined, and the latter two groups did not differ from each other. There were no differences on any of the other variables. The authors reported a number of within-group differences, but space limitations preclude a discussion of those findings. Overall, these treatments appeared effective. The authors concluded that all treatments were equally effective and, given the small number of between-group differences, this appears to be an accurate interpretation. Although SIT treatment was described as a purely cognitive treatment, the substantial imaginal rehearsal component, which inherently involves imaginal exposure, confounds the use of cognitive and traditional behavioral treatments, making it difficult to disentangle the therapeutic components. The 1-month follow-up provides only minimal information on the durability of treatment effects.

Heimberg et al. (1990) compared the effects of a combined cognitive and behavioral intervention to a placebo treatment. Forty-nine social phobics were treated in 12 group sessions. The cognitive-behavioral treatment (CBT) consisted of education about anxiety; identification, analysis, and disputation of problematic cognitions; exposure to group-simulated phobic situations; and homework assignments of exposure and cognitive restructuring. The placebo condition (PT) consisted of didactic presentations focused on various aspects of anxiety, and group discussion about difficult situations and methods of coping. At posttreatment and 6-month follow-up, the CBT group had significantly greater improvement on ratings of phobic severity. A considerably larger number of CBT patients also manifested clinical improvement on composite indexes. At posttreatment, the CBT patients had significantly lower anticipatory and performance ratings of subjective units of distress (SUDS) in a behavioral simulation, and the differences at follow-up were maintained for the performance SUDS ratings. There were no group differences on maximum anxiety ratings or ratio of positive to negative thoughts at posttreatment, but the CBT group was superior at follow-up. Finally, there were no differences at posttreatment or follow-up on any instruments included in the self-report battery. In summary, between-group differences were found on 4 of 11 outcome variables at posttreatment and on 5 of 11 at follow-up. The variables on which differences were found were important and central, and therefore suggestive of the superiority of CBT over PT, as the authors concluded. Given the study design and the inclusion of both cognitive and behavioral treatment strategies, no conclusions about the relative merits of any individual CBT component can be drawn.

Mattick and Peters (1988) compared the effectiveness of guided exposure with cognitive restructuring (GE/CR) and without it (GE) for 51 DSM-III social phobics. Treatment consisted of six group sessions. The GE treatment consisted of hierarchical, gradual, therapist-assisted exposure that continued until habituation occurred. For patients in the GE/CR condition, rational restructuring procedures (identifying problematic thoughts, analyzing and reevaluating situations) were applied during the exposure sessions. Both groups received homework assignments consistent with their treatment assignment.

At posttreatment, there were no differences between the groups. However, at 3-month follow-up, the GE/CR group showed significantly fewer difficulties than the GE group. The authors then conducted two orthogonal planned contrasts: (a) differences between the treatments from pretreatment to "after-treatment" (posttreatment and follow-up combined) and (b) differences between the treatments from posttreatment to follow-up, using pre-SAD scores as a covariate. In the first contrast, the GE/CR group was significantly superior on 2 of 11 variables: less avoidance of the highest 10 hierarchy items and lower ratings on the Fear Questionnaire target phobia scale. No significant differences were found for the second contrast. Endstate functioning and improvement ratings at posttreatment were not reported; however, at follow-up, the GE/CR group had significantly higher composite ratings for both indexes. The authors concluded that these data indicated the superiority of the combined treatment approach for social phobia. However, the lack of between-group differences at posttreatment on the majority of individual outcome measures does not seem to support this conclusion. As with most of the other studies, the treatment and the follow-up period were relatively short. No actual behavioral measures of social phobia were included.

In a follow-up investigation designed to more clearly address the specific role of cognitive therapy, cognitive restructuring only (CR), guided exposure only (GE), and their combination (COMB) were compared to a waiting-list control (WLC) group (Mattick et al., 1989). The sample consisted of 43 social phobics, treated in weekly group sessions for 6 weeks. CR consisted of both rational restructuring and rational-emotive therapy. It is important to note that patients in the CR condition were discouraged from entering phobic situations, and a treatment integrity check indicated that this group engaged in significantly fewer exposure experiences than the others. The GE condition was identical to that of Mattick and Peters (1988). The COMB treatment consisted of assessing the reality of fears and evaluations in the exposure situations. Dependent variables included an individualized, hierarchical Behavioral Avoidance Test (BAT), an extensive self-report battery, and two composite variables: endstate functioning and improvement, generated using the 3-month follow-up data. Data analytic procedures were quite complicated and included 3×4 repeated-measures analysis of variance (treatment group by time) and planned orthogonal contrasts. Pretreatment scores were compared to posttreatment and follow-up scores combined, and then posttreatment scores were compared to follow-up scores. Several additional planned orthogonal contrasts included comparisons of the WLC group versus the three treatment groups; the CR group versus the EX and COMB groups; and the EX group versus the COMB group.

The three treatment groups improved significantly more than the WLC on all variables except the FNE and the Irrational Beliefs Test (IBT). Within the three treatment groups, there were no significant differences on the composite indexes. The EX and COMB groups were significantly superior to the CR group on the BAT variables. However, the CR group was significantly more improved than the EX and COMB groups on the majority of the self-report instruments. The specific contrast of the COMB and the EX groups revealed that, from posttreatment to follow-up, the COMB group continued to show improvement on the BAT and one self-report instrument, whereas the EX group did not. (Numerous within-group changes were reported, but the reader is referred to the original report for those findings.) The authors concluded, primarily based on within-group differences, that the COMB and CR treatments were superior to the EX-only group. This conclusion seems questionable, given the lack of differences on the more conservative between-group analyses, including those on the endstate functioning and improvement indexes. Of particular concern is the unconventional combination of post-treatment and follow-up scores used in the analysis. Finally, although the authors concluded that changes in the cognitive variables might be mediators of the treatment effects, this conclusion is suspect, inasmuch as the treatment groups did not differ from the WLC group at posttreatment on the commonly accepted "cognitive" measures, the FNE and the IBT. As for most of the other studies, the treatment in this study was relatively short. However, the design provided the only clear comparisons of exposure and cognitive treatments currently available.

THE ISSUE OF SUBTYPES

To improve the efficacy of the various behavioral or cognitive-behavioral treatments, two studies examined the role of specific patient characteristics in treatment outcome. Based on the three-system model of fear (Lang, 1968), one might hypothesize that a treatment tailored to an individual's response profile may be more effective. Ost et al. (1981) compared social skills training (SST) and applied relaxation training (ART) in the treatment of 32 social phobics. Prior to treatment, patients were determined to be high physiological/low behavioral reactors or high behavioral/low physiological reactors, based on an analogue social interaction. Patients from each category were randomly assigned to each treatment group. Treatment consisted of 10 to 12 weekly sessions. ART consisted of progressive muscle relaxation, "release only" relaxation, cue-controlled relaxation, and differential relaxation, followed by the systematic use of relaxation during role play of social situations. The SST condition addressed both general social skills and individual problematic situations. Training consisted of instruction, modeling, role play, and feedback.

The results indicated that there was not a significant *across-treatments* difference between the physiological and behavioral reactors on the improvement index. However, within-group changes indicated that the behavioral reactors who received SST improved more than those who received ART on 6 of the 10 outcome measures, the majority of which assessed skill or subjective distress rather than autonomic response. In contrast, the physiological reactors who received ART improved more than those who received SST on 3 of the 10 outcome measures. Furthermore, when contrasting the two treatment groups who received treatment matched to their reaction pattern with the two groups who did not, the matched groups had significantly greater overall change than did the nonmatched groups. The authors concluded that these data supported their hypothesis that matching patient response to specific interventions would enhance treatment outcome, although this appears to be valid only for skills-deficient patients treated with SST.

In a similar investigation, Jerremalm et al. (1986) compared the effects of ART and self-instructional training (SIT) for 38 social phobic patients who were either high physiological/low cognitive or low physiological/high cognitive reactors, based on their responses during a social interaction. Within each response pattern, patients were randomly assigned to ART or SIT; a subset group was assigned to a waiting-list control (WLC) condition. The ART condition was the same as in Ost et al. (1981). The SIT treatment consisted of a modified version of stress-inoculation training, without the relaxation component. For the physiological reactors, the ART group differed from the WLC group on only the heart rate and behavioral ratings. Differences between the treatment groups favored SIT, suggesting that it was superior for the physiological reactors. These results are not consistent with the hypothesis. For the cognitive reactors, ART was only minimally different from the WLC. The comparison of the two active treatments indicated that SIT was superior to ART. In summary, the results of this study were not supportive of the hypothesis that these treatments would have differential effects for the physiological and cognitive reactor types. The authors concluded that the hypothesis was accurate for the cognitive reactors because of the superiority of SIT for this group on one of the three measures from the behavioral assessment and three of the seven self-report inventories. However, not only do these differences seem moderate at best, but the same pattern emerged for the physiological reactors. Also, the ART condition did not produce significant differences from the WLC on the majority of outcome measures. Overall, these results were not consistent with the hypothesized interaction effect but rather seemed to support a main effect for treatment outcome. Specifically, SIT was superior to ART, and ART was not significantly different from the WLC. Unfortunately, these data were not analyzed in a factorial design, and such a conclusion actually was not tested. However, in both studies, ART appeared to result in inferior treatment results. Finally, despite the lack of positive findings in this study, the general questions regarding subtypes of social phobics and differences in treatment among the subtypes are important and are in need of further investigation. Preliminary results from our ongoing investigation illustrate the potential importance of considering subtypes when evaluating treatment response. As depicted in Table 2.5, the generalized social phobics were more severe than the specific social phobics at pretreatment on every measure of psychopathology except one. Although they appeared to be improved at posttreatment, their scores (with two exceptions) were still higher than the *pretreatment* scores of the specific subtype.

TABLE 2.5 Comparison of Pretreatment (Pre) and Posttreatment (Post) Scores for Specific and Generalized Social Phobia Subtypes (Patients Treated with Flooding)

	Specific	Generalized
Self-Report		
SPAI: Difference Score		
Pre	*72.9*	110.8
Post	48.1	*94.3*
STAI:		
State		
Pre	*32.3*	40.0
Post	30.3	*47.4*
Trait		
Pre	*30.4*	46.8
Post	31.3	*44.2*
SAD		
Pre	*7.7*	20.6
Post	3.3	*18.2*
FNE		
Pre	*13.0*	25.11
Post	13.4	*22.11*
FQ: Social Phobia		
Pre	*10.6*	21.4
Post	3.0	*15.3*
Behavioral Assessment		
Speech Length		
Pre	*371.4*	284.7
Post	526.2	*478.4*
SUDS		
Pre	*4.4*	6.9
Post	2.1	*4.6*
SISST:		
Positive		
Pre	*41.8*	26.8
Post	52.8	*35.3*
Negative		
Pre	*41.6*	51.9
Post	25.0	*32.1*
Speech Pulse		
Pre	*98.3*	123.9
Post	93.3	*100.4*
Independent Evaluator Ratings		
Hamilton Anxiety Scale		
Pre	*18.0*	24.0
Post	6.0	*17.0*
CGI Severity		
Pre	*3.9*	4.6
Post	2.0	*3.3*
Avoidance Rating		
Pre	*3.6*	3.6
Post	0.8	*1.9*

Case Description

The Anxiety Disorders Clinic at Western Psychiatric Institute and Clinic has an active treatment program for social phobia. The core of this program is flooding, which is currently being evaluated in a large treatment outcome study. The following case illustrates the use of flooding in the treatment of social phobia. Following the description of the patient and the intervention procedures, several issues regarding the implementation of the treatment program will be discussed.

Patient Description

The patient was a 28-year-old single male who was self-referred for treatment of public speaking fears. He had a lifelong history of shyness and difficulty meeting new people; however, these problems only became significant when he gained a position as a litigating attorney and had to speak in court. He avoided public speaking situations whenever possible, fearing that others would see him as unsophisticated, uneducated, and incompetent. On occasions when he could not avoid public speaking, he experienced many somatic symptoms prior to and during the engagement, including rapid heart beat, trembling of his hands and legs, blushing, sweating, nausea, dizziness, chest pain, difficulty breathing, and difficulty concentrating. His distress was so severe that he had seriously considered a career change so that he would not have to speak in front of others.

After the initial assessment, it became clear that this patient also experienced significant fear of general social interactions. He avoided talking to new people, those in authority, and particularly females, whenever possible. These situations were most difficult for him when he stated his opinion or defended his views in front of others. He avoided eating or writing in public, riding public transportation, and standing in crowded elevators or laundromats, because of fears that others would evaluate him negatively and notice his anxiety. In such situations, his symptoms were identical to those he experienced when faced with public speaking but were of lesser severity. To decrease his anxiety in social situations, he often drank 5 to 10 beers at bars or parties. He had gotten into fights when drinking and had been arrested for driving while under the influence of alcohol. The diagnosis was social phobia, generalized subtype.

Treatment

The treatment plan consisted of flooding (exposure), wherein the patient was exposed to the salient fear cues within the relevant situations. During treatment sessions, he was exposed to the fear cues within the context of a habituation paradigm (i.e., until his subjective anxiety level, as reported on a 1 to 8 SUDS scale, returned to the baseline, or near baseline, level). Thus, the length of the sessions was determined by the patient's response. Flooding was conducted twice per week for the first 8 weeks and then assigned for homework for an additional 4 weeks; 20 treatment sessions were conducted. Initially, flooding was conducted imaginally. Beginning with session 10, in vivo flooding was instituted, first with therapist assistance and then without the therapist's presence. The imaginal flooding scene was designed to address *all* of the pertinent cues related to the patient's fear, as follows:

> You are walking into the courtroom where you have spoken many times. As you look around, you see the judge on the bench and the jury off to the side. The rest of the room is filled with colleagues from your firm, your boss, well-respected attorneys from other firms, and attorneys with whom you attended law school. As you approach the center of the courtroom to begin your presentation, you see that all attention is focused on you. You try to begin to speak, but

words are not coming out of your mouth. Slowly, some words start to come out, but you are so nervous you are not sure what you are saying. Your mind has gone blank and you cannot think of what to say next. As you speak, your legs and hands are shaking quite hard. It is clearly visible to others. Your heart is beating faster and faster and there is a tightness in your chest. The lump in your throat and the difficulty you are having catching your breath make it harder and harder to keep speaking. As you look around the room, you can clearly see the disapproving stares. These people can tell how nervous you are and they are all questioning your competence. They are thinking that you look like an uneducated hick who never should have become an attorney. Your boss sees how poorly you are doing and thinks that he will probably have to suggest that you change jobs. As you continue to talk, your hands and forehead become visibly sweaty and your voice, your hands, and your legs continue to shake. You start to feel light-headed and nauseous. Everyone looks either bored or amazed at how you could be doing such a poor job, but you have no choice but to continue speaking.

Initially, this patient experienced difficulty with the imaginal flooding procedure. For example, during the first session, his subjective anxiety rose to 8 (on a 1 to 8 SUDS scale), where it remained for at least 25 minutes. Suddenly, he then appeared to have stopped responding completely, as if he had fallen asleep. Upon questioning by the therapist, the patient reported that he must have fainted during the flooding session. Actually, he had "escaped" from the distress elicited by the imaginal scene by ceasing participation in the imaginal exposure. The therapist discussed the parallel between his behavior in the flooding session and his usual pattern of escaping or avoiding other such situations and pointed out that, despite his distress, he would not benefit from the treatment if he continued to escape from the imaginal exposure procedures.

In subsequent imaginal sessions, the patient's SUDS ratings showed a more characteristic response pattern, with anxiety increasing to the highest SUDS level of 8 and then decreasing in a gradual manner over a 110-minute period. At times, the patient still "escaped" the scene for brief periods of time and had to be instructed to resume the imaginal exposure. As often happens, the initial imaginal sessions revealed new information regarding the fear complex, and these cues were added to the scene. After 8 imaginal sessions, his anxiety peaked at 5 and decreased to 1 within 45 minutes. At that point, in vivo flooding was introduced and alternated with continued imaginal flooding. During the in vivo flooding, the patient was instructed to stand and speak in front of a panel of three people (not including the therapist). He responded to questions about law, politics, and his views on several controversial issues. Across 4 in vivo sessions, his peak anxiety level decreased from 5 to 4 (see Figure 2.1).

After 4 weeks of alternating imaginal and in vivo sessions, therapist assistance during the flooding sessions was discontinued. The patient was instructed to conduct self-guided exposure. Specific situations that he had avoided previously were assigned (e.g., talking to his boss about particular cases, approaching a review board about cases, talking to females in bars without having any alcohol, and talking to strangers on a bus). In each case, he was instructed not to prematurely escape the situation (e.g., discontinue conversations before their natural end); whenever possible, he was to stay in the situation until his anxiety decreased. He was able to enter most of the situations. Whenever he did so, he reported a decrease in his fear and anxiety about entering the situation again. Some situations required strong encouragement from the therapist and assurances that his anxiety would eventually decrease and that the situations would become gradually easier.

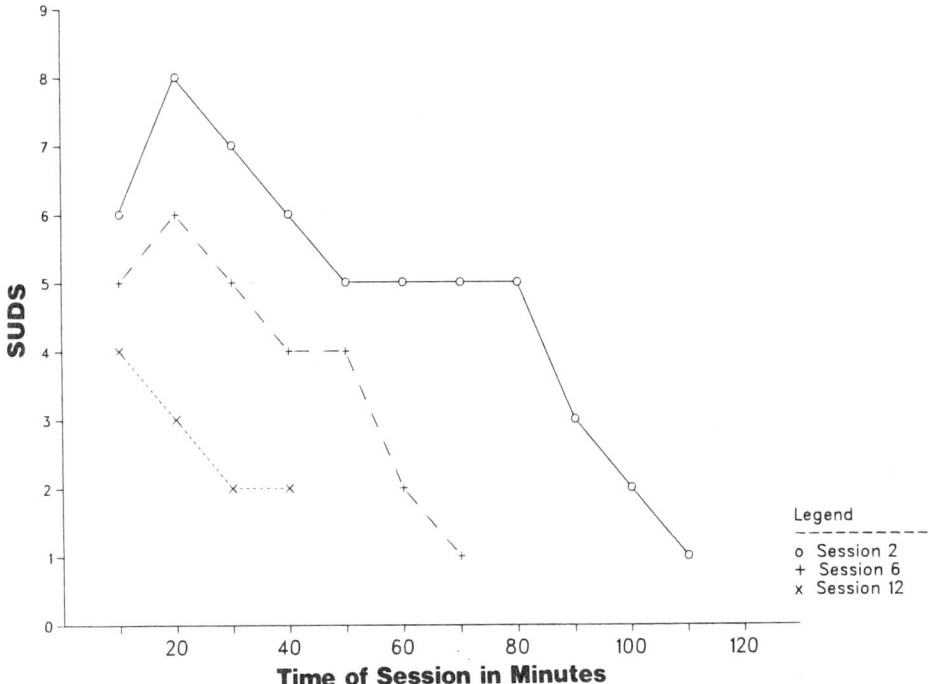

Figure 2.1. Within-and between-session extinction using flooding. *Note.* Reprinted by permission of Methuen & Co. Publishers, from *The Structure of Human Abilities* (p. 22) by P. E. Vernon, 1960.

After 4 weeks of self-guided exposure, he showed a significant increase in the number of situations he could enter, and he was feeling less anxiety than prior to treatment. He was able to identify and to enter situations that he usually had avoided or escaped, and was pleased with his progress. Treatment was terminated at this point with the understanding that any remaining discomfort that continued should eventually decrease with further self-guided exposure and should eventually decrease. At posttreatment, he was able to complete a 10-minute speech; prior to treatment, he had chosen to terminate the speech early (i.e., escaped from the task). His SUDS rating during the task decreased from a pretreatment rating of 4 to a posttreatment rating of 2. At 3-month follow-up, he was entering many more social situations and typically experienced anxiety levels of 1 to 3. His Social Phobia and Anxiety Inventory (SPAI) score had decreased from 115 to 85, his SAD score had decreased from 24 to 10, and his FNE score had decreased from 25 to 6. His social phobia score on the Fear Questionnaire had decreased from 18 to 11.

This case demonstrates both the severity of social dysfunction often found in someone seeking treatment for "public speaking" fear, and some of the difficulties that can occur when implementing a flooding program. Many patients can become severely distressed even when the exposure is conducted in an imaginal format, and often will attempt to escape or minimize their distress by limiting their participation in the treatment session. Usually, the reaction is not as extreme as in this patient, who pretended to faint in order to stop the session. However, some patients will endeavor to control their anxiety by imagining only the least distressing parts of the scene or by deliberately imagining themselves "coping well" with the phobic stimulus. These practices are subtle (or perhaps not so subtle) means of escape and interfere with the extinction process. As happened in this case, they can be managed with careful explanation and vigilance on the part of the therapist. The patient was improved markedly as a result of the behavioral treatment, but in all likelihood would need to continue to place himself in formerly anxiety-producing situations in order to maintain his treatment gains. For many individuals, these situations frequently present themselves, and specific efforts to seek out opportunities are not necessary. Other patients need to make special arrangements in order to continue their practice. Membership in civic organizations, Toastmasters, or Dale Carnegie classes is often useful in this regard. In essence, the effective use of this type of treatment for social phobia requires a high degree of clinical and technical expertise as well as considerable creativity.

Pharmacological Treatment

The empirical studies examining the effectiveness of drugs for the treatment of social phobia are even fewer than those in the existing behavioral literature. Although the extant studies used relatively small samples and most suffered from a number of serious methodological flaws, they serve to provide some initial guidance in the use of pharmacological agents. There are a number of case studies and small open clinical trials, but this review will be limited to group studies that involve the use of DSM-III or DSM-III-R diagnosed social phobics.

As a result of their reported effectiveness in treating social anxiety among mixed phobic states (Solyom, Solyom, & LaPierre, 1981; Tyrer, Candy, & Kelly, 1973), monoamine oxidase inhibitors (MAOIs) have received considerable attention as a potential treatment for social phobia. Liebowitz and his colleagues published a series of reports describing the treatment of social phobics with the MAOI drug phenelzine. In summarizing these findings, Liebowitz et al. (1988) reported a response rate of 62% for phenelzine compared to 25% for placebo. Similarly, Versiani, Mundim, Nardi, and Liebowitz (1988) reported that 18 patients were considered marked responders, 4 moderate responders, and 6 nonresponders to phenelzine. One of the difficulties with interpreting the results of these studies is that the judgment of improvement was based on global clinical ratings. Accepting the results as they are reported, it appears that phenelzine was effective for 50 to 60% of social phobics.

A second class of drugs that have been used in treating social phobia is the beta-blockers. Early reports indicating that these drugs suppressed performance anxiety—and in some cases enhanced performance (particularly among musicians)—provided the basis for considering this group of drugs as a potential treatment for social phobia (Gossard, Dennis, & Debush, 1984; Neftel et al., 1982). Beta-blockers have been shown to have only modest effects with pervasive anxiety states but they have a potent effect on the somatic symptoms associated with anxiety (Tyrer & Lader, 1974). Many of the somatic symptoms experienced by social phobics primarily are mediated by the beta-adrenergic system (Gorman & Gorman, 1987)—a fact that provides a stronger theoretical rationale for using beta-blockers as a treatment for social phobics.

In the Liebowitz et al. (1988) study, one group of patients received atenolol. The response rate for this drug was reported to be 32%, not much different from the 25% placebo response rate. However, when the patients were divided into generalized and specific subtypes, the atenolol response rate for the specific subtype was 50%. In an ongoing study in our clinic, Turner et al. (1991) also found a 25% improvement rate for atenolol. When divided by specific and generalized subtype, improvement rates of 50% and 9.5% respectively were obtained. These studies suggest that if atenolol has a role in the treatment of social phobia, it is likely to be for the specific subtype only.

At least two studies have examined the relative efficacy of behavior therapy (or cognitive-behavior therapy) and pharmacotherapy. Clark and Agras (1991) compared buspirone, a combination of buspirone and a group cognitive-behavioral treatment (CBT), CBT with placebo, and placebo alone, in treating 34 musicians with stage fright who met DSM-III criteria for social phobia. When the two CBT treatment groups were compared to the drug-treatment-only groups, the CBT groups were significantly more improved on a number of dependent variables. Buspirone was essentially no different from placebo. Interestingly, in a number of cases, including the posttreatment to 1-month follow-up assessment, the CBT-plus-placebo group did best (i.e., better than the CBT-plus-buspirone group). This result suggests that buspirone actually may serve to decrease the effectiveness of CBT. The lack of positive findings for buspirone is consistent with our clinical experience, which indicates that this drug appears to be of limited value in treating any of the anxiety disorders.

Turner et al. (1991) examined the effectiveness of flooding, atenolol, and placebo in a sample of 75 social phobics. In addition, a nonrandomized group of patients was treated with combined atenolol and flooding. The results indicated that the flooding treatment was significantly better than atenolol and placebo on composite indexes of improvement and endstate status. Atenolol and placebo essentially resulted in similar, nonsignificant effects. This pattern of results was maintained over a 6-month follow-up interval. Visual inspection of response curves indicated that the combined flooding and atenolol group responded essentially the same as the flooding-only group, suggesting that flooding was the active component of the treatment. When the subjects were divided into specific and generalized subtypes, both atenolol and flooding were more effective for the specific subtype, but flooding was still significantly superior to atenolol. Although less effective for the generalized subtype, flooding clearly was the most effective treatment.

There have been a number of other smaller reports on the use of the newer high-potency benzodiazepines (e.g., alprazolam and clonazepam) in the treatment of social phobia. However, the number of patients involved is so small that we have elected not to describe them in any detail here. There is some indication that these drugs might be of use in the treatment of social phobia, but a definitive conclusion will have to await further study. One problem with these drugs is that they have a considerable addictive potential (psychological and physiological). Alprazolam, in particular, can have very dangerous side effects and it is not entirely clear that these drugs can be withdrawn safely. Appropriate caution should be exercised.

SUMMARY OF TREATMENT FINDINGS

The most consistent finding is that, whether delivered individually or in groups, interventions consisting of exposure and/or more cognitively oriented procedures appear to be superior to no treatment, placebo control groups, or drugs. Various methods of exposure seem to be effective, suggesting that the exact procedure may not be the most important factor. Similarly, the myriad cognitive methods all seem to be efficacious. Current comparisons of behavioral and cognitive-behavioral interventions are difficult because, with the exception of one study, all the interventions include significant components of exposure. In the study where a comparison was appropriate (Mattick et al., 1989), there were few differences between the treatments, although the results were difficult to interpret because of the unconventional data analytic strategy. Therefore, it is still very unclear whether augmentation in the form of cognitive strategies increases the effectiveness of more traditional behavioral treatments.

The studies examining the effectiveness of drugs in the treatment of social phobia have produced the following results:

1. Phenelzine appears to be effective for approximately 50 to 60% of social phobics. However, it is not entirely clear how effectiveness was determined in the studies leading to this figure (Liebowitz et al., 1988).
2. Atenolol produces essentially the same response rate as does placebo. However, it is somewhat more effective for the specific subtype. An examination of the effect of atenolol on social phobics with autonomic nervous system reactivity versus those without reactivity would be interesting. One might hypothesize that atenolol should be more effective for the reactors.
3. The comparisons of flooding or cognitive-behavioral treatments to drugs conducted so far show the drugs to be less effective, but additional well-designed studies that take patient variables into account are needed.
4. Preliminary results suggest that at least one drug (buspirone) may have decreased the effectiveness of cognitive-behavioral treatment, rather than facilitating its effects.

A major limitation in evaluating the effectiveness of current treatments is that follow-up data exist only for short intervals, if at all. Because the durability of these interventions is unknown, an overall evaluation of their worth is impossible. On a related point, several studies (Butler et al., 1984; Heimberg et al., 1990) have documented that even when interventions did not appear to be significantly different from control groups at posttreatment, they were so at follow-up. In these studies, continued exposure to the feared situations during the follow-up period may have been the crucial variable. These findings indicate that a treatment program longer than the typical 6 to 12 treatment sessions may be necessary to achieve maximum benefit and to promote permanent treatment gains, and that longer-term follow-up periods are desirable.

The population of social phobics is not homogeneous, as was noted in the discussion of the clinical syndrome. A number of potentially significant dimensions, including the issue of subtypes, the presence of other Axis I and II disorders, and the patterns of autonomic nervous system reactivity have been identified. Early studies by Öst and his colleagues attempted to improve treatment response by constructing subgroups of patients based on response characteristics (matching the treatment to cognitive or physiological responsiveness), an approach that appeared only somewhat effective. However, matching treatments with various response patterns or clinical profiles is worthy of further study.

The issue of subtypes is an important and continuing one for the treatment of social phobia. The relevant dimension, however, may not be the pattern of emotional distress but rather the pervasiveness of the patient's fears. Data from the Liebowitz et al. (1988) study suggested that MAOIs were superior for the generalized subtype, but MAOIs and beta-blockers were equally effective for the specific subtype. Furthermore, data from our current investigation (Turner et al., 1991) have indicated that a 20-session behavioral treatment program may be less effective for social phobics with the generalized subtype. Both of these studies indicated that the generalized subtype may represent a group particularly refractory to treatment, and that continuing to group all social phobics together in outcome studies may obscure meaningful parameters predictive of treatment outcome.

Finally, avoidant personality disorder is another important variable to examine in treatment outcome studies. Despite its obvious classification difficulties, this condition becomes important because the current diagnostic criteria allow social phobia and avoidant personality disorder to be diagnosed concurrently, and the two syndromes as currently defined are very similar. It is unclear exactly where the boundary between these two disorders lies. There are data to support the conclusion that, when both conditions are present in social phobics, the syndrome is much more severe. Moreover, our clinical impression is that the presence of avoidant personality disorder, or of significant features of this disorder, complicates treatment and may dictate alternative approaches. Currently, several alternatives to enhance treatment outcome are being explored in our clinic.

REFERENCES

American Psychiatric Association. (1980). *Diagnostic and statistical manual of mental disorders* (3rd ed.). Washington, DC: Author.

American Psychiatric Association. (1987). *Diagnostic and statistical manual of mental disorders* (3rd ed. rev.). Washington, DC: Author.

Amies, P. L., Gelder, M. G., & Shaw, P. M. (1983). Social phobia: A comparative clinical study. *British Journal of Psychiatry, 142,* 174–179.

Beck, A. T. (1976). *Cognitive therapy and the emotional disorders.* New York: International Universities Press.

Beidel, D. C. (1988). Psychophysiological assessment of anxious emotional states in children. *Journal of Abnormal Psychology, 97,* 80–82.

Beidel, D. C., & Turner, S. M. (1986). A critique of the theoretical bases of cognitive behavior theories and therapies. *Clinical Psychology Review, 6,* 177–197.

Beidel, D. C., Turner, S. M., & Dancu, C. V. (1985). Physiological, cognitive and behavioral aspects of social anxiety. *Behaviour Research and Therapy, 23,* 109–117.

Butler, G., Cullington, A., Munby, M., Amies, P., & Gelder, M. (1984). Exposure and anxiety management in the treatment of social phobia. *Journal of Consulting and Clinical Psychology, 52,* 642–650.

Clark, D. B., & Agras, S. (1991). The assessment and treatment of performance anxiety in musicians. *American Journal of Psychiatry, 148,* 598–605.

Emmelkamp, P. M. G., Mersch, P. P., Vissia, E., & van der Helm, M. (1985). Social phobia: A comparative evaluation of cognitive and behavioral interventions. *Behaviour Research and Therapy, 23,* 365–369.

Falloon, I. R. H., Lloyd, G. G., & Harpin, R. E. (1981). The treatment of social phobia: Real life rehearsal with nonprofessional therapists. *Journal of Nervous and Mental Disease, 169,* 180–184.

Gorman, J. M., & Gorman, L. F. (1987). Drug treatment of social phobia. *Journal of Affective Disorders, 13,* 183–192.

Gossard, D., Dennis, C., & Debush, R. F. (1984). Use of beta-blocking agents to relieve stress of presentation at an international cardiology meeting: Results of a survey. *American Journal of Cardiology, 54,* 240–241.

Heimberg, R. G., Hope, D. A., Dodge, C. S., & Becker, R. E. (1990). DSM-III-R subtypes of social phobia: Comparison of generalized social phobics and public speaking phobics. *Journal of Nervous and Mental Disease, 178,* 172–179.

Heimberg, R. G., Dodge, C. S., Hope, D. A., Kennedy, C. R., Zollo, L., & Becker, R. E. (1990). Cognitive behavioral treatment of social phobia: Comparison to a credible placebo control. *Cognitive Therapy and Research, 178,* 172–179.

Jerremalm, A., Jansson, L., & Ost, L. (1986). Cognitive and physiological reactivity and the effects of different behavioral methods in the treatment of social phobia. *Behaviour Research and Therapy, 24,* 171–180.

Kagan, J., Reznick, J. S., & Snidman, N. (1988). Biological bases of childhood shyness. *Science, 240,* 167–171.

Kagan, J., Reznick, J. S., Snidman, N., Gibbons, X. X., and Johnson, M. O. (1988). Childhood derivatives of inhibition and lack of inhibition to the unfamiliar. *Child Development, 59,* 1580–1589.

Klass, E. T., DiNardo, P. A., & Barlow, D. H. (1989). DSM-III-R personality diagnoses in anxiety disorder patients. *Comprehensive Psychiatry, 30,* 251–258.

Lang, P. J. (1968). Fear reduction and fear behavior: Problems in treating a construct. In J. M. Shlien (Ed.), *Research in psychotherapy, Vol. 3.* Washington, DC: American Psychological Association.

Liebowitz, M. R., Gorman, J. M., Fyer, A. J., & Klein, D. F. (1985). Social phobia. *Archives of General Psychiatry, 42,* 729–736.

Liebowitz, M. R., Gorman, J. M., Fyer, A. J., Campeas, R., Levin, A. P., Sandberg, D., Hollander, E., Papp, L., & Goetz, D. (1988). Pharmacotherapy of social phobia: An interim report of a placebo controlled comparison of phenelzine and atenolol. *Journal of Clinical Psychiatry, 49,* 252–257.

Lucock, M. P., & Salkovskis, P. M. (1988). Cognitive factors in social anxiety and its treatment. *Behaviour Research and Therapy, 26,* 297–302.

Marks, I. M. (1970). The classification of phobic disorders. *British Journal of Psychiatry, 116,* 377–386.

Marks, I., & Gelder, M. G. (1966). Different onset ages in varieties of phobias. *American Journal of Psychiatry, 123,* 218–221.

Mattick, R. P., & Peters, L. (1988). Treatment of severe social phobia: Effects of guided exposure with and without cognitive restructuring. *Journal of Consulting and Clinical Psychology, 56,* 251–260.

Mattick, R. P., Peters, L., & Clarke, J. C. (1989). Exposure and cognitive restructuring for severe social phobia. *Behavior Therapy, 20,* 3–23.

Mineka, S. (1985). Animal models of anxiety-based disorders: Their usefulness and limitations. In A. H. Tuma & J. D. Maser (Eds.), *Anxiety and the anxiety disorders* (pp. 199–244). Hillsdale, NJ: Erlbaum.

Neftel, K. A., Adler, R. H., Kappell, L., Rossi, M., Dolder, M., Kaser, H. E., Bruggesser, H. H., & Vorkauf, H. (1982). Stage fright in musicians: A model illustrating the effects of beta-blockers. *Psychosomatic Medicine, 44,* 461–469.

Öhman, A. (1986). Face the beast and fear the face: Animal and social fears as prototypes for evolutionary analyses of emotion. *Psychophysiology, 23,* 123–145.

Öst, L. G. (1987). Age of onset in different phobias. *Journal of Abnormal Psychology, 96,* 223–229.

Öst, L. G., Jerremalm, A., & Johansson, J. (1981). Individual response patterns and the effects of different behavioral methods in the treatment of social phobia. *Behaviour Research and Therapy, 19,* 1–16.

Pollard, C. A., & Henderson, J. G. (1988). Four types of social phobia in a community sample. *Journal of Nervous and Mental Disease, 176,* 440–445.

Reich, J., & Yates, W. (1988). A pilot study of treatment of social phobia with alprazolam. *American Journal of Psychiatry, 145,* 590–594.

Sanderson, W. C., Rapee, R. M., & Barlow, D. H. (1987). The DSM-III-R revised anxiety disorder categories: Descriptors and patterns of comorbidity. Paper presented at the annual meeting of the Association for Advancement of Behavior Therapy, Boston, MA.

Solyom, C., Solyom, L., & LaPierre, Y. (1981). Phenelzine and exposure in the treatment of phobias. *Biological Psychiatry, 16,* 239–247.

Spitzer, R. L., Williams, J. B. W., Gibbon, M., & First, M. B. (1988). *Structured clinical interview for DSM-III-R Axis II Personality Disorders.* Biometrics Research Department, New York State Psychiatric Institute.

Stravynski, A., Marks, I., & Yule, W. (1982). Social skills problems in neurotic outpatients: Social skills training with and without cognitive modification. *Archives of General Psychiatry, 39,* 1378–1385.

Suomi, S. J. (1986). Anxiety in young nonhuman primates. In R. Gittelman (Ed.), *Anxiety disorders of childhood* (pp. 1–23). New York: Guilford.

Torgersen, S. (1983). Genetic factors in anxiety disorders. *Archives of General Psychiatry, 40,* 1085–1089.

Turner, S. M., & Beidel, D. C. (1985). Empirically derived subtypes of social anxiety. *Behavior Therapy, 16,* 384–392.

Turner, S. M., Beidel, D. C., Borden, J. W., Stanley, M. A., & Jacob, R. G. (1991). Social phobia: Axis I and II correlates. *Journal of Abnormal Psychology.*

Turner, S. M., Beidel, D. C., Dancu, C. V., & Keys, D. J. (1986). Psychopathology of social phobia and comparison to avoidant personality disorder. *Journal of Abnormal Psychology, 95,* 389–394.

Turner, S. M., Beidel, D. C., & Larkin, K. T. (1986). Situational determinants of social anxiety in clinic and nonclinic samples: Physiological and cognitive correlates. *Journal of Consulting and Clinical Psychology, 54,* 523–527.

Turner, S. M., McCann, B. S., Beidel, D. C., & Mezzich, J. B. (1986). DSM-III classification of anxiety disorders: A psychometric study. *Journal of Abnormal Psychology, 95,* 168–172.

Turner, S. M., Beidel, D. C., & Jacob, R. G. (1991). *Pharmacological and behavioral treatment of social phobia.* Unpublished manuscript, University of Pittsburgh.

Turner, S. M., Beidel, D. C., & Townsley, R. M. (1990). Social phobia: Relationship to shyness. *Behaviour Research and Therapy, 28,* 497–505.

Turner, S. M., Beidel, D. C., & Townsley, R. M. (in press). Social phobia: A comparison of specific and generalized subtypes and avoidant personality disorder. *Journal of Abnormal Psychology.*

Tyrer, P., Candy, J., & Kelly, D. A. (1973). A study of the clinical effects of phenelzine and placebo in the treatment of phobic anxiety. *Psychopharmacologia, 32,* 237–254.

Tyrer, P. J., & Lader, M. H. (1974). Response to propranolol: Diazepam in somatic and psychic anxiety. *British Medical Journal, 2,* 14–16.

Versiani, M., Mundim, F. D., Nardi, A. E., & Liebowitz, M. R. (1988). Tranylcypromine in social phobia. *Journal of Clinical Psychopharmacology, 8,* 279–283.

Zimbardo, P. G., Pilkonis, P. A., & Norwood, R. M. (1975). The social disease called shyness. *Psychology Today, 8,* 68–72.

CHAPTER 3

Cognitive-Behavioral Treatment of Panic Disorder, Agoraphobia, and Generalized Anxiety Disorder

MICHELLE G. CRASKE, RONALD M. RAPEE, and DAVID H. BARLOW

Few areas have witnessed more rapid and startling advances in approaches to behavioral treatment than the anxiety disorders. During the 1980s, we developed a number of efficient and productive treatments for the variety of anxiety disorders that so frequently confront clinicians. Some of the more significant advances have been made in treatment of the anxiety states, including panic disorder and generalized anxiety disorder. Little evidence existed previously for the effectiveness of psychological treatments for these disorders; their high prevalence accounts in part for the very high rates of prescription of benzodiazepines and other anxiolytics (Barlow, 1988). With new treatments for panic disorder and generalized anxiety disorder, the 1990s may see benzodiazepines and other pharmacological approaches replaced by specific, powerful, and effective cognitive-behavioral techniques. For certain cases, combinations of pharmacological and behavioral approaches may be the most desirable treatment.

This chapter presents cognitive-behavioral approaches to the treatment of panic disorder, agoraphobia, and generalized anxiety disorder; many of the approaches were devised in our own setting. For each disorder, an outline of the features of the clinical syndrome and presenting characteristics precedes description of the treatment procedures and their efficacy. Proposed mechanisms of action of successful treatments are described in brief for each treatment procedure. The most recent advances in cognitive-behavioral treatments are emphasized.

PANIC DISORDER AND AGORAPHOBIA

Clinical Syndrome

Features

In the most recent edition of the DSM-III-R (American Psychiatric Association, 1987), panic attacks are defined as acute episodes of intense fear or discomfort, associated on at least one occasion with 4 of 13 physical and cognitive symptoms (the presence of fewer than 4 symptoms may not necessarily represent a functionally different phenomenon) (Barlow & Craske, 1989). The criteria for panic disorder (PD) specify that at least one attack must be "unexpected," and that the attacks must have occurred at least 4 times within 4 weeks, or have been followed by at least 1 month of apprehension about their recurrence. (Revisions to the criteria may be forthcoming with the projected publication of DSM-IV in 1992–1993.) The main defining features are (a) the experience of a sudden rush of intense fear or discomfort for no apparent reason, which is distinct from gradually building anxious arousal and from phobic reactions to clearly discernible, circumscribed stimuli; and (b) apprehension about the attacks.

The symptoms reported most frequently during panic attacks include dizziness, unsteadiness or faintness, palpitations or tachycardia, trembling/shaking, parasthesias, sweating, and fears of going crazy and losing control (Barlow et al., 1985; Oei, Craske, Rapee, DiNardo, & Barlow, 1989, unpublished raw data; Rapee, Craske, & Barlow, 1990). The frequency with which panic attacks occur varies considerably over time, and symptoms experienced during panic attacks vary considerably from one attack to another (Rapee, Craske, & Barlow, 1990). However, fluctuations in frequency and symptomatology may be artifacts of nonstandardized and/or liberal definitions of panic attacks.

Several typologies have been suggested for the description of panic attacks (Barlow, 1988; Klein & Klein, 1989; Sheehan & Sheehan, 1983). Barlow (1988) suggested a 2 × 2 typology, comprising cued–uncued and expected–unexpected dimensions. In this typology, cue refers to an event that has a demonstrated functional relationship with the occurrence of panic. Cues may be internal (e.g., images, bodily sensations, and cognitions) or external. Cued panics are panics that have a discriminable cue. A cued, expected panic might be experienced while waiting in line, when a panic was fully anticipated on that particular occasion. A cued, unexpected panic might also be experienced while waiting in line, when a panic was minimally anticipated on that particular occasion. An uncued, expected panic is exemplified by a generalized expectancy of panicking, although not in association with any specific cue (e.g., "I know that I am going to panic some time today, but I do not know when"). Uncued, unexpected panics are "out of the blue" attacks.

Street, Craske, and Barlow (1989) observed the following distribution of 100 attacks from PD subjects:

	Percent
Uncued/unexpected	12.5
Uncued/expected	1.4
Cued/unexpected	18.1
Cued/expected	68.1

Among the general population, 6 to 12% report having experienced a panic attack that occurred for no apparent reason (Brown, Cash, & Deagle, 1988; Craske & Krueger, 1990; Norton, Dorward, & Cox, 1980; Rapee, Ancis, & Barlow, 1988; Salge, Beck, & Logan, 1988; Telch, Lucas, & Nelson, 1989). However, only 2 to 6% meet criteria for panic disorder (PD) or panic disorder with agoraphobia (PDA). What differentiates infrequent panickers from those who go on to develop PD? Barlow (1988) has conceptualized the significant variable as anxious apprehension over the experience of panic. Associated with panic-apprehension are features such as heightened chronic arousal, body vigilance or selectivity of attention, and cognitive misappraisals of bodily cues, which are believed to result in a maintained pattern of continuing panic and apprehension. Persons with PD/PDA do tend to misappraise bodily symptoms as threatening (Chambless, Caputo, Bright, & Gallagher, 1984; Reiss, Peterson, Gursky, & McNally, 1986), report more arousal symptomatology (Holt & Andrews, 1989), and be more interoceptively aware (Ehlers & Margraf, 1989) than other anxiety disorder groups.

Agoraphobic avoidance is specified in the DSM-III-R nosology as avoidance, or endurance with distress, of situations from which escape might be difficult or in which help is unavailable in the event of a panic attack or of developing symptoms that could be incapacitating or embarrassing (e.g., loss of bowel control). Typical situations include shopping in malls, waiting in lines, attending movie theaters, traveling by car or bus, visiting crowded restaurants and stores, and being alone. Three levels of avoidance are specified to reflect differing levels of restriction on mobility: mild, moderate, and severe (the truly "housebound" agoraphobic).

Agoraphobics who seek treatment most often report a history of panic attacks. Avoidance usually develops following the occurrence of an initial panic attack (Craske & Barlow, 1990; Noyes et al., 1986; Pollard, Pollard, & Corn, 1989; Swinson, 1986; Thyer, Himle, Curtis, Cameron, & Nesse, 1985). In contrast, epidemiological survey data (e.g., Epidemiological Catchner Area Study (ECA); Weissman, Leaf, Blazer, Boyd, & Florio, 1986) show that agoraphobia occurs proportionately more often in the absence of panic. It is as yet unclear whether the discrepancy between community and clinic samples is an artifact of the method of questioning or whether differences exist, but the presence of panic attacks increases the likelihood that help will be sought (Boyd, 1986; Weissman, et al., 1986).

Persons experiencing panic disorder (PDs) or panic disorder with agoraphobia (PDAs) are equally apprehensive of the experience of panic attacks (Adler, Craske, Kirschenbaum, & Barlow, 1989), but PDAs tend to report higher expectancies for panicking in "agoraphobic-type" situations (Craske, Burton, & Barlow, 1988; Telch et al., 1989). PDs and PDAs share many characteristics, such as duration of the disorder, age of onset, symptom profiles, proportion of each type of attack (i.e., cued/uncued and expected/unexpected), and panic frequency (see Craske & Barlow, 1988, for a review). Both groups are equally fearful of panic sensations in the absence of feared external situations (Craske & Barlow, 1989). The proportion of female sufferers increases as the degree of avoidance intensifies (Reich, Noyes, & Troughton, 1987; Sanderson, Rapee, & Barlow, 1987; Thyer et al., 1985). Finally, many PDs do not develop agoraphobic avoidance patterns. Subtle and covert forms of avoidance may occur across PD and PDA groups to the same extent. These forms of avoidance include attempted distraction from bodily sensations; nonparticipation in activities that elicit sensations similar to panic sensations, such as caffeine consumption, emotional arousal, or cardiovascular exertion; and proximity to safety cues such as medical facilities and medication.

Features of Presentation

PDs and PDAs seek treatment typically around the age of 34 years. The mean age of onset ranges from 23 to 29 years (Breier, Charney, & Heninger, 1986; Craske & Barlow, 1990; Noyes et al., 1986). A large percent (approximately 72%; Craske & Barlow, 1990) report the presence of identifiable stressors around the time of the first panic attack, but their number does not differ from the number of stressors experienced by other anxiety groups or control subjects. PD/PDAs have been found to rate stressful events as more impactful (Pollard et al., 1989; Rapee, Litwin, & Barlow, 1990; Roy-Byrne, Geraci, & Uhde, 1986). Approximately 50% report having experienced "panicky" feelings at some time before their first panic attack, suggesting that the onset may be either insidious or acute (Craske & Barlow, 1990). Approximately 80% of PDAs and approximately 57% of PDs are female (Reich et al., 1987; Thyer et al., 1985).

Sanderson, DiNardo, Rapee, and Barlow (in press) found that, of 55 PD/PDAs, 22% experienced additional diagnostic features of social phobia and 13% experienced additional diagnostic features of generalized anxiety disorder; of these, 40% were in relation to simple phobia, 2% in relation to obsessive-compulsive disorder, 11% in relation to major depressive episodes, and 18% in relation to dysthymia. The group of PD/PDAs differed from other principally diagnosed anxiety disorder groups in terms of the following patterns of comorbidity: PD/PDAs evidenced substantially fewer socially phobic features than did persons with generalized anxiety disorder (GADs), substantially fewer major depressive features than persons with obsessive-compulsive disorder (OCDs), and substantially more simple phobic features than any other group.

A high proportion of PD/PDAs seeks medical treatment. Even in a select sample of 190 PD/PDAs attending a psychological clinic (Center for Stress and Anxiety Disorders, Albany), 50.5% reported the use of anxiolytics, 2.6% reported the use of antidepressants, and 2.6% reported the use of beta-blockers (Oei et al., unpublished raw data). Rapee (1985a, 1985b) noted that PDs were more likely to seek medical help than were GADs.

Cognitive-Behavioral Interventions for Agoraphobia

Nonpharmacological treatment of agoraphobia began in the 1960s with systematic desensitization (SD). The nonpharmacological treatment for panic attacks did not begin until the 1970s, at which time stress management techniques were implemented. In the 1980s, significant advances were made in the nonpharmacological treatments specific to panic disorder, and refinements were made in the treatments for agoraphobia.

Systematic Desensitization

SD is rarely used now as a treatment for agoraphobia. The SD approach for agoraphobia entailed devising a hierarchy of situations that were typically avoided, and then repetitiously pairing progressive muscle relaxation with imaginal exposure to the different situations. As with all methods of SD, the theoretical basis was one of counterconditioning. Early studies of the effectiveness of SD for agoraphobia did not provide strong evidence for its efficacy (Gelder, Marks, & Wolff, 1967; Gillan & Rachman, 1974). Therapeutic effects were no greater than results from psychotherapy controls (Emmelkamp, 1982; Gelder & Marks, 1966; Marks, 1971). Some researchers have suggested that SD's results are not very different from exposure treatments at follow-up assessments (Mathews et al., 1976; Munby & Johnston, 1980), although follow-up status may be a function of self-directed exposure by members of SD groups (Barlow, 1988).

In summary, SD is not considered a very useful treatment for agoraphobia. Imaginal rehearsal has been used to prepare for in vivo exposure when clients are unwilling to attempt even the most graduated form of in vivo exposure, or require practice with items too impractical to conduct in vivo (e.g., aircraft). The efficacy of such a preparatory approach is untested, and the additional benefit of relaxation under these conditions is unknown.

Relaxation

Early research established very little efficacy of relaxation procedures in isolation from other procedures for the treatment of phobic avoidance (Gillan & Rachman, 1974). The application of relaxation during exposure to agoraphobic situations will be addressed in more detail next.

Direct in Vivo Exposure Therapy

The treatment procedure of choice for agoraphobic avoidance is the method of exposure—repeated confrontation with, or approach to, the object that is avoided. Outcome results, as reviewed by Jansson and Ost (1982) and by others, are as follows. When dropouts are excluded, 60 to 70% of agoraphobics who complete treatment show some clinical improvement, which is maintained (on average) 4 years or more (Burns, Thorpe, & Cavallaro, 1986; Cohen, Monteiro, & Marks, 1984; Hafner, 1976; Jansson, Jerremalm, & Ost,

1986; Jansson & Ost, 1982; Marks, 1971; Munby & Johnston, 1980). The median dropout rate is 12% (Barlow & Waddell, 1985), with a range as high as 25 to 40% under certain conditions (Jansson & Ost, 1982; Zitrin, Klein, & Woerner, 1980). Of those who complete treatment, 30 to 40% fail to benefit; of the remaining 60 to 70%, a substantial proportion may not attain clinically meaningful levels of functioning. The percentage of those who are classified as high end-state (i.e., minimal or no symptoms) ranges from 15 to 50%. As many as 50% who have benefited clinically may relapse, although usually the relapse is transient and is followed by a return to clinical gains (Munby & Johnston, 1980).

Given these qualifications to the efficacy of exposure-based treatments, attempts to improve efficacy continue, through examination of the following procedural variables: massed versus spaced exposure, graduated versus intensive exposure, therapist-directed versus self-directed exposure, extinction of fear versus controlled escape or quality of performance variables, focus of attention versus distraction during exposure, use of coping strategies to target panic attacks and panic-apprehension. The most recent findings relevant to each variable will be addressed.

Massed versus spaced exposure. At its most intensive level, exposure therapy may be conducted 3 to 4 hours a day, 5 days a week. Long, continuous sessions are generally considered more effective than shorter or interrupted sessions (Chaplin & Levine, 1981; Marshall, 1985; Stern & Marks, 1973).

The optimal rate at which exposure sessions should be conducted is unclear. Foa, Jameson, Turner, and Payne (1980) compared 10 weekly sessions with 10 daily sessions of in vivo exposure therapy for 11 agoraphobics (counterbalanced crossover design). Short-term superior effects were apparent following massed treatment. However, Barlow (1988) suggested that spaced exposure is preferred for the following reasons: dropout rates are generally higher with massed exposure (Emmelkamp & Ultee, 1974; Emmelkamp & Wessels, 1975); relapse rates may be higher following massed exposure (Hafner, 1976; Jansson & Ost, 1982); and rapid changes are more stressful for the phobic's family.

Chambless (1989) reported results that are not consistent with some of these predictions. In her study, 36 subjects (approximately half of whom were agoraphobic and the remainder were simple phobics) were assigned to massed or spaced exposure. All subjects received 10 sessions of graduated in vivo exposure, and training in respiratory control, distraction techniques, and paradoxical intention. Spaced exposure was conducted weekly and massed exposure was conducted daily. The two conditions were equally effective in the short term and at 6-month follow-up. There was no trend toward a differential dropout rate or toward differential relapse rates over the 6-month follow-up period. However, because massed exposure was not acceptable for some subjects who did not agree to random assignment, a sample bias was created. In addition, Chambless pointed out that her results may lack generalization: spaced exposure was usually interspersed with homework assignments, which may have increased outcome efficacy. Chambless concluded by suggesting that the choice for massed versus spaced exposure is the decision of the therapist and client.

Graduated versus intensive exposure. In vivo exposure is conducted typically in a graduated format, progressing from least to most difficult hierarchy items. Feigenbaum (1988) reported short-term and long-term outcomes from intensive versus graduated exposure treatment conditions. All training sessions were conducted in a massed format over the course of 6 to 10 consecutive days; no avoidance was allowed, nor did clients have control over the duration or sequence of their exposure tasks. Exposure proceeded from therapist-accompanied to self-directed. One group received ungraded exposure (n = 25), beginning with the most feared items from avoidance hierarchies. Another group received graded exposure (n = 23), beginning with the least feared hierarchy items. The sample was severely agoraphobic: approximately one third were housebound at initial assessment. At posttreatment and 8 months later, the conditions proved to be equally effective, although the graded group reported the training period to be more distressing. Ungraded exposure was clearly superior at the 5-year follow-up assessment: 76% of the intensive group versus 35% of the graded group reported themselves to be completely free of symptoms. In an extension of the study, 104 new subjects were added to the intensive exposure format and evaluated 5 years later. Of the total of 129 subjects, 78% were reportedly completely symptom-free 5 years later. This dramatic set of results suggests that an intensive approach is most beneficial when conducting massed exposures. The extent to which the outcome generalizes to spaced exposure formats is unknown, and information regarding subject acceptance was not provided. Both massed and intensive exposure may be acceptable to fewer people, but, for those who consent, the outcome is likely to be as effective—if not more effective—than spaced or graduated exposure.

Therapist-directed versus self-directed exposure. Several self-help manuals that outline self-directed exposure methods are available (Marks, 1978; Mathews, Gelder, & Johnston, 1981; Weeks, 1976). Ghosh and Marks (1987), Mathews et al. (1981), and Jannoun, Munby, Catalan, and Gelder (1980) have found that structured, manualized programs, with minimal therapist contact, are as effective as more intensive therapist contact, although the results are less promising with severe (housebound) agoraphobics (Holden, O'Brien, Barlow, Stetson, & Infantino, 1983). More recently, McNamee, O'Sullivan, Lelliott, and Marks (1989) compared telephone-guided exposure treatment (n = 13) with telephone-guided relaxation treatment (n = 10) for housebound agoraphobics. Subjects had no face-to-face contact with therapists. Superior rates of success were found with the exposure treatment, particularly at the 32-week follow-up. However, gains were not comparable to those usually obtained with therapist-guided exposure, and 50% of the exposure group dropped from treatment, as did 20% of the relaxation group.

The results indicate that self-help or telephone-guided treatments may be of some value to persons who are unable to travel to treatment centers, but the same subsample of severe agoraphobics is probably the least likely to benefit from these treatments. The greatest value of such procedures may lie in their provision of steps toward reaching treatment centers where therapist-assisted exposure can be conducted.

Family members have been incorporated into exposure-based treatment programs for several reasons: prompting of self-directed exposure practise, modification of maladaptive communications patterns, and reduction of background stress. Involvement of significant others in all aspects of assessment and treatment has been shown to produce results superior to the exclusion of significant others (Barlow, O'Brien, & Last, 1984); this finding is particularly evident 2 years following treatment (Cerny, Barlow, Craske, & Himadi, 1987). In this treatment, couples participated in a group treatment and were instructed in methods of exposure practices. Spouses were taught to serve as coaches for the practice of exposure tasks, helping in their design and in the application of anxiety-control strategies. In contrast, Cobb, Mathews, Childs-Clarke, and Blowers (1984) reported that a home-based treatment program that included the spouse in all phases of assessment and treatment was no more effective than a home-based treatment that did not include the spouse. However, the authors' observation that spouses of the latter group actually showed considerable interest in treatment procedures raises the possibility that they participated in the treatment program. The addition of communication training to exposure conducted in a couples format has been found to enhance gains from exposure procedures (Arnow, Taylor, Agras, & Telch, 1985).

Much attention has been given to the issue of marital satisfaction and how it pertains to treatment outcome (e.g., Bland & Hallam, 1981; Craske, Burton, & Barlow, 1988; Emmelkamp, 1980; Himadi, Cerny, Barlow, Cohen, & O'Brien, 1986; Milton & Hafner, 1979). The results have been contradictory. There is no reliable evidence to suggest that marital satisfaction worsens as a function of phobic improvement, or that pretreatment measures of marital satisfaction predict degree of phobic improvement.

Extinction of fear versus controlled escape. A golden rule of in vivo exposure has been the continuation of an exposure trial until anxiety reduces markedly (Marks, 1978). Similarly, the emotional processing model outlined by Foa and Kozak (1986) posits that long-term fear reduction is dependent on activation of high levels of arousal and within-session fear reduction.

Marshall (1985) observed substantial benefit from longer periods of exposure, in which time was allowed for complete anxiety reduction. In contrast, Emmelkamp (see Emmelkamp, 1982, for a review) has demonstrated repeatedly the value of exposure treatment in which subjects are instructed to terminate exposure when anxiety reaches "unduly high" levels. Agras, Lieterberg, and Barlow (1968) obtained successful results with a similar procedure, called *reinforced practice.* De Silva and Rachman (1984) and Rachman, Craske, Tallman, and Solyom (1986) obtained equally effective results whether subjects escaped exposure tasks when anxiety reached 70 on a 0-to-100 point scale (as long as escape was followed by return to the situation), or were instructed to remain in the situation until anxiety peaked and was then reduced by at least 50%. Interestingly, the "escape" group reported more perceived control and less fear during exposure than the no-escape group, suggesting that maximal fear elicitation was not essential for therapeutic benefit.

The model of therapeutic change described by Bandura (1977, 1988) and Williams (1988) emphasizes performance accomplishment or self-efficacy, as opposed to fear reduction or habituation. A mastery approach is taken in accord with the recognition that exposure therapy entails not only a simple approach to a stimulus, but also the way in which the stimulus is approached. Unadaptive, defensive behaviors that inhibit the development of self-efficacy and result in performance achievement attributed to protective behaviors, instead of to personal capabilities, are corrected. For example, subjects are taught to drive in a relaxed position at the wheel and to walk across a bridge without holding the rail. Guided mastery has been shown to produce more effective results than "stimulus exposure" treatment (Bandura, Jeffrey, & Wright, 1974; Williams, Turner, & Peer, 1985).

Williams and Zane (1989) compared mastery exposure and stimulus exposure of agoraphobics who were very anxious in specific situations but did not avoid them (n = 26). The mastery group improved most, in terms of anxiety measures; and the finding was maintained at follow-up assessment. Moreover, the mastery subjects tended to report the least anxiety during exposure, again suggesting that high levels of anxiety arousal during exposure are not prerequisite for therapeutic benefit. Similarly, Michelson, Mavissakalian, Marchione, Dancu, and Greenwald (1986) found that level of anxiety during exposure explained 30 to 50% of the variance in their outcome data; individuals who experienced lower anxiety tended to respond more favorably overall.

Williams (1988) suggested that therapist presence is necessary for the modification of unadaptive, defensive behaviors. This rationale may in part explain the poorer results obtained with self-help and minimal therapist contact approaches for severely avoidant agoraphobics. However, the "stimulus" exposure conditions may lack generalizability to the way in which exposure programs (self- or therapist-directed) are typically conducted. Williams and Zane (1989) did not include the usual verbal-cognitive components to exposure treatment, but their results highlight the importance of behavioral guidance during exposure practices, especially given the pervasiveness of subtle forms of avoidance (i.e., defensive, protective behaviors).

Rachman (1984) emphasized the protective value of safety signals, including certain behaviors (e.g., traveling familiar routes), objects, and people. In contrast to removal of the safety signals, Rachman suggested that exposure treatment might be facilitated by incorporating safety signals. For example, instead of entering a supermarket while the therapist waits outside, clients might walk toward a safety signal (the therapist) waiting inside the supermarket. Sartory, Master, and Rachman (1989) compared a safety signal exposure approach (n = 9) to standard therapist-directed exposure (n = 10) for the treatment of agoraphobia. Four graduated exposure treatment sessions were conducted in the client's home environment over a period of 2 weeks. Two weeks of homework assignments followed. A small advantage was achieved by the safety signal condition, particularly in the homework-assignments phase. Although the results were preliminary, they suggest the value of considering alternative methods of conducting exposure treatment.

Focus of attention versus distraction. It has been suggested that exposure is most functional when attention is directed fully toward the phobic object and internal and external sources of distraction are minimized (Borkovec, 1976; Foa & Kozak, 1986). Distraction may be viewed as a defensive behavior similar to that described by Williams and Zane (1989). Distraction techniques have been shown to weaken long-term outcome results from the treatment of obsessive-compulsive disorder (OCD) (Foa & Kozak, 1986; Grayson, Foa, & Steketee, 1982).

Craske, Street, and Barlow (1989) treated agoraphobics in small groups for 11 sessions. Self-directed exposure followed therapist-directed exposure. An instructional manipulation was conducted. In one condition (n = 16), subjects were instructed to monitor bodily sensations and thoughts throughout in vivo exposures and to use thought-stopping and focusing self-statements to interrupt distraction. In a second condition (n = 14), subjects were taught to engage in specific distraction tasks (e.g., word rhymes, spelling) during in vivo exposures and to use thought-stopping and distracting self-statements to interrupt focusing of attention on feared bodily sensations and images. The treatment groups did not differ at posttreatment nor at follow-up assessment. However, consistent with the findings from OCD subjects, the focused exposure group improved significantly from posttreatment to follow-up, in contrast to a slightly deteriorating trend in the distracted exposure group. In light of preawareness selectivity of attention processes, it is unlikely that an instructional manipulation sufficiently controlled focus of attention. Nevertheless, this clinical test suggested that instructions to focus or self-distract from feared sensations and thoughts during in vivo exposures may yield comparable short-term results. A stronger advantage may develop for focused exposure after treatment completion.

Use of coping strategies. Various anxiety-control strategies have been employed as means of reducing levels of anxiety during in vivo exposure. These include cognitive methods such as distraction, coping self-statements (e.g., instructing oneself to stay in the situation, accept the feelings, and discount unrealistic beliefs), and paradoxical intention (e.g., confronting and exaggerating fearful imagery). Physical coping strategies include relaxation and medication.

One approach to the use of coping strategies stems from emotional processing theory. Foa and Kozak (1986) suggested that the experience of extreme anxiety during exposure may interfere with attentional processes and disrupt effective learning. Hence, coping strategies may be helpful, especially those that contribute to habituation and the development of nonfearful interpretations of "what may happen" during exposure. The contrasting view is to use coping techniques to prevent the experience of anxiety during exposure. As described above, the necessity of experiencing maximal anxiety during exposure is unclear.

The various coping strategies alone are not effective forms of treatment for agoraphobic avoidance. The ineffectiveness of relaxation training was mentioned earlier. Emmelkamp, Kuipers, and Eggeraat (1978) compared the effectiveness of a set of cognitive strategies (such as challenging irrational beliefs about perceived catastrophic consequences of anxiety, reinforcing and task-oriented self-statements, and imaginal rehearsal of entering feared situations) with prolonged in vivo exposure. The treatment was intensive (5 sessions per week). Within the constraints of a brief treatment, cognitive techniques were found to be of very limited usefulness in comparison to in vivo exposure. Over a follow-up interval, the effects of self-statement training may markedly improve (Emmelkamp & Mersch, 1982), possibly due to self-initiated exposure practice (Barlow, 1988).

The combination of cognitive strategies with in vivo exposure has been shown to be effective (Vermilyea, Boice, & Barlow, 1984). However, the extent to which cognitive strategies enhance the efficacy of in vivo exposure has been questioned (Emmelkamp & Mersch, 1982; Michelson, Mavissakalian, & Marchione, 1985; Williams & Rappaport, 1983). Similarly, relaxation does not seem to enhance the efficacy of in vivo exposure (Jansson et al., 1986; Michelson et al., 1985). Strategies designed specifically to control panic attacks (described in more detail later), such as interoceptive exposure and breathing retraining, have not been found to contribute significantly to the effects obtained from in vivo exposure (deRuiter, Rijken, Garssen, & Kraaimaat, 1989).

However, attrition rates have been found to rise twice as high in exposure-alone conditions (Michelson et al., 1985). The major value of coping strategies may be their facilitation of compliance with exposure instructions. Michelson et al. (1986) reported the amount of self-directed exposure practice conducted in each treatment group from the 1985 study: exposure alone, exposure plus relaxation, and exposure plus paradoxical intention. Those who received relaxation training practiced exposure more frequently than any other group during treatment and at follow-up assessment.

Practice has been shown to relate positively to degree of improvement (Barlow et al., 1984; Craske, Burton, & Barlow, 1988; Vermilyea et al., 1984). The finding that, despite more practice, relaxation did not enhance the efficacy of exposure treatment suggests that although relaxation may be a motivator for exposure practice, it may also slow the process through which anxiety control is achieved.

In contrast to the many indications of failure to enhance the efficacy of in vivo exposure, Michelson (1989) reported a different set of results from a comparison of the following three treatment conditions: in vivo exposure, in vivo exposure plus progressive muscle relaxation, and exposure plus cognitive restructuring. The latter condition was found to be significantly more effective on a wide range of avoidance and panic measures at posttreatment and at follow-up. The full report of these findings may prove to be very important.

Prediction and Mechanisms of Change

Hypothesized mechanisms of fear and avoidance reduction include cognitive reattribution or a change in the meaning structure, physiological habituation, development of self-efficacy, and development of affective control. Development of predictability has also been emphasized. Southworth and Kirsch (1988) have shown that expectancy regarding therapeutic gain influences results from exposure therapy: "Repeated exposures to the feared situation provides clients with experiential feedback that confirms their expectancies for reduced fear and thereby strengthens expectations of their improvement" (Southworth & Kirsch, 1988, p. 114). They compared a group of subjects who were informed that exposure tasks were part of treatment with another group who were informed that equivalent tasks were part of assessment. The "treatment" group showed significantly more gain in approach behavior. The same effects have been observed with dental phobics by Gauthier, Laberge, Freve, and DuFour (1986).

Rachman and colleagues (Rachman & Levitt, 1985; Rachman, Levitt, & Lopatka, 1988; Rachman & Lopatka, 1986; Rachman, Lopatka, & Levitt, 1988) have demonstrated the importance of predictability in another sense. They have shown that agoraphobics typically overestimate the degree of fear experienced in specific situations. Overestimation of degree of avoidance situations during behavioral testing is typical also (Craske, Rapee, & Barlow, 1988). The degree to which a given situation is avoided relates very strongly to the degree to which panic or fear is expected to occur in the situation. Furthermore, one trial of unexpected fear/panic tends to increase the expectancy that fear/panic will occur in subsequent exposures. With repeated exposures, predictions become more accurate, but the process of disconfirmation is slow and overestimation tends to continue. Rachman and Bichard (1988) suggested that therapeutic effects occur through disconfirmation of overprediction, particularly since, regardless of expectations, actual fear levels reduce with repeated exposures.

The experience of unexpected fear/panic seems to be very crucial to the psychopathology of PD/PDA. Several researchers have suggested that relapse following successful reduction in agoraphobic avoidance is related to the reoccurrence of panic (Arnow et al., 1985; Craske, Street, & Barlow, 1989; Sartory et al., 1989). The development of methods by which panic can be controlled has advanced considerably in the past 5 years. These developments were necessary because in vivo exposure procedures targeting agoraphobic avoidance did not reliably control panic attacks (Arnow et al., 1985; Michelson et al., 1985; Stern & Marks, 1973).

Cognitive-Behavioral Interventions for Panic

A multicomponent approach was used initially for the treatment of free-floating anxiety or nonsituational anxiety. For example, in an uncontrolled study, Gitlin et al. (1985) treated 11 patients with PD, using 6 to 32 sessions entailing education about panic attacks, relaxation training, diaphragmatic breathing training, in vivo exposure, and assertiveness training. Ten of the patients were free of panic at postassessment and 5 months later (according to telephone contact). In two controlled studies, the effects of similar multicomponent treatments were shown to be superior to the passage of time alone for the control of panic attacks (Barlow et al., 1984; Waddell, Barlow, & O'Brien, 1984). More recently developed treatment components can be divided into panic management approaches and exposure approaches. The panic management approaches include somatic and cognitive techniques. The somatic techniques include breathing retraining, applied relaxation, and vagal innervation techniques.

Panic Management: Somatic Techniques

Breathing retraining. One of the earliest, most dramatic, but uncontrolled reports of the nonpharmacological treatment of panic attacks was by Clark, Salkovskis, and Chalkley (1985). They developed a cognitive-behavioral treatment that emphasized breathing retraining. Several researchers have examined the efficacy of breathing retraining, given the similarity of hyperventilatory symptoms to those that characterize panic attacks for 50 to 60% of PD/PDAs. However, recent research has shown that symptom report is considerably discrepant from physiology, and that hyperventilation physiology may not play a major role (Holt & Andrews, 1989).

In the conception of panic attacks that emphasizes hyperventilation, panic attacks are viewed as stress-induced, respiratory changes that either provoke fear because they are perceived as frightening, or augment fear already elicited by other stimuli (Clark et al., 1985). Kraft and Hoogduin (1984) found that 6 biweekly sessions of breathing retraining and progressive relaxation reduced the frequency of panic attacks from 10 to 4 per week. However, the treatment was no more effective than either repeated hyperventilation and control of symptoms by breathing into a bag, or identification of life stressors and problem solving. Two case reports have described the successful application of breathing retraining in the context of cognitively based treatments, where patients are taught to reinterpret sensations as not dangerous (Rapee, 1985a; Salkovskis, Warwick, Clark, & Wessels, 1986). As mentioned earlier, Clark et al. (1985) reported a larger-scale, although uncontrolled, study in which 18 panickers received 2 weekly sessions of respiratory control and cognitive reattribution training. Panic attacks were reduced markedly in that brief period of time. Salkovskis et al. (1986) gave 9 panicking patients 4 weekly sessions of forced hyperventilation, corrective information, and breathing retraining, after which in vivo exposure was provided if necessary. Panic attack frequency was reduced, on average, from 7 to 3 per week after respiratory control training.

Unfortunately, results from respiratory control training programs are difficult to interpret. First, because subjects have been selected typically on the basis of exhibiting hyperventilatory symptoms, the extent to which the findings generalize to those who do not experience hyperventilatory symptoms is unclear. Second, deRuiter et al. (1989), using similarly selected subjects, did not replicate the efficacy of a combination of breathing retraining and cognitive restructuring. Third, breathing retraining protocols typically include cognitive restructuring and interoceptive exposure which, as will be described, have been shown to be very effective treatments for panic attacks. Therefore, it is difficult to ascribe the results primarily to respiratory control measures.

Applied relaxation. This form of relaxation has shown promising results as a treatment for panic attacks. Applied relaxation entails training in progressive muscle relaxation (PMR) until the subject is skilled in the use of cue-control procedures, at which point the relaxation skill is applied when practicing items from an individualized hierarchy of anxiety-provoking tasks. A theoretical basis for the use of relaxation has not been elaborated beyond the provision of a somatic counterresponse to the muscular tension that is likely to occur during the expression of anxiety and fear. However, evidence from other sources does not lend support to this notion (Rupert, Dobbins, & Mathew, 1981). Others have suggested that, to the extent that relaxation provides a sense of control or mastery, fear and anxiety are reduced (Bandura, 1977; Rice & Blanchard, 1982). With applied forms of relaxation, the procedures and mechanisms accountable for therapeutic gains are indeterminable, given the involvement of exposure procedures.

Barlow, Craske, Cerny, and Klosko (1989) compared applied PMR (n = 10), interoceptive exposure and cognitive restructuring (n = 15), and their combination (n = 16) to a waiting-list control condition (n = 15), for the treatment of PD with mild or no avoidance. PMR was applied to the practice of items from an individualized hierarchy of anxiety-provoking situations. Although PMR did not as effectively reduce panic attacks as did the other active treatment conditions, 60% of the PMR group achieved a panic-free status by the end of the 15-week program. However, the attrition rate was significantly higher (33%) in the PMR condition. When dropouts were included in the analysis and were assumed to continue to panic, the proportion of the PMR group who were panic-free reduced to 40%, which was not significantly different from the result (30%) with the waiting-list control group.

Öst (1988) reported considerably more favorable results with the implementation of applied PMR for the control of panic attacks. When he compared applied PMR (n = 8) to PMR (n = 8), 100% of the first group were panic-free after 14 sessions, in comparison to approximately 72% of the second group. Furthermore, the results of the first group were maintained at follow-up (approximately 19 months after treatment completion), while maintenance occurred for 57% of the second group. All of the applied PMR group were classified as high end-state at follow-up, in comparison to 25% of the PMR group. It is important to note that Ost's applied PMR condition included exposure to interoceptive cues, which are highly salient to PD responding, and integral targets for the interoceptive exposure procedures included in the study by Barlow et al. (1989). The exclusion of interoceptive hierarchy items from the applied PMR condition in the Barlow et al. (1989) study may account for the discrepant results between the two studies.

Vagal innervation. Another somatic control technique has been developed by Sartory and Olajide (1988). Vagal innervation entails teaching control of heart rate through various massage techniques. These include stimulation of vagal receptors by massaging the carotid, or pressing on one eye during expiration, or exerting pressure on the chest. In a preliminary investigation, 9 generalized anxiety disorder patients who experienced distinct "spontaneous" panic attacks were treated. Cognitive restructuring and progressive muscle relaxation training were provided to a control group. The experimental group also received vagal innervation training.

The results were suggestive of a slight advantage to the experimental condition, although the groups did not differ with respect to panic frequency. The authors suggested that vagal innervation may provide a greater sense of perceived control than relaxation procedures.

Panic Management: Cognitive Restructuring

Cognitive treatments that focus on correcting misappraisals of bodily sensations as threatening began with Beck's (1985) extension of his cognitive model of depression to anxiety and panic. In this approach, cognitive therapy is conducted in conjunction with behavioral techniques, although the effective mechanism of change is assumed to lie in the cognitive realm. In an uncontrolled study, Beck (1988) treated 25 PD patients with cognitive techniques in combination with interoceptive and in vivo exposure for an average of 17 individual sessions. The panic response was eliminated in 17 patients who did not have additional diagnoses of personality disorder, at posttreatment and 12-month assessments. However, it is difficult to attribute the outcome to cognitive procedures, given the inclusion of specific behavioral treatment procedures.

Preliminary reports from studies ongoing in Oxford (Clark, 1989) and Marburg (Margraf, 1989) have suggested that cognitive procedures conducted in isolation from exposure procedures are highly effective means of controlling panic attacks. The full results from these studies may prove to be very important.

Interoceptive Exposure

The purpose of interoceptive exposure, as with exposure to external phobic stimuli, is to disrupt or weaken associations between specific bodily cues and panic reactions. The theoretical basis for the implementation of interoceptive exposure is one of fear extinction, given the conceptualization of panic attacks as "conditioned" or learned alarm reactions to salient bodily cues (Barlow, 1988). Interoceptive exposure is conducted through procedures that induce panic-type sensations reliably, such as cardiovascular exercise, inhalations of carbon dioxide, spinning, and hyperventilation. The exposure is conducted using a graduated format. In early studies, Bonn, Harrison, and Rees (1971) and Haslam (1974) observed successful reduction in reactivity with repeated infusions of sodium lactate (a drug that produces panic-type bodily sensations, as does caffeine ingestion and yohimbine), although panic attack measures were not recorded. Griez and van den Hout (1986) compared the effectiveness of 6 sessions of repeated carbon dioxide inhalations over the course of 2 weeks and a 2-week regimen of propranolol (a beta-blocker chosen because it suppresses symptoms that are induced by carbon dioxide inhalations). The inhalation treatment resulted in a mean reduction from 12 to 4 panic attacks, which was superior to the results from propranolol, and in significantly greater reductions in reported fear of sensations. A 6-month follow-up assessment suggested maintenance of treatment gains, although panic frequency was not noted.

In the first controlled study of behavioral treatments for panic disorder, as described earlier, Barlow, Craske, Cerny, and Klosko (1989) compared the following four conditions: applied PMR, interoceptive exposure and cognitive restructuring, their combination, and a waiting-list control. Interoceptive exposure entailed repeated exposures using induction techniques such as forced hyperventilation, spinning, and cardiovascular effort. The two conditions entailing interoceptive exposure and cognitive restructuring were significantly superior to applied PMR and waiting-list conditions, in terms of panic frequency. Fully 87% of those two treatment groups were free of panic at posttreatment. These patterns seem to be maintained up to 24 months following treatment completion (Craske, Brown, & Barlow, 1991).

Summary of Cognitive-Behavioral Treatments for Panic and Agoraphobia

Several points can be made concerning the cognitive-behavioral treatment for panic and agoraphobia. First, in vivo exposure remains the treatment of choice for agoraphobic avoidance, although variations in the means by which exposure is conducted have been investigated recently to suggest the following possibilities. Massed exposure may be as effective as spaced exposure, and intense exposure may be as effective as graded exposure, both in the short term and the long term. Evocation of high levels of anxiety during exposure and continuation in the exposure setting until anxiety levels reduce may not be necessary for effective treatment outcome. The ways in which tasks are approached are important to consider, because distraction and continued defensive behaviors may mitigate the benefit of exposure practice. Self-directed exposure can be very effective, although more severe agoraphobia may warrant more therapist-directed procedures. Inclusion of significant others in the treatment program seems to enhance treatment outcome. The value of somatic and cognitive coping strategies may lie primarily in decreasing attrition rates and increasing compliance with exposure practice demands. However, specific coping skills may result in superior outcome from exposure-based therapy.

Second, cognitive-behavioral treatments have been shown to be very effective for the control of panic attacks, both in the short term and, more importantly, up to 2 years following treatment completion. The panic control procedures include respiratory control training, applied relaxation and other methods of somatic control; cognitive restructuring, and introceptive exposure. This has been a major advancement, given that, until fairly recently, panic attacks were considered to be most appropriately treated with pharmacotherapy.

Questions that remain to be answered include the ways in which treatments targeting agoraphobic avoidance complement treatments targeting panic attacks. In addition, the combination of such cognitive-behavioral procedures with anxiolytic medications warrants further investigation.

GENERALIZED ANXIETY DISORDER (GAD)

Clinical Syndrome

Generalized anxiety disorder (GAD), one of the least common anxiety disorders presenting to general outpatient clinics or specialist anxiety centers (Barlow, 1988), is the second most common anxiety problem found in the general population (see Barlow, 1988). When GAD is a widespread problem, why do GAD sufferers rarely seek help, in comparison to those who experience panic attacks? Possibly because these patients are rarely referred to specialty clinics by primary care physicians, who often prescribe anxiolytics. A principal diagnosis of GAD accounts for about 10% of anxiety clinic samples (Barlow, 1988); GAD is commonly found to accompany other anxiety disorders and depressive disorders (Barlow, Blanchard, Vermilyea, Vermilyea, & DiNardo, 1986; Breslau, 1985). An understanding of the nature and treatment of this disorder is likely to be important for the behavior therapist.

The diagnosis of GAD is often poorly understood, probably because of the changes that occurred between the DSM-III and the DSM-III-R. The DSM-III-R removed the residual status assigned to GAD in the DSM-III and tightened the criteria to make GAD an active diagnosis. As specified in the DSM-III-R diagnostic criteria, the central feature of GAD is a tendency to worry excessively. A number of somatic symptoms are specified, but, because these symptoms do not appear to be specific to GAD (Barlow et al., 1986), they are somewhat less important in the differential diagnosis of GAD.

By definition, the anxiety characteristic of GAD does not revolve around a circumscribed stimulus, but it is a fallacy to describe the anxiety as "free-floating." The anxious apprehension characteristic of GAD is typically focused on a number of varying but specific stimuli, all of which represent a potential threat (Rapee, 1990).

As mentioned, GAD patients are conceptualized as chronic worriers. The most common areas of worry include family, money, work, illness, and "minor things" (Sanderson & Barlow, 1989). These areas are obviously very "normal" and few differences appear between GAD and normal worries. However, one study suggested that GAD patients are more likely to worry about health than are nonanxious controls and that GAD patients view their worries as less controllable (Craske, Rapee, Jackel, & Barlow, 1989). This latter feature may be particularly important: a perceived lack of control over worrying may be partly responsible for its distressing nature (Barlow, 1988). Providing a sense of control over the tendency to worry may be an important component of treatment and there is likely to be an emphasis on controllability of worry in the forthcoming DSM-IV definition of GAD.

The diagnosis of GAD appears to contain a number of difficulties. Studies investigating the reliability of the diagnosis have varied tremendously, providing kappas between 0.27 and 0.79 (DiNardo, Rapee, Moras, & Barlow, 1990; Mannuzza et al., 1990; Riskind, Beck, Berchick, Brown, & Steer, 1987). Methodological differences may account for some of these discrepancies, but much of the variability may occur as a result of different emphases within the diagnosis. Specifically, it appears that the diagnosis of GAD based on somatic symptomatology is very unreliable while a diagnosis focused on worry over life circumstances provides far higher agreement (Rapee, 1990).

Despite the good agreement among clinicians in diagnosing areas of worry, some problems inherent in the DSM-III-R definition of GAD still need to be addressed. One of the main difficulties in diagnosing GAD concerns the extent to which the worry is excessive or unrealistic. The DSM-III-R provides no guidelines for making this decision, which can be very subjective. For example, a 31-year-old secretary reported worrying about whether she had made an error in every piece of work she typed. This worry was obviously excessive. The same woman reported worrying about whether she would ever become pregnant. The fact that she had been trying to become pregnant for the previous 6 months made it difficult to decide whether that worry was excessive. She appeared to be having difficulty becoming pregnant, so it could be argued that the worry was quite reasonable. The DSM needs to include operational criteria that will help clinicians to define excessiveness. These definitional issues are being addressed in DSM-IV.

Some questions have been raised about the validity of GAD as a diagnostic entity (Rapee, 1990). Probably the best response to such questions is the fact that, although the reliability of GAD is not especially high, it is well above chance. In addition, some studies have demonstrated differences in terms of the presentation of GAD and PD (Anderson, Noyes, & Crowe, 1984; Hibbert, 1984; Rapee, 1985b). Research into the nature of GAD is still lacking, but there is some evidence to suggest that it is a valid entity (Rapee, 1990).

Features of Presentation

GADS who present for treatment are typically slightly older than many other anxiety disorder patients, perhaps reflecting the somewhat lower distress level associated with this disorder. Most studies indicate an age of presentation in the 40s (Craske, Rapee, Jackel, & Barlow, 1989; Rapee, 1985b; Sanderson & Barlow, 1989). Females predominate, as they do for most anxiety disorders, but the sex distribution is less extreme than for many disorders. Approximately 60% of GADs are female (Craske, Rapee, Jackel, & Barlow, 1989; Rapee, 1985b).

The mean age of onset is in the middle to late teen years (Barlow et al., 1986; Rapee, Sanderson, & Barlow, 1988). Calculating a mean age of onset for GAD may be quite misleading; a large number of subjects report having the problem "all of their lives" (Barlow et al., 1986). Even when individuals report an approximate age of onset, many cannot remember a specific time when the problem began and instead report that the disorder built gradually (Rapee, 1985b). Some GADs relate the onset of problematic levels of anxiety to times when new responsibilities were acquired, such as having children or entering the workforce. It is likely that many GADs have some degree of generalized anxiety for most of their lives but that, for some, the anxiety becomes impairing or extreme at stressful times or in response to various maturational or lifestyle changes.

GAD is often associated with high levels of social anxiety (Rapee, Sanderson, & Barlow, 1988) and, more specifically, with an additional diagnosis of social phobia. GAD patients commonly experience depressive disorders (Breslau, 1985). GAD itself is a common additional diagnosis for other anxiety or affective disorders (Barlow et al., 1986).

On presentation to a mental health practitioner, GADs patients are somewhat less likely to be taking psychotropic medications than are PDs/PDAs. This may be a result of the fact that GAD can be less distressing than many other disorders. Or, because GADs are less able to ascribe their anxiety to a specific circumscribed stimulus, and the content of their worries is similar to that of most people, they may be less likely to seek help, although they are very distressed. Compared to persons with panic disorder, GADs are more likely to seek "alternative" help—such as bibliotherapy, acupuncture, and relaxation tapes—than to seek conventional medical assistance (Rapee, 1985b). When GADs are given medication (commonly from a general practitioner), benzodiazepines are usually prescribed on an as-needed basis. It has been suggested that such medication habits may interfere with behavioral therapy, because clients may attribute control to the drug rather than to themselves.

Cognitive-Behavioral Interventions for GAD

Relaxation

The use of relaxation techniques for the reduction of chronic anxiety began with the seminal work of Jacobson (1938). His particular technique, known as *deep muscle relaxation,* involved the systematic tensing and relaxing of distinct muscle groups (although Jacobson himself focused more on relaxing and less on tensing than more recent versions). It is assumed that the individual learns to detect subtle increases in tension before it reaches intense levels, and, through various feedback mechanisms, subjective anxiety is reduced. The technique as originally proposed by Jacobson (1938) involved a larger number of separate muscle groups than more recent versions of the procedure utilize. One of the most widely used protocols, developed by Bernstein and Borkovec (1973), begins with 16 different muscle groups. With practice, the individual reduces this to 8 and then to 4 muscle groups. Ultimately, the subject acquires "cue-controlled" relaxation or recall of a relaxed state in response to mental repetition of the word "relax."

Since the development of deep muscle relaxation, many other relaxation techniques have emerged, the most popular of which is meditation (Benson, Beary, & Carol, 1974). The purpose of meditation is to control the mental aspects of anxiety (such as worry) by learning to focus attention on neutral images. Few studies have compared differences among forms of relaxation, and, at present, there is little empirical reason for selecting one over the other. In fact, techniques overlap tremendously. Most relaxation techniques involve both a peripheral physiological focus and a mental control focus.

Despite the original theoretical underpinnings of relaxation techniques, it is unclear how they work. The mechanism seems to be not purely one of muscle tension reduction. Following the suggestion that reduction of muscle tension is important to the control of chronic anxiety, a number of studies have used biofeedback to maximize this process, thus supposedly maximizing anxiety reduction. However, biofeedback does not appear to be any more effective than simple relaxation for the reduction of anxiety (Rice & Blanchard, 1982). The degree to which muscle tension is reduced does not seem to be related to the degree of anxiety reduction (Rupert et al., 1981), and it has been suggested that relaxation operates through expectation or demand, or by enhancing the sense of control (Barlow, 1988; Rice & Blanchard, 1982). Many subjects who are treated with relaxation report that they have learned to worry less, suggesting perhaps that relaxation also produces an attitudinal shift.

Regardless of the mechanism of action, most studies seem to demonstrate that relaxation is of value to the reduction of chronic anxiety. Only four studies have utilized relaxation in isolation from other procedures for the treatment of GAD (Blowers, Cobb, & Mathews, 1987; Borkovec et al., 1987; Borkovec & Mathews, 1988; Rapee & Barlow, 1988). These studies have demonstrated that relaxation is an effective means for reducing generalized anxiety. However, the value of relaxation alone compared to relaxation plus other techniques is not yet clear. Blowers et al. (1987) found that relaxation alone was not as effective as relaxation plus cognitive restructuring, and Borkovec et al. (1987) found that relaxation plus nondirective therapy was not as effective as relaxation plus cognitive restructuring. In contrast, Borkovec and Mathews (1988) found no differences between relaxation plus nondirective therapy, relaxation plus cognitive therapy, and relaxation plus imaginal exposure. Preliminary results from an ongoing study (Rapee & Barlow, 1988) seem to indicate no difference between relaxation alone and relaxation plus cognitive restructuring; clients were encouraged to apply their relaxation, as a coping skill, to the management of anxiety-provoking situations, thus incorporating an in vivo exposure component. Many of the important clinical issues associated with relaxation delivery were covered in an excellent early paper by Borkovec and Sides (1979). Two major issues were identified as essential to the production of maximum therapeutic gains. First, it seems important that a number of therapy sessions be devoted to relaxation. The authors found that successful studies utilized an average of 4.5 sessions of relaxation and unsuccessful studies used significantly less. Second, teaching of relaxation directly by the therapist rather than through the sole use of tapes appears crucial. Tapes may form a valuable adjunct in some cases, but training by the therapist followed by client practice is likely to produce the greatest benefits.

Extensive homework training is important to relaxation, as it is to any behavioral technique. An interesting study by Hoelscher, Lichstein, and Rosenthal (1984) demonstrated that anxiety reduction was significantly correlated with the amount of relaxation practice measured objectively but was not correlated with self-reported relaxation practice. This study raises a particularly important issue: GAD (and many other) patients typically overreport the amount of relaxation practice they engage in. Given that homework practice is important to the success of relaxation, it would seem vital to stress the necessity of honest, accurate monitoring and possibly to engage the cooperation of a significant other as a "practice cue." Another important issue related to relaxation is credibility and understanding of the technique.

If the mechanism of relaxation treatment involves attitudinal shift or development of a sense of control, then credibility will obviously be important and an extensive and detailed rationale will be valuable.

Cognitive Restructuring

A key study conducted by Butler and Mathews (1983) investigated the type of cognitive distortions involved in GAD. Three related problems were identified for GAD patients:

1. They tended to interpret ambiguous situations in a threatening manner. For example, in response to the item "You are awakened by a noise in the middle of the night," they were more likely than normals to choose the "burglar" response category.
2. They rated the likelihood of threatening events happening to themselves (but not to others) as much more probable.
3. They rated negative events as more costly than did normal controls.

A number of "clinical" authors have pointed to various cognitive distortions made by GADs. For example, Beck and Emery (1985) highlight the importance of "all-or-none thinking," "black-and-white thinking," and "catastrophizing." Most of those features are broadly similar to the increased likelihood and increased cost of negative events identified by Butler and Mathews (1983). Thus, cognitive restructuring for GAD should be aimed at teaching patients how to reassess the probability and consequences of threatening events in a more realistic fashion.

One study has examined the treatment of generally anxious subjects using cognitive restructuring as described by Beck and Emery (Durham & Turvey, 1987). The results demonstrated large posttreatment benefits from cognitive restructuring, with around 50% of subjects improving markedly. These results were maintained at 6-month follow-up, at which point the cognitive restructuring condition was superior to a mixed behavioral treatment without cognitive restructuring. It should be noted, however, that techniques such as exposure were included within the cognitive restructuring treatment.

Another study has included a cognitive restructuring condition in the treatment of GAD (Rapee & Barlow, 1988). Cognitive restructuring (which also included some exposure) has resulted in marked improvements but no more so than relaxation or combined treatment. At least some subjects (for whom we have data) have maintained their gains for up to 2 years. As described earlier, at least two studies have demonstrated that cognitive restructuring provides benefits over and above relaxation alone (Blowers et al., 1987; Borkovec et al., 1987).

A number of cognitive restructuring techniques have been developed (Beck & Emery, 1985; Ellis & Harper, 1975; Meichenbaum, 1975) and the question may arise as to which is better. To date, there have been few comparisons of different styles of cognitive restructuring and it is unknown whether one is better than another. In light of the cognitive biases characteristic of generalized anxiety, described earlier, it would seem essential for treatment procedures to address overestimates of threat. Possibly, the cognitive therapies may target the same cognitive biases but employ different frameworks and methodologies.

Duration of treatment is likely to be another important issue. Empirical investigations have not yet been conducted with cognitive restructuring. This is a difficult technique for clients to master, and one of the most likely reasons for treatment failure is too little within-session attention. Extensive homework practice is essential, and cognitive restructuring lends itself well to in vivo practice.

Exposure

It is often thought that GAD is not amenable to in vivo exposure, given its lack of focus on specific cues. However, as mentioned previously, this "free-floating" description of GAD is a fallacy. Exposure is not only possible but is likely to be a major aspect of treatment.

The most important step in applying exposure to GAD is to identify the feared stimuli. Because feared stimuli in GAD patients tend to be highly idiosyncratic, exposure hierarchies must be designed for each individual. However, a number of themes tend to recur—fears of making mistakes, distress over lack of neatness, and obsessive punctuality. Social anxieties and specific minor phobias are common. Some of the exposure exercises that we have used include intentionally being late to functions or meetings, leaving a mess in the house or a bed unmade, asking for more responsibility at work, intentionally making a few mistakes at work, and not jumping up immediately when the baby cries. To date, there have been no investigations of the effects of exposure alone in GAD, but exposure is often included in successful combined packages (Butler, Cullington, Hibbert, Klimes, & Gelder, 1987; Rapee & Barlow, 1988).

Other Techniques

A number of other techniques commonly used in stress management would seem to be of value for the treatment of GAD but have not yet been empirically investigated. These include assertiveness training, time management, and problem solving.

As mentioned above, many GAD patients are socially anxious. Assertiveness seems to be a major problem for them (Rapee, Sanderson, & Barlow, 1988). To a large extent, assertiveness training can be viewed as an extension of cognitive restructuring and in vivo exposure. However, more specific attention to increasing assertiveness may be an important treatment component.

Another difficulty often encountered by GAD patients is a feeling of time pressure. This can be due to one or both of two reasons: a genuine overcommitment due to lack of assertiveness and perfectionism, or a perceived lack of time as part of the distorted cognitive process. In either case, training in systematically organizing time can be a valuable exercise for GAD patients, to allow them to complete their tasks more efficiently and to "sleep easier" knowing that there is time for everything.

Because of GAD patients' overestimations of consequences, practical solutions to relatively minor problems often elude them. D'Zurilla and Goldfried (1971) described a problem-solving technique in which clients "brainstorm" to generate as many solutions as possible and then rank-order these from most to least practical. Much of this procedure will be covered by regular cognitive restructuring, and problem solving is an extension of this technique. However, problem solving can often help to indicate a specific plan of action, in addition to reorganizing the interpretation of events.

SUMMARY OF COGNITIVE-BEHAVIORAL TREATMENT FOR PANIC, AGORAPHOBIA, AND GENERALIZED ANXIETY DISORDER

The treatments for panic disorder (PD), with and without agoraphobia (PDA), and generalized anxiety disorder (GAD) have advanced considerably in recent years, in concert with advances in conceptualizations of each disorder. The conceptualization and treatment for GAD are, in general, less advanced than for PD/PDA, although similar courses of development are apparent in at least three areas. First, identification of the precise cues that elicit fearful and anxious states has assumed a central role. Recognition of the extent to which bodily sensations serve as cues for triggering panic attacks has led to the implementation of interoceptive exposure fear reduction techniques, somatic symptom reduction techniques, and tailoring of cognitive procedures to correct misappraisals of bodily sensations for the control of PD. Similarly, recognition of the importance of specific foci of excessive worry (such as finances, safety of family members, or making mistakes) has led to the implementation of specific cognitive restructuring procedures and exposure techniques for the control of GAD.

Second, exposure principles are incorporated in the treatment of agoraphobic avoidance, panic attacks, and generalized anxiety, although their implementation is at a different stage of development for each anxiety problem. For agoraphobic avoidance, exposure principles continue to be employed with regard to feared and avoided situations, and detailed examination of the various parameters of in vivo exposure, such as duration, scheduling, and intensity of practices, has been conducted. For panic attacks, exposure has been more recently employed with regard to feared and avoided bodily sensations. The overall efficacy of interoceptive exposure techniques has been demonstrated, although exploration of the various parameters is yet to be conducted. For generalized anxiety, the value of exposure principles for correcting excessive worry tendencies has only just been recognized, and the efficacy of exposure procedures has not as yet been tested in isolation from other procedures.

Third, the degree to which different treatment procedures are more effective in isolation or in combination with other procedures remains a source of continuing research interest for all three types of anxiety problems. For example, the benefit of adding cognitive restructuring to in vivo exposure procedures for the reduction of agoraphobic avoidance is unclear, as is the benefit from the combination of relaxation and cognitive restructuring over each one in isolation for the control of generalized anxiety. Another area significant to all three anxiety disorders concerns the mechanisms through which treatment approaches exert their efficacy, although the development of a perception of control seems to be applicable in each case.

CONCLUSION

Additional improvements in the efficacy of treatment will probably have to await a deeper and fuller understanding of the nature of anxiety and panic. This in turn might allow more fruitful theorizing on processes of anxiety reduction and affective change. For example, we have speculated elsewhere (e.g., Barlow, 1988) that essential processes of anxiety reduction will include three major changes. First would be a blocking of any action tendencies associated with inappropriate emotions. Panic is the basic emotion of fear, firing inappropriately. In the case of fear, this strategy would involve blocking of escapist action tendencies; in the case of anxiety, it would involve interfering with the preparatory coping set that seems to be characterized by chronic hyperarousal. This is most obvious clinically in the processes of vigilance and scanning and of the autonomic hyperactivity that characterizes general anxiety or "anxious apprehension."

A second essential target for change would be increasing perceptions of control, which are considered to play a crucial role in the process of anxiety. Specifically, experiencing the world as unpredictable and uncontrollable seems to comprise the core of negative affect associated with anxiety (Barlow, 1988).

The third essential target for change would involve altering distortions in informational processing, particularly as manifested in self-focused attention (Craske & Barlow, 1990). This would be the "neurotic self-preoccupation" that has long been noticed by clinicians but has not been systematically studied in terms of anxiety reduction. Some cognitive therapies are beginning to target this process in anxiety more directly, but much work needs to be done.

In this conceptualization of affective therapy (Barlow, 1988), directly altering hot apprehensive cognitions and other cognitive schemata associated with anxiety might be helpful but not necessarily essential to affective change. Similarly, instilling more appropriate coping skills and attending to social support available to the patient would also be helpful, as would reducing chronic physiological overreactivity by either relaxation or drugs.

REFERENCES

Adler, C., Craske, M. G., Kirschenbaum, S., & Barlow, D. H. (1989). "Fear of panic": An investigation of its role in panic occurrence, phobic avoidance, and treatment outcome. *Behaviour Research and Therapy, 27,* 391–396.

Agras, W. S., Lieterberg, H., & Barlow, D. H. (1968). Social reinforcement in the modification of agoraphobia. *Archives of General Psychiatry, 19,* 423–427.

American Psychiatric Association (1987). *Diagnostic and statistical manual of mental disorders* (3rd ed. rev.). Washington, DC: Author.

Anderson, D. J., Noyes, R., Jr., & Crowe, R. R. (1984). A comparison of panic disorder and generalized anxiety disorder. *American Journal of Psychiatry, 141,* 572–575.

Arnow, B. A., Taylor, C. B., Agras, W. S., & Telch, M. J. (1985). Enhancing agoraphobia treatment outcome by changing couple communication patterns. *Behavior Therapy, 16,* 452–467.

Bandura, A. (1977). Self-efficacy: Toward a unifying theory of behavioral change. *Psychological Review, 84,* 191–215.

Bandura, A. (1988). Self-efficacy conception of anxiety. *Anxiety Research, 1,* 77–98.

Bandura, A., Jeffrey, R. W., & Wright, C. L. (1974). Efficacy of participant modeling as a function of response induction aids. *Journal of Abnormal Psychology, 83,* 56–64.

Barlow, D. H. (1988). *Anxiety and its disorders: The nature and treatment of anxiety and panic.* New York: Guilford.

Barlow, D. H., Blanchard, E. B., Vermilyea, J. A., Vermilyea, B. B., & DiNardo, P. A. (1986). Generalized anxiety and generalized anxiety disorder: Description and reconceptualization. *American Journal of Psychiatry, 143,* 40–44.

Barlow, D. H., Cohen, D., Waddell, M., Vermilyea, J., Klosko, J., Blanchard, E. B., & DiNardo, P. A. (1984). Panic and generalized anxiety disorders: Nature and treatment. *Behavior Therapy, 15,* 431–449.

Barlow, D. H., & Craske, M. G. (1989). "Unexpected" panic and DSM-IV. Anxiety disorders workgroup taskforce, DSM-IV, American Psychiatric Association.

Barlow, D. H., Craske, M. G., Cerny, J. A., & Klosko, J. S. (1989). Behavioral treatment of panic disorder. *Behavior Therapy, 20,* 261–282.

Barlow, D. H., O'Brien, G. T., & Last, C. G. (1984). Couples treatment of agoraphobia. *Behavior Therapy, 15,* 41–58.

Barlow, D. H., Vermilyea, J. A., Blanchard, E. B., Vermilyea, B. B., DiNardo, P. A., & Cerny, J. A. (1985). The phenomenon of panic. *Journal of Abnormal Psychology, 94,* 320–328.

Barlow, D. H., & Waddell, M. T. (1985). Agoraphobia. In D. H. Barlow (Ed.), *Clinical handbook of psychological disorders: A step-by-step treatment manual.* New York: Guilford.

Beck, A. T. (1985). Theoretical perspectives on clinical anxiety. In A. H. Tuma & J. D. Maser (Eds.), *Anxiety and the anxiety disorders.* Hillsdale, NJ: Erlbaum.

Beck, A. T. (1988). Cognitive approaches to panic disorder: Theory and therapy. In S. Rachman & J. D. Maser (Eds.), *Panic: Psychological perspectives.* Hillsdale, NJ: Erlbaum.

Beck, A. T., & Emery, G. (1985). *Anxiety disorders and phobias: A cognitive perspective.* New York: Basic Books.

Benson, H., Beary, J. F., & Carol, M. P. (1974). The relaxation response. *Psychiatry, 37,* 37–46.

Bernstein, D. A., & Borkovec, T. D. (1973). *Progressive relaxation training.* Champaign, IL: Research Press.

Bland, K., & Hallam, R. S. (1981). Relationship between response to exposure and marital satisfaction in agoraphobics. *Behaviour Research and Therapy, 19,* 335–338.

Blowers, C., Cobb, J., & Mathews, A. (1987). Generalized anxiety: A controlled treatment study. *Behaviour Research and Therapy, 25,* 493–502.

Bonn, J. A., Harrison, J., & Rees, W. (1971). Lactate-induced anxiety: Therapeutic application. *British Journal of Psychiatry, 119,* 468–470.

Borkovec, T. (1976). Physiological and cognitive processes in the regulation of anxiety. In G. Schwartz & D. Shapiro (Eds.), *Consciousness and self-regulation: Advances in research Vol. 1,* 26–312. New York: Plenum.

Borkovec, T. D., & Mathews, A. M. (1988). Treatment of nonphobic anxiety disorders: A comparison of nondirective, cognitive, and coping desensitization therapy. *Journal of Consulting and Clinical Psychology, 56,* 877–884.

Borkovec, T. D., Mathews, A. M., Chambers, A., Ebrahimi, S., Lytle, R., & Nelson, R. (1987). The effects of relaxation training with cognitive restructuring or nondirective therapy and the role of relaxation-induced anxiety in the treatment of generalized anxiety. *Journal of Consulting and Clinical Psychology, 55,* 883–888.

Borkovec, T. D., & Sides, J. K. (1979). Critical procedural variables related to the physiological effects of progressive relaxation: A review. *Behaviour Research and Therapy, 17,* 119–125.

Boyd, H. H. (1986). Use of mental health services for the treatment of panic disorder. *American Journal of Psychiatry, 143,* 1569–1574.

Breier, A., Charney, D. S., & Heninger, G. R. (1986). Agoraphobia with panic attacks. *Archives of General Psychiatry, 43,* 1029–1036.

Breslau, N. (1985). Depressive symptoms, major depression, and generalized anxiety: A comparison of self-reports on CES-D and results from diagnostic interviews. *Psychiatry Research, 15,* 219–229.

Brown, T. A., Cash, T. F., & Deagle, E. A. (1988). *Prevalence and phenomenology of panic in nonclinical samples: Additional findings and methodological considerations.* Poster presented at 22nd Annual Convention, Association for the Advancement of Behavior Therapy, New York.

Burns, L. E., Thorpe, G. L., & Cavallaro, L. A. (1986). Agoraphobia eight years after behavioral treatment: A follow-up study with interview, self-report, and behavioral data. *Behavior Therapy, 17,* 580–591.

Butler, G., Cullington, A., Hibbert, G., Klimes, I., & Gelder, M. (1987). Anxiety management for persistent generalised anxiety. *British Journal of Psychiatry, 151,* 535–542.

Butler, G., & Mathews, A. (1983). Cognitive processes in anxiety. *Advances in Behaviour Research and Therapy, 5,* 51–62.

Clark, D. (1989, June). Paper presented at the 1st World Congress of Cognitive Therapy, Oxford, England.

Clark, D., Salkovskis, P., & Chalkley, A. (1985). Respiratory control as a treatment for panic attacks. *Journal of Behavior Therapy and Experimental Psychiatry, 16,* 23–30.

Cerny, J. A., Barlow, D. H., Craske, M. G., & Himadi, W. G. (1987). Couples treatment of agoraphobia: A two-year follow-up. *Behavior Therapy, 18,* 401–415.

Chambless, D. L. (1989, November). *Spacing of exposure sessions in the treatment of phobia.* Poster presented at 22nd Annual Convention, Association for the Advancement of Behavior Therapy, New York.

Chambless, D., Caputo, G., Bright, P., & Gallagher, R. (1984). Assessment of fear in agoraphobics: The Body Sensations Questionnaire and the Agoraphobic Cognitions Questionnaire. *Journal of Consulting and Clinical Psychology, 52,* 1090–1097.

Chaplin, E. W., & Levine, B. A. (1981). The effects of total exposure duration and interrupted versus continued exposure in flooding therapy. *Behavior Therapy, 12,* 360–368.

Cobb, J. P., Mathews, A. M., Childs-Clarke, A., & Blowers, C. M. (1984). The spouse as co-therapist in the treatment of agoraphobia. *British Journal of Psychiatry, 144,* 282–287.

Cohen, S. D., Monteiro, W., & Marks, I. M. (1984). Two-year follow-up of agoraphobics after exposure and imipramine. *British Journal of Psychiatry, 144,* 276–281.

Craske, M. G., & Barlow, D. H. (1988). A review of the relationship between panic and avoidance. *Clinical Psychology Review, 8,* 667–685.

Craske, M. G., & Barlow, D. H. (1989, November). *Salience of bodily area in the assessment and treatment of panic disorder with agoraphobia.* Paper presented at 23rd Annual Convention, Association for Advancement of Behavior Therapy, Washington, DC.

Craske, M. G., & Barlow, D. H. (1990). Contribution of cognitive psychology to assessment and treatment of anxiety. In P. Martin (Ed.), *Handbook of behavior therapy and psychological science.* New York: Pergamon.

Craske, M. G., Bran, T. A., & Barlow, D. H. (1991). Behavioral treatment of panic disorder: A two-year follow-up. *Behavior Therapy, 22,* 289–304.

Craske, M. G., Burton, T., & Barlow, D. H. (1988). Relationships among measures of communication, marital satisfaction and exposure during couples treatment of agoraphobia. *Behaviour Research and Therapy, 27,* 131–140.

Craske, M. G., & Krueger, M. (1990). The prevalence of nocturnal panic in a college population. *Journal of Anxiety Disorders, 4,* 125–139.

Craske, M. G., Rapee, R. M., & Barlow, D. H. (1988). The significance of panic-expectancy for individual patterns of avoidance. *Behavior Therapy, 19,* 577–592.

Craske, M. G., Rapee, R. M., Jackel, L., & Barlow, D. H. (1989). Qualitative dimensions of worry in DSM-III-R generalized anxiety disorder subjects and nonanxious controls. *Behaviour Research and Therapy, 27,* 397–402.

Craske, M. G., Street, L., & Barlow, D. H. (1989). Instructions to focus upon or distract from internal cues during exposure treatment for agoraphobic avoidance. *Behaviour Research and Therapy, 27,* 663–672.

deRuiter, C., Rijken, H., Garssen, B., & Kraaimaat, F. (1989). Breathing retraining, exposure and a combination of both, in the treatment of panic disorder with agoraphobia. *Behaviour Research and Therapy, 27,* 647–656.

deSilva, P., & Rachman, S. J. (1984). Does escape behavior strengthen agoraphobic avoidance? A preliminary study. *Behaviour Research and Therapy, 22,* 87–91.

DiNardo, P. A., Rapee, R. M., Moras, K., & Barlow, D. H. (1990). Kappa co-efficients for DSM-III-R anxiety disorders. Manuscript in preparation.

Durham, R. C., & Turvey, A. A. (1987). Cognitive therapy vs. behaviour therapy in the treatment of chronic general anxiety. *Behaviour Research and Therapy, 25,* 229–234.

D'Zurilla, T. J., & Goldfried, M. R. (1971). Problem solving and behavior modification. *Journal of Abnormal Psychology, 78,* 107–126.

Ehlers, A., & Margraf, J. (1989). The psychophysiological model of panic attacks. In P. M. G. Emmelkamp (Ed.), *Anxiety disorders: Annual series of European research in behavior therapy.*

Ellis, A., & Harper, R. A. (1975). *A new guide to rational living.* Englewood Cliffs, NJ: Prentice-Hall.

Emmelkamp, P. M. G. (1980). Agoraphobics' interpersonal problems: Their role in the effects of exposure in vivo therapy. *Archives of General Psychiatry, 37,* 1303–1306.

Emmelkamp, P. M. G. (1982). *Phobic and obsessive-compulsive disorders: Theory, research, and practice.* New York: Plenum.

Emmelkamp, P. M. G., Kuipers, A. C. M., & Eggeraat, J. G. (1978). Cognitive modification versus prolonged exposure in vivo: A comparison with agoraphobics as subjects. *Behaviour Research and Therapy, 16,* 33–41.

Emmelkamp, P. M. G., & Mersch, P. P. (1982). Cognition and exposure in vivo in the treatment of agoraphobia: Short-term and delayed effects. *Cognitive Therapy and Research, 6,* 77–88.

Emmelkamp, P. M. G., & Ultee, K. A. (1974). A comparison of "successive approximation" and "self-observation" in the treatment of agoraphobia. *Behavior Therapy, 5,* 606–613.

Emmelkamp, P. M. G., & Wessels, H. (1975). Flooding in imagination vs. flooding in vivo: A comparison with agoraphobics. *Behaviour Research and Therapy, 13,* 7–15.

Feigenbaum, W. (1988). Long-term efficacy of ungraded versus graded massed exposure in agoraphobics. In I. Hand & H. Wittchen (Eds.), *Panic and phobias: Treatments and variables affecting course and outcome.* Berlin: Springer-Verlag.

Foa, E. G., Jameson, J. S., Turner, R. M., & Payne, L. L. (1980). Massed vs. spaced exposure sessions in the treatment of agoraphobia. *Behaviour Research and Therapy, 18,* 333–338.

Foa, E. B., & Kozak, M. S. (1986). Emotional processing of fear: Exposure to corrective information. *Psychological Bulletin, 99,* 20–35.

Gauthier, J., Laberge, B., Freve, A., & DuFour, L. (1986). The contribution of therapeutic expectancies to exposure in the behavioral treatment of fear. Unpublished manuscript.

Gelder, M. G., & Marks, I. M. (1966). Severe agoraphobia: A controlled prospective trial of behavior therapy. *British Journal of Psychiatry, 112,* 309–319.

Gelder, M. G., Marks, I. M., & Wolff, H. H. (1967). Desensitization and psychotherapy in the treatment of phobic states: A controlled inquiry. *British Journal of Psychiatry, 113,* 53–73.

Ghosh, A., & Marks, I. M. (1987). Self-directed exposure for agoraphobia: A controlled trial. *Behavior Therapy, 18,* 3–16.

Gillan, P., & Rachman, S. J. (1974). An experimental investigation of desensitization in phobic patients. *British Journal of Psychiatry, 124,* 392–401.

Gitlin, B., Martin, M., Shear, K., Frances, A., Ball, G., & Josephson, S. (1985). Behavior therapy for panic disorder. *Journal of Nervous and Mental Disease, 173,* 742–743.

Grayson, J. B., Foa, E. B., & Steketee, G. (1982). Habituation during exposure treatment: Distraction versus attention-focusing. *Behaviour Research and Therapy, 20,* 323–328.

Griez, E., & van den Hout, M. A. (1986). CO_2 inhalation in the treatment of panic attacks. *Behaviour Research and Therapy, 24,* 145–150.

Hafner, R. J. (1976). Fresh symptom emergence after intensive behavior therapy. *British Journal of Psychiatry, 129,* 378–383.

Haslam, M. T. (1974). The relationship between the effect of lactate infusion on anxiety states and their amelioration by carbon dioxide inhalation. *British Journal of Psychiatry, 125,* 88–90.

Hibbert, G. A. (1984). Ideational components of anxiety: Their origin and content. *British Journal of Psychiatry, 144,* 618–624.

Himadi, W., Cerny, J. A., Barlow, D. H., Cohen, S. L., & O'Brien, G. T. (1986). The relationship of marital adjustment to agoraphobia treatment outcome. *Behaviour Research and Therapy, 24,* 107–115.

Hoelscher, T. J., Lichstein, K. L., & Rosenthal, T. L. (1984). Objective versus subjective assessment of relaxation compliance among anxious individuals. *Behaviour Research and Therapy, 23,* 187–193.

Holden, A. E. O., O'Brien, G. T., Barlow, D. H., Stetson, D., & Infantino, A. (1983). Self-help manual for agoraphobia: A preliminary report of effectiveness. *Behavior Therapy, 14,* 545-556.

Holt, P., & Andrews, G. (1989). Hyperventilation and anxiety in panic disorder, social phobia, GAD, and normal controls. *Behaviour Research and Therapy, 27,* 453-460.

Jacobson, E. (1938). *Progressive relaxation.* Chicago: University of Chicago Press.

Jannoun, L., Munby, M., Catalan, J., & Gelder, M. (1980). A home-based treatment program for agoraphobia: Replication and controlled evaluation. *Behavior Therapy, 11,* 294-305.

Jansson, L., Jerremalm, A., & Öst, L.-G. (1986). Follow-up of agoraphobic patients treated with exposure in vivo or applied relaxation. *British Journal of Psychiatry, 149,* 486-490.

Jansson, L., & Öst, L.-G. (1982). Behavioral treatments for agoraphobia: An evaluative review. *Clinical Psychology Review, 2,* 311-336.

Klein, D. F., & Klein, H. M. (1989). The substantive effects of variations in panic measurement and agoraphobia definition. *Journal of Anxiety Disorders, 3,* 45-56.

Kraft, A. R., & Hoogduin, C. A. (1984). The hyperventilation syndrome: A pilot study of the effectiveness of treatment. *British Journal of Psychiatry, 145,* 538-542.

Mannuzza, S., Fyer, A. J., Martin, L. Y., Gallops, M. S., Endicott, J., Gorman, J., Liebowitz, M. R., & Klein, D. F. (1989). Reliability of anxiety assessment: I. Diagnostic agreement. *Archives of General Psychiatry, 46,* 1093-1101.

Margraf, J. (1989, June). Comparative efficacy of cognitive, exposure and contained treatments for panic disorder. Paper presented at the 1st World Congress of Cognitive Therapy, Oxford, England.

Marks, I. M. (1971). Phobic disorders four years after treatment: A prospective follow-up. *British Journal of Psychiatry, 118,* 683-686.

Marks, I. M. (1978). *Living with fear.* New York: McGraw-Hill.

Marshall, W. L. (1985). The effects of variable exposure in flooding therapy. *Behavior Therapy, 16,* 117-135.

Mathews, A. M., Gelder, M. G., & Johnston, D. W. (1981). *Agoraphobia: Nature and treatment.* New York: Guilford.

Mathews, A. M., Johnston, D. W., Lancashire, M., Munby, M., Shaw, P. N., & Gelder, M. G. (1976). Imaginal flooding and exposure to real phobic situations: Treatment outcome with agoraphobic patients. *British Journal of Psychiatry, 129,* 362-371.

McNamee, G., O'Sullivan, G., Lelliott, P., & Marks, I. M. (1989). Telephone-guided treatment for housebound agoraphobics with panic disorder: Exposure vs. relaxation. *Behavior Therapy, 20,* 491-497.

Meichenbaum, D. (1975). Self-instructional methods. In F. H. Kanfer and A. P. Goldstein (Eds.), *Helping people change.* Sydney: Pergamon.

Michelson, L. (1989, November). *Cognitive-behavioral treatments of panic disorder with agoraphobia: A comparative outcome investigation.* Paper presented at the 23rd Annual Convention, Association for Advancement of Behavior Therapy, Washington, DC.

Michelson, L., Mavissakalian, M., & Marchione, K. (1985). Cognitive and behavioral treatments of agoraphobia: Clinical, behavioral, and psychophysiological outcomes. *Journal of Consulting and Clinical Psychology, 53,* 913-925.

Michelson, L., Mavissakalian, M., Marchione, K., Dancu, C., & Greenwald, M. (1986). The role of self-directed in vivo exposure practice in cognitive, behavioral and psychophysiological treatments of agoraphobia. *Behavior Therapy, 17,* 91-108.

Milton, F., & Hafner, J. (1979). The outcome of behavior therapy for agoraphobia in relation to marital adjustment. *Archives of General Psychiatry, 36,* 807-911.

Munby, J., & Johnston, D. W. (1980). Agoraphobia: The long-term follow-up of behavioural treatment. *British Journal of Psychiatry, 137,* 418-427.

Norton, G. R., Dorward, J., & Cox, B. J. (1980). Factors associated with panic attacks in nonclinical subjects. *Behavior Therapy, 17,* 239-252.

Noyes, R., Crowe, R. R., Harris, E. L., Hamra, B. J., McChesney, C. M., & Chaudhry, D. R. (1986). Relationship between panic disorder and agoraphobia: A family study. *Archives of General Psychiatry, 227*-232.

Oei, T., Craske, M. G., Rapee, R. M., DiNardo, P. A., & Barlow, D. H. (1989). [Factor structure of the DSM-III-R symptoms for panic attacks]. Unpublished raw data.

Öst, L.-G. (1988). Applied relaxation vs. progressive relaxation in the treatment of panic disorder. *Behaviour Research and Therapy, 26,* 13–22.

Pollard, C. A., Pollard, H. J., & Corn, K. J. (1989). Panic onset and major events in the lives of agoraphobics: A test of contiguity. *Journal of Abnormal Psychology, 98,* 318–321.

Rachman, S. J. (1984). Agoraphobia: A safety-signal perspective. *Behaviour Research and Therapy, 22,* 59–70.

Rachman, S. J., & Bichard, S. (1988). The overprediction of fear. *Clinical Psychology Review, 8,* 303–312.

Rachman, S. J., Craske, M. G., Tallman, K., & Solyom, C. (1986). Does escape behavior strengthen agoraphobic avoidance? A replication. *Behavior Therapy, 17,* 366–384.

Rachman, S. J., & Levitt, K. (1985). Panics and their consequences. *Behaviour Research and Therapy, 23,* 585–600.

Rachman, S. J., Levitt, K., & Lopatka, C. (1988). Experimental analyses of panic III—claustrophobic subjects. *Behaviour Research and Therapy, 26,* 41–52.

Rachman, S. J., & Lopatka, C. (1986). Match and mismatch in the prediction of fear—I & II. *Behaviour Research and Therapy, 24,* 387–393.

Rachman, S. J., Lopatka, C., & Levitt, K. (1988). Experimental analyses of panic II—panic patients. *Behaviour Research and Therapy, 26,* 41–52.

Rapee, R. M. (1985a). A case of panic disorder treated with breathing retraining. *Behavior Therapy and Experimental Psychiatry, 16,* 63–65.

Rapee, R. M. (1985b). Distinctions between panic disorder and generalized anxiety disorder: Clinical presentation. *Australian and New Zealand Journal of Psychiatry, 19,* 227–232.

Rapee, R. M. (1990). *Generalized anxiety disorder: A review of clinical features and theoretical concepts.* Manuscript submitted for publication.

Rapee, R. M., Ancis, J., & Barlow, D. H. (1988). Emotional reactions to physiological sensations: Panic disorder patients and non-clinical SS. *Behaviour Research and Therapy, 26,* 265–269.

Rapee, R. M., & Barlow, D. H. (1988). *Cognitive restructuring and relaxation in the treatment of generalized anxiety disorder: A controlled study.* Paper presented at the 22nd Annual Convention, Association for the Advancement of Behavior Therapy, New York.

Rapee, R. M., Craske, M. G., & Barlow, D. H. (1990). Subject-described features of panic attacks using a new self-monitoring form. *Journal of Anxiety Disorders, 4,* 171–181.

Rapee, R. M., Litwin, E. M., & Barlow, D. H. (1990). Impact of life events on subjects with panic disorder and on comparison subjects. *American Journal of Psychiatry, 147,* 640–644.

Rapee, R. M., Sanderson, W. C., & Barlow, D. H. (1988). Social phobia features across the DSM-III-R anxiety disorders. *Journal of Psychopathology and Behavioral Assessment, 10,* 287–299.

Reich, J., Noyes, R., & Troughton, E. (1987). Dependent personality disorder associated with phobic avoidance in patients with panic disorder. *American Journal of Psychiatry, 144,* 323–326.

Reiss, S., Peterson, R. A., Gursky, D. M., & McNally, R. J. (1986). Anxiety sensitivity, anxiety frequency and the prediction of fearfulness. *Behaviour Research and Therapy, 24,* 1–8.

Rice, K. M., & Blanchard, E. B. (1982). Biofeedback in the treatment of anxiety disorders. *Clinical Psychology Review, 2,* 557–577.

Riskind, J. H., Beck, A. T., Berchick, R. J., Brown, G., & Steer, R. A. (1987). Reliability for DSM-III diagnoses of major depression and generalized anxiety disorder using the structured clinical interview for DSM-III. *Archives of General Psychiatry, 44,* 817–820.

Roy-Byrne, P. P., Geraci, M., & Uhde, T. W. (1986). Life events and the onset of panic disorder. *American Journal of Psychiatry, 143,* 1424–1427.

Rupert, P. A., Dobbins, K., & Mathew, R. J. (1981). EMG biofeedback and relaxation instructions in the treatment of chronic anxiety. *American Journal of Clinical Biofeedback, 4,* 52–61.

Salge, R., Beck, G., & Logan, A. C. (1988). A community survey of panic. *Journal of Anxiety Disorders, 2,* 157–167.

Salkovskis, P., Warwick, H., Clark, D., & Wessels, D. (1986). A demonstration of acute hyperventilation during naturally occurring panic attacks. *Behaviour Research and Therapy, 24,* 91–94.

Sanderson, W. C., & Barlow, D. H. (1989). *Domains of worry within the DSM-III-Revised generalized anxiety disorder category: Reliability and description.* Manuscript submitted for publication.

Sanderson, W. C., DiNardo, P. A., Rapee, R. M., & Barlow, D. H. (in press). Syndrome co-morbidity in patients diagnosed with a DSM-III-Revised anxiety disorder. *Journal of Abnormal Psychology.*

Sanderson, W. S., Rapee, R. M., & Barlow, D. H. (1987, November). *The DSM-III-Revised anxiety disorder categories: Description and patterns of comorbidity.* Poster presented at 20th Annual Convention, Association for the Advancement of Behavior Therapy, Boston.

Sartory, G., Master, D., & Rachman, S. J. (1989). Safety-signal therapy in agoraphobics: A preliminary test. *Behaviour Research and Therapy, 27,* 205–209.

Sartory, G., & Olajide, D. (1988). Vagal innervation techniques in the treatment of panic disorder. *Behaviour Research and Therapy, 26,* 431–434.

Sheehan, D. V., & Sheehan, K. H. (1983). The classification of phobic disorders. *International Journal of Psychiatric Medicine, 12,* 243–266.

Southworth, S., & Kirsch, I. (1988). The role of expectancy in exposure-generated fear reduction in agoraphobia. *Behaviour Research and Therapy, 26,* 113–120.

Stern, R. S., & Marks, I. M. (1973). Brief and prolonged flooding: A comparison of agoraphobic patients. *Archives of General Psychiatry, 28,* 270–276.

Street, L., Craske, M. G., & Barlow, D. H. (1989). Sensations, cognitions and the perception of cues associated with expected and unexpected panic attacks. *Behaviour Research and Therapy, 27,* 189–198.

Swinson, R. P. (1986). Reply to Kleiner. *The Behavior Therapist, 9,* 110–128.

Telch, M. J., Lucas, J. A., & Nelson, P. (1989). Nonclinical panic in college students: An investigation of prevalence and symptomatology. *Journal of Abnormal Psychology, 98,* 300–306.

Thyer, B. A., Himle, J., Curtis, G. C., Cameron, O. G., & Nesse, R. M. (1985). A comparison of panic disorder and agoraphobia with panic attacks. *Comprehensive Psychiatry, 26,* 208–214.

Vermilyea, J. A., Boice, R., & Barlow, D. H. (1984). Rachman and Hodgson (1974) a decade later: How do desynchronous response systems relate to the treatment of agoraphobia? *Behaviour Research and Therapy, 22,* 615–621.

Waddell, M., Barlow, D. H., & O'Brien, G. T. (1984). A preliminary investigation of cognitive and relaxation treatment of panic disorder: Effects on intense anxiety vs. "background" anxiety. *Behaviour Research and Therapy, 22,* 393–402.

Weeks, C. (1976). *Simple, effective treatment of agoraphobia.* New York: Hawthorne.

Weissman, M. M., Leaf, P. J., Blazer, D. G., Boyd, J. H., & Florio, L. (1986). The relationship between panic disorder and agoraphobia: An epidemiological perspective. *Psychopharmacology Bulletin, 43,* 787–791.

Williams, S. L. (1988). Addressing misconceptions about phobia, anxiety, and self-efficacy: A reply to Marks. *Journal of Anxiety Disorders, 2,* 277–289.

Williams, S. L., & Rappaport, J. A. (1983). Cognitive treatment in the natural environment for agoraphobics. *Behavior Therapy, 14,* 299–313.

Williams, S. L., Turner, S. M., & Peer, D. F. (1985). Guided mastery and performance desensitization treatments for severe acrophobia. *Journal of Consulting and Clinical Psychology, 53,* 237-247.

Williams, S. L., & Zane, G. (1989). Guided mastery and stimulus exposure treatments for severe performance anxiety in agoraphobics. *Behaviour Research and Therapy, 27,* 237-245.

Zitrin, C. M., Klein, D. F., & Woerner, M. G. (1980). Behavior therapy, supportive psychotherapy, imipramine, and phobias. *Archives of General Psychiatry, 37,* 63-72.

CHAPTER 4

Obsessive-Compulsive Disorder

MELINDA A. STANLEY

Obsessive-compulsive disorder (OCD), one of the most severe and chronic of the anxiety disorders, traditionally was thought of as a rare disorder that was generally refractory to treatment. However, recent advances in behavior therapy and pharmacotherapy have improved significantly the prognosis for OCD. Behavioral treatment consisting of exposure (flooding) and response prevention has been described by some as the treatment of choice for OCD (Foa, Steketee, & Ozarow, 1985; Turner & Beidel, 1988). An overall improvement rate of 70% is generally reported. Pharmacological interventions with antidepressants also have produced promising results (Towlin, Leckman, & Cohen, 1987). The drugs most frequently used to treat OCD are clomipramine and fluoxetine, both of which are antidepressants with strong serotonergic activity.

This chapter's review of various aspects of the behavioral treatment of OCD begins with a description of the clinical syndrome and a review of assessment strategies. The current status of theory and research regarding flooding and response prevention is then surveyed, and procedures associated with implementation of this intervention are described. Relevant clinical issues are also discussed, as are alternative behavioral interventions. Finally, a case example of a treatment program is described, and directions for further research are addressed. Pharmacotherapy of OCD is not addressed except as it relates to treatment with flooding and response prevention.

DESCRIPTION OF THE CLINICAL SYNDROME

OCD is characterized by the presence of either obsessions or compulsions. An obsession is any thought, image, urge, or impulse that is intrusive, unwanted, persistent, and uncontrollable. Patients typically perceive obsessions as senseless, excessive, and distressful. Although obsessions are defined by the nature of a thought, many similar themes occur. The most common of these is a fear of contamination (Akhtar, Wig, Verma, Pershad, & Verma, 1975). Some patients describe a specific fear of contracting and/or spreading a disease such as cancer or AIDS; others describe a vague fear of just not being clean enough. Other obsessions frequently reported are fear of causing a disastrous event (e.g., the death or injury of another person as a result of an automobile accident), violent or sexual images or urges (e.g., images of stabbing someone or engaging in sexual activity with strangers), and religion-related thoughts or images (e.g., repetitive thoughts of the word "Satan"). A small subgroup of patients reports a less common obsession involving fears of negative evaluation (Stanley, Turner, & Borden, 1990).

Compulsions are ritualistic, stereotypic, or repetitive actions that typically accompany obsessional ideation. Patients generally perceive compulsions to be senseless and excessive, but they nevertheless are unable to resist completing the acts. The most common types of compulsive rituals involve repetitive cleaning or checking (Rachman, 1985); typical symptoms include ritualistic handwashing or housecleaning, and checking and rechecking of locks, windows, or work-related tasks. Cleaning rituals typically accompany obsessional fears of contamination, whereas repetitive checking usually occurs along with fears of being responsible for some impending disaster.

Compulsions need not be overt, motoric acts; rather, for some patients, ritualistic activity occurs cognitively. For example, a patient recently seen in our clinic reported that, following any "bad" thought about another person, he had to think of a list of friends' names in a particular order, pairing each name with the name of another "good" person. If the act was interrupted before completion, the patient had to begin the series again, in order to reduce his anxiety about his original "bad" thought. This symptom pattern has been characterized as cognitive ritual.

Regardless of whether compulsive activity occurs overtly or cognitively, completion of rituals usually reduces or wards off anxiety associated with obsessions (Barlow, 1988; Rachman, 1985; Turner & Beidel, 1988). Thus, one way to conceptualize rituals is as escape or avoidance mechanisms. At times, however, patients report no such relief from anxiety following compulsive activity. Under these circumstances, continued anxiety may result from the patient's inability to control ritualistic behavior (Turner & Beidel, 1988).

Although obsessions and compulsions typically are perceived as senseless, a small subset of patients denies the excessive nature of their actions. For example, a patient recently assessed in our clinic maintained the belief, in the face of disconfirming evidence, that he actually could contract AIDS by drinking from a soda can that might have been touched by an infected person. Patients with this belief pattern are said to exhibit "overvalued ideation." As described below, these individuals are somewhat difficult to treat with flooding and response prevention.

Another subset of OCD patients appears to have obsessions alone, without motoric rituals (Akhtar et al., 1975). A variant of OCD known as "primary obsessional slowness" also has been described (Rachman, 1974). Although slowness at times accompanies other ritualistic behavior, patients with this syndrome take an excessive amount of time to perform normal daily routines (e.g., dressing, bathing) without performing repetitive, ritualistic actions. Distinct obsessions also are absent in this syndrome, and a decrease in anxiety following completion of the behaviors is not characteristic. Hence, there is some suggestion that primary obsessional slowness may represent a variant of obsessive-compulsive personality rather than a form of OCD (Turner & Beidel, 1988).

Recent epidemiological data have suggested that OCD is much more common than previously believed, with lifetime prevalence rates ranging from 2 to 3% (Karno, Golding, Sorenson, & Burnam, 1988). These figures are 40 to 50% higher than previous estimates. Onset of the disorder typically occurs between late adolescence and the mid-20s, although patients usually report premorbid obsessional symptoms. Onset often is associated with significant life events such as childbirth, medical illness, or change in employment. Gender ratios suggest that the disorder is slightly more common in females (Karno et al., 1988), although the frequency of female patients with primary washing compulsions far outweighs that of males (Rachman & Hodgson, 1980). The course of the disorder is chronic, with frequent exacerbations during periods of stress (Turner & Beidel, 1988). Even following treatment, OCD symptoms are rarely completely absent. The more typical course is for treatment to reduce symptoms to a degree that allows the patient to function more effectively in social, work, and family activities.

A significant level of distress is associated with OCD, and patients often experience general anxiety and depression. Such distress is exemplified by the higher scores produced by OCD patients on a variety of instruments when compared to the scores of other anxiety patients (Turner, McCann, Beidel, & Mezzich, 1986). Overlap with other DSM-III-R Axis I diagnostic categories (e.g., depression, other anxiety disorders) also is common (Rachman, 1985; Turner & Beidel, 1988), and OCD patients almost always report family, social, and occupational difficulties.

ASSESSMENT STRATEGIES

Clinical Interviews

Clinical interviews with OCD patients are unique in that these individuals are often quite secretive, usually out of fear of embarrassment about symptoms or fear that talking about symptoms will make them worse (Turner & Beidel, 1988). The interviewer can handle secrecy by asking questions that indicate knowledge of typical symptoms and by reacting in a calm, nonjudgmental manner when bizarre symptoms are described. Often, detailed questions that provide examples of symptoms make a patient feel more comfortable about reporting unusual fears or behaviors. Detailed questioning also is useful for eliciting the information needed to develop a behavioral treatment plan. For example, if a patient describes any amount of excessive washing, it is important to ask about specific rituals in a number of areas: personal hygiene (e.g., bathroom, dressing, and bathing activities), housecleaning (e.g., use of particular cleaning substances, order of cleaning activities), laundry (e.g., washing of items in preparation for laundering clothes, amount of soap used, rewashing of clean clothing), and avoidance of contaminated areas of the patient's surroundings. Within any of these areas, vague questions about rituals (e.g., "What housecleaning rituals do you have?") are unlikely to yield essential information about the nature, frequency, or duration of rituals. Rather, asking patients to detail their actions during certain activities (e.g., "Tell me precisely what you do when you take a shower.") or to give specific information (e.g., "How many showers do you take each day?" or "How much time do you spend showering daily?") will elicit more useful descriptions.

Structured clinical interviews also can be helpful. One such instrument is the Yale–Brown Obsessive-Compulsive Inventory (YBOC; Goodman et al., 1989), which provides a checklist that can be used to help identify obsessive-compulsive symptoms. The YBOC allows for quantitative clinical ratings of time spent with obsessions and compulsions, interference and distress associated with each, and ability to resist and control symptoms. Initial psychometric data are adequate (Goodman et al., 1989), and the YBOC has been used as a repeated measure in pharmacological treatment outcome studies (e.g., Pato, Zohar-Kadouch, Zohar, & Murphy, 1988).

Self-Report Inventories

The two most commonly used questionnaires for the assessment of OCD are the Maudsley Obsessional-Compulsive Inventory (MOC; Hodgson & Rachman, 1977) and the Leyton Obsessional Inventory

(LOI; Cooper, 1970). These scales utilize true–false formats to provide quantitative estimates of OCD symptoms, but the LOI also assesses obsessive-compulsive personality traits and requires that patients make Likert-type ratings to assess interference and resistance of symptoms. The LOI thus provides a fairly detailed evaluation of a variety of OCD symptoms; however, the MOC is a briefer inventory that is much simpler to administer and score.

Behavioral Observation

An additional method that is useful for circumventing the secrecy of OCD patients is to observe them in their home environments. As discussed below, flooding and response prevention typically are initiated with a home visit. Although this visit serves to institute some of the treatment procedures, it is also an essential evaluation session. By asking the patient to progress through certain normal daily routines, the clinician is able to observe numerous ritualistic behaviors that otherwise might go unreported. For example, we recently initiated treatment with the patient (described above) who reported a fear of developing AIDS through contact with a variety of stimuli. Only during a visit to his home did we learn of his need to microwave foodstuffs prior to eating them. After preparing breakfast, the patient reported that his food had gotten cold and indicated a desire to reheat it in the microwave. Very little questioning was required to learn the significance of this act, and its correction was immediately incorporated into his treatment. A home visit can enable the clinician to make a more complete list of ritualistic behaviors to be incorporated into the behavioral treatment plan.

Behavioral observation also can occur in the clinician's office by placing the patient in situations wherein urges to perform rituals occur (e.g., seat the patient in a room with "contaminated" substances; ask the patient to perform a behavior that typically is checked and rechecked). The patient's ability to approach the feared substance and/or refrain from ritualistic behaviors can be observed, and reports of subjective distress under a variety of conditions can be obtained.

Self-Monitoring

Daily record keeping can be useful in assessing the pervasity of symptoms. Quantitative ratings of frequency and duration can be used to evaluate the initial severity of symptoms and to assess treatment efficacy. Daily self-monitoring also can provide qualitative information about the nature of symptoms, precipitating variables, and degree of distress. To accomplish these goals, patients should be provided with a written form upon which to record the variables of interest. This form might be a standard recording device or an individualized adaptation that fits a particular patient's symptom picture. Patients may be asked to complete a single form each day (Turner & Beidel, 1988) or to use a time-sampling method such that symptoms are recorded at equal intervals throughout the day (Barlow, 1988).

Self-monitoring alone can modify OCD symptoms. Some patients report exacerbations due to increased attention to symptoms; others exhibit a reactive response in which symptoms decrease. Rosenberg and Upper (1983) suggested that self-monitoring exacerbates the symptoms of OCD patients with checking compulsions. However, their case study involved a patient with somewhat atypical obsessions and rituals, whose symptoms were treated with a variety of interventions over a 19-week period. Although details were brief, the patient seemed similar to the subgroup of OCD patients with schizotypal features described by Stanley et al. (1990). Specifically, the patient's primary obsession revolved around his appearance and a fear of negative evaluation rather than a fear of being held responsible for some disastrous event, as is typical of most "checkers." It is as yet unclear whether members of this subgroup respond differently to any of the interventions used by Rosenberg and Upper (1983). Thus, conclusions regarding the reactivity of self-monitoring in OCD patients are limited. In general, my clinical experience has been that any symptom changes (positive or negative) that occur in response to self-monitoring procedures are temporary.

Psychophysiological Assessment

Psychophysiological assessment in OCD has not received the empirical attention that it deserves. However, a few available studies have shown increased skin conductance fluctuations after touching a "contaminated" object (Hornsveld, Kraaimaat, & van Dam-Baggen, 1979), and increased pulse associated with obsessive imagery and flooding or contact with contamination (Hodgson & Rachman, 1977; Rabavilas & Boulougouris, 1974). Some evidence further suggests that these indexes are reduced following performance of rituals (Hodgson & Rachman, 1977; Hornsveld et al., 1979). However, this area is well-deserving of further empirical attention.

Despite limited empirical data, psychophysiological assessment can be useful clinically to identify specific fear cues and to evaluate anxiety responses during treatment. Specifically, during behavioral observation, simple measures of heart rate or respiration frequency may provide information regarding the anxiety that accompanies contact with various stimuli, and in so doing may corroborate or expand information provided by the patient. During treatment, psychophysiological assessment can assist the clinician in determining when anxiety responses have returned to baseline levels (i.e., habituation has occurred).

FLOODING AND RESPONSE PREVENTION—CURRENT THEORY AND RESEARCH

Current Status of Theory

As noted above, flooding and response prevention are considered to be the treatments of choice for OCD (Foa et al., 1985). Intervention consists of two components: exposure to the feared stimuli and prevention of ritualistic responses that typically serve to reduce anxiety. This combination of strategies is based theoretically on Mowrer's (1939) two-stage theory of the learning of fear (Dollard & Miller, 1950). Mowrer proposed that learning occurs in two stages:

1. A neutral stimulus elicits fear as a result of classical conditioning;
2. Avoidance or escape behaviors, which develop as a result of the fear, tend to persist and to maintain fear, given the negative reinforcement that occurs when these behaviors reduce anxiety.

In the case of OCD, higher-order conditioning presumably causes numerous thoughts, images, persons, and objects to become associated with the fear. Consequently, a wide array of ritualistic thoughts and behaviors develops and provides avoidance or escape mechanisms.

Although limitations of Mowrer's theory have been noted (Foa et al., 1985), application of this perspective to OCD implies that treatment should entail procedures both to reduce anxiety and to prevent negative reinforcement of rituals. The combination of flooding and response prevention addresses both of these needs. Specifically, flooding involves intense exposure to feared stimuli until anxiety is reduced, and response prevention involves assisting the patient in stopping all ritualistic activity, thus eliminating the negative reinforcement associated with avoidance or escape. In cases wherein performance of rituals serves to increase anxiety (possibly due to negative evaluation; Turner & Beidel, 1988), response prevention also serves to eliminate anxiety.

Empirical data have supported the proposition that exposure and response prevention have differential treatment effects. For example, Steketee, Foa, and Grayson (1982) treated OCD patients who had washing rituals with exposure (flooding) alone, response prevention alone, or combined treatment. During exposure alone, patients were kept in contact with "contaminated" stimuli, but were allowed to wash whenever they chose. Immediately following washing, however, patients were "recontaminated." Patients treated with response prevention alone were prevented from washing excessively, but were allowed to avoid "contaminated" stimuli as they wished. Results revealed that exposure-only patients experienced significantly less anxiety when in contact with feared substances than did the response prevention patients, but the latter group showed significantly less time spent in completing washing rituals. Combined treatment led to improvement in both areas. Thus, exposure (or flooding) appeared to serve an anxiety-reducing function whereas response prevention-only reduced rituals. Foa et al. (1985) concluded that, during response prevention alone, patients are likely to refrain from rituals by avoiding contact with feared stimuli. Given such a situation, ritualistic behavior is likely to recur following exposure to "contaminated" substances.

A further point of theoretical interest involves the mechanism(s) through which flooding reduces anxiety. Flooding typically leads to habituation, a phenomenon defined by decreases in physiological, subjective, or behavioral measures of anxiety following repetitive exposure. Extinction theories propose that this anxiety reduction results from repeated exposure that is not followed by the feared aversive consequences (e.g., an OCD patient is exposed to a contaminant but neither the patient nor members of his or her family develop a feared disease). Within-session habituation, which occurs during a single session of exposure, has been demonstrated for OCD patients with regard to both heart rate and subjective anxiety (Foa, Grayson, & Steketee, 1982; Grayson, Foa, & Steketee, 1986). Between-session habituation, which occurs across sessions, typically is evident as peak anxiety responses and/or the length of time required for within-session habituation decreases over time. This phenomenon has been observed in OCD patients during both in vivo (Foa et al., 1982) and imaginal (Foa & Chambless, 1978) flooding. In order for between-session habituation to occur, within-session habituation must have occurred (Foa, 1979), although achieving the latter does not guarantee the former. In an attempt to explain the apparent independence of these two phenomena, Foa et al. (1985) proposed that within-session habituation involves responses of the autonomic nervous system whereas between-session habituation requires cognitive processing. This hypothesis requires further empirical attention.

Other perspectives have been proposed to explain the anxiety-reduction mechanism(s) of exposure. An emotional processing explanation, based on the bioinformational theory of affect proposed by Lang (1979), was elaborated by Foa and Kozak (1986). This model suggests that anxiety is represented via a cognitive "network" of information about threatening events or stimuli, responses to those stimuli (e.g., behavioral, physiological), and the meanings attached to each. Foa and Kozak (1986) proposed that, in order to reduce anxiety, all elements of this fear network need to be accessed and replaced with new, incompatible information. Flooding is effective, therefore, when it includes exposure to all stimulus and response cues and when it provides incompatible information (e.g., feared consequences do not occur following exposure; anxiety responses dissipate with time).

Another explanation of the effects of exposure comes from Bandura's (1977) self-efficacy theory. This model proposes that enhancement of self-efficacy expectancies, or perceptions of self-competence, is the mechanism by which all fear-reduction treatment is effective. According to this model, flooding is effective to the extent that it increases patients' judgments of their abilities to perform fear-related behaviors.

Empirical support for each of these perspectives is mixed (Barlow, 1988), and further investigation into the mechanisms of anxiety reduction through exposure certainly is a fertile area for empirical study.

Current Status of Treatment Outcome Research

The earliest attempt to utilize flooding and response prevention in the treatment of OCD was reported by Meyer (1966). In the two cases reported in Meyer's paper, patients were exposed to anxiety-provoking situations for extended periods of time while being prevented 24 hours a day from performing rituals. Both patients experienced significant reduction in obsessional and compulsive symptoms. In a subsequent series of studies with inpatients at the Maudsley Hospital in London, the combination of flooding and response prevention was compared to treatment with relaxation (Hodgson, Rachman, & Marks, 1972; Rachman, Marks, & Hodgson, 1973). In these studies, patients received one of three variants of flooding and response prevention: (a) gradual, in vivo exposure to feared stimuli following a therapist's modeling of the behavior; (b) in vivo exposure without therapist modeling; or (c) in vivo exposure with therapist modeling. In general, flooding and response prevention demonstrated a 75% improvement rate (75% of patients were improved or much improved), with treatment gains largely intact at 2-year follow-up. Treatment with relaxation had very few beneficial effects. Although flooding with therapist modeling appeared to demonstrate superior outcome at 6-month follow-up, patients in the three groups exhibited equivalent outcome 2 years posttreatment.

Similar improvement rates have been demonstrated in other studies. Roper, Rachman, and Marks (1975) reported that 8 of 10 "washers" were improved following 15 daily sessions of flooding and response prevention. Boersma, Den Hengst, Dekker, and Emmelkamp (1976) treated 13 patients in their homes (also with 15 sessions of flooding) and reported that 77% were improved or symptom-free at posttreatment and follow-up. In a meta-analysis of treatment outcome studies involving 50 patients, Foa et al. (1983b) categorized patients with treatment gains of 70% (or more) as much improved, those with gains between 30% and 70% as improved, and those with fewer gains as failures. Summary statistics indicated that following treatment with flooding and response prevention, 58% of patients were much improved, 38% were improved, and 4% were failures. At follow-up (which ranged from 3 months to 3 years), 59% were much improved, 17% were improved, and 24% failed to maintain treatment gains.

In a subsequent analysis, Foa et al. (1985) examined data from over 200 patients treated with flooding and response prevention and found a similar outcome pattern. Specifically, 51% of patients were symptom-free or much improved at posttreatment, 39% were moderately improved, and 10% showed no treatment gains. By follow-up, the failure rate had increased to 24%. Nevertheless, Foa et al. (1985) concluded from their review that combined flooding and response prevention is the treatment of choice for OCD.

Treatment Variations

A number of variations in flooding and response prevention procedures have been investigated empirically. Some of these include the mode of presentation of stimuli (imaginal versus in vivo), whether exposure is gradual or rapid, duration of exposure, and the therapist's role.

Early studies suggested that in vivo exposure was superior to imaginal presentation of stimuli (Rabavilas, Boulougouris, & Stefanis, 1976). However, in these trials, the content of the exposure did not vary with the mode of stimulus presentation (e.g., imaginal exposure asked patients to imagine tangible stimuli). As Foa et al. (1985) pointed out, the primary fear for all OCD patients is not accessed most effectively via tangible stimuli. For example, if a patient's primary fear is of some imagined disaster (as is true for most patients with checking compulsions), the fear should be accessed most effectively through imagination. Foa, Steketee, Turner, and Fischer (1980) reported that OCD patients with checking compulsions were more likely to maintain treatment gains during a follow-up period if treatment included imaginal flooding. Thus, it appears that imaginal flooding is important for patients with fears of disastrous consequences that cannot be produced in vivo. As Turner and Beidel (1988) suggested, imaginal flooding also may be useful for patients with cognitive avoidance that interferes with in vivo exposure. For these patients, repetitively focusing their attention on imagined feared consequences may help to decrease such avoidance.

Another variation in exposure procedures involves whether exposure occurs in a gradual or rapid manner. Empirical data from Hodgson and Rachman (1977) suggested that treatment outcome was similar for patients treated with gradual or rapid exposure, but that patients felt more comfortable with the former procedure. Other data have suggested that high initial levels of subjective fear correlated with decreased levels of habituation (Foa, Grayson, Steketee, & Doppelt, 1983a). Thus, moderate levels of anxiety associated with exposure may be optimal (Foa et al., 1985), although specific definitions of mild, moderate, and high are lacking and therefore make this proposition difficult to apply to treatment (Barlow, 1988). On the basis of clinical experience, Turner and Beidel (1988) reported that rapid exposure is most efficacious, given the pervasiveness with which OCD patients experience fear and perform rituals.

Duration of exposure sessions is another area in which variations in procedure have been investigated. Empirical and clinical data have supported the position that long exposure sessions are more beneficial, particularly when exposure is being conducted in an in vivo fashion (Rabavilas et al., 1976; Turner & Beidel, 1988). However, the most crucial variables appear to be the total amount of exposure provided and the length of the interval between treatment sessions (Foa et al., 1985). Thus, frequent exposure sessions separated by small time intervals are probably most effective.

Finally, the therapist's role in flooding and response prevention has been debated. In one study, the therapist's presence during exposure did not have a significant effect on treatment outcome (Emmelkamp & van Kraanen, 1977). However, some kind of supervised response prevention typically improves outcome (Mills, Agras, Barlow, & Mills, 1973), probably because of its effect on compliance. The therapist can point out ritualistic behaviors that the patient is either unaware of or reluctant to give up (Turner & Beidel, 1988). Further, patient ratings of the therapist's attitude or method of conducting sessions correlated with treatment outcome (Rabavilas, Boulougouris, & Perissaki, 1979). Thus, the therapist is not indispensable, particularly during initial exposure sessions.

Patient Characteristics That Influence Treatment Outcome

An initial characteristic that will influence the efficacy of flooding and response prevention is the patient's willingness to engage in what often is a very stressful and time-consuming intervention (Foa et al., 1985). Even when patients cooperate fully with treatment, some fail to respond. Variables that have been associated with poor response include age at symptom onset, level of pretreatment depression, and presence of overvalued ideation (Foa, 1979; Foa et al., 1983a). Foa et al. (1985) proposed that age at symptom onset (which is negatively correlated with treatment outcome) may interact with treatment inasmuch as age of onset has some relationship to personality, although this is as yet an untested hypothesis. Depression has been proposed to interfere with treatment outcome, given its effect on within-session habituation, which may occur as a result of depressed patients' enhanced reactivity to feared stimuli (Foa et al., 1985). Overvalued ideation seems to interfere with between-session habituation, possibly because of the cognitive processing that is required in that process. Some data have suggested that the addition of cognitive therapy to the treatment of patients with overvalued ideation is useful (Salkovskis & Warwick, 1985).

Retrospective data have suggested that schizotypal personality features predict poor treatment response (Jenike, Baer, Minichiello, Schwartz, & Carey, 1986). However, this proposition has yet to be tested in a prospective fashion. Factors generally not associated with treatment outcome include severity of symptoms and general level of anxiety (Foa et al., 1983b).

IMPLEMENTATION OF FLOODING AND RESPONSE PREVENTION

Pretreatment Issues

Before beginning a program of flooding and response prevention, a number of issues need to be addressed (Turner & Beidel, 1988). First, the patient should receive a full medical examination to rule out any physical factors that might interfere with or be exaggerated by treatment (e.g., cardiovascular problems, ulcerative colitis). If any of these conditions exist, the therapist should consider postponing treatment until further medical attention is paid to these problems or implementing the treatment in a gradual fashion. Second, the patient should be evaluated for depressive symptomatology. If the patient exhibits severe depressive symptoms, consideration should be given to an antidepressant trial prior to initiation of flooding and response prevention. Third, any use of alcohol or anxiolytics should be discontinued so that anxiety is not blocked by these agents during behavioral treatment.

Prior to initiation of treatment, the therapist also needs to make a decision regarding the need for inpatient intervention. Turner and Beidel (1988) reviewed some of the reasons one might decide to begin with inpatient treatment:

1. Detoxification is required.
2. Distance would prevent the patient from attending daily outpatient sessions.

3. Response prevention could not be implemented in the home.
4. Medical difficulties and/or severe depressive symptomatology (e.g., suicidal ideation) require more intensive attention.

Once these preliminary issues have been addressed and the decision has been made to offer flooding and response prevention, it is useful to spend some time educating the patient about OCD and the treatment. Patients often are unaware of the nature, chronicity, and prevalence of the disorder, and therefore benefit from a brief explanation of OCD and a very general discussion of the behavioral theories upon which flooding and response prevention are based. Although most patients will not grasp these theories initially, this discussion can serve to set realistic expectations for the disorder and the outcome of treatment. Patients need to know that, even with extensive treatment, some symptoms of the disorder are likely to remain. They also should be told the time commitment that will be required throughout different phases of flooding, and the need for continued work to maintain and control symptoms. Before any intervention is begun, the patient must agree to expend the extensive demands of the treatment.

Next, a list of specific stimuli that elicit fear must be made, in order to determine the precise nature of flooding sessions (e.g., imaginal versus in vivo). A detailed list of ritualistic behaviors should be created, for a matchup of specific response prevention instructions. The therapist should remain flexible, modifying these interventions as necessary, but it is important to begin with as accurate an assessment of stimuli and responses as is possible, given a reasonable time frame.

Treatment Issues

Treatment typically begins with a home visit. During this visit, the therapist assists the patient in completing all response prevention tasks (e.g., taking a shower within a specified time limit, washing hands a limited number of times, refraining from checking doors or windows upon leaving the house), and evaluates the need for revisions in the response prevention program based on newly observed ritualistic behaviors. Family members are instructed to refrain from any behaviors that assist the patient's ritualistic endeavors. For example, a patient recently treated in our clinic required that her husband be seated in exactly the same place when she left a room as he had been when she entered the room. During our first visit to their home, the husband was instructed not to comply with such requests. Enlisting family assistance in flooding and response prevention can be essential but can also create increased tension in relationships that already are quite strained. Thus, the method by which the assistance is requested and the responsibility given to family members must be determined on an individualized, clinical basis.

Following initiation of response prevention, a program of 10 consecutive, daily flooding sessions is conducted. The nature of these sessions should be determined on an individualized basis, and the length of each will depend on the amount of time required for within-session habituation. Habituation is determined by observing physiological, behavioral, and subjective indexes of anxiety, and the session is stopped only when measures return to baseline levels. Usually, sessions of approximately 2 hours are sufficient, although some flooding sessions can last many hours. After 10 flooding sessions, evidence of significant between-session habituation should be apparent. For flooding and response prevention to be effective, both within- and between-session habituation must occur.

After 10 daily flooding sessions have been completed, the frequency of sessions can be decreased to two or three times a week and the patient should begin to assume more responsibility for self-exposure. At this point—or earlier, if patient characteristics allow—transfer of responsibility for exposure may be facilitated by the use of audiotapes of flooding sessions (Salkovskis, 1983). Frequency of sessions usually can be reduced further after an additional two to four weeks.

In an inpatient setting, procedures are similar, but 24-hour supervised response prevention can be utilized and flooding can be conducted more than once per day. Usually, a 3-week hospital stay is required to get obsessive-compulsive symptoms under reasonable control. At discharge, however, an intensive program of outpatient work, including at least one home visit, is required to generalize treatment gains to the home setting. Videotapes can be useful for this purpose. For one inpatient with severe fears of contaminating her home with food particles, videotapes of the patient's home were used to enhance the utility of inpatient imaginal flooding and to prepare the patient for her return home (Beidel, Turner, & Allgood-Hill, 1986).

Maintenance of Treatment Gains

An intense period of flooding and response prevention typically gets obsessive-compulsive symptoms under some control. However, without an extended maintenance period of treatment, relapse is inevitable. For patients who begin to assume responsibility for self-exposure, sessions can become briefer and can focus primarily on assigning and evaluating self-exposure tasks. When OCD symptoms are under good control, treatment should begin to address residual symptoms (e.g., generalized anxiety, or family/social/employment difficulties). If patients do not learn to manage these residual symptoms, relapse is likely to occur when stress levels increase. Treatment at this stage can include a variety of interventions—social skills training, relaxation training, cognitive therapy, or family/marital treatment. (See "Other Behavioral Interventions," below.) In general, a period of one or two years is necessary for the full treatment of OCD.

RELEVANT CLINICAL ISSUES

Patient Management

How to handle patients' secrecy, and the importance of educating the patient regarding the nature and treatment of OCD were among the strategies described earlier; others also deserve attention. First, patients are often ambivalent regarding treatment. I concur with Turner and Beidel's (1988) suggestion that patients should not be pressured into accepting treatment. Because flooding and response prevention can be extremely stressful and require a significant amount of patient motivation, the patient must agree to participate of his or her own accord. Patients should not be treated solely at the request of a family member. Treatment should be embarked upon only if the patient understands that treatment is needed and agrees to follow the program as required.

Second, it is important *not* to provide the patient with any anxiety-reduction strategies during flooding sessions. It is tempting to do so when patients are in a significant amount of distress, but such strategies run counter to the habituation/extinction model upon which flooding is based. Although some contradictory data exist, it is generally believed that the patient's attention should remain focused on the fear cues, because distraction can reduce the extent of habituation (Grayson et al., 1986).

Third, with regard to response prevention, again I concur with Turner and Beidel (1988) that patients should never be required to perform behaviors that the therapist would not be willing to do. For example, patients should never be required to perform unsanitary behaviors such as putting their hands into toilets or eating without washing their hands first. They should not be asked to perform unsafe behaviors such as leaving their front doors unlocked or switching on heated appliances (e.g., irons, coffee pots) when they will be away from home. Patients should never be physically forced to perform any behaviors; they must be willing to engage in the treatment plan of their own accord. If patients continue to refuse to perform required behaviors, the treatment plan should be stopped.

Finally, the therapist should assume a confident and directive approach that challenges the patient to perform new behaviors while simultaneously conveying an understanding attitude regarding the patient's difficulties. An empirical study by Rabavilas et al. (1979) reported that patients who perceived their therapist as understanding, encouraging, challenging, and explicit improved more than did those who saw the clinician as permissive and tolerant.

Matching Treatment with Patient Characteristics

As noted above, not all OCD patients respond to flooding and response prevention. In particular, both severely depressed patients and those with overvalued ideation require additional interventions. The former group benefits from addition of antidepressant medication and the latter may require cognitive therapy.

Other subgroups who may not respond well to flooding and response prevention include patients with cognitive rituals only, obsessions only, or primary obsessional slowness. Empirical data on these subgroups are generally lacking, but it has been proposed that patients with cognitive rituals only would benefit from flooding and response prevention if alternative procedures are used to block cognitive rituals (e.g., thought stopping, discussed in the next section). The problem with this approach is its reliance on patient self-report concerning when cognitive rituals are or are not occurring. Twenty-four-hour supervised response prevention—which often is optimal, given failure of a patient's self-supervised response prevention—might provide no advantage for these patients, if they are unwilling or unable to report cognitive rituals. Patients with obsessions only should benefit from flooding alone, although it has been suggested that most patients who appear to have obsessions alone probably manifest some kind of cognitive ritual (Foa et al., 1985). Finally, primary obsessional slowness can be treated by giving patients strict time limits within which to perform daily activities (Turner & Beidel, 1988). However, it is important to ensure that such a syndrome is not accompanied by other OCD symptoms (e.g., overt or cognitive rituals), intellectual deficiency, or other organic impairment.

OTHER BEHAVIORAL INTERVENTIONS

Systematic desensitization, a treatment useful for a number of other anxiety disorders, has proven ineffective in the treatment of OCD (e.g., Cooper, Gelder, & Marks, 1965). However, other interventions do have some impact under certain circumstances. As noted above, cognitive therapy may be beneficial for patients with overvalued ideation (Salkovskis & Warwick, 1985), and a blocking procedure called thought stopping may be useful for some patients. In the thought-stopping procedure, a cognition (either a cognitive ritual or an obsession) is paired with the shouting of the word "stop." Eventually, the patient is able merely to think the word "stop" and cease the maladaptive cognitive activity. In some cases, thought stopping can be useful for decreasing obsessional thoughts (e.g., Turner, Holzman, & Jacob, 1983) and for the prevention of cognitive rituals (Foa et al., 1985).

Alternative behavioral interventions serve most often merely as adjuncts to flooding and response prevention. However, they become most useful during a maintenance phase of treatment, when patients are taught to consolidate treatment gains and prevent relapse. Because onset and relapse of OCD often occur during periods of stress, patients need to learn strategies for keeping anxiety at a minimal level and for handling increases in stress. Interventions during this phase might involve accepting some limitations (e.g., not trying to perform a job that has excessive amounts of responsibility), or learning new ways to handle stressful situations through relaxation training or cognitive-behavioral therapy. Social skills training also can help patients guard against relapse by providing them with skills to handle difficult situations. Finally, marital or family treatment often is necessary to rebuild relationships that have been strained by the presence of OCD. Such treatment may provide social supports against which OCD symptoms will be less likely to recur.

CASE EXAMPLE OF FLOODING AND RESPONSE PREVENTION

Description of the Patient

The patient was a 21-year-old, white, single male with a one-year history of obsessions and compulsions surrounding a fear of contracting AIDS. Onset of the disorder followed a report from an ex-girlfriend that she had contracted chlamydia. The patient received treatment for this disease and had an HIV test that returned negative. Over the next few months, his fear about developing AIDS increased and he had two additional HIV tests, both of which were negative. The patient reported no homosexual relationships, nor had he ever received blood transfusions or used IV drugs. Within 3 months after the original report of chlamydia, the patient had developed obsessional fears about contracting and spreading AIDS as a result of touching certain objects, eating in public, and breathing the air around a person who might be infected. In accordance with these fears, the patient developed numerous rituals and avoidance behaviors, including the following: refusal to eat outside of his own home or at a table with family members present, refusal to eat anything with his hands, repetitive handwashing, excessive rinsing of clean dishes before use, avoidance of substances exposed to the air (e.g., top of the toilet-paper roll, toothpaste from the top of the tube), and dressing and showering rituals.

The patient expressed some overvalued ideation—that is, a belief that he actually might contract AIDS and die from contact with an inanimate object. The extent of this belief, however, was not apparent prior to initiation of treatment. At the initial evaluation, the patient reported a 5% belief that he could actually develop AIDS through the types of activities he feared. In accordance with his symptoms, the following treatment plan was developed.

Response Prevention

Treatment began with a home visit during which the following response prevention activities were practiced and prescribed:

1. *Grooming*: Take only one shower per day. Spend no more than 10 minutes in the shower. Spend no more than 2 minutes getting dressed. Use one bar of soap until it is gone. Brush teeth no more than twice per day, using no more than 45 seconds for this activity. Use toothpaste from the top of the tube. Share a

bathroom with another family member, and use toilet paper from the top of the roll.
2. *Cleaning*: Wash hands only before meals and after using the bathroom. Spend no more than 30 seconds at each washing. Use dishes out of cabinets, without extra rinsing or washing. Do not wash clothes until you have worn them for at least one day.
3. *Eating*: Eat at least 3 meals a day, one of which should be eaten with another family member present. At each meal, eat at least one serving of food with your hands. Family members should not prepare any food in a special manner due to fear of AIDS.

Flooding

Following the home visit, a combination of in vivo and imaginal flooding was initiated. The patient was asked to drink from a cola can that had been obtained by the clinician from a vending machine in the treatment building. After taking a sip and holding the can in his hand, the patient was asked to imagine the following scene until within-session habituation occurred.

> Picture what you have just done. You have drunk from a cola can. Picture in your mind the can as you were bringing it closer to your lips; you could almost see the AIDS germs crawling around on the can. You were not given time to inspect the can thoroughly before you drank, so the germs must surely be in your system right now. They have flowed down your throat, into your digestive system, and soon will enter your blood stream.
>
> Keep your eyes closed and again move the can closer to your mouth. Notice your chest getting tighter and tighter, your teeth clenching, and your hand shaking. You cannot stop thinking about where that cola came from. Someone had to touch it to put it in the machine—maybe it has been sitting on a counter for a while. Maybe another patient touched it. If so, that person might have been a homosexual or a drug abuser—or recently had sex with someone in one of those categories. Everyone is not nearly as careful with germs as you have become, and that person or one of us might even have the disease already.
>
> Bring the cola can closer and closer to your lips. As you do, see in your mind even more AIDS germs just covering the can—they're crawling on it. The germs there seem to be attracting other germs—like magnets—that are hovering in the air. Your cola is swarming with germs that may, even as you breathe, be entering your body.
>
> Take a swallow. Feel the AIDS germs moving down your esophagus into your stomach and into your blood stream. They're now oozing everywhere inside your body. There is no way you can ever get them out now. Imagine as the days go by you begin to feel weaker and weaker. As you walk around your house, touching the few things you need to, you realize that anyone who comes within a few feet of you is likely to get the disease from you. You are a carrier—you are not only destined to die yourself, but you also are transmitting the disease with every breath to your brother, your mother, and your father. Each of them soon will begin to suffer with the symptoms of the disease. You have already begun to notice how your body has started to weaken. Your nose runs continually and you cannot stop coughing. You can't seem to catch your breath as easily these days. Your gums begin to hurt, your hair loses its luster, and you can't keep food down. Your energy is zapped, your skin hurts, and you keep losing weight.
>
> Your parents begin to show similar signs. Picture them as they are taking care of you. See them each day getting weaker and weaker. They begin to have trouble breathing and start coughing, just as you have done. You think to yourself over and over that it is your fault. They have contracted this deadly disease because of something you did.

Patient Response

The flooding scene elicited both subjective and physiological anxiety that demonstrated some habituation within sessions.

However, over the course of a number of days of flooding, between-session habituation did not occur as expected, even with modifications of the flooding scene to incorporate other possible primary fears (e.g., fear that others would think he was homosexual, given his contraction of AIDS; guilt about being sexually active premaritally; fear that others would reject him because he had been promiscuous). During subsequent discussions with the patient, it became apparent that overvalued ideation was more extreme than originally believed. Thus, flooding and response prevention were terminated and alternative interventions were discussed with the patient. Both pharmacotherapy and cognitive therapy were offered, but the patient decided to postpone treatment of any kind.

In this case, both in vivo and imaginal exposure were used to access the patient's primary fear of developing and spreading AIDS. The imaginal scene utilized visual, tactile, physiological, and response cues to elicit and maintain this fear. The exposure was successful in this regard, but between-session habituation failed to occur, presumably because of the patient's relatively strong belief that he actually might develop AIDS as a result of the behaviors he avoided.

PHARMACOTHERAPY AND BEHAVIORAL TREATMENT

A complete review of pharmacotherapy for OCD is beyond the scope of this chapter, but an overview of the utility of drug treatment in combination with behavior therapy deserves some attention. The drugs of choice for the treatment of OCD are the serotonergic antidepressants; clomipramine and fluoxetine are used most frequently. In a number of trials, clomipramine has produced greater improvement in obsessional symptoms than placebo (e.g., Jenike, Baer, et al., 1989; Mavissakalian, Turner, Michelson, & Jacob, 1985). Although fluoxetine has been studied less thoroughly, data addressing its efficacy in treating OCD also have been positive (e.g., Turner, Jacob, Beidel, & Himmelhoch, 1985). Data regarding the relative utility of clomipramine and other antidepressants have been inconsistent (Turner & Beidel, 1988), and no studies have yet addressed this issue with regard to fluoxetine.

A primary problem with the use of pharmacotherapy alone in the treatment of OCD concerns the high relapse rate upon withdrawal of medication. Ananth (1986) reported that as many as 70% of patients relapse following discontinuation of medication. In a more recent report, 89% of patients showed significant recurrence of obsessional symptoms after clomipramine was replaced by placebo for a 7-week period (Pato et al., 1988). Thus, treatment with medication alone is far from optimal.

However, the use of medication in combination with behavior therapy is often quite effective and, in some cases, the addition of medication is essential. As noted above, patients with severe depressive symptomatology fail to respond to flooding and response prevention. For these patients, an adequate trial of antidepressant medication is essential to improve affective state prior to initiation of flooding and response prevention. There are some data to suggest that OCD patients with severe depression benefit most from pharmacotherapy, perhaps indicating that antidepressants may be effective in this disorder primarily through their mood-altering properties (Marks, Sterm, Mawson, Cobb, & McDonald, 1980; Turner, Beidel, Stanley, & Jacob, 1988). However, other studies have found no correlation between pretreatment levels of depression and improvement in obsessive-compulsive symptoms after clomipramine or fluoxetine (Ananth, Pecknold, Van Den Steen, & Engelsmann, 1981;

Jenike, Buttolph, Baer, Ricciardi, & Holland, 1989). Thus, the extent to which these drugs have specific antiobsessional properties is as yet uncertain.

In studies that have examined the effects of both clomipramine and behavior therapy, combined treatment seems to be most efficacious (Amin, Ban, Pecknold, & Klingner, 1977; Marks et al., 1980). In one report that compared the effects of these two interventions, clomipramine and behavior therapy were equally effective with regard to improvement in obsessional symptoms, but behavior therapy had a greater effect on compulsions (Solyom & Sookman, 1977). In a comparison of fluoxetine and behavior therapy, the latter intervention seemed to have a more specific effect on obsessions and compulsions, whereas fluoxetine was most useful for patients with severe pretreatment depression (Turner et al., 1988). However, these comparisons suffered from methodological difficulties (e.g., small sample size, or short treatment duration), and as Christensen, Hadzi-Pavlovic, Andrews, and Mattick (1987) pointed out, a controlled, randomized trial comparing antidepressant medication, behavioral treatment, and combined treatment is sorely needed.

Despite the lack of strong empirical data regarding the relative effects of pharmacotherapy and behavioral treatment, the available data and clinical experience suggest that antidepressant medication is an important adjunct to flooding and response prevention for at least a subset of OCD patients.

DIRECTIONS FOR FUTURE RESEARCH

As noted throughout this chapter, unanswered questions exist in a number of areas. First, the mechanisms of flooding and response prevention are as yet uncertain. Extinction theories and the prevention of negative reinforcement have provided the most popular explanations; other, more cognitively based theories, such as Foa and Kozak's (1986) emotional processing model and Bandura's (1977) self-efficacy theory, provide alternative mechanism hypotheses. Support for each of these positions is mixed (Barlow, 1988), and the specific roles of physiological, behavioral, and cognitive variables in the process of anxiety reduction are unclear at present. This area is a fertile arena for further work.

Second, other questions regarding mechanisms surround the fact that depressed patients and those with overvalued ideation generally do not fare as well with behavior therapy. Foa et al. (1985) proposed that the former group fails to demonstrate within-session habituation because of increased physiological reactivity to feared stimuli, and the latter group exhibits deficits in cognitive processing that interfere with between-session habituation. These propositions are in accord with the hypothesis that mechanisms of within-session habituation occur in the autonomic nervous system whereas those of between-session habituation rely on cognitive processing. These are interesting propositions, but they definitely require additional empirical attention.

Finally, more research is needed to investigate the application of flooding and response prevention procedures for patients with cognitive rituals, obsessions without rituals, and primary obsessional slowness. It is not clear that these procedures are ineffective with these subgroups, although there is some suggestion that modifications in procedures, as well as the addition of adjunctive interventions, may be required in order to apply behavioral treatment most effectively to these subgroups. Other subgroups also are in need of further study. For example, a prospective study to examine the impact of schizotypal personality features on treatment outcome is needed. If this variable is associated with poor response, again we need to examine modifications and/or adjunctive interventions that will improve prognosis for this group.

REFERENCES

Akhtar, S., Wig, N. H., Verma, V. K., Pershad, D., & Verma, S. K. (1975). A phenomenological analysis of symptoms in obsessive-compulsive neurosis. *British Journal of Psychiatry, 127,* 342-348.

Amin, M. M., Ban, T. A., Pecknold, J. C., & Klingner, A. (1977). Clomipramine (Anafranil) and behavior therapy in obsessive-compulsive and phobic disorders. *Journal of International Medical Research, 5* (Suppl. 5), 33-37.

Ananth, J. (1986). Clomipramine: An antiobsessive drug. *Canadian Journal of Psychiatry, 31,* 253-258.

Ananth, J., Pecknold, J., Van Den Steen, N., & Engelsmann, F. (1981). Double-blind comparative study of clomipramine and amitriptyline in obsessive neurosis. *Progress in Neuro-Psychopharmacology and Biological Psychiatry, 5,* 257-262.

Bandura, A. (1977). Self-efficacy: Toward a unifying theory of behavioral change. *Psychological Review, 84,* 191-215.

Barlow, D. H. (1988). *Anxiety and its disorders: The nature and treatment of anxiety and panic.* New York: Guilford.

Beidel, D. C., Turner, S. M., & Allgood-Hill, B. (1986). The use of videotape exposure sessions in the treatment of obsessive-compulsive disorder. Paper presented at the Association for the Advancement of Behavior Therapy Annual Convention, Chicago.

Boersma, K., Den Hengst, S., Dekker, J., & Emmelkamp, P. M. G. (1976). Exposure and response prevention: A comparison with obsessive-compulsive patients. *Behaviour Research and Therapy, 14,* 19-24.

Christensen, H., Hadzi-Pavlovic, D., Andrews, G., & Mattick, R. (1987). Behavior therapy and tricyclic medication in the treatment of obsessive-compulsive disorder: A quantitative review. *Journal of Consulting and Clinical Psychology, 55,* 701-771.

Cooper, J. E. (1970). The Leyton Obsessional Inventory. *Psychological Medicine, 1,* 48-64.

Cooper, J. E., Gelder, M. G., & Marks, I. M. (1965). Results of behavior therapy in 77 psychiatric patients. *British Medical Journal, 1,* 1222-1225.

Dollard, J., & Miller, N. E. (1950). *Personality and psychotherapy: An analysis in terms of learning, thinking and culture.* New York: McGraw-Hill.

Emmelkamp, P. M. G., & van Kraanen, J. (1977). Therapist-controlled exposure in vivo: A comparison with obsessive-compulsive patients. *Behaviour Research and Therapy, 15,* 491-495.

Foa, E. B. (1979). Failure in treating obsessive-compulsives. *Behaviour Research and Therapy, 17,* 169-176.

Foa, E. B., & Chambless, D. L. (1978). Habituation of subjective anxiety during flooding in imagery. *Behaviour Research and Therapy, 16,* 391-399.

Foa, E. B., Grayson, J. B., & Steketee, G. (1982). Depression, habituation, and treatment outcome in obsessive-compulsives. In J. C. Boulougouris (Ed.), *Practical applications of learning theories in psychiatry.* New York: Wiley.

Foa, E. B., Grayson, J. B., Steketee, G. S., & Doppelt, H. G. (1983a). Treatment of obsessive-compulsives: When do we fail? In E. B. Foa and P. M. G. Emmelkamp (Eds.), *Failures in behaviour therapy.* New York: Wiley.

Foa, E. B., Grayson, J. B., Steketee, G. S., Doppelt, H. G., Turner, R. M., & Latimer, P. R. (1983b). Success and failure in the behavioral treatment of obsessive-compulsives. *Journal of Consulting and Clinical Psychology, 51,* 287-297.

Foa, E. B., & Kozak, M. S. (1986). Emotional processing of fear: Exposure to corrective information. *Psychological Bulletin, 99,* 20-35.

Foa, E. B., Steketee, G. S., & Ozarow, B. J. (1985). Behavior therapy with obsessive-compulsives: From theory to treatment. In M. Mavissakalian, S. M. Turner, and L. Michelson (Eds.), *Obsessive-compulsive disorder: Psychological and pharmacological treatment* (pp. 49–129). New York: Plenum.

Foa, E. B., Steketee, G., Turner, R. M., & Fischer, S. C. (1980). Effects of imaginal exposure to feared disasters in obsessive-compulsive checkers. *Behaviour Research and Therapy, 18,* 449–455.

Goodman, W. K., Price, L. H., Rasmussen, S. A., Mazure, C., Fleischmann, R. L., Hill, C. L., Heninger, G. R., & Charney, D. S. (1989). Part I. Yale-Brown Obsessive-Compulsive Scale: Development, use, and reliability. *Archives of General Psychiatry, 46,* 1006–1011.

Grayson, J. B., Foa, E. B., & Steketee, G. (1986). Exposure in vivo of obsessive-compulsives under distracting and attention-focusing conditions: Replication and extension. *Behaviour Research and Therapy, 24,* 475–479.

Hodgson, R. J., & Rachman, S. (1977). Obsessional-compulsive complaints. *Behaviour Research and Therapy, 15,* 389–395.

Hodgson, R. J., Rachman, S., & Marks, I. M. (1972). The treatment of chronic obsessive-compulsive neurosis: Follow-up and further findings. *Behaviour Research and Therapy, 10,* 181–189.

Hornsveld, R. H. J., Kraaimaat, F. W., & van Dam-Baggen, R. M. J. (1979). Anxiety/discomfort and handwashing in obsessive-compulsive and psychiatric control patients. *Behaviour Research and Therapy, 17,* 223–228.

Jenike, M. A., Baer, L., Minichiello, W. E., Schwartz, C. E., & Carey, R. J., Jr. (1986). Coexistent obsessive-compulsive disorder and schizotypal personality disorder: A poor prognostic indicator. *Archives of General Psychiatry, 43,* 296.

Jenike, M. A., Baer, L., Summergrad, P., Weilburg, J. B., Holland, A., & Seymour, R. (1989). Obsessive-compulsive disorder: A double-blind placebo controlled trial of clomipramine in 27 patients. *American Journal of Psychiatry, 146,* 1328–1330.

Jenike, M. A., Buttolph, L., Baer, L., Ricciardi, J., & Holland, A. (1989). Open trial of fluoxetine in obsessive-compulsive disorder. *American Journal of Psychiatry, 146,* 909–911.

Karno, M., Golding, J. M., Sorenson, S. B., & Burnam, A. (1988). The epidemiology of obsessive-compulsive disorder in five US communities. *Archives of General Psychiatry, 45,* 1094–1099.

Lang, P. J. (1979). A bio-informational theory of emotional imagery. *Psychophysiology, 16,* 495–512.

Marks, I. M., Sterm, R. S., Mawson, D., Cobb, J., & McDonald, R. (1980). Clomipramine and exposure for obsessive-compulsive rituals: I. *British Journal of Psychiatry, 136,* 1–25.

Mavissakalian, M., Turner, S. M., Michelson, L., & Jacob, R. G. (1985). Tricyclic antidepressants in obsessive-compulsive disorder: II. Antiobsessional or antidepressant agents? *American Journal of Psychiatry, 142,* 572–576.

Meyer, V. (1966). Modification of expectations in cases with obsessional rituals. *Behaviour Research and Therapy, 4,* 273–280.

Mills, H. L., Agras, W. S., Barlow, D. H., & Mills, J. R. (1973). Compulsive rituals treated by response prevention. *Archives of General Psychiatry, 28,* 524–527.

Mowrer, O. (1939). A stimulus-response analysis of anxiety and its role as a reinforcing agent. *Psychological Review, 46,* 553–565.

Pato, M. T., Zohar-Kadouch, R., Zohar, J., & Murphy, D. L. (1988). Return of symptoms after discontinuation of clomipramine in patients with obsessive-compulsive disorder. *American Journal of Psychiatry, 145,* 1521–1525.

Rabavilas, A. D., & Boulougouris, J. C. (1974). Physiological accompaniments of ruminations, flooding, and thought-stopping in obsessive patients. *Behaviour Research and Therapy, 12,* 239–243.

Rabavilas, A. D., Boulougouris, J. C., & Perissaki, C. (1979). Therapist qualities related to outcome with exposure in vivo in neurotic patients. *Journal of Behavior Therapy and Experimental Psychiatry, 10,* 293–299.

Rabavilas, A. D., Boulougouris, J. C., & Stefanis, C. (1976). Duration of flooding sessions in the treatment of obsessive-compulsive patients. *Behaviour Research and Therapy, 14,* 349–355.

Rachman, S. (1974). Primary obsessional slowness. *Behaviour Research and Therapy, 12,* 9–18.

Rachman, S. J. (1985). An overview of clinical and research issues in obsessional-compulsive disorders. In M. Mavissakalian, S. M. Turner, and L. Michelson (Eds.), *Obsessive-compulsive disorder: Psychological and pharmacological treatment* (pp. 1–47). New York: Plenum.

Rachman, S. J., & Hodgson, R. J. (1980). *Obsessions and compulsions.* Engelwood Cliffs, NJ: Prentice-Hall.

Rachman, S., Marks, I. M., & Hodgson, R. (1973). The treatment of obsessive-compulsive neurotics by modelling and flooding in vivo. *Behaviour Research and Therapy, 11,* 463–471.

Roper, G., Rachman, S., & Marks, I. M. (1975). Passive and participant modeling in exposure treatment of obsessive-compulsive neurotics. *Behaviour Research and Therapy, 13,* 271–279.

Rosenberg, H., & Upper, D. (1983). Problems with stimulus/response equivalence and reactivity in the assessment and treatment of obsessive-compulsive neurosis. *Behaviour Research and Therapy, 21,* 177–180.

Salkovskis, P. M. (1983). Treatment of an obsessional patient using habituation to audiotaped ruminations. *British Journal of Clinical Psychology, 22,* 311–313.

Salkovskis, P. M., & Warwick, H. M. C. (1985). Cognitive therapy of obsessive-compulsive disorder: Treating treatment failures. *Behavioural Psychotherapy, 13,* 243–255.

Solyom, L., & Sookman, D. (1977). A comparison of clomipramine hydrochloride (Anafranil) and behavioral therapy in the treatment of obsessive neurosis. *Journal of International Medical Research, 5* (Suppl. 5), 49–61.

Stanley, M. A., Turner, S. M., & Borden, J. W. (1990). Schizotypal features in obsessive-compulsive patients. *Comprehensive Psychiatry, 31,* 511–518.

Steketee, G. S., Foa, E. B., & Grayson, J. B. (1982). Recent advances in the treatment of obsessive-compulsives. *Archives of General Psychiatry, 39,* 1365–1371.

Towlin, K. E., Leckman, J. F., & Cohen, D. J. (1987). Drug treatment of obsessive-compulsive disorder: A review of findings in the light of diagnostic and metric limitations. *Psychiatric Developments, 1,* 25–50.

Turner, S. M., & Beidel, D. C. (1988). *Treating obsessive-compulsive disorder.* New York: Pergamon.

Turner, S. M., Beidel, D. C., Stanley, M. A., & Jacob, R. G. (1988). A comparison of fluoxetine, flooding, and response prevention in the treatment of obsessive-compulsive disorder. *Journal of Anxiety Disorders, 2,* 219–225.

Turner, S. M., Jacob, R. G., Beidel, D. C., & Himmelhoch, J. (1985). Fluoxetine treatment of obsessive-compulsive disorders. *Journal of Clinical Psychopharmacology, 5,* 207–212.

Turner, S. M., Holzman, A., & Jacob, R. G. (1983). Treatment of compulsive looking by thought-stopping. *Behavior Modification, 7,* 576–582.

Turner, S. M., McCann, B. S., Beidel, D. C., & Mezzich, J. B. (1986). DSM-III classification of the anxiety disorders: A psychometric study. *Journal of Abnormal Psychology, 95,* 168–172.

CHAPTER 5

Behavioral Treatment of Post-Traumatic Stress Disorder

TERENCE M. KEANE, ROBERT J. GERARDI, STEPHEN J. QUINN, and BRETT T. LITZ

Exposure to life-threatening events, or traumas, leaves an indelible mark on all who survive. For the vast majority of people, there is an initial period of psychological instability from which most recover. Typically, this recovery period lasts from one to three months. Individuals then begin to engage normally in activities and reconstitute healthy interpersonal relationships. However, for a subgroup of people exposed to traumatic events, recovery is a more protracted experience; for an even smaller group, persistent symptoms of psychopathology emerge.

Post-traumatic stress disorder (PTSD) is the diagnostic classification that best describes the constellation of symptoms resulting from exposure to traumatic experience of an extreme nature. PTSD is the most extreme reaction that individuals can have to such events. The disorder is characterized by three classes of symptoms: re-experiencing events that occurred during the trauma, numbing and avoidance, and chronic hyperarousal (DSM-III-R; American Psychiatric Association, 1987). Re-experienced phenomena include nightmares, intrusive thoughts of the traumatic event, and a preoccupation with the event and its aftermath. Numbing and avoidance refer to two related but separate problems. Numbing is the emotional response that follows prolonged periods of high stress and is described by patients as an inability to feel any positive emotions toward individuals or activities. Avoidance is a behavioral symptom involving an individual's efforts to remain in safe areas and not to approach things that are reminiscent of the traumatic event. Finally, symptoms of hyperarousal, both physiological and subjective, complete the symptom picture of PTSD. The most salient of the arousal symptoms include sleep disturbance and startle reaction.

Associated with PTSD are a wide range of other psychological and social problems. Anxiety, depression, and guilt are prominent clinical features of the disorder. Complicating the symptom picture for many individuals is the presence of alcohol or drug abuse, mechanisms frequently used by traumatized people in efforts to manage their distress (Keane, Gerardi, Lyons, & Wolfe, 1988). Marital problems and divorce, vocational impairment, and interpersonal alienation are social problems that can ensue (Nezu & Carnevale, 1987; Resick, Calhoun, Atkeson, & Ellis, 1981; Roberts et al., 1982; Solomon, Mikulincer, & Avitzur, 1988).

In summary, severely traumatized individuals suffer a wide range of psychological and social problems that may result in functional impairment across the major life areas. Rates of criminal victimization, including rape, are rising, as are the frequencies of natural and technological disasters. Many countries remain at war, and generations of citizens have been exposed to the horrors of war in this and other countries. Automobile, train, airplane, and boating accidents occur daily in our society. Each of these events can result in death and destruction and, for those who survive, there are psychological consequences of the exposure to these extreme events. PTSD in its full form and in its variants is, therefore, a major challenge to public health in the United States and across the world.

The purpose of this chapter is to outline an integrated approach to the treatment of PTSD that attempts to address the various symptoms associated with traumatic stress disorders.

PREVALENCE OF POST-TRAUMATIC STRESS DISORDER

Progress in the study of PTSD has been considerable since the introduction of the disorder into the diagnostic nomenclature in 1980 (DSM-III; American Psychiatric Association, 1980). Perhaps most significant has been the completion of several epidemiological studies estimating prevalence rates for PTSD in the general population and in specific subsections of the population. These estimates of PTSD have been instrumental in the development of service delivery programs and the enhancement of support for both research on the parameters of the disorder and education for practitioners and students in the mental health professions.

Epidemiological Catchment Area Study

The National Institute of Mental Health, in collaboration with investigators at five sites across the country (i.e., the Epidemiological Catchment Area Study (ECA), New Haven, Baltimore, North Carolina, St. Louis, and Los Angeles), studied the prevalence rates of some 40 different mental health disorders. Unfortunately, PTSD was examined only at the St. Louis site (Helzer, Robins, & McEvoy, 1987). This study was conducted using the Diagnostic Interview Schedule (DIS) as the sole diagnostic instrument. The DIS asks specific questions about each mental health diagnosis to determine whether a person meets criteria for a disorder. Lay interviewers were responsible for conducting face-to-face interviews. In this study, 1 percent of the general population reached criteria for a lifetime diagnosis of PTSD, a figure representing some 2.4 million cases. However, it is not clear how valid these findings are, because the DIS has been noted to lead to spurious diagnostic estimates.

National Vietnam Veterans Readjustment Study

In 1984, Congress created historic legislation when it requested a study of the psychological and social consequences of the Vietnam War. This study, known as the National Vietnam Veterans Readjustment Study (NVVRS), was unique in at least two important ways. It was the first time that any country sought to comprehensively understand the psychological and social consequences of a war (and in particular the rates of PTSD and other major psychological disorders). Secondly, this was the first nationwide probability sampling procedure employed in an epidemiological study of mental health in the United States. This study also contained several important design features. For example, it included not simply the target group of interest (Vietnam theater veterans), but also critical comparison groups: Vietnam-era veterans and civilians. Sampling strategies involved oversampling of blacks, Hispanics, and women so that inspection of PTSD rates by minority group membership could be accomplished. The measurement of PTSD included lay diagnostic interviews, psychological tests, and clinical interviews sequenced in a multistage manner described by Dohrenwend and Shrout (1981).

Results from the study indicated that 15.2% of the 3.14 million males who served in Vietnam have PTSD today. This percentage represents some 479,000 cases. Lifetime prevalence rates for PTSD were 30.9% among males. For blacks, the current rate of PTSD was observed to be 20.6%, and among Hispanics the rate was 27.9%. The differences in prevalence among minority groups were significant when compared to the rate among whites (i.e., 13.7%), thus stimulating the Department of Veterans Affairs (DVA) to develop additional PTSD programs with minority group emphases. Further data analyses of the minority group findings indicated that the differential rate of PTSD among blacks was directly attributable to higher levels of combat exposure. Similarly, combat exposure also was a major contributor to the higher rates of PTSD among Hispanics. These data are being analyzed further to examine other factors responsible for the higher rate of PTSD seen in Hispanic Vietnam veterans.

There also were significant findings among the theater veterans (i.e., those who served in Vietnam), era veterans (i.e., those who were in the military during that era but did not go to Vietnam), and civilian comparison groups. Among the males, era veterans had a 2.5% prevalence rate and civilians reported a 1.2% prevalence rate. When evaluating the effects of exposure to war-zone stressful events, the NVVRS found that the males exposed to high war-zone stress had a current rate of PTSD of 35.8%.

For women who served in Vietnam, the effects were equally as striking. The current rate of PTSD was estimated to be 8.5% of the population. This compared with 1.1% of the era veterans and 0.3% of the civilians. Those women who were exposed to high levels of war-zone stress had a 17.5% rate of PTSD today. Overall, the lifetime PTSD rate for these women was found to be 26.9%.

The findings of the NVVRS and the ECA studies provide unequivocal support for the high rate of PTSD in our society. In the ECA study of the general population, PTSD was estimated to have at least a 1% prevalence rate (using data from the St. Louis site). This is equivalent to the rate of schizophrenia in the general population. The report of PTSD rates in the NVVRS was even more sobering. When specific high-risk populations were examined, the rate of PTSD was found to be extremely high. Other findings regarding civilian-related PTSD from studies of the Buffalo Creek Disaster (Gleser, Green, & Winget, 1981), the Mount St. Helens explosion (Shore, Tatum, & Vollmer, 1986), criminal victimization (Kilpatrick, Saunders, Veronen, Best, & Von, 1987), and rape (Kilpatrick, Veronen, & Resick, 1979) support the need for consideration of psychological consequences of major stressful life events. Many research studies have found that there are predictable vulnerabilities (e.g., previous psychological problems) to the development of PTSD once one is exposed to extreme life stressors, but there is now ample evidence to suggest that even the most healthy and well-adjusted persons, when exposed to traumatic stressors, can develop the symptoms of PTSD (Keane, 1989).

PSYCHOLOGICAL TREATMENT OF PTSD

Behavioral treatments of PTSD are based on conceptual models positing that trauma-related cues represent formerly neutral stimuli that have been powerfully conditioned during a state of high arousal and/or life threat (Foa, Steketee, & Rothbaum, 1989; Keane, Zimering, & Caddell, 1985; Kilpatrick et al., 1979). Common to all behavioral treatments for PTSD is some level of exposure to these cues with the prevention of characteristic avoidance responses (Fairbank & Nicholson, 1987). Exposure and response prevention result in changes in the value or valence of these stimuli through deconditioning, extinction, or the learning of new, incompatible coping behaviors.

Two types of treatment for PTSD predominate in the current literature: exposure and stress management, in various forms. During exposure therapy (direct therapeutic exposure, systematic desensitization, flooding, implosive therapy), a patient is repeatedly exposed to the fear stimulus while in the safety of the therapeutic relationship, until a reduction in anxiety is achieved. In stress management, the focus is usually on teaching patients new skills to manage their trauma-induced fears and anxiety. However, stress management techniques also entail some degree of exposure to feared or avoided stimuli. Using stress management, characteristic avoidance behaviors are challenged by competing cognitive and behavioral coping responses and arousal management strategies. Therapeutic exposure and stress management are not mutually exclusive treatments and are generally used conjointly in individual cases. The empirical data suggest that both treatments are associated with positive treatment outcomes in both veteran and nonveteran populations (Boudewyns & Hyer, 1990; Cooper & Clum, 1989; Frank et al., 1988; Keane, Fairbank, Caddell, & Zimering, 1989; Resick, Jordan, Girelli, Hutter, & Marhoeffer-Dvorak, 1988).

STRESS MANAGEMENT

Stress management approaches for PTSD consist of multiple components that are tailored to fit the clinical aspects of individual cases. Treatment components commonly used to treat PTSD include relaxation training, thought stopping, self-dialogue, communication training, problem solving, assertiveness training, and the identification and disputation of specific cognitive distortions. Upon concluding the initial assessment, targets for intervention are chosen in consultation with the patient. These target symptoms can be matched with one or more of the cognitive-behavioral components. For example, relaxation training may be helpful for the arousal symptoms of PTSD. Thought stopping and self-dialogue may be utilized to address intrusive thoughts of the trauma or to reduce reactivity to intrusions. Treating the numbing and avoidance components of this disorder may require the systematic use of additional training components. The interpersonal areas of functioning probably require some combination of communication training, problem solving, and assertiveness training.

Stress Inoculation Training (SIT), a stress management approach developed by Meichenbaum and his colleagues (Meichenbaum & Jaremko, 1983), has been used extensively in the treatment of PTSD among civilians (Kilpatrick et al., 1979; Veronen & Kilpatrick, 1983). This broad-based treatment package targets maladaptive responses to everyday stressors as well as idiosyncratic maladaptive reactions to stimuli reminiscent of the trauma. SIT typically occurs in three phases. In the *education* phase, patients are taught a conceptualization for their present difficulties and for the proposed treatment. In the *skill acquisition* phase, patients are instructed in a variety of skills (e.g., assertiveness, relaxation, anger control, modification of self-statements, and cognitive appraisals regarding trauma-related information), in order to modify their coping repertoires. Finally, in the *rehearsal and application* phase, patients practice these new skills in fear-producing, but safe, situations in therapy. Patients also practice these new skills in homework assignments that are designed to maximize self-efficacy expectations and success experiences. SIT fosters a reduction in the isolation and withdrawal often seen in PTSD by increasing social supports and adaptive requests for contacts with significant others.

A discussion of all possible combinations of PTSD problems and therapeutic approaches is beyond the scope of the present chapter. Instead, it is suggested that clinicians use the examples given here as a conceptual framework for their own problem solving in designing and implementing effective treatment packages for individual patients. In the clinic, each case is unique in its manifestation of symptoms, interpersonal problems, and emotional reactions, and should be analyzed and treated as such.

Case A

This case illustrates the use of stress management in treating a case of combat-related PTSD. D.P. was a male Vietnam veteran referred to the PTSD unit of his local DVA Medical Center. D.P. reported feeling extremely stressed over the past six months because of problems on his job. He complained of sleep disturbance, angry outbursts, intrusive thoughts, nightmares, and avoidance of movies, books, and television shows associated with Vietnam. He also was experiencing marital difficulties, constriction of affect, and numbing of emotions. Since his discharge from the military, D.P. had avoided discussing Vietnam (his friends over the past 20 years were unaware that D.P. had even been in the military), and he stated that he did not want to discuss Vietnam in treatment. Respecting his wishes, treatment began by addressing sleep disturbance and interpersonal difficulties. D.P. learned progressive muscle relaxation and began using the technique to prepare for sleep, to get back to sleep after awakening, and at times throughout the day when he felt himself becoming stressed.

Interpersonal difficulties were then addressed in couples sessions using communication and problem-solving skills. D.P. and his wife had developed a relatively noncommunicative style over a number of years. Mrs. P. complained about a lack of intimacy in their relationship and being overburdened with decisions that were better made by both of them. In therapy, the couple learned to listen to one another and to give constructive positive and negative feedback.

As is common among combat veterans with PTSD, D.P. was afraid of his anger, even though he had not been violent in over 17 years. To address this concern, he was taught several strategies for anger control. For example, D.P. was given permission by the therapist to remove himself from a situation or discussion that created stress for him. He was taught to request a time and place to later continue working on that specific problem. This allowed D.P. to work on problem-solving skills while titrating his exposure to aversive, arousing circumstances. Initially, problem solving was conducted only during the session; however, after several weeks, the couple began problem solving at home, and reviewed the contracts and solution processes in the following session. As D.P. learned a variety of new skills that enhanced his ability to manage his stress and his interpersonal problems, he became less defensive about Vietnam and began to address those issues more directly in therapy.

DIRECT THERAPEUTIC EXPOSURE (DTE)

Exposure-based treatments have a long history in the technology available to behavior therapists (Barlow, 1988). A direct outgrowth of conditioning theories of psychopathology, exposure treatments have demonstrated their effectiveness in reducing fear and avoidance in a variety of anxiety disorders. Because it is not always possible to conduct in vivo exposure with PTSD patients, direct therapeutic exposure with these individuals is often accomplished using imaginal procedures.

Numerous case studies (Black & Keane, 1982; Fairbank & Keane, 1982; Keane & Kaloupek, 1982; Kipper, 1977; McCaffrey & Fairbank, 1985; Mueser & Butler, 1987; Rychtarik, Silverman, Van Landingham, & Prue, 1984) have reported positive outcomes of DTE in the treatment of PTSD. Additionally, several randomized controlled studies have been conducted on the use of imaginal exposure with PTSD (Boudewyns & Hyer, 1990; Cooper & Clum, 1989; Keane et al., 1989). Although these studies lend some support to the use of DTE, comparative studies have not been conducted, and it is not yet clear that DTE is more effective than other treatments for PTSD.

CONDUCTING DTE

The clinician should attend to several issues prior to initiating DTE. First, the therapist should assess the patient's ability to tolerate increases in within-session emotion as well as temporary exacerbation of symptoms. The therapist should also be aware of other factors that may threaten treatment compliance or interfere with effective within-session habituation (e.g., current substance abuse or dependence, or other current life stressors).

The therapist can minimize the chances of dropout or noncompliance by spending some time preparing the patient for therapy. Individuals with PTSD typically attempt to avoid thoughts and emotions associated with traumatic events, and many enter treatment only after their attempts at avoidance have been unsuccessful. Therefore, it is important for patients to learn about PTSD and to understand why they are now being asked to intentionally expose themselves to these painful memories.

The therapist can improve compliance by providing the patient with information about what to expect in treatment. Many, if not all, patients undergoing DTE experience an increase in symptoms that may last for several weeks before any reduction in symptoms is seen. Patients should know that increases in symptoms are temporary and not a sign of a treatment failure. Predicting symptom increases before they occur will prevent patients from leaving treatment with the mistaken belief that therapy was making them worse. It is also advisable to educate other treatment providers and significant others about the treatment and the possible short-term negative side effects.

The therapist should try to obtain as many details about the traumatic event as possible. Revealing the details can be very difficult for a patient who has never talked about the trauma. The therapist should ask the patient to be as specific as possible, taking into account the patient's ability to tolerate the ensuing anxiety. Many PTSD patients believe that what they have experienced is too terrible to discuss and that they themselves are reprehensible because of the experience. Accordingly, it is important to remain supportive and nonjudgmental when discussing a patient's trauma. The therapist should also be aware of his or her own emotional reactions at hearing about a patient's traumatic event (Haley, 1974). The therapist may empathize with the patient, but strong emotional responses by the therapist may be misinterpreted and precipitate a crisis for the patient. Control of one's emotional responses can be especially difficult for therapists who have not worked with traumatized patients. Arranging some type of formal supervision (with either a senior colleague or a peer) to discuss an individual's reactions to hearing about horrifying traumatic experiences is recommended.

In the form of DTE used in our program, prior to beginning, several sessions are spent teaching the patient progressive muscle relaxation. The importance of practicing the relaxation is stressed, because the relaxation will be used to manage some of the feelings that arise during the session. When the patient has achieved some mastery of the relaxation procedure, the imagery work can begin.

Each exposure session begins with progressive muscle relaxation. After several minutes of relaxation, the therapist asks the patient to imagine that they are back at the time of the trauma. Beginning at some point before the traumatic event, the patient is asked to picture and describe (in the first person, present tense) the traumatic event in as much detail as can be reported. The patient proceeds through the scene slowly, allowing for exposure to as many of the stimulus and response cues associated with the traumatic event as possible. The therapist's task is to keep the narrative focused on the traumatic event and to prevent the patient from escaping or avoiding. Periodically, the therapist should ask the patient to rate his or her level of anxiety on a subjective units-of-distress scale. This allows the therapist to assess which stimulus and/or response elements are most distressing to the patient and to determine when the patient has experienced some reduction in anxiety. In contrast to systematic desensitization, there is no attempt by the therapist to minimize the patient's anxiety during the exposure.

Patients differ in the amount of structure they require from the therapist in order to participate in imagery-based therapies. Some patients seem to be very good imagers and proceed through the scene with very little assistance from the therapist. Others have great difficulty imagining the event and require more active guidance from the therapist. The therapist should be flexible in altering the technique to match the patient's style while focusing on the main objective (i.e., exposing the patient to the stimulus and response cues associated with the traumatic event).

Several common avoidance behaviors are seen during an exposure session. Some patients may try to avoid the trauma by racing through the memory, providing a "description" of the event rather than trying to relive it. Other patients may appear unable or unwilling to proceed any further with the memory. These are easily observed behaviors and require the therapist to be more active in setting the pace. A more difficult problem arises when the patient omits reporting some aspect of the memory. This may occur because a patient does not yet have full access to the memory (i.e., psychogenic amnesia), in which case the patient will most likely access more of the memory with repeated exposures. However, PTSD patients may also intentionally withhold from the therapist the most distressing elements of the trauma. Here again, with repeated exposure, more details of the trauma may emerge.

Case B

John was a 40-year-old Vietnam War army veteran who was referred to the PTSD program when he complained of intense anxiety when thinking about Vietnam and nightmares about combat experiences. During the assessment, John revealed several discrete combat events that he re-experienced through intrusive thoughts and images. He also reported having a recent minor automobile accident when a helicopter flying overhead triggered a "flash-back." After completing the assessment, John and his therapist discussed DTE in some detail, and John agreed to a trial of DTE.

Several sessions were spent detailing John's traumatic combat experiences. In one incident, he narrowly missed boarding a helicopter that he observed crash and burst into flames, killing all aboard.

John's unit was ordered to the crash site, where he stood guard and helped recover the charred bodies of the helicopter crew. In a second incident, John nearly drowned when crossing a river. On that same day, John was in a firefight, received a shrapnel wound to his face, and lost the sight in one eye. He was med-evacked out of the field and spent the next year recuperating in military hospitals.

After the details of John's traumatic events were obtained, several sessions were devoted to learning progressive muscle relaxation. John requested to begin DTE with the helicopter crash, currently the most distressing event for him. The first session of DTE began with several minutes of progressive muscle relaxation. John was then instructed to imagine and describe the helicopter crash in as much detail as possible. Continuous heart rate was obtained with a psychophysiological polygraph, and John made periodic anxiety (0–10) ratings. He became very anxious during the session (this was apparent in increased anxiety ratings and heart rate) and required much support and encouragement. The session ended with progressive muscle relaxation and a brief discussion of John's experience with DTE. John was encouraged to practice the relaxation at home and to avoid any stressful situations if possible. When he returned to the next session, he said that he had been increasingly anxious and irritable all week, and he expressed some reservations about continuing the DTE. The therapist reminded John that it was common for people in DTE to feel worse before they feel better. John was reassured by this and agreed to continue DTE. During the second session, he was again very emotional during the imagery, and he reported more details of the event than he had in the first session. By the end of the session he appeared calmer, and he stated that he felt much more relaxed than at the beginning of the session. By the third session, John was familiar with the procedure and he was able to imagine the event with little guidance from the therapist. The therapist intervened only to focus John on the more distressing parts of the event, in which he had to handle the bodies of the helicopter crew. By the seventh session of DTE, John had achieved significant within-session reductions in anxiety. This was reflected in reductions in both his SUDS ratings and his heart rate. Additionally, John reported having fewer re-experiencing symptoms, feeling more relaxed and confident, and being less socially avoidant.

The focus of the therapy shifted to the two remaining traumatic events. The DTE with the second trauma proceeded in much the same way as before, except that John was now much less apprehensive about the procedure. While working on the third traumatic memory, John experienced several life stressors, which resulted in a marked increase in symptoms. He appeared more anxious and depressed, and he reported increased avoidance of work and social activities. He reported some increase in re-experiencing symptoms, but these symptoms were still much less severe than pretreatment levels. At this point, a decision was made to discontinue DTE until John's acute problems were resolved. A stress management approach was employed to deal with the effects of the current stressors. John's avoidance behaviors were viewed as strategies to avoid anxiety, and he agreed to expose himself to those things he was avoiding. Several specific avoidance behaviors were targeted (e.g., making business phone calls), and John successfully completed several homework assignments by engaging in these behaviors. These successes resulted in immediate increases in self-efficacy and some decreases in symptomatology. The current treatment plan calls for John to continue with stress management until some of his current difficulties resolve.

At that point, John and his therapist will decide jointly about the need for further DTE.

RELAPSE PREVENTION

Regardless of the type of treatment employed, traumatic events can continue to affect individuals' lives. The most notable lasting effect of traumatization is that affected individuals appear to have an increased vulnerability to stress. This vulnerability can be in response to situations or events related to the trauma (e.g., Fourth of July fireworks for a combat veteran) or to other life events that would be stressful for anyone (e.g., being laid off a job, divorce, loss of a loved one, etc.). Prior to terminating treatment, the therapist can discuss the issue of relapse with the patient and teach the patient some relapse prevention skills.

Although the relapse prevention model was developed for use in the treatment of addictive behaviors (Marlatt & Gordon, 1985), it is readily applied to PTSD. Patients can learn to anticipate unique high-risk situations and plan to implement specific appropriate coping responses. In this way, patients can reduce the likelihood of an acute exacerbation of PTSD symptoms and the use of maladaptive coping efforts (e.g., substance abuse). Additionally, relapse prevention in the treatment of PTSD patients can foster:

1. Recognition that the trauma has changed them in lasting but manageable ways;
2. Positive expectations about personal efficacy in high-risk stressful situations, particularly situations that are reminiscent of the trauma;
3. Better recovery from stress reactions to life events (versus the belief that stress reactions won't occur at all);
4. Self-reward for effective coping with stressful life events.

CONCLUSIONS

Trauma occupies an increasingly prominent position in the etiology of psychopathology. PTSD, both civilian- and military-related, represents a significant challenge to mental health delivery systems. Individuals with PTSD present with a complex assortment of symptoms, ranging from physiological to interpersonal, that can be quite resistant to treatment. Given the complexity of this disorder, no single treatment approach addresses all the needs of traumatized individuals. Rather, it is necessary to employ a combination of treatments to effectively treat PTSD.

Although controlled research on the behavioral treatment of PTSD is still in its infancy, behavior therapy appears to have much to offer individuals with the disorder. Stress management approaches that target specific skills deficits can improve an individual's ability to cope with current stressful demands. Additionally, imaginal or in vivo exposure can be helpful in reducing the frightening re-experiencing symptoms. When used in conjunction, these treatment approaches can significantly ameliorate the pervasive and often devastating impact of traumatic events.

REFERENCES

American Psychiatric Association. (1980). *Diagnostic and statistical manual of mental disorders* (3rd ed.). Washington, DC: Author.

Barlow, D. H. (1988). *Anxiety and its disorders: The nature and treatment of anxiety and panic.* New York: Guilford.

Black, J. L., & Keane, T. M. (1982). Implosive therapy in the treatment of combat related fears in a World War II veteran. *Journal of*

Behavior Therapy and Experimental Psychiatry, 13, 163-165.

Boudewyns, P. A., & Hyer, L. (1990). Physiological response to combat memories and preliminary treatment outcome in Vietnam veteran PTSD patients treated with direct therapeutic exposure. *Behavior Therapy, 21,* 63-87.

Cooper, N. A. & Clum, G. A. (1989). Imaginal flooding as a supplementary treatment for PTSD in combat veterans: A controlled study. *Behavior Therapy, 20,* 381-391.

Dohrenwend, B. D., & Shrout, P. B. (1981). Toward the development of a two-stage procedure for case identification and classification in psychiatric epidemiology. *Research in Community and Mental Health, 2,* 295-323.

Fairbank, J. A., & Keane, T. M. (1982). Flooding for combat-related stress disorders: Assessment of anxiety reduction across traumatic memories. *Behavior Therapy, 13,* 499-510.

Fairbank, J. A., & Nicholson, R. A. (1987). Theoretical and empirical issues in the treatment of post-traumatic stress disorder in Vietnam veterans. *Journal of Clinical Psychology, 43,* 44-55.

Foa, E. B., Steketee, G., & Rothbaum, B. O. (1989). Behavioral/cognitive conceptualizations of post-traumatic stress disorder. *Behavior Therapy, 20,* 155-176.

Frank, E., Anderson, B., Stewart, B. D., Dancu, C., Hughes, C., & West, D. (1988). Efficacy of cognitive behavior therapy and systematic desensitization in the treatment of rape trauma. *Behavior Therapy, 19,* 403-420.

Gleser, G. C., Green, B. L., & Winget, C. (1981). *Buffalo Creek revisited: Prolonged psychosocial effects of disaster.* New York: Simon & Schuster.

Haley, S. (1974). When the patient reports atrocities. *Archives of General Psychiatry, 30,* 191-196.

Helzer, J. E., Robins, L. N., & McEvoy, L. (1987). Post-traumatic stress disorder in the general population. *New England Journal of Medicine, 317,* 1630-1634.

Keane, T. M. (1989). Post-traumatic stress disorder: Current status and future directions. *Behavior Therapy, 20,* 149-153.

Keane, T. M., Fairbank, J. A., Caddell, J. M., & Zimering, R. T. (1989). Implosive (flooding) therapy reduces symptoms of PTSD in Vietnam veterans. *Behavior Therapy, 20,* 245-260.

Keane, T. M., Gerardi, R. J., Lyons, J. A., & Wolfe, J. (1988). The interrelationship of substance abuse and PTSD: Epidemiological and clinical considerations. In M. Galanter (Ed.), *Recent developments in alcoholism, Vol. VI.* New York: Plenum.

Keane, T. M., & Kaloupek, D. G. (1982). Imaginal flooding in the treatment of a posttraumatic stress disorder. *Journal of Consulting and Clinical Psychology, 50,* 138-140.

Keane, T. M., Zimering, R. T., & Caddell, J. M. (1985). A behavioral formulation of posttraumatic stress disorder in Vietnam veterans. *The Behavior Therapist, 8,* 9-12.

Kilpatrick, D. G., Saunders, B. E., Veronen, L. J., Best, C. L., & Von, J. M. (1987). Criminal victimization: Lifetime prevalence, reporting to police and psychological impact. *Crime and Delinquency, 33,* 479-489.

Kilpatrick, D. G., Veronen, L. J., & Resick, P. A. (1979). The aftermath of rape: Recent empirical findings. *American Journal of Orthopsychiatry, 49,* 658-669.

Kipper, D. A. (1977). Behavior therapy for fears brought on by war experiences. *Journal of Consulting and Clinical Psychology, 45,* 216-221.

Marlatt, G. A., & Gordon, J. R. (1985). *Relapse prevention.* New York: Guilford.

Meichenbaum, D., & Jaremko, M. E. (1983). *Stress reduction and prevention.* New York: Plenum.

McCaffrey, R. J., & Fairbank, J. A. (1985). Behavioral assessment and treatment of accident-related posttraumatic stress disorder: Two case studies. *Behavior Therapy, 16,* 406-416.

Mueser, K. T., & Butler, R. W. (1987). Auditory hallucinations in combat-related chronic post-traumatic stress disorder. *American Journal of Psychiatry, 144,* 299-302.

Nezu, A., & Carnevale, G. (1987). Interpersonal problem solving and coping reactions of Vietnam veterans with posttraumatic stress disorder. *Journal of Abnormal Psychology, 96,* 155–157.

Resick, P., Calhoun, K., Atkeson, B., & Ellis, E. (1981). Social adjustment in victims of sexual assault. *Journal of Consulting and Clinical Psychology, 49,* 705–712.

Resick, P. A., Jordan, C. G., Girelli, S. A., Hutter, C. K., & Marhoeffer-Dvorak, S. (1988). A comparative study of behavioral group therapy for sexual assault victims. *Behavior Therapy, 19,* 385–401.

Roberts, W. R., Penk, W. E., Gearing, M. L., Robinowitz, R., Dolan, M. P., & Patterson, E. T. (1982). Interpersonal problems of Vietnam veterans with symptoms of posttraumatic stress disorder. *Journal of Abnormal Psychology, 91,* 444–450.

Rychtarik, R. G., Silverman, W. K., Van Landingham, W. P., & Prue, D. M. (1984). Treatment of an incest victim with implosive therapy: A case study. *Behavior Therapy, 15,* 410–420.

Shore, J., Tatum, E., & Vollmer, W. (1986). Psychiatric reactions to disaster: The Mount St. Helens Experience. *American Journal of Psychiatry, 143,* 590–595.

Solomon, Z., Mikulincer, M., & Avitzur, E. (1988). Coping, locus of control, social support, and combat-related posttraumatic stress disorder: A prospective study. *Journal of Personality and Social Psychology, 55,* 279–285.

Veronen, L. J., & Kilpatrick, D. G. (1983). Stress management for rape victims. In D. Meichenbaum & M. E. Jaremko (Eds.), *Stress reduction and prevention.* New York: Plenum.

CHAPTER 6

Unipolar Depression

W. EDWARD CRAIGHEAD, DONALD D. EVANS, and CLIVE J. ROBINS

Depression is a rather ubiquitous label that is applied to a dysphoric mood state, a set of symptoms (a syndrome), or a clinical disorder (e.g., Major Depression). This chapter focuses on the treatment of the clinical disorder of Major Depression, which in DSM-III-R (American Psychiatric Association, 1987) is a subtype of Mood Disorders. Major Depression is also frequently called unipolar depression, to distinguish it from Bipolar Disorder (manic-depression). In this chapter, Major Depression will be referred to simply as *depression,* even though there is also a diagnosable milder and chronic form of depression labeled dysthymia. The DSM-III-R diagnostic criteria for a Major Depressive episode are:

A. At least five of the following symptoms have been present during the same two-week period and represent a change from previous functioning; at least one of the symptoms is either (1) depressed mood, or (2) loss of interest or pleasure. (Do not include symptoms that are clearly due to a physical condition, mood-incongruent delusions or hallucinations, incoherence, or marked loosening of associations.)

(1) depressed mood (or can be irritable mood in children and adolescents) most of the day, nearly every day, as indicated either by subjective account or observation by others

(2) markedly diminished interest or pleasure in all, or almost all, activities most of the day, nearly every day (as indicated either by subjective account or observation by others of apathy most of the time)

(3) significant weight loss or weight gain when not dieting (e.g., more than 5% of body weight in a month), or decrease or increase in appetite nearly every day (in children, consider failure to make expected weight gains)

(4) insomnia or hypersomnia nearly every day

(5) psychomotor agitation or retardation nearly every day (observable by others, not merely subjective feelings of restlessness or being slowed down)

(6) fatigue or loss of energy nearly every day

(7) feelings of worthlessness or excessive or inappropriate guilt (which may be delusional) nearly every day (not merely self-reproach or guilt about being sick)

(8) diminished ability to think or concentrate, or indecisiveness, nearly every day (either by subjective account or as observed by others)

(9) recurrent thoughts of death (not just fear of dying), recurrent suicidal ideation without a specific plan, or a suicide attempt or a specific plan for committing suicide.

B. (1) It cannot be established that an organic factor initiated and maintained the disturbance.
   (2) The disturbance is not a normal reaction to the death of a loved one (Uncomplicated Bereavement).
      Note: Morbid preoccupation with worthlessness, suicidal ideation, marked functional impairment or psychomotor retardation, or prolonged duration suggest bereavement complicated by Major Depression.
C. At no time during the disturbance have there been delusions or hallucinations for as long as two weeks in the absence of prominent mood symptoms (i.e., before the mood symptoms developed or after they have remitted).
D. Not superimposed on Schizophrenia, Schizophreniform Disorder, Delusional Disorder, or Psychotic Disorder NOS. (pp. 222–223)

Depression is a personal and social problem of significant proportions. During their lifetimes, about one in five people in the United States will experience an episode of depression sufficient to warrant diagnosis and treatment, and 3 to 5% of the population will be hospitalized and treated for depression and its sequelae (Craighead, Kennedy, Raczynski, & Dow, 1984). Although depression was once viewed as a mid-life and older-person problem, its prevalence among young adults and even among children is now widely accepted (see Rutter, Izard, & Read, 1986). Depression has negative economic and interpersonal effects as it impacts on daily functioning, and its frequent and severe health implications have been recently documented (Wells et al., 1989).

Because of the human suffering and misery created by depression, from the time of Hippocrates to the present (see Styron, 1990), it has occupied a prominent position among popular and scientific writers. In the later part of the 19th century, Kraepelin gave depression a permanent home among psychiatric diagnostic entities by dividing psychoses into schizophrenic and manic-depressive disorders (including bipolar and unipolar depression). Earlier in this century, psychoanalytic (Abraham, 1911; Freud, 1917/1956) and neoanalytic models and treatments of depression were prevalent.

There was a shift to biological explanations of the etiology of depression with the advent of somatic interventions such as the treatment of depression with psychotropic medications during the 1950s and the increased use of electroseizure therapy (EST). This biological focus became paramount in the 1960s and 1970s as extensive research on biological approaches to the etiology and treatment of depression emerged (Ballenger, 1988; Williams, Katz, & Shield, 1972). This increase in biological focus was accompanied by the declining influence of psychoanalytic thinking and the virtual absence of alternative psychological models of depression. In the 1970s, however, the rapidly developing fields of behavior therapy and cognitive-behavior therapy (Craighead, 1982) offered four somewhat overlapping, but independent, models that proposed explanations for the development of depression and suggested therapy programs. These included Lewinsohn's (1974) socioenvironmental model, Beck's (1974, 1976) cognitive model, Seligman's (1975) learned helplessness model and its reformulation (Abramson, Seligman, & Teasdale, 1978), and a self-control model most clearly stated by Rehm (1977). Over the past decade, these writers, and others working within this general theoretical domain, have gradually become more similar in their explanations of depression and the treatment programs derived from their models. As Rehm (in press) recently observed about therapies based on these models:

The programs are quite complex and most are composed of multiple units, lessons or modules that overlap and duplicate one another. In addition, there are variations in the application of the same program from one researcher to another, and even in the research clinics of the originators, the programs have evolved and changed. In many instances the effect is that the programs have become more similar to one another. When closely examined the basic structures of most of the programs show surprising parallels. Many of the programs contain similar procedures though the rationale and the label for the procedure may vary from one program to another. (p. 3)

The purpose of this chapter is to summarize and review the treatment outcome studies that have been derived from these behavioral and cognitive-behavioral models of depression. We will first provide a brief overview of the psychopathology of depression from this theoretical perspective, note methods of assessing depression, discuss the etiology of depression, and relate these findings to the intervention procedures. We will then review the treatment outcome studies, and subsequently note the major current issues and possible directions for future outcome research in the treatment of Major Depression.

PSYCHOPATHOLOGY OF DEPRESSION

The common symptoms of depression, not all of which will be experienced by every depressed individual, can be categorized in four groups: emotional-motivational, biological, behavioral, and cognitive symptoms. In describing these symptoms, we will note, where applicable, how they interface with the DSM-III-R diagnostic criteria.

Emotional Symptoms

The most obvious emotional symptom of depression is depressed or dysphoric mood; however, this is not present in about 20% of depressed patients (Beck, 1967). There is also significant *anxiety* in about 50% of the cases, and there may also be feelings of *anger* or *irritability*. For these feelings to be considered significant, they should clearly be present nearly every day for most of the day. Other frequent emotional-motivational symptoms are loss of ability to experience pleasure and loss of interest in formerly pleasurable activities; these symptoms tend to be seen in more severe or melancholic depressions. Other emotional symptoms considered indicative of melancholia are a lack of reactivity of mood to environmental events and diurnal variation of mood, with a worsening in the morning.

Biological Symptoms

Several symptoms of Major Depression appear to reflect dysregulations of biological systems. These include a decrease in weight and/or appetite, not due to dieting, or, less frequently (about 15%), an increase in weight or appetite. Similarly, sleep may be disrupted, which decreases the total hours slept, and early morning awakening may be a frequent aspect of the sleep disturbance. Again, in a minority of cases (10 to 15%), one sees an increase in sleep. A very common symptom of depression is fatigue. Some individuals do not even report depressed mood, but do complain of fatigue; upon further questioning, they fulfill a number of other symptom criteria for depression.

All-night sleep recordings of severely depressed individuals frequently show a decreased latency of REM sleep, an increase in REM density, and a decrease in stage IV sleep (Ballenger, 1988). Another commonly used tool for assessing biological dysregulation in depression is the dexamethasone suppression test (Carroll, et al., 1981). Administration of dexamethasone to nondepressed individuals results in a temporary suppression of cortisol output. Many depressed individuals, especially those with severe or melancholic depressions (Evans & Nemeroff, 1987), fail to show this suppression or escape from it early, which is thought to indicate over-activation of the hypothalamic-pituitary-adrenal axis. It has been known for some time that changes in neurotransmitter systems, particularly norepinephrine and serotonin, also occur in depression. Recent research demonstrates that, contrary to earlier suggestions, it is not just a question of too little or too much of a given neurotransmitter, but rather some "failure of regulation or buffering of these systems" (Siever & Davis, 1985, p. 1017).

Behavioral Symptoms

In severe depressions, there may be observable psychomotor retardation or agitation. Not mentioned as a criterion in DSM-III-R, but commonly seen in depression, are decreased levels of activity in general, and social withdrawal in particular. These may be seen as secondary to loss of interest or of pleasure. Frequent crying spells are common in depression, although some severely depressed persons report no longer being able to cry. Finally, suicidal behavior may be a symptom of depression.

Cognitive Symptoms

Two classes of cognitive symptoms are prominent in depression: cognitive-intellectual deficits and social-cognitive changes. Commonly experienced cognitive-intellectual deficits include difficulty in concentrating, indecisiveness, and poor short-term memory.

The changes in social cognition have been described by Beck (1976) as a "negative cognitive triad"—the depressed person's negative view of the self, the world, and the future. Beck proposed that the most proximal determinant of depressed mood and other depressive symptoms is the presence of negative thoughts about these three areas. Because the patient frequently is not immediately aware of them, these thoughts are called "automatic thoughts." They are believed to reflect the operation of underlying cognitive structures or schemata that influence what we attend to, how we encode it, and what we later remember.

With regard to the self, Hammen and Krantz (1976) documented that depressed persons evaluate themselves in a negative manner. DSM-III-R lists feelings of worthlessness and guilt, nearly every day, as symptoms of Major Depression, and the related symptom of low self-esteem in the case of dysthymia. Such negative self-evaluations have been proposed by Beck (1976) and others to reflect the operation of organized cognitive schemata that result in a negative selective bias when encoding and recalling information. This hypothesis has been supported in a series of studies by Kuiper and his colleagues (e.g., Derry & Kuiper, 1981).

With regard to the negative view of the world, depressed individuals often see their existence as bleak. Although it is true that depression often occurs in the context of negative life experiences, depressed persons also process these experiences in a way that minimizes positive aspects and maximizes negative ones (Beck, 1976).

The negative view of the future can be described as a sense of hopelessness and futility, which is listed in DSM-III-R as a criterion for dysthymia. In the extreme, this hopelessness can give rise to thoughts about death and suicidal ideation, listed as a criterion for Major Depression.

ASSESSMENT OF DEPRESSION

The symptoms of depression are best assessed by means of a structured interview, of which several are in common use in research, including the Schedule for Affective Disorders and Schizophrenia (Endicott & Spitzer, 1978), the Diagnostic Interview Schedule (Robins, Helzer, Croughan, & Ratcliff, 1981), and the Structured Clinical Interview for DSM-III-R—Patient (Spitzer, Williams, Gibbon, & First, 1989). These rely both on the patient's self-report and on interview-based observations of behavior. Such comprehensive interviews are relatively time-consuming, usually lasting 1 to 2 hours. Initial screening for depression, as well as ongoing assessment of its severity, can be obtained by use of self-administered questionnaires such as the Beck Depression Inventory (Beck, Rush, Shaw, & Emery, 1979) or interviewer rating scales such as the Hamilton Depression Rating Scale (Hamilton, 1960) or the Montgomery and Asberg Depression Rating Scale (Montgomery & Asberg, 1979).

INITIATING AND MAINTAINING VARIABLES (ETIOLOGY) OF DEPRESSION

As noted earlier, several cognitive-behavioral theories about the causes of depression have guided research over the past two decades. These theories will not be discussed in detail here, but potential etiological or maintaining factors will be described under the headings of the Environment and three Person factors: cognition, behavior, and biology (see Craighead, 1990).

Environmental Factors

Three classes of environmental factors have been the focus of considerable recent research: discrete life events, chronic strains, and social support. There is a clearly documented relationship between depression and a high frequency of recent negative life events (Brown & Harris, 1989), but causality is difficult to demonstrate because reports of recent life events have been retrospective and consequently open to negatively biased depressive recall.

More minor daily events or "hassles" have been found to be related to depressive symptoms (e.g., Monroe, 1983). However, such minor events may not be related to *clinical* depression. Brown and Harris (1978) found that 89% of onset cases of depression in a community sample reported having suffered a severe event or chronic difficulty in the previous nine months; this compared with only 30% of noncases. In contrast, minor events did not discriminate cases from noncases.

Depressed persons report receiving less social support from their environments than do nondepressed people (Billings, Cronkite, & Moos, 1983), which may in part be a function of the increased frequency of distressed marriages and family relationships (Rounsaville, Weissman, Prusoff, & Herceg-Baron, 1979). Brown and Harris (1978) found that the incidence of depression in working-class women under stress increased fourfold if the women reported the lack of a confidant. Although it is quite clear that social support deficits are related to depression, one is again faced with the problem of determining causality, because depressed behavior itself could decrease social support.

Cognitive and Personality Factors

Two prominent theoretical models have emphasized the importance of cognitive factors in depression. Beck's (1967) model suggests that persons vulnerable to depression have dysfunctional schemata, or attitudes about themselves and the world, that may be latent at most times but become activated by relevant impinging stressors. At such times, these schemata lead to negatively biased processing of incoming information, which in turn leads to depressive symptoms. The attributional reformulation of the learned helplessness model of Abramson, Seligman, and Teasdale (1978) suggests that persons vulnerable to depression have a tendency to attribute the causes of negative events to internal, stable, and global factors. When relevant stressors occur, this attributional style leads the individual to make such explanations for the specific event or events, which in turn leads to a sense of hopelessness and symptoms of depression. Thus, both of these models incorporate a cognitive diathesis which, in interaction with stressful events, leads to particular perceptions of events, and hence to depression.

Measures of dysfunctional attitudes and attributional style have usually been considered measures of relatively stable traits that confer vulnerability to depression. However, many studies have found that scores on such measures significantly decrease—often to the level of nondepressed individuals (Hollon, Kendall, & Lumry, 1986; Peselow, Robins, Block, Barouche, & Fieve, 1990)—when patients are in remission, demonstrating that they are heavily influenced by the depressed state. Although this has been taken as a challenge to cognitive theories, it should be borne in mind that these cognitive theories, particularly that of Beck (1967), claim that, in the nondepressed state, such attitudes may be present but latent. They would, therefore, require activation by stressful events in order to be readily assessed. The fact that such measures fluctuate with the depressed state is therefore to be expected. Perhaps the issue of state vs. trait is a false dichotomy. A recent study by Miranda and Persons (1988) found that individuals with a history of depressive episodes endorsed more dysfunctional attitudes than did those without such a history, but only if they were currently in a negative mood state, indicating that dysfunctional attitudes may indeed be a trait, but also may be dependent on mood state for their expression.

Unfortunately, the great majority of studies to date have not adequately tested the cognitive models regarding the etiology of depression (Alloy, Hartlage, & Abramson, 1988). Several studies that have examined the interaction of dysfunctional attitudes or a depressive self-schema with the frequency of negative life events have failed to find an effect of this interaction on depressive symptoms (Hammen, Marks, DeMayo, & Mayol, 1985; Robins & Block, 1989; Robins, Block, & Peselow (in press-a). In contrast, Olinger, Kuiper, and Shaw (1987) did find a relation to depression of the interaction between dysfunctional attitudes and reported occurrence of events specifically related to those attitudes. This suggests that it may be relatively specific matches between person characteristics and event characteristics that are important in depression, or at least in reactive depressions.

One line of research on specific person–event matches has concerned two personality dimensions, referred to by Beck (1983) as sociotropy and autonomy, and by Blatt, D'Afflitti, and Quinlan (1976) as dependency and self-criticism. According to these theorists, highly dependent or sociotropic individuals are particularly vulnerable to negative interpersonal losses, whereas highly autonomous or self-critical individuals are particularly vulnerable to experiences of failure or lack of control. Several recent studies have supported this hypothesis (Hammen et al., 1985; Hammen, Ellicott, Gitlin, & Jamison, 1989; Robins, in press; Robins & Block, 1988).

Behavioral Factors

Two classes of behavioral factors have been examined for their potential etiological role in depression: social skills and skills for coping with stressful life events. Consistent with this, Lewinsohn and his colleagues have found that depressed individuals are less skilled in a group situation and are unassertive (Youngren &

Lewinsohn, 1980). Jacobson and Anderson (1982) found that, in interactions with a confederate, depressed subjects made more negative self-references and more unsolicited self-disclosures. Coyne (1976) and Gotlib and Robinson (1982) have reported that the interpersonal behavior of depressed subjects elicits negative reactions in their interaction partners. It is likely that such negative reactions of others may lead the depressed individual to feel socially isolated or rejected, which may in turn maintain the depression. As with our discussion of cognitive and environmental factors, however, the interpersonal behavioral problems seen in depression may be a cause of depression, an effect, or both.

The other major behavioral factor examined in research has been coping skills. Because the relationship between stressful life events and depression is only a relatively weak one, a number of investigators have suggested that the manner in which the individual copes with these events may be a critical factor. Several studies (e.g., Billings et al., 1983; Coyne, Aldwin, & Lazarus, 1981) have found that, in coping with stressful events, depressed subjects show less problem-solving behavior; more seeking of information; help-seeking; wishful thinking; acceptance of the situation; and emotional release strategies. Again, it is not clear that these types of strategies play a causal role. In fact, Parker and Brown (1982) have shown that coping strategies are very dependent on the depressive state. Furthermore, differences in coping strategies could be largely a function of exposure to different types of stressors.

Biological Factors

Biological dysregulation occurs particularly in melancholic, endogenous, psychotic, or otherwise severe depressions. We do not know whether, in these depressions, biology also plays a greater etiologic role, though it seems likely that this is the case. One potential biological diathesis is that neurotransmitter receptor sites in certain brain areas, such as the limbic system, may be persistently subsensitive and therefore constitute a vulnerability marker, even in the absence of an acute depressive episode (Siever & Davis, 1985).

Part of the reason for believing that a biological diathesis may exist in some individuals comes from genetic studies. Data from several family concordance studies (e.g., Weissman et al., 1984) show strong evidence for heritability of Major Depressive disorder. Torgersen (1986) found much higher concordance rates for Major Depression in monozygotic twins than in dizygotic twins.

Combination of Factors

In most cases, depression probably occurs as a result of interactions among a number of the factors that have been described, including biological vulnerability; personal resources such as dysfunctional attitudes, attributional style, social skills, and problem-solving skills; environmental stressors such as severe events, daily hassles, and chronic strains; and environmental resources such as social support.

How is it that psychosocial and biological factors add to or interact with one another in causing depression? Akiskal and McKinney (1973) suggested that several possible causes, such as early object loss, current loss of reinforcement, helplessness, and biogenic amine depletion, all result in a "final common pathway" of "a reversible, functional derangement in the diencephalic mechanisms of reinforcement" (p. 26). A somewhat different view, presented by Craighead (1980, 1990), is that "depression may be a polydimensional phenomenon, with each dimension possibly having its own cause(s) and etiological pattern(s)" (1980, p. 24). There are some indications that depressions with a stronger biological component may have less of a cognitive or psychological component and vice versa. For example, Robins, Block, & Peselow (in press-b) found that nonendogenous depressed patients scored higher than endogenous patients on dysfunctional attitudes and recent life events. It is not being suggested that depressions should necessarily be dichotomized in this manner, but that depressions may vary according to the *degree* of biological and psychosocial influences.

Implications for Treatment

The relationship between treatment options and etiological factors is not a one-to-one correspondence. Appropriate choice of treatments is better made based on the environment, symptoms, dysfunctions, and deficits found during this and prior episodes of depression, prior treatment response, and family history data. The two major classes of treatment are biological (somatic) and psychosocial.

The most commonly used *biological treatment* is antidepressant medications, and the most commonly used class of antidepressant drugs is the tricyclics. Less commonly used are the monoamine oxidase inhibitors. Several new drugs that do not fall into either of these classes have been developed, such as trazodone (Desyrel), fluoxetine (Prozac), and bupropion (Wellbutrin). In difficult-to-treat cases, the effects of these medications may be augmented by lithium carbonate or other medication regimens (Heninger, Charney, & Sternberg, 1983). Electroseizure therapy (EST) is used most often in patients who, in addition to having a particular symptom profile, have failed to respond to antidepressant medications. The most effective *psychosocial treatments* have included behavioral, cognitive, and cognitive-behavioral therapies. The next section of this chapter will review and discuss the empirical research evaluating the effectiveness of these psychosocial treatments when they are used alone or in conjunction with antidepressant medications.

COGNITIVE AND BEHAVIORAL TREATMENTS FOR DEPRESSION

The complex nature of clinical depression has contributed to diversity among cognitive and behavioral treatments for depression. For purposes of discussion, these interventions have been divided into those that are mostly behavioral in origin and those that are primarily cognitive; this distinction is clearly artificial. All treatment programs for depression identified as cognitive or behavioral have elements of both, and the classification into behavioral and cognitive is based on the relative emphasis within each treatment program.

Behavioral Treatments

Several behavioral interventions for depression have been proposed and tested. Representative treatments include activity training, social skills training, and behavioral marital therapy.

Activity Training

One of the first behavioral treatment programs for depression was developed by Lewinsohn (1974). He assumed that depression is caused by a reduction in response-contingent positive reinforcement, an increase in aversive experiences, or a combination of both factors. It was hypothesized that the fundamental shift in an individual's experience could be due to the environment, inadequate skills to obtain reinforcers and reduce aversive experiences, or reduced reinforcing value of positive events and increased aversive value for negative events. Hoberman and Lewinsohn (1985) recently described their treatment model, in which the role of thoughts, feelings, and behavior, and their reciprocal interaction (Bandura, 1977), were explicitly acknowledged. However, Hoberman and Lewinsohn maintained that the feelings and thoughts associated with depression can be modified most effectively by behavior change.

On beginning this treatment program, patients are presented with a rationale about the connection between behavior and feelings. They then monitor events and affect to clarify the connection between them and mood, and to identify targets for behavioral intervention.

Progressive relaxation training is introduced early in the treatment. It is included to reduce anxiety, which magnifies the impact of negative events and reduces the reinforcing value of positive events. It also allows patients an early success. Interestingly, when relaxation training was used as a control condition in a study comparing it with amitriptyline, behavior therapy, and short-term psychodynamic psychotherapy (McLean & Hakstian, 1979), relaxation fared better than short-term psychotherapy and was equally effective to drug therapy. The general behavioral program was the most effective of all treatments. Following relaxation skills training, the treatment focuses on reducing aversive events. Application of relaxation skills, stress-management training, assertiveness training, and modification of dysfunctional thoughts are all included. In this module, a departure is made from strictly behavioral techniques, and a number of cognitive techniques are introduced.

The treatment is concluded by teaching patients to increase the number and quality of pleasant activities. This is the heart of the treatment and the best known part of the overall program. The initial step is the establishment of realistic goals for increasing the number of pleasant events. Patients are then taught to increase their enjoyment of events by applying their previously learned cognitive and behavioral skills. Finally, they choose activities associated with positive moods and develop specific plans to increase the likelihood they will actually engage in the activities. Social activities receive special attention, and the goals become progressively higher as the program continues to completion.

Lewinsohn's behavioral approach to treating depression has been shown to be effective when administered individually (Brown & Lewinsohn, 1984; Lewinsohn, Sullivan, & Grosscup, 1982) or in psychoeducational groups (Brown & Lewinsohn, 1984; Steinmetz, Lewinsohn, & Antonuccio, 1983) with no differences between the modalities of therapy (Teri & Lewinsohn, 1986). Both the Coping with Depression Course (group therapy) and the individual treatment based on this model are broadly based behavioral programs rather than narrowly focused pleasant/unpleasant event interventions.

Social Skills Training

A well-designed and comprehensive social skills approach to treating depression has been developed by Bellack, Hersen, and Himmelhoch (1981). This program assumes an overabundance of negative interpersonal events and a relative lack of positive interpersonal events as causative factors in depression. The functional aspects of depression, such as receiving attention, sympathy, and support for depression-related behaviors, are targets for change. Their change allows patients to have more positive and self-enhancing social interactions.

Social skills include the familiar components of assertion training, such as refusing unreasonable requests, expressing disapproval, making requests, and compromise and negotiation. Also included are positive assertion skills such as giving compliments, expressing affection, offering approval and praise, and making apologies. A third component is conversational skill, which is composed of initiating a conversation, asking questions, providing information, reinforcing others, and ending conversations. These three skill areas are evaluated in a variety of contexts, including interactions with strangers, friends, family, fellow workers, or schoolmates. The therapist uses didactic training, experiential training (modeling, guided practice, role playing), and eventual testing in the natural environment to ensure that the skills are implemented.

In addition to the skills training content, three other components are explicitly included in each session. The first of these is social perception training. Accurate perception of others is taught by the therapist didactically and practiced during the role-playing activities. The second component is practice of the newly learned behavioral skills. The authors strongly emphasize the necessity of repetition to ensure application and maintenance. The final component is self-evaluation and self-reinforcement, which is included because of the tendency for depressed patients to evaluate themselves more negatively than is warranted by their performance (Nelson & Craighead, 1981; Rehm, 1977). Patients are taught to evaluate their own performance and they are provided with corrective feedback when they grade themselves too harshly. They are also taught to reinforce themselves with positive self-statements when they do well.

Evidence for the efficacy of social skills training in the treatment of depression was provided by Hersen, Bellack, Himmelhoch, and Thase (1984). They compared four groups: (a) social skills training plus pill placebo, (b) social skills training plus amitriptyline, (c) amitriptyline, and (d) psychotherapy plus pill placebo. They found all treatments to be effective with no differences among them on outcome measures of depression. There was, however, an additional advantage for the subjects receiving social skills training in that they showed more improvement on measures of social interaction.

Behavioral Marital Therapy

Investigators in both O'Leary's and Jacobson's laboratories (Beach & O'Leary, 1986; Jacobson, Holtzworth-Monroe, & Schmaling, 1989) have proposed behavioral marital therapy as a viable treatment for depression. It has been demonstrated to be effective in the treatment of marital discord (Beach & Bauserman, 1990). The rationale for marital intervention as a treatment of depression rests on the assumption that marital discord is either causative or related to maintenance of a depressed state. Approximately 50% of couples seeking marital therapy have at least one spouse who is depressed (Beach, Jouriles, & O'Leary, 1985). This high correspondence has also been found in the families of patients seeking treatment for depression (Rounsaville et al., 1979), where a 50% level of comorbid marital discord has also been observed.

In a dyadic setting with the couple, behavioral marital therapy applies many of the components previously outlined for individuals in activity and social skills therapies. These include increasing positive behaviors, decreasing negative behaviors, improving communication skills, and setting realistic goals and expectations for the relationship. Increasing insight into the causes of the marital problems, improving problem-solving skills, and correcting misperceptions of the other spouse are also included as treatment goals.

Studies that have compared behavioral marital therapy and cognitive behavior therapy in treating depression have shown that behavioral marital therapy is equal to cognitive behavior therapy in relieving depressive symptoms (Beach & O'Leary, 1986; Jacobson et al., 1989; O'Leary & Beach, in press). However, the reverse has not been found; as a group, subjects successfully treated with cognitive therapy do not show increases in marital satisfaction. Therefore, behavioral marital therapy may be the treatment of choice for those couples with both problems. These data also suggest that untreated marital discord may be a factor in unsuccessful individual treatment.

Cognitive Therapy

As with the behavioral programs, no attempt will be made to list all cognitive approaches or techniques to treating depression. The representative treatment chosen is Beck's cognitive therapy. Cognitive therapy is a relatively short-term, symptom-focused treatment for unipolar depression (Beck et al., 1979; Sacco & Beck, 1985). It is based on Beck's model, which assumes that depression results from maladaptive beliefs or schemas. These in turn lead to a series of related automatic thoughts that are negative, contain logical errors, and are organized around certain themes such as social evaluation, family conflict, and work performance. The maladaptive beliefs and negative automatic thinking maintain the negative cognitive triad consisting of a negative view of self, the world, and the future. The goal of cognitive therapy is to retrain the individual to think more logically and realistically and to modify fundamental underlying beliefs.

Cognitive therapy begins with a presentation of the model to the patients, which helps them to understand the relationships among cognition, behavior, and emotion. Collaborative relationships with the patients are fostered. Patients are taught to view themselves as personal scientists involved in identifying and evaluating automatic thoughts and underlying assumptions.

Further understanding of the relationships among situations, emotions, and cognitions is accomplished through self-monitoring on a daily record of dysfunctional thoughts (Beck et al., 1979). After patients have learned to self-monitor adequately, they begin to evaluate their thoughts for logical errors, which may include: arbitrary inference, selective abstraction, overgeneralization, magnification and minimization, personalization, and all-or-none thinking (Beck, 1976). They are then taught to substitute more reasonable thoughts for automatic negative thoughts.

The final component of the treatment is the identification and modification of automatic thought patterns or themes, which are hypothesized to be reflective of maladaptive beliefs or "silent assumptions." They could include beliefs such as "I'm no good," "I have to be perfect," or "I have to be liked by everyone." After silent assumptions are identified, patients are instructed to engage in testing their validity. When patients reach this stage, therapists continue to help with problem solving, designing appropriate testing of assumptions, and promoting practice of newly learned skills. It is hoped that, by the end of treatment, patients will independently continue this hypothesis-testing process.

Research efforts in nondrug treatments of depression were given a particularly significant boost with the publication of data by Rush, Beck, Kovacs, and Hollon in 1977, suggesting that cognitive therapy for depression could equal or surpass the effectiveness of antidepressant medication. Cognitive therapy patients, when compared to patients receiving imipramine, showed greater decreases in depressive symptoms, were less likely to drop out of treatment, and were less likely to reenter treatment during a 6-month follow-up. Although these findings have been criticized (Becker & Schuckit, 1978), a number of studies since then have found cognitive therapy equal to drug therapy (American Psychiatric Association, 1989).

Given two treatments of demonstrated efficacy, namely antidepressants and cognitive therapy, a logical step in the research effort was to test the combination of these treatments. Surprisingly, there is little evidence to support the addition of medication to subjects treated with cognitive therapy, or vice versa (Beck, Hollon, Young, Bedrosian, & Budenz, 1985; Murphy, Simons, Wetzel, & Lustman, 1984).

A recent report by Hollon et al. (1989) again reaffirmed the equality of cognitive therapy and tricyclic antidepressants administered singly. Some evidence for a slight advantage for combined treatment was also observed. In conducting this study, the investigators addressed criticisms of previous work:

1. The effect was replicated outside of Beck's group;
2. Clinician ratings were added to self-report and were conducted blindly;
3. Blood plasma levels of drugs and adherence to protocol for psychotherapy were monitored;
4. Drugs were not withdrawn before final treatment outcome ratings were conducted.

The recent reported NIMH Treatment of Depression collaborative research program (Elkin et al., 1989) compared cognitive-behavioral therapy (CBT), interpersonal psychotherapy (IPT), imipramine, and pill placebo. The results of this study generally support the equality of CBT and IPT with imipramine. There was some indication that imipramine and IPT were more effective with severely depressed patients and CBT worked better with more mildly depressed patients. However, interpretations of the results are clouded by site differences, with one site favoring CBT with severely depressed patients and others favoring IPT. There also was a treatment by marital status confound, which may have affected the results of this study.

If cognitive therapy and drug therapy are equally effective and drug therapy is less expensive, why continue doing cognitive therapy? The answer becomes clear when factors other than immediate treatment outcome are considered. Tricyclic antidepressants have potentially dangerous side effects that are not tolerated by some patients. In large quantities, they also provide the means for a successful suicide. The most promising data supporting the continued use of cognitive therapy have come from the follow-up reports of the outcome studies. Rush et al. (1977) reported that group differences were maintained at 6-month follow-up and that more imipramine-treated subjects had sought additional treatment. However, by 1 year (Kovacs, Rush, Beck, & Hollon, 1981), the group differences were maintained only for self-rated depression.

Other studies have found differential relapse rates in favor of cognitive-behavior therapy to be a more lasting effect. A 1-year follow-up study by Simons, Murphy, Levine, and Wetzel (1986) showed a lower relapse rate for subjects treated with cognitive therapy than for subjects treated with antidepressants. Two-year follow-up data from another study (Blackburn, Eunson, & Bishop, 1986) replicated this finding. In the latter study, patients were continued on their medication for at least 6 months, yet the groups that received cognitive therapy or cognitive therapy plus pharmacotherapy were less likely to relapse than the pharmacotherapy-only group.

A recent 2-year follow-up of the patients treated in the Hollon et al. study (Evans et al., 1989) provides the clearest picture regarding relapse. After treatment completion, half of the medication-only subjects were withdrawn from their medication. A 2-year follow-up was conducted on the resultant four groups: medication withdrawn posttreatment, medication continued for 1 year, cognitive-behavior therapy, cognitive-behavior therapy combined with drug treatment (drug withdrawn at posttreatment). At 2 years, 50% of the group whose medication was withdrawn posttreatment had relapsed, most within the first 4 months after treatment (a figure comparable to most other studies). For the other groups, the numbers who relapsed were 27%, 20%, and 15%, respectively, for the continued medication, cognitive-behavior therapy, and combined cognitive-behavior therapy and medication conditions. It is observable from these data that both cognitive-behavior therapy and continued medication therapy can help prevent relapse.

CURRENT STATUS AND RECOMMENDATIONS

Based on the reviewed outcome studies with outpatients diagnosed as suffering from Major Depression, it seems reasonable to conclude that about two-thirds can be successfully treated with behavior therapy and/or cognitive therapy; perhaps either would be more felicitously titled cognitive-behavior therapy (CBT). The same can be concluded about antidepressant medications, such as imipramine, nortriptyline, and others that have been adequately evaluated in clinical trials. Interpersonal psychotherapy (IPT) also appears to be an equally effective short-term intervention for depression. There are insufficient outcome data from clinical trials to allow any empirically based conclusions regarding the effectiveness of any other forms of psychotherapy for the treatment of depression.

Short-term CBT also appears to produce lasting effects, because its 1-year and 2-year follow-up relapse rates are very low. Indeed, the relapse rates following successful treatment with 16 to 20 sessions of CBT given over a course of 3 months are among the lowest of those produced by any treatments or combinations of treatments for Major Depression. The lasting effects of IPT have not been adequately evaluated, but will soon be known when the NIMH Psychotherapy Collaborative Outcome follow-up data are published. Short-term (3-month) treatment with antidepressant medications, although equally effective with CBT and IPT, has repeatedly produced very minimal long-term effects; relapse rates nearly always exceed 50%. If short-term medication treatment is employed, it needs to be combined with short-term psychotherapy such as CBT in order to produce acceptable relapse rates. Current data *suggest* that the most effective outpatient treatment for unipolar depression is the combination of long-term (up to 15 months) antidepressant medication with short-term CBT.

All the clinical trials reported in this chapter were conducted with outpatients. Depressed subjects who were psychotic or imminently suicidal were excluded from these studies. Recent *preliminary* data, however, support the use of CBT with more severely depressed inpatients. Bowers (1990) has effectively combined CBT with medications in an inpatient setting. Thase (in press) has successfully treated 13 of 16 endogenous depressed inpatients with CBT without concurrent antidepressant medications. These preliminary results need replication in broader-based clinical trials, but do provide further encouraging support for the effectiveness of CBT as an intervention for depression.

Who comprise the one-third nonresponders to these therapies for depression? Craighead (1990) has suggested that they are: (a) bipolar individuals who have not yet suffered a manic episode, so they currently might be diagnosed with Major Depression; (b) individuals with more complicated and severe biological dysregulation difficulties (data summarized by Belsher and Costello (1988) support this idea); and (c) individuals with concomitant Axis II personality disorders, especially narcissistic, histrionic, and borderline types. In fact, the latter group may need long-term, more maintenance-oriented CBT as described by Linehan (in press).

Research on psychopathology, etiology, and treatment of depression suggest at least three important future directions for psychosocial intervention research. The *role of emotion* or feeling has been conspicuously absent from treatments designed for this "mood" disorder. Incorporation of this domain into CBT would perhaps allow for a broader effect on the components or symptoms of this disorder. Linehan's (in press) dialectical behavior therapy and Craighead's (1990) emotional restructuring procedure represent steps to incorporate specific feeling-change efforts into CBT. Second, *maintenance therapies* need to be developed and evaluated. These could be based on currently effective CBT procedures, but integrated into long-term maintenance strategies. Kupfer, Frank, and Perel (1989) are currently evaluating creative treatment maintenance strategies with IPT and antidepressant medication. Because social support is an important factor both in the development of depression and in relapse following successful treatments (see Belsher & Costello, 1988), *treatments that emphasize increasing social support,* such as behavioral marital therapy, need further evaluation. Behavioral family therapy (Wells, 1985) and CBT group therapy are other interventions that focus on social support but have not yet been adequately and systematically evaluated as interventions or maintenance treatments for depression.

REFERENCES

Abraham, K. (1911). Notes on the psychoanalytic investigation and treatment of manic-depressive insanity and allied conditions. In *Selected papers of Karl Abraham.* London: Institute of Psychoanalysis and Hogarth Press, 1927.

Abramson, L. Y., Seligman, M. E. P., & Teasdale, J. (1978). Learned helplessness in humans: Critique and reformulation. *Journal of Abnormal Psychology, 87,* 49–74.

Akiskal, H. S., & McKinney, W. T. (1973). Depressive disorders: Toward a unified hypothesis. *Science, 182,* 20–29.

Alloy, L. B., Hartlage, S., & Abramson, L. Y. (1988). Testing the cognitive diathesis-stress theories of depression: Issues of research design, conceptualization and assessment. In L. B. Alloy (Ed.), *Cognitive processes in depression.* New York: Guilford.

American Psychiatric Association. (1987). *Diagnostic and statistical manual of mental disorders* (3rd ed. rev.). Washington, DC: Author.

American Psychiatric Association. (1989). *Treatments of psychiatric disorders: A task force report of the American Psychiatric Association: Vol. 3* (pp. 1834–1846). Washington, DC: Author.

Ballenger, J. C. (1988). Biological aspects of depression: Implications for clinical practice. In A. J. Frances and R. E. Hales (Eds.), *Review of psychiatry: Vol. 7* (pp. 169–212). Washington, DC: American Psychiatric Press.

Bandura, A. (1977). *Social learning theory.* Englewood Cliffs, NJ: Prentice-Hall.

Beach, S. R. H., & Bauserman, S. A. K. (1990). Enhancing the effectiveness of marital therapy. In F. D. Fincham and T. N. Bradbury (Eds.), *The psychology of marriage* (pp. 349–374). New York: Guilford.

Beach, S. R. H., Jouriles, E., & O'Leary, K. D. (1985). Extramarital sex: Impact on depression and commitment in couples seeking marital therapy. *Journal of Sex and Marital Therapy, 11,* 99–108.

Beach, S. R. H., & O'Leary, K. D. (1986). The treatment of depression occurring in the context of marital discord. *Behavior Therapy, 17,* 43–49.

Beck, A. T. (1967). *Depression: Clinical, experimental, and theoretical aspects.* New York: Harper and Row.

Beck, A. T. (1974). The development of depression: A cognitive model. In R. J. Friedman & M. M. Katz (Eds.), *The psychology of depression: Contemporary theory and research* (pp. 3–27). New York: Winston-Wiley.

Beck, A. T. (1976). *Cognitive therapy and the emotional disorders.* New York: International University Press.

Beck, A. T. (1983). Cognitive therapy of depression: New perspectives. In P. J. Clayton & J. E. Barrett (Eds.), *Treatment of depression: Old controversies and new approaches* (pp. 265–290). New York: Raven Press.

Beck, A. T., Hollon, S. D., Young, J. E., Bedrosian, R. C., & Budenz, D. (1985). Treatment of depression with cognitive therapy and amitriptyline. *Archives of General Psychiatry, 42,* 142–158.

Beck, A. T., Rush, A. J., Shaw, B. F., & Emery, G. (1979). *Cognitive therapy of depression: A treatment manual.* New York: Guilford.

Becker, J., & Schuckit, M. A. (1978). The comparative efficacy of cognitive therapy and pharmacotherapy in the treatment of depressions. *Cognitive Therapy and Research, 2,* 193–197.

Bellack, A. S., Hersen, M., & Himmelhoch, J. M. (1981). Social skills training for depression: A treatment manual. *Journal Supplement Abstract Service Catalog of Selected Documents in Psychology, 10,* 92.

Belsher, G., & Costello, C. G. (1988). Relapse after recovery from unipolar depression: A critical review. *Psychological Bulletin, 104,* 84–96.

Billings, A. G., Cronkite, R. C., & Moos, R. H. (1983). Social-environmental factors in unipolar depression: Comparisons of depressed patients and nondepressed controls. *Journal of Abnormal Psychology, 92,* 119–134.

Blackburn, I. M., Eunson, K. M., & Bishop, S. (1986). A two-year naturalistic follow-up of depressed patients treated with cognitive therapy, pharmacotherapy and a combination of both. *Journal of Affective Disorders, 10,* 67–75.

Blatt, S. J., D'Afflitti, J. P., & Quinlan, D. M. (1976). Experiences of depression in normal young adults. *Journal of Abnormal Psychology, 85,* 383–389.

Bowers, W. A. (1990). Treatment of depressed inpatients: Cognitive therapy plus medication, relaxation plus medication, and medication alone. *British Journal of Psychiatry, 156,* 73–78.

Brown, G. W., & Harris, T. O. (1978). *Social origins of depression: A study of psychiatric disorder in women.* New York: Free Press.

Brown, G. W., & Harris, T. O. (1989). Depression. In G. W. Brown and T. O. Harris (Eds.), *Life events and illness* (pp. 49–93). New York: Guilford.

Brown, R. A., & Lewinsohn, P. M. (1984). A psychoeducational approach to the treatment of depression: Comparison of group, individual and minimal contact procedures. *Journal of Consulting and Clinical Psychology, 52,* 774–783.

Carroll, B. J., Feinberg, M., Greden, J. K., Tarika, K., Albala, A. A., Hasktt, R. F., James, N. M. I., Kronfol, Z., Lohr, N., Steiner, M., DeVigne, J. P., & Young, E. (1981). A specific laboratory test for the diagnosis of melancholia. *Archives of General Psychiatry, 38,* 15–22.

Coyne, J. C. (1976). Depression and the response of others. *Journal of Abnormal Psychology, 85,* 186–193.

Coyne, J. C., Aldwin, C., & Lazarus, R. S. (1981). Depression and coping in stressful episodes. *Journal of Abnormal Psychology, 90,* 439–447.

Craighead, W. E. (1980). Away from a unitary model of depression. *Behavior Therapy, 11,* 122–128.

Craighead, W. E. (1982). A brief clinical history of cognitive-behavior therapy with children. *School Psychology Review, 11,* 5–13.

Craighead, W. E. (1990). There's a place for us: All of us. *Behavior Therapy, 21,* 3–23.

Craighead, W. E., Kennedy, R. E., Raczynski, J. M., & Dow, M. G. (1984). Affective disorders—unipolar. In S. M. Turner and M. Hersen (Eds.), *Adult psychopathology: A behavioral perspective* (pp. 184–244). New York: Wiley.

Derry, P. A., & Kuiper, N. A. (1981). Schematic processing and self-reference in clinical depression. *Journal of Abnormal Psychology, 4,* 286–297.

Elkin, I., Shea, M. T., Watkins, J. T., Imber, S. D., Sotsky, S. M., Collins, J. F., Glass, D. R., Pilkonis, P. A., Leber, W. R., Docherty, J. P., Fiester, S. J., & Parloff, M. B. (1989). National Institute of Mental Health treatment of depression collaborative research program: General effectiveness of treatments. *Archives of General Psychiatry, 46,* 971–982.

Endicott, J., & Spitzer, R. L. (1978). A diagnostic interview: The Schedule for Affective Disorders and Schizophrenia. *Archives of General Psychiatry, 35,* 837–844.

Evans, D. L., & Nemeroff, C. B. (1987). The clinical use of the dexamethasone suppression test in DSM-III affective disorders: Correlation with the severe depressive subtypes of melancholia and psychosis. *Journal of Psychiatric Research, 21,* 185–194.

Evans, M. D., Hollon, S. D., DeRubeis, R. J., Piasecki, J. M., Grove, W. M., Garvey, M. J., & Tuason, V. B. (1989). *Differential relapse following cognitive therapy, pharmacotherapy, and combined cognitive-pharmacotherapy for depression.* Manuscript submitted for publication.

Freud, S. (1956). Mourning and melancholia. In J. Strachey (Ed. and Trans.), *The standard edition of the complete psychological works of Sigmund Freud* (Vol. 14). London: Hogarth Press. (Original work published 1917)

Gotlib, I. H., & Robinson, L. A. (1982). Responses to depressed individuals: Discrepancies between self-report and observer-rated behavior. *Journal of Abnormal Psychology, 91,* 231–240.

Hamilton, M. (1960). A rating scale for depression. *Journal of Neurology, Neurosurgery, and Psychiatry, 23,* 56–62.

Hammen, C., Ellicott, A., Gitlin, M., & Jamison, K. R. (1989). Sociotrophy/autonomy and vulnerability to specific life events in patients with unipolar depression and bipolar disorders. *Journal of Abnormal Psychology, 98,* 154–160.

Hammen, C. L., & Krantz, S. (1976). Effect of success and failure on depressive cognitions. *Journal of Abnormal Psychology, 85,* 577–586.

Hammen, C., Marks, T., DeMayo, R., & Mayol, A. (1985). Self-schemas and risk for depression: A prospective study. *Journal of Personality and Social Psychology, 49,* 1147–1159.

Heninger, G. R., Charney, D. S., & Sternberg, D. E. (1983). Lithium carbonate augmentation of antidepressant treatment. *Archives of General Psychiatry, 40,* 1335–1342.

Hersen, M., Bellack, A. S., Himmelhoch, J. M., & Thase, M. E. (1984). Effects of social skill training, amitriptyline, and psychotherapy in unipolar depressed women. *Behavior Therapy, 15,* 21–40.

Hoberman, H. M., & Lewinsohn, P. M. (1985). The behavioral treatment of depression. In E. E. Beckham & W. R. Leber (Eds.), *Handbook of depression: Treatment, assessment & research.* Homewood, IL: Dorsey Press.

Hollon, S. D., DeRubeis, R. J., Evans, M. D., Wiemer, M. J., Garvey, M. J., Grove, W. M., & Tuason, V. B. (1989). *Cognitive therapy, pharmacotherapy, and combined cognitive-pharmacotherapy in the treatment of depression.* Manuscript submitted for publication.

Hollon, S. D., Kendall, P. C., & Lumry, A. (1986). Specificity of depressotypic cognitions in clinical depression. *Journal of Abnormal Psychology, 95,* 52–59.

Jacobson, N. S., & Anderson, E. A. (1982). Interpersonal skill and depression in college students: An analysis of the timing of self-disclosures. *Behavior Therapy, 13,* 271–282.

Jacobson, N. S., Holtzworth-Munroe, A., & Schmaling, K. B. (1989). Marital therapy and spouse involvement in the treatment of depression, agoraphobia, and alcoholism. *Journal of Consulting and Clinical Psychology, 57,* 5–10.

Kovacs, M., Rush, A. J., Beck, A. T., & Hollon, S. D. (1981). Depressed outpatients treated with cognitive therapy or pharmacotherapy. *Archives of General Psychiatry, 38,* 33–39.

Kupfer, D. J., Frank, E., & Perel, J. M. (1989). The advantage of early treatment intervention in recurrent depression. *Archives of General Psychiatry, 46,* 771–775.

Lewinsohn, P. M. (1974). Clinical and theoretical aspects of depression. In K. S. Calhoun, H. E. Adams, & K. M. Mitchell (Eds.), *Innovative treatment methods in psychopathology* (pp. 63–120). New York: Wiley.

Lewinsohn, P. M., Sullivan, J. M., & Grosscup, S. J. (1982). Behavior therapy: Clinical applications. In A. J. Rush (Ed.), *Short-term psychotherapies for the depressed patient* (pp. 50–87). New York: Guilford.

Linehan, M. M. (in press). Dialectical behavior therapy in groups: Treating borderline personality disorders and suicidal behavior. In C. M. Brody (Ed.), *Women in groups.* New York: Springer.

McLean, P. D., & Hakstian, A. R. (1979). Clinical depression: Comparative efficacy of outpatient treatments. *Journal of Consulting and Clinical Psychology, 47,* 818–836.

Miranda, J., & Persons, J. B. (1988). Dysfunctional attitudes are mood-state dependent. *Journal of Abnormal Psychology, 97,* 76–79.

Monroe, S. M. (1983). Major and minor life events as predictors of psychological distress: Further issues and findings. *Journal of Behavioral Medicine, 6,* 189–205.

Montgomery, S. A., & Asberg, M. (1979). A new depression scale designed to be sensitive to change. *British Journal of Psychiatry, 134,* 382–389.

Murphy, G. E., Simons, A. D., Wetzel, R. D., & Lustman, P. J. (1984). Cognitive therapy and pharmacotherapy. *Archives of General Psychiatry, 41,* 33–41.

Nelson, R. E. & Craighead, W. E. (1981). Tests of a self-control model of depression. *Behavior Therapy, 12,* 123–129.

O'Leary, K. D., & Beach, S. H. R. (in press). Marital therapy: A viable treatment for depression and marital discord. *American Journal of Psychiatry.*

Olinger, L. J., Kuiper, N. A., & Shaw, B. F. (1987). Dysfunctional attitudes and stressful life events: An interactive model of depression. *Cognitive Therapy and Research, 11,* 25–40.

Parker, G. B., & Brown, L. B. (1982). Coping behaviors that mediate between life events and depression. *Archives of General Psychiatry, 39,* 1386–1391.

Peselow, E. D., Robins, C. J., Block, P., Barouche, F., & Fieve, R. R. (1990). Dysfunctional attitudes in depressed patients before and after clinical treatment and in normal control subjects. *American Journal of Psychiatry, 147,* 439–444.

Rehm, L. P. (1977). A self-control model of depression. *Behavior Therapy, 8,* 787–804.

Rehm, L. P. (in press). Psychotherapies for depression. In K. Schlesinger and B. Bloom (Eds.), *Proceedings of the First Boulder Symposium on Clinical Psychology: Depression.* Hillsdale, NJ: Erlbaum.

Robins, C. J. (in press). Congruence of personality and life events in depression. *Journal of Abnormal Psychology.*

Robins, C. J., & Block, P. (1988). Personal vulnerability, life events, and depressive symptoms: A test of a specific interactional model. *Journal of Personality and Social Psychology, 54,* 847–852.

Robins, C. J., & Block, P. (1989). Cognitive theories of depression viewed from a diathesis-stress perspective: Evaluations of the models of Beck and of Abramson, Seligman, and Teasdale. *Cognitive Therapy and Research, 13,* 297–313.

Robins, C. J., Block, P., & Peselow, E. D. (in press-a). Cognition and life events in major depression: A test of the mediation and interaction hypotheses. *Cognitive Therapy and Research.*

Robins, C. J., Block, P., & Peselow, E. D. (in press-b). Endogenous and nonendogenous depressions: Relations to life events, dysfunctional attitudes, and event perceptions. *British Journal of Clinical Psychology.*

Robins, L. N., Helzer, J. E., Croughan, J., & Ratcliff, K. S. (1981). National Institute of Mental Health Diagnostic Interview Schedule. Its history, characteristics and validity. *Archives of General Psychiatry, 38,* 381–389.

Rounsaville, B. J., Weissman, M. M., Prusoff, B. A., & Herceg-Baron, R. L. (1979). Marital disputes and treatment outcome in depressed women. *Comprehensive Psychiatry, 20,* 483–490.

Rush, A. J., Beck, A. T., Kovacs, M., & Hollon, S. (1977). Comparative efficacy of cognitive therapy and pharmacotherapy in the treatment of depressed outpatients. *Cognitive Therapy and Research, 1,* 17–37.

Rutter, M., Izard, C. E., & Read, P. B. (Eds.) (1986). *Depression in young people: Developmental and clinical perspectives.* New York: Guilford.

Sacco, W. P., & Beck, A. T. (1985). Cognitive therapy of depression. In E. E. Beckham & W. R. Leber (Eds.), *Handbook of depression: Treatment, assessment & research* (pp. 3–38). Homewood, IL: Dorsey Press.

Seligman, M. E. P. (1975). *Helplessness: On depression, development, and death.* San Francisco: Freeman.

Siever, L. J., & Davis, K. L. (1985). Overview: Toward a dysregulation hypothesis of depression. *American Journal of Psychiatry, 142,* 1017–1031.

Simons, A. D., Murphy, G. E., Levine, J. L., & Wetzel, R. D. (1986). Cognitive therapy and pharmacotherapy for depression: Sustained improvement over one year. *Archives of General Psychiatry, 43,* 43–48.

Spitzer, R. L., Williams, J. B. W., Gibbon, M., & First, M. B. (1989). *Structured clinical interview for DSM-III-R—patient edition.* New York: Biometric Research Department, New York State Psychiatric Institute.

Steinmetz, J. L., Lewinsohn, P. M., & Antonuccio, D. (1983). Prediction of individual outcome in a group intervention for depression. *Journal of Consulting and Clinical Psychology, 51,* 331–337.

Styron, W. (1990). *Darkness visible: A memoir of madness.* New York: Random House.

Teri, L., & Lewinsohn, P. M. (1986). Individual and group treatment of unipolar depression: Comparison of treatment outcome and identification of predictors of successful treatment outcome. *Behavior Therapy, 17,* 215–228.

Thase, M. E. (in press). Cognitive behavior therapy of endogenous depression. Part 2. Preliminary findings in 16 unmedicated patients. *Behavior Therapy.*

Torgersen, S. (1986). Genetic factors in moderately severe and mild affective disorders. *Archives of General Psychiatry, 43,* 222–226.

Weissman, M. M., Gershon, E. S., Kidd, K. K., Prusoff, B. A., Leckman, J. F., Dibble, E., Hamovit, J., Thompson, W. D., Pauls, D. L., & Guroff, J. J. (1984). Psychiatric disorders in the relatives of probands with affective disorders: The Yale–National Institute of Mental Health Collaborative Study. *Archives of General Psychiatry, 41,* 13–21.

Wells, K. B., Stewart, A., Hays, R. D., Burnam, A., Rogers, W., Daniels, M., Berry, S., Greenfield, S., & Ware, J. (1989). The functioning and well-being of depressed patients: Results from the medical outcomes study. *Journal of the American Medical Association, 262,* 914–919.

Wells, K. G. (1985). Behavioral family therapy. In M. Hersen and A. S. Bellack (Eds.), *Dictionary of behavior therapy* (pp. 25–30). New York: Plenum.

Williams, T. A., Katz, M. M., & Shield, J. A. (1972). *Recent advances in the psychobiology of the depressive illnesses* (DHEW Publication No. HSM 70-9053). Washington, DC: U.S. Government Printing Office.

Youngren, M. A., & Lewinsohn, P. M. (1980). The functional relation between depression and problematic interpersonal behavior. *Journal of Abnormal Psychology, 89,* 333–341.

CHAPTER 7

Behavioral Intervention with Personality Disorders

IRA D. TURKAT

The 1990s offer significant hope for the advancement of behavior therapy in the management of the personality disorders. According to the American Psychiatric Association's Task Force Report on the treatment of psychiatric disorders, "the behavioral literature suggests that some behaviors in personality disorders can be modified with lasting results" (American Psychiatric Association, 1989, p. 2656). Behavior therapists should be delighted that the American Psychiatric Association (an organization with a subgroup of members who have often been skeptical and frequently hostile to the idea that behavior therapy has anything useful to offer in the management of the personality disorders) would make such a statement. However, many behavior therapists would question the American Psychiatric Association Task Force's conclusion, because if one looks for a body of sound scientific data to support this statement, it is unavailable at the present time. There is no question that the behavioral literature at large has documented that certain behaviors associated with personality disorders can be changed, with long-lasting results, but studies demonstrating such improvement among a specific, well-defined personality disorder syndrome do not exist. Nonetheless, given that there was once a time when many behavior therapists themselves questioned whether personality disorders even existed, the conclusion of the American Psychiatric Association Task Force should be viewed positively because it suggests a maturing of psychiatric opinion.

An important aspect of the Task Force's report is that it acknowledges that resources are available to modify many of the behavioral patterns associated with personality disorders. With this conclusion in mind, it is hoped that some of the information and ideas reported in this chapter will serve to stimulate interest among behavior therapists in working with these neglected yet highly prevalent disorders.

This chapter will focus on a variety of important issues that apply to the literature on personality disorders in general. Following a discussion of general issues, each DSM-III-R (American Psychiatric Association, 1987) personality disorder will be reviewed in accord with the DSM-III-R cluster scheme. For each personality disorder, a brief history of the diagnostic entity will be provided, along with a short review of pertinent diagnostic attributes. These will be followed by a discussion of behavioral strategies for treatment and presentation of a typical clinical case. (The word *typical* should be emphasized, because certain personality disordered cases presented will reveal shortcomings that clinicians face constantly.) Given space limitations, more thorough evaluation of the literature can be found elsewhere (e.g., American Psychiatric Association, 1989; Liebowitz, Stone, & Turkat, 1986; Turkat, 1990; Turner & Turkat, 1988).

GENERAL ISSUES

As noted above, there was a time when behavior therapists questioned the existence of personality disorders. This was no doubt partly attributable to the lack of data supporting behavioral consistency of the type necessitated by the concept of personality syndromes (e.g., Mischel, 1968). Also, in many respects, this was a function of a suspect diagnostic system (see Turkat & Levin, 1984). For present purposes, we will assume that the specific personality disorders as presented in DSM-III-R do in fact exist clinically.

Determining the prevalence of the personality disorders is extremely difficult because of the lack of epidemiological data. However, there are estimates that anywhere from 20 to 80 percent of psychiatric patients seen in clinics present with a personality disorder. The DSM-III (American Psychiatric Association, 1980) field trials indicated that approximately 50 to 60 percent of patients studied had at least one personality disorder diagnosis. However, any conclusion based on these data, as well as others, must be tempered by the notoriously low reliability for personality diagnoses. Yet, clinicians and researchers alike agree that the personality disorders are highly prevalent.

Although the personality disorders represent the largest class of psychiatric disorders, the literature on these syndromes is relatively young, for several reasons. First, the DSM-III personality disorders contain several diagnostic entities that did not exist prior to 1980. Further, of the disorders that have been retained since then, the criteria have changed substantially. An additional problem, as noted above, is that the reliability of personality disorder diagnosis has traditionally been a significant problem. Unfortunately, although the bases of diagnosis appeared to improve somewhat with the publication of the DSM-III, the appearance of DSM-III-R rekindled the issue because its diagnostic overlap is quite problematic (Blashfield & Breen, 1989). Finally, although 50 to 60 percent of psychiatric patients may receive a personality disorder diagnosis, two major problems remain, from a research perspective. First, numerous Axis I disorders (e.g., bulimia, depression, etc.) may be present as well. Second, there are 11 specific types of personality disorders. In any particular setting, it may prove difficult at times to generate a sufficient number of any one type of personality disorder for large-scale group research. An excellent example is the paranoid personality. Such cases have been demonstrated empirically to resist participating in research (Turkat & Banks, 1987), and clinicians resist referring such cases for scientific investigation (Thompson-Pope & Turkat, 1989).

Despite the impediments, the number of research studies on the personality disorders is growing at an impressive rate. Unfortunately, there is still very little of this work in the behavior therapy literature. Rather, the bulk of studies on the personality disorders may be found in mainstream psychiatry journals. A handful of behavior therapists are actively working in the area, and the efforts of some of these individuals will be reported here. Also, the National Institute of Health has established a program for the personality disorders, in conjunction with the Affective and Anxiety Disorders Program.

DSM-III-R organizes the personality disorders into three clusters. Cluster A includes the paranoid personality disorder, schizoid personality disorder, and schizotypal personality disorder. This cluster is often referred to as the "odd cluster" because individuals with these disorders presumably present eccentricity, weirdness, etc. Cluster B consists of the "dramatic" personality disorders: the antisocial personality disorder, borderline personality disorder, narcissistic personality disorder, and histrionic personality disorder. Cluster C personality disorders include the avoidant personality disorder, dependent personality disorder, obsessive-compulsive personality disorder, and passive-aggressive personality disorder. These pathologies are grouped as such because of anxious and fearful attributes.

CLUSTER A PERSONALITY DISORDERS

Paranoid Personality Disorder

The paranoid personality disorder has appeared in every edition of the *Diagnostic and Statistical Manual of Mental Disorders* (American Psychiatric Association, 1952, 1968, 1980, 1987). At the same time, it is the least researched personality disorder (Thompson-Pope & Turkat, 1989; Turkat, 1985; Turkat & Banks, 1987). There are several reasons for this state of affairs. First, paranoid personality disorders are rarely institutionalized and hence are not readily available to participate in research. Second, even if such cases were available to participate in research, studies have shown that these patients are reluctant to do so and clinicians treating such patients are reluctant to refer them. Finally, given the guarded and suspicious nature of these individuals, there may be a subset who present in ways that lead clinicians to misdiagnose them.

Despite the lack of research, there is no shortage of opinion on the treatment outcome with paranoid personality disorder. This is best exemplified by the American Psychiatric Association's Task Force Report on treatment of psychiatric disorders, which concluded that "behavioral therapies have no demonstrative role in the treatment of paranoid personality" (American Psychiatric Association, 1989, p. 2710). Interestingly, Turkat has argued that certain paranoid personality disorders can in fact be treated successfully with behavior therapy (Turkat, 1985; 1990; Turkat & Maisto, 1985).

It should be noted that, although the American Psychiatric Association's Task Force Report downplays any role for behavior therapy, it does state that "it is important to emphasize that patients with paranoid personalities are treatable" (American Psychiatric Association, 1989, p. 2711).

From clinical experience, Turkat has proposed two critical target areas for behavioral intervention with paranoid personality disorders: decreasing sensitivity to criticism and improving the patient's social skills repertoire. In regard to the former, various behavioral anxiety management strategies (e.g., biofeedback, relaxation, in vivo exposure) matched to the individual case (Meyer & Reich, 1978) have been employed. In regard to modifying social behavior, four key areas have been identified: social attention, information processing, response emission, and feedback. These areas are addressed through a variety of behavioral social skills training modalities such as modeling, instruction, rehearsal, and role playing. Many of these individuals must first be taught how to decrease their sensitivity to criticism before they can take advantage of the constructive criticism that is provided in social skills training.

Case Illustration

A 37-year-old divorced caucasian female presented with multiple complaints, including difficulties relating with others, absence of close friends, intense anger, jealous feelings, and varied depressive symptomatology. Of immediate concern to the patient was a current conflict with a superior at work. She noted that through her history she had always had "an enemy at the office." The patient was abused in her history and generally had significant difficulty trusting others. She was highly suspicious, easily provoked toward anger, and constantly on guard for attack. At one time in her life, she had thought that she was "a witch." The patient was treated over a 15-month period with a variety of methods, including anxiety management to fear of criticism, anger control training, and social skills training. When therapy was terminated, she was asymptomatic, had developed several satisfactory relationships, and had recently transferred to a new position in another state. Several months following her transfer, the patient called long-distance for advice on handling some adjustment difficulties. Following a few telephone conversations, no further contact was necessary.

Although it cannot be concluded that this strategy would work in every case of paranoid personality disorder, the case does illustrate that these patients are treatable. Moreover, it shows the viability of behavioral treatments.

Schizoid Personality Disorder

Like the paranoid personality disorder, the schizoid personality disorder first appeared in the initial *Diagnostic and Statistical Manual of Mental Disorders* (American Psychiatric Association, 1952). Also, as with its counterpart, there is no research available to suggest that we know how to treat the schizoid personality. However, unlike the paranoid personality, behavior therapists have yet to provide any useful case reports on successful treatment of this disorder.

The schizoid personality disorder is characterized by a basic indifference to social relationships. Such individuals have a restrictive range of emotional experience and expression, are loners, and appear relatively content that way. Clinically, such cases rarely seek treatment out of their own initiative (Turkat, 1990). The more typical circumstance is for such an individual to have gone through a change that causes a problem for someone else. Turkat (1990) discussed the case of a schizoid personality who was content to spend most of her time home alone, reading. Unfortunately, she developed a visual disorder, which precluded her ability to read. Her home was subsequently hit by a tornado, and these events seemed to contribute to a depression that prevented the patient from keeping up with household chores. This state of affairs was intolerable to the patient's husband and she eventually was hospitalized.

The American Psychiatric Association Task Force Report on treatment of psychiatric disorders (American Psychiatric Association, 1989) suggested that behavior therapy may prove useful with a subset of schizoid personalities in regard to "modification of maladaptive behavior patterns" (p. 2716). Unfortunately, in order to make such a statement, one has to assume that individuals who are generally uninterested in developing emotional and social attachments now have a motivation to change their behavior. As noted elsewhere (Liebowitz et al., 1986), until a method is found that enables the clinician to help motivate the schizoid personality to desire behavior change, it is unlikely that behavior therapy (or for that matter, *any* therapy) will be of much value. Yet, there are a number of strategies in the behavioral literature that have demonstrated effectiveness in increasing motivation (e.g., token economies), and one would hope that they are applicable to the schizoid personality.

Case Illustration

The patient was a 75-year-old caucasian female who had never married, and who had been a dietician in the armed forces for 25 years. The patient had no previous psychiatric history. She described herself as a loner who preferred it "to be that way." She was pressured by her sister to see the author of this chapter. According to the patient, prior to 1½ years before, all had been well in her life. However, at that time, a routine physical examination revealed a rapid heart rate. She went to a cardiologist on the advice of her sister. She was hospitalized for a "thorough evaluation" and discharged on six medications. During the next 1½ years, she experienced several episodes of hospitalization for medication side effects. Eventually, she transferred to a new physician. Reportedly, this physician was horrified, removed all the other medications, and placed her on one (lanoxin). At the present time, while feeling physically better, she was bitter for "losing a whole year out of my life." She was sleeping more than usual, complaining of boredom, and was easily irritated. As noted above, she historically preferred to be alone and thus there was no evidence of social withdrawal. It appeared to the author that the patient had functioned without psychiatric difficulty during her previous 70-plus years of life despite having significant schizoid traits. It was hypothesized that the present symptomatology was related to an adjustment reaction and that, more than likely, these symptoms would abate over time without intervention. The patient was offered this viewpoint as well as an option for behaviorally oriented symptomatic relief. She chose the former and a 3-month follow-up indicated the patient was symptom-free.

Schizotypal Personality Disorder

The schizotypal personality disorder was first introduced into the diagnostic code with DSM-III (American Psychiatric Association, 1980). However, the concept has been around for a long time. (An excellent discussion of theoretical issues was recently presented in the *Journal of Personality Disorders,* which focused on the contributions of Paul Meehl (Chapman, 1990; Holtzman, 1990; Meehl, 1990; Siever, 1990; Widiger, 1990).)

Diagnostically, the schizotypal personality disorder is characterized by deficits in interpersonal relations, marked most notably by peculiarities in thought, self-presentation, and behavior. Such cases may have extreme social anxiety, odd thoughts and perceptions, no close friends, and inappropriate speech and affect. Paranoid ideation and/or suspiciousness often accompanies the presenting picture.

Behavioral case reports on schizotypal personality disorder are hard to come by. The American Psychiatric Association Task Force Report on the treatment of psychiatric disorders speculated that "the re-educative approach necessary to work with schizotypal patients may at times have to be reinforced after the manner of behavior modification therapy" (American Psychiatric Association, 1989, p. 2724).

In the treatment of a female schizotype reported by Turkat (1990), the primary difficulty, which seemed to be generating other symptoms, was the patient's lack of confidence in her own judgment skills. Objective testing indicated that there was nothing wrong with the patient's judgment skills. However, because of her lack of confidence in evaluating her own ideas, she would entertain numerous ideas from others, many of which were strange. This patient was taught first how to differentiate between a description and an inference. She was then instructed how to become a good "behavioral observer." She had frequent homework assignments that focused on analyzing things descriptively and not inferentially; she also read scientific papers on operational description. After the patient had progressed along these lines, she was taught methods for evaluating the validity of a concept. First, the patient would attempt an operational definition of the concept and follow it with a description of several attributes that consensually would be felt to be strong indicators of that concept. She would then compare these indicators of the concept to the present circumstance, to assess the validity of a judgment. Turkat (1990) reported that once the patient had acquired this skill, much of her schizotypal presentation was reduced markedly.

Case Illustration

A 29-year-old married caucasian female nurse presented with pervasive ideas of reference, interpersonal particularities, and social isolation. She previously had been seen by a psychiatrist who attempted to provide medication, which she refused. She also had been seen previously by a mental health counselor, with no positive results. The patient's ideas of reference had become so intense of late that she would avoid watching television (because individuals on the shows would be making "gestures" that indicated to the patient that they were mocking her and that they knew her intimately) and avoid talking around others ("because others know what I am going to say and they may distort it"), as well as generally engaging in a variety of "self-protective behaviors." Despite these particularities, the patient was functioning adequately as a mother (she was currently not engaged in the practice of nursing). Her husband (a dentist) and she and their son resided in a rural area, which limited interaction with others. The patient was not interested in any form of medication or hospitalization. She was not suicidal or hallucinating, and, despite attaching "special meanings" to things, she was functioning adequately. The patient was seen in nine outpatient sessions. Attempts were made to teach the patient how to evaluate and dispute her disturbing thoughts, and each week she reported improvement in controlling her ideas of reference and related behaviors. After the eighth session, she abruptly terminated treatment. Two months later, the patient appeared for another treatment session and stated that she now had her husband "watching out for other people's gestures." Despite the relapse, she did not return for further treatment. Four months later, the patient sent this author a Christmas card.

CLUSTER B PERSONALITY DISORDER

Antisocial Personality Disorder

The most frequently researched personality disorder is the antisocial personality disorder. Volumes of scientific data have been generated on this personality pathology, and most are pessimistic about its modification. In fact, the American Psychiatric Association Task Force Report on treatment of psychiatric disorders noted that "the treatment of antisocial personality, and of related antisocial syndromes, is an unpopular topic in psychiatry" (American Psychiatric Association, 1989, p. 2742).

Diagnostically, the antisocial personality has gone through substantial revision. Earlier definitions focused on the negative, interpersonal attributes of impulsivity, self-gratification, ruthlessness, and so on. More recent formulations (American Psychiatric Association, 1980, 1987) have focused more on the "criminal personality." To be diagnosed as antisocial personality disorder, an individual must demonstrate evidence of a conduct disorder before the age of 15, by indicators such as truancy, using a weapon in fights, forcing someone into sexual activity, and/or physical cruelty to animals, people, or property. After demonstration of a conduct disorder, the individual must show irresponsible and antisocial behavior, including inability to maintain employment, violations of the law, repeated physical fighting, defaulting on debts, lying, and being reckless regarding his or her own and others' personal safety. Given these attributes, it is not surprising that many researchers and clinicians develop negative attitudes toward the antisocial personality disorder.

In light of the diagnostic issues, the American Psychiatric Association Task Force Report noted that ". . . most of the literature concerning antisocial personality or behavior does not relate to the DSM-III-R definition at all. Therefore, much of what has been written regarding treatment has an unknown relationship to the population identified by DSM-III-R" (American Psychiatric Association, 1989, p. 2743).

There is much literature on the use of behavioral interventions for modifying specific behaviors that are often associated with antisocial actions. Unfortunately, there have yet to appear manuscripts in which successful behavioral interventions have been reported with DSM-III or DSM-III-R diagnosed antisocial personality disorders. Cognitive behavioral treatment of conduct-disorder children has been reported (e.g., Kazdin, Bass, Siegel, & Thomas, 1989). Also, Sutker and her associates (Brantley & Sutker, 1984; Sutker & Allain, 1983; Sutker, Archer, & Kilpatrick, 1981; Sutker & King, 1985) have provided the most optimistic treatment-relevant manuscripts to date. First and foremost, Sutker argued that to deny patients genuine concern and professional treatment is in many respects inhumane. According to Sutker, in order to treat such cases, the therapist must advocate open-mindedness and unbiased attitudes. Then, by performing proper behavior analyses and case formulations, she argued, one should build on the patient's strengths within the context of a supportive therapeutic relationship (Sutker & King, 1985).

Turkat (1990) reviewed different subtypes of antisocial personality disorders and reported on two major, formulated, primary problem targets for intervention in select cases. The first was anger management: a hierarchy of anger-eliciting stimuli is generated and then a competing response is trained (e.g., cognitive distraction, deep relaxation, etc.), in line with individualized matching of treatment procedures as outlined by Meyer and Reich (1978) for anxiety management. The second target was impulse control training: a hierarchy is developed of stimuli that elicit urges to act impulsively. The therapist then teaches competing responses that help the patient delay acting on the impulse. Turkat (1990) noted that the most common competing response he has used in impulse control training is "systematic distraction." This may involve internal distraction strategies (e.g., doing multiplication tables) or external distraction strategies (e.g., turning a radio on at loud volume). Unfortunately, while the above recommendations for behavioral intervention may prove useful, there are no data available to suggest their adoption. Nevertheless, a number of behavioral techniques appear plausible. What is required is a concerted effort at evaluating these strategies by properly trained behavior therapists. It is clear that a great deal of creativity will be required.

Case Illustration

A 31-year-old caucasian male was seen on an inpatient unit, following voluntary admission. The patient stated that he "wanted to get in touch with his feelings," but a more detailed analysis revealed that he was in considerable legal difficulty and was hoping to prevent going to jail. The patient had a 20-year history of cocaine abuse as well as participation in the manufacturing and selling of various illegal drugs, such as "angel dust." The patient also noted that he frequently engaged in street fights and highly expensive impulsive acts, such as getting on a plane to eat lunch in the Bahamas even though the next day he would be broke. He had been arrested as many as 15 times, most recently for significant and repeated violation of parole coupled with possession of a stolen Jaguar and carrying a concealed weapon. The patient's history revealed numerous difficulties with impulse control and conflict with authority, including school suspension, frequent fighting, and selling drugs. One hypothesis was that, if the patient was to change his impulsive style, he would need to be in a highly structured inpatient program for a significant length of time. He was not interested. Accordingly, the patient shortly discharged himself from the hospital and went to face the possibility of a lengthy jail term.

Borderline Personality Disorder

The term "borderline" has been traditionally a "wastebasket" category (Turkat & Levin, 1984). The concept was first introduced as a diagnostic entity for personality pathology in DSM-III (American Psychiatric Association, 1980). Since that time, there has been a significant amount of literature on various anomalies referred to as "borderline," some of which has applied to the borderline personality disorder. In fact, there have been a handful of behaviorally oriented manuscripts on the treatment of such cases (Linehan, 1987; Turkat, 1990; Turner, 1989).

The diagnosis of borderline personality disorder is highlighted by instability of mood, interpersonal relationships, and self-image. These individuals may present with recurring suicidal threats and gestures, self-mutilating behavior, rapid shifts in mood, impulsivity, identity uncertainty, and intense interpersonal relationships.

Linehan (1987) devised a behaviorally oriented approach focusing on key borderline personality disorder characteristics, such as suicidal behaviors. Patients are seen in individual and group therapy sessions that employ behavioral rehearsal and skill acquisition strategies. Although there are no treatment outcome data to date, the approach is currently under evaluation for its efficacy.

Pharmacotherapy has proven useful with certain borderline personality disorder cases (Cowdry & Gardner, 1988). Recently, Turner (1989) reported the use of a combined cognitive-behavioral and alprazolam treatment of borderline personality disorder. The behavioral approach aimed to modify ". . . the patient's behavioral, affective and cognitive dysregulations" as opposed to the idea that the clinician should ". . . restructure the personality of the individual or . . . cure the personality disorder, per se" (Turner, 1989, p. 478). Four DSM-III-R defined borderline personality disorders were treated with medication, flooding, covert rehearsal, cognitive therapy, and medication. Although the author noted that the report suffered methodologically from validity threats that are associated with case studies, the fact that the intervention resulted in reductions in target symptoms and other psychopathology indicators suggests that future evaluation of the methods should be encouraged.

Turkat reported that many cases of borderline personality disorder seem to have a basic defect in problem-solving abilities (Turkat, 1990; Turkat & Levin, 1984; Turkat & Maisto, 1985). However, the nature of the problem-solving deficits may vary from case to case. For example, some individuals are inept at seeing "a middle ground" in anything, which thereby compromises problem-solving abilities. Other patients' problem-solving skills may be interfered with by intense emotions. Accordingly, behavioral interventions for modifying aspects of borderline personality disorder problem-solving deficiencies relate to the specific hypothesized components involved with each particular case. First, Turkat (1990) outlined four areas in which behavioral strategies have been employed for borderline personality disorder patients. He reported clinical benefit with use of basic problem-solving training in line with the format devised by Goldfried and D'Zurilla (D'Zurilla & Goldfried, 1971; Goldfried & Davidson, 1976). A flow sheet for clinical use has been devised (Turkat & Calhoun, 1980) and used with certain borderline personality disorder patients.

It has been reported that certain borderline personality disorder patients have considerable difficulty forming concepts. Accordingly, Turkat (1990) outlined a method by which such patients may be provided formal training in concept formation. Additionally, many borderline personalities tend to see things in either "all good or all bad" views; training in how to view the "middle ground" through instructions and rehearsal has been reported to be of benefit. Because some borderline personality disorder patients seem to process information slowly, Turkat (1990) reported using practice trials with increasingly complex problems and a goal of improving processing speed. Finally, Turkat (1990) reported having certain patients practice problem solving following the induction of a negative mood state artificially (e.g., having the patient view a tape of crippled children, imaginably evoking anger, etc.). It is clear that little is known about the nature of borderline personality disorders and that behavioral analytic and formulative strategies can play a unique role in elucidating relevant parameters. Furthermore, behavioral interventions appear to be particularly well suited for treating many of the deficiencies noted.

Case Illustration

A 27-year-old pregnant caucasian female first presented in my outpatient office worried whether her "brain was going dead." She had a history of multiple and frequent psychiatric hospitalizations for depression. Upon presentation to me, she was severely depressed, and psychotic features were noted (e.g., she was hearing voices of her aunt and sister screaming at her). She was hospitalized, and eventually had an abortion and electroconvulsive therapy (ECT). She was treated as an outpatient following this hospitalization, but not for any significant length of time because of repeated episodes requiring hospitalization and further ECT. She was on a variety of medications, including antidepressants and neuroleptics. When the patient was taken on by a second psychiatrist, she was removed from neuroleptic medication and received anxiety-relieving agents. At this point, psychotic features remitted and she became a candidate for outpatient treatment. The patient's difficulties were conceptualized as a severe problem-solving deficit with numerous features. Accordingly, she received behavioral treatments along this line, including basic problem-solving training, categorization management, concept formation training, processing-speed exercises, attentional training, and extensive support. She is presently still in treatment (now on a once-monthly basis), and, as of this writing, almost one year has passed without rehospitalization. This is the longest hospitalization-free period for this patient in years.

Histrionic Personality Disorder

The histrionic personality (formerly referred to as the hysterical personality) has received much attention in the psychoanalytic literature but has been ignored largely by behaviorally oriented therapists. In regard to treatment investigations, the disorder has been ignored by virtually everyone.

The DSM-III-R histrionic personality disorder is characterized by excessive emotionality and attention seeking. Diagnostic attributes include constantly seeking reassurance, approval, and praise; inappropriate seductiveness; exaggerated emotional expression; self-centeredness; and vagueness. In reviewing their behavioral approach to the treatment of histrionic personality disorder, Brantley and Callon (1985) argued that treatment procedure selection must be based on an individualized case formulation. Using one case of histrionic personality disorder as an illustration, Brantley and Callon (1985) discussed the use of social skills training and argued that implementation of standardized/packaged social skills training programs would fail with such cases. Again, however, behavioral interventions would appear to have promise for treating some of the abnormalities associated with this syndrome.

Turkat (1990; Turkat & Levin, 1984; Turkat & Maisto, 1985) used empathy training with several histrionic personality disorder patients. Clinically, the results were mixed. The goal of empathy training is to have the histrionic patient learn to focus on reading others' feelings and intentions correctly and at the same time decrease his or her own self-centeredness. Basic social skills such as active listening, paraphrasing, reflection, and so on are taught with modeling, role playing, and videotaped feedback.

Case Illustration

A 29-year-old caucasian female, who had been treated for bulimia previously by another psychologist and a psychiatrist, presented with numerous difficulties in addition to active bulimia. The patient described herself as moody and insecure; she liked to be the center of attention, needed a lot of reassurance, and had stormy "up-and-down relationships" with people "for years." It was noticed that the patient was bored easily, very defensive, and dramatic. Analysis of the clinical picture identified inept social behavior as the primary trigger for the multitude of difficulties she was experiencing. This seemed especially true as a trigger for her bulimic episodes. The patient was first treated with social skills training, with an emphasis on acquiring empathic capabilities. This involved typical behavioral social skills training procedures. Unfortunately, she was unable to comply over any reasonable period of time. Every few sessions, she would present with a new problem, demanding immediate resolution. Following the inability to successfully implement formulation-based behavior therapy, the patient did not wish to be referred elsewhere and insisted on symptomatic treatment for her various difficulties. These included direct attempts at the bulimia as well. The patient developed a pattern of regularly attending therapy sessions and then not appearing for significant lengths of time. In each instance, she returned in crisis and did not wish to be referred elsewhere. After two years of struggling (although obviously not seen regularly during this time span), the patient finally agreed that therapy with the current writer was not successful and that different avenues should be pursued.

Narcissistic Personality Disorder

The narcissistic personality disorder was first introduced into the official diagnostic code with the publication of DSM-III (American Psychiatric Association, 1980). Although an extensive literature on "narcissism" in general exists, narcissistic personality disorder as defined in DSM-III-R is difficult to find. Like the term "borderline," the label "narcissistic" has been quite abused. Descriptions of psychoanalytic approaches are plentiful and behavioral treatment approaches are notably absent. In fact, the behavioral literature on narcissistic personality disorder is best exemplified by the American Psychiatric Association Task Force Report on the treatment of psychiatric disorders (1989): behavior therapy is not even mentioned.

The DSM-III-R narcissistic personality disorder is characterized by pervasive grandiosity, lack of empathy, and a hypersensitivity to the evaluation of others. Common diagnostic indicators include interpersonal exploitation, exaggerated self-importance, preoccupation with fantasies of success and power, and an inability to identify and experience how others feel. Turkat and Maisto (1985) reported on the treatment of a narcissistic personality disorder by utilization of impulse control training. Although this patient showed marked gains during treatment, she terminated prematurely and it is unclear whether the behavioral intervention had any long-lasting impact.

Case Illustration

The patient was a 22-year-old, extremely attractive caucasian female who presented with numerous difficulties. Her presenting complaint was: "I'm not in life where I should be, I'm not pleasing my parents." She stated that she had difficulty getting close to people, and that she always seemed to have to provide an "onstage appearance"; she was not feeling "up to it anymore." The patient further described herself: "I'm a bitch 99% of the time, I don't want to be nice unless I have to get something." She agreed that she was egocentric and nonempathic. Additionally, the patient had a positive history for alcohol and cocaine abuse. She presented significant depressive symptomatology and reported throwing temper tantrums three times per week. Without any close friends, the patient indicated that she spent approximately 3 hours per day daydreaming about being the center of attention and being a "great horseman." Related to the above, the patient was easily bored, and frequently would pick up men for the "thrill of it." She described situations in which she would enter a bar, quickly scan for the most attractive man in the room, become excited, and try to pick him up. If she failed, she became quite depressed. Often, however, when she succeeded, she was disappointed in the sexual interaction. She was unable to develop relationships beyond superficial interaction. The patient's difficulties were formulated as being the product of a significant sensation-seeking dysfunction. The patient's pervasive impression management skills were viewed as secondary to the core sensation-seeking difficulty. At the time treatment began (and throughout her history), the patient had no responsibilities at all. She was living at home with her parents, following college. Treatment was therefore focused on developing control over her sensation-seeking difficulty. Fortunately, she was capable of experiencing guilt once the consequences of her behaviors were pointed out. However, she rarely if ever naturally self-induced guilt but experienced it when others (e.g., parents) created conditions for it. Accordingly, a behavioral program was devised in which the patient was taught how to self-induce guilt and then to practice doing so in a hierarchical fashion to sensation-seeking-related imaginal and in vivo stimuli. The patient was treated in 36 behavior therapy sessions. At the termination of treatment, she had developed a close relationship, was working as a paralegal, and was free of all presenting symptoms. A 4-year follow-up revealed the patient to be married, running her own paralegal business, and extremely happy both from her own report and from an independent report from her mother.

Anyone remotely familiar with this disorder and its treatment will recognize this as a significant treatment success. Whether the strategy would work with others remains to be seen, but this case certainly provides a glimmer of hope.

CLUSTER C PERSONALITY DISORDERS

Avoidant Personality Disorder

The avoidant personality disorder was introduced into the diagnostic taxonomy in the DSM-III; the DSM-III-R later characterized the disorder as a pervasive pattern of social discomfort and fear of negative evaluation (American Psychiatric Association, 1980, 1987). Individuals with this disorder are easily hurt by disapproval, avoid development of social relationships unless guaranteed acceptance, and fear being embarrassed. Turner and his associates (Turner, Beidel, Dancu, & Keys, 1986) have shown that individuals with avoidant personality disorder can reliably be differentiated from individuals with social phobia.

Given the attributes of avoidant personality, it should come as no surprise that behaviorally oriented anxiety management strategies have been used with such cases clinically (Turkat, 1990; Turkat & Maisto, 1985). In the first research study to evaluate behavioral treatment for avoidant personality disorder, Alden (1989) evaluated the effects of a 10-week group treatment program. Four groups were compared: one group received gradual exposure combined with progressive relaxation; a second group received interpersonal skills training (e.g., listening/attending skills, assertiveness); a third group received all of the previously mentioned modalities with a greater emphasis on developing intimate relationships; and a fourth group received no treatment. Participants in the treatment groups demonstrated significantly greater improvement than did the control subjects. It appeared that the gradual exposure/relaxation procedures worked just as well without including the skills training. Of interest is Alden's (1989) finding that the significant improvement still did not bring the avoidant subjects up to the normative comparison level when treatment ended. However, to expect a 10-week program to completely override a person's entire life history for a pervasive disorder like a personality pathology is unrealistic. Importantly, this study demonstrated that a short-term, behaviorally oriented, fear reduction approach to modifying avoidant personality disorder can meet with significant success, compared to no treatment.

Case Illustration

A 19-year-old caucasian female of small physical stature (4′10″) presented herself at my university office after hearing me give a guest lecture in one of her classes. The patient related that she had Hodgkin's disease, had received chemotherapy, and had decided that she would rather die than return for treatment. The patient had developed severe conditioned nausea from the chemotherapy. For example, if she heard a voice on the radio that sounded like the nurse who administered the chemotherapy, she would become nauseated. The stimuli had become so numerous that the patient reported feeling nauseated almost all of the time. Additionally, she was intensely shy and wanted to be accepted by others, yet had no close friends. An examination of her psychological functioning led to a formulated hypersensitivity to negative evaluation as the major culprit. The chemotherapy-related nausea certainly contributed to the patient's decision to not return for treatment for Hodgkin's disease, but her unsuccessful social life contributed significantly as well. It was hypothesized that the patient would not return for Hodgkin's disease treatment unless improvement in her social capabilities seemed possible. It also was reasoned that if the patient's conditioned nausea could be reduced, then she would be more likely to return to chemotherapy sessions. Accordingly, the patient was first taught deep muscular relaxation. Next, while deeply relaxed, the patient imagined nausea-related stimuli and brought on her nausea-related discomfort. She then practiced relaxing it away under these controlled conditions. A hierarchy was constructed and in vivo items were utilized. Toward the higher end of the hierarchy, the patient practiced relaxing deeply with the therapist in the chemotherapy room, on days when chemotherapy was not administered. Eventually, she returned to chemotherapy utilizing the relaxation procedures. Following restoration of chemotherapy sessions, the patient's anxiety management was directed toward social evaluation. Three years following termination of behavior therapy, the patient was in full remission from Hodgkin's disease, happily married, and a proud mother.

Dependent Personality Disorder

The dependent personality disorder first appeared in the DSM-I (American Psychiatric Association, 1952) as a subtype of the passive-aggressive personality disorder. Despite this considerable history, only a handful of case reports on the disorder can be found and research studies on treatment have yet to appear.

The DSM-III-R (American Psychiatric Association, 1987) dependent personality disorder is characterized by a pervasive pattern of dependent and submissive behavior. Clinical indicators include having difficulty making everyday decisions without excessive amounts of reassurance from others; permitting others to make important decisions; agreeing with people even when one believes the other people are wrong; difficulty initiating projects; and being easily hurt by disapproval.

Only one case report could be found on the behavioral treatment of a dependent personality disorder. Turkat & Carlson (1984) initially treated a woman who appeared to have an adjustment reaction to her daughter's recent diagnosis of diabetes mellitus. The authors were unable to account for why the mother had an excessive reaction. Symptomatic treatment was initiated and it appeared to succeed. However, at the first instance of increasing the length of time between therapy sessions, the patient returned in full relapse. The case was then reanalyzed and it was hypothesized that the patient was hypersensitive to making independent decisions and that diagnostically she fit the criteria for dependent personality disorder. Behavioral treatment consisted of an anxiety management approach to the fear of making independent decisions. Not only did this treatment lead to a diminution of systematically gathered anxiety ratings but the gains (which were correlated with clinical reports of improvement) were maintained at an 11-month follow-up. In reviewing this particular case, the American Psychiatric Association Task Force Report on treatment of psychiatric disorders (American Psychiatric Association, 1989) stated:

> [A]lthough involving only one patient, this report is striking in that treatment was based on a formulation of a common mechanism for a wide variety of the patient's dependent features. The behavioral formulation is also compatible with a psychodynamic view. Further study of the efficacy of behavioral therapy for dependent personality disorder may be fruitful. (p. 2769)

Despite the Task Force's comment on the similarity to psychodynamic formulations, it has been pointed out elsewhere (Turkat, 1982; Turkat & Meyer, 1982) that a behavioral case formulation is quite different from a psychodynamic case formulation.

Case Illustration

A 29-year-old caucasian female presented with anxiety and depressive symptomatology following her twin sister's recent move away from home to the Persian Gulf (during peacetime). The patient had no previous psychiatric history. Additionally, a few months before coming to see me, the patient's grandmother (with whom she was close) had died. Currently, she found herself constantly worrying about her boyfriend's leaving her, despite evidence to the contrary. Her functioning at work had deteriorated, as had her relationship with her boyfriend and with other friends.

The patient's current symptomatology and history supported a formulation of a fear of being emotionally alone, which was recently exacerbated by the departures of important reassurance figures in her life. She was treated with behavioral anxiety management procedures based on a hierarchy of fear of being emotionally abandoned. She was treated in 29 sessions and the problem was successfully resolved. There was no evidence of relapse over a 5-year period.

Obsessive-Compulsive Personality Disorder

Despite considerable history, there continues to be much confusion about the obsessive-compulsive personality disorder. Much of this confusion is due to the muddling of the picture by patients who have obsessive-compulsive personality disorder versus patients who do not have the personality disorder but rather have obsessive-compulsive disorder. The former is associated with personality traits of perfectionism, inflexibility, preoccupation with details, rules, unreasonable insistence that others follow his or her way of doing things, overconscientiousness, and restricted affect. Obsessive-compulsive disorder is characterized by repetitive cognitive and/or motor acts which the individual cannot control. Often the confusion stems from using the terms "obsessive-compulsive," "compulsive," and "obsessive," interchangeably. In fact, the American Psychiatric Association Task Force Report on treatment of psychiatric disorders (1989) clearly reflects this confusion: In its review of behavioral treatment for obsessive-compulsive personality disorder, the Report focuses on the behavioral treatment of obsessive-compulsive disorder (e.g., motor rituals).

The gains made in the treatment of obsessive-compulsive disorder by behaviorally oriented clinicians are quite impressive, but there has yet to appear a case report by a behavior therapist on successful treatment of obsessive-compulsive personality disorder. However, many obsessive-compulsive disorder patients have both conditions, and a recent report indicated that many social phobics do as well (Turner, Beidel, Borden, Stanley, & Jacob, in press). To date, there has been little attention to the personality features when associated with these other disorders.

Case Illustration

A 59-year-old caucasian female was referred by a gastroenterologist for vomiting episodes of unknown etiology. Analysis of the patient's presenting difficulties revealed significant overcontrolling tendencies and compulsive organizational behavior (no evidence of obsessions or rituals). The patient had been taught all her life to suppress emotions and to control everything around her. When presented with highly stressful stimuli demanding an emotional response (i.e., suicidal death of her brother), vomiting began. Diagnostically, the patient appeared to have an obsessive-compulsive personality disorder and generalized anxiety disorder. The vomiting seemed secondary to an inordinate fear of being out of control. Treatment of this case involved behavioral anxiety management strategies to the fear of being out of control. The patient's treatment over a 3-month period resulted in complete elimination of the presenting symptomatology.

Passive-Aggressive Personality Disorder

The passive-aggressive personality disorder was first described in the DSM-I (American Psychiatric Association, 1952). Although the disorder has been recognized for a considerable length of time, research investigations on treatment efficacy have yet to appear. The DSM-III-R

(American Psychiatric Association, 1987) characterizes the passive-aggressive personality disorder as a pervasive pattern of passive resistance to demands for adequate social and occupational performance. Such individuals procrastinate, become sulky or irritable when pressed to do something, deliberately work slowly, or just plain forget to do the things they were supposed to do.

Assertiveness training has been advocated as one behavioral treatment for passive-aggressive personality (Perry & Flannery, 1982). Unfortunately, the most common type of passive-aggressive personality disorder does not view himself or herself as having the problem; rather, someone else has "forced" the patient to come to therapy (Turkat, 1990). This leads to significant and usually fatal treatment resistance.

The American Psychiatric Association Task Force Report on treatment of psychiatric disorders (1989) gave other behavioral accounts of approaches to treating passive-aggressive personality disorder. Plout and Platt (cf. American Psychiatric Association, 1989) appeared to support the use of various behavioral strategies such as role playing, videotape feedback, and instructions to achieve assertive related goals as noted in the Task Force Report (American Psychiatric Association, 1989). Also, Burns and Epstein focused on the patient's thoughts regarding "seeing the worst in everything." The Task Force Report suggested that this cognitive approach seemed to be a useful "prelude" to assertiveness training.

Case Illustration

A 15-year-old caucasian female with cystic fibrosis since 7 months of age was referred following a suicidal gesture. The gesture was precipitated by a problem with her boyfriend. The mother was also very concerned about the patient's noncompliance with medication, manipulativeness, inability to comply with responsibilities at home, and general "stubbornness." In addition to the above, the patient was legally blind, had a severe learning disability, and was not expected to live past age 30. Her parents had been divorced for the past 12 years. It appeared that the patient was engaging in a wide range of passive-aggressive behaviors, and treatment was aimed at modifying her social deficiencies. Behavior therapy focused on three key areas. First, a therapeutic relationship was established in which no responsibilities were given to the patient initially and then requirements were gradually introduced. Passive-aggressive maneuvers were approached in a supportive but firm manner. Second, the patient was provided individual social skills training for direct expression capabilities. Third, she participated in a carefully designed social skills training group for adolescents, to practice appropriate behaviors. The patient was treated for more than 9 months. Significant gains in handling demands and rules were noted, along with an improvement in overall social functioning. Both parents independently confirmed a significant increase in the patient's self-esteem and confidence.

CONCLUDING COMMENTS

A variety of behavioral approaches exist generally for psychiatric disorders (Turner & Calhoun, 1981), and the same is true for the personality disorders (Turner & Turkat, 1988). Technological, formulation-based, and behavioral approaches for personality disorder management have been advocated (Liebowitz et al., 1986; Pretzer & Fleming, 1989; Turkat, 1990; Turkat & Maisto, 1985; Turner & Turkat, 1988). Scientific evidence to support behavioral intervention is lacking in most cases, but there are numerous suggestions that appear promising. In fact, some may argue that there is more evidence for the efficacy of behavior therapy than any other modality. Accordingly, I conclude with Turner and Turkat's (1988) observations that:

> In the absence of a solid research foundation, behavioral therapy offers as viable an intervention approach to these complex and poorly understood disorders as any other therapeutic system. We hope that future research will reveal some set of intervention methods to be clinically valuable with specific disorders of personality. (p. 345)

REFERENCES

Alden, L. (1989). Short-term structured treatment for avoidant personality disorder. *Journal of Consulting and Clinical Psychology, 57,* 756-764.

American Psychiatric Association. (1952). *Diagnostic and statistical manual of mental disorders.* Washington, DC: Author.

American Psychiatric Association. (1968). *Diagnostic and statistical manual of mental disorders* (2nd ed.). Washington, DC: Author.

American Psychiatric Association. (1980). *Diagnostic and statistical manual of mental disorders* (3rd ed.). Washington, DC: Author.

American Psychiatric Association. (1987). *Diagnostic and statistical manual of mental disorders* (3rd ed. rev.). (DSM-III-R) Washington, DC: Author.

American Psychiatric Association. (1989). *Treatment of psychiatric disorders: A Task Force Report of the American Psychiatric Association.* Washington, DC: Author.

Blashfield, R. K., & Breen, N. J. (1989). Face validity of the DSM-III-R personality disorders. *American Journal of Psychiatry, 146,* 1575-1579.

Brantley, P. J., & Callon, E. B. (1985). Histrionic personality: A behavioral formulation. In I. D. Turkat (Ed.), *Behavioral case formulation* (pp. 205-251). New York: Plenum.

Brantley, P. J., & Sutker, P. B. (1984). Antisocial behavior disorders. In H. E. Adams & P. B. Sutker (Eds.), *Comprehensive handbook of psychopathology* (pp. 439-478). New York: Plenum.

Chapman, L. J. (1990). Meehl's theory of schizotaxi, schizotypi and schizophrenia. *Journal of Personality Disorders, 4,* 111-115.

Cowdry, R. W., & Gardner, D. L. (1988). Pharmacotherapy of borderline personality disorder. *Archives of General Psychiatry, 45,* 111-119.

D'Zurilla, T., & Goldfried, N. (1971). Problem solving and behavior modification. *Journal of Abnormal Psychology, 78,* 107-126.

Goldfried, N. R., & Davidson, G. C. (1976). *Clinical behavior therapy.* New York: Holt, Rinehart & Winston.

Holtzman, P. S. (1990). Comments on Paul Meehl's: Toward an integrated theory of schizotaxi, schizotypi, and schizophrenia. *Journal of Personality Disorders, 4,* 100-105.

Kazdin, A. E., Bass, D., Siegel, T., & Thomas, C. (1989). Cognitive-behavioral therapy and relationship therapy in the treatment of children referred for antisocial behavior. *Journal of Consulting and Clinical Psychology, 57,* 522-535.

Liebowitz, M. R., Stone, M. H., & Turkat, I. D. (1986). Treatment of personality disorders. In A. J. Frances & R. E. Hales (Eds.), *American Psychiatric Association annual review* (pp. 356-393). Washington, DC: American Psychiatric Press.

Linehan, M. (1987). Dialectical behavior therapy for borderline personality disorder: Theory and method. *Bulletin of the Menninger Clinic, 51,* 261-276.

Meehl, P. E. (1990). Toward an integrated theory of schizotaxi, schizotypi, and schizophrenia. *Journal of Personality Disorders, 4,* 1-99.

Meyer, V., & Reich, B. (1978). Anxiety management: The marriage of physiological and cognitive variables. *Behavior Research and Therapy, 16,* 177-182.

Mischel, W. (1968). *Personality and assessment.* New York: Wiley.

Perry, J. C., & Flannery, R. B. (1982). Passive-aggressive personality disorder: Treatment implications of a clinical typology. *Journal of Nervous and Mental Disease, 170,* 164-173.

Pretzer, J., & Fleming, B. (1989). Cognitive-behavioral treatment of personality disorders. *The Behavior Therapist, 12,* 105-109.

Siever, L. J. (1990). Commentary on: Toward an integrated theory of schizotaxi, schizotypi and schizophrenia. *Journal of Personality Disorders, 4,* 116-119.

Sutker, P. B., & Allain, A. N. (1983). Behavior and personality assessment in men labeled adaptive sociopaths. *Journal of Behavioral Assessment, 5,* 65-79.

Sutker, P. B., Archer, R. P., & Kilpatrick, D. G. (1981). Sociopathy and antisocial behavior: Theory and treatment. In S. M. Turner, K. S. Calhoun, & H. E. Adams (Eds.), *Handbook of clinical behavior therapy* (pp. 665-712). New York: Wiley.

Sutker, P. B., & King, A. R. (1985). Antisocial personality disorder. In I. D. Turkat (Ed.), *Behavioral case formulation* (pp. 115-153). New York: Plenum.

Thompson-Pope, S. K., & Turkat, I. D. (1989). Paranoia about paranoid personality research. *Journal of Clinical Psychology, 50,* 310.

Turkat, I. D. (1982). Behavior-analytic consideration of alternative clinical approaches. In P. Wachtel (Ed.), *Resistance: Psychodynamic and behavioral approaches* (pp. 251-257). New York: Plenum.

Turkat, I. D. (1985). Formulation of paranoid personality disorder. In I. D. Turkat (Ed.), *Behavioral case formulation* (pp. 161-198). New York: Plenum.

Turkat, I. D. (1990). *The personality disorders: A psychological approach to clinical management.* New York: Pergamon.

Turkat, I. D., & Banks, D. S. (1987). Paranoid personality and its disorder. *Journal of Psychopathology and Behavioral Assessment, 9,* 295-304.

Turkat, I. D., & Calhoun, J. F. (1980). The problem-solving flow chart. *The Behavior Therapist, 3,* 21.

Turkat, I. D., & Carlson, C. R. (1984). Symptomatic versus data based formulation of treatment: The case of dependent personality. *Journal of Behavioral Therapy and Experimental Psychology, 15,* 153-160.

Turkat, I. D., & Levin, R. A. (1984). Formulation of personality disorders. In H. E. Adams & P. B. Sutker (Eds.), *Comprehensive handbook of psychopathology* (pp. 495-522). New York: Plenum.

Turkat, I. D., & Maisto, S. A. (1985). Application of the experimental method to the formulation and modification of personality disorders: In D. H. Barlow (Ed.), *Clinical handbook of psychological disorders* (pp. 503-570). New York: Guilford.

Turkat, I. D., & Meyer, V. (1982). The behavior-analytic approach. In P. Wachtel (Ed.), *Resistance: psychodynamic and behavioral approaches* (pp. 157-184). New York: Plenum.

Turner, R. M. (1989). Case study evaluations of a bio-cognitive behavioral approach for the treatment of borderline personality disorder. *Behavior Therapy, 19,* 477-489.

Turner, S. M., Beidel, D. C., Borden, J., Stanley, M. A., & Jacob, R. G. (in press). Social phobia: Axis I and II correlates. *Journal of Abnormal Psychology.*

Turner, S. M., & Calhoun, K. S. (1981). Historical perspectives and current issues in behavior therapy. In S. M. Turner, K. S. Calhoun & H. E. Adams (Eds.), *Handbook of clinical behavior therapy* (pp. 1-11). New York: Wiley.

Turner, S. M., & Turkat, I. D. (1988). Behavior therapy and the personality disorders. *Journal of Personality Disorders, 2,* 342-349.

Widiger, T. A. (1990). A commentary on: Toward an integrated theory of schizotaxi, schizotypi, and schizophrenia. *Journal of Personality Disorders, 4,* 106-110.

CHAPTER 8

Behavioral Interventions in Schizophrenia

ALAN S. BELLACK, RANDALL L. MORRISON, and KIM T. MUESER

Schizophrenia is one of the most severe and debilitating mental illnesses, resulting in a tremendous emotional and interpersonal impact on patients and their families. It is accompanied by extreme financial costs, including those involved in both inpatient and outpatient care, as well as lost productivity and earned income. Despite considerable research aimed at understanding its etiology and improving treatment, schizophrenia remains enigmatic, and although there have been improvements in treatment, more needs to be done. There is not, nor does it currently appear likely that there will ever be, a single curative treatment for the disorder. Rather, combined pharmacologic and psychosocial intervention remains the treatment of choice. In this chapter, we will first provide an overview of those symptoms and characteristics of the disorder which impinge most markedly on patients' ability to respond to psychosocial interventions. We will then review those behavioral treatment strategies which have been shown in controlled trials to provide benefit for the schizophrenic patient.

THE NATURE OF SCHIZOPHRENIA

To design and implement effective behavioral interventions for schizophrenia, it is essential to understand the social and environmental factors impinging on the schizophrenic patient as well as the symptoms and possible etiology. Schizophrenia is a pernicious, debilitating disorder that has profound consequences for the patient, the family, and the social environment in which the patient lives. It is characteristically a multiply handicapping, life-long disorder. Only a small proportion of patients have a substantial recovery with a return to premorbid levels of functioning (Strauss & Carpenter, 1981). The majority have residual handicaps even when the primary symptoms are well-controlled. As many as one-third of schizophrenics appear to have a minimal recovery; they have continual residual symptoms and remain substantially dysfunctional throughout their adult life. Even patients who have a "good" outcome can be expected to have notable handicaps and periodic exacerbations. Relapse

---

Preparation of this chapter was supported by NIMH grants MH38636 and MH39998.

is a natural part of the illness for most patients, rather than a sign of treatment failure.

Beginning in the 1950s, the locus of treatment for schizophrenia shifted from long-term stays in state hospitals to short-term stays in community hospitals, interspersed with outpatient programs such as day hospitals at community mental health centers (Goldman, Adams, & Taube, 1983). As a by-product of this shift, there has been a tremendous increase in hospital readmissions. Roughly 70% of current psychiatric admissions involve patients with a previous history of hospitalization (Sharfstein, 1984). Patients entering a psychiatric hospital in the 1950s could expect a multiyear stay; current patients can expect to have multiple admissions of several days to several weeks. Schizophrenics in the United States may accumulate as many as 500,000 hospital admissions per year (Goldman, 1984). This figure would be even higher if current commitment laws were more lenient.

Unfortunately, the current system of acute hospitalization and community treatment has not enabled most schizophrenics to achieve an adequate level of functioning. The vast majority are chronically unemployed, with little hope of finding work. They remain dependent on the social service system for money, food, and shelter. Only a small proportion of ex-patients are capable of living independently, and most require some form of supervised living arrangements (Goldstrom & Manderscheid, 1981). Of those who do live on their own, a great many live in run-down apartments or rooming houses in decaying areas of cities. A large number have no residence whatsoever, and as many as one-half of the 2 million homeless people in the United States are chronically mentally ill (Cordes, 1984).

Most chronic patients have a poor quality of life, aside from housing (Goldstrom & Manderscheid, 1981). They are easy prey for street criminals and are disproportionately victims of crime. A majority of patients cannot perform basic tasks of daily living. Fewer than 60% are able to independently perform household chores, prepare meals, or maintain an adequate diet, and fewer than 50% can manage their own money or take medication as prescribed. Chronic patients frequently suffer from poor physical health and have shortened life expectancies. They also fail to take advantage of social and recreational opportunities available in the community, because they lack the money, skills, or motivation to participate in such activities. Many are socially isolated and spend endless hours sleeping, walking the streets, or sitting in community mental health center dayrooms.

Medication plays an essential role in the overall treatment of schizophrenia, but it is far from a panacea. As many as 50% of schizophrenics may not receive appreciable benefit from neuroleptics, either because they do not have a notable clinical response or because they do not take medication as prescribed (Gardos & Cole, 1976). Of those who do respond, 25 to 30% can be expected to relapse within 1 year, and as many as 50% within 2 years (Hogarty et al., 1979). Neuroleptics have their most demonstrable effect on positive symptoms, such as thought disorder, hallucinations, and delusions. However, they often do not appreciably reduce negative symptoms, such as apathy, anergia, and social withdrawal (Carpenter, Heinrichs, & Alphs, 1985). Similarly, they do not enhance skills of daily living or markedly improve quality of life (Diamond, 1985).

The mental health system has traditionally been geared to the treatment of acute disorders that are quickly and permanently resolved. The "up and out" philosophy of treatment, characteristic of most mental health programs, is not only ineffective for schizophrenics but may actually increase stress and precipitate relapse (Schooler & Spohn, 1982).

Schizophrenia is a chronic disorder and must be viewed from the same perspective as renal disease, juvenile diabetes, Down syndrome, and other chronic physical/neurological illnesses. These disorders require long-term, multidimensional treatment. The goals of intervention for these conditions are: managing symptoms, teaching living and coping skills, and enhancing quality of life—not "curing" the illness. A similar approach is required for the treatment of schizophrenia.

The chronic illness model provides a valuable perspective on the needs of the schizophrenic patient. It is not appropriate to think of "treatment" in the traditional sense of the patient coming to the clinic for brief visits to receive a single intervention for a limited period of time. Treatment per se is only one element of a multicomponent system of services, each of which has an essential role in the overall care of the patient (Bellack, 1989; Test, 1984). Behavior therapy, or any other treatment, cannot be effective if the patient does not have a place to live, adequate nutrition and health care, and a means for economic support.

Behavioral strategies can be critical in the management of symptoms and reduction of relapse (see below). They also can make significant contributions to the implementation of pharmacotherapy (Bellack, 1986; Wallace, Boone, Donahoe, & Foy, 1985), as well as to rehabilitation and improvements in quality of life (Anthony & Nemec, 1984). Behavior therapy may not produce the demonstrable changes associated with treatment of anxiety disorders or depression, but it is no less valuable for the treatment of schizophrenia. In fact, given the magnitude of the need and the dearth of other effective treatments, it is essential for behavior therapists to focus their expertise on this population.

The etiology and pathogenesis of schizophrenia are not known. The most widely accepted working hypothesis is the stress-vulnerability model (Zubin & Spring, 1977). Schizophrenic symptoms are thought to emerge as a result of the combined influence of psychobiological vulnerability and environmental stress. "Vulnerability" is a sensitivity or predisposition to decompensate under stress and experience a range of psychotic symptoms. It is hypothesized to result largely from genetic and developmental factors, and varies in degree across affected individuals.

Stressors are environmental events that impact negatively on an individual, including life events (Rabkin, 1980), negative ambient family emotion (Koenigsberg & Handley, 1986), or an unstructured, impoverished environment (Wing & Brown, 1970; Wong et al., 1987). Intraorganismic factors, such as physical illness and the effects of psychostimulants or hallucinogens, can also serve as significant stressors (Mueser et al., 1990). The impact of stress is modulated by a person's coping skills, including social skills, problem-solving skills, skills needed for daily living (such as using public transportation and managing money), and basic self-care skills (such as personal hygiene and grooming). Coping skills can help to circumvent potential stressors entirely, as well as to decrease the severity and duration of their impact.

TREATMENT STRATEGIES

The stress-vulnerability model has important implications for developing treatment interventions to improve the outcome of the illness. To be effective, treatments for schizophrenia must modify at least one of the three constructs presumed to influence outcome: (a) biological vulnerability; (b) environmental stress; or (c) coping skills that mediate the noxious effects of stress. Behavior modification can play a key role in each of these domains. Vulnerability is assumed to be a result of genetic and biological factors, although it can be lowered by antipsychotic medications and increased by alcohol or drug abuse. Behavioral interventions may influence vulnerability by increasing compliance with medication regimens; for example, patients can be instructed regarding the effects of medication and trained in the social skills needed for discussion of medication issues with their physician (Boczkowski, Zeichner, & DeSanto, 1985). Conceptually, the deleterious effects of substance abuse can be minimized by application of any number of behavioral techniques developed for the treatment of addictive disorders, but there are no data to support this hypothesis.

Environmental stress can be decreased by a variety of different behavioral interventions. One significant form of stress is hostile, critical, or intrusive family interactions (Hooley, 1985). As will be discussed below, behavioral family therapy has proven to be effective in teaching family members strategies for communicating in a less stressful manner and solving everyday problems associated with the multiple handicaps of schizophrenia. Similarly, stress in nonfamily environments, such as day treatment programs, board-and-care homes, and foster homes, can be minimized by providing rehabilitation programming that remediates deficits and teaches skills for independent living. Stress can result from environmental overstimulation, but chronic understimulation, a lack of structure, and an absence of social contacts can also produce stress and can lead to an increase in symptoms (Rosen, Sussman, Mueser, Lyons, & Davis, 1981; Wong et al., 1987). Interventions can minimize understimulation by adequately structuring social rehabilitation programs and by teaching skills, such as leisure and recreation skills, to enable patients to meaningfully structure their own time.

The third strategy commonly used to improve the outcome of schizophrenia is to enhance coping skills. Two approaches have been applied to bolster patients' ability to cope with stress:

1. Teaching social skills, to enable patients to obtain instrumental and social needs and to reduce interpersonal conflict;
2. Applying behavioral self-management techniques, to reduce psychotic symptoms.

Chronic symptoms, such as persistent auditory hallucinations and delusions of control, are often extremely stressful, and behavioral self-management methods can sometimes be helpful in reducing the frequency or intensity of these symptoms.

A vast array of behavioral interventions has been utilized to improve the outcome of schizophrenia, but relatively few interventions have been systematically studied and replicated. The impact of many methods on widely accepted domains of the illness (e.g., relapse rate, social adjustment) remains to be demonstrated. For example, the Paul and Lentz (1977) study on the effects of the token economy on chronic patients is one of the most important and widely cited studies ever conducted on behavior therapy. This study generated dramatic findings in support of the efficacy of a token economy program for a severely impaired inpatient population, including improvements in adaptive behavior, decreased need for medication, increased rates of discharge into the community, and community survival. Although this method continues to be the treatment of choice for many severely ill schizophrenics, these results have never been replicated in another setting. A broad range of different cognitive-behavioral strategies has been applied successfully in the treatment of psychotic symptoms, including systematic desensitization (Slade, 1972), aversive conditioning (Turner, Hersen, & Bellack, 1977), covert sensitization (Moser, 1974), contingency management (Liberman, Wallace, Teigen, & Davis, 1974), overcorrection (Sumner,

Mueser, Hsu, & Morales, 1974), thought stopping (Fisher & Winkler, 1975), self-monitoring (Adams, Malatesta, Brantley, & Turkat, 1981), self-instructional training (Bentall, Higson, & Lowe, 1987), and cognitive restructuring of irrational beliefs (Perris, 1989). These reports have almost all been on individual cases; some have used controlled single-case designs with others being uncontrolled. These successes notwithstanding, no research has documented the efficacy or feasibility of these behavioral methods for the broader population for schizophrenic patients. Moreover, schizophrenics generally have significant impairments in attention and information processing, even under low stress (Neuchterlein & Dawson, 1984). It seems unlikely that they would be able to implement strategies that place a premium on self-control, planning, and adaptive problem solving (Bellack, Morrison, & Mueser, 1989). At present, only two approaches to behavior therapy of schizophrenia have been supported by research that is both controlled and replicated: social skills training and behavioral family therapy. These findings represent significant advances: neither of these interventions had been supported by even a single controlled study as recently as 10 years ago. Thus, we will focus here on describing recent developments in these treatments for schizophrenia.

BEHAVIORAL FAMILY THERAPY

One major consequence of the shift in treatment from state psychiatric hospitals to the community has been a dramatic increase in the number of schizophrenic patients living in the homes of relatives. Estimates of the percentage of noninstitutionalized psychiatric patients living with relatives are high, ranging from 58 to 73 percent (Goldman, 1982; Minkoff, 1978). As families have assumed an increased responsibility for caring for a schizophrenic relative, they have also experienced economic and psychological hardships in coping with the stressful behavior of a chronically ill and sometimes disruptive patient at home (Dearth, Labenski, Mott, & Pellegrini, 1986; Hoenig & Hamilton, 1966). Negative symptoms, such as social isolation and lack of motivation, are particularly troublesome to family members, who are more prone to criticize patients for these behaviors than for positive symptoms such as delusions and hallucinations (Leff & Vaughn, 1985). The burden of the illness on the family acts as a potent stressor on relatives and can lead to excessive criticism or emotional overinvolvement directed toward the patient. These communications, referred to as "expressed emotion" (EE), have been found to substantially increase patients' risk for symptomatic relapses (Koenigsberg & Handley, 1986). In fact, following discharge from a hospital, patients returning to homes characterized by high EE are 2 to 3 times more likely to have a relapse than patients returning to low-EE homes or to community residences (Hooley, 1985).

Behavioral family therapy has emerged over the past 10 years as an important treatment approach for modifying negative affect directed toward the patient by the family, and for reducing the burden of the illness on the family. Two different behavioral interventions with families have been developed and have received empirical support, one by Falloon and his colleagues (Falloon et al., 1988; Falloon, Boyd, & McGill, 1984; Mueser, 1989), and one by Barrowclough and Tarrier (1987) and Tarrier et al. (1989). Both approaches provide education to family members about the nature of schizophrenia, strive to minimize stress on all family members, and aim to enhance patient functioning. The two methods differ in the strategies they employ to change the behavior of family members. Falloon's approach focuses on changing behavior primarily through teaching specific interpersonal skills using social skills training methods. Barrowclough and Tarrier's method provides stress management training and goal setting to improve patients' social and vocational functioning, and does not target specific interpersonal skills for modification. No studies have yet documented that one or more of these various treatment components are more critical than others.

Intervention Procedures

The family therapy approach described here combines didactic education with skills training in a semistructured format. The treatment can be divided into five sequential stages, although material from each stage is repeated as needed throughout the course of treatment: family assessment, education about schizophrenia, communication skills training, problem-solving training, and special problems.

Treatment is conducted in the home when possible, to enhance the generalization of newly acquired skills into the family's natural environment and to give the clinician a picture of the environment that serves as a backdrop for problem-solving efforts. Meeting with the family in their own home also conveys the therapist's concern and involvement, stemming possible family resistance to therapy and increasing compliance.

Family Assessment

Behavioral assessment of the family is an ongoing process that both precedes and is interwoven throughout treatment. The goal of assessment is to identify (a) the assets and deficits of individual members of the family as a whole, and (b) the role that specific problem behaviors play in the functioning of the family. Information for assessment is obtained through conducting individual interviews, observing family members' interaction while participating in family sessions, and noting the performance of family members on specific problem-solving tasks.

During interviews conducted with each member of the family, the understanding of schizophrenia and perceptions of its burden are assessed, and short-term goals are formulated for all participating family members. These goals are reviewed and revised routinely during therapy. Problem-solving assessments in which family members attempt to solve a problem together in the absence of the therapist are conducted before therapy and throughout treatment, to track the acquisition of problem-solving skills taught in the sessions. The use of communication skills, whether prompted in role play or spontaneous, by each member during treatment sessions is recorded by the therapist to monitor the learning of these skills, which are critical to successful family problem-solving.

Education about Schizophrenia

It is assumed that most family members lack accurate information about schizophrenia. False beliefs and misperceptions likely increase feelings of guilt and fear and result in unwarranted hostility toward the patient. Thus, all family members, including the patient, are given a short course on the illness. During the educational sessions, the ill relative is encouraged to take the role of the "expert" and to describe to the family his or her experience with the symptoms. The impact of the illness on the patient and the relatives is elicited, and problems of management are discussed.

Common misconceptions about the causes of schizophrenia are refuted, such as: people with the illness have a "split personality." Families learn about how schizophrenia is diagnosed, its characteristic signs and symptoms, its prevalence and course, genetic and biological theories, and the role of stress in triggering symptom exacerbations in vulnerable persons. Patients and family members are taught to recognize possible prodromal signs of relapse. The effects of neuroleptic medications in reducing acute symptoms and prevention of relapses are emphasized, as are characteristic side effects and the use of side-effect medications. The availability and appropriate utilization of community resources, such as psychiatric hospitals, day treatment centers, vocational programs, and social agencies, are addressed, depending on the individual family's needs. This material is covered in the first three or four sessions, using didactic presentation, discussion, posters, and handouts.

Communication Skills Training

Communication in many families with a schizophrenic relative is marked by high levels of criticism, hostility, mind reading, and intrusiveness. Each of these behaviors can be highly stressful for patients and nonill relatives alike. Communication skills training is designed to decrease stress in the family by teaching attentive listening skills, effective ways for expressing positive and negative feelings, and how to request for changes in behavior in a nonhostile manner. Training in these behaviors emphasizes direct, brief, verbal communications that identify a specific behavior of the other person (either commenting on a behavior or requesting one) and that express the speaker's feeling about that behavior. The initial phase focuses on empathic listening and the expression of positive feelings. The goal of this phase of treatment is to create a warm milieu in which family members are able to recognize and reward specific positive behaviors in one another.

Training in communication skills is conducted using the same procedures employed in social skills training: providing a rationale for the importance of the skill, modeling, role playing, coaching, social reinforcement and corrective feedback, repeated role playing, and homework assignments. Communication deficits are assessed in an ongoing fashion throughout the therapy. Well-ingrained patterns require repeated prompting from the therapist and ongoing rehearsal of new behaviors.

Problem-Solving Training

The main tenet of behavioral family therapy is that improvements in family problem-solving skills will lessen the ambient stress in the family by improving the ability of all the members to attain personal goals and buffer the noxious effects of exogenous stressors. Training in problem solving consists of teaching a set of sequential steps for resolving problems that minimizes negative emotional undercurrents while maximizing the identification, evaluation, and implementation of optimal solutions. The steps of problem solving include the following:

1. Define the problem to everyone's satisfaction.
2. Brainstorm a list of potential solutions to the problem.
3. Evaluate the advantages and disadvantages of each solution.
4. Choose the best solution or combination of solutions. Compromise between solutions if necessary.
5. Formulate a plan for how to implement the solution.
6. Review progress on implementing the solution and reinforce approximations toward attaining the goal.

Early in problem-solving training, the therapist demonstrates the different steps by chairing the sessions and recording the progress made. This role is gradually relinquished to family members as the therapist progressively gives the family responsibility for conducting its own problem-solving sessions. Family members take turns "chairing" the family discussion, including leading the discussion, and recording the definition of the problem, alternative solutions, and the steps for implementing the solutions. As family members gradually become more active in solving their own problems together, they are instructed to conduct weekly family problem-solving meetings between therapy sessions. Crises are handled by using the problem-solving approach, rather than having the therapist make decisions for the family. The therapist steps in to chair the session only if the family's skills are not sufficient or if the problem is too difficult. The end goal of behavioral family therapy is for families to conduct their own weekly problem-solving sessions in the absence of the therapist and for these sessions to focus on removing current stressors and achieving individual and family goals. It should be emphasized that the goal is to alter the entire family's ability to solve problems, *not* to simply help the family "manage" the patient.

Special Problems

When family members have acquired good problem-solving skills, attention turns to working on special problems that remain and have not responded to family problem-solving. This phase involves teaching any of a wide range of behavioral techniques, such as contingency contracting for mutually desired behavior changes, cognitive-behavioral modification for depression or anxiety, social skills training for social inadequacy, token economy programs for enhancing constructive daily activity, and relaxation and/or exposure treatments for anxiety problems. Usually, the entire family is involved in implementing these strategies and monitoring their effects, although in some cases the therapist can work with one member individually.

Empirical Support

The clinical efficacy of behavioral family therapy has been strongly supported in two controlled studies. Falloon et al. (1985) and Falloon, McGill, Boyd, & Pedersen (1987) compared this intervention with individual treatment and case management. All patients were living with high-EE relatives and were treated with antipsychotic medication by psychiatrists who were blind to their treatment assignment. Family treatment was provided in the family's home once per week for the first 3 months, biweekly for the next 6 months, and monthly for 15 months. At the 2-year point, only 17% of the patients receiving family treatment had relapsed, compared to 83% of the individually treated patients. Family treated patients also had a lower rate of rehospitalization and greater gains in social and vocational functioning. The family treatment was also successful in reducing the burden of the illness on the relatives and in decreasing critical and intrusive statements made by family members to the patient during problem-solving discussions.

Several replication studies are currently under way, including the National Institute of Mental Health Collaborative Study on the Treatment of Schizophrenia (Schooler, Keith, Severe, & Matthews, in press). Recently, a variation on behavioral family therapy has been described and validated in a controlled clinical trial (Barrowclough & Tarrier, 1987; Tarrier et al., 1989). These studies also provide support for the general behavioral approach. Two-year relapse rates of patients living with high-EE relatives were significantly lower in patients receiving the behavioral family treatment (33%) than in those receiving routine treatment (59%).

The two studies referred to above (Falloon et al., 1985, 1987) demonstrated significant treatment effects for behavioral family therapy as compared to less or no psychosocial intervention. These findings represent important clinical advances, but the precise role of behavioral methods in improving outcome remains to be determined. Two nonbehavioral family interventions have been reported to reduce relapse rates of schizophrenics in controlled studies similar to the ones performed on behavioral treatment, suggesting that education alone may be an important factor in the treatment of families (Hogarty, Anderson, & Reiss, 1987; Leff, Kuipers, Berkowitz, & Sturgeon, 1985). Future research will need to directly compare behavioral interventions with purely educational treatments for families, to evaluate the importance of behavioral methods for enabling families to manage a schizophrenic relative more effectively.

SOCIAL SKILLS TRAINING

Social skills training involves the use of a range of interventions in order to enhance patients' interpersonal competence. To respond in a socially skillful manner, an individual must accurately perceive the meaning of cues provided by the interpersonal context, and emit context-appropriate verbal and nonverbal responses. Thus, social skill is situation-specific, and the ability to "read" social cues, including the affect states and motives of other persons, is central to interpersonal competence. Individuals differ across situations and over time, as well as from one another, in terms of interpersonal abilities. Some part of this variance is the result of differences in previous learning opportunities/experiences; a major factor in social competence in any given interpersonal context is the individual's past experience in similar contexts. Few, if any, persons invariably respond in the "right" or maximally effective way across the range of social situations that they encounter. We are all prone to occasionally misinterpreting social cues. At times, our abilities to respond in a socially competent manner might be compromised by factors of physical or emotional health. It is difficult, for example, to be particularly conversant while experiencing a toothache, or after having been reprimanded by one's boss. Finally, we all may come upon social situations that tax our abilities to remain socially facile—for example, in trying to console a close friend over the death of a loved one when we may literally feel at a loss for words. However, because of the chronic impact of schizophrenia, accurate interpretation of most affective cues may be beyond the abilities of many schizophrenic patients. Schizophrenics may be chronically anhedonic, and/or disinterested in being conversant or socially outgoing. Finally, social interactions beyond the most elementary level may require skills that exceed the abilities of many schizophrenic patients. It was once felt that these sorts of social impairments among schizophrenics almost invariably resulted from faulty learning opportunities, but it is now recognized that interpersonal dysfunction is multiply determined. Assuredly, the lack of an opportunity to use or practice certain interpersonal abilities may relate to some social deficits among some schizophrenics. An illness as disabling as schizophrenia will invariably interfere with experiences that normally shape interpersonal development. For example, premorbid social withdrawal and emotional detachment may emerge at a young age and effectively eliminate many learning opportunities. Periodic rehospitalizations as the illness progresses can produce further isolation from the natural teaching community. Because of such restricted social opportunities, the schizophrenic individual may be rendered incompetent across a range of interpersonal contexts. However, social dysfunction may also occur in relation to factors other than restricted opportunities for social learning and/or a restricted repertoire of interpersonal abilities. Non-skill factors associated with interpersonal performance in general, and schizophrenic psychopathology in particular, are presented in Table 8.1.

TABLE 8.1 Nonskill Factors Associated with Interpersonal Performance

Motivational/Cognitive Factors
  Reinforcement history
  Values; goals; expectancies
  Self-evaluation

Nonclinical Affect States
  Anxiety; anger; sadness

Other Organic/Physical Factors
  Physical attractiveness
  Motor skill; physical fitness

Schizophrenic Psychopathology
  Information-processing deficits
    attentional disturbances
    adverse cognitive effects of neuroleptic regimens
    affect recognition
  Negative symptoms

The role of cognitive and/or information-processing impairments in the social dysfunction of schizophrenic patients has received considerable attention. In particular, extensive emphasis recently has been placed on the ability to accurately decode visual and auditory affective cues. It has been demonstrated that many schizophrenic patients may lack the information-processing abilities to perform affective decoding tasks, and that organic pathology may underlie this dysfunction (e.g., Feinberg, Rifkin, Schaffer, & Walker, 1986; Novic, Luchins, & Perline, 1984; Walker, McGuire, & Bettes, 1984). Such limits in information-processing abilities may have implications for the efficacy of social skills training with schizophrenic patients. Similarly, social dysfunction may be intricately related to negative symptomatology (Carpenter et al., 1985). Although even nonnegative syndrome patients may exhibit marked social dysfunction, the social impairment associated with the negative syndrome may be particularly pernicious and, again, related to organic deficits. Thus, increasing emphasis has been placed on the evaluation of the social disabilities of schizophrenic patients in relation to the context of the patient's other symptomatology. For example, in considering the interpersonal dysfunction of a newly diagnosed, young schizophrenic, an assessment should consider attentional and perceptual abilities and motivational factors as well as social skills per se. Problems in any of these general areas would need to be better specified in order to develop adequate interventions. For example, if the patient's cognitive abilities were found to be markedly impaired, options would include increasing or decreasing the patient's neuroleptic dose (cognitive impairment could result from poorly controlled psychotic symptoms *or* medication side effects). In sum, the patient's social skills should be evaluated within the context of associated factors that can affect performance, including longitudinal fluctuation in major psychiatric symptoms.

A preliminary goal of social skills assessment with schizophrenic patients is to begin to determine whether the social dysfunction exhibited by a patient results from factors that are likely to minimize the impact of social skills training. An overmedicated patient will respond poorly to training efforts, and his or her social disabilities may lessen or change as a more appropriate medical regimen is achieved. A grossly psychotic and agitated patient may obtain only minimal benefit from training. However, in remission, he or she may exhibit a narrower range of social impairments.

After some preliminary determination that social skills training is appropriate for a patient, a detailed evaluation of the deficits that the patient exhibits in different social situations must be conducted, with the goal of identifying specific skill areas—overt response and/or social perception skills—on which training will be focused. Separate assessment procedures have been developed for each of these two skill areas.

Assessment of Overt Response Skills

Table 8.2 indicates the range of behaviors that is usually evaluated. *Expressive elements* include verbal and nonverbal parameters involved in communicating a message. Poverty of speech and/or poverty of content (symptoms that are especially prominent in the negative syndrome) can severely impair social performance. *Paralinguistic elements* are the voice parameters that serve to qualify a verbal message. Many schizophrenics exhibit blunted emotional tone and will require direct training in expressive tonality. *Nonverbal behavior* refers to bodily positions and movements during social interaction. Some typical nonverbal difficulties among schizophrenic patients include diminished facial responsiveness, minimal eye contact, and restricted bodily movements and gestures (kinesics). A final category of social response skill is *Interactive balance,* including response timing, turn taking, and social reinforcement. Psychiatric patients may, for example, exhibit inappropriately long response latencies when they are asked a question, causing others to feel uncomfortable. They may also be ignorant of the give-and-take of conversational interaction and may try to inject statements at inopportune moments. Social reinforcement refers to cues that indicate attention and interest (e.g., head nodding, "um-hm," occasional smiles).

Competent social performance is characterized not only by the correct execution of individual response elements, but also by the integration of those elements into complex behavioral repertoires. Conversational skills, assertive skills, heterosocial (i.e., dating) skills, and vocational skills are examples of the complex repertoires that constitute skillful interpersonal behavior. Schizophrenics may exhibit deficits in all of these areas, and all have been the target of social skills training programs for these patients.

To train a patient in the use of complex response skills repertoires, the repertoires must be reduced to some intermediate complexity. As an example, consider training in basic conversational skills. Table 8.3 lists some of the skills required to carry on a conversation. Distinct abilities are required to initiate, maintain, and end a conversation. However, even greater specificity is required to teach patients specific conversational responses (see Table 8.4). Only when the responses in Table 8.3 are reduced to sufficient detail

TABLE 8.2 Overt Response Components of Social Skills

Expressive Elements
  Speech content
  Paralinguistic elements
    voice volume
    pace
    pitch
    tone
  Nonverbal behavior
    proxemics
    kinesics
    gaze (eye control)
    facial expression

Interactive Balance
  Response timing
  Turn taking
  Social reinforcement

TABLE 8.3 Conversational Skills

Initiating Conversations
  Initiating a brief conversation with an acquaintance
  Initiating a brief conversation with a stranger
  Social telephone calls

Maintaining Conversations
  Asking questions
  Providing information
  Social reinforcement
  Social perception

Ending Conversations
  Timing
  How to break it off
  Goodbyes
  Judging when the partner wants to leave

TABLE 8.4 Initiating a Conversation

1. Make contact (smile and say, "Hello, [name].")
2. Ask a general question ("How have you been?")
3. Ask a specific question or answer a question from the other person.
4. When it is time to leave, give a reason for leaving and say goodbye ("I have an appointment . . . .")

can a patient be trained to use them as they relate to conversational abilities. Similar groupings and specification of skills would be conducted for training on assertive, heterosocial, and job skills.

Assessment Procedures

Were it not for the time and expense involved, a very complete social assessment could be provided by direct observation of the patient's behavior in his or her natural environment. Some direct observation may be possible, and both clinical staff and significant others of the patients can often provide important insights into the patient's social dysfunction, but direct observation is typically not possible across the range of social interactions that may be of interest. Therefore, other assessment techniques have been developed. The most widely used procedure is the role-play test.

A role-play test involves a brief enactment of a social interaction as if the scene were really occurring. In a typical test, a situation is described to the patient, and the therapist, playing the role of another person in the scene, issues a verbal prompt. The patient is instructed to respond to the prompt as realistically as possible, and the therapist extends the interaction for one or two more interchanges. For example, a scene description might be as follows: "Imagine you are home watching television when your roommate walks in and changes the channel without asking. He says, 'Let's watch this channel for a while.'" Following the patient's response, the therapist might continue: "You've been watching your shows all day. This one is better, anyway." Once again, the patient would be asked to respond to the therapist's prompt.

Assessment of Social Perception Skills

Social perception and/or receptive elements of social skill refer to abilities involved in the perception of the meaning of interpersonal communications. Effective social interaction is dependent on the ability to detect, interpret, and respond appropriately to what are often subtle interpersonal cues. A range of cues is involved, from nonverbal affect states to more complex indicators of intent. For example, to accurately interpret the affective state of others, an individual must be able to "read" nonverbal cues, including both facial displays of affect and auditory affect cues. In many instances, the process of deciding on an appropriate response to the relevant interpersonal cues may not involve a calculated decision, but there are some situations in which social problem-solving skills may be relevant (Bellack et al., 1989). The individual must consider various response possibilities and decide on the most effective alternative. An important prerequisite for this ability is focused attention—the individual must be able to attend to complex interpersonal cues of affect and/or intent, and must accurately decode the meaning of these cues. Because attentional impairments are common among schizophrenic patients (Cromwell, 1978; Kornetsky & Orzack, 1978; Wohlberg & Kornetsky, 1973) and may be particularly severe among negative syndrome patients (Andreasen, 1982; Green & Walker, 1984), many patients will require extensive training to attend to relevant interpersonal cues.

Considerable effort has been devoted to the development and standardization of affect recognition assessment measures. In this research, facial and vocal affect recognition have been conceptualized as specific, right-hemisphere-mediated, information-processing abilities. Regarding facial cues, investigators have developed assessment tasks that are intended to differentiate facial affect and facial identity recognition. Several investigations have been conducted to evaluate whether schizophrenic patients exhibit a differential deficit in facial affect recognition versus facial identity recognition (Feinberg et al., 1986; Novic et al., 1984; Walker et al., 1984). Results indicate that, although schizophrenics are impaired on a broader range of facial-perception skills than other psychiatric groups, it is in the area of emotion discrimination and recognition that they show the greatest deficit. These studies offer methodological advances over earlier investigations of "social perception" in schizophrenia, yet several concerns remain. Stimuli have varied across studies. No investigations have yet considered lateralization patterns in affect recognition studies with schizophrenics. Virtually no attention has been given to the possible impact of medication on affect recognition. Finally, the relationship of affect recognition performance to other measures of social skill has not been adequately considered.

Social Skills Training Procedures

The most common training protocol is the response acquisition approach. In this protocol, treatment proceeds by training on each deficient response element (one at a time, in order of increasing difficulty). Specific responses should be attacked in an order that maximizes the patient's success throughout training (i.e., based on what the patient can most easily learn at each point). The strategy of focusing on response elements one at a time and ensuring continuing success throughout treatment is especially important for patients with attentional difficulties. Training can be telescoped when the patient is less disturbed or when it has proceeded to a point where many responses are generalized across situations.

Training consists of five techniques:

- Instruction;
- Modeling;
- Role play;
- Feedback and social reinforcement;
- Practice.

Instruction

The first step in presenting a new skill is to provide a rationale and instruction for its use. For example, when addressing the common problem of poor eye contact, the therapist might say: "If people are going to know that you are serious, you should look at them when you speak. Try to look me in my eyes when you answer me."

Modeling

After explaining the new skill, the therapist models its use. Immediately prior to the demonstration, the therapist should draw attention to important components (e.g., "Watch how I nod sometimes while I am listening"). The enactment should be brief and to the point. Extended demonstrations may exceed the patient's attentional abilities or draw his or her attention to extraneous behavior. The skill may have to be demonstrated repeatedly for some patients.

Role Play

After the skill has been modeled, the patient is asked to try to mimic the therapist's behavior in a brief role-play interaction. This is a most important component of social skills training, because simply talking about and/or viewing skillful behavior is unlikely to impart those skills to the patient. Using the same scenario that was used to model the skill, the patient attempts to implement the skill in role play with the therapist. After the patient masters the minimal components of the skill, the therapist can generate more complex role plays. Although the learning abilities of individual patients will vary, in most cases extended practice and repetition will be necessary.

Feedback and Social Reinforcement

The therapist should provide feedback and positive reinforcement following every role play. The feedback should be specific and should focus initially on the positive aspects of the patient's response. This principle should be adhered to even when the patient's performance is grossly deficient. Only after the patient's attempt is appropriately praised should suggestions for change be provided. For example, the therapist might say: "You did a good job looking at my eyes when you first started to speak. This time, try to do even more of that." A patient who experiences frequent feelings of success and receives prodigious praise and encouragement is more likely to retain the motivation required to practice social skills to proficiency than one who receives only suggestions for improvement.

Homework

Role-play interactions provide an opportunity to learn and practice new skills, but additional practice or homework between sessions is required in order for those skills to generalize to other settings. Patients are routinely assigned to use the skills acquired in a particular session with other individuals, prior to the next session. Specific assignments, such as "Ask your roommate to help you play cards tonight," are more likely to be completed than vague assignments such as "Try requesting things from people." The assignment should be one that is likely to meet with success. The therapist should be reasonably certain that the patient is capable of carrying out the assignment and that it stands a good chance of receiving a favorable response. At the beginning of each session, the homework assignments from the preceding session are reviewed and any problems that have arisen are resolved before proceeding to a new skill.

Training is typically conducted in a group format, involving between 6 and 10 patients. Groups typically meet 3 times per week or daily. The duration of training will vary as a function of the syllabus. Usually, a minimum of 1 month must be devoted to a particular compound skill repertoire. Groups are best conducted by two therapists, because it is difficult for one person to teach social skills and maintain control of the group. Moreover, the use of two therapists can greatly facilitate the modeling of new social skills.

Empirical Support

Perhaps the most significant developments in social skills training for schizophrenics have been concerned with social validation of target behaviors and evaluation of combined treatment packages that have included social skills training. These developments have been spurred in part by ongoing concerns regarding the generalization and maintenance of social skills training effects. The extent to which effects of social skills training generalize to nontraining environments, and persist following training, has been a concern for some time (Morrison & Bellack, 1984). Social validation involves selecting component behaviors for training, as well as performance criterion levels for the behaviors, based on an assessment of the interpersonal skills of "normal" nonpsychiatric persons in the community. The rationale for this approach is that training behaviors to criterion levels will permit the behaviors to more easily come under the control of environmental contingencies, thus facilitating both generalization and maintenance. Holmes, Hansen, and St. Lawrence (1984) provided group training focusing on conversational components and speech content to chronic psychiatric patients enrolled in a partial hospitalization program. Following training, the frequency of targeted component behaviors increased to socially validated criterion levels. Training effects generalized to unfamiliar, nonpsychiatric conversational partners, and were maintained throughout a 7-month follow-up.

However, even investigations of this sort fail to address the issue of whether these new skills provide a clinically meaningful difference. The purpose of psychosocial interventions for chronically impaired patients is to facilitate better adjustment in the community and, ultimately, to prevent or postpone relapse. Unfortunately, Holmes et al. (1984) did not address relapse. A frequent criticism of social skills training with chronic patients has been that changes in social skills repertoires "do not often result in substantial differences in patients' quality of life" (Wallace, 1982, p. 60).

Bellack, Turner, Hersen, and Luber (1984) used a 12-week day hospital program supplemented by comprehensive social skills training to treat chronic schizophrenics. Patient performance was assessed using a battery of self-report and behavioral measures, and was compared to that of chronic schizophrenics who received only day hospital treatment. Both groups improved at posttreatment. However, during a 6-month follow-up, patients who had received social skills training either continued to improve or maintained their gains on most measures; patients receiving day hospital treatment alone either maintained gains or lost them. Finally, almost half of the patients in both groups were hospitalized at least once during the year following treatment. Thus, the findings suggest that social skills training did little to forestall relapse.

Subsequent findings (Liberman, Mueser, & Wallace, 1986) indicated that schizophrenics who received intensive (12 hours per week) social skills training as inpatients evidenced better functioning, spent less time hospitalized, and had fewer symptomatic relapses 2 years after treatment than a comparable group that had received holistic health treatment during the index hospitalization. That the findings reported by Bellack et al. (1984) and Liberman et al. (1986) are discordant with regard to the prevention of relapse may be attributable to differences in the skills training protocols and/or to characteristics of the patients. With regard to treatment, the skills training procedures utilized by Liberman et al. were more intensive. This factor should receive further consideration in relationship to treatment outcome.

Data reported by Hogarty et al. (1986) attest to the importance of possible interactions between social skills training and specific patient characteristics. These investigators examined the effects of social skills training, family psychoeducation, and maintenance medication in the aftercare treatment of schizophrenic and schizoaffective patients. Both social skills training and family treatment, administered in conjunction with medication, resulted in a significant reduction in first-year relapse rates relative to control subjects (maintenance neuroleptic treatment). Furthermore, combined treatment (social skills training and family psychoeducation) reduced first-year relapse to 0 percent (among 17 subjects receiving combined treatment). Finally, the effects of social skills training were apparently somewhat mitigated among patients discharged in a psychotic state. Three patients in the social skills training condition experienced a Type II relapse, defined by the authors as a "severe clinical exacerbation of persistent psychotic symptoms" (p. 636).

Social Perception Training

The mastery of individual response skills does not guarantee their effective use in social situations. In addition to training in overt response skills, patients usually must be taught when and where to use them. These abilities require that the patient attend to and correctly interpret interpersonal and contextual cues. For example, a patient who has mastered the ability to initiate a conversation may also need to learn that it can be unwise to use that skill with someone who displays an extremely unreceptive facial expression.

Training in social perception does not follow a separate, structured sequence of activities, but is typically integrated with response training. The objective is to train the patient to attend to and interpret interpersonal cues that signify the feelings and motives of other individuals and contextual variables that determine the appropriateness of various responses. This training can be accomplished during role plays by introducing subtle variations in the therapist's behavior and inquiring into the possible meanings of those variations. For example, during role plays of casual conversation, the therapist can exhibit nonverbal cues indicating a lack of interest and a desire to leave (e.g., glance at watch, look at door). After each role play, patients can be questioned about possible interpretations of and acceptable responses to such behavior. With respect to contextual cues, training is through didactic means. A portion of each session can be devoted to discussing the social rules that govern the acceptable use of the skills under consideration.

Wallace (1982) has developed a program intended to improve the information-processing skills of schizophrenic patients. Patients are taught to accurately receive and process incoming stimuli, and to subsequently send effective verbal and nonverbal responses. The distinctive component of this approach is its emphasis on interpersonal stimulus processing, or problem solving, during which patients are taught to generate various response options, weigh the value of those options, and devise an appropriate response implementation strategy. This approach has proven to be effective with many schizophrenic patients, and it appears to offer a practical means of addressing the information-processing deficits of schizophrenics with negative symptoms.

With the increasing emphasis on facial affect recognition, it is likely that a technology for the (re)training of facial affect recognition will be developed. Several possible strategies for this sort of training exist. Training can be modeled after procedures that have been used for retraining cognitive skills in the rehabilitation of brain-injured patients (cf. Goldstein & Rutven, 1983).

CONCLUSIONS

The two approaches to behavior therapy of schizophrenia that have been systematically evaluated relate to interpersonal symptoms of the disorder. The interpersonal disabilities experienced by most schizophrenic patients are pronounced and limiting. However, the application of behavior therapy techniques to the social symptoms of the disorder has shown particular promise. The impact of combined behavioral family therapy and social skills training, as suggested by the Hogarty et al. (1986) study, when used in conjunction with appropriate medication strategies, holds promise for enhancing patients' quality of life. Furthermore, from a clinical research perspective, behavioral assessment protocols may prove to play a role in the further substantiation of existing subdiagnostic classification schemata as specific interpersonal deficits are shown to characterize particular schizophrenic subtypes.

However, further research is needed to refine the use of behavior therapy techniques with schizophrenic patients, including careful evaluation of predictors of outcome. For example, the data reported by Hogarty et al. (1986) indicated that persistent psychotic symptoms, and/or a prolonged period to achieve stabilization following an acute psychotic episode, may be an important predictor of outcome. Other considerations may relate to particular pharmacologic treatment regimens and/or pharmacologic response, because neuroleptics can produce adverse cognitive effects that might, at least temporarily, impair patients' ability to maximally benefit from psychosocial training procedures. Much greater attention needs to be directed toward the relationship of specific behavioral manifestations of the disorder to treatment response.

REFERENCES

Adams, H. E., Malatesta, V., Brantley, P. J., & Turkat, I. D. (1981). Modification of cognitive processes: A case study of schizophrenia. *Journal of Consulting and Clinical Psychology, 49,* 460-464.

Andreasen, N. D. (1982). Negative symptoms in schizophrenia. *Archives of General Psychiatry, 39,* 784-788.

Anthony, W. A., & Nemec, P. B. (1984). Psychiatric rehabilitation. In A. S. Bellack (Ed.), *Schizophrenia: Treatment, management, and rehabilitation.* Orlando: Grune & Stratton.

Barrowclough, C., & Tarrier, N. (1987). A behavioural family intervention with a schizophrenic patient: A case study. *Behavioural Psychotherapy, 15,* 252-271.

Bellack, A. S. (1986). Schizophrenia: Behavior therapy's forgotten child. *Behavior Therapy, 17,* 199-214.

Bellack, A. S. (1989). A comprehensive model for treatment of schizophrenia. In A. S. Bellack (Ed.), *A clinical guide for the treatment of schizophrenia* (pp. 1-22). New York: Plenum.

Bellack, A. S., Morrison, R. L., & Mueser, K. T. (1989). Social problem solving in schizophrenia. *Schizophrenia Bulletin, 15,* 101-116.

Bellack, A. S., Turner, S. M., Hersen, M., & Luber, R. F. (1984). An examination of the efficacy of social skills training for chronic schizophrenic patients. *Hospital and Community Psychiatry, 35,* 1023-1028.

Bentall, R. P., Higson, P. J., & Lowe, C. F. (1987). Teaching self-instructions to chronic schizophrenic patients: Efficacy and generalization. *Behavioral Psychotherapy, 15,* 58-76.

Boczkowski, J. A., Zeichner, A., & DeSanto, N. (1985). Neuroleptic compliance among chronic schizophrenic outpatients: An intervention outcome report. *Journal of Consulting and Clinical Psychology, 53,* 666-671.

Carpenter, W. T., Jr., Heinrichs, D. W., & Alphs, L. D. (1985). Treatment of negative symptoms. *Schizophrenia Bulletin, 11,* 440-452.

Cordes, C. (1984). The plight of the homeless mentally ill. *APA Monitor, 15,* 1-13.

Cromwell, R. L. (1978). Attention and information processing: A foundation for understanding schizophrenia? In L. C. Wynne, R. L. Cromwell, & S. Matthysse (Eds.), *The nature of schizophrenia: New approaches to research and treatment* (pp. 219-224). New York: Wiley.

Dearth, N., Labenski, B. J., Mott, M. E., & Pellegrini, L. M. (1986). *Families helping families: Living with schizophrenia.* New York: Norton.

Diamond, R. (1985). Drugs and the quality of life: The patient's point of view. *Journal of Clinical Psychiatry, 46,* 29-35.

Falloon, I. R. H., Boyd, J. L., & McGill, C. W. (1984). *Family care of schizophrenia: A problem-solving approach to the treatment of mental illness.* New York: Guilford.

Falloon, I. R. H., Boyd, J. L., McGill, C. W., Williamson, M., Razani, J., Moss, H. B., Gilderman, A. M., & Simpson, G. M. (1985). Family management in the prevention of morbidity of schizophrenia. Clinical outcome of a two year longitudinal study. *Archives of General Psychiatry, 42,* 887-896.

Falloon, I. R. H., McGill, C. W., Boyd, J., & Pedersen, J. (1987). Family management in the prevention of morbidity of schizophrenia: Social outcome of a two-year longitudinal study. *Psychological Medicine, 17,* 59-66.

Falloon, I. R. H., Mueser, K. T., Gingerich, S., Rapaport, S., McGill, C., & Hole, V. (1988). *Workbook for behavioural family therapy.* London: Barns Inc.

Feinberg, T. E., Rifkin, A., Schaffer, C., & Walker, E. (1986). Facial discrimination and emotional recognition in schizophrenia and affective disorders. *Archives of General Psychiatry, 43,* 276-279.

Fisher, E. B., Jr., & Winkler, R. C. (1975). Self-control over intrusive experiences. *Journal of Consulting and Clinical Psychology, 6,* 911-916.

Gardos, G., & Cole, J. O. (1976). Maintenance antipsychotic therapy: Is the cure worse than the disease? *American Journal of Psychiatry, 133,* 32-36.

Goldman, H. H. (1982). Mental illness and family burden: A public health perspective. *Hospital and Community Psychiatry, 33,* 557-560.

Goldman, H. H. (1984). Epidemiology. In J. A. Talbott (Ed.), *The chronic mental patient: Five years later* (pp. 15-31). Orlando: Grune & Stratton.

Goldman, H. H., Adams, N. H., & Taube, C. A. (1983). Deinstitutionalization: The data demythologized. *Hospital and Community Psychiatry, 34,* 129-134.

Goldstein, G., & Rutven, L. (1983). *Rehabilitation of the brain-damaged adult.* New York: Plenum.

Goldstrom, I. D., & Manderscheid, R. W. (1981). The chronically mentally ill: A descriptive analysis from the uniform client data instrument. *Community Support Service Journal, 2,* 4-9.

Green, M., & Walker, E. (1984). Susceptibility to backward masking in positive versus negative symptom schizophrenia. *American Journal of Psychiatry, 141,* 1273-1275.

Hoenig, J., & Hamilton, M. W. (1986). The schizophrenic patient in the community and his effect on the household. *International Journal of Social Psychiatry, 12,* 165-176.

Hogarty, G. E., Anderson, C. M., & Reiss, D. J. (1987). Family psychoeducation, social skills training, and medication in schizophrenia: The long and short of it. *Psychopharmacology Bulletin, 23,* 12-13.

Hogarty, G. E., Anderson, C. M., Reiss, D. J., Kornblith, S. J., Greenwald, D. P., Javna, C. D., & Madonia, M. J. (1986). Family psycho-education, social skills training and maintenance chemotherapy: I. One year effects of a controlled study on relapse and expressed emotion. *Archives of General Psychiatry, 45,* 797-805.

Hogarty, G. E., Schooler, N. R., Ulrich, R., Mussare, F., Ferro, P., & Herron, E. (1979). Fluphenazine and social therapy in the aftercare of schizophrenic patients. *Archives of General Psychiatry, 36,* 1283-1294.

Holmes, M. R., Hansen, D. G., & St. Lawrence, J. S. (1984). Conversational skills training with aftercare patients in the community: Social validation and generalization. *Behavior Therapy, 15,* 84-100.

Hooley, J. (1985). Expressed emotion: A review of the critical literature. *Clinical Psychology Review, 5,* 119-140.

Koenigsberg, H. W., & Handley, R. (1986). Expressed emotion: From predictive index to clinical construct. *American Journal of Psychiatry, 143,* 1361-1373.

Kornetsky, C., & Orzack, M. H. (1978). Physiologic and behavioral correlates of attention dysfunction in schizophrenic patients. In L. C. Wynne, R. L. Cromwell, & S. Matthysse (Eds.), *The nature of schizophrenia: New approaches to research and treatment* (pp. 196-204). New York: Wiley.

Leff, J., Kuipers, L., Berkowitz, R., & Sturgeon, D. (1985). A controlled trial of social intervention in the families of schizophrenic patients: Two year follow-up. *British Journal of Psychiatry, 146,* 594-600.

Leff, J., & Vaughn, C. (1985). *Expressed emotion in families.* New York: Guilford.

Liberman, R. P., Mueser, K. T., & Wallace, C. J. (1986). Social skills training for schizophrenic individuals at risk for relapse. *American Journal of Psychiatry, 143,* 523-526.

Liberman, R. P., Wallace, C., Teigen, J., & Davis, J. (1974). Interventions with psychotic behaviors. In K. S. Calhoun, H. E. Adams, & K. M. Mitchell (Eds.), *Innovative treatment methods in psychopathology* (pp. 323-412). New York: Wiley.

Minkoff, K. (1978). A map of chronic mental patients. In J. A. Talbott (Ed.), *The chronic mental patient.* Washington, DC: American Psychiatric Association.

Morrison, R. L., & Bellack, A. S. (1984). Social skills training. In A. S. Bellack (Ed.), *Schizophrenia: Treatment, management, and rehabilitation.* Orlando: Grune & Stratton.

Moser, A. J. (1974). Covert punishment of hallucinatory behavior in a psychotic male. *Journal of Behavior Therapy and Experimental Psychiatry, 5,* 297-299.

Mueser, K. T. (1989). Behavioral family therapy. In A. S. Bellack (Ed.), *A clinical guide for the treatment of schizophrenia* (pp. 207-236). New York: Plenum.

Mueser, K. T., Yarnold, P. R., Levinson, D. F., Singh, H., Bellack, A. S., Kee, K., Morrison, R. L., & Yadalam, K. G. (1990). Prevalence of substance abuse in schizophrenia: Demographic and clinical correlates. *Schizophrenia Bulletin, 16,* 31-56.

Neuchterlein, K. H., & Dawson, M. E. (1984). Information processing and attentional functioning in the developmental course of schizophrenic disorders. *Schizophrenia Bulletin, 10,* 160-203.

Novic, J., Luchins, D. J., & Perline, R. (1984). Facial affect recognition in schizophrenia: Is there a differential deficit? *British Journal of Psychiatry, 144,* 533-537.

Paul, G. L., & Lentz, R. J. (1977). *Psychosocial treatment of chronic mental patients: Milieu versus social-learning programs.* Cambridge, MA: Harvard University Press.

Perris, C. (1989). *Cognitive therapy with schizophrenic patients.* New York: Guilford.

Rabkin, J. G. (1980). Stressful life events and schizophrenia: A review of the research literature. *Psychological Bulletin, 87,* 408-425.

Rosen, A. J., Sussman, S., Mueser, K. T., Lyons, J. S., & Davis, J. M. (1981). Behavioral assessment of psychiatric inpatients and normal controls across different environmental contexts. *Journal of Behavioral Assessment, 3,* 25-36.

Schooler, N., Keith, S., Severe, J., & Matthews, S. (in press). Acute treatment response and short term outcome in schizophrenia: First results of the NIMH treatment strategies in schizophrenia study. *Psychopharmacology Bulletin.*

Schooler, N., & Spohn, H. E. (1982). Social dysfunction and treatment failure in schizophrenia. *Schizophrenia Bulletin, 8,* 85-98.

Sharfstein, S. S. (1984). Sociopolitical issues affecting patients with chronic schizophrenia. In A. S. Bellack (Ed.), *Schizophrenia: Treatment, management, and rehabilitation* (pp. 113-132). Orlando: Grune & Stratton.

Slade, P. D. (1972). The effects of systematic desensitization on auditory hallucinations. *Behaviour Research and Therapy, 10,* 85-91.

Sumner, J. H., Mueser, S. T., Hsu, L., & Morales, R. G. (1974). Overcorrection treatment for radical reduction of aggressive-disruptive behavior in institutionalized mental patients. *Psychological Reports, 35,* 655-662.

Strauss, J. S., & Carpenter, W. T., Jr. (1981). *Schizophrenia.* New York: Plenum.

Tarrier, N., Barrowclough, C., Vaughn, C., Bamrah, J. S., Porceddu, K., Watts, S., & Freeman, H. A community trial of a behavioural intervention with families to reduce relapse. *British Journal of Psychiatry, 154,* 625-628.

Test, M. A. (1984). Community support programs. In A. S. Bellack (Ed.), *Schizophrenia: Treatment, management, and rehabilitation* (pp. 347-373). Orlando: Grune & Stratton.

Turner, S. M., Hersen, M., & Bellack, A. S. (1977). Effects of social description, stimulus interference, and aversive conditioning on auditory hallucinations. *Behavior Modification, 1,* 249-258.

Walker, E., McGuire, M., & Bettes, B. (1984). Recognition and identification of facial stimuli by schizophrenics and patients with affective disorders. *British Journal of Psychiatry, 23,* 37-44.

Wallace, C. J. (1982). The social skills training project of the Mental Health Clinical Research Center for the Study of Schizophrenia. In J. F. Curran and P. M. Monti (Eds.), *Social skills training: A practical handbook for assessment and treatment* (pp. 57-89). New York: Guilford.

Wallace, C. J., Boone, S. E., Donahoe, C. P., & Foy, D. W. (1985). The chronically mentally disabled: Independent living skills training. In D. H. Barlow (Ed.), *Clinical handbook of psychological disorders: A step-by-step treatment manual* (pp. 462–501). New York: Guilford.

Wing, J. K., & Brown, G. W. (1970). *Institutionalization and schizophrenia.* London: Cambridge University Press.

Wohlberg, G., & Kornetsky, C. (1973). Sustained attention in remitted schizophrenics. *Archives of General Psychiatry, 28,* 533–537.

Wong, S. E., Terranova, M. D., Bowen, L., Zarete, T., Massel, H. K., & Liberman, R. P. (1987). Providing independent recreational activities to reduce stereotypic vocalizations in chronic schizophrenics. *Journal of Applied Behavior Analysis, 20,* 77–81.

Zubin, J., & Spring, B. (1977). Vulnerability—A new view of schizophrenia. *Journal of Abnormal Psychology, 86,* 103–126.

CHAPTER 9

Behavioral Approaches to Sexual Dysfunction

J. GAYLE BECK

The past three decades have witnessed substantial progress in the understanding and treatment of male and female sexual dysfunctions, largely because of the contributions of early behavior therapists (e.g., Wolpe, 1958) and the application of learning principles to human sexual behavior. Not surprisingly, the primary tenet of broad-based sex therapy is drawn directly from behavioral theory, specifically the assumption that sexual dysfunctions are learned as the result of an array of psychophysiological, cognitive, and behavioral processes. Although the current practice of sex therapy often includes interventions derived from nonbehavioral approaches, the foundations of sex therapy have remained grounded in behavior therapy.

In considering behavioral approaches to sexual dysfunction, it is important to note that the term "sexual dysfunction" does not connote a unitary disorder, but rather comprises a collection of disorders occurring at various points during the sexual arousal response. Because sexual arousal involves physical as well as emotional responses, a current listing of sexual dysfunctions includes disorders of sexual desire, arousal, and orgasm (see Table 9.1). This delineation is based on Masters and Johnson's (1966) description, which differentiated four phrases of the sexual response cycle: excitement, plateau, orgasm, and resolution. Although the notion of discrete phases of sexual responding has been questioned both conceptually (Robinson, 1976) and empirically (Rosen & Beck, 1988), the distinction between sexual arousal and orgasm has remained viable and useful in treatment. Most recently, recognition of the importance of sexual desire as a separate aspect of sexual functioning has been highlighted by Lief (1977) and Kaplan (1979), thus expanding the domain of sexual dysfunctions to include disorders characterized by low motivation for sexual interaction and lack of sexual interest.

A clear distinction often cannot be drawn between the sexual problems of "normal" and clinical populations. For example, Frank, Anderson, and Rubinstein (1978) reported that, among a sample of 100 happily married couples who were not seeking sex therapy, 40% of the men reported erectile or ejaculatory dysfunctions and 63% of the women reported arousal or orgasmic dysfunctions. In highlighting the complexity of human sexual behavior, these figures also indicate that multiple criteria must be used in diagnosing sexual dysfunction and evaluating the effects of sex therapy.

156 Behavioral Approaches to Sexual Dysfunction

TABLE 9.1 A Current Listing of the Sexual Dysfunctions

Disorders of Sexual Desire

- *Hypoactive sexual desire disorder*
  A persistent or recurrent lack of sexual fantasies or desire for sexual activity, which is unusual in the context of the individual's life circumstances and is a source of distress to the individual or their partner.
- *Sexual aversion disorder*
  Persistent aversion, repugnance, fear, and avoidance of most or all sexual contact with a partner.

Disorders of Sexual Arousal

- *Male erectile disorder*
  Either recurrent inability to attain or maintain an erection until completion of sexual activity or a persistent lack of subjective sexual excitement and pleasure during sexual activity.
- *Female sexual arousal disorder*
  Either recurrent inability to attain or maintain the vaginal lubrication-vasocongestion response until completion of sexual activity or a persistent lack of subjective sexual excitement and pleasure during sexual activity.

Disorders Involving Pain During Sexual Activity

- *Vaginismus*
  Recurrent involuntary spasm of the musculature of the outer third of the vagina that interferes with coitus.
- *Dyspareunia*
  Persistent genital pain in either a male or female before, during, or after sexual intercourse.

Disorders of Sexual Orgasm

- *Inhibited female orgasm*
  A recurrent delay in, or absence of, orgasm in a female following normal sexual excitement during activity that is judged to be adequate in focus, intensity, and duration.
- *Inhibited male orgasm*
  A recurrent delay in, or absence of, orgasm in a male following normal sexual excitement during activity that is judged to be adequate in focus, intensity, and duration.
- *Premature ejaculation*
  Recurrent ejaculation with minimal sexual stimulation or shortly after penetration and before the man desires it.

THE SEXUAL DYSFUNCTIONS

Within each form of sexual dysfunction, several distinctions traditionally are drawn in assessment and classification. Based originally on Masters and Johnson's (1970) formulations, sexual problems can be classified as *primary,* indicating that the individual has never enjoyed an interval of adequate sexual functioning; *secondary,* connoting that the sexual dysfunction followed a period of adequate functioning; or *situational,* implying that the sexual problem occurs only under specific circumstances, such as with a particular partner. These distinctions have important prognostic value for some of the sexual dysfunctions to be discussed below, such as female orgasmic dysfunction and male arousal difficulties.

In assessing the range of sexual dysfunctions, it is critical for the behavior therapist to ensure that an organic etiology is not present prior to embarking on a course of behavioral sex therapy. There is accumulating evidence that many cases of erectile dysfunction and retarded ejaculation in males, and low sexual arousal and dyspareunia in females, are either caused by physical factors or develop as the result of medication side effects. Currently, the strategies available for the differential diagnosis of organic and psychogenic factors in male sexual dysfunction are considerably more refined, relative to those used in the evaluation of female dysfunction (e.g., Fracher, Leiblum, & Rosen, 1981; Krane, Goldstein, & DeTejada, 1989). However, a careful physical assessment is a necessary component of pretreatment assessment for all individuals presenting with sexual dysfunction.

Disorders of Sexual Desire

Sexual desire disorders are a relatively new addition to classification schemes for the sexual dysfunctions. By definition, hypoactive sexual desire is diagnosed when an individual reports a persistent and pervasive lack of motivation for sexual activity, which is a source of distress for either the individual or his or her partner (DSM-III-R; American Psychiatric Association, 1987). In evaluating complaints of low desire, it is mandatory to rule out current coexisting psychopathology (e.g., depression) and medical factors such as hyperprolactinemia. Recent studies of low sexual desire, however, indicate that the lifetime prevalence of affective disorder among individuals with low sexual desire is twice that of the normal population, and, often, the initial episode of depression coincided with or preceded the onset of low sexual desire (Schreiner-Engel & Schiavi, 1986). Women with low desire also may report severe symptoms of premenstrual syndrome.

Although theories concerning disorders of sexual desire are abundant (e.g., Leiblum & Rosen, 1988), empirical data are scant. Nutter and Condron (1983, 1985) reported that both males and females with low sexual desire fantasize less during sexual activity, masturbation, and general daydreaming than do normal controls, although the content of sexual fantasies is identical. Females with low desire reported a frequency of masturbation to orgasm similar to that of controls; males with low desire reported *more frequent* masturbation. Typically, when a woman presents with low sexual desire, the frequency of sexual activity with her partner is not unusually low, reflecting traditional sex role prescriptions concerning the initiation and acquiescence with sexual requests. However, when a man reports low desire, the frequency of sexual contact often is reduced drastically, and may occur only when the female partner initiates the activity. Given the complex interaction between sexual desire and sexual behavior, consideration of general relationship functioning is necessary in a complete behavioral analysis of low desire. Sexual desire discrepancies between partners may reflect unspoken resentments, difficulties in the distribution of power within the relationship, and other problems in marital functioning.

A somewhat different form of desire disorder, termed sexual aversion, refers to repugnance, fear, or disgust associated with sexual activity. Unlike low sexual desire, sexual aversion is characterized by these extreme emotional reactions and active avoidance of sexual situations. Often, sexual aversion is the result of trauma, such as rape (e.g., Masters, 1986), and may be better conceptualized as a form of post-traumatic stress disorder. For example, Masters presented the case of a 37-year-old man who was sexually assaulted at gunpoint by two women. In addition to being forced to have intercourse, the man was beaten about the genitals and rectum. Within 6 months of the assault, he had become increasingly anxious when his wife attempted to discuss his lack of sexual interest, and he would experience nausea and sometimes vomit if his wife tried to initiate sexual activity. He had not attempted masturbation since the assault, nor had he made any sexual overtures to his wife. Unlike the typical case of low sexual desire, this case illustrates the benefit of including assessment for post-traumatic stress disorder in cases of sexual aversion,

Disorders of Sexual Arousal

In both males and females, problems of low sexual arousal are characterized by a lack of responding early in the sexual response process: failure to achieve or sustain an erection in the male, and lack of adequate vaginal lubrication and vasoengorgement in the female. Considerably more is known about male erectile dysfunction than about female arousal disorders, which tend to co-occur with orgasmic dysfunction.

A collection of organic factors has been documented as causal in erectile failure, including neurogenic impairment (resulting from spinal-cord injury, diabetes mellitus, or alcoholism, for example), vascular impairment (from atherosclerosis, hypertension, pelvic trauma, or pelvic irradiation), endocrine abnormalities (particularly disturbances of the pituitary and thyroid), and drug side effects (Krane et al., 1989; Tiefer & Melman, 1989). A comprehensive medical evaluation should include a series of examinations, such as nocturnal penile tumescence testing, hormonal assays, vascular testing using injections of vasoactive agents such as papaverine or protaglandin E_1, and determination of penile sensory thresholds. In particular, the role of pharmacological agents used to treat various diseases, such as hypertension, should be carefully evaluated, because erectile dysfunction is a frequent side effect, particularly among older men (Leiblum & Segraves, 1989).

In the absence of a documented organic cause for erectile failure, many men with low sexual arousal report distracting preoccupation with their sexual performance, worry and other negative emotional states associated with sexual situations, and fears concerning their inability to satisfy a partner (Barlow, 1986; Beck, 1987; Beck & Barlow, 1984). Although an occasional instance of erectile difficulty is normal for most men, those who report persistent arousal dysfunctions are more likely to exaggerate the significance of erectile failure and overestimate what constitutes "normal" sexual functioning. Over time, a man may stop initiating sexual contact, for fear of failure and embarrassment. Thus, the differential diagnosis of low sexual desire and low sexual arousal warrants exploration of the motivation behind infrequent sexual contact. Fagan, Schmidt, Wise, and Derogatis (1988) reported that, among a representative sample of men with erectile failure, 18% were diagnosed with concurrent substance abuse disorders and 22% were given personality disorder diagnoses, following DSM-III criteria. Each of these diagnostic dimensions indicates a poor prognosis for treatment and suggests that treatment formulation first should address related factors that interfere with sexual functioning.

Overall, less is known about arousal disorders in women than in men, particularly regarding the role of organic factors in impairing vasocongestion and vaginal lubrication in women. An estrogen deficiency may be causal in reports of poor lubrication and difficulties in becoming aroused among postmenopausal women who are not on replacement hormones (Swartzman & Leiblum, 1987). Less is known concerning the impact of hypertension, diabetes, and medication side effects on female sexual functioning as compared with male sexual functioning, although preliminary reports suggest that the sexual side effects of these various organic factors are more variable for women than they are for men (Jensen, 1981).

Psychological factors similar to those noted in erectile dysfunction frequently are present for women with arousal deficits. Some women may report adequate physical responding but indicate an absence of subjective sexual arousal, although the opposite pattern also can be present. The fact that the subjective and physical components of arousal do not covary is not a marker of sexual dysfunction in women (Rosen & Beck, 1988), although this response discordance can be useful in treatment formulation. Occasionally, low sexual arousal can be attributed to ignorance about sexual functioning, strict religious beliefs, or the partner's lack of sexual skill, although these factors are less prevalent clinically than they were 20 years ago, when sex therapy was a relatively new treatment approach. At present, many women presenting with arousal disorders indicate relative sophistication concerning sexuality, gleaned from the popular press and self-help books. This clearly makes the task of the behavior therapist more challenging. Additionally, there is agreement that secondary arousal dysfunctions in women are less responsive to treatment than primary arousal dysfunctions (Everaerd, 1983) and frequently are related to more general relationship difficulties.

Two sexual dysfunctions that differ in form from arousal difficulties but affect responding at the beginning of the sexual arousal process are vaginismus and dyspareunia. Within the current nosological scheme (DSM-III-R; American Psychiatric Association, 1987), these are termed sexual pain disorders. Vaginismus involves spastic contraction of the female circumvaginal muscles when penetration is attempted. For some women, vaginismus occurs with nonsexual contacts as well, such as during a gynecological examination. LoPiccolo and Stock (1987) noted that vaginismus may be presented by women who were molested as children and, in these cases, usually is accompanied by low arousal and difficulties reaching orgasm. Treatment approaches for vaginismus have proven quite effective, as outlined below. Dyspareunia may be difficult to distinguish from vaginismus in women, because painful penetration is the primary complaint in both disorders. A pelvic examination is necessary for the differential diagnosis of these two disorders: women with vaginismus may show characteristic vaginal vasospasm which is absent in women with dyspareunia. In all cases, dyspareunia is the result of a physical problem such as a vaginal lesion or (in males) a chronic urinary tract infection. Sandberg and Quevillon (1987) noted that psychological factors often are present in cases of dyspareunia, in addition to organic factors. Dyspareunia appears to be considerably more common in women than in men (Masters & Johnson, 1970).

Disorders of Sexual Orgasm

Orgasmic dysfunctions take slightly different forms in males and females, although interruption of the orgasmic response is the central complaint for both sexes. Men may present with premature ejaculation, which involves extremely rapid, uncontrolled ejaculation; or retarded ejaculation, an inability to ejaculate (usually intravaginally) despite adequate sexual stimulation. Premature ejaculation usually is reported by younger men who have a low frequency of partner contact and may be hypervigilant to their own level of arousal (Speiss, Geer, & O'Donohue, 1984). Occasionally, a man may present with a normal orgasmic response and with concerns that arise from media depictions of superhuman performance, but these cases are no longer common in sex therapy practice. Fortunately, premature ejaculation is one of the more readily treated sexual dysfunctions.

The same statement cannot be made concerning retarded ejaculation, however. In 1979, Munjack and Kanno reviewed the literature on retarded ejaculation, concluding that there were few objective reports of etiology and treatment outcome available. Unfortunately, this state of affairs continues today. Several different models have been proposed to account for a failure to achieve orgasm in males, including speculations related to a preference for autoerotic stimulation and exceedingly narrow stimulus control over orgasm, because of a masturbatory style that is incompatible with partner stimulation. Additionally, high doses of certain psychotropic medications (e.g., phenothiazines) and alcohol may be causal in retarded ejaculation (Schover & Jensen, 1988). Although various organic conditions, such as spinal-cord injury or the side effects of genital surgery such as radical prostatectomy or cystectomy, may reduce the intensity of orgasmic pleasure, retarded ejaculation is not diagnosed in these cases. As will be outlined, treatment of retarded ejaculation reflects the present uncertain understanding of this disorder.

Difficulty in achieving orgasm is one of the most frequent sexual complaints of women. Depending on the survey methodology used, 7 to 30% of nonclinical samples have been reported to have never experienced orgasm. Factors such as failure to express sexual needs, anxiety concerning sexual functioning (perhaps related to prior sexual trauma), lack of privacy, time constraints traceable to career and family demands, and inadequate sexual skills all have been identified as important in orgasmic dysfunction in women. Organic factors often are not involved, with the exception of antidepressant medications (Shen & Sata, 1983). Generally, anorgasmia is followed by a complaint of low sexual arousal, which is related to the orgasmic dysfunction. Although cases of primary orgasmic dysfunction respond easily to intervention, this is most likely due to the greater incidence of relationship problems that co-occur with secondary orgasmic dysfunction. A somewhat typical case of secondary orgasmic dysfunction was described by Beck (1985), involving Sarah, a woman with a 13-year history of anorgasmia; its onset followed the development of agoraphobia. Although Sarah had been successfully treated for the anxiety disorder, a number of relationship and communication problems remained and interfered with her ability to relax during sexual contact. Additionally, her husband, Bill, had developed premature ejaculation, originally intended to reduce his wife's discomfort by abbreviating what appeared to be an unpleasant experience for her. Successful resolution of this case required interventions designed to affect both sexual and marital changes, as is often the case with secondary anorgasmia.

BEHAVIORAL TREATMENT OF SEXUAL DYSFUNCTION

General Prognostic Factors

Irrespective of the particular form of dysfunction, several general factors have been identified as predictors of treatment outcome and attrition, assuming the absence of organic contributions to the dysfunction. The presence of psychopathology, particularly affective disorder, is a poor prognostic indicator, as is a strained marital relationship. Hawton and Catalan (1986) demonstrated that both therapist and client ratings of the quality of the relationship are the best indicators of treatment response; other data have shown that marital distress predicts premature termination and failure to comply with behavioral homework. Previous sexual experience does not appear to determine treatment outcome, with the possible exception of a lack of previous experience serving as a favorable predictor for women with vaginismus (Hawton & Catalan, 1986). As discussed previously, primary dysfunctions in women respond more favorably to treatment relative to secondary dysfunctions. For men, the duration of dysfunction appears to be a better predictor of treatment response, with more chronic problems showing greater resistance to change. Men with acute onset dysfunctions appear to respond more favorably to treatment relative to men with insidious onset disorder (Beck, 1990).

Behavioral Intervention Strategies

In conceptualizing the treatment of sexual dysfunction, interventions can be grouped into two categories. The first category includes those which often are used for all of the sexual disorders described above. These strategies are derived from large-scale sex therapy programs, such as Masters and Johnson's (1970) landmark clinic. These interventions have formed the backbone of sex therapy, as will be described in the next section. The second type of intervention includes approaches that have evolved for the treatment of specific disorders and are not applied in other cases. Table 9.2 provides a guide to the use of both forms of interventions, although, for any particular case, the specific interventions chosen should follow from a careful pretreatment assessment and behavioral formulation of problem areas. The separation of general and specific interventions is not intended to imply that a package treatment strategy should be applied to any given case. Individuals with sexual dysfunctions present complex problems that require thoughtful formulation of individual treatment goals.

General Interventions

The foundation of current sex therapy rests on Masters and Johnson's (1970) conceptualization of etiological factors in sexual dysfunction, which includes a lack of adequate information about the sexual response, negative sexual attitudes, a history

TABLE 9.2. Behavioral Strategies and Target Goals

Treatment Strategy	Target Goal
General Interventions	
Ban on intercourse	To interrupt the negative cycle of sexual interactions
Nongenital pleasuring	To increase sensual contact and reduce performance pressure
Sensate focus	To shift cognitive focus to pleasurable physical sensations To enhance communication
Systematic desensitization	To reduce anxiety
Skill training (self-help manuals, demonstration films)	To increase knowledge of sexual anatomy and physiology, to improve sexual technique
Communication training	To improve dyadic problem-solving and facilitate expression of sexual needs and desires
Interventions for Specific Disorders	
Directed masturbation	To improve the consistency and quality of orgasm (female orgasmic dysfunction)
Kegel exercises	To increase PC muscle strength, with indirect effect of improving orgasmic potential (female orgasm dysfunction, retarded ejaculation)
Vaginal dilators and relaxation	To diminish contraction of the vaginal muscles (vaginismus)
Stop-go/squeeze technique	To facilitate voluntary control of ejaculation (premature ejaculation)
Vibrator stimulation	To enhance erotic sensations (retarded ejaculation)
Role plays Facilitation of insight Cognitive restructuring	To address factors contributing to low sexual desire (provisional)

of sexual encounters that have been unarousing and frustrating, and anxiety concerning the quality of one's sexual performance. The initial step used in treatment is to place a ban on intercourse, with the goals of removing performance pressures and interrupting the self-fulfilling cycle of negative sexual experiences. Although there are no empirical data on the therapeutic value of this instruction, it is useful in removing the onus of sexual initiation from one partner and helping to reformulate the problem as a couples problem. Because most therapeutic interventions require active participation from both members of the couple, strategies designed to reduce labeling one partner as "dysfunctional" and the other as "uninvolved" include interviewing techniques and the assignment of homework to both partners.

Sensate focus and nongenital pleasuring constitute a major ingredient of the general interventions. Sensate focus exercises involve instructions to attend to the wide variety of physical sensations arising from the partner's touch. Couples are instructed to alternate the roles of giver and receiver and to experiment with different verbal and nonverbal forms of communicating their likes and dislikes. These instructions are practiced in the context of nongenital pleasuring, with the goal of reducing performance anxiety and helping the couple to establish new patterns that will be arousing.

Although the mechanism of action of these interventions is conceptualized as anxiety reduction, there are data to suggest that low sexual arousal may not be maintained by anxiety per se (e.g., Barlow, 1986; Beck & Barlow, 1984). From a programmatic line of studies exploring the effects of increased physiological arousal and cognitive factors on sexual responding in men with erectile dysfunction, it appears that a process akin to worry (or preoccupation with physical responding and the partner's reaction) and a shift in attention away from erotic cues may maintain problems of low sexual arousal and, possibly, orgasmic difficulties. Although replication of these studies with female subjects has yet to be undertaken, these data indicate that sensate focus and nongenital pleasuring may achieve therapeutic effects by interrupting this cognitive attentional process and helping the individual to refocus on erotic thoughts and cues. Additionally, the process of gradually introducing more intimate forms of sexual contact is akin to self-paced gradual exposure, as employed in the treatment of phobias and other anxiety disorders. Empirical examination of variations of this approach have yet to be undertaken.

Another treatment approach that is based on an anxiety-reduction model is systematic desensitization. Although most useful for cases where marked anxiety is present, systematic desensitization has been applied to the full range of sexual dysfunctions (Caird & Wincze, 1977), with the noted effects of anxiety reduction, increased orgasmic frequency (for women), and improved sexual communication. Given that anxiety may not play a central role in maintaining most sexual disorders, particularly low sexual arousal, it is difficult to account for the efficacy of systematic desensitization. At present, this approach is not used widely, except in cases where sexual anxiety is prominent (sexual aversion).

Another component of the general interventions involves sex education and is designed to improve sexual skills by expanding an individual's knowledge of the sexual response, sexual technique, and communication skills. It is cost-effective to use self-help books as the medium for providing accurate information to clients, as well as for helping to establish greater understanding of the diversity of "normal" sexual behaviors. Books by Zilbergeld (1978), Barbach (1975), and Schover (1984) have proven useful and are written in a style that does not offend or ridicule clients. The use of demonstration films can assist in refining sexual skills and can be used with an individual or couple. To facilitate communication skills, in-session exercises targeting specific ways to share feelings and to give and receive feedback are used. To illustrate, in the case of Sarah and Bill, described earlier, communication training was used to address a chronic lack of communication and to help the couple articulate discrepancies in their expectations of one another. At first, Sarah and Bill were most comfortable with discussions concerning changes in their sexual relationship. In later sessions, the focus of communication training was expanded to include their use of leisure time and Bill's long-standing concerns over Sarah's ability to cope with increased independence. (Greater detail of the process of integrating communication training with sex therapy techniques with this couple can be found in Beck (1985).) To date, no studies have examined the unique contribution of these skill-building interventions, although these approaches have been included as one component of treatment in empirical studies of the efficacy of sex therapy (reviewed below).

Frequently, through the use of these interventions, previously denied relationship conflicts surface, given the stipulation that the couple reciprocate pleasuring and experiment with new forms of communication. For example, Rust, Golombok, and Collier (1988) reported that marital dissatisfaction correlates highly with sexual problems, particularly male erectile dysfunction and premature ejaculation. Although behavioral sex and marital therapy share some common elements, the clinical decision to address marital problems or to focus on the sexual dysfunction can be difficult. Unfortunately, there are no conclusive guidelines for this decision process. The empirical data are mixed; some studies demonstrate positive transfer from treating marital distress to increased sexual satisfaction (and vice versa), while other studies show no generalization effects. Most sex therapists will attempt to intervene first with sexual problems, unless general discord within the relationship precludes the couple from effectively participating in homework assignments.

In considering the efficacy of the general intervention strategies, it is important to note that most available studies have examined the effects of these interventions when delivered *in toto,* relative to various control conditions. Thus, the only statements concerning efficacy that can be made are rather general, with more refined understanding of the impact of specific treatment components awaiting further research. Across studies, these strategies appear to lead to improvement in approximately 66% of clients (e.g., Crown & D'Ardenne, 1982; Kilmann & Auerbach, 1979; Mills & Kilmann, 1982). Unfortunately, clinical practice has tended to advance far ahead of research validation, resulting in large gaps in our knowledge. For example, there are few established guidelines for matching specific components of the general interventions with client characteristics. Thus, what is known of the advantages and disadvantages of each technique tends to be culled from clinical observation rather than empirical examination. However, while use of these intervention approaches may not be necessary in all cases, it would appear that the general intervention strategies are effective for many types of sexual dysfunction. Specific issues involving long-term outcome, premature termination, failure to adhere to homework assignments, and definition of treatment success (and failure) will be discussed below.

Interventions Designed for Specific Disorders

In addition to the backdrop of general interventions, particular treatment strategies are used to address many of the sexual dysfunctions.

Directed Masturbation

The most effective approach for orgasmic dysfunction in women, particularly primary dysfunction, is a program developed by LoPiccolo and Lobitz (1972). The basic components of this program include self-exploration and body awareness, development of sexual fantasy, and directed masturbation exercises, as outlined in a self-help book (Heiman & LoPiccolo, 1988). Because masturbation is the most probable method for a woman to reach orgasm, this program leads the woman through a guided series of activities designed to increase her awareness of genital sensations, expand her range of erotic imagery, and help her to identify types of stimulation that are arousing. At the outset, these activities are done alone, with introduction of the sexual partner in the later stages. Throughout this program, the goal of female orgasm during intercourse is deemphasized, because this is not always realistic.

Empirical studies of this program indicate a high success rate for primary orgasmic dysfunction. For example, LoPiccolo and Stock (1986) reported that 95% of women participating in this program achieved orgasm through masturbation, with 40% reporting orgasm during intercourse following the program. When Riley and Riley (1978) compared directed masturbation with a combined sensate focus and supportive psychotherapy approach, the results indicated that directed masturbation was the superior treatment approach. Recently, Morokoff and LoPiccolo (1986) demonstrated that directed masturbation can be delivered in a minimal therapist–self-help format without a loss of effectiveness.

Directed masturbation also has been delivered in a group format, using groups ranging from 4 to 10 in size. Variations within this format indicate that one therapist is as effective as two; that the gender of the therapist does not affect outcome; and that massed and spaced sessions generally are equally effective (Libman, Fichten, & Brender, 1985). Although questions remain concerning the use of group treatment—such as the need to include male partners, the ideal number of treatment sessions, and the effects of mixing women who have primary and secondary orgasmic dysfunctions—the consensus across empirical studies indicates that this format is a cost-effective means of treating orgasmic dysfunction, for clients without severe psychopathology or significant relationship problems.

Kegel Exercises

Kegel's (1952) proposal, that increased strength of the pubococcygeus (PC) muscle surrounding the vagina contributes to an increased frequency and intensity of orgasm, led to the development of PC-strengthening exercises. These are performed daily in the treatment of female orgasmic dysfunction and male retarded ejaculation. Although clinical reports support the value of Kegel exercises, empirical data do not indicate a consistent relationship between PC muscle strength and orgasmic potential in women (Chambless et al., 1984). It is possible that Kegel exercises achieve their reported positive effects by increasing the client's awareness of genital sensations and, possibly, by interrupting distracting thoughts, much like sensate focus exercises. Given that Kegel exercises are a simple intervention to implement (see Table 9.3), there is no rationale against their use, although their efficacy may be questionable.

Vaginal Dilators

Because vaginismus is the result of contraction of the vaginal musculature caused by a fear of penetration, the recommended treatment approach involves a combination of relaxation and progressive dilation of the vagina. A key therapeutic ingredient

TABLE 9.3 Outline of Practice for Kegel Exercises

Slow Kegels—Tighten the PC muscle and hold it as you do when you stop the flow of urine for a slow count of 3. Then relax the muscle.

Quick Kegels—Tighten and relax the PC muscle as rapidly as you can. At first it will feel like a flutter. You will gradually gain more control.

Pull in/push out—Pull in the entire pelvic area as though trying to suck up water into the genitals. Then push out or bear down as if trying to push the imaginary water out. (This exercise will use a number of stomach or abdominal muscles as well as the PC muscle.)

Repetitions—At first do 10 of these exercises (one set) 3 times a day (3 exercises × 10 times × 3 times a day = 90 total exercises to start). Each week add 5 more times to each exercise. Example: Week 2: 3 sets × 15 times × 3 times a day; Week 3: 3 sets × 20 times × 3 times a day; Week 4: 3 sets × 25 times × 3 times a day. Keep doing 3 sets a day.

You can help yourself remember to do the exercises by associating them with some activity you do every day: talking on the phone, watching television, waiting in line, or lying in bed. Think of activities that don't require much moving around.

Don't worry if your muscles seem to get tired easily at first; that's normal for exercising any new muscle group. Rest between sets for a few seconds and start again. Remember to keep breathing naturally.

Women can place one or two fingers into the vagina and men one finger on each side of the base of the penis in order to feel the movement and strength of the muscle. You may also watch the movement by looking at your genitals in a hand mirror. Doing these things with your Kegels will help you learn them more rapidly.

---

of dilation is that the rate and diameter of the dilators chosen are under the woman's control. Efficacy rates appear similar whether dilation is performed in the gynecologist's office (by the physician), by the partner, or by the woman herself, using dilators graded in diameter and slowly increasing in size as the woman becomes less fearful of penetration. If the couple is patient in using this approach, without rushing the rate of progress, the treatment of vaginismus with dilators is highly effective, with an estimated 100% success rate. This figure conceals the fact that poor compliance or dropout from a program of dilation may indicate an unreported sexual trauma or general relationship distress.

Stop-Go/Squeeze Technique

Another highly effective intervention is the squeeze technique, also termed the stop-go or pause technique. This approach is used in the treatment of premature ejaculation and is designed to help the man to develop a greater awareness of arousing sensations prior to ejaculation. In the squeeze technique, the man is stimulated to a high level of arousal, at which point pressure is applied beneath the coronal ridge of the penis, effectively reducing arousal and postponing ejaculation. The stop-go technique follows the same principle, except the couple is instructed to "pause" (instead of squeeze) and engage in nongenital pleasuring. It is possible that this approach achieves the reported 90 to 98% effectiveness rates through a counter-conditioning extinction process of crowding the threshold (Gutherie, 1952). To date, we have no real understanding of the mechanism of action of the squeeze technique, although it can be taught with equal effectiveness in individual or group formats. An additional advantage of this intervention is its utility with men who do not currently have a sexual partner. In these instances, transfer of ejaculatory control to sex with a partner usually occurs.

Vibrator Stimulation

Although at present there are few clear guidelines for the treatment of retarded ejaculation, LoPiccolo (1977) suggested the use of vibrator stimulation to enhance erotic sensations for men with this disorder.

To date, no empirical data are available on the effectiveness of this approach.

Interventions for Low Sexual Desire: A Challenge

Despite the attention that sexual desire disorders have attracted in the literature, we currently have few guidelines for the effective treatment of these problems. The most complete approach developed to date has been described by Friedman and Hogan (1985). This treatment included four elements, specifically:

- Exercises designed to heighten emotional awareness (using role plays and other approaches drawn from the Gestalt school of psychotherapy);
- The use of traditional insight-oriented interventions to highlight factors within the relationship that maintain low desire;
- Cognitive restructuring for thoughts that interfere with sexual contact;
- Behavioral strategies designed to increase arousal, such as sensate focus and nongenital pleasuring exercises, as described above.

In this program, these elements are tailored to the particular couple, as needed. The program is based on the following assumptions:

- Low desire is maintained by a lack of affective awareness;
- Insight into the reasons for the dysfunction is valuable;
- Both members of the couple need to be actively involved in treatment;
- A series of graded sexual tasks is important for restoring adequate sexual functioning. Interestingly, no distinction is drawn between low sexual desire and sexual aversion by Friedman and Hogan.

To illustrate, these authors described the case of Ann and Bob, who presented with a 7-year history of intermittent sexual problems, including premature ejaculation and erectile failure on Bob's part and inhibited arousal on Ann's part. Bob's pattern of low desire had developed approximately 1 year prior to therapy. Following a thorough assessment, it was hypothesized that six factors maintained these problems: Bob's performance anxiety over attaining an erection; communication dysfunction; disagreement over whether to have children (the couple was not using contraception); their mutual history of other sexual dysfunctions; Bob and Ann's guilt over "letting go" during sex; and a lack of sexual attraction to Ann. Friedman and Hogan provided a session-by-session outline of interventions that stemmed from the four treatment elements described above (heightening emotional awareness, facilitating insight, cognitive restructuring, and behavioral strategies). With this couple, the beginning stages of therapy focused on providing insight, with introduction of cognitive restructuring beginning at week 4. The latter stages of therapy included more in-depth discussion of communication problems and several Gestalt exercises designed to reduce guilt. Sensate focus and directed masturbation were integrated throughout the course of the 15-week program. Although this approach has not been used extensively, one outcome study (Schover & LoPiccolo, 1982) showed positive results. Given that sexual desire does not seem to be affected by other behavioral sex therapy approaches, continued development of effective interventions appears warranted.

Combining Behavioral Sex Therapy and Medical Treatment Approaches

In the past decade, numerous advances in the medical treatment of sexual dysfunction have been made, particularly for erectile dysfunction. Before considering the integration of sex therapy with medical (and surgical) interventions, a brief review of these treatments is necessary. Perhaps the most widely publicized medical intervention for erectile dysfunction is the surgical placement of a prosthetic device within the cavernosal tissue of the penis, which permits penile rigidity sufficient for intercourse. Various models of penile prostheses currently are available, including a semirigid device and a multicomponent hydraulic inflatable device, which allows tumescence and detumescence as saline is pumped in and out of rods implanted in the penis (Krane et al., 1989). Although the risks of mechanical failure and extrusion vary by the type of device used, many couples report increased sexual satisfaction postoperatively, for intervals up to 4 years (Tiefer & Melman, 1989).

A related technique, designed for men with neurologically based erectile dysfunction, involves intracavernosal injections of papervine or another smooth-muscle relaxant. The man is taught how to inject a predetermined dose of these medications, which produce an erection lasting between 30 minutes and 1 hour. Possible side effects include infection; development of fibrotic nodules, which may create penile curvature; hypotension; and disturbance of liver function (Krane et al., 1989). To date, there are no long-term studies of the effects of intracavernosal injection therapy. For men with erectile dysfunction caused by vascular impairment, microvascular bypass surgery and/or ligation of the venous drainage system can be performed. Widely varying rates of success have been reported with these techniques, and careful screening of candidates for surgery is recommended (Krane et al., 1989). No long-term studies have been reported for these techniques.

The final intervention that has been developed for men with erectile dysfunction involves vacuum constriction devices, which consist of a vacuum source connected to a plastic cylinder that is placed over the flaccid penis. The pressure in the cylinder creates tumescence, which then is maintained via constriction bands, placed at the base of the penis. Potential complications include ejaculatory difficulties and penile pain. Given the relative novelty of this procedure, little is known concerning negative side effects and long-term course.

Hormonal imbalances or deficiencies are corrected via exogenous hormone administration, for both men and women. Although increases in vaginal vasocongestion have been difficult to document in women receiving such treatment (Myers & Morokoff, 1986), the effects on sexual functioning appear to be positive. For cases of prolactin-secreting tumors of the pituitary, radiation or surgical removal, followed by hormone replacement, appears effective in restoring hormonal balance.

Although these medical interventions vary with respect to the degree of invasiveness, involvement of the individual in enacting the procedure, relative risks and benefits, and potential side effects, most writers consider integration of sex therapy techniques as vital in their successful implementation (Schover, 1989). For example, one clinic noted that, if psychogenic factors are relevant in maintaining erectile dysfunction, papervine autoinjection therapy tends to be rejected or regarded as unsatisfactory (Althof et al., 1988). Organically based sexual dysfunctions tend to produce disturbances in self-esteem, body image, communication patterns, and feelings of trust and intimacy. In keeping with this observation, Schover (1989) outlined a brief sexual counseling approach for individuals with chronic illness. Sex education, cognitive-behavioral methods to dispel maladaptive sexual attitudes, sensate focus exercises, techniques for overcoming physical handicaps, and brief marital therapy were included. Schover suggested that most individuals will benefit from 2 to 5 treatment sessions, indicating that sex therapy can be a briefer intervention when used in conjunction with medical treatments. As with other forms of behavioral sex therapy, inclusion of the partner is desired, particularly with those medical interventions that require partner support or assistance (e.g., the inflatable prothesis, autoinjection therapy).

Issues in the Clinical Practice of Behavioral Sex Therapy

As with any behavioral intervention, a number of issues arise in the clinical application of sex therapy. In the face of impressive efficacy rates at the end of therapy, questions can be raised about the long-term outcome of sex therapy. Originally, Masters and Johnson (1970) reported excellent outcomes 5 years after sex therapy, with nearly all couples sustaining positive changes. However, Masters and Johnson followed only cases judged to be treatment successes, thus biasing their results. Additionally, doubt has been raised concerning their choice of outcome statistics (Zilbergeld & Evans, 1980). Subsequent reports have indicated less positive long-term outcomes, suggesting that improvement of target problems often is not sustained over time, particularly for disorders of low sexual desire. Unfortunately, many of the available studies of this issue suffer from methodological problems, such as low response rates, biased samples (only couples with good outcome consented to be followed), and reliance on postal questionnaires rather than interviews. A prospective follow-up study that provided perhaps the best indicator of long-term outcome was reported recently by Hawton, Catalan, Martin, and Fagg (1986). In this report, 140 couples who had entered sex therapy 1 to 6 years earlier were interviewed; of this sample, 61% had completed treatment, during an average of 15 therapy sessions. Therapist ratings of posttreatment outcome suggested that, in 58% of the cases, the presenting problem was resolved or much improved; in 42%, the problem was unresolved or worsened. All couples were included in the follow-up regardless of whether they had completed treatment.

The results of this report are particularly interesting because it is suggested that specific sexual dysfunctions have different long-term outcomes. Follow-up was possible in 106 (75%) of the couples, and, in most cases, both members of the couple were assessed. Gains made by couples originally presenting with erectile dysfunction were well maintained, but the long-term outcome for premature ejaculation was relatively poor. For the female sexual dysfunctions, the long-term outcome for couples originally presenting with low sexual desire was poor, particularly given the fact that posttreatment changes often were marginal. Couples who presented with vaginismus reported excellent long-term outcomes. Unfortunately, the number of cases with female orgasmic dysfunction, retarded ejaculation, and inhibited sexual desire in males was too small to derive meaningful outcome information. Closer examination of factors that predicted long-term outcome indicated that a history of psychiatric treatment or psychiatric disorder was correlated with poorer outcome, while the communication skills of the couple at pretreatment and a positive overall relationship predicted better outcome. Although these data were derived from National Health Service settings in the U.K., which have different referral patterns from those in the United States, there are few reasons to suspect that different long-term outcome rates would be obtained in other countries.

A related issue in considering the long-term effects of behavioral sex therapy is the untreated course of the sexual dysfunctions. Specifically, it has been argued that any form of therapy can be judged effective only to the extent that a greater proportion of individuals receiving treatment are improved, relative to those improving without intervention (Landis, 1937). Although reliable data are not available for all of the sexual disorders discussed here, Segraves, Knopf, and Camic (1982) reported that 12.5% to 15% of men evaluated but not treated for erectile dysfunction experienced remission of their problem over a 1-year interval. A briefer duration of erectile dysfunction tended to be associated with remission. DeAmicis, Goldberg, LoPiccolo, Friedman, and Davies (1984) addressed a similar question for both men and women who were evaluated but not treated for sexual dysfunction. Although over half of this sample indicated that they subsequently had sought and received some form of treatment during the 3-year interval following initial assessment, the results indicated that treatment (unspecified) did not significantly influence females' sexual functioning, and males who had received therapy experienced greater sexual difficulties than those who had not sought intervention. Overall, women reported improvement over time, particularly with problems of low sexual arousal and anorgasmia. Men, in contrast, reported a mixed course: premature ejaculation and erectile dysfunction improved over time, but most cases of retarded ejaculation and low sexual interest were judged as either unchanged or worse. More information is required concerning the untreated course of each of the sexual dysfunctions prior to forming any conclusions regarding the long-term effectiveness of behavioral sex therapy.

It is not uncommon for the sex therapist to note that some proportion of clients drops out of treatment prior to receiving a complete course of behavioral treatment. A review of available treatment studies (Zimmer, 1987) indicates a dropout rate of approximately 30% across both private practices and sex therapy clinics. Premature termination is a common occurrence in sex therapy. The most typical reason offered for dropout from therapy is relationship problems. Some decisions to seek sex therapy may constitute an attempt to avoid a more serious relationship problem. In these cases, premature termination usually is preceded by considerable resistance to intervention, particularly homework assignments and in-session exercises. In other cases, it appears that the sexual dysfunction represents the sole remaining aspect of the relationship; it is not unusual for these individuals to terminate therapy once the topic of separation and divorce has been raised and decided upon. In handling these issues, it is critical for the therapist to avoid being placed in the role of "judge," in order to prevent the establishment of coalitions. As with behavioral marital therapy, the therapist must be constantly aware of the shifting emotional interplay within the couple and of individual attempts to coerce a partner through the therapeutic medium.

Occasionally, premature termination results from individual problems. For example, Everaerd (1983) described the case of a man who prematurely terminated treatment for secondary erectile dysfunction. He had been married twice previously, and both wives had died of uterine cancer. With his present partner, he reported consistent erectile problems. A pretreatment assessment indicated that incomplete grieving and a fear of recurrence of cancer in his sexual partner were probable maintaining factors; however, the client rejected this formulation and insisted that he did not wish to discuss his former wives, but rather simply to restore his erectile functioning. He left therapy and, presumably, would not have been compliant with treatment suggestions had he remained. Other examples of individual factors that influence dropout from treatment include a past history of trauma, extreme unassertiveness, and an undisclosed extramarital relationship. To date, we have few guidelines to differentiate individual and relationship factors that predict dropout, although lack of compliance with therapeutic instructions probably serves as the best warning indicator that premature termination may occur.

A final issue of relevance in the clinical use of sex therapy is the definition of treatment success. Given the wide range of sexual behaviors that are considered normal, as well as the fact that couples who define themselves as sexually functional report a high prevalence of the problems discussed here (Frank et al., 1978), the use of preestablished criteria for treatment successes is untenable. Rather, it appears necessary to rely on multiple indices, including client satisfaction with sexual functioning; reports of functioning in relevant behavioral domains (desire, arousal, and orgasm); and therapist ratings of the couple's communication skills, overall relationship quality, and sexual functioning. Given that sexual difficulties are likely to recur at some point following treatment, whether because of transient life stresses or a tendency for the couple to return to former patterns of sexual interaction, it is important to include an assessment of the couple's ability to address and problem-solve issues that influence sexual functioning. For example, Hawton et al. (1986) reported that, among cases judged as treatment successes, adaptive coping strategies often were employed when sexual problems recurred, including the reintroduction of sensate focus exercises, accepting the sexual problem as a passing phase, and reading a self-help book.

SUMMARY AND FUTURE DIRECTIONS

Throughout this chapter, a number of areas in need of further study were highlighted, particularly with reference to differential diagnosis of psychogenic and organic factors in the etiology of dysfunction, treatment parameters, and the mechanism of action of many of the interventions involved in behavioral sex therapy. What is obvious from these issues is that the clinical use of sex therapy has been shown to be effective, yet many questions remain. Unfortunately, empirical studies of sex therapy have become less numerous in recent years, creating the false impression that we know all that we need to know concerning these interventions. In certain respects, the formal recognition of disorders of sexual desire offers the opportunity for renewed vigor in this field, given the fact that traditional sex therapy often is not effective for these clients. For example, the possibility of examining the interaction of pharmacological and behavioral interventions for low desire states would appear to be a fruitful area for future research, as well as allowing greater sophistication in the development of sex therapy techniques. In light of our current knowledge of sexual behavior and existing clinical needs, the next three decades are likely to hold as many exciting developments as the previous three have. There is no doubt that behavioral principles and treatment strategies will continue to play a central role in this process.

REFERENCES

Althof, S. E., Turner, L. A., Levine, S. B., Risen, C. B., Bodner, D., Kursh, D., & Resnick, M. I. (1988). *Why do so many people drop out from injection therapy for impotence? The view after two years.* Paper presented at the Society for Sex Therapy and Research, New York.

American Psychiatric Association. (1987). *Diagnostic and statistical manual of mental disorders* (3rd ed. rev.). Washington, DC: Author.

Barbach, L. G. (1975). *For yourself: The fulfillment of female sexuality.* New York: Signet.

Barlow, D. H. (1986). Causes of sexual dysfunction: The role of anxiety and cognitive interference. *Journal of Consulting and Clinical Psychology, 54,* 140–148.

Beck, J. G. (1985). Secondary orgasmic dysfunction: Modifying sexual and marital scripts. In M. Hersen and C. G. Last (Eds.), *Behavior therapy casebook* (pp. 185–199). New York: Springer.

Beck, J. G. (1987). Self-generated distraction in erectile dysfunction: The role of attentional processes. *Advances in Behavior Research and Therapy, 8,* 205–221.

Beck, J. G. (1990). Brief psychotherapy for the sexual dysfunctions. In R. A. Wells and V. J. Giannetti (Eds.), *Handbook of the brief psychotherapies* (pp. 461–492). New York: Plenum.

Beck, J. G., & Barlow, D. H. (1984). Current conceptualization of sexual dysfunction: A review and an alternative perspective. *Clinical Psychology Review, 4,* 363–378.

Caird, W., & Wincze, J. P. (1977). *Sex therapy.* New York: Harper & Row.

Chambless, D. L., Sultan, F. E., Stern, T. E., O'Neill, C., Garrison, S., & Jackson, A. (1984). Effects of pubococcygeal exercise on coital orgasm in women. *Journal of Consulting and Clinical Psychology, 52,* 114–118.

Crown, S., & D'Ardenne, P. (1982). Symposium on sexual dysfunction: Controversies, methods, results. *British Journal of Psychiatry, 140,* 70–77.

DeAmicis, L. A., Goldberg, D. C., LoPiccolo, J., Friedman, J., & Davies, L. (1984). Three-year follow-up of couples evaluated for sexual dysfunction. *Journal of Sex and Marital Therapy, 10,* 215–228.

Everaerd, W. T. A. M. (1983). Failures in treating sexual dysfunctions. In E. B. Foa and P. M. G. Emmelkamp (Eds.), *Failures in behavior therapy* (pp. 392–405). New York: Wiley.

Fagan, P. J., Schmidt, C. W., Jr., Wise, T. N., & Derogatis, L. R. (1988). Sexual dysfunction and dual psychiatric diagnoses. *Comprehensive Psychiatry, 29,* 278–284.

Fracher, J. C., Leiblum, S. R., & Rosen, R. C. (1981). Recent advances in the comprehensive evaluation of erectile dysfunction. *International Journal of Mental Health, 10,* 110–121.

Frank, E., Anderson, C., & Rubenstein, D. (1978). Frequency of sexual dysfunction in "normal" couples. *New England Journal of Medicine, 299,* 111–115.

Friedman, J. M., & Hogan, D. R. (1985). Sexual dysfunction: Low sexual desire. In D. H. Barlow (Ed.), *Clinical handbook of psychological disorders* (pp. 417–461). New York: Guilford.

Gutherie, E. R. (1952). *The psychology of learning.* New York: Harper & Row.

Hawton, K., & Catalan, J. (1986). Prognostic factors in sex therapy. *Behaviour Research and Therapy, 24,* 377–385.

Hawton, K., Catalan, J., Martin, P., & Fagg, J. (1986). Long-term outcome of sex therapy. *Behaviour Research and Therapy, 24,* 665–675.

Heiman, J. R., & LoPiccolo, J. (1988). *Becoming orgasmic.* Englewood Cliffs, NJ: Prentice-Hall.

Jensen, S. B. (1981). Diabetic sexual dysfunction: A comparative study of 160 insulin-treated diabetic men and women and an age-matched control group. *Archives of Sexual Behavior, 10,* 493–504.

Kaplan, H. S. (1979). *Disorders of desire.* New York: Brunner/Mazel.

Kegel, A. (1952). Sexual functions of the pubococcygeus muscle. *Western Journal of Surgery, 60,* 521–524.

Kilmann, P. R., & Auerbach, R. (1979). Treatments of premature ejaculation and psychogenic impotence: A critical review of the literature, *Archives of Sexual Behavior, 8,* 81–100.

Krane, R. J., Goldstein, I., & DeTejada, I. S. (1989). Impotence. *New England Journal of Medicine, 321,* 1648–1659.

Landis, C. A. (1937). A statistical evaluation of psychotherapeutic methods. In L. E. Hinsie (Ed.), *Concepts and problems of psychotherapy* (pp. 155–165). New York: Columbia University Press.

Leiblum, S. R., & Rosen, R. C. (Eds.). (1988). *Sexual desire disorders.* New York: Guilford.

Leiblum, S. R., & Segraves, R. T. (1989). Sex therapy with aging adults. In S. R. Leiblum and R. C. Rosen (Eds.), *Principles and practice of sex therapy* (2nd ed.; pp. 352–381). New York: Guilford.

Libman, E., Fichten, C. S., & Brender, W. (1985). The role of therapeutic format in the treatment of sexual dysfunction: A review. *Clinical Psychology Review, 5*, 103–117.

Lief, H. I. (1977). Inhibited sexual desire. *Medical Aspects of Human Sexuality, 7*, 94–95.

LoPiccolo, J. (1977). Direct treatment of sexual dysfunction in the couple. In J. Money & H. Musaph (Eds.), *Handbook of sexology* (pp. 1227–1244). New York: Elsevier/North Holland.

LoPiccolo, J., & Lobitz, W. C. (1972). The role of masturbation in the treatment of orgasmic dysfunction. *Archives of Sexual Behavior, 2*, 163–171.

LoPiccolo, J., & Stock, W. (1986). Treatment of sexual dysfunction. *Journal of Consulting and Clinical Psychology, 54*, 158–167.

LoPiccolo, J., & Stock, W. (1987). Sexual counseling in gynecological practice. In Z. Rosenwaks, F. Benjamin, & M. Stone (Eds.), *Basic gynecology*. New York: Macmillan.

Masters, W. H. (1986). Sexual dysfunction as an aftermath of sexual assault of men by women. *Journal of Sex and Marital Therapy, 12*, 35–45.

Masters, W. H., & Johnson, V. E. (1966). *Human sexual response*. Boston: Little, Brown.

Masters, W. H., & Johnson, V. E. (1970). *Human sexual inadequacy*. Boston: Little, Brown.

Mills, K. H., & Kilmann, P. R. (1982). Group treatment of sexual dysfunction: A review of the outcome literature. *Journal of Sex and Marital Therapy, 8*, 259–296.

Morokoff, P. J., & LoPiccolo, J. (1986). A comparative evaluation of minimal therapist contact and 15-session treatment for female orgasmic dysfunction. *Journal of Consulting and Clinical Psychology, 54*, 294–300.

Munjack, D. J., & Kanno, P. H. (1979). Retarded ejaculation: A review. *Archives of Sexual Behavior, 8*, 139–150.

Myers, L. S., & Morokoff, P. J. (1986). Physiological and subjective sexual arousal in pre- and postmenopausal women and postmenopausal women taking replacement therapy. *Psychophysiology, 23*, 283–292.

Nutter, D., & Condron, M. K. (1983). Sexual fantasy and activity patterns of females with inhibited sexual desire versus normal controls. *Journal of Sex and Marital Therapy, 9*, 276–282.

Nutter, D. E., & Condron, M. K. (1985). Sexual fantasy and activity patterns of males with inhibited sexual desire and males with erectile dysfunction versus normal controls. *Journal of Sex and Marital Therapy, 11*, 91–98.

Riley, A. J., & Riley, G. J. (1978). A controlled study to evaluate directed masturbation in the management of primary orgasmic failure in women. *British Journal of Psychiatry, 133*, 404–409.

Robinson, P. (1976). *The modernization of sex*. New York: Harper & Row.

Rosen, R. C., & Beck, J. G. (1988). *Patterns of sexual arousal*. New York: Guilford.

Rust, J., Golombok, S., & Collier, J. (1988). Marital problems and sexual dysfunction: How are they related? *British Journal of Psychiatry, 152*, 629–631.

Sandberg, G., & Quevillon, R. P. (1987). Dyspareunia: An integrated approach to assessment and diagnosis. *Journal of Family Practice, 24*, 66–69.

Sarrel, P. M., & Masters, W. H. (1982). Sexual molestation of men by women. *Archives of Sexual Behavior, 11*, 117–131.

Schover, L. (1984). *Prime time: Sexual health for men over fifty*. New York: Holt, Rinehart, & Winston.

Schover, L. R. (1989). Sexual problems in chronic illness. In S. R. Leiblum and R. C. Rosen (Eds.), *Principles and practice of sex therapy* (2nd ed.; pp. 319–351). New York: Guilford.

Schover, L. R., & Jensen, S. B. (1988). *Sexuality and chronic illness: A comprehensive approach*. New York: Guilford.

Schover, L., & LoPiccolo, J. (1982). Treatment effectiveness for dysfunctions of sexual desire. *Journal of Sex and Marital Therapy, 8*, 179–197.

Schreiner-Engel, P., & Schiavi, R. C. (1986). Lifetime psychopathology in individuals with low sexual desire. *Journal of Nervous and Mental Disease, 174*, 646–651.

Segraves, R. T., Knopf, J., & Camic, P. (1982). Spontaneous remission in erectile impotence. *Behaviour Research and Therapy, 20*, 89–91.

Shen, W. W., & Sata, L. S. (1983). Inhibited female orgasm resulting from psychotropic drugs: A clinical review. *Journal of Reproductive Medicine, 28,* 497–499.

Spiess, W. F., Geer, J. H., & O'Donohue, W. T. (1984). Premature ejaculation: Investigation of factors in ejaculatory latency. *Journal of Abnormal Psychology, 93,* 242–245.

Swartzman, L., & Leiblum, S. (1987). Changing perspectives on the menopause. *Journal of Psychosomatic Obstetrics and Gynecology, 6,* 11–24.

Tiefer, L., & Melman, A. (1989). Comprehensive evaluation of erectile dysfunction and medical treatments. In S. R. Leiblum and R. C. Rosen (Eds.), *Principles and practice of sex therapy* (2nd ed.; pp. 207–236). New York: Guilford.

Wolpe, J. (1958). *Psychotherapy by reciprocal inhibition.* Stanford, CA: Stanford University Press.

Zilbergeld, B. (1978). *Male sexuality.* Toronto: Bantam Books.

Zilbergeld, B., & Evans, M. (1980). The inadequacy of Masters and Johnson. *Psychology Today, 14,* 29–43.

Zimmer, D. (1987). Motivational issues in premature termination of treatment for sexual dysfunction. *Sexual and Marital Therapy, 2,* 153–161.

CHAPTER 10

Behavior Therapy with Paraphilic Disorders

RICHARD D. MCANULTY and HENRY E. ADAMS

Increased media coverage of cases of child molestation and rape have fostered public and professional awareness of aberrant sexual proclivities. As a consequence, mental health professionals are increasingly being consulted for assistance in the disposition of sexual offenders. Psychologists' involvement may include diagnostic evaluations and treatment implementation. Regardless of area of specialty, at some time in their career, most psychologists will encounter a patient accused of perpetrating a sexual crime.

The latest version of the official psychiatric nomenclature (DSM-III-R; American Psychiatric Association, 1987) defines the essential feature of sexual deviations, or paraphilic disorders, as "recurrent intense sexual urges and sexually arousing fantasies generally involving either (1) nonhuman objects, (2) the suffering or humiliation of oneself or one's partner, (3) children or other nonconsenting persons" (p. 279). It is emphasized that paraphilic arousal deviates from the norm and may interfere with a person's ability to engage in "reciprocal, affectionate sexual activity" (p. 279). This latest revision in the formulation and classification of sexual deviations represents a significant departure from previous ones. In DSM-II (American Psychiatric Association, 1968), sexual deviations were classified as personality disorders on the basis of inferred processes underlying the overt sexual behavior. The earliest classification schemes were clearly based on the prevailing psychoanalytic theory (e.g., Fenichel, 1945).

Changes in psychiatric nomenclature have paralleled the increased acceptance of behavioral formulations of paraphilias. In behavioral terms, the problem in sexual deviations entails deviant sexual arousal, which is acquired through specific conditioning experiences (Barlow, 1974; Evans, 1968; McGuire, Carlisle, & Young, 1965). According to McGuire et al. (1965), the repeated pairing of fantasized or actual sexual stimuli with orgasm strengthens the sexually arousing properties of the stimulus. Sexual fantasies are assumed to instigate and determine the type of sexual behavior (Abel & Blanchard, 1974; Evans, 1968; Money, 1986). Hence, the target behaviors in behavior therapy are deviant sexual fantasies and behaviors as well as any variables that may contribute to their maintenance, such as heterosocial fears and skills deficits (Barlow, 1974, 1977).

One of the most influential behavioral models of sexual deviations is that presented by Barlow (1974, 1977). Deviant sexual arousal commonly is associated with a number of behavioral excesses and deficits that interfere with an individual's ability to engage in adaptive and socially approved sexual behavior. According to this model, the following areas require assessment: (a) patterns of sexual arousal, (b) heterosexual behavior, (c) heterosocial behavior, and (d) gender role behavior. Ignoring any of these crucial components of sexual behavior will result in a simplistic and incomplete intervention that is unlikely to be therapeutically successful (Adams & Sturgis, 1978). A number of the early behavioral treatment studies of paraphilias suffered from a restricted and narrow focus, but the trend in recent years has been to employ multicomponent interventions designed to address deficits in all of these areas as needed (e.g., Abel et al., 1984; Marshall & Barbaree, 1988). A recent emphasis in the behavioral treatment of sexual deviations entails the use of relapse prevention strategies (Laws, 1989). Because relapse is common in treated sexual offenders, relapse prevention seems most appropriate and merits empirical study.

In this chapter, assessment and modification of deviant sexual proclivities will be discussed from a behavioral perspective. The discussion is organized to address interventions appropriate to the problem areas listed above. The focus is on case formulation, a necessary process in adapting the treatment procedures to the individual's problems. Legal and ethical issues in working with sex offenders are addressed, and data on the efficacy of behavior therapy with sexual deviations are presented.

Because sexual deviations are seen almost exclusively in males, the discussion does not address the treatment of sexual deviation in females. Furthermore, because social norms and professional attitudes toward homosexuality have changed significantly, as evidenced by the removal of homosexuality from the official psychiatric nomenclature, the modification of homosexuality will receive only minimal coverage.

ASSESSMENT OF DEVIANT SEXUAL BEHAVIOR

A comprehensive, multimodal assessment of each targeted behavior is a prerequisite to efficacious interventions, and continuous assessment is necessary in order to evaluate effectiveness (Ciminero, Calhoun, & Adams, 1986). Multimodal assessment, the hallmark of behavior therapy, is critical for case formulation and for evaluating treatment outcome. Three modalities have traditionally been assessed: subjective report, behavioral ratings, and psychophysiological parameters.

Individuals who engage in aberrant sexual behaviors are notoriously difficult patients. In most cases, they are coerced into treatment by the courts or family members. Treatment may be perceived as the least aversive alternative for many of these patients, who are commonly facing criminal prosecution and suffering from social/familial alienation. These factors contribute to the importance of gathering as much information as possible, including criminal records. Individuals charged with sexual offenses frequently deny the validity of these accusations (McAnulty, Adams, & Andrew, 1989), which presents unique ethical and legal challenges in addition to complicating the assessment process. Although these issues are beyond the scope of this discussion, they are problems that any professional treating sexual offenders will face at some point. The circumstances surrounding the allegations of a sexual offense should be considered carefully because they may be relevant to case formulation and treatment selection (McAnulty & Adams, 1990). Accusations of a sexual offense are not infallible diagnostic signs of a paraphilia.

Even those individuals who admit to having deviant sexual interests may tend to minimize their problem. This was clearly illustrated in a study by Abel, Becker, Cunningham-Rathner, Rouleau, and Murphy (1987), who found that sexual offenders who were assured complete confidentiality and freedom from prosecution admitted to having large numbers of victims. Homosexual pedophiles admitted to having sexually abused an average of 150.2 victims (Abel et al., 1987); most of these offenses were undetected by officials. Hence, self-report measures (e.g., self-monitoring and questionnaires) may be of limited usefulness in assessing individuals for whom there may be serious consequences for admitting to engaging in aberrant sexual practices.

Assessment of Sexual Arousal

A multitude of measures of sexual arousal is currently available. Evaluation of sexual arousal should include measurement of an individual's responsiveness to deviant and normal stimuli. Questionnaires are the most commonly used measures, although their usefulness with this population is limited. Subjective reports in the form of self-monitoring have clear applications in the assessment and treatment of deviant sexual arousal. For obvious ethical and legal reasons, the direct observation of sexual behavior is not feasible. Therefore, there have been few applications of behavioral observation in measuring deviant sexual arousal. Finally, psychophysiological methods are among the most valid measures of sexual arousal (Adams, McAnulty, & Iezzi, 1990; Rosen & Beck, 1988).

The most widely used questionnaire is the Minnesota Multiphasic Personality Inventory (MMPI; Hathaway & McKinley, 1967). This instrument is not a measure of sexual arousal but rather of general psychopathology. Nevertheless, the MMPI continues to be used routinely with sexual offenders, in spite of its lack of sensitivity to the vagaries of sexual deviations (Adams et al., 1990; Erickson, Luxenberg, Walbek, & Seely, 1987). A more efficient method of assessing an individual's sexual arousal is by way of interview and self-monitoring of sexual urges, fantasies, and behavior. The latter method is an especially appropriate treatment outcome measure when used in conjunction with other measures such as psychophysiological techniques. However, the validity of self-report measures must be corroborated with other methods.

Self-monitoring typically requires the individual to record the occurrence of a specific behavior (e.g., deviant urges) as well as the events preceding and following the behavior of interest. Detailed data on the parameters of the situations in which the behaviors occur are essential for a functional analysis (Kanfer & Saslow, 1969). For a pedophile, this monitoring would entail recording all urges and fantasies involving children, with detailed information on the circumstances surrounding the urges. Additionally, the individual would be instructed to report any sexual urges centering on adult partners as well as all incidents of sexual activity including masturbation and masturbatory fantasies.

Although a number of psychophysiological responses occur in conjunction with sexual arousal (e.g., activation of cardiovascular and electrodermal systems, and pupillary dilation), none of these is as specific to male sexual arousal as penile erection (Zuckerman, 1971). For this reason, the measurement of penile tumescence in response to specific sexual stimuli is the preferred method for assessing sexual preference (Adams et al., 1990; Langevin, 1983; Rosen & Beck, 1988). Two classes of transducers are used to monitor erections during assessment: volumetric or circumferential devices. Both transducers have been used extensively, but the circumferential gauges are less cumbersome, can be attached by the patient, and are apparently less susceptible to movement artifacts (Rosen & Keefe, 1978; Wheeler & Rubin, 1987).

The typical procedure in penile plethysmography consists of placing the subject in a laboratory setting where the measurement device is attached to the penis. Testing consists of presenting various neutral and sexually explicit stimuli while continuously monitoring changes in penile tumescence. Changes in tumescence are channeled into an amplifier and are recorded on hardcopy records such as chart-paper. Penile erection is typically quantified on a percentage erection scale (Barlow, Becker, Leitenberg, & Agras, 1970) or in terms of absolute changes in penis size (Freund, 1963). The test stimuli entail color slides of nudes of various age groups, videotaped films, audiotaped scripts, and fantasy. The audiotaped scripts offer the advantage of being individualized for the subjects' erotic idiosyncrasies (for a typical script, see Abel, Barlow, Blanchard, & Guild, 1977; Abel, Blanchard, Becker, & Djenderedjian, 1978).

The ultimate goal in penile plethysmography is to determine which stimuli elicit sexual arousal for the individual. For case formulation and treatment purposes, it is essential to assess sexual responsiveness to deviant *and* to nondeviant cues. Ideally, a broad range of sexual stimuli is presented, in addition to cues selected on the basis of the patient's subjective report and presenting problem.

Assessment of Gender Behavior

Gender behavior is probably the least understood of the four major components of sexual behavior. Barlow (1977) defined a disturbance in gender role as "some degree of incongruence between one's biological and genetic sex and the behavior accompanying that sex as defined by a given culture" (p. 494). Langevin (1983) emphasized the distinction between gender behavior and gender identity. For example, a male may engage in activities traditionally associated with the feminine gender, such as sewing (gender behavior), without having a strong desire to be a female (gender identity). Engaging in cross-gender behaviors is not necessarily problematic, whereas cross-gender identification typically is. Gender identity disturbances have been clearly established in transsexualism and in some cases of homosexuality (Langevin, 1983). Gender identity problems are not necessarily associated with transvestism, in spite of overt appearances.

The Sex Role Inventory (Bem, 1974) measures orientation to masculine and female gender roles by requiring respondents to choose items for self-description. Masculine items include such terms as "aggressive" and "ambitious," whereas feminine items involve such words as "affectionate" and "cheerful." Freund, Nagler, Langevin, Zajac, and Steiner (1974) developed the Feminine Gender Identity Scale, which was found to successfully discriminate between transsexual and homosexual males (Freund, Langevin, Satterberg, & Steiner, 1977). The transsexual males scored higher on feminine gender identity and there was minimal overlap between groups.

The assessment of gender role behavior through observation of overt behavior is typically implemented via behavioral checklists and coding systems. Barlow, Reynolds, and Agras (1973) approached the assessment of gender role behavior by directly assessing the motor behaviors of standing, sitting, and walking for both sexes. According to Barlow (1974), females tend to sit with their lower back close to the back of a chair and cross their legs by resting one leg on the knee of the other. Conversely, males tend to sit with the lower back further away from the back of the chair and are more likely to cross their legs by resting one ankle on the knee of the other leg. Barlow (1977) argued that females display greater diversity in motor behaviors than do males, who exhibit a restricted range of stereotypically masculine behaviors.

Assessment of Heterosocial Skills

Although theoreticians of psychoanalytic and behavioral schools have argued that heterosocial skills deficits are etiologically relevant to sexual deviations, there have been relatively few empirical tests of this hypothesis. Several questionnaires exist to assess heterosocial competence. The Survey of Heterosocial Interactions (Twentyman & McFall, 1975) and the Social Activity Questionnaire (Christensen & Arkowitz, 1974) provide measures of anxiety in social situations and of dating frequency and experience. These have primarily been standardized on college student populations, and their applicability to paraphiliacs has yet to be demonstrated.

The most sophisticated studies have used multimodal assessments that include self-report measures, behavioral observation of role-play scenes, ratings by trained observers, and psychophysiological measures. Overholser and Beck (1986) compared rapists and pedophiles with three control conditions: low socioeconomic status (SES) community volunteers, heterosocially anxious college males, and incarcerated non-sex offenders. The multimodal assessment included naturalistic and role-play heterosocial interactions, a physiological measure of anxiety during role play, judge ratings, and self-report measures. Both sexual offender groups were found to be less socially skilled than the community volunteers in the role play. The community subjects and college students displayed a higher percentage of socially skilled behaviors than the rapists and pedophiles. However, the college students were rated as the most anxious during role play. In role play requiring assertiveness, the rapists evidenced the highest physiological levels of anxiety. Finally, the pedophiles reported the greatest concern with negative evaluations by others, viewed themselves as the least assertive of all groups, and held the most conservative stereotypes of women. Other studies have also demonstrated that sexual deviants tend to have heterosocial deficits (Segal & Marshall, 1985; Stermac & Quinsey, 1986), although these impairments do not always differentiate sexual offenders from other psychiatric groups.

One element of heterosocial functioning that has received little attention is heterosocial perception, the ability to accurately read cues in heterosocial and other situations. Deficits in social perception may mediate social inadequacy in some cases (Arkowitz, 1981; Bellack & Morrison, 1982). Lipton, McDonel, and McFall (1987) found that rapists were less accurate cue readers in a first-date situation than were violent and nonviolent nonrapists from the same correctional facility.

Heterosocial skills are directly measured by evaluating specific behaviors that presumably comprise heterosocial skills. Ideally, such an assessment would entail behavioral observation in role play and in naturalistic settings. Barlow, Abel, Blanchard, Bristow, and Young (1977) created the Heterosocial Skills Checklist (HSC) as an instrument to assess social skills from four categories: voice, form of conversation, affect, and motor behavior. Each category requires performance ratings in several areas; affect includes such behaviors as appropriateness of facial expression, eye contact, and laughter. The instrument was found to successfully differentiate socially competent high school and college students from socially inadequate sexual deviants. The total score, form of conversation, and affect categories were the best discriminators. However, it is unclear whether the HSC is useful for finer discriminations. Furthermore, the selected categories may not adequately sample the range of behaviors comprising heterosocial skills.

Assessment of Heterosexual Skills

Heterosexual skills entails sexual knowledge, attitudes, and skills necessary for successfully initiating and maintaining a sexual encounter. Assessment of heterosexual skills is essential for evaluating the patient's ability to function adaptively in a sexual relationship with an appropriate partner. Although empirical studies are limited, it is widely believed that individuals with paraphilic disorders are deficient in knowledge about normal sexual functioning and lacking in sexual skills. Furthermore, many of these individuals hold dysfunctional beliefs and attitudes about sexual functioning. Failure to address these deficits could interfere with successful sexual reorientation.

Assessment of heterosexual behaviors is typically accomplished via clinical interview. The focus in the interview is on sexual history, beginning with early sexual experiences, source of sexual knowledge, parental attitudes about sex, religious upbringing, peer group norms, and dating history. Additionally, it is essential to obtain detailed information on deviant and nondeviant sexual experiences. Related topics of assessment include masturbatory fantasies, knowledge of male and female anatomy, and knowledge of techniques for pleasuring an appropriate partner.

THE ROLE OF CASE FORMULATION

Although technological approaches to behavior therapy, which match standard treatment techniques to type of deviant response, have been repeatedly advocated, there are a number of problems with this approach (Haynes, 1988; Nelson, 1988; Turkat, 1988). The major difficulties are the failure to recognize the heterogeneity of diagnosis categories and the vagaries of individual cases. For example, pedophiles may hold certain common characteristics, but in each case there are many unique aspects that may greatly influence treatment outcome. Thus, in order to enhance the probability of successful interventions, it is necessary to adapt the treatment regimen to the individual's specific strengths and deficits.

To truly understand a patient's unique problems, a careful case formulation is essential. According to Wolpe and Turkat (1985), a valid and thorough case formulation clarifies the relationship among a patient's presenting complaints, traces the course of these problems, and allows the prediction of future behavior under specific stimulus conditions. The parameters of all presenting problems, including antecedent and maintaining events, require identification for effective intervention. After a detailed case formulation is constructed, selection of the most appropriate intervention is possible.

Clinical case management is a process that begins with a comprehensive assessment leading to testable hypotheses. The ensuing case formulation provides the basis for the design of an appropriate treatment program. In most cases, actual implementation should follow a presentation of the case formulation and discussion of treatment options with the patient. In addition to eliciting patient compliance, this presentation may yield useful information, even when the patient disagrees with the case formulation (which may require a re-evaluation of the hypotheses and treatment program). Treatment implementation, the next phase, requires ongoing monitoring of behavior. If there is no evidence of behavioral change, then a modification of the case formulation and treatment program is required. The final phase is follow-up and relapse prevention. The multitude of interventions summarized in the following section are designed to be implemented only after a careful determination of appropriateness on a case-by-case basis.

MODIFICATION OF DEVIANT SEXUAL AROUSAL

Elimination of Deviant Sexual Arousal

The primary procedures used to eliminate deviant sexual arousal are collectively referred to as aversion therapy. Aversion therapy involves the pairing of an unpleasant stimulus with the deviant stimulus that elicits sexual arousal, the ultimate goal being to weaken the bond between the conditioned deviant stimulus and sexual arousal (Rachman & Teasdale, 1969). According to Wolpe (1982), aversion therapy is most appropriate for the modification of "autonomic habits" such as sexual arousal. Wolpe (1982) argued that "the intent of aversion therapy is to diminish the habit strength of the target response through inhibiting it by the competition of the aversive agent" (p. 258), a process that he called "reciprocal inhibition."

Several conditioning paradigms have been employed for aversive therapy, such as classical fear conditioning, punishment, escape, and avoidance conditioning. However, most applications bear more similarities than differences. In his review of the literature on behavioral reorientation of pedophiliacs, Kelly (1982) noted that some form of aversive conditioning was employed in 78% of all treatment studies, making it the most commonly used technique among over 20 different treatment procedures.

Despite the widespread use of aversive therapy in the treatment of sexual deviations, it remains controversial (e.g., Marks, 1976). In fact, few therapeutic techniques have generated more debate than aversive treatment procedures. Most of the opponents of aversion therapy have challenged its usage on ethical and moral grounds, citing concerns over the potential for haphazard implementations and abuse. All therapeutic techniques should be performed in a manner that produces expedient and maximal success while minimizing unnecessary distress.

The usefulness and efficacy of aversive treatment techniques, when correctly administered, has been noted by many behavioral scientists (Azrin & Holtz, 1966; Barlow, 1974; Marks, Rachman, & Gelder, 1965; Wolpe, 1982). The overall efficacy of aversive therapy in eliminating or reducing deviant sexual urges is influenced by a number of variables. With homosexual subjects, successful suppression of homosexual urges has ranged from 30% (McConaghy, 1969; Bancroft, 1969) to 60% (Feldman & MacCullough, 1971). An important variable in predicting homosexual subjects' response to aversive therapy appears to be the extent of prior heterosexual experience. Homosexual subjects with minimal or no previous heterosexual experience appear to be quite resistant to change (e.g., Feldman & MacCullough, 1971). Among transvestites and fetishists, those who have some degree of heterosexual adjustment and few gender identity problems appear to be the best candidates for aversion therapy (Gelder & Marks, 1969; Marks & Gelder, 1967). Interestingly, masochism does not appear to be a contraindication for aversive therapy (Marks et al., 1965). Pedophiles who exhibit clear patterns of sexual responsiveness to child cues during penile plethysmographic evaluation should also be considered for aversion therapy (Marshall & Barbaree, 1988).

Other studies using aversion therapy with sexual deviates have produced less impressive results. Quinsey, Bergersen, and Steinman (1976) obtained significant yet relatively small changes in the sexual preferences of 10 pedophiles treated with an aversive conditioning paradigm. Callahan and Leitenberg (1973) also reported limited success in their treatment study using aversion procedures. Consequently, a number of variables appear to moderate the efficacy of aversive techniques and these should be considered in making treatment selections. Assessment results should be carefully considered in evaluating the appropriateness of aversion therapy for each patient. The blind and routine implementation of aversion therapy is irresponsible and unethical.

The major types of aversive therapy are summarized in the following sections.

Faradic Aversion

Faradic or electrical aversion involves the use of a mild but painful electrical shock as the aversive stimulus. Advantages of this procedure include the ability to precisely control the frequency, timing, and intensity of the aversive stimulus. However, the shock units typically are not portable. When they are portable, the opportunity for the patient to self-administer the aversive stimulus in the natural environment enhances the probability of success.

Feldman and MacCullough (1971) compared an anticipatory avoidance learning paradigm to a fear conditioning paradigm with groups of 10 homosexual subjects. The control group received traditional psychotherapy. The experimental conditions were equally effective (improvement in 60% of cases) and superior to the control condition (20% of cases improved). Unfortunately, penile tumescence measures of improvement were not used.

Abel, Levis, and Clancy (1970) employed a standard aversive conditioning paradigm with 3 exhibitionists, 2 transvestites, and 1 masochist. The aversion trials were followed by avoidance conditioning trials in which shock could be avoided by verbalizing normal sexual behavior. Follow-up at 18 weeks revealed no significant penile tumescence to deviant cues used during conditioning trials and generalization to novel deviant cues. Erections to nondeviant cues were essentially unchanged.

Marks and Gelder (1967) treated 2 fetishists and 3 transvestites with faradic aversion. Electrical shock was paired with fantasies and the actual deviant stimuli (e.g., wearing panties). All subjects revealed elimination of deviant fantasies and of penile erections to the deviant stimuli after the aversive conditioning. Subjective reports corroborated these findings. The length of follow-up was unclear. In a subsequent investigation, the authors (Gelder & Marks, 1969) found that transsexuals with gender identity disturbances did not improve markedly with aversive therapy.

Compared to other aversive procedures, electrical aversion is relatively simple to implement. However, individual differences in pain tolerance dictate that the shock level be individually determined. The ideal intensity is set at or just above the patient's pain threshold, in order to obtain rapid improvements. Shock intensity is periodically varied in an unpredictable manner, to prevent habituation. The appropriateness of faradic aversion and any other aversive technique must be determined through a thorough evaluation of the patient's psychological and medical status. Electrical aversion is contraindicated for patients with cardiovascular disease.

Chemical and Olfactory Aversion

Chemical aversion therapy involves pairing an aversive physiological state such as nausea or vomiting with the deviant stimulus. Scoline, a curarizing drug, causes paralysis, requires the use of life-support equipment to prevent asphyxiation, and necessitates medical support. A problem with all chemical aversion is high patient dropout rates because of the highly aversive nature of the procedures. Olfactory aversion entails the use of a noxious odor such as valeric acid, which has been likened to the smell of rotten eggs. Other odoriferous chemical agents include aromatic ammonia, which produces burning sensations in the nose and throat. A clear advantage of some types of olfactory aversion is portability, which permits the patient to conduct sessions at home and in the natural environment, when deviant urges occur.

Morganstern, Pearce, and Linford-Rees (1965) treated 13 transvestites by administering injections of apomorphine and having them cross-dress while experiencing the drug-induced nausea. Each subject underwent 39 total sessions. Follow-up ranged from 8 months to 4 years. Cross-dressing was completely eliminated in 7 of 13 subjects; the remaining subjects showed improvements but periodic relapses.

Several problems are inherent in the use of chemical aversion. First, individuals differ greatly in the speed and intensity of their reactions to the drugs. As a consequence, precise control of the pairings is not possible, and there is a risk of using a backward conditioning paradigm if the nauseating sensations follow rather than precede the presentation of the deviant stimulus. Second, the possibility of side effects is greater than with most other aversion techniques. In many cases, the requirement of medical support is costly and impractical. Finally, patient reactions to the treatment may range from dropping out prematurely to becoming aggressive and hostile (Morganstern et al., 1965).

Olfactory aversion therapy has mostly been used in conjunction with other aversion techniques such as covert sensitization (e.g., Maletzky, 1974). However, a few case studies have documented the effectiveness of exclusive olfactory aversion. Laws, Meyer, and Holmen (1978) treated a sexual sadist with valeric acid for 8 weeks. The chemical agent was self-administered by the patient while viewing slides depicting sadistic activities. Erectile responses to the deviant cues were eliminated and responsiveness to normal stimuli was unaltered. These results were maintained at 8-month follow-up.

Earls and Castonguay (1989) used ammonia to eliminate deviant sexual arousal in a 17-year-old incarcerated bisexual pedophile. Pretreatment baseline assessments revealed no change in erections to child cues over a 6-month interval without treatment. A total of 20 aversion sessions was implemented. A penile plethysmography follow-up at 1 year revealed a marked decrease in responsiveness to child cues while tumescence to adult cues remained high.

Olfactory aversive therapy appears to be a promising technique for eliminating deviant sexual arousal. However, more empirical data are needed. Difficulties with controlling the parameters of the aversive stimulus may occur, as with other chemical agents. However, the technique is simple, portable, and easily self-administered after adequate patient training.

Covert Sensitization

Covert sensitization requires that the patient pair noxious imagery with deviant sexual fantasies. The noxious images and scenes serve as the aversive stimulus. The appeal of this technique lies in its acceptability to patients, reduced risks of side effects and patient dropout, and accessibility (Cautela & Wisocki, 1971). Furthermore, covert sensitization directly targets fantasies that are closely tied to overt sexual behavior (McGuire et al., 1965). Sensitization scenes are constructed from the information provided by the patient concerning sexually arousing stimuli. The aversive component of the scenes typically consists of vivid descriptions of images of vomiting, drinking urine, or public embarrassment (for a typical sensitization script, see Brownell, Hayes, & Barlow, 1977; Cautela & Wisocki, 1971).

Barlow, Leitenberg, and Agras (1969) used an A-B-A reversal design to evaluate the effectiveness of covert sensitization with a pedophilic and a homosexual subject. Subjective reports suggested that the attractiveness of the deviant stimuli decreased when the noxious scenes were paired with them and increased when the aversive scenes were removed. Electrodermal responses corroborated these findings for one subject. Therefore, the covert sensitization procedure appeared to account for observed changes.

Brownell et al. (1977) treated 2 exhibitionists, 1 pedophile, 1 sadist, and 1 transvestite with covert sensitization. All subjects evidenced significant reductions in their deviant arousal as measured by frequency of urges, card sort, and penile plethysmography. These gains were maintained at 6 months and corroborated by the patients' spouses for 4 of the 5. The reductions in responsiveness to deviant stimuli were not accompanied by increased arousal to nondeviant stimuli, which necessitated an additional treatment technique for 2 subjects. This finding suggests that normal and deviant sexual arousal may be functionally independent and, therefore, both should be systematically assessed in all cases (Brownell & Barlow, 1976).

Although covert sensitization has been shown to be effective in reducing deviant sexual arousal in several small investigations, it is not without limitations. The major criticism is that a number of patients are unable to successfully visualize the aversive scenes (Laws et al., 1978; Maletzky & George, 1973). Maletzky (1974) has tried to remedy that problem by incorporating olfactory aversion in a procedure dubbed "assisted" covert sensitization. Another potential limitation is that the therapist ultimately has little control over the technique.

Shame Aversion

The aversive stimulus in shame aversion is shame or embarrassment. The technique has been almost exclusively applied to exhibitionists and consists of having them engage in genital exposure and verbalize their cognitions in front of an audience. According to Wickramasekera (1972, 1976), shame aversion is indicated for the treatment of exposers who are introverted, moralistic, and nonassertive. It is not appropriate in cases where there are clear sociopathic features (Wickramasekera, 1976). The goal of the technique is to eliminate the exhibitionist's private and autistic fantasies, which are believed to mediate the genital exposure, and to replace these with embarrassment and fear. The audience consists of several females who are selected on the basis of their similarity to the exposer's preferred victims. The audience members are trained to stare expressionlessly at the patient, thereby removing any reinforcement from victim reactions and enhancing anxiety. While exposing, the patient is instructed to verbalize his fantasies, verbalize an introspective dialogue between him and his penis, describe bodily sensations, and verbalize what he thinks the female viewers are thinking and feeling. The impact of the procedure is enhanced by videotaping the session for future viewing.

Wickramasekera (1976) treated 16 exhibitionists with 1 to 4 sessions of shame aversion. Follow-up ranged from 3 months to 7 years. None of the patients reported any relapses or was re-arrested for exposing. Temporary side effects of the treatment included anxiety, depression, nightmares, and erectile failure in some cases. According to Wickramasekera (1976), these problems spontaneously remitted within 5 weeks. Some patients tend to dissociate during the exposure session, thereby reducing the impact of the procedure. Insisting that the patient attend to the physical realities of the situation (e.g., by having him describe his sensations and the characteristics of the observers) serves to diminish this escape response. One limitation of the shame aversion procedure is that it is taxing to the patient and other participants (Wickramasekera, 1976).

Serber (1971) successfully applied the technique to a case of transvestism. However, applications to other sexual deviations are limited. Shame aversion appears to be an innovative approach to eliminating deviant sexual arousal and merits further empirical study. However, it has several serious problems in some cases. If it serves to increase arousal rather than embarrass the patient, it may aggravate the problem. Further studies are needed to elucidate the value of the procedure and identify its limitations.

Masturbatory Satiation

Masturbatory satiation (Marshall, 1973; 1979) is a method of decreasing deviant arousal by having the patient masturbate to deviant fantasies for prolonged periods (usually 1 to 2 hours). The rationale is that, after the initial orgasm, the repeated exposure to deviant fantasies without accompanying sexual arousal and pleasure will weaken the arousing properties of the stimulus. Alford, Morin, Atkins, and Schoen (1987) subsequently relabeled the technique "masturbation extinction" because the presumed mechanism for effectiveness involves repeated presentations of deviant stimuli (conditioned stimuli) in the absence of sexual excitement and orgasm (unconditioned stimuli).

Several controlled case studies support the effectiveness of masturbation extinction as a method of reducing deviant arousal. Marshall (1979) described the successful elimination of pedophilic and fetishistic arousal in one subject, using a multiple baseline design. Heterosexual arousal was enhanced by the addition of an orgasmic reconditioning procedure. Similar results were replicated with another pedophile for whom aversion therapy was ineffective (Marshall, 1973). Marshall and Lippens (1977) subsequently reported similar findings with a third case. Alford et al. (1987) successfully treated a pedophile with masturbatory extinction. The gains were maintained at 1-year follow-up.

Masturbatory satiation or extinction appears to be a promising technique designed to decrease deviant sexual arousal. Although the technique is described as "boring" by patients (e.g., Marshall & Lippens, 1977), it is less controversial than the use of painful methods such as faradic aversion. Therefore, this procedure may be more acceptable to some patients and professionals. Another advantage is that it can readily be used by compliant patients at home. However, there have been no treatment outcome studies in which masturbation was used as the sole intervention. As with most other techniques discussed so far, combinations of methods appear to offer the most viable treatments for sexual deviations.

INCREASING HETEROSEXUAL AROUSAL

As previously noted, modifying deviant sexual arousal does not ensure an increase in responsiveness to normal sexual stimuli (Barlow, 1973; Brownell, Hayes, & Barlow, 1977). Techniques that are specifically designed to enhance heterosexual arousal are indicated in cases where the patient demonstrates significant responsiveness to deviant stimuli but minimal arousal to normal stimuli. Because most of the literature has focused on increasing heterosexual arousal, this discussion will follow suit, although it seems reasonable that these techniques may also be applicable to enhancing homosexual arousal.

Because it appears that gender preferences are more salient than age preferences (e.g., Freund, Watson, & Rienzo, 1988), for pedophiles the optimal treatment may require reorientation to adult partners of the same sex as the preferred partners, rather than cross-gender reorientation. For example, with a homosexual pedophile, increasing sexual arousal to adult males may be more successful than attempting to increase arousal to adult females.

Aversion Relief

Aversion relief involves pairing a heterosexual stimulus with the termination of an aversive stimulus. The technique has been commonly used in conjunction with aversion therapy because of convenience. The goal in aversion relief is to associate the heterosexual stimuli with escape from noxious stimulation, thereby bestowing reinforcing properties on the heterosexual stimuli. The relief stimulus may be verbal, such as verbalizing heterosexual interests, or pictorial, usually in the form of heterosexual slides (Barlow, 1974).

Thorpe, Schmidt, Brown, and Castell (1964) introduced the technique of aversion relief with sexual deviations in a treatment study with 3 homosexuals, 1 transvestite, and 1 fetishist. Subjects were required to read aloud words that served as stimuli for deviant sexual arousal. Electrical shock was paired with each word. The last word of each series was a heterosexual term, which signaled the end of the shock sequence. Therefore, the heterosexual words were associated with relief from shock. At termination of treatment, all subjects reported an increase in heterosexual interests; unfortunately, no additional outcome measures were used and no follow-up was completed. Thorpe et al. (1964) argued that aversion relief operates either by inhibiting heterosexual anxiety or reinforcing heterosexual approach behavior.

Feldman and MacCullough (1965) used an escape conditioning paradigm in treating homosexual patients. Slides of seminude and nude males were shown, and the patients were told that they could terminate the electrical shock whenever they no longer found the slides sexually arousing. Shock onset occurred 8 seconds after each slide was presented, and the shock intensity was gradually increased until the patient pressed a switch to remove the slide. Slides of nude females were presented upon termination of the male slide, signaling shock-free relief periods. Feldman and MacCullough (1971) claimed that aversion relief operates by reducing heterosexual anxiety.

Abel et al. (1970) also used aversion relief in their clinical replication series. However, there was no measurable effect because heterosexual responsiveness did not increase, although deviant arousal decreased as measured by penile plethysmography. Most of the support for the effectiveness of aversion relief is anecdotal, inasmuch as controlled treatment outcome studies are lacking. Barlow's (1973, 1974) conclusion that experimental evidence does not support the effectiveness of aversion relief still appears to be valid.

Shaping

Shaping involves the contingent provision of positive reinforcers for successive approximations of the target response. Quinn, Harbison, and McAllister (1970) and Harbison, Quinn, and McAllister (1970) used a shaping procedure in treating homosexual patients. After using aversion therapy to decrease homosexual arousal, patients underwent a period of dehydration. A lime drink was presented contingently on (a) increases in duration and elaboration of heterosexual fantasies, and (b) increased penile erection to slides and pictures of nude females. The results revealed an increase on both measures of heterosexual arousal and a decrease in attitudinal scores toward homosexual stimuli during the course of treatment. Unfortunately, no follow-up measures of extralaboratory sexual behavior were reported.

In an interesting application of shaping, Quinsey, Chaplin, and Carrigan (1980) evaluated a biofeedback conditioning procedure with child molesters. Colored lights were used to signal to patients whether they had reached the criterion amount of penile tumescence. Tumescence to child stimuli was shifted downward and tumescence to adult heterosexual stimuli was shifted upward. The success criteria were initially set at one-third of each patient's pretreatment maximal erection to a stimulus category (i.e., child and adult female). Each successive approximation shift required a 30% increase or decrease in the patient's current amount of penile erection. Eighteen pedophiles were assigned to a biofeedback condition, an electrical aversion condition, or a combined biofeedback–aversion condition. Posttreatment results revealed that the combined biofeedback–punishment was the most effective: 5 of the 6 subjects showed significant improvements. No follow-up data were reported.

Shaping appears to be a potentially useful technique for increasing heterosexual responsiveness. However, applications of shaping as the sole treatment procedure are questionable. The few studies upholding the usefulness of shaping procedures have also employed aversion therapy. Thus, it is unclear how useful this procedure would be when used alone.

Fading

The technique of fading traces its roots to the operant procedure of errorless discrimination (Terrace, 1966). Fading involves the introduction or "fading in" of a nonarousing stimulus (e.g., heterosexual cues) while the patient is sexually aroused, usually by the presentation of the preferred deviant stimulus. The purpose of the technique is to gradually condition sexually arousing properties to a formerly nonarousing stimulus by association with a stimulus with positive valence. Barlow and Agras (1973) developed a technology that allowed one slide to be superimposed onto another. Using an adjustable transformer, the investigators could selectively increase the brightness of a female slide while simultaneously decreasing the brightness of a male slide.

In a series of three controlled case studies with homosexual subjects, Barlow and Agras (1973) faded in female stimuli contingent on the subject's maintaining 75% of a full erection. A series of 20 steps was employed, beginning with 100% male brightness and ending with 100% female brightness. A reversal design was used in which the female slides were faded out and the male slides faded back in. During this period, subject reports of heterosexual responsiveness decreased sharply. Although the fading technique was successful in increasing verbal report and penile measures of heterosexual arousal, 2 of the 3 subjects required heterosocial skills training.

Because no efforts are made to decrease deviant arousal with fading, it remains unclear whether the technique is sufficient. One could feasibly develop an increase in heterosexual responsiveness while also maintaining deviant arousal (possibly becoming bisexual, in the case of the homosexual subjects). Few data have been generated through the use of this strategy, and more empirical data are needed to evaluate its usefulness.

Exposure

Exposure as a method of increasing heterosexual arousal simply involves the presentation to explicit heterosexual stimuli in order to elicit heterosexual arousal.

Herman and colleagues (Herman, 1971; Herman, Barlow, & Agras, 1974) used exposure in case studies with 2 homosexuals and 1 pedophile. In the first phase of treatment, subjects were shown films of a nude, seductive female for 10 minutes daily. A movie of a nude male was presented during the control phase. The female exposure was reinstated in the final phase. Heterosexual responsiveness increased during the female exposure conditions and decreased during the male exposure phase. Interestingly, homosexual arousal did not change except for one patient who had previously undergone aversion therapy. Follow-up assessments ranging from 3 months to 1 year revealed that 2 subjects were experiencing difficulties with heterosexual relations in spite of continued heterosexual arousal. Used alone, the few data available do not suggest that this is a viable strategy.

The reason for change in exposure remains uncertain (Barlow, 1974). One possibility is that it is functionally equivalent to flooding and serves to decrease heterosexual anxiety, which inhibits heterosexual arousal. Another possibility is that exposure provides novel material which, if subsequently used in masturbatory fantasies, functions to enhance heterosexual arousal (Barlow, 1973, 1974). Exposure therapy as a treatment strategy with sexual deviates has not been fully explored.

Orgasmic Reconditioning

Orgasmic reconditioning refers to a group of techniques designed to enhance heterosexual arousal by pairing heterosexual stimuli with orgasm. It is also referred to as masturbation training and masturbatory conditioning. The rationale for orgasmic reconditioning is based on the assumption that stimuli acquire sexually arousing properties through their pairing with pleasurable sensations, namely sexual arousal and orgasm (Evans, 1968; McGuire et al., 1965). Several laboratory analogue studies seem to support this view. Rachman (1966) paired slides of women's boots with slides of a nude female. The 3 heterosexual subjects exhibited significant increases in penile tumescence to the boots after the conditioning trials. These findings were replicated by Rachman and Hodgson (1968) with 5 additional subjects. Anecdotal support for these notions was offered in a series of 45 paraphiliacs by McGuire et al. (1965) and in another series by Evans (1968).

The term "orgasmic reconditioning" has been used in reference to two different techniques. As originally used, orgasmic reconditioning (Marquis, 1970) required the patient to masturbate using deviant stimuli until the point of ejaculatory inevitability, at which time the patient was to switch to appropriate heterosexual fantasy. Over successive sessions, the patient was instructed to switch to heterosexual fantasy backward in time from the point of orgasm until he could ultimately use these fantasies from the beginning of masturbation. In the early phases of treatment, patients may lose their arousal and erection during the switch to normal fantasy. If arousal is lost, the patient is instructed to use his preferred deviant fantasy to achieve a high level of arousal and to then return to the heterosexual fantasy.

Case studies by Marquis (1970) and Davison (1968) reported success in using orgasmic reconditioning with sadomasochistic patients, but treatment did not rely on the technique exclusively. One of the few attempts to evaluate the effectiveness of orgasmic reconditioning was conducted by Conrad and Wincze (1976). Three homosexuals and 1 pedophile underwent 40 sessions of orgasmic reconditioning using visual and/or fantasized stimuli. Subjective reports suggested significant increases in heterosexual arousal, but penile measures revealed no change in sexual preferences. The pedophile received an additional phase of electrical aversion without notable improvement. At this juncture, findings on the use of orgasmic reconditioning as a technique for increasing heterosexual arousal are inconclusive.

Desensitization Techniques

The rationale for the application of desensitization techniques (Wolpe, 1958) is based on the hypothesis that heterosexual anxiety inhibits heterosexual arousal for some paraphiliacs. It is only applicable to cases where heterosexual anxiety is determined to be contributing to the individual's social inadequacy. If this is the case, eliminating heterosexual fears should result in an increase in sexual arousal to heterosexual stimuli. Several methods of implementing desensitization have been used: (a) imaginal, (b) in vivo, and (c) video desensitization.

The goal in imaginal desensitization is to counteract anxiety-provoking images with an antagonistic response such as relaxation (Wolpe, 1982). Typically, training begins by targeting the least feared stimuli, progressing gradually to the most anxiety-provoking scenes. In a case of heterosexual anxiety, treatment might begin by teaching the patient to relax while imagining himself greeting a female, and progress to imagined scenes of intimacy while on a date with a female partner. Fear hierarchies are constructed with the patient, based on thematically related stimuli that elicit anxiety.

Bancroft (1970) compared systematic desensitization to heterosexual scenes to aversion therapy with two groups of 15 homosexuals. Outcome measures included subjective reports of heterosexual and homosexual behavior and penile plethysmography data. No differences between treatments were noted in heterosexual arousal at the end of treatment and at 6-month follow-up. However, homosexual arousal decreased only in the aversion therapy condition. Subjects were separated into improved and unimproved groups, based on reports of behavior at follow-up. Those subjects rated as improved evidenced more heterosexual arousal than the unimproved subjects. However, neither treatment condition produced dramatic results: only 30% of subjects were rated as improved.

In vivo desensitization substitutes engaging in the actual behaviors for imagined scenes. This procedure obviously requires a partner. A few case studies have documented the use of in vivo desensitization. Cooper (1963) successfully treated a fetishist with a combination of olfactory aversion and in vivo desensitization. The latter procedure was implemented by instructing the patient to lie in bed naked with his wife until relaxed. He was then encouraged to gradually follow a series of steps culminating with sexual intercourse. The patient was instructed not to advance to a higher step until completely relaxed during all previous steps. Gray (1970) combined covert sensitization with this procedure in treating a homosexual male. Other investigators (e.g., Barlow & Agras, 1973; Wickramasekera, 1968) have successfully used in vivo desensitization without aversion therapy.

Video desensitization, like the imaginal and in vivo variants of the technique, involves relaxation training, hierarchy construction, and graduated exposure to the anxiety-provoking stimuli. However, video desensitization entails visual presentations of the feared stimuli. This application is derived from research demonstrating that exposure to models engaging in feared or phobic behavior successfully reduces anxiety of the observers (Bandura, Blanchard, & Ritter, 1969; Bandura & Menlove, 1968). Caird and Wincze (1977) prepared an extensive library of 140 video cassettes depicting a wide variety of sexual interactions. The content of the 4-minute films ranged from couples merely talking to explicit depictions of heterosexual intercourse. The videos were presented in hierarchical fashion after the patient was instructed to imagine himself as the male model and the video actress as his partner.

The technique of systematic desensitization and its variants appears to be a promising method of reducing heterosexual anxiety in sexual deviations. The implementation of the technique should be dictated by case formulation. For patients who exhibit clear signs of heterosexual anxiety, this technique may be useful. Unfortunately, there is a lack of empirical evidence evaluating the efficacy of desensitization with this population.

MODIFICATION OF GENDER ROLE BEHAVIOR

As previously noted, the subject of gender role behavior in sexual deviations largely has been ignored, particularly in the behavioral treatment literature. Such an observation is disconcerting, given the data showing that gender identity disturbances are poor prognostic signs (Gelder & Marks, 1969; Langevin, 1983).

Barlow et al. (1973) employed modeling and videotape feedback in modifying the inappropriate gender role behaviors of a 17-year-old transsexual, after aversion therapy had failed to suppress homosexual arousal. Pretreatment measures revealed that the patient's motor behaviors were almost exclusively feminine. Using a multiple baseline design, several classes of motor behavior were targeted, beginning with sitting. After sitting was successfully modified, standing and walking were sequentially addressed. The components of gender behavior were broken down and taught step-by-step. Appropriate gender behaviors were modeled by a male therapist and rehearsed by the patient. Feedback and contingent reinforcement were used to shape approximations of appropriate gender behaviors. The final trial of each session was videotaped for future viewing.

The stability of each class of effeminate behaviors until systematically treated suggests that the behavioral procedures accounted for the changes. Modifying the patient's gender role behaviors did not decrease his homosexual arousal. Sexual orientation did not change until aversion therapy, which had been previously unsuccessful, was reinitiated. Interestingly, increases in heterosexual arousal enhanced the patient's masculine role behaviors. Although positive result were reported, this case suggests that the primary disturbance in transsexuals is gender identity disorder rather than simple deviant arousal.

Rekers and Varni (1977) used similar techniques to modify inappropriate gender role behaviors in children. However, aside from these studies, there are few published studies directed at the modification of gender role behaviors.

MODIFICATION OF HETEROSOCIAL FUNCTIONING

Deficits in heterosocial skills have long been recognized as important factors in understanding sexual deviations (Quinsey, 1977). An important distinction must be made between skills deficits and performance inhibition (Arkowitz, 1981; Bellack & Morrison, 1982). In the latter case, the individual possesses the requisite skills but his fears inhibit adequate performance. The former case involves a failure to acquire the skills necessary for heterosocial functioning. In actual practice, the distinction is difficult and a careful assessment is indicated. Whereas heterosocial fears are best treated via anxiety reduction techniques (e.g., desensitization), social skills deficits require a skills acquisition treatment program.

Although there have been few studies that relied exclusively on social skills training to treat paraphilias, most multicomponent treatment programs incorporate a social skills training module (e.g., Abel et al., 1984; Marshall & Barbaree, 1988). These multicomponent programs do not permit the evaluation of the efficacy of an isolated technique. However, the abundant literature on heterosocial skills training with nondeviant males offers findings that should be applicable to the modification of heterosocial functioning in paraphilias. The bulk of the following discussion is drawn from reviews of heterosocial skills techniques by Curran (1977), Curran and Monti (1982), and Bellack and Morrison (1982).

Self-Reinforcement

Rehm and Marston (1968) reasoned that many males who experience anxiety in heterosocial situations actually possess an adequate behavioral repertoire. They hypothesized that increasing anxious males' approach of females by self-reinforcement would serve to reduce heterosocial anxiety and enhance the subjects' sense of self-efficacy. Twenty-four college students who complained of discomfort in dating situations were randomly assigned to one of three groups: (a) self-reinforcement, (b) nonspecific therapy control (nondirective counseling), (c) contact control (instructed to think about the problems and possible solutions but without suggestions from the therapist). Subjects in the self-reinforcement group were asked to construct a hierarchy of in vivo heterosocial interactions, to monitor their performance in light of their individualized goals, and to reward themselves with self-approval contingently on successful interactions. Outcome measures included self-ratings of anxiety, monitoring of dating frequency, and behavioral measures of heterosocial skills.

Results revealed that only the self-reinforcement group experienced a significant decrease in self-reported anxiety. Additionally, these subjects recorded the greatest increase in dating frequency from baseline. However, the behavioral measure that entailed observer ratings of anxiety, adequacy of response, and latency of response did not differentiate groups at 7- to 9-month follow-up. Thus, the self-reinforcement appeared to reduce subjective reports of heterosocial anxiety but no changes were noted on the behavioral measures chosen to sample heterosocial skills. This result may not be completely unexpected, because there was no emphasis on skills acquisition.

Response Practice

This approach is most appropriate for heterosocially anxious males who possess adequate behavioral repertoires but need practice in learning how and when to utilize their skills. This approach rests on the assumption that repeated exposure to heterosocial encounters will result in the enhanced use of heterosocial skills and decreased anxiety.

Martinson and Zerface (1970) examined the impact of practice dating on subsequent dating and comfort. Twenty-four males were randomly assigned to a 5-week practice dating condition, individual counseling, or a delayed treatment control group. All subjects reported having had no dates during the month preceding the study and described themselves as anxious in dating situations. The practice dating condition entailed a series of semistructured dates with female confederates. Results suggested that the practice dating condition was more effective than the other conditions in reducing subjective reports of fear of dating, and more effective than the control condition in increasing dating frequency. No significant posttreatment differences were found on measures of general manifest anxiety.

Christensen and Arkowitz (1974) found that a practice dating program that incorporated a feedback exchange from dating partners successfully decreased heterosocial anxiety in addition to increasing dating frequency and skills. Bellack and Morrison (1982) noted that practice should entail the assignment of specific homework and be designed to maximize success (i.e., reinforcement).

The use of response practice as a means of ensuring generalization of acquired skills has been advocated (Bellack & Morrison, 1982). However, Curran (1977) cautioned that arranged dates could be experienced as failures and consequently increase heterosocial fears. Careful partner matching may be useful in minimizing that risk (Curran, 1977). In summary, in vivo response practice that is carefully selected and monitored should probably be used as a component of heterosocial skills training where possible.

Response Acquisition

The response acquisition model of social skills training consists of a combination of behavioral techniques designed to facilitate the acquisition of requisite skills. These treatment packages typically are comprised of such techniques as instruction, modeling, behavioral rehearsal, feedback, and reinforcement (Bellack & Morrison, 1982; Curran & Monti, 1982). This model remains the most commonly used approach to the modification of heterosocial skills deficiencies (Bellack & Morrison, 1982).

As Curran (1977) noted, many of the early investigations of social skills training with minimally dating males are methodologically flawed. Problems range from questionable subject selection procedures to the lack of follow-up data. Furthermore, several studies failed to use multimodal measures of treatment outcome. Nevertheless, several studies uphold the usefulness of social skills training for enhancing heterosocial competence.

Curran and colleagues (Curran, 1975; Curran & Gilbert, 1975; Curran, Gilbert, & Little, 1976) conducted a series of comparative treatment outcome studies that provides support for the effectiveness of heterosocial skills training. The social skills package generally included instruction, modeling, behavioral rehearsal, coaching, video and group feedback, and in vivo response practice. Target skills consisted of giving and receiving compliments, nonverbal communication, assertiveness, and "feelings talk." Additionally, subjects were taught strategies for appropriately handling silence during interactions, planning and soliciting dates, improving appearance, and dealing with physical intimacy problems.

Curran (1975) compared social skills training with systematic desensitization, an attention placebo condition, and a waiting-list control group. Male and female subjects were recruited through advertisement. Both social skills training and desensitization were superior to the other conditions in modifying ratings of anxiety and of skill in a role-play task. No follow-up data were reported. Curran and Gilbert (1975) subsequently compared social skills training, systematic desensitization, and a waiting-list control condition. Both treatment conditions evidenced significant posttreatment decreases in heterosocial anxiety as measured by subjective reports and role-play ratings. At 6-month follow-up, the social skills training recipients were rated as more socially skilled than subjects in the other groups. Both treatment conditions were associated with increases in dating during and after treatment. Curran et al. (1976) demonstrated that social skills training is superior to a sensitivity training condition in improving heterosocial competence.

Curran (1977) concluded that the previous studies demonstrate that the response acquisition approach to heterosocial skills training is effective. The major limitations of these studies are their lack of psychophysiological measures of anxiety and of direct measures of transfer of treatment gains to the natural environment, and the absence of validity data on some of the assessment instruments (Curran, 1977). Other potential problems include their reliance on college students and their exclusive focus on dating skills, which are but one component of heterosocial competence.

It should be noted that positive results have also been reported with anxiety reduction strategies and cognitive therapy techniques (Bellack & Morrison, 1982). Heterosocial skills deficits may result from a variety of problems, and careful assessment results and case formulation should dictate the most appropriate intervention.

As a final note, several cases of sexual deviation have been successfully treated with assertiveness training (e.g., Edwards, 1972; Stevenson & Wolpe, 1960). Subjects are typically taught assertiveness as a means of reducing heterosocial anxiety and enhancing heterosocial competence. Wolpe (1982) defines assertive behavior as "the appropriate expression of any emotion other than anxiety toward another person" (p. 118). According to Wolpe (1982), heterosocial anxieties may be causally related to sexual deviations; hence, reducing the anxiety should be the focus of treatment in those cases. However, the usefulness of this approach as the sole treatment in the treatment of sexual deviancy has not been empirically evaluated.

MODIFICATION OF HETEROSEXUAL SKILL DEFICIENCIES

A therapist working with a paraphilic patient often assumes the role of a sex educator and permission-giver. If an appropriate female partner is available for the patient, recruiting her involvement and assistance can be most beneficial. The actual content of heterosexual skills training is determined by the specific needs of the patient; however, some discussion of human reproductive anatomy and physiology is usually included, and sexual techniques are often reviewed. A problem commonly encountered in evaluating an individual's sexual knowledge is the tendency to deny or minimize sexual skills deficits. A variety of cultural and peer-group influences leads many males to believe that an admission of sexual ineptitude is a sign of generalized inadequacy and questionable masculinity. Therefore, the therapist should be sensitive, uncritical, and supportive in addressing sexual difficulties.

Topics of discussion may cover: typical sequences of various heterosexual behaviors, from initial advances to foreplay and subsequent sexual intercourse; behaviors that facilitate arousal in one's partner; demographic data on human sexual behavior; and the effects of age, drugs, alcohol, anxiety, and illness on sexual functioning. It is often helpful to augment instruction, guidance, reassurance, and advice with educational aids, such as nontechnical but authoritative reading materials (e.g., Comfort, 1972; McCrary, 1973). Many materials that were initially designed for treating sexually dysfunctional males may be useful adjuncts for modifying heterosexual skills deficits (e.g., Zilbergeld, 1978).

Excessively restrictive attitudes toward sexuality may change when the therapist, an authority figure, condones or labels as "normal" sexual activity and fantasies previously considered taboo by the patient. As Kolvin (1967) noted, sexual education, counseling, and reassurance may alone generate behavior change. However, modification of heterosexual skills deficits typically requires in vivo sexual interactions to be completed by the patient with the assistance of a supportive partner. This is accomplished by way of between-session practice by the patient of the behaviors discussed with the therapist during office sessions. A structured approach combining education and homework assignments may be beneficial to many patients.

Unfortunately, many patients requiring heterosexual skills training lack a sexual partner. This obviously makes the use of in vivo learning experience difficult. In an attempt to meet the needs of patients who lack a partner, several therapists and clinics have experimented with sexual group therapy, in which all patients are without partners. The format might include the presentation of erotic materials, erotic stimulation between members, and emphasis on masturbation (Kaplan, 1974). Others have resorted to nudity and massages between patient and therapist (Hartman & Fithian, 1972). These practices raise a multitude of ethical and legal questions. Sexual relationships between therapist and patient constitute a violation of professional ethical standards for psychologists and physicians. Moreover, they undoubtedly raise questions of a negative nature in the mind of the public. Finally, there is no empirical study of such procedures.

Masters and Johnson (1970) employed trained surrogate partners in treating sexually dysfunctional males and reported positive results. However, the use of sexual surrogates for therapeutic purposes remains highly controversial and poses ethical and legal questions, perhaps even more so since the emergence of new sexual diseases. Proponents of therapy using sexual surrogates argue that, if appropriately used, this approach presents fewer risks than the alternative of having no partner, which may lead to recidivism and the victimization of innocent persons. In the final analysis, the use of sexual surrogates should be based on an estimation of potential benefits while carefully weighing potential hazards, including consideration of professional ethics, laws, personal values, and the availability of other options.

RELAPSE PREVENTION

Figures on rates of recidivism of treated sexual offenders (e.g., Furby, Weinrott, & Blackshaw, 1989; Marshall & Barbaree, 1988) suggest that many patients evidence significant short-term treatment benefits; however, long-term maintenance is often less than optimal. Relapse prevention consists of a cognitive-behavioral program designed to maintain treatment gains. The relapse prevention model was originally developed to minimize the likelihood of relapse following the treatment of addictive behaviors such as alcoholism. In sexual deviations, according to this model (Laws, 1989; Pithers, Marques, Gibat, & Marlatt, 1983), the determinants of a relapse consist of exposure to a high-risk situation followed by a failure to cope adaptively, which leads to deviant fantasies. The recurrence of deviant fantasies ("lapse") in turn is interpreted by the individual as a loss of control (dubbed the "abstinence violation effect"), which sets the stage for full-blown recidivism ("relapse").

The intervention begins by addressing possible misconceptions about treatment. Patients are informed that occasional recurrences of deviant fantasies are to be expected and are not necessarily indications of treatment failure. Treatment of sexual deviation is reconceptualized to the patient as a means of increasing personal control over his deviant behavior rather than as a cure. Relapse prevention requires the identification of situations in which relapse has occurred in the past or is likely to occur in the future. Pithers, Kashima, Cumming, Beal, and Buell (1988) reported that negative mood states were the most common precursors to sexual aggression among rapists and pedophiles. The patient is taught to recognize high-risk situations, and coping skills training is implemented (e.g., stimulus control, anger management). Finally, cognitive restructuring is used to counteract the abstinence violation effect.

The relapse prevention model as a component in the treatment of sexual deviations is intuitively appealing. This strategy is still new, and empirical data supporting its effectiveness are limited. However, in our opinion, most individuals who require treatment for sexual deviation would probably benefit from relapse prevention interventions. For a discussion of the model and implementations of relapse prevention with this population, the reader is referred to Laws (1989) and Marshall, Laws, and Barbaree (1990).

LEGAL AND ETHICAL CONSIDERATIONS

Clinicians working with sex offenders face a number of legal issues. First, because many deviant sexual acts are criminal offenses, therapists are bound by duties to warn and protect potential victims. Furthermore, most states have enacted legislation that limits the boundaries of privileged communication in cases where a patient admits to his therapist that he has committed child molestation. In such cases, the therapist's failure to report the offense may lead to criminal liability. The outpatient treatment of sex offenders poses dilemmas that should be carefully evaluated. Cooperation with legal authorities by the therapist should be understood and formalized by all concerned parties as a condition of treatment. In most cases, consideration should be given to temporarily removing the offender from his natural environment in order to reduce the chances of recidivism, especially in cases of incest. A discussion of issues pertaining to expert testimony is beyond the scope of this chapter. The interested reader is referred to Shapiro's (1984) text on psychological evaluation and expert testimony.

Ethical considerations require finding a balance between treatment aversiveness and effectiveness. The ideal treatment combines optimal efficacy with minimal discomfort to the patient. This issue is particularly relevant to applications of aversive therapy. Case formulation should dictate the optimal course of treatment. In any case, the therapist's first obligation is to potential victims.

Other ethical dilemmas center on such issues as the use of sexual surrogates to enhance heterosexual arousal, and the use of explicit sexual materials during assessment and treatment. Ethical considerations have greatly influenced the state of research in evaluating the efficacy of behavior therapy with paraphiliacs. For obvious legal and ethical reasons, the use of waiting-list control conditions is rarely if ever possible. Furthermore, chances of recidivism may preclude using treatment control conditions, the effectiveness of which is uncertain (or, worse yet, conditions that have proven ineffective). A clear understanding of these issues is essential for any therapist undertaking treatment with sex offenders.

CONCLUSIONS AND FUTURE DIRECTIONS

Over the past two decades, significant advances have been made in the treatment of sexual deviations. A departure from exclusive reliance on a single technique, such as aversion therapy, is evident; the present trend favors multicomponent treatments. Unfortunately, there is a paucity of controlled treatment outcome experiments with paraphiliacs. The majority of studies consist of single-case designs or small, uncontrolled trials. There are many inherent difficulties in using untreated control conditions as well as in relying on procedures that are of unknown efficacy.

In his review of the literature, Kelly (1982) concluded that behavior therapy was fairly effective in treating pedophilia. More recently, Marshall, Jones, Ward, Johnston, and Barbaree (1991) noted that behavior therapy techniques were useful with pedophiles and exhibitionists but not rapists. Marshall and Barbaree (1988) conducted one of the few comparative treatment outcome studies with pedophiles and reached several conclusions. Sixty-eight child molesters were treated in an outpatient, behaviorally based, multicomponent program and compared to 58 pedophiles who were not treated (because of their refusal or inability to attend). Treated patients evidenced significant reductions in deviant arousal and lower recidivism rates than the untreated group. Follow-up at intervals ranging from 1 to 11 years revealed that over 34% of untreated subjects had recidivated, compared to 13% of treated subjects. This study represents one of the few controlled treatment studies in which behavior therapy was compared to a no-treatment control condition. The addition of a systematic relapse prevention component may have further reduced recidivism, a hypothesis that merits empirical study. Marshall and Barbaree (1988) found that offender age (younger than 40) and perpetration of genital–genital contact were poor prognostic signs for the pedophiles. Further, if a patient's sexual behavior is consistent with his sexual values, the prognosis may be poor. Behavioral change occurs only in motivated individuals.

The behavioral treatment of sexual deviations presents many challenges. However, data on efficacy suggest that behavior therapy is promising and merits more empirical study (Marshall et al., 1991). In fact, no other approach to the treatment of sexual deviations has yielded comparable results. Future research is needed to enhance understanding of the parameters of specific paraphilias in order to ultimately match interventions to individual patient needs.

REFERENCES

Abel, G. G., Barlow, D. H., Blanchard, E. B., & Guild, D. (1977). The components of rapists' sexual arousal. *Archives of General Psychiatry, 34,* 895–903.

Abel, G. G., Becker, J. V., Cunningham-Rathner, J., Rouleau, J. L., Kaplan, M., & Reich, J. (1984). *The treatment of child molesters: Treatment manual.* Atlanta: Authors.

Abel, G. G., Becker, J. V., Cunningham-Rathner, J., Rouleau, J. L., & Murphy, W. D. (1987). Self-reported sex crimes of nonincarcerated paraphiliacs. *Journal of Interpersonal Violence, 2,* 2–25.

Abel, G. G., Blanchard, E. B. (1974). The role of fantasy in the treatment of sexual deviation. *Archives of General Psychiatry, 30,* 467–475.

Abel, G. G., Blanchard, E. B., Becker, J. V., & Djenderedjian, A. (1978). Differentiating sexual aggressives with penile measures. *Criminal Justice and Behavior, 5,* 315–332.

Abel, G. G., Levis, D. J., & Clancy, J. (1970). Aversion therapy applied to taped sequences of deviant behavior in exhibitionism and other sexual deviations: A preliminary report. *Journal of Behavior Therapy and Experimental Psychiatry, 1,* 59–66.

Adams, H. E., McAnulty, R. D., & Iezzi, A. (1990). *Assessment of deviant sexual arousal: A review of the literature.* Manuscript submitted for publication.

Adams, H. E., & Sturgis, E. T. (1978). Status of behavioral reorientation techniques in the modification of homosexuality: A review. *Psychological Bulletin, 84,* 1171–1188.

Alford, G. S., Morin, C., Atkins, M., & Schoen, L. (1987). Masturbatory extinction of deviant sexual arousal: A case study. *Behavior Therapy, 18,* 265–271.

American Psychiatric Association. (1968). *Diagnostic and statistical manual of mental disorders* (2nd ed.). Washington, DC: Author.

American Psychiatric Association. (1987). *Diagnostic and statistical manual of mental disorders* (3rd ed. rev.). Washington, DC: Author.

Arkowitz, H. (1981). Assessment of social skills. In M. Hersen & A. S. Bellack (Eds.), *Behavioral assessment: A practical handbook* (2nd ed.; pp. 296–327). New York: Pergamon.

Azrin, N. H., & Holtz, W. C. (1966). Punishment. In W. K. Honig (Ed.), *Operant behavior: Areas of research and application* (pp. 380–447). New York: Appleton-Century-Crofts.

Bancroft, J. (1969). Aversion therapy of homosexuality: A pilot study of 10 cases. *British Journal of Psychiatry, 115,* 1417–1431.

Bancroft, J. A. (1970). A comparative study of aversion and desensitization in the treatment of homosexuality. In L. E. Burns & J. L. Worsley (Eds.), *Behavior therapy in the 70's.* Bristol, England: Wright.

Bandura, A., Blanchard, E. B., & Ritter, R. (1969). The relative efficacy of desensitization and modeling approaches for inducing behavioral, affective, and attitudinal changes. *Journal of Personality and Social Psychology, 13,* 173–199.

Bandura, A., & Menlove, F. L. (1968). Factors determining vicarious extinction of avoidance behavior through symbolic modeling. *Journal of Personality and Social Psychology, 8,* 99–108.

Barlow, D. H. (1973). Increasing heterosexual responsiveness in the treatment of sexual deviation: A review of the clinical and experimental evidence. *Behavior Therapy, 4,* 655–761.

Barlow, D. H. (1974). The treatment of sexual deviation: Toward a comprehensive behavioral approach. In K. S. Calhoun, H. E. Adams, & K. M. Mitchell (Eds.), *Innovative treatment methods in psychopathology* (pp. 121–147). New York: Wiley.

Barlow, D. H. (1977). Assessment of sexual behavior. In A. R. Ciminero, K. S. Calhoun, & H. E. Adams (Eds.), *Handbook of behavioral assessment* (pp. 461–508). New York: Wiley.

Barlow, D. H., Abel, G. G., Blanchard, E. B., Bristow, A. R., & Young, L. D. (1977). A heterosocial skills checklist for males. *Behavior Therapy, 8,* 229–239.

Barlow, D. H., & Agras, W. S. (1973). Fading to increase heterosexual responsiveness in homosexuals. *Journal of Applied Behavior Analysis, 6,* 355–367.

Barlow, D. H., Becker, R., Leitenberg, H., & Agras, W. S. (1970). A mechanical strain gauge for recording penile circumference change. *Journal of Applied Behavior Analysis, 3,* 73–76.

Barlow, D. H., Leitenberg, H., & Agras, W. S. (1969). Experimental control of sexual deviation through manipulation of the noxious scene in covert sensitization. *Journal of Abnormal Psychology, 74,* 596–601.

Barlow, D. H., Reynolds, E. H., & Agras, W. S. (1973). Gender identity change in a transsexual. *Archives of General Psychiatry, 28,* 569–579.

Bellack, A. S., & Morrison, R. L. (1982). Interpersonal dysfunction. In A. S. Bellack, M. Hersen, & A. E. Kazdin (Eds.), *International handbook of behavior modification and therapy* (pp. 717–747). New York: Plenum.

Bem, S. L. (1974). The measurement of psychological androgyny. *Journal of Consulting and Clinical Psychology, 42,* 155–162.

Brownell, K. D., & Barlow, D. H. (1976). Measurement and treatment of two sexual deviations in one person. *Journal of Behavior Therapy and Experimental Psychiatry, 7,* 349–354.

Brownell, K. D., Hayes, S. C., & Barlow, D. H. (1977). Patterns of appropriate and deviant sexual arousal: The behavioral treatment of multiple sexual deviations. *Journal of Consulting and Clinical Psychology, 45,* 1144–1155.

Caird, W. K., & Wincze, J. P. (1977). *Sex therapy: A behavioral approach.* Hagerstown, MD: Harper & Row.

Callahan, E. I., & Leitenberg, H. (1973). Aversion therapy for sexual deviation: Contingent shock and covert sensitization. *Journal of Abnormal Psychology, 81,* 60–73.

Cautela, J. R., & Wisocki, P. A. (1971). Covert sensitization for the treatment of sexual deviations. *The Psychological Record, 21,* 37–48.

Christensen, A., & Arkowitz, H. (1974). Preliminary report on practice dating and feedback as treatment for college dating problems. *Journal of Counseling Psychology, 21,* 92–95.

Ciminero, A. R., Calhoun, K. S., & Adams, H. E. (1986). *Handbook of behavioral assessment* (2nd ed.). New York: Wiley.

Comfort, A. (1972). *The joy of sex.* New York: Crown.

Conrad, S. R., & Wincze, J. P. (1976). Orgasmic reconditioning: A controlled study of its effects upon the sexual arousal and behavior of adult male homosexuals. *Behavior Therapy, 7,* 155–166.

Cooper, A. A. (1963). A case of fetishism and impotence treated by behavior therapy. *British Journal of Psychiatry, 109,* 649–652.

Curran, J. P. (1975). An evaluation of a skills training program and a systematic desensitization program in reducing dating anxiety. *Behaviour Research and Therapy, 13,* 65–68.

Curran, J. P. (1977). Skills training as an approach to the treatment of heterosexual-social anxiety: A review. *Psychological Bulletin, 84,* 140–157.

Curran, J. P., & Gilbert, F. S. (1975). A test of the relative effectiveness of a systematic desensitization program and an interpersonal skills training program with date anxious subjects. *Behavior Therapy, 6,* 510–521.

Curran, J. P., Gilbert, F. S., & Little, L. M. (1976). A comparison between behavioral training and sensitivity training approaches to heterosexual dating anxiety. *Journal of Counseling Psychology, 23,* 190–196.

Curran, J. P., & Monti, P. M. (1982). *Social skills training: A practical handbook for assessment and treatment.* New York: Guilford.

Davison, G. (1968). Elimination of a sadistic fantasy by a client-controlled counter-conditioning technique: A case study. *Journal of Abnormal Psychology, 63,* 84–90.

Earls, C. M., & Castonguay, L. G. (1989). The evaluation of olfactory aversion for a bisexual pedophile with a single-case multiple baseline design. *Behavior Therapy, 20,* 137–146.

Edwards, N. B. (1972). Case conference: Assertive training in a case of homosexual pedophilia. *Journal of Behavior Therapy and Experimental Psychiatry, 3,* 55–63.

Erickson, W. D., Luxenberg, M. G., Walbek, N. H., & Seely, R. K. (1987). Frequency of MMPI two-point code types among sex offenders. *Journal of Consulting and Clinical Psychology, 55,* 566–570.

Evans, D. R. (1968). Masturbatory fantasy and sexual deviation. *Behaviour Research and Therapy, 6,* 17–19.

Feldman, M. P., & MacCullough, M. J. (1965). The application of anticipatory avoidance learning and the treatment of homosexuality: Theory, technique and preliminary results. *Behaviour Research and Therapy, 2,* 165.

Feldman, M. P., & MacCullough, M. J. (1971). *Homosexual behavior: Therapy and assessment.* Oxford, England: Pergamon.

Fenichel, O. (1945). *The psychoanalytic theory of the neuroses.* New York: Norton.

Freund, K. (1963). A laboratory method for diagnosing predominance of homo- and hetero-erotic interest in the male. *Behaviour Research and Therapy, 1,* 85–93.

Freund, K., Langevin, R., Satterberg, J., & Steiner, B. (1977). Extension of the gender identity scale for males. *Archives of Sexual Behavior, 6,* 507–519.

Freund, K., Nagler, E., Langevin, R., Zajac, Y., & Steiner, B. (1974). Measuring feminine gender identity in homosexual males. *Archives of Sexual Behavior, 3,* 249–260.

Freund, K., Watson, R., & Rienzo, D. (1988). Signs of feigning in the phallometric test. *Behaviour Research and Therapy, 26,* 105–112.

Furby, L., Weinrott, M. R., & Blackshaw, L. (1989). Sex offender recidivism: A review. *Psychological Bulletin, 105,* 3–30.

Gelder, M. G., & Marks, I. M. (1969). Aversion treatment in transvestism and transsexualism. In R. Green & J. Money (Eds.), *Transsexualism and sex reassignment* (pp. 383–413). Baltimore: Johns Hopkins.

Gray, J. J. (1970). Case conference: Behavior therapy in a patient with homosexual fantasies and heterosexual anxieties. *Journal of*

Behavior Therapy and Experimental Psychiatry, 1, 225–232.

Harbison, J. J., Quinn, J. T., & McAllister, H. (1970). An attempt to shape human penile response. *Behaviour Research and Therapy, 9,* 286–290.

Hartman, W. A., & Fithian, M. A. (1972). *Treatment of sexual dysfunction.* Long Beach, CA: Center for Marital and Sexual Studies.

Hathaway, S. R., & McKinley, J. C. (1967). *Minnesota Multiphasic Personality Inventory manual.* New York: Psychological Corporation.

Haynes, S. N. (1988). Causal models and the assessment-treatment relationship in behavior therapy. *Journal of Psychopathology and Behavioral Assessment, 10,* 171–183.

Herman, S. H. (1971). *An experimental analysis of two methods of increasing heterosexual arousal in homosexuals.* Unpublished doctoral dissertation, University of Mississippi.

Herman, S. H., Barlow, D. H., & Agras, W. S. (1974). An experimental analysis of exposure to "elicit" heterosexual stimuli as an effective variable in changing arousal patterns in homosexuals. *Behaviour Research and Therapy, 12,* 315–345.

Kanfer, F. H., & Saslow, G. (1969). Behavioral diagnosis. In C. M. Franks (Ed.), *Behavior therapy: Appraisal and status* (pp. 417–444). New York: McGraw-Hill.

Kaplan, H. S. (1974). *The new sex therapy.* New York: Brunner-Mazel.

Kelly, R. J. (1982). Behavioral reorientation of pedophiliacs: Can it be done? *Clinical Psychology Review, 2,* 387–408.

Kolvin, I. (1967). Aversion imagery treatment in an adolescent. *Behaviour Research and Therapy, 5,* 245–248.

Langevin, R. (1983). *Sexual strands: Understanding and treating sexual anomalies in men.* Hillsdale, NJ: Erlbaum.

Laws, D. R. (1989). *Relapse prevention with sex offenders.* New York: Guilford.

Laws, D. R., Meyer, J., & Holmen, M. L. (1978). Reduction of sadistic sexual arousal by olfactory aversion: A case study. *Behaviour Research and Therapy, 16,* 281–285.

Lipton, D. N., McDonel, E. C., & McFall, R. M. (1987). Heterosocial perception in rapists. *Journal of Consulting and Clinical Psychology, 55,* 17–21.

Maletzky, B. M. (1974). "Assisted" covert sensitization in the treatment of exhibitionism. *Journal of Consulting and Clinical Psychology, 42,* 34–40.

Maletzky, B. M., & George, F. S. (1973). The treatment of homosexuality by "assisted" covert sensitization. *Behaviour Research and Therapy, 8,* 460–463.

Marks, I. M. (1976). Management of sexual disorders. In H. Leitenberg (Ed.), *Handbook of behavior modification and behavior therapy* (pp. 255–300). Englewood Cliffs, NJ: Prentice-Hall.

Marks, I. M., & Gelder, M. G. (1967). Transvestism and fetishism: Clinical and psychological changes during faradic aversion. *British Journal of Psychiatry, 113,* 711–729.

Marks, I. M., Rachman, S., & Gelder, M. G. (1965). Methods for assessment of aversion treatment in fetishism with masochism. *Behaviour Research and Therapy, 3,* 253–258.

Marquis, J. N. (1970). Orgasmic reconditioning: Changing sexual choice through controlling masturbatory fantasies. *Journal of Behavior Therapy and Experimental Psychiatry, 1,* 263–271.

Marshall, W. L. (1973). The modification of sexual fantasies: A combined treatment approach to the reduction of deviant sexual arousal. *Behaviour Research and Therapy, 11,* 557–564.

Marshall, W. L. (1979). Satiation therapy: A procedure for reducing deviant sexual arousal. *Journal of Applied Behavior Analysis, 12,* 377–389.

Marshall, W. L., & Barbaree, H. E. (1988). The long-term evaluation of a behavioral treatment program for child molesters. *Behaviour Research and Therapy, 26,* 499–511.

Marshall, W. L., Jones, R., Ward, T., Johnston, P., & Barbaree, H. E. (1991). Treatment outcome with sex offenders. *Clinical Psychology Review, 11,* 465–485.

Marshall, W. L., Laws, D. R., & Barbaree, H. E. (1990). *Handbook of sexual assault.* New York: Plenum.

Marshall, W. L., & Lippens, K. (1977). The clinical value of boredom: A procedure for reducing inappropriate sexual interests. *The Journal of Nervous and Mental Disease, 165,* 283–287.

Martinson, W. D., & Zerface, J. P. (1970). Comparison of individual counseling and a social program with non-daters. *Journal of Counseling Psychology, 17,* 36–40.

Masters, W. H., & Johnson, V. E. (1970). *Human sexual inadequacy.* Boston: Little, Brown.

McAnulty, R. D., & Adams, H. E. (1990). Patterns of sexual arousal of alleged child molestors involved in custody disputes. *Archives of Sexual Behavior, 19,* 541–556.

McAnulty, R. D., Adams, H. E., & Andrew, M. (1989, November). *Characteristics of individuals who deny the validity of child molestation allegations.* Paper presented at the meeting of the Association for the Advancement of Behavior Therapy, Washington, DC.

McConaghy, N. (1969). Subjective and penile plethysmograph responses following aversion relief and apomorphine aversion therapy for homosexual impulses. *British Journal of Psychiatry, 115,* 723–730.

McCrary, J. L. (1973). *Human sexuality.* New York: Van Nostrand Reinhold.

McGuire, R. J., Carlisle, J. M., & Young, B. G. (1965). Sexual deviations as conditioned behaviour: A hypothesis. *Behaviour Research and Therapy, 2,* 185–190.

Money, J. (1986). *Lovemaps: Clinical concepts of sexual/erotic health and pathology, paraphilia, and gender transposition in childhood, adolescence, and maturity.* New York: Irvington.

Morganstern, F. S., Pearce, J. F., & Linford-Rees, W. (1965). Predicting the outcome of behavior therapy by psychological tests. *Behaviour Research and Therapy, 3,* 191–200.

Nelson, R. O. (1988). Relationships between assessment and treatment within a behavioral perspective. *Journal of Psychopathology and Behavioral Assessment, 10,* 155–170.

Overholser, J. C., & Beck, S. (1986). Multimethod assessment of rapists, child molesters, and three control groups on behavioral and psychological measures. *Journal of Consulting and Clinical Psychology, 54,* 682–687.

Pithers, W. D., Kashima, K. M., Cumming, G. F., Beal, L. S., & Buell, M. M. (1988). Relapse prevention of sexual aggression. In R. A. Prentky & V. L. Quinsey (Eds.), *Human sexual aggression: Current perspectives* (pp. 244–260). New York: Annals of the New York Academy of Sciences.

Pithers, W. D., Marques, J. K., Gibat, C. C., & Marlatt, A. (1983). Relapse prevention with sexual aggressives: A self-control model treatment and maintenance of change. In J. G. Greer & I. R. Stuart (Eds.), *The sexual aggressor: Current perspectives on treatment* (pp. 214–239). New York: Van Nostrand Reinhold.

Quinn, J. T., Harbison, J. J., & McAllister, H. (1970). An attempt to shape penile responses. *Behaviour Research and Therapy, 8,* 212–216.

Quinsey, V. L. (1977). The assessment and treatment of child molesters: A review. *Canadian Psychological Review, 18,* 204–220.

Quinsey, V. L., Bergersen, S. G., & Steinman, C. M. (1976). Changes in physiological and verbal responses of child molesters during aversion therapy. *Canadian Journal of Behavioral Science, 8,* 202–212.

Quinsey, V. L., Chaplin, T. C., & Carrigan, W. F. (1980). Biofeedback and signaled punishment in the modification of inappropriate sexual age preferences. *Behavior Therapy, 11,* 567–576.

Rachman, S. (1966). Sexual fetishism: An experimental analogue. *The Psychological Record, 16,* 293–296.

Rachman, S. J., & Hodgson, R. J. (1968). Experimentally induced sexual fetishism: Replication and development. *Psychological Record, 18,* 25–27.

Rachman, S. J., & Teasdale, J. (1969). *Aversion therapy and behaviour disorders: An analysis.* London: Routledge & Kegan Paul.

Rehm, L. P., & Marston, A. R. (1968). Reduction of social anxiety through modification of self-reinforcement: An instigation therapy technique. *Journal of Consulting and Clinical Psychology, 32,* 565–574.

Rekers, G. A., & Varni, J. W. (1977). Self-monitoring and self-reinforcement process in a pre-transsexual boy. *Behaviour Research and Therapy, 10,* 211–216.

Rosen, R., & Beck, G. (1988). *Patterns of sexual arousal: Psychophysiological processes and clinical applications.* New York: Guilford.

Rosen, R. C., & Keefe, F. J. (1978). The measurement of human penile tumescence. *Psychophysiology, 15,* 366–376.

Segal, Z. V., & Marshall, W. L. (1985). Heterosexual social skills in a population of rapists and child molesters. *Journal of Consulting and Clinical Psychology, 53,* 55–63.

Serber, M. (1971). Shame aversion therapy. *Journal of Behavior Therapy and Experimental Psychiatry, 1,* 213–215.

Shapiro, D. L. (1984). *Psychological evaluation and expert testimony.* New York: Van Nostrand Reinhold.

Stermac, L. E., & Quinsey, V. L. (1986). Social competence among rapists. *Behavioral Assessment, 8,* 171–185.

Stevenson, I., & Wolpe, J. (1960). Recovery from sexual deviations through overcoming non-sexual neurotic responses. *American Journal of Psychiatry, 116,* 739–742.

Terrace, H. S. (1966). Stimulus control. In W. K. Honig (Ed.), *Operant behavior: Areas of research and application* (pp. 271–344). New York: Appleton-Century-Crofts.

Thorpe, J. G., Schmidt, E., Brown, P. T., & Castell, D. (1964). Aversion relief therapy: A new method for general application. *Behaviour Research and Therapy, 2,* 71–82.

Turkat, I. D. (1988). Issues in the relationship between assessment and treatment. *Journal of Psychopathology and Behavioral Assessment, 10,* 185–197.

Twentyman, C. T., & McFall, R. M. (1975). Behavioral training of social skills in shy males. *Journal of Consulting and Clinical Psychology, 43,* 384–395.

Wheeler, D., & Rubin, H. B. (1987). A comparison of volumetric and circumferential measures of penile erection. *Archives of Sexual Behavior, 16,* 289–299.

Wickramasekera, I. (1968). The application of learning theory to a case of sexual exhibitionism. *Psychotherapy: Theory, Research, & Practice, 5,* 108–112.

Wickramasekera, I. (1972). A technique for controlling a certain type of sexual exhibitionism. *Psychotherapy: Theory, Research, & Practice, 9,* 207–210.

Wickramasekera, I. (1976). Aversive behavior rehearsal for sexual exhibitionism. *Behavior Therapy, 7,* 167–176.

Wolpe, J. (1958). *Psychotherapy by reciprocal inhibition.* Stanford: Stanford University Press.

Wolpe, J. (1982). *The practice of behavior therapy* (3rd ed.). New York: Pergamon.

Wolpe, J., & Turkat, I. D. (1985). Behavioral formulation of clinical cases. In I. D. Turkat (Ed.), *Behavioral case formulation* (pp. 5–36). New York: Plenum.

Zilbergeld, B. (1978). *Male sexuality.* Boston: Little, Brown.

Zuckerman, M. (1971). Physiological measures of sexual arousal in the human. *Psychological Bulletin, 25,* 297–327.

CHAPTER 11

Substance Abuse

JALIE A. TUCKER, RUDY E. VUCHINICH, and KAREN K. DOWNEY

This chapter focuses on empirically supported behavioral treatments for alcohol and drug abuse. It begins with a brief sketch of behavioral models of substance abuse, especially as contrasted with more traditional approaches, and then outlines the general assessment and treatment implications of the behavioral view. The treatments are then described, with more attention directed toward the clinical procedures than to details of the supporting empirical evidence. The final section outlines several unresolved issues relevant to the advancement of behavioral treatments of substance abuse.

BEHAVIORAL MODELS OF SUBSTANCE ABUSE

The addiction-as-disease perspective has been a dominant force for at least 60 years and has had a salutary effect by making treatment more widely available. Pattison, Sobell, and Sobell (1977) described this view in detail as applied to alcohol abuse; the same basic ideas have been generalized to other addictions. From this perspective, substance abuse is caused by forces "inside" the individual, in the form of either a biological or a psychological deficiency. Affected persons are viewed as inevitably susceptible to the addicting properties of alcohol or drugs, and substance use is considered primarily driven by physiological factors and impervious to environmental influence.

This perspective continues to dominate service delivery. However, by the 1970s, rescarch (Griffiths, Bigelow, & Liebson, 1974; Marlatt, Demming, & Reid, 1973; Mello & Mendelson, 1965) had demonstrated the perspective's inadequacy as well as the viability of the radically different behavioral perspective. In general, the behavioral approach maintains that substance abuse arises from and is maintained through the individual's commerce with the environment. Contemporary behavioral research on substance abuse is bifurcated along theoretical borders corresponding to behavior analytic (e.g., Griffiths, Bigelow, & Henningfield, 1980; Vuchinich & Tucker, 1988) and cognitive behavioral or social learning (e.g., Blane & Leonard, 1987; Marlatt & Gordon, 1985) perspectives. Despite some important differences in assumptions about the controlling variables of substance abuse, both views share other critical assumptions that distinguish them from the disease model. First, both regard alcohol and drugs as powerful reinforcers capable of maintaining self-administration, with behavior analysts and cognitive behaviorists preferring to view them as positive and negative reinforcers, respectively. Second, both views consider alcohol and drug self-administration to be dependent on the historical and current environmental context of substance availability. Behavior analysts characterize that context directly in terms of environmental variables; cognitive behaviorists characterize it indirectly in terms of the effects of the environment on internal states (e.g., anxiety).

GENERAL TREATMENT IMPLICATIONS

Characterizing alcohol and drugs as reinforcers, the consumption of which is dependent on environmental contexts, is very different from assuming that the controlling variables of substance abuse lie in some biological, personality, or other stable individual characteristic. The disease and behavioral views of addiction thus entail very different conceptualizations of the treatment process. Disease-based treatments do not focus directly on changing relevant behavior, but instead attempt to induce lifelong abstinence by inculcating clients with an internally consistent, persuasive framework that in most cases removes personal responsibility for their addiction (e.g., it is attributed to a biological predisposition). This approach is undoubtedly compatible with the personal experience of some substance abusers, but it neglects the variability observed in substance abuse problems across individuals and overlooks how substance abuse is embedded in individuals' overall life circumstances and varies with changing conditions. Behavioral treatments are built on empirical covariation between patterns of substance abuse and the surrounding environment, and thus focus on the substance use behaviors directly and on how they vary with changing conditions in the natural environment. The goal of treatment is to decrease clients' preference for substance use while simultaneously increasing preference for other activities that will support long-term adaptive functioning. The specific areas of functioning adversely affected by substance use will vary among clients, as will patterns of substance use and abuse, and necessitate that treatment be individualized.

The related principles of the context-dependence of substance use and treatment individualization have implications for treatment goal selection that are not consistent with the disease perspective, which focuses on lifelong abstinence as the only possible goal regardless of circumstances. Behavioral approaches view substance abuse as lying on a continuum of dysfunction with respect to both substance use and the presence and nature of related life problems. It thus follows that (a) goal selection is not limited only to eliminating substance use, but also must entail changes in areas of functioning related to the substance abuse, and (b) some individuals can reasonably be expected to engage in nonproblem substance use. The latter statement is controversial and may not apply to some illegal drugs, but it is an empirical fact with respect to alcohol consumption (Miller & Hester, 1986a) and is a basic assumption of methadone maintenance for opiate addiction. Few clinicians, behavioral or otherwise, would advocate nonabstinence for the majority of clients. Nevertheless, outcome research indicating that a small but clinically significant proportion of clients succeed in moderation drinking (Miller & Hester, 1986a) shows that such outcomes are possible. This is a relevant finding because abstinence is rejected by some clients (e.g., early problem drinkers) or is not supported by their environment. As discussed later, the task ahead is to identify predictor variables that reliably identify who can and cannot attain a moderation goal.

Behavioral and traditional treatments also differ on the value of inpatient and outpatient treatment. To facilitate lasting change, behavioral treatments aim to modify problem behavior in the environments in which it is maintained by natural contingencies of reinforcement. This is better accomplished by outpatient treatment, which can be preceded with hospitalization in appropriate cases. Traditional treatments appear to make little distinction between treatment settings, apart from cost considerations. Perhaps because of the dominance of physicians in inpatient settings, most inpatient programs adhere to traditional treatment approaches, with postdischarge care often limited to infrequent aftercare visits and/or recommendations to attend A.A. or N.A. This method of treatment delivery reduces the probability of maintenance of treatment gains, and, at least with respect to alcohol treatment, little evidence exists that inpatient treatment produces better long-term outcomes than outpatient treatment or that lengthier treatment results in superior outcomes (Miller & Hester, 1986b). Hospitalization certainly is appropriate when clients are physically compromised, at risk for serious health complications during withdrawal, engaged in highly destructive behaviors, or living in highly stressful environments. Otherwise, outpatient treatment, including physician-managed detoxification, is a reasonable, cost-effective alternative that provides a better vehicle for promoting permanent behavior change.

GENERAL ASSESSMENT IMPLICATIONS

The disease view of addiction implies a treatment-relevant diagnostic scheme that categorizes clients based on identifiable symptoms. Such a scheme is contained in the DSM-III-R (American Psychiatric Association, 1987) criteria for psychoactive substance use disorders. A basic distinction is made between abuse and dependence. Up to nine symptoms characterize dependence, including tolerance, withdrawal symptoms, interference in fulfilling responsibilities, and decreased involvement in valued activities because of substance use. A diagnosis of abuse is appropriate when individuals are not dependent but show continued maladaptive use, despite substance-related problems, for a month or longer.

These criteria are useful for determining that a problem exists, but are incomplete with respect to providing the following information needed for behavioral treatments:

1. A detailed history of the quantity, frequency, and temporal patterning of individuals' substance use, particularly during the preceding year, which ascertains the level and variability of use and whether clients had periods of abstinence or moderate use. Particularly important are the conditions under which individuals do and do not engage in substance use and abuse, which may include environmental contexts and private events or states. Also assessed are past quit attempts, whether treatment-assisted or not, and the variables that influenced their outcome.

2. A comprehensive evaluation of life functioning in areas such as intimate, family, and social relations; vocational functioning; financial status; legal problems; and physical health, with emphasis on identifying for individual clients areas that are impaired by substance use and may require specific treatment interventions. Also assessed are consequences of substance use that the client views as positive.

3. An identification of valued activities that compete with substance use or whose probability of receipt increases with abstinence or reduced use.

4. An overall level of client motivation and resources and the extent to which his or her environment will support various treatment goals, including, but not limited to, those related to substance use.

Donovan and Marlatt (1988) discussed specific assessment procedures for collecting this information. The important point here is that behavioral treatment requires that the client and the therapist understand how the client's substance use is embedded in his or her broader life circumstances and how problem use covaries with environmental conditions and with changes in the availability of important reinforcers in the client's life. As is true in all behavior therapies, assessment continues throughout treatment and can lead to important revisions in treatment methods and goals. A central example of this in the substance use area occurs when a client relapses during treatment, which is an important learning opportunity and should be examined nonjudgmentally, to understand the conditions that place the client at risk for substance use (Marlatt & Gordon, 1985).

BEHAVIORAL TREATMENT PROCEDURES

Treatments That Focus Exclusively on Substance Use

The aversion and cue exposure treatments described in this section seek to alter substance use behaviors only and are not directly concerned with modifying related life problems. Thus, they may be most appropriately used as a means of initially suppressing problem substance use, but maintenance of treatment gains may well require additional interventions. These procedures also share a common conceptual focus on the role of classical conditioning in substance abuse disorders.

Aversion Therapies, Including Covert Sensitization

Aversion treatments pair substance-relevant stimuli (e.g., the sight or taste of alcohol) with noxious stimuli (e.g., nausea-inducing drugs), presumably to produce a conditioned aversion to the substance-related stimuli. Subsequent reductions in substance use are hypothesized to depend on the strength of the conditioned aversion. In the most commonly used method with alcoholics, a nausea-inducing drug such as emetine hydrocloride is administered in a medically supervised setting, and beverage cues are presented during the resulting nausea and vomiting. Because the time course of the drug effect is difficult to control, and because of risks associated with drug administration, painful but safe levels of shock have been investigated as an alternative conditioning agent. Although shock is more controllable and generally safer, research indicates that it is less effective for alcoholism than using nausea-inducing drugs. This difference is interpreted as being caused by the greater biological preparedness of taste and gustatory cues to be conditionable to nausea- and emesis-producing stimuli. This issue has not been adequately investigated with other substance disorders, which usually have employed electrical aversion.

Although aversion treatment of alcoholism using nausea-inducing drugs usually suppresses consumption for the first several months after treatment, its several disadvantages include the following:

1. It must be conducted in a carefully monitored medical setting and is contraindicated by certain medical conditions (e.g., gastrointestinal or cardiac problems);
2. Like other treatments based on aversion or punishment, generalization of treatment gains usually requires additional procedures (e.g., contingency contracting) that address contingencies of reinforcement maintaining substance use in the natural environment;
3. If effective alternative treatments exist that rely on positive reinforcement or extinction, ethical considerations argue strongly for their use;
4. Research has not strongly supported the predicted relationship between the strength of the conditioned aversion and posttreatment drinking, except for measures of aversion based on cardiac response (Cannon, Baker, Gino, & Nathan, 1986).

Because of these concerns, covert sensitization recently has been investigated as an alternative imagery-based aversion treatment, and encouraging results have been obtained for alcoholism (Clarke & Hayes, 1984; Elkins, 1980) and other substance disorders (Copemann, 1977; Polakow, 1975). Based on the work of Cautela (1970), covert sensitization entails the imaginal pairing of substance use scenes with highly unpleasant events and sometimes is accompanied by noxious odors, such as from valeric acid. Aversion relief procedures also may be included, during which the client terminates the unpleasant scenes contingent on imagining an appropriate response such as refusing drug use or leaving the drug use environment.

Rimmele, Miller, and Dougher (1989) described how to implement covert sensitization, which requires development of realistic scenes involving clients' substance use that are paired with sensitization scenes of highly unpleasant consequences of substance use. Their example of a sensitization scene illustrates the vividness of the images required:

You finish the first sip of beer, and you . . . notice a funny feeling in your stomach . . . . Maybe another drink will help. . . . As you tip it back . . . that funny feeling in your stomach is stronger, and you feel like you will have to burp. . . . You swallow again, trying to force it down, but it doesn't work. You can feel the gas coming up. . . . You swallow more, but suddenly your mouth is filled with a sour liquid that burns the back of your throat, and goes up your nose. . . . [you] spew the liquid all over the counter and sink. You can tell that it is . . . chunks of food and brownish vomit. . . . You can smell the sour odor of the beer and the stench of the vomit. . . . You feel your stomach contract, and your throat fills with more burning vomit. . . . Your stomach heaves uncontrollably, and vomit spews out of your mouth into the sink, splashing back up into your face. You can see the chunks of food and the vomit oozing down the drain, and you notice that there are spots of blood in the vomit as well. . . . your stomach won't quit heaving. Now greenish bile is in your mouth. . . . Your eyes are watering, and your nose and throat are burning. . . . The stench from the sink is almost unbearable, the sour odor of vomit, half-digested food and beer. That smell triggers another heave in your stomach, but there is nothing left to come up. (p. 135)

As this example shows, covert sensitization, like all imagery-based treatments, depends on client effectiveness in constructing, maintaining, and terminating imaginal stimuli, which is a potential limitation. Otherwise, covert sensitization has many advantages over other aversion methods (e.g., relative safety, ease of implementation in a variety of settings) and is unique in incorporating stimulus events in clients' natural environments related to substance use. Although it is not as well evaluated as earlier aversion treatments and reports of its use with drug addicts are limited largely to single-case studies or studies in which covert sensitization was one of several treatment components (reviewed by Childress, McLellan, & O'Brien, 1985a), several well-conducted outcome studies with alcoholics have supported the procedure (Elkins, 1980; Elkins & Murdock, 1977). The latter research indicates, however, that clients who develop a conditioned aversion quickly in treatment (e.g., in 2 to 6 sessions) achieve better long-term outcomes.

Cue Exposure and Response Prevention

A common notion in both the alcohol and drug literatures is that environmental stimuli associated repeatedly with substance use or with substance withdrawal can, through a classical conditioning process, come to serve as conditioned stimuli for further substance use (reviewed by Baker, Morse, & Sherman, 1987; Niaura, et al., 1988). Although disagreement exists about the nature of the conditioned response (i.e., whether it represents a conditioned withdrawal syndrome or functions as positive incentive motivation to consume drugs), this general view has led to the development of exposure-based treatments of alcohol (e.g., Rankin, Hodgson, & Stockwell, 1983) and drug (e.g., O'Brien, Ehrman, & Ternes, 1986) abuse that are very similar to behavioral treatments of obsessive-compulsive disorders (see Foa & Kozak, 1986). As applied to substance abuse, clients are exposed to substance-related stimuli and are prevented from or strongly encouraged not to engage in substance use. With repeated exposure, urges to engage in substance use presumably are extinguished, which should reduce substance use when clients encounter the stimuli in their natural environments.

Rankin et al. (1983) described the technique with inpatient alcoholics who were given a "priming" dose of alcohol and then placed in close proximity to alcoholic beverages for 45 minutes. Clients were encouraged to hold the drink, place it to their lips, and smell the alcohol. Exposure resulted in reports of a decreased desire to drink, and, during behavioral tests assessing the length of time taken to drink a standard amount of alcohol, the experimental group had longer durations than a control group. However, no differences were found on physiological indexes thought to reflect the conditioned response undergoing extinction, and the long-term effects of treatment on drinking in the natural environment were not evaluated. Similar strategies have been used with cocaine abusers (O'Brien et al., 1988). As in Rankin et al. (1983), exposure reduced reports of cocaine cravings, but drug use after treatment was not evaluated.

Until reliable effects on posttreatment substance use are demonstrated apart from case studies (cf. Childress et al., 1985a), this must be regarded as an important qualification of the approach. Moreover, studies of substance use relapse and reports of conditioned withdrawal symptoms and cravings have not shown a strong relationship between these variables (Tucker, Vuchinich, & Harris, 1985) and thus are not particularly encouraging about the role of conditioned responses in drug self-administration. Niaura et al. (1988) also summarized several treatment parameters that require clarification, including the timing of exposure in relation to drug withdrawal or drug use during treatment, the length and frequency of exposure sessions to assure habituation and extinction, and cue selection and the method of cue presentation. For example, with opiate addicts, cue exposure that involved drug injections led to a high rate of attrition despite cash inducements to continue (O'Brien, Greenstein, Ternes, McLellan, & Grabowski, 1979), whereas use of a graduated hierarchy of drug-related stimuli, with optional self-injections, reduced attrition (Childress, McLellan, & O'Brien, 1985b). Because of these undecided issues, cue exposure treatments should be viewed as experimental but worthy of continued evaluation.

Comprehensive Operant Treatment Approaches

The three approaches described here are more comprehensive than aversion and exposure treatments and address substance use behaviors and related life problems. Because they rely primarily on reward or extinction and deal with substance abuse in the environments in which it occurs, they do not suffer the ethical concerns associated with aversion procedures, nor is generalization of treatment gains as salient an issue.

Behavioral Self-Control Training (BSCT)

BSCT is a well-researched, reward-based treatment (Hester & Miller, 1989a; Maisto & Caddy, 1981) that is especially suited for outpatient use. It is distinguished by its educational approach of training clients to become effective behavior analysts of the contingencies maintaining their substance disorder. Interventions made at three levels can be adapted to the needs of individual clients:

1. Stimulus control procedures aimed at eliminating environmental stimuli associated with substance misuse;
2. Modification of the topography or temporal patterning of substance use in ways that minimize intoxication or other negative consequences;
3. Modification of the consequences of substance use and related behaviors, to reinforce reduced substance use and increased involvement in adaptive behaviors.

Stimulus control procedures involve initial assessment, usually through self-monitoring, of the environmental conditions or private events that precede or occur with substance misuse. The client then restricts all substance use to a single set of highly circumscribed stimuli. Eventually, that stimulus array will be eliminated as well, but this will likely require contingency management procedures that modify the consequences of substance use.

Although BSCT was developed in the context of training moderation drinking, interventions that modify the topography or temporal patterning of substance use are useful regardless of the treatment goal. Even in abstinence-oriented programs, most clients engage in some substance use, and such interventions assist in limiting the quantity of use, or use in situations or at times when the risk of negative consequences is high (e.g., driving while intoxicated). Interventions may include: (a) having clients agree to ingest a less preferred beverage or drug (e.g., methadone rather than heroin) if substance use occurs; (b) training clients to use external cues to monitor intoxication levels (e.g., counting sips of alcoholic beverages); and (c) having clients agree to restrict any substance use to times and situations that minimize negative consequences (this intervention overlaps with the stimulus control procedures).

Contingency management procedures administered by the client or by designated others (e.g., family members) typically are used to modify the consequences of substance use and related behaviors. As in all such programs, target behaviors and goals should be (a) specified in observable, unambiguous terms; (b) broken into small units so that they occur frequently, to allow multiple reinforcement opportunities; and (c) revised as behavior change occurs, so that long-term goals are shaped incrementally. Reinforcers should be delivered quickly following the target behavior and should be readily accessible, inexpensive, and tailored to the client's preference structure. Reinforcers might include quiet time alone each day and social events that do not involve substance availability. The Premack principle also can be used to identify effective reinforcers; that is, a low probability behavior can be reinforced by a higher probability behavior. For example, for a sedentary problem drinker with goals of quitting drinking and getting in shape, attendance at an evening exercise class as a way of filling time previously spent drinking could be reinforced by subsequent engagement in a preferred sedentary activity (e.g., time spent in the sauna and pool).

Outcome evaluations have been favorable over follow-up intervals lasting up to 2 years with outpatient problem drinkers (reviewed by Hester & Miller, 1989a), and, although the complete BSCT program has not been widely evaluated with drug abusers, contingency management is the most widely researched treatment for drug abuse and is strongly supported. With problem drinkers, no differences have been noted when BSCT was implemented in group versus individual formats (Miller, Pechacek, & Hamburg,

1981) or in therapist-directed treatment versus bibliotherapy (Miller & Taylor, 1980). For bibliotherapy, the self-directed program of Miller and Munoz (1982) is recommended. What are currently lacking are dismantling studies that evaluate the necessity of including the many components of BSCT. This qualification notwithstanding, BSCT is a viable, reward-based procedure for clients who can be treated as outpatients and, as summarized by Hester and Miller (1989a), ". . . should be available as one option among many within a treatment program wishing to serve a broad range of problem drinkers." (p. 147).

Contingency Management

The reinforcement component of BCST has been successfully used alone in treating drug addicts (Bigelow, Stitzer, & Liebson, 1984; Stitzer, Bigelow, & McCaul, 1985) and, to a lesser extent, alcoholics (Miller, 1975; Miller, Hersen, Eisler, & Watts, 1974). Usually, the client and therapist come to a written agreement about scheduling consequences for target behaviors that are administered by the therapist or by designated others, rather than by the client, although this is not necessarily a critical distinction. In some instances, such as at methadone clinics, the contingencies are established on a clinic-wide basis and are not individually negotiated, or they may be implemented as a token economy (Glosser, 1983).

Contingency contracting has been successfully implemented with heroin addicts maintained on methadone (Dolan, Black, Penk, Robinowitz, & DeFord, 1986; Magura, Casriel, Goldsmith, Strug, & Lipton, 1988), cocaine abusers (Anker & Crowley, 1982; Kleber & Gawin, 1984; Resnick & Resnick, 1986), and polydrug abusers (Crowley, 1984). With heroin addicts maintained on methadone, common problems are clients' continued use of opiates and noncompliance with aspects of the treatment program, such as attending the clinic each day to receive methadone, providing drug-free urinalyses, or participating in components aimed at increasing adaptive functioning (e.g., vocational counseling). Incentives that have successfully increased these target behaviors include methadone take-home privileges, wherein clients who meet behavior goals are given methadone for self-administration outside the clinic setting (McCaul, Stitzer, Bigelow, & Liebson, 1984; Stitzer, et al., 1977), or clients are given control over their dosage of methadone (Stitzer, Bigelow, & Liebson, 1979). Interestingly, giving alcoholics control over disulfiram administration similarly reduces alcohol use (Duckert & Johnsen, 1987). Monetary and material incentives also have been used with some success with heroin addicts in methadone treatment (Magura, Casriel, Goldsmith, & Lipton, 1987).

With respect to cocaine abuse, Anker and Crowley (1982) effectively reduced drug use by having clients write letters admitting their problem to employers, licensing boards, and related groups. The therapist mailed the letters only if a positive urinalysis was obtained. Crowley (1984) described a case showing how this contingency was used in an overall treatment program with a cocaine abuser:

A 30-year-old single professional woman had snorted 0.5–3 gm of cocaine almost daily for 3 months, while using . . . a variety of other drugs. After a car wreck, she began to abstain. Eight days later, fearing the great attractiveness of cocaine, she entered treatment to help assure continued abstinence . . . . The patient saw loss of her professional license and her job as the probable outcomes of continued use.

Her therapist recommended a contingency contract to use fear of license loss as a motivator toward abstinence. She wrote a letter to her state licensing board confessing her drug abuse and surrendering her license. . . . In a written contract she directed the therapist to obtain urine samples and to mail the letter if any sample contained drugs or if she failed to provide a scheduled sample. . . . the patient then used therapy sessions to dispose of her extensive drug paraphernalia, to list her drug-using contacts and make plans to end those relationships, and to develop new strategies for problematic relationships with men and her parents. She remained free of . . . drugs of abuse (except for alcohol and marijuana), repeatedly renewing the initial 3-month contract for a total of 12 months. By that time she felt the inherent rewards of her drug-free life outweighed the combined benefits and costs of resuming drug use . . . . She has continued in psychotherapy for 19 more months without urinalyses. She has taken no more cocaine, has completed a course of post-graduate training, and no longer associates with underworld figures. (pp. 69–70)

The encouraging results obtained for contingency management with severe drug abusers are not without qualifications. First, contracting appears more successful for nondrug-related goals (e.g., clinic attendance) than for drug-related goals (e.g., drug-free urinalyses). Second, contract effectiveness seems to vary directly with the severity of the scheduled consequences (Anker & Crowley, 1982; Magura et al., 1987), but, at the same time, aversive consequences may result in higher treatment dropout rates (Yaguchi, Stitzer, Bigelow, & Liebson, 1988) and raise ethical concerns. Third, contingency management tends to be effective only so long as the contingencies are in effect (Stitzer, Bigelow, Liebson, & Hawthorne, 1982), and, with heroin addiction, only so long as clients receive methadone at the clinic (McCaul et al., 1984), which raises questions about the long-term maintenance of treatment gains. Finally, contingency management seems most effective for older clients who have lengthy histories of both addiction and methadone maintenance and lower pretreatment levels of drug use (Dolan et al., 1986). Although these qualifications indicate the need for further research to maximize the effectiveness of contingency management, it presently is the best available treatment for severe drug abuse.

Community Reinforcement Approach (CRA)

Hunt and Azrin (1973) pioneered a comprehensive operant treatment program for highly debilitated alcoholics, to reduce drinking and to increase adaptive functioning. The program has evolved since its development with inpatient alcoholics to include outpatients and procedures that ensure client use of disulfiram. Sisson and Azrin (1989) described the CRA as currently including the following components:

1. Disulfiram use is facilitated by having the spouse or other intimate monitor and verbally reinforce the client's daily use.
2. For clients involved in an intimate relationship, the client and partner participate in "reciprocity marriage counseling" to increase communication skills and mutually rewarding interactions.
3. Unemployed clients participate in a "Job Club," where they analyze their work history and skills, are instructed about employment-seeking strategies, and then set behavioral goals aimed at securing work (e.g., making 10 calls a day to potential employers).
4. Social and recreational activities that do not involve alcohol availability are identified, and clients without such options can attend the program's "United Club," which is a dry bar available on weekends.
5. Clients receive training on how to refuse drinks and to control urges to drink.

The CRA is strongly supported in well-controlled research conducted by Azrin

(1976) and his colleagues (Azrin, Sisson, Meyers, & Godley, 1982; Hunt & Azrin, 1973). Of particular note are the findings of Azrin et al. (1982), who showed that disulfiram assurance alone resulted in near total abstinence for clients who were married or living with their monitor, but was not an adequate individual treatment for single clients, who benefited from the addition of other CRA components. The complete program has not been widely evaluated by other investigators, although several individual components have received support (Hall, Loeb, & Allen, 1984; Keane, Foy, Nunn, & Rychtarik, 1984; Mallams, Godley, Hall, & Meyers, 1982).

Treatment of Life–Health Dysfunction Related to Substance Abuse

A major assumption of behavioral treatments is that substance abuse often is related in complex ways with functioning in other areas. In such cases, treating only the substance abuse will likely be inadequate, and abstinence will not ensure recovery in other areas unless they also are treated. Although such interventions must be individualized, interventions in several areas of functioning have been well researched with substance abuse clients, including marital and family therapy, social skills training, stress management, and vocational interventions. Vocational strategies were described previously under comprehensive operant treatments. Interventions in the remaining areas are described here.

Marital and Family Therapy

Although the marriages and families of substance abusers have been characterized along numerous dimensions (e.g., psychodynamically; see Paolino & McCrady, 1977), behavioral treatments focus on how family members may maintain the substance abuse through contingent reinforcement and seek to modify the family's behavior in ways that reward abstinence and involvement in satisfying activities, including family interactions, that do not entail substance use. O'Farrell and Cowles (1989) and Todd (1984) provided excellent discussions of marital and family therapy for alcohol and drug abusers, respectively.

In the program developed for alcoholics by O'Farrell and his colleagues (e.g., O'Farrell, 1986; O'Farrell & Cutter, 1984), interventions are sequentially introduced to motivate the client to engage in treatment, to produce rapid decreases in alcohol abuse and engagement in dangerous behaviors such as family violence, and then to improve family communication and life-style patterns in ways that support long-term family stability and client abstinence. The program is highly structured and relies on behavioral contracts among family members. For example, disulfiram contracts like those employed in the CRA may be used; "time-out" agreements may be implemented to reduce the potential for violence during conflicts, especially when the client is intoxicated; and family members may agree to reward positive changes and to ignore, rather than to criticize, problem behaviors. Similarly structured methods and goals are used to increase positive family interactions and problem-solving skills.

Outcome research generally has shown a positive relationship between improved family and marital functioning and reduced substance use (Miller, Hedrick, & Taylor, 1983; Stanton & Todd, 1982). Studies that specifically evaluated family or marital interventions indicated that they effectively motivate initial client commitment to treatment (Sisson & Azrin, 1986), improve relationships, and reduce substance use during the first 6 months following treatment initiation (McCrady et al., 1986). Heroin withdrawal conducted at home with family involvement appears to be a relatively successful alternative to inpatient detoxification (Todd, 1984). However, the data are more equivocal about the long-term effectiveness of the interventions, particularly with respect to maintaining reductions in substance use.

Social Skills Training

Social situations often involve alcohol or drug availability, requiring clients to avoid valued interactions that involve substance use or to learn ways of refusing use. Avoidance is reasonable for some, but, even in such cases, developing new social contacts that do not involve substance availability comprises an important treatment goal. The nondrinkers' social club of the CRA is one method of encouraging this goal, and A.A. and related groups probably serve a similar function.

Because of the ubiquity of drugs (especially alcohol) in social situations, it is desirable to train clients in refusing substance use in social contexts. The usual method, which has been widely used with alcoholics, is through social skills training aimed at effective drink refusal. Alcoholics are not generally deficit in social skills (Twentyman, et al., 1982), but can benefit from structured interventions based on a role-play approach that train them to resist social pressure to drink (Chaney, O'Leary, & Marlatt, 1978; Freedberg & Johnston, 1981).

Chaney (1989) described the procedures involved in social skills training, which usually is conducted in small groups (cf. Monti, Abrams, Kadden, & Cooney, 1989, regarding a more general skills training program). Role-play situations are devised that resemble high-risk situations for substance use in clients' natural environments. Effective responses are modeled by the therapist(s) and then rehearsed by each client, who receives constructive feedback from the group. Client progress typically is assessed by repeated administration of a standardized role-play task (Chaney et al., 1978).

Social skills training improves client performance on measures of social skills. Several, but not all (Oei & Jackson, 1982) outcome studies have shown favorable reductions in alcohol use during the posttreatment interval. In reviewing this research, Chaney (1989) concluded that ". . . the strongest evidence for the efficacy of social skill training comes from studies conducted in the context of inpatient alcohol programs in which there are additional treatment components. . ." (p. 219). Thus, for appropriately selected clients with demonstrated skills deficits, including skills training as one component of a comprehensive treatment program is warranted. It is reasonable to assume that skills training would also be effective with drug abusers, but controlled studies with this population are lacking.

Stress Management

Stress, anxiety, and related constructs have long been viewed as etiologic in the development of alcohol and drug problems. Research support for this premise, however, is quite inconsistent (Cappell & Greeley, 1987), and it is clear that chronic, heavy substance use increases anxiety. Reasonable interpretations of this equivocal literature are that (a) a small percentage of substance abusers have dual diagnoses with some type of anxiety disorder, and (b) at least with respect to alcohol, individual differences exist in the degree to which consumption reduces indexes of stress (Sher, 1987). For the limited number of clients in these categories, stress management procedures, such as those described by Stockwell and Town (1989), may be a useful part of comprehensive treatment programs, but such procedures alone are unnecessary or insufficient treatment in most cases. Anxiety also may be a treatment issue during substance withdrawal for physically dependent clients, but will probably be managed pharmacologically (e.g., with librium) on a short-term basis only, because of the risks of dangerous drug interactions.

Although stress management, relaxation, or biofeedback techniques have been included in broad-spectrum behavioral treatments of alcohol (Freedberg & Johnston, 1978) and drug (Rawson, Glazer, Callahan, & Liberman, 1979) abuse, dismantling studies are rare, so their specific contribution is difficult to evaluate. The evidence implies a more consistent effect of techniques on indexes of anxiety and life functioning than on alcohol (Freedberg & Johnston, 1978) and drug (Khatami, Mintz, & O'Brien, 1977) use. Moreover, Rosenberg (1979; discussed in Miller & Hester, 1986a) highlights the importance of selecting clients according to pretreatment anxiety status; only highly anxious alcoholics evidenced reduced alcohol consumption from relaxation training. Thus, like marital and family therapy and social skills training, stress management procedures should only be included in an overall treatment plan when clients' presenting complaints suggest their utility.

Relapse Prevention (RP)

Initial reductions in substance abuse can be achieved by several treatment methods, but maintaining long-term change is much more difficult and may be influenced by different variables than those producing the initial change. For example, early in treatment, clients may be able to avoid situations involving substance availability; on a long-term basis, this is probably unrealistic, and learning to deal effectively with situations associated with past substance misuse may be quite important for long-term success. This is the rationale for RP training (Annis & Davis, 1989; Marlatt & Gordon, 1985), which represents an important shift in treatment emphasis that builds on research indicating the powerful influence of the post-treatment environment on long-term treatment outcomes (Tucker, Vuchinich, & Gladsjo, 1990–91).

The RP programs developed by Marlatt and by Annis differ somewhat in the guiding conceptualization of relapse determinants and in the specific interventions used, but share a focus (a) on training clients in coping skills to deal with emotions, cognitions, and environments associated with past substance misuse, (b) on viewing substance use episodes as learning opportunities for understanding the determinants of clients' relapses, and (c) on minimizing the extent of substance use when it does occur. Marlatt's approach involves cognitive restructuring aimed at reducing the "abstinence violation effect" experienced after initial substance use, which is a complex sequence of cognitive and affective changes thought to motivate further use. Also employed are strategies derived from BSCT and related skills training procedures to foster effective coping responses in the high-risk situations for substance use.

Annis used Marlatt's (1978) classification system of relapse determinants to develop the Inventory of Drinking Situations (IDS), which evaluates the extent to which clients' alcohol use during the past year was associated with eight different situations (e.g., unpleasant emotions, social pressure to drink, conflict with others). From this information, a hierarchy of risk situations is developed, and treatment entails progressive in vivo exposure to the situations from low to high risk, which presumably increases clients' self-efficacy expectations for resisting future substance use in the situations. Clients' coping responses also are evaluated, with a goal of ensuring that they develop a wide range of responses.

Support for Marlatt's RP program has been mixed (Curry, Marlatt, Gordon, & Baer, 1988; Hall, Rugg, Tunstall, & Jones, 1984; Ito, Donovan, & Hall, 1988), but, as noted by Curry et al. (1988), outcome studies with negative findings often combined RP with several treatment components that were conceptually unrelated; better controlled studies comparing RP alone with other standard treatments or in combination with relevant behavioral treatments clearly are needed. Outcome studies of Annis' program are limited to those conducted by the author and her colleagues (see Annis & Davis, 1989). These data are quite encouraging and yield an empirical basis for treatment matching. In a 6-month follow-up of 83 alcohol clients (Annis, Davis, Graham, & Levinson, 1987), those who received RP versus a more traditional outpatient treatment showed significant reductions in daily drinking, but only if they initially had a differentiated IDS profile, indicating variability in drinking patterns across the eight risk situations. Clients with a generalized profile lacking such variability did not differ as a function of type of treatment.

UNRESOLVED ISSUES AND FUTURE DIRECTIONS

These behavioral treatments enjoy empirical support relative to no treatment or to more conventional interventions, but this is not to say that they are effective in an absolute sense. Relapse rates remain disturbingly high regardless of treatment orientation, so there is plenty of room for improvement even in treatments that currently are the best the field has to offer. As our understanding of addictive disorders improves, we can expect this knowledge to be incorporated into the design of future treatments that are more effective. Although it is difficult to predict where the next "breakthrough" will occur, this final section discusses several areas where conceptual and empirical advances could have a significant impact on future behavioral treatments of addictive disorders.

The Role of the Post-Treatment Environment in Treatment Outcome

Long-term treatment outcome studies (e.g., Polich, Armor, & Braiker, 1981) have shown (a) that individual clients show considerable variability in outcome status at different assessment points, and (b) that this variability seems related more to life circumstances during the posttreatment interval (e.g., marital and vocational status, life-event occurrences) than to treatment-specific factors, including the type and duration of treatment and the treatment goals (cf. Tucker et al., 1990-91). Such findings question the role of treatment-specific factors in determining long-term outcomes and underscore the importance of understanding the contextual determinants of relapse and recovery during the posttreatment interval.

Marlatt's (1978; Marlatt & Gordon, 1985) influential work on relapse anticipated this focus on the posttreatment environment. Although his specific relapse model and RP procedures have not been consistently supported, this work has had an extremely important reorienting effect on clinical research and practice: It has directed attention away from straightforward treatment outcome evaluations that are concerned only with the percentage of clients in different outcome status groups at discrete follow-up points and toward describing the temporal dynamics of individual clients' substance use over time and how variability in use after treatment is related to changing environmental circumstances.

As discussed in Tucker et al. (1990-91), the status of the several models of relapse (Baker et al., 1987; Marlatt, 1978; Vuchinich & Tucker, 1988) is ambiguous—in part because of a lack of research, but also because characterizations of the relevant environmental variables are currently inadequate. Thus, although the posttreatment environment has emerged from several lines of research as highly influential on long-term outcomes, and this knowledge has potential for facilitating effective treatment, exploiting it in therapeutic interventions will require more detailed measurement and explication of the relevant relationships.

Recovery without Treatment

Similar issues apply to the process of recovery from substance abuse without professional treatment or participation in self-help groups. Although research is limited, natural recovery has been associated with environmental circumstances similar to those that appear related to relapse and recovery with treatment assistance (Tuchfield, 1981; Vaillant & Milofsky, 1982). This work also has found that the recovery process is lengthy and evolves over time, and that focusing on a single, discrete quit attempt, with or without treatment, may obscure influential variables whose effects operate over longer intervals (Prochaska & DiClemente, 1986; Schachter, 1982). For example, certain changes may motivate a quit attempt (e.g., arrests, physical problems related to drug use), but long-term success may depend on reinforcing decreases in such problems after quitting or on a degree of stability existing in individuals' life circumstances that supports continued maintenance efforts (Tucker, Vuchinich, Gladsjo, Hawkins, & Sherrill, 1989).

These findings suggest that time-limited treatments be viewed as one of many environmental influences that may be brought to bear on substance abuse, but that treatment alone is unlikely to produce permanent behavior change unless changes also occur in natural contingencies that maintain substance abuse and abstinence. Further clarification of the circumstances that support natural resolution and the strategies employed by successful self-quitters will likely have important implications for treatment-assisted change.

Treatment Matching and the Search for Matching Variables

The notion that matching client problems with appropriate interventions will produce better outcomes is a basic principle of any clinical endeavor and quite consistent with a behavioral approach. The controlled drinking controversy has provided impetus for recent concern with treatment matching. If abstinence and moderation outcomes are both entertained as potential goals, then an obvious step toward resolving the controversy is to identify pretreatment variables that allow effective client matching to goals and the tailoring of treatment procedures to facilitate those goals. Some initial enthusiasm existed for using measures of problem severity, such as the degree of alcohol dependence, as the basis of matching, with less severe problems being regarded as more appropriate for less intensive treatment and a moderation goal. This hypothesis has not been uniformly supported (Sanchez-Craig & Wilkinson, 1987), but has encouraged development of effective minimal interventions for early problem drinkers (Heather, 1989). Another interesting finding is that clients who choose their treatment approach and goal from among several alternatives evidence better outcomes than clients without such options (Sanchez-Craig & Wilkinson, 1987).

Matching research also has raised two general conceptual issues:

1. Should the client characteristics used for matching be based on personality and psychopathology or on parameters of clients' substance abuse?
2. Should matching variables be conceptualized as mutually exclusive categories or as dimensions reflecting continuous variables?

Although less clear about the latter issue, Morey, Skinner, and Blashfield (1984; Skinner, 1982) argued strongly for matching criteria based on substance use variables, even though extant research has emphasized personality and psychopathology variables (e.g., MMPI profiles) or diagnostic categories according to DSM-III-R criteria. The latter approach has not been highly successful, but development of matching procedures based on substance use parameters is in its infancy.

Currently lacking and more consistent with a behavioral approach are matching criteria based on more fine-grained aspects of clients' pretreatment substance use patterns, such as the daily temporal patterning of use during the pretreatment year, and the negative consequences of use in different areas of functioning. Developing such criteria probably would have considerable positive effects on selecting from among available behavioral treatments. An unresearched possibility is that some of the environmental variables mentioned in the sections on the posttreatment environment and on natural recovery may have promise as potentially important matching criteria.

The Problem of Technology Transfer

When a substance abuser enters treatment in the United States today, he or she probably will not receive any of the behavioral treatments discussed in this chapter and instead will receive inpatient treatment based on the disease model. This situation exists despite the empirical support for behavioral treatments and the lack of support for treatments that constitute standard practice (Miller & Hester, 1986a, 1986b). Not only is there a need for more effective treatments, but the question of why the substantial empirical work on behavioral treatments of substance abuse has had so little impact on clinical practice also must be addressed. Several authors (Marlatt, 1987; Miller, 1987; Sobell & Sobell, 1984) have speculated on possible reasons, including but not limited to:

1. The economic hegemony achieved by disease-based programs early in the development of service delivery in this country, and the monetary incentives for resisting changes in treatment orientation;

2. Widespread public acceptance of the disease view of addictions, probably because of its lengthy history, visibility, and consistency with certain cultural values;

3. Differences in professional training about addictions; the disease orientation predominates in medical professions and the behavioral orientation predominates only among a subset of psychologists.

The problem also can be viewed as one of ensuring effective technology transfer, which is not unique to the substance abuse field and has been important in many areas of psychology, including behavior therapy and behavior analysis. Pennypacker's (1986) cogent analysis of the problem may be instructive for the current stalemate in the addictions area (cf. Miller, 1987). He argued that academic scientists are not well-prepared in the financial and entrepreneurial skills necessary to take a product to market, nor do universities effectively support such activities. As a result, when scientists develop an effective technology, they probably will fail to bring the product to market or will lose control over its implementation. When portions of the technology are co-opted into systems dominated by individuals lacking expertise in behavior analysis, this risks removing the technology's effective elements and its basis for competition in the marketplace. Thus, for example, the effectiveness of RP training may be seriously undermined when it is co-opted into disease-oriented programs (cf. Curry et al., 1988).

Pennypacker further argued that behaviorally oriented scientists must apply their skills in behavior analysis to the transfer process itself, which essentially requires identifying and manipulating contingencies of reinforcement that operate throughout the process. The behavioral analysis cannot end with the "science" of technology development, because data alone are not a necessary or sufficient condition for technology transfer, as the behavioral substance abuse field is all too aware. Marketplace economics will be the final arbiter of success, but the behavioral product, to be competitive, must not be diluted before it operates within the market. Product control by behavioral scientists is essential.

The practical significance of this view is evidenced by Pennypacker's own experience of developing a scientifically grounded behavioral technology for breast self-exam within a university system and then marketing the technology through his own company (Mammacare, Inc.; see Pennypacker & Iwata, in press). Like the dominance of disease-oriented programs in substance abuse treatment, the breast self-exam field is dominated by the training program of the American Cancer Society, which is much less effective with respect to small-lump detection than the Mammacare method, but is widely accepted and practiced. What is highlighted already by the Mammacare experience is the importance of disseminating behavioral knowledge in a controllable manner to service delivery systems and of resisting rapprochement with empirically unsupported treatments if this undermines the effectiveness of behavioral treatments. To that end, Hester and Miller's (1989b) recent volume clearly describing how to conduct empirically supported behavioral treatments of substance abuse is an excellent start. However, greater activism in marketing such treatments will likely be required if they are to gain their deserved place based on data in the treatment delivery system. The increased accountability for healthcare dollars in the 1990s offers a favorable opportunity for such activism, and, on humanitarian grounds, a strong argument can be made for providing a greater diversity of treatments that better match the diversity of substance abuse problems experienced by individual clients.

REFERENCES

American Psychiatric Association (1987). *Diagnostic and statistical manual of mental disorders* (3rd ed. rev.). Washington, DC: Author.

Anker, A. L., & Crowley, T. J. (1982). Use of contingency contracts in specialty clinics for cocaine abuse. In L. S. Harris (Ed.), *Problems of drug dependence, 1981: Proceedings of the 43rd annual scientific meeting, the Committee on Problems of Drug Dependence* (NIDA Research Monograph No. 41, pp. 452–459). Washington, DC: U.S. Government Printing Office.

Annis, H. M., & Davis, C. S. (1989). Relapse prevention. In R. K. Hester & W. R. Miller (Eds.), *Handbook of alcoholism treatment approaches: Effective alternatives* (pp. 170–182). New York: Pergamon.

Annis, H. M., Davis, C. S., Graham, M., & Levinson, T. (1987). *A controlled trial of relapse prevention procedures based on self-efficacy theory.* Unpublished manuscript, Addiction Research Foundation, Toronto, Ontario.

Azrin, N. H. (1976). Improvements in the community-reinforcement approach to alcoholism. *Behaviour Research and Therapy, 14,* 339–348.

Azrin, N. H., Sisson, R. W., Meyers, R., & Godley, M. (1982). Alcoholism treatment by disulfiram and community reinforcement therapy. *Journal of Behavior Therapy and Experimental Psychiatry, 13,* 105–112.

Baker, T. B., Morse, E., & Sherman, J. E. (1987). The motivation to use drugs. In P. C. Rivers (Ed.), *Nebraska symposium on motivation: Alcohol and addictive behavior, Vol. 34* (pp. 257–323). Lincoln: University of Nebraska Press.

Bigelow, G. E., Stitzer, M. L., & Liebson, I. A. (1984). The role of behavioral contingency management in drug abuse treatment. In J.

Grabowski, M. L. Stitzer, & J. E. Henningfield (Eds.), *Behavioral intervention techniques in drug abuse treatment* (NIDA Research Monograph No. 46, pp. 36–52). Washington, DC: U.S. Government Printing Office.

Blane, H. T., & Leonard, K. E. (Eds.) (1987). *Psychological theories of drinking and alcoholism.* New York: Guilford.

Cannon, D. S., Baker, T. B., Gino, A., & Nathan, P. E. (1986). Alcohol-aversion therapy: Relation between strength of aversion and abstinence. *Journal of Consulting and Clinical Psychology, 54,* 825–830.

Cappell, H., & Greeley, J. (1987). Alcohol and tension reduction: An update on research and theory. In H. T. Blane & K. E. Leonard (Eds.), *Psychological theories of drinking and alcoholism* (pp. 15–44). New York: Guilford.

Cautela, J. R. (1970). The treatment of alcoholism by covert sensitization. *Psychotherapy: Theory, Research, & Practice, 7,* 86–90.

Chaney, E. F. (1989). Social skills training. In R. K. Hester & W. R. Miller (Eds.), *Handbook of alcoholism treatment approaches: Effective alternatives* (pp. 206–221). New York: Pergamon.

Chaney, E. F., O'Leary, M. R., & Marlatt, G. A. (1978). Skill training with alcoholics. *Journal of Consulting and Clinical Psychology, 46,* 1092–1104.

Childress, A. R., McLellan, A. T., & O'Brien, C. P. (1985a). Behavioral therapies for substance abuse. *International Journal of the Addictions, 20,* 947–969.

Childress, A. R., McLellan, A. T., & O'Brien, C. P. (1985b). Assessment and extinction of conditioned withdrawal-like responses in an integrated treatment for opiate dependence. In L. S. Harris (Ed.), *Problems of drug dependence, 1984: Proceedings of the 46th annual scientific meeting, the Committee on Problems of Drug Dependence* (NIDA Research Monograph No. 55, pp. 202–210). Washington, DC: U.S. Government Printing Office.

Clarke, J. C., & Hayes, D. (1984). Covert sensitization, stimulus relevance and the equipotentiality premise. *Behaviour Research and Therapy, 22,* 451–454.

Copemann, C. D. (1977). Treatment of polydrug abuse by covert sensitization: Some contraindications. *International Journal of the Addictions, 12,* 17–23.

Crowley, T. J. (1984). Contingency contracting treatment of drug-abusing physicians, nurses, and dentists. In J. Grabowski, M. L. Stitzer, & J. E. Henningfield (Eds.), *Behavioral intervention techniques in drug abuse treatment* (NIDA Research Monograph No. 46, pp. 68–83). Washington, DC: U.S. Government Printing Office.

Curry, S. J., Marlatt, G. A., Gordon, J., & Baer, J. S. (1988). A comparison of alternative theoretical approaches to smoking cessation and relapse. *Health Psychology, 7,* 545–556.

Dolan, M. P., Black, J. L., Penk, W. E., Robinowitz, R., & DeFord, H. A. (1986). Predicting the outcome of contingency contracting for drug abuse. *Behavior Therapy, 17,* 470–474.

Donovan, D. M., & G. A. Marlatt (Eds.) (1988). *Assessment of addictive behavior.* New York: Guilford.

Dukert, P., & Johnsen, J. (1987). Behavioral use of disulfiram in the treatment of problem drinking. *International Journal of the Addictions, 22,* 445–454.

Elkins, R. L. (1980). Covert sensitization and alcoholism: Contributions of successful conditioning to subsequent abstinence maintenance. *Addictive Behaviors, 5,* 67–89.

Elkins, R. L., & Murdock, R. P. (1977). The contribution of successful conditioning to abstinence maintenance following covert sensitization (verbal aversion) treatment of alcoholism. *IRCS Medical Science: Psychology & Psychiatry: Social and Occupational Medicine, 5,* 167.

Foa, E. B., & Kozak, M. J. (1986). Emotional processing of fear: Exposure to corrective information. *Psychological Bulletin, 99,* 20–35.

Freedberg, E. J., & Johnston, W. E., (1978). *The effects of relaxation training within the context of a multi-modal alcoholism treatment program for employed alcoholics* (Substudy no. 988). Toronto, Ontario: Addiction Research Foundation.

Freedberg, E. J., & Johnston, W. E. (1981). Effects of assertion training within the context of a multi-modal alcoholism treatment program for employed alcoholics. *Psychological Reports, 48,* 379–386.

Glosser, D. S. (1983). The use of a token economy to reduce illicit drug use among methadone maintenance clients. *Addictive Behaviors, 8,* 93–104.

Griffiths, R. R., Bigelow, G. E., & Henningfield, J. E. (1980). Similarities in animal and human drug-taking behavior. In N. K. Mello (Ed.), *Advances in substance abuse: Behavioral and biological research, Vol. 1* (pp. 1–90). Greenwich, CT: JAI Press.

Griffiths, R. R., Bigelow, G. E., & Liebson, I. (1974). Suppression of ethanol self-administration in alcoholics by contingent time-out from social interactions. *Behaviour Research and Therapy, 12,* 327–334.

Hall, S. M., Loeb, P. C., & Allen, T. (1984). The Job Seekers' Workshop: A skill training program for drug treatment clients. In J. Grabowski, M. L. Stitzer, & J. E. Henningfield (Eds.), *Behavioral intervention techniques in drug abuse treatment* (NIDA Research Monograph No. 46, pp. 115–130). Washington, DC: U.S. Government Printing Office.

Hall, S. M., Rugg, D., Tunstall, C., & Jones, R. T. (1984). Preventing relapse to cigarette smoking by behavioral skill training. *Journal of Consulting and Clinical Psychology, 52,* 372–382.

Heather, N. (1989). Brief intervention strategies. In R. K. Hester & W. R. Miller (Eds.), *Handbook of alcoholism treatment approaches: Effective alternatives* (pp. 93–116). New York: Pergamon.

Hester, R. K., & Miller, W. R. (1989a). Self-control training. In R. K. Hester & W. R. Miller (Eds.), *Handbook of alcoholism treatment approaches: Effective alternatives* (pp. 141–149). New York: Pergamon.

Hester, R. K., & Miller, W. R. (Eds.) (1989b). *Handbook of alcoholism treatment approaches: Effective alternatives.* New York: Pergamon.

Hunt, G. M., & Azrin, N. H. (1973). A community-reinforcement approach to alcoholism. *Behaviour Research and Therapy, 11,* 91–104.

Ito, J. R., Donovan, D. M., & Hall, J. J. (1988). Relapse prevention in alcohol aftercare: Effects on drinking outcome, change process, and aftercare attendance. *British Journal of Addiction, 83,* 171–181.

Keane, T. M., Foy, D. W., Nunn, B., & Rychtarik, R. G. (1984). Spouse contracting to increase antabuse compliance in alcoholic veterans. *Journal of Clinical Psychology, 40,* 340–344.

Khatami, M., Mintz, J., & O'Brien, C. P. (1977). Biofeedback-mediated relaxation in narcotic addicts. *Behavior Therapy, 8,* 968–969.

Kleber, H. D., & Gawin, F. H. (1984). Cocaine abuse: A review of current and experimental treatments. In J. Grabowski (Ed.), *Cocaine: Pharmacology, effects, and treatment of abuse.* (NIDA Research Monograph No. 50, pp. 111–129). Washington, DC: U.S. Government Printing Office.

Magura, S., Casriel, C., Goldsmith, D. S., & Lipton, D. S. (1987). Contracting with clients in methadone treatment. *Social Casework, 68,* 485–493.

Magura, S., Casriel, C., Goldsmith, D. S., Strug, D. L., & Lipton, D. S. (1988). Contingency contracting with polydrug-abusing methadone patients. *Addictive Behaviors, 13,* 113–118.

Maisto, S. A., & Caddy, G. R. (1981). Self-control and addictive behavior: Present status and prospects. *International Journal of the Addictions, 16,* 109–133.

Mallams, J. H., Godley, M. D., Hall, G. M., & Meyers, R. A. (1982). A social-systems approach to resocializing alcoholics in the community. *Journal of Studies on Alcohol, 43,* 1115–1123.

Marlatt, G. A. (1978). Craving for alcohol, loss of control, and relapse: A cognitive-behavioral analysis. In P. E. Nathan, G. A. Marlatt, & T. Løberg (Eds.), *Alcoholism: New directions in behavioral research and treatment* (pp. 271–314). New York: Plenum.

Marlatt, G. A. (1987). Research and political realities: What the next twenty years hold for behaviorists in the alcohol field. *Advances in Behaviour Research and Therapy, 9,* 165–171.

Marlatt, G. A., Demming, B., & Reid, J. B. (1973). Loss of control drinking in alcoholics: An experimental analogue. *Journal of Abnormal Psychology, 81,* 233–241.

Marlatt, G. A., & Gordon, J. R. (Eds.). (1985). *Relapse prevention.* New York: Guilford.

McCaul, M. E., Stitzer, M. L., Bigelow, G. E., & Liebson, I. A. (1984). Contingency management interventions: Effects on treatment outcome during methadone detoxification. *Journal of Applied Behavior Analysis, 17,* 35–43.

McCrady, B. S., Noel, N. E., Abrams, D. B., Stout, R. L., Nelson, H. F. & Hay, W. M. (1986). Comparative effectiveness of three types of spouse involvement in outpatient behavioral alcoholism treatment. *Journal of Studies on Alcohol, 47,* 459–467.

Mello, N. K., & Mendelson, J. H. (1965). Operant analysis of drinking patterns of chronic alcoholics. *Nature, 206,* 43–46.

Miller, P. M. (1975). A behavioral intervention program for chronic public drunkenness offenders. *Archives of General Psychiatry, 32,* 915–918.

Miller, P. M., Hersen, M., Eisler, R. M., & Watts, J. G. (1974). Contingent reinforcement of lowered blood/alcohol levels in an outpatient chronic alcoholic. *Behaviour Research and Therapy, 12,* 261–263.

Miller, W. R. (1987). Behavioral alcohol treatment advances: Barriers to utilization. *Advances in Behaviour Research and Therapy, 9,* 145–164.

Miller, W. R., Hedrick, K. E., & Taylor, G. A. (1983). Addictive behaviors and life problems before and after behavioral treatment of problem drinkers. *Addictive Behaviors, 8,* 403–412.

Miller, W. R., & Hester, R. K. (1986a). The effectiveness of alcoholism treatment: What research reveals. In W. R. Miller & N. Heather (Eds.), *Treating addictive behaviors: Processes of change* (pp. 121–174). New York: Plenum.

Miller, W. R., & Hester, R. K. (1986b). Inpatient alcoholism treatment: Who benefits? *American Psychologist, 41,* 794–805.

Miller, W. R., & Munoz, R. F. (1982). *How to control your drinking* (rev. ed.). Albuquerque, NM: University of New Mexico Press.

Miller, W. R., Pechacek, T. F., & Hamburg, S. (1981). Group behavior therapy for problem drinkers. *International Journal of the Addictions, 16,* 827–837.

Miller, W. R., & Taylor, C. A. (1980). Relative effectiveness of bibliotherapy, individual and group self-control training in the treatment of problem drinkers. *Addictive Behaviors, 5,* 13–24.

Monti, P. M., Abrams, D. B., Kadden, R. M., & Cooney, N. L. (1989). *Treating alcohol dependence.* New York: Guilford.

Morey, L. C., Skinner, H. A., & Blashfield, R. K. (1984). A typology of alcohol abusers: Correlates and implications. *Journal of Abnormal Psychology, 93,* 408–417.

Niaura, R. S., Rohsenow, D. J., Binkoff, J. A., Monti, P. M., Pedraza, M., & Abrams, D. B. (1988). Relevance of cue reactivity to understanding alcohol and smoking relapse. *Journal of Abnormal Psychology, 97,* 133–152.

O'Brien, C. P., Childress, A. R., Arndt, I. O., McLellan, A. T., Woody, G. E. & Maany, I. (1988). Pharmacological and behavioral treatments of cocaine dependence: Controlled studies. *Journal of Clinical Psychiatry, 49* (Suppl.), 17–22.

O'Brien, C. P., Ehrman, R., & Ternes, J. (1986). Classical conditioning in human opioid dependence. In S. R. Goldberg & I. P. Stolerman (Eds.), *Behavioral analysis of drug dependence* (pp. 329–356). Orlando, FL: Academic Press.

O'Brien, C. P., Greenstein, R., Ternes, J., McLellan, T., & Grabowski, J. (1979). Unreinforced self-injections: Effects of rituals and outcome in heroin addicts. In L. S. Harris (Ed.), *Problems of drug dependence, 1979: Proceedings of the 41st annual scientific meeting, the Committee on Problems of Drug Dependence* (NIDA Research Monograph No. 27, pp. 275–281). Washington, DC: U.S. Government Printing Office.

Oei, T. P. S., & Jackson, P. R. (1982). Social skills and cognitive behavioral approaches to the treatment of problem drinking. *Journal of Studies on Alcohol, 43,* 532–547.

O'Farrell, T. J. (1986). Marital therapy in the treatment of alcoholism. In N. S. Jacobson & A. S. Gurman (Eds.), *Clinical handbook of marital therapy* (pp. 513–535). New York: Guilford.

O'Farrell, T. J., & Cowles, K. S. (1989). Marital and family therapy. In R. K. Hester & W. R. Miller (Eds.), *Handbook of alcoholism treatment approaches: Effective alternatives* (pp. 183–205). New York: Pergamon.

O'Farrell, T. J., & Cutter, H. S. G. (1984). Behavioral marital therapy couples groups for male alcoholics and their wives. *Journal of Substance Abuse Treatment, 1,* 191–204.

Paolino, T. J., Jr., & McCrady, B. S., (1977). *The alcoholic marriage: Alternative perspectives.* New York: Grune & Stratton.

Pattison, E. M., Sobell, M. B., & Sobell, L. C. (1977). *Emerging concepts of alcohol dependence.* New York: Springer.

Pennypacker, H. S. (1986). The challenge of technology transfer: Buying in without selling out. *The Behavior Analyst, 9,* 147–156.

Pennypacker, H. S., & Iwata, B. M. (in press). Mammacare: A case history in behavioral medicine. In P. Blackman & H. LeJeune (Eds.), *Behavior analysis in theory and practice: Contributions and controversies.* Hillsdale, NJ: Erlbaum.

Polakow, R. L. (1975). Covert sensitization treatment of a probationed barbiturate addict. *Journal of Behavior Therapy and Experimental Psychiatry, 6,* 53–54.

Polich, J. M., & Armor, D. J., & Braiker, H. B. (1981). *The course of alcoholism: Four years after treatment.* New York: Wiley.

Prochaska, J. O., & DiClemente, C. C. (1986). Toward a comprehensive model of change. In W. R. Miller & N. Heather (Eds.), *Treating addictive behaviors: Processes of change* (pp. 3–27). New York: Plenum.

Rankin, H., Hodgson, R., & Stockwell, T. (1983). Cue exposure and response prevention with alcoholics: A controlled trial. *Behaviour Research and Therapy, 21,* 435–446.

Rawson, R. A., Glazer, M., Callahan, E. J., & Liberman, R. P. (1979). Naltrexone and behavior therapy for heroin addiction. In N. A. Krasnegor (Ed.), *Behavioral analysis and treatment of substance abuse* (NIDA Research Monograph No. 25, pp. 26–43). Washington, DC: U.S. Government Printing Office.

Resnick, R. B., & Resnick, E. (1986). Psychological issues in the treatment of cocaine abuse. In L. S. Harns (Ed.), *Problems of drug dependence, 1985: Proceedings of the 47th annual scientific meeting, The Committee on Problems of Drug Dependence* (NIDA Research Monograph No. 67, pp. 290–294). Washington, DC: U.S. Government Printing Office.

Rimmele, C. T., Miller, W. R., & Dougher, M. J. (1989). Aversion therapies. In R. K. Hester & W. R. Miller (Eds.), *Handbook of alcoholism treatment approaches: Effective alternatives* (pp. 128–140). New York: Pergamon.

Rosenberg, S. D. (1979). *Relaxation training and a differential assessment of alcoholism.* Unpublished doctoral dissertation, California School of Professional Psychology, San Diego, CA. (University Microfilms No. 8004362).

Sanchez-Craig, M., & Wilkinson, D. A. (1987). Treating problem drinkers who are not severely dependent on alcohol. *Drugs and Society, 1,* 39–67.

Schachter, S. (1982). Recidivism and self-cure of smoking and obesity. *American Psychologist, 37,* 436–444.

Sher, K. (1987). Stress response dampening. In H. T. Blane & K. E. Leonard (Eds.), *Psychological theories of drinking and alcoholism* (pp. 227–271). New York: Guilford.

Sisson, R. W., & Azrin, N. H. (1986). Family-member involvement to initiate and promote treatment of problem drinkers. *Journal of Behavior Therapy and Experimental Psychiatry, 17,* 15–21.

Sisson, R. W., & Azrin, N. H. (1989). The community reinforcement approach. In R. K. Hester & W. R. Miller (Eds.), *Handbook of alcoholism treatment approaches: Effective alternatives* (pp. 242–258), New York: Pergamon.

Skinner, H. A. (1982). Statistical approaches to the classification of alcohol and drug addiction. *British Journal of Addiction, 77,* 259–273.

Sobell, M. B., & Sobell, L. C. (1984). The aftermath of heresy: A response to Pendery et al.'s critique of "Individualized Behavior

Therapy for Alcoholics." *Behaviour Research and Therapy, 22,* 412–440.

Stanton, M. D., & Todd, T. C. (1982). *The family therapy of drug abuse and addiction.* New York: Guilford.

Stitzer, M. L., Bigelow, G. E., Lawrence, C., Cohen, J., D'Lugoff, B., & Hawthorne, J. W. (1977). Medication take-home as a reinforcer in a methadone maintenance program. *Addictive Behaviors, 2,* 9–14.

Stitzer, M. L., Bigelow, G. E., & Liebson, I. (1979). Reducing benzodiazepine self-administration with contingent reinforcement. *Addictive Behaviors, 4,* 245–252.

Stitzer, M. L., Bigelow, G. E., Liebson, I. A., & Hawthorne, J. W. (1982). Contingent reinforcement for benzodiazepine-free urines: Evaluation of a drug abuse treatment intervention. *Journal of Applied Behavior Analysis, 15,* 493–503.

Stitzer, M. L., Bigelow, G. E., & McCaul, M. E. (1985). Behavior therapy in drug abuse treatment: Review and evaluation. In R. S. Ashery (Ed.), *Progress in the development and cost-effective treatment for drug abusers.* (NIDA Research Monograph No. 58, pp. 31–49). Washington, DC: U.S. Government Printing Office.

Stockwell, T., & Town, C. (1989). Anxiety and stress management. In R. K. Hester & W. R. Miller (Eds.), *Handbook of alcoholism treatment approaches: Effective alternatives* (pp. 222–230). New York: Pergamon.

Todd, T. C. (1984). A contingency analysis of family treatment and drug abuse. In J. Grabowski, M. L. Stitzer, & J. E. Henningfield (Eds.), *Behavioral intervention techniques in drug abuse treatment* (NIDA Research Monograph No. 46, pp. 104–114). Washington, DC: U.S. Government Printing Office.

Tuchfield, B. S. (1981). Spontaneous remission in alcoholics: Empirical observations and theoretical implications. *Journal of Studies on Alcohol, 42,* 626–641.

Tucker, J. A., Vuchinich, R. E., & Gladsjo, J. A. (1990–91). Environmental influences on relapse in substance use disorders. *International Journal of the Addictions, 25,* 1017–1050.

Tucker, J. A., Vuchinich, R. E., Gladsjo, J. A., Hawkins, J., & Sherrill, J. T. (1989, November). *Environmental influences on natural recovery from alcohol problems without treatment.* Presented at the meeting of the Association for the Advancement of Behavior Therapy, Washington, DC.

Tucker, J. A., Vuchinich, R. E., & Harris, C. V. (1985). Determinants of substance abuse relapse. In M. Galizio & S. A. Maisto (Eds.), *Determinants of substance abuse: Biological, psychological, and environmental factors* (pp. 383–421). New York: Plenum.

Twentyman, C. T., Greenwald, D. P., Greenwald, M. A., Kloss, J. D., Kovalski, M. B., & Zibung-Hoffman, P. (1982). An assessment of social skills deficits in alcoholics. *Behavioral Assessment, 4,* 317–326.

Vaillant, G. E., & Milofsky, E. S. (1982). Natural history of male alcoholism. IV. Paths to recovery. *Archives of General Psychiatry, 39,* 127–133.

Vuchinich, R. E., & Tucker, J. A. (1988). Contributions from behavioral theories of choice to an analysis of alcohol abuse. *Journal of Abnormal Psychology, 97,* 181–185.

Yaguchi, M., Stitzer, M. L., Bigelow, G. E., & Liebson, I. A. (1988). Contingency management in methadone maintenance: Effects of reinforcing and aversive consequences on illicit polydrug use. *Drug and Alcohol Dependence, 22,* 1–7.

PART TWO

Childhood Disorders

CHAPTER 12

Behavioral Treatment of Childhood Anxiety Disorders

GRETA FRANCIS

The purpose of this chapter is to provide a selected overview of behavioral treatment approaches for anxiety disorders in children and adolescents. When applicable, pharmacological interventions also are discussed. Although the clinical and research literature on mild to moderate fears is large, there are relatively few studies of clinic-referred youngsters with anxiety disorders. The scope of this chapter is limited to a discussion of the treatment of anxiety disorders in clinic-referred children and adolescents.

The term "anxiety disorders" encompasses a number of heterogeneous anxiety problems. DSM-III-R (American Psychiatric Association, 1987) described three different anxiety disorders specific to children and adolescents: separation anxiety disorder, overanxious disorder, and avoidant disorder. In addition, children and adolescents may receive anxiety diagnoses that are not specific to children, including simple phobia, social phobia, panic disorder with or without agoraphobia, obsessive-compulsive disorder, and post-traumatic stress disorder.

The literature on the treatment of anxiety disorders in children consists primarily of descriptive uncontrolled work. There is growing support in the research literature for the existence of anxiety disorders in youth, but very few empirical investigations of treatment outcome exist. Only a small number of single-case design studies and an even smaller number of group studies can be found.

Few factors have been shown *empirically* to influence treatment selection or outcome with anxiety-disordered children. Hypothesized factors include age and/or cognitive maturity of the child, involvement of the parent or school, severity and pervasiveness of symptoms, extent of avoidance behavior, and source of the anxiety. Of these, the factor probably most frequently used in making treatment selection is the source of the anxiety. "Source" is used here to describe that toward which the child's anxiety is directed (i.e., what the child is afraid of). For example, in a child with anxiety-based school refusal, the source of anxiety might be separation from the parents or fear of speaking in public.

When treating an anxiety-disordered child, it is critical that a comprehensive functional analysis be completed, in order to identify the source of the anxiety. The problem of school refusal highlights this need. Children may refuse to attend school for a variety of reasons. To select appropriate treatment interventions, it is necessary to delineate the factors antecedent or consequent to the school refusal behavior. Kearney and Silverman (1988) proposed a functional model of assessment and treatment of school refusal that allows for identification of the variables influencing school refusal. These authors developed the School Refusal Assessment Scale (SRAS) to measure avoidance of specific or general fearfulness, escape from aversive social situations, attention-seeking or separation-anxious behavior, and tangible reinforcement.

Because treating children with anxiety disorders often is labor-intensive, there is a need for therapist availability and flexibility, to better the chances that the child will be successful in completing treatment tasks. It is difficult, if not impossible, to treat children with anxiety disorders—especially young children—without working closely with their parents. If the child's anxiety is problematic in school, it often is necessary to forge working relationships with teachers, guidance counselors, and school psychologists. Frequently, it is beneficial to maintain frequent phone contact with the child, parent, or school in between scheduled sessions. Treatment may consist of lengthy sessions several times per week. There may also be a need to accompany the child into the home or school, in order to instruct parents or teachers to implement treatment techniques.

The treatment strategies used for children with anxiety disorders mirror those used for adults with anxiety disorders. These include various methods of exposure; relaxation; and operant, modeling, and cognitive treatments. Often, the treatment strategies used are multicomponent in nature. According to Ollendick (1979), the element common to most treatment packages for anxious children is exposure. In the following sections, each of the childhood anxiety disorders will be discussed briefly, and current behavioral treatments will be considered. Finally, a discussion of pharmacotherapy, particularly in conjunction with behavior therapy, will be provided.

SEPARATION ANXIETY DISORDER

Separation anxiety disorder is characterized by marked distress related to separation of the child from major attachment figures or the home. Children with separation anxiety disorder may evidence worry about their own or their parents' safety, reluctance to attend school or other activities away from parents, and reluctance to sleep alone or away from home. In addition, these children may display somatic concerns at separation times, clinginess with parents, anxiety in anticipation of separation, and distress while separated from parents. Some evidence suggests that separation anxiety disorder is more common in clinic-referred females and youngsters of lower socioeconomic status (Last, Hersen, Kazdin, Finkelstein, & Strauss, 1987).

Francis, Last, and Strauss (1987) investigated the symptoms of separation anxiety disorder in a sample of 45 outpatient youngsters diagnosed with separation anxiety disorder. They found that young children (ages 5 to 8 years) evidenced more symptoms than did older children (ages 9 to 12 years). One hundred percent of young children received a diagnosis of separation anxiety disorder based on having met *more than* the minimum three diagnostic criteria; the same was true for only 69 percent of older children. Adolescents (ages 13 years and above) did not differ from either young or older children; 75% presented with more than three symptoms. In addition, there was some evidence that young children demonstrated different symptoms than did older children or adolescents. Young children were more likely to report nightmares involving separation and excessive distress upon separation. Much has been written about separation anxiety disorder, but little in the way of empirical research exists. Hence, the psychopathology of this condition is poorly understood. For additional information on the syndrome, the reader is referred to Ollendick and Huntzinger (1990).

Behavioral Treatment

There have been very few reports in the literature of the treatment of clearly separation-anxious children. Mansdorf and Lukens (1987) described the use of a cognitive-behavioral approach for the treatment of two separation-anxious children and their parents. Both children refused to attend school and previously had failed to respond to treatment with a tricyclic-antidepressant. The authors completed an assessment of the self-statements of both the children and their parents, and determined already existing consequences for nonattendance at school. Treatment consisted of self-instruction training for the child, cognitive restructuring for the parent, and environmental restructuring in which parental reinforcement was made contingent on school attendance. In addition, children were returned gradually to school. The goal of treatment was to promote the use of coping cognitions by the children and their parents. For example, one child reported a worry: "The kids in school make fun of me." This inhibiting cognition was replaced with the following coping cognition: "That's their problem, not mine." Similarly, the parents of this child expressed their concern: "My child is sick so I shouldn't push." This inhibiting cognition was replaced with the following coping cognition: "This is the way to help." Results indicated that both children were able to remain alone in school all day after 4 weeks of treatment. Moreover, at 3-month follow-up, these treatment gains were maintained. Although this study needs to be replicated with a larger sample and longer follow-up, it stands as a promising and efficient approach to the treatment of separation anxiety involving both the child and parent.

Peterson (1987) described a treatment program consisting of relaxation, cognitive coping strategies, imagery, a reward system, and graduated exposure, for the treatment of separation anxiety in an 8-year-old girl. The child was afraid to be alone at home for even a few seconds and exhibited intense anticipatory anxiety about separation. She and her mother participated in 8 treatment sessions in which the child was taught deep muscle relaxation, positive imagery, and coping statements (e.g., "I can do it"). In addition, the mother instituted a reward system to increase time spent alone at home. Over the course of treatment, the child was able to spend gradually increasing periods of time alone at home while using the above-mentioned techniques. By the end of treatment, she was able to tolerate time alone at home without distress. Her self-reported anxiety while alone at home decreased, and her perceived ability to remain alone at home increased.

OVERANXIOUS DISORDER

The hallmark of overanxious disorder is excessive or unrealistic worry. In contrast to the relatively circumscribed worries indicative of separation anxiety disorder, the worries of overanxious-disorder children tend to be pervasive and may involve a variety of social, athletic, and academic situations. The child with overanxious disorder may worry about both past and future events and be excessively concerned with his or her performance in academic, athletic, or social situations. In addition, the child may express vague somatic complaints, evidence extreme self-consciousness, require excessive reassurance, and complain of tenseness or an inability to relax. Strauss, Lease, Last, and Francis (1989) found relatively equal numbers of males and females in their clinic sample of youngsters with overanxious disorder. When compared to children with separation anxiety disorder, children with overanxious disorder were more likely to be from families of middle-upper socioeconomic status (Last, Strauss, & Francis, 1987).

Strauss et al. (1989) studied age differences in symptom expression, in a clinic sample of 55 children diagnosed with overanxious disorder. The authors compared children (ages 5 to 11 years) and adolescents (ages 12 to 19 years) on symptom ratings and self-report inventories. Although adolescents were more likely to describe unrealistic concern about the appropriateness of their past behavior than were younger children, there were no differences in the rates at which they described other overanxious symptoms. However, adolescents presented with a greater number of symptoms than did children. Finally, overanxious adolescents reported significantly more anxiety and depression using self-report questionnaires.

Behavioral Treatment

There are no reports in the research literature about the treatment of overanxious disorder. However, Strauss (1988) presented a case study of the treatment of overanxious disorder in an 11-year-old girl (Ashley). Ashley worried excessively about most future and past events. She was perfectionistic and often sought reassurance as to the correctness of her academic and social behavior. She was extremely self-conscious and had difficulty relaxing. A multimethod assessment was conducted, including self-report inventories and teacher-rating scales. Ashley described herself on self-report questionnaires as anxious, fearful, sad, and lonely. Her teachers characterized her as anxious, withdrawn, and socially neglected among her classmates.

Treatment consisted of a package based on interventions used successfully with generalized anxiety disorder in adults. The treatment package included relaxation techniques, cognitive restructuring, and assertiveness training. Ashley was seen for a total of 25 individual treatment sessions over a 6-month period. The initial phase of treatment consisted of training in deep muscle relaxation. A reward system was added to encourage Ashley to practice relaxation exercises at home. She reported no reduction in anxiety or worrying following completion of the relaxation training. During this initial phase of treatment, Ashley also self-monitored cognitions and subjective anxiety. Cognitive rehearsal and cognitive restructuring were used to modify her maladaptive thoughts. She was taught to replace maladaptive thoughts with coping thoughts, such as "I know that I am as good as the other kids." In addition, Ashley was taught to modify her faulty thinking by identifying and challenging cognitive errors, such as catastrophizing thoughts. According to the author, progress in cognitive therapy was slow. However, once Ashley grasped the concept that her thinking was affecting her behavior, her progress quickened. The final phase of treatment consisted of assertiveness training. Role-play practice sessions were used to increase assertive responding and initiations of social interactions. For example, Ashley practiced refusing unreasonable requests and calling peers on the telephone. Strauss reported that this multicomponent treatment package was effective in modifying Ashley's overanxious symptomatology. At the end of treatment, Ashley no longer met DSM-III criteria for overanxious disorder. Her self-reported anxiety, fear, sadness, and loneliness also decreased. At 3 months posttreatment, both Ashley and her parents reported that treatment gains had been maintained.

AVOIDANT DISORDER

Children with avoidant disorder are described as excessively shy around unfamiliar people, so much so as to interfere with social functioning in peer relationships. However, such children do value interpersonal involvement. That is, they evidence appropriate relationships with familiar people or express the wish to have friendships with peers.

Avoidant disorder has been mentioned rarely in the literature. Cantwell and Baker (1987) found avoidant disorder to be the most common diagnosis in their sample of young language-disordered children. In an attempt to examine the diagnosis of avoidant disorder in a clinic sample of anxiety-disordered youngsters, Francis, Last, and Strauss (1990) found roughly equal numbers of males and females receiving the diagnosis of avoidant disorder. Avoidant disorder frequently was associated with other DSM-III-R anxiety disorders and rarely occurred as the child's only diagnosis.

Behavioral Treatment

There are no published reports of the treatment of Avoidant Disorder. Because peer relationships are thought to be impaired in children with avoidant disorder, treatment strategies aimed at remediating social isolation may be beneficial; however, this remains an empirical question.

PHOBIAS

The diagnosis of phobia in children is similar to its diagnosis in adults. The phobic child must show persistent fear, avoidance or endurance coupled with intense anxiety, recognition that the fear is excessive or unreasonable, and impairment in day-to-day functioning or distress about having the fear. Phobias are characterized as simple or social. Common simple phobias in children include fears of animals and medical procedures; common social phobias include fears of speaking and eating in public.

Studies of subclinical fears indicate a change in the type and number of fears over the course of childhood and adolescence (Graziano, DeGiovanni, & Garcia, 1979; MacFarlane, Allen, & Honzik, 1954). For example, young children tend to demonstrate more and different fears than do older children and adolescents. Although there appears to be an age-related decrease in reported fears of imaginary creatures, the dark, and animals, there is an age-related increase in social fears (Agras, Chapin, & Oliveau, 1972; Bauer, 1976; Maurer, 1965).

Generally, it has been found that girls report more fear and anxiety than do boys (Abe & Masui, 1981; Anderson, Williams, McGee, & Silva, 1987; Lapouse & Monk, 1958; Richman, Stevenson, & Graham, 1975). However, as Graziano et al. (1979) pointed out, it is unclear whether the higher rate of fears reported for girls reflects a greater prevalence of fearfulness in girls or a greater willingness by girls and their parents or teachers to report fears.

Children on varying socioeconomic status (SES) levels have been found to differ in the number and type of fear reported. Children from lower SES levels report more fears and worries than do children from higher SES levels (Angelino, Dollins, & Mech, 1956; Lapouse & Monk, 1959). Moreover, these researchers found that low SES children were more likely to report fears of rats and drunks, whereas higher SES children were more likely to report fears of car accidents.

Behavioral Treatment

There have been a large number of articles published on the behavioral treatment of *school* phobia. Behavioral approaches such as contingency contracting (Welch & Carpenter, 1970), in vivo exposure (Garvey & Hegrenes, 1966), imaginal exposure (Galloway & Miller, 1978), and various combinations of the above (Ayllon, Smith, & Rogers, 1970; Lazarus, Davison, & Polefka, 1965; Miller, 1972) reportedly have been effective in the treatment of school refusal. Unfortunately, this literature is plagued by a number of methodological problems that preclude definitive statements about treatment effectiveness. These methodological problems include inadequately defined samples, lack of controlled treatment outcome studies, and failure to use objective and standard assessment procedures. Somewhat surprisingly, there have been few advances in the school refusal treatment literature of late. A notable exception is a study by Kearney and Silverman (in press), which will be discussed next.

Miller, Barrett, Hampe, and Noble (1972) conducted a group study of the treatment of childhood phobias. Although their sample consisted of children with various types of phobias, the majority (69%) presented with school phobia. Children were randomly assigned to one of three treatment conditions: waiting-list control, systematic desensitization, or psychotherapy. Outcome measures included parent and clinician ratings of improvement, as well as parent checklists measuring the child's general fearfulness. When considering *parental* reports of improvement, results indicated that both active treatment conditions were more effective than the waiting-list control, with no significant difference between the two treatment conditions. In contrast, *clinician* ratings of improvement were no different among the three conditions.

Several methodological problems are present in the Miller study. First, there were a number of similarities between the two treatment conditions. Both the psychotherapy condition and the systematic desensitization condition included the use of operant techniques in which the parents were instructed to modify their contingencies for "fearful" behavior. For example, in both conditions, parents were instructed to remove daytime television watching if their child refused to attend school. Second, no clear report was given about the severity of the children's phobias. There was little information available about the presence of phobic avoidance. Third, the outcome measures used were problematic. The authors reported that they were unable to keep the nontreating clinician who made improvement ratings blind to treatment condition. In addition, there was no direct measure of treatment effectiveness. The parent checklists provided information regarding general fearfulness; however, no direct measures of fear or avoidance were given. Although Miller and colleagues advanced the literature by presenting a controlled group study of the treatment of childhood fears, methodological problems make interpretation of the results difficult.

The second group study of the treatment of school refusal was conducted by Blagg and Yule (1984). The authors compared behavioral treatment, inpatient hospitalization, and home tutoring plus psychotherapy for a group of school phobic children. The majority of the children in the sample were between 11 and 14 years of age. Behavioral treatment consisted of frequent contact with school personnel, operant strategies (e.g., parents praised school attendance while ignoring physical complaints in the morning before school), and in vivo flooding. The inpatient hospitalization condition consisted of the physical separation of the parent and child, therapeutic milieu, possible pharmacotherapy, and discharge planning around school placement. In the home tutoring condition, the child was permitted to remain at home while receiving educational tutoring and psychotherapy. Children were not assigned randomly to treatment conditions; rather, these treatment groups were naturally occurring.

Blagg and Yule collected a number of measures of overall emotional adjustment, as well as a record of school attendance. Following treatment, 93.3% of the children in the behavioral treatment condition attended school without significant problems. This is in marked contrast to the success rates for inpatient hospitalization (37.5%) and home tutoring (10%). In addition, children in the behavioral treatment condition evidenced improvement on measures of self-esteem and extroversion. Behavioral treatment was found to be much less time-consuming than other treatment. Children in the behavioral treatment condition received an average of 2.53 weeks of treatment as compared with 45.3 weeks for inpatient hospitalization and 72.1 weeks for home tutoring. These results yield support for the efficacy of in vivo flooding plus operant procedures in the treatment of school phobia. However, the study is not without methodological problems, including the lack of random assignment to treatment conditions.

In the child anxiety literature, the only study using treatment matching was conducted by Kearney and Silverman (in press). Using results of a functional analysis, they prescribed treatment for youngsters with school refusal behavior. The authors used systematic desensitization to treat children with specific fearfulness or general overanxiousness. Cognitive behavior therapy and/or modeling was used for children avoidant of aversive social situations. Differential reinforcement of other behaviors was used for children who were thought to be attention-seeking or separation-anxious. Finally, contingency contracting was used for children who avoided school because of significant rewards for nonattendance. The extent to which treatment was focused on the child or parent varied according to the source of the problem. Results indicated that 6 of the 7 subjects improved (i.e., attended school consistently) in accordance with their prescriptive treatments. Although preliminary, this study represents an innovative approach to treatment that highlights the importance of conducting a functional analysis. The notion of prescriptive treatment for school refusal behavior is especially appealing, given the large number of variables that influence such behavior.

Virtually no information is available about the treatment of *social* phobias in children. This is in contrast to a large literature on the treatment of social withdrawal in children. Francis and Ollendick (1990) conducted a case study of the treatment of an adolescent with social phobia, using graduated exposure. The subject was a 16-year-old female with a lengthy history of school avoidance coupled with avoidance of many other social situations (e.g., parties, stores). Her extensive avoidance was not caused by a fear of panicking; rather, she feared embarrassment and humiliation. For example, she became very anxious about having to take the trash outside to the dumpster and would spend hours "getting ready" prior to going outside. She was diagnosed with social phobia: generalized type. Self-report assessment questionnaires revealed that the youngster reported significant depressive and anxiety symptoms as well as intense social-evaluative fears. There was no evidence of a social skills deficit as assessed by a behavioral role-play test.

Using a graduated in vivo exposure approach, a hierarchy was developed. Each week the adolescent completed homework assignments drawn from the hierarchy. The least anxiety-provoking hierarchy items were "going to a shopping mall with someone," "going to a small department store with someone," and "standing in line at a fast food place with someone." The most anxiety-provoking items were "taking the trash outside without getting ready first" and "going to school all day." Over the course of 3 months, she was exposed gradually to a number of social situations. She practiced such tasks as taking the trash to the dumpster after getting ready for no more than 30 minutes; riding the bus with someone; going early to a movie and waiting; and going to a shopping mall alone. The gradual exposure program appeared to be helpful in decreasing her social-evaluative anxiety. By the end of treatment, she completed her high school equivalency degree (GED), enrolled in a community college, confronted the majority of social situations with minimal anxiety, and reported significantly fewer symptoms of depression, anxiety, and fear. Key factors involved in this patient's treatment were adequate diagnostic assessment, including a functional analysis of target behaviors; selection of treatment based on the results of the assessment; active involvement of the patient in development of the hierarchy and determination of homework assignments; and continuous assessment of treatment progress.

Relaxation and operant techniques have been used as part of multicomponent treatment packages for childhood *simple* phobias. For example, Graziano and colleagues (Graziano & Mooney, 1980, 1982; Graziano, Mooney, Huber, & Ignasiak, 1979) used relaxation and operant strategies in combination with cognitive self-control training to treat young children who were afraid of the dark. In their controlled group study, Graziano and Mooney (1980) treated 17 children with severe nighttime fears. Their control group consisted of 16 children who participated in the assessments but did not receive treatment. Subjects were assigned randomly to experimental or control conditions. Children in the experimental group ranged in age from 6.2 to 12.3 years, with an average age of 4.9 years. Children in the control group ranged in age from 6 years to 13.5 years, with an average age of 5.2 years. The entire sample evidenced nighttime fears for an average of longer than 2 years.

Children and their parents were seen for a total of 5 sessions. Assessments were completed during the first and fifth sessions, and the remaining 3 sessions were devoted to treatment. Experimental and control groups participated in a 7-day baseline phase during which nighttime behaviors were monitored. Both children and their parents monitored "fearless nighttime behavior." Fearless nighttime behavior consisted of the child's going to bed within 20 minutes of an instruction to do so, sleeping in his or her own room with the lights and radio off, and not complaining at bedtime or throughout the night. The experimental group then participated in 3 weeks of family self-control training. Posttreatment assessment was conducted for both groups.

Treatment consisted of groups for parents and children. During the child-focused group treatment, children were taught to relax, imagine a pleasant scene, and say: "I am brave. I can take care of myself when I am alone. I can take care of myself when I am in the dark." They were instructed to practice these skills each night. During the parent-focused group treatment, parents were instructed to initiate their child's practice session each evening. In addition, parents monitored their child's progress and used an operant strategy to provide immediate rewards for nonfearful behavior. Children were given "bravery" tokens by their parents each morning and evening. The tokens were to be used toward a party at a popular fast-food restaurant.

Results indicated that children in the experimental group evidenced significant improvement in nighttime fears compared to control group children. Treated children were fearful on fewer nights, fell asleep faster, went to bed faster, were more willing to go to bed, and evidenced fewer "delay" tactics.

Graziano and Mooney (1982) followed up many of the children in their 1980 study for approximately 3 years after discontinuation of treatment. They administered questionnaires that asked parents whether their child was still afraid at bedtime or had developed any new problems. Results indicated that 23 of 34 children were reported to have maintained their improvement, 8 of 34 were reported "still to be afraid but much less so," and 3 of 34 were reported to evidence significant nighttime fears. The majority of children were reported not to have developed any additional problems.

The studies of Graziano and colleagues provide support for the use of relaxation and operant strategies in combination with cognitive self-control strategies for the treatment of severe nighttime fears in young children. Of note, Graziano's study is one of the very few controlled group studies of treatment outcome in the child anxiety literature.

Pharmacological Treatment

Tricyclic antidepressants have been used to treat phobias involving school refusal. Gittelman-Klein and Klein (1971) conducted a double-blind placebo controlled study using imipramine or placebo to treat 35 youngsters with school refusal. Children were included in the study if they refused to attend school for 2 weeks or exhibited marked distress while in school. The presence of significant depressive symptomatology did not exclude youngsters from participation. Subjects were randomly assigned to imipramine or placebo conditions. Medication dosage ranged from 100 to 200 mg per day. All subjects received a psychosocial intervention aimed at increasing school attendance. Results indicated that imipramine was superior to placebo in promoting return to school. Of the youngsters in the imipramine condition, 81% began to attend school regularly as compared to 47% of youngsters in the placebo condition. Global improvement also was reported to be more apparent with imipramine treatment.

A number of problems with the Gittelman-Klein and Klein study (1971) make interpretation of the findings difficult. First, although the authors postulated that imipramine was successful in treating "separation anxiety," subjects were selected on the basis of school refusal rather than separation anxiety per se. Second, the study contained a number of children with significant depressive symptomatology. As such, treatment gains with imipramine may have been a function of the drug's antidepressant effect. Finally, there was improvement in school attendance for a substantial number of children in the placebo condition. Thus, the extent to which imipramine alone would be helpful in treating school refusal is not clear.

A second study of pharmacologic treatment of anxiety-based school refusal was conducted by Bernay et al. (1981). These authors performed a double-blind trial of clomipramine and placebo. Subjects were selected on criteria similar to those used by Gittelman-Klein and Klein (1971), and depressed children were not excluded from participation. Medication or placebo therapy occurred in conjunction with individual therapy and case management. Results revealed that both groups improved from baseline to the end of treatment, with no significant difference between treatment groups. Interpretation of these results is hampered by problems similar to those delineated above in reference to the Gittelman-Klein and Klein study.

PANIC DISORDER

Panic disorder with or without agoraphobia may be diagnosed in children and adolescents using the adult criteria specified in DSM-III-R. Panic disorder without agoraphobia is characterized by spontaneous anxiety attacks, consisting of multiple physiological symptoms, in the absence of significant avoidance behavior. In contrast, the diagnosis of panic disorder with agoraphobia requires both spontaneous anxiety attacks and significant avoidance behavior. Agoraphobics are believed to avoid situations because of fear of having a panic attack.

There have been reported cases of panic disorder with and without agoraphobia in children and adolescents (e.g., Black & Robbins, 1990; Last & Strauss, 1989). In the past, many youngsters with symptoms of panic disorder may have been given the label of "hyperventilation syndrome" when seen by their pediatricians (Herman, Stickler, & Lucas, 1981).

Behavioral Treatment

There have been very few reports of the treatment of agoraphobia in youngsters. This is somewhat surprising, given that the typical age of onset for agoraphobia is late adolescence or early adulthood (O'Brien & Barlow, 1984). Two published treatment studies of agoraphobia that involved adolescent subjects will be discussed (Barlow & Seidner, 1983; Kolko, 1984). Barlow and Seidner (1983) conducted multicomponent group treatment—including panic management strategies, cognitive restructuring, and graduated exposure—to treat three adolescent agoraphobics. Subjects evidenced significant impairment in school attendance related to their agoraphobic symptoms. Assessments included weekly hierarchy ratings by both the adolescent and his or her parent, as well as questionnaires designed to tap parent–adolescent communication. Pretreatment, midtreatment, posttreatment, and follow-up assessments were conducted.

Results indicated that two of the three adolescents evidenced significant improvement over the course of treatment and at the 6-month follow-up assessment. In both cases, there were marked decreases in hierarchy anxiety ratings and evidence of improved parent–adolescent communication. The third subject exhibited no change in agoraphobic behavior over the course of treatment.

Barlow and Seidner hypothesized that inclusion of the parent, like inclusion of the spouse when treating adult agoraphobics, was an important factor contributing to treatment success. They noted that their adolescent subjects had difficulty tolerating any anxiety during practice sessions, despite the presentation of a detailed treatment rationale. This reaction is unlike that of adult agoraphobics, who generally accept that their fears are irrational. In this way, adolescents were said to resemble adult agoraphobics with overvalued ideation, who typically do not respond positively to treatment (Foa, 1979). As the authors pointed out, this argues for the inclusion of a parent in the treatment of adolescent agoraphobia, in order to provide necessary in vivo support and encouragement.

Kolko (1984) described the treatment of an adolescent agoraphobic using paradoxical instruction. The 16-year-old female subject complained of panic attacks and required physical accompaniment to go outside the home. Treatment was evaluated using an AB design with follow-up. During baseline, an assessment was conducted and a hierarchy was developed. Assessment included self-reported anxiety ratings during exposure to the hierarchy, and self-report measures of anxiety and fear. At pretest, the subject was able to complete only 1 of 10 hierarchy tasks. Treatment consisted of paradoxical instruction and in vivo exposure. Essentially, the adolescent was instructed to approach each situation on the hierarchy while focusing all of her attention on the associated fear, thoughts, and physiological symptoms.

Results revealed that the adolescent reported less fear and avoidance to all items on the hierarchy following completion of treatment. At posttest and follow-up, she was able to complete all 10 hierarchy tasks and reported decreased anxiety levels in all situations. In addition, reductions of emotional sensitivity, state and trait anxiety, and fear were observed using self-report questionnaires.

OBSESSIVE-COMPULSIVE DISORDER

Obsessive-compulsive disorder (OCD) in children and adolescents virtually is identical to the disorder in adults. The essential feature of obsessive-compulsive disorder is repetitive disturbing thoughts and/or behavioral rituals. The interruption of these thoughts or rituals typically causes extreme distress. Common obsessions are thoughts of doubt, dying, or contamination. Common compulsions include washing, checking, touching, and counting rituals. Childhood obsessive-compulsive disorder is a rare and debilitating psychiatric problem. Estimates of the prevalence of obsessive-compulsive disorder in children have been placed at less than 2% of childhood disorders (Hollingsworth, Tanguay, Grossman, & Pabst, 1980; Judd, 1965).

Behavioral Treatment

The literature offers a few accounts of the behavioral treatment of childhood obsessive-compulsive disorder. The majority of available studies have employed flooding and response prevention (Bolton, Collins, & Steinberg, 1983; Mills, Agras, Barlow, & Mills, 1973; Stanley, 1980). The combination of flooding and response prevention has been studied extensively with obsessive-compulsive adults and has been found to be the treatment of choice (Steketee & Foa, 1985).

As an example, Mills and colleagues (1973) described the use of response prevention to treat a 15-year-old hospitalized boy who evidenced elaborate bedtime and morning rituals. Following a 12-day baseline, response prevention was applied to his bedtime rituals. The adolescent was told that he would no longer be allowed to engage in the bedtime rituals. During the response prevention phase, a staff member remained with the adolescent in his bedroom during the night. Within 10 days, bedtime rituals stopped. In addition, the authors noted a concomitant decrease in morning rituals, even though morning rituals had not been a target of treatment. During the return to baseline phase, the staff member no longer remained in the room with the adolescent during the night. The adolescent continued to refrain from exhibiting any bedtime or morning rituals during this time. According to the authors, treatment gains were maintained for approximately 8 weeks following discharge; however, the adolescent then began to engage in a new series of bathing rituals. Further outpatient treatment, which consisted of response prevention implemented by the parents, reportedly was successful in reducing the bathing rituals.

Extinction procedures also have been used in the treatment of childhood obsessive-compulsive disorder. Hallam (1974) noted that compulsive reassurance seeking often is a problem in children with obsessive-compulsive disorder. He described the use of extinction to treat a 15-year-old hospitalized female with a 3-year history of repetitive questions about whether people were saying nasty things about her.

In an attempt to expand on Hallam's (1974) work, Francis (1988) conducted a within-series single-case study of the use of extinction to treat an 11-year-old boy who had obsessive-compulsive disorder. The child was seen on an outpatient basis and treatment was implemented by the parents. The child presented with an acute exacerbation of obsessive worries about death and dying, as well as compulsive reassurance-seeking behavior. He frequently voiced fears of dying from various diseases and persistently asked questions such as: "Am I going blind?" "Do you think I will throw up?" "Am I going to die?" The parents were instructed to monitor reassurance-seeking behavior 4 times per day. During the 8-day baseline phase, parents were instructed to respond in their usual way to the child's reassurance seeking. During the 8-day extinction phase, parents were instructed to ignore all reassurance-seeking questions by looking/turning away and redirecting the conversation. The therapist maintained frequent phone contact with the family during this phase. The return to baseline phase lasted for 5 days and consisted of a return to attending to the reassurance-seeking behavior at a time when a number of family members were ill. Of note, the family illness persisted for another 5 days following the end of this phase. The return to extinction phase lasted for 20 days and consisted of reimplementation of extinction procedure. A 1-month follow-up assessment was conducted in which the parents monitored the child's behavior for 3 days.

Results indicated that the extinction procedure was successful in decreasing the frequency of reassurance-seeking behavior to zero within 6 days. During the withdrawal of extinction, the child's behavior worsened dramatically, and reassurance seeking was occurring at rates higher than those seen during baseline. Once extinction was reimplemented, the frequency of reassurance-seeking behavior fell to zero within 12 days and remained at zero for 9 consecutive days and at the 1-month follow-up.

It is important to emphasize that the available single-case treatment studies of childhood obsessive-compulsive disorder have reported short-term treatment success. Given the chronic and disabling nature of obsessive-compulsive disorder, future researchers need to evaluate the long-term efficacy of such treatment strategies.

Pharmacological Treatment

Clomipramine is the only pharmacological treatment that has been evaluated systematically for OCD youngsters (Flament et al., 1985; Leonard, Swedo, Rapoport, Coffey, & Cheslow, 1988; Rapoport, Elkins, & Mikkelson, 1980). Flament et al. (1985) conducted a double-blind crossover-design study comparing clomipramine and placebo. Subjects included 19 OCD youngsters between the ages of 10 and 18 years (mean age = 14.5 years) who had experienced significant OCD symptoms for at least 1 year. The average duration of illness was 4 years. Children with psychosis, mental retardation, or primary affective disorder were excluded from the study. All youngsters but one had a past history of psychiatric treatment, and one half of the sample had not responded to previous treatment with tricyclic antidepressants. Youngsters participated in a 1-week baseline monitoring phase followed by 10 weeks of clomipramine or placebo, each of which was administered for 5 weeks. The mean dose of clomipramine was 141 mg per day. Children and their parents also received supportive psychotherapy. No formal behavior therapy was conducted. Results indicated that clomipramine treatment yielded a decrease in obsessional behavior that was independent of baseline depression levels, though not a full recovery of obsessive symptoms. At the end of clomipramine treatment, 26% of the youngsters were described as unchanged or only slightly improved, 64% were described as moderately or much improved, and 10% were described as symptom-free. There was no change in global measures of depression or anxiety. Because the authors provided no information about the kind of compulsive behaviors exhibited by the youngsters, it is not possible to assess the effect of clomipramine on compulsive behavior.

Leonard et al. (1988) conducted a double-blind crossover study comparing clomipramine and desmethylimipramine (DMI). Twenty-one OCD youngsters between the ages of 8 and 19 years participated in the study. Subjects had an average symptom duration of 2.7 years, and reportedly were not significantly depressed. Treatment was conducted on an outpatient basis and consisted of a 2-week single-blind placebo phase followed by 2 consecutive 5-week trials of clomipramine or DMI increased to 3 mg/kg. Ongoing assessments of obsessive-compulsive symptomatology, depression, and side effects were conducted. Results indicated that clomipramine was superior to DMI in alleviating OCD symptoms. These differences were observed by the third week of treatment. DMI produced little or no improvement from baseline, and relapse was apparent within 2 weeks when DMI followed clomipramine.

The other pharmacological agent for childhood OCD that has been described in the clinical literature is fluoxetine. Riddle, Hardin, King, Scahill, and Woolston (1990) reported preliminary clinical experience using fluoxetine to treat youngsters with OCD. Subjects included 5 boys and 5 girls between the ages of 8 and 15 years, 6 of whom presented with primary Tourette's syndrome (TS). Four of the OCD/TS youngsters were being treated concurrently with other medications. Treatment consisted of an open trial of fluoxetine. Five youngsters were characterized as responders, as indicated by "much improved" ratings by their clinician. Each of the responders was on a dose of 20 mg/day and treatment lasted between 4 and 20 weeks. A common adverse side effect, seen in 4 of the subjects (all but 1 were nonresponders), was behavioral agitation defined by increased motor activity and pressured speech. As the authors readily acknowledge, data in this study must be viewed cautiously, given the lack of a placebo control condition. The authors reported anecdotally that all 5 responders have continued on fluoxetine. In fact, they described rapid decompensation in the one child whose medication was discontinued temporarily.

POST-TRAUMATIC STRESS DISORDER

Children and adolescents may present with symptoms indicative of post-traumatic stress disorder (PTSD). The essential feature of PTSD is continued distress following an unusual and markedly distressing event (e.g., natural disaster, physical abuse). The continued distress is manifested by re-experiencing of the traumatic event, avoidance of situations associated with the event, and persistent symptoms of increased arousal.

Behavioral Treatment

There have been a small number of reports of the behavioral treatment of childhood PTSD (Saigh, 1986a, 1986b, in press). Saigh described the use of flooding in the treatment of three children with war-related PTSD. In brief, treatment consisted of the presentation of flooding scenes in which children were instructed to imagine the precise details of each traumatic scene. For example, in the case of a 6-year-old boy who had been exposed to a bomb blast (Saigh, 1986a), anxiety-provoking scenes included hearing a loud explosion and seeing people injured, approaching the shopping area in which the explosion had occurred, and observing a man carrying an injured child. During each scene, the child was asked to rate his anxiety level. The author reported that flooding was effective in decreasing self-reported anxiety during flooding scenes. In addition, the child completed pre- and posttreatment behavioral approach tests that required him to return to the shopping center where the explosion had occurred. By the time of his 6-month posttreatment follow-up assessment, the child was able to complete 95% of the behavioral approach test criteria as compared to completing only 45% of the criteria prior to treatment.

SUMMARY

The *empirical* study of anxiety disorders in children and adolescents has just begun. Much of the current treatment literature consists of uncontrolled, single-subject, multicomponent treatment packages. As such, no definitive statements can be made regarding the efficacy of behavior therapy or pharmacological interventions for childhood anxiety in clinic populations. The literature suggests that exposure, relaxation, operant, and cognitive strategies may be used effectively to treat anxiety disorders in clinic populations of anxious children and adolescents. Moreover, there is suggestive evidence that clomipramine may be beneficial in the treatment of childhood OCD. There is an immediate need for adequately controlled treatment studies. The studies highlighted in this chapter represent a base on which further investigations can be built.

REFERENCES

Abe, K., & Masui, T. (1981). Age-sex trends of phobic and anxiety symptoms in adolescents. *British Journal of Psychiatry, 138,* 297–302.

Agras, S., Chapin, H. H., & Oliveau, D. (1972). The natural history of phobia. *Archives of General Psychiatry, 26,* 315–317.

American Psychiatric Association. (1987). *Diagnostic and statistical manual of mental disorders* (3rd ed. rev.). Washington, DC: Author.

Anderson, J. C., Williams, S., McGee, R., & Silva, P. A. (1987). DSM-III disorders in preadolescent children. *Archives of General Psychiatry, 44,* 69–76.

Angelino, H., Dollins, J., & Mech, E. V. (1956). Trends in the "fear and worries" of school children as related to socioeconomic status and age. *Journal of Genetic Psychology, 89,* 263–276.

Ayllon, T., Smith, D., & Rogers, M. (1970). Behavioral management of school phobia. *Journal of Behavior Therapy and Experimental Psychiatry, 1,* 125–138.

Barlow, D. H., & Seidner, A. L. (1983). Treatment of adolescent agoraphobia: Effects on parent–adolescent relations. *Behaviour Research and Therapy, 21,* 519–526.

Bauer, D. H. (1976). An exploratory study of developmental changes in children's fears. *Journal of Child Psychology and Psychiatry, 17,* 69–74.

Berney, T., Kolvin, I., Bhate, S. R., Garside, R. F., Jeans, J., Kay, B., & Scarth, L. (1981). School phobia: A therapeutic trial with clomipramine and short-term outcome. *British Journal of Psychiatry, 138,* 110–118.

Black, B., & Robbins, D. R. (1990). Panic disorder in children and adolescents. *Journal of the American Academy of Child and Adolescent Psychiatry, 29,* 36–44.

Blagg, N. R., & Yule, W. (1984). The behavioral treatment of school refusal—A comparative study. *Behaviour Research and Therapy, 22,* 119–127.

Bolton, D., Collins, S., & Steinberg, D. (1983). The treatment of obsessive-compulsive disorder in adolescence: A report of 15 cases. *British Journal of Psychiatry, 142,* 456-464.

Cantwell, D. P., & Baker, L. (1987). The prevalence of anxiety in children with communication disorders. *Journal of Anxiety Disorders, 1,* 239-248.

Flament, M. F., Rapoport, J. L., Berg, C. J., Sceery, W., Kilts, C., Mellstrom, B., & Linnoila, M. (1985). Clomipramine treatment of childhood obsessive-compulsive disorder. *Archives of General Psychiatry, 42,* 977-983.

Foa, E. B. (1979). Failure in treating obsessive-compulsives. *Behaviour Research and Therapy, 17,* 169-176.

Francis, G. (1988). Childhood obsessive-compulsive disorder: Extinction of compulsive reassurance-seeking. *Journal of Anxiety Disorders, 2,* 361-366.

Francis, G., Last, C. G., & Strauss, C. C. (1987). Expression of separation anxiety disorder: The roles of age and gender. *Child Psychiatry and Human Development, 18,* 82-89.

Francis, G., Last, C. G., & Strauss, C. C. (1990). *Avoidant disorder in children and adolescents.* Unpublished manuscript.

Francis, G., & Ollendick, T. (1990). Anxiety disorders. In E. L. Feindler & G. R. Kalfus (Eds.), *Casebook in adolescent behavior therapy.* New York: Springer.

Galloway, D., & Miller, A. (1978). The use of graded in vivo flooding in the extinction of children's phobias. *Behavioral Psychotherapy, 6,* 7-10.

Garvey, W. P., & Hegrenes, J. R. (1966). Desensitization techniques in the treatment of school phobia. In B. B. Wolman, J. Egan, & A. O. Ross (Eds.), *Handbook of treatment of mental disorders in childhood and adolescence.* Englewood Cliffs, NJ: Prentice-Hall.

Gittelman-Klein, R., & Klein, D. F. (1971). Controlled imipramine treatment of school phobia. *Archives of General Psychiatry, 25,* 204-207.

Graziano, A., DeGiovanni, I. S., & Garcia, K. (1979). Behavioral treatment of children's fears: A review. *Psychological Bulletin, 86,* 804-830.

Graziano, A. M., & Mooney, K. C. (1980). Family self-control instruction for children's nighttime fear reduction. *Journal of Consulting and Clinical Psychology, 48,* 206-213.

Graziano, A. M., & Mooney, K. C. (1982). Behavioral treatment of "night fears" in children: Maintenance of improvement at 2½ to 3 years follow up. *Journal of Consulting and Clinical Psychology, 50,* 398-399.

Graziano, A. M., Mooney, K. C., Huber, C., & Ignasiak, D. (1979). Self-control instruction for children's fear reduction. *Journal of Behavior Therapy and Experimental Psychiatry, 10,* 221-227.

Hallam, R. S. (1974). Extinction of ruminations: A case study. *Behavior Therapy, 5,* 565-568.

Herman, S., Stickler, G., & Lucas, A. (1981). Hyperventilation syndrome in children and adolescents: Long-term follow-up. *Pediatrics, 67,* 183-187.

Hollingsworth, C., Tanguay, P., Grossman, L., & Pabst, P. (1980). Long-term outcome of obsessive-compulsive disorder in childhood. *Journal of the American Academy of Child Psychiatry, 19,* 134-144.

Judd, L. L. (1965). Obsessive-compulsive neurosis in children. *Archives of General Psychiatry, 12,* 136-143.

Kearney, C. A., & Silverman, W. K. (1988). *Measuring the function of school refusal behavior: The School Refusal Assessment Scale (SRAS).* Paper presented at the annual meeting of the Association for the Advancement of Behavior Therapy, New York.

Kearney, C. A., & Silverman, W. K. (in press). A preliminary analysis of a functional model of assessment and treatment for school refusal behavior. *Behavior Modification.*

Kolko, D. J. (1984). Paradoxical instruction in the elimination of avoidance behavior in an agoraphobic girl. *Journal of Behaviour Therapy and Experimental Psychiatry, 15,* 51-57.

Lapouse, R., & Monk, M. A. (1958). An epidemiologic study of behavior characteristics in children. *American Journal of Public Health, 48,* 1134-1144.

Lapouse, R., & Monk, M. A. (1959). Fears and worries in a representative sample of children. *American Journal of Orthopsychiatry, 29*, 803–818.

Last, C. G., Hersen, M., Kazdin, A. E., Finkelstein, R., & Strauss, C. C. (1987). Comparison of DSM-III separation anxiety and overanxious disorders: Demographic characteristics and patterns of comorbidity. *Journal of the American Academy of Child Psychiatry, 26*, 527–531.

Last, C. G., & Strauss, C. C. (1989). Panic disorder in children and adolescents. *Journal of Anxiety Disorders, 3*, 87–95.

Last, C. G., Strauss, C., & Francis, G. (1987). Comorbidity among childhood anxiety disorders. *Journal of Nervous and Mental Disease, 175*, 726–730.

Lazarus, A. A., Davison, G. C., & Polefka, D. (1965). Classical and operant factors in the treatment of school phobia. *Journal of Abnormal Psychology, 70*, 225–229.

Leonard, H. L., Swedo, S. E., Rapoport, J. L., Coffey, M. L., & Cheslow, D. L. (1988). Treatment of childhood obsessive-compulsive disorder with clomipramine and desmethylimipramine: A double-blind crossover comparison. *Psychopharmacological Bulletin, 24*, 93–95.

MacFarlane, J. N., Allen, L., & Honzik, M. P. (1954). *A developmental study of the behavior problems of normal children between 21 months and 14 years.* Berkeley: University of California Press.

Mansdorf, I. J., & Lukens, E. (1987). Cognitive-behavioral psychotherapy for separation-anxious children exhibiting school phobia. *Journal of the American Academy of Child and Adolescent Psychiatry, 26*, 222–225.

Maurer, A. (1965). What children fear. *Journal of Genetic Psychology, 106*, 265–277.

Miller, L. C., Barrett, C. L., Hampe, E., & Noble, H. (1972). Factor structure and childhood fears. *Journal of Consulting and Clinical Psychology, 39*, 264–268.

Miller, P. (1972). Severe separation anxiety in two preschool children: Successfully treated by reciprocal inhibition. *Journal of Nervous and Mental Disease, 154*, 457–460.

Mills, H. L., Agras, W. S., Barlow, D. H., & Mills, J. R. (1973). Compulsive rituals treated by response prevention: An experimental analysis. *Archives of General Psychiatry, 38*, 524–529.

O'Brien, G. T., & Barlow, D. H. (1984). Agoraphobia. In S. M. Turner (Ed.), *Behavioral theories and treatment of anxiety* (pp. 143–185). New York: Plenum.

Ollendick, T. H. (1979). Fear reduction techniques with children. In M. Hersen, R. M. Eisler, & P. M. Miller (Eds.), *Progress in behavior modification, Vol. 8.* Orlando: Academic Press.

Ollendick, T. H. & Huntzinger, R. M. (1990). Separation anxiety disorder in children. In M. Hersen and C. G. Last (Eds.), *Handbook of child and adult psychopathology. A longitudinal perspective.* New York: Pergamon.

Peterson, L. (1987). Not safe at home: Behavioral treatment of a child's fear of being alone at home. *Journal of Behavior Therapy and Experimental Psychiatry, 18*, 381–385.

Rapoport, J., Elkins, R., & Mikkelson, E. (1980). Clinical controlled trial of clomipramine in adolescents with obsessive-compulsive disorder. *Psychopharmacological Bulletin, 16*, 61–63.

Richman, N., Stevenson, J. E., & Graham, P. J. (1975). Prevalence of behavior problems in three-year-old children: An epidemiologic study in a London borough. *Journal of Child Psychology and Psychiatry, 16*, 277–287.

Riddle, M. A., Hardin, M. T., King, R., Scahill, L., & Woolston, J. L. (1990). Fluoxetine treatment of children and adolescents with Tourette's and Obsessive Compulsive Disorders: Preliminary clinical experience. *Journal of the American Academy of Child and Adolescent Psychiatry, 29*, 45–48.

Saigh, P. A. (1986a). In vitro flooding in the treatment of a 6-year-old boy's post-traumatic stress disorder. *Behaviour Research and Therapy, 6*, 685–688.

Saigh, P. A. (1986b, August). *In vitro flooding of a childhood post-traumatic stress disorder.* Paper presented at the annual meeting of the American Psychological Association. Washington, DC.

Saigh, P. A. (in press). In vitro flooding of a childhood post-traumatic stress disorder: A systematic replication. *Professional School Psychology.*

Stanley, L. (1980). Treatment of ritualistic behavior in an eight-year-old girl by response prevention: A case report. *Journal of Child Psychology and Psychiatry, 21,* 85–90.

Steketee, G., & Foa, E. B. (1985). Obsessive-compulsive disorder. In D. H. Barlow (Ed.), *Clinical handbook of psychological disorders* (pp. 69–144). New York: Guilford.

Strauss, C. C. (1988). Overanxious disorder. In M. Hersen & C. G. Last (Eds.), *Child behavior therapy casebook* (pp. 19–29). New York: Plenum.

Strauss, C. C., Lease, C. A., Last, C. G., & Francis, G. (1989). Overanxious disorder: An examination of developmental differences. *Journal of Abnormal Child Psychology, 16,* 433–443.

Welch, M. W., & Carpenter, C. (1970). Solution of school phobia by contingency contracting. *School Applications of Learning Theory, 2,* 11–17.

CHAPTER 13

Behavioral Treatment of Childhood Depression

CYNTHIA L. FRAME, SHIRLEY L. ROBINSON, and ELIZABETH CUDDY

The treatment of childhood depression is a topic of recent origin. Thirty years ago, depression in children was not thought to exist; 15 years ago, the first empirical treatment study with depressed children had yet to be published. Given this framework, the reader will soon realize that a great deal of knowledge has been acquired in a short period of time. However, in comparison with various types of adult psychopathology, our information base about the efficacious treatment of childhood depression lags far behind. Basic research on the characteristics and correlates of childhood depression is also rather scant, but is increasing. The intent of this chapter is to provide a guide to the conduct of behavior therapy with depressed children and adolescents by examining the findings of existing intervention research, as well as the implications for treatment suggested by theory, basic research, and/or clinical experience.

BRIEF HISTORICAL OVERVIEW

The basic behavioral theories of depression are discussed elsewhere in this volume, but it is necessary to consider briefly the role that various theoretical viewpoints have played in the history of mental health professionals' view of childhood depression. As mentioned above, as late as the 1950s, depression in childhood was not considered to be a viable diagnosis. Psychoanalytic theory, the prevailing framework of the time, basically proposed that adult depressive disorder stemmed from guilt produced by the superego. The theory further asserted that children do not develop strong superegos until adolescence or later. Thus, children were generally viewed as *incapable* of experiencing the type of depressive disorder displayed by adults (Rie, 1966), and childhood depression was neither studied nor treated.

Theorizing about child depression since the 1960s has passed through at least four more phases. First, some professionals began to assert that children could experience behavioral problems that were the "equivalent" of adult depression (e.g., Cytryn & McKnew, 1974). Also termed "masked" depression, this disorder was proposed to include a variety of internalizing and externalizing symptoms, from anxiety to delinquency. As will be discussed below, the basic notion that children might evince symptoms of a disorder differently from adults is a valid one and deserves consideration. However, the concept of masked depression, as defined by any of a number of other behavior problems, rendered both clinical and research work nearly impossible; for example, how was one to distinguish "real" temper tantrums from masked depression? The concept of masked depression, however, did serve to lend credibility to the entity of childhood depressive disorder.

Another line of thinking was more accepting of the possibility that depression with adult-like symptoms could occur in childhood, but was less concerned with the problem. Proponents of this view claimed that, although children might indeed display symptoms of depressive disorder, mental health professionals need not be very concerned, because these problems were normal developmental phenomena that would dissipate over time (Lefkowitz & Burton, 1978). There was considered to be little or no need to diagnose or treat childhood depression.

A totally different viewpoint was represented by the writers of DSM-III (American Psychiatric Association, 1980), who stated that not only could depression be diagnosed in children, but its symptomatology would appear almost identical to that of adult depression. A slightly modified version of this viewpoint will be presented in greater detail in the next section, where childhood depression is defined according to DSM-III-R (American Psychiatric Association, 1987). The DSM-III-R version of the concept forms the basis for most current research and treatment in the area.

Finally, developmental psychopathologists are currently making a case for yet another view of childhood depression, one that encompasses ideas from each of the three viewpoints presented above (Cantwell, 1990). According to the developmental approach, childhood depression is viewed as a hypothetical construct tied to a group of observable symptoms. The operational definition of the construct, it is proposed, must be determined empirically across the age span. Some of the symptoms comprising the disorder may be the same as those displayed by adults with depressive disorder; others may be unique to depressed children of a particular developmental stage. Any of the symptoms alone may be a normal developmental phenomenon that precludes diagnosis or treatment; however, various combinations or frequencies of symptoms may be indicative of psychopathology at different ages. Although this approach appears to be both valid and promising, it still awaits most of the proposed empirical underpinnings.

Where and how childhood depression fits into the greater picture of developmental psychopathology is unclear at the present time. It is well-documented that most adults diagnosed with depressive disorder do *not* appear to have suffered from depression during childhood (Rutter, 1986b). Yet, recent research demonstrates that depressive disorder in childhood, as diagnosed by DSM-III-R type criteria, is not transient; a single episode lasts for 7 to 9 months on average, and about two-thirds of depressed youngsters experience recurrence of the disorder prior to adulthood (Kovacs, 1989; McGee & Williams, 1988). According to community surveys, the prevalence of childhood depression lies somewhere between 2% and 10% in the general population, a rate lower than that for adult depression (Anderson, Williams, McGee, & Silva, 1987; Cantwell, 1990; Kashani et al., 1987). In these ways, it is not at all clear that childhood depression is an early expression of adult affective disorder. However, childhood depression occurs frequently enough, and is of sufficient severity and duration, that it definitely is an entity worthy of professional attention, regardless of its relation to the adult disorder.

DEFINITION OF CHILDHOOD DEPRESSION

For purposes of this chapter, the definition of depression in childhood will rely primarily on the criteria outlined by DSM-III-R for the unipolar mood (affective) disorder termed Major Depression. Although it is quite possible that children may also experience the other mood disorders, such as dysthymic disorder or mania, less is known about their childhood manifestations, and they will not be considered here. This chapter will concentrate on the treatment of Major Depression in childhood.

A major depressive episode, according to DSM-III-R, may be diagnosed in children if there has been at least a 2-week duration of predominantly depressed mood; severe loss of interest or pleasure; and/or irritability. In addition, at least four of the following symptoms must be present: weight change or failure to make expected developmental weight gains; sleep problems; psychomotor agitation or retardation; fatigue; low self-esteem or excessive guilt; concentration problems; and recurrent suicidal thoughts or actions. Finally, DSM-III-R notes that prepubertal children may also display somatic concerns, auditory hallucinations, and/or anxiety; adolescents may exhibit emotionality, antisocial behavior, and/or substance abuse. In childhood, the disorder has most often been found to occur with equal frequency in boys and girls (Kashani et al., 1983), but has occasionally been seen more often in boys (McGee & Williams, 1988; Rutter, 1986b). After puberty, however, depression is found more often in females than in males, as it is in adulthood (Carlson & Cantwell, 1980; Mezzich & Mezzich, 1979).

Recent developmental research indicates that, in fact, differing prominent depressive symptoms by age and gender may exist. Younger children (up to age 10) are more likely to demonstrate sadness, vegetative signs, social withdrawal, and somatic complaints as symptoms of depression; older children and adolescents admit to more cognitive symptoms such as guilt, poor self-esteem, difficulty concentrating, and suicidal ideation (McConville, Boag, & Purohit, 1973; Puig-Antich, 1982; Ushakov & Girich, 1971). In addition, grade school boys, but not male preschoolers, tend to evince suicidal talk as part of their constellation of depressive symptoms; grade school girls, as opposed to female preschoolers, display anxiety and thoughts of persecution in addition to the typical depressive features (Achenbach & Edelbrock, 1983).

Diagnosing depression in children younger than 8 or 10 may be quite difficult, because of younger children's more limited ability to introspect, to describe abstract ideas, to use time frames meaningfully, and to engage in metacognition (Cantwell, 1990; Rutter, 1986a). Young children have difficulty reporting, for example, how they feel about themselves, whether their thinking is different from usual, and how long they have been experiencing distress. This is probably part of the explanation for the lower rate of cognitive symptoms in younger children's depressions: children experience difficulty recognizing and reporting such phenomena. As a result, diagnosis of depression in younger children tends to rely on behavioral observations of depressed affect and vegetative signs, and on significant others' reports of depressive symptomatology.

It should be clear to the reader by this point that one must differentiate among the single *symptom* of depressed mood, the *syndrome,* or cluster of symptoms involving depressed mood, and the *disorder,* or syndrome plus social/educational impairment, when assessing whether a child is experiencing depression requiring professional attention. The symptom of depressed mood, when occurring in isolation, is generally considered to be a normal reaction of limited duration, to a variety of environmental stimuli—a reaction that does not generally necessitate the types of intervention to be described here. The presence of the full disorder almost always indicates a need for treatment. In clinical settings, children may be seen who have a depressive syndrome but do not display enough symptoms or impairment to qualify for a DSM-III-R diagnosis. It would appear that these children would benefit greatly from treatments designed for use with depressed children. Until more sophisticated research is available to suggest better alternatives, it is recommended that the behavior therapist use the available treatments for any child who demonstrates significant prolonged distress and/or impaired social or educational functioning apparently related to depressive symptomatology.

FEATURES OF DEPRESSION AS TARGETS FOR INTERVENTION

Interestingly, although a comprehensive approach to treating childhood depression would be expected to concentrate on the entire group of symptoms comprising the disorder, most behavioral interventions have concentrated on producing change in individual symptoms, or even associated features of the disorder. In considering specific behavioral targets for intervention with depressed children, behaviorists have tended to focus on the DSM symptoms of depressed affect and low self-esteem, and the associated feature of social withdrawal. In addition, they have extended adult depression research findings to children, assuming that cognitive correlates of adult depression, such as perceived lack of control and cognitive distortions (including helplessness attributions and hopelessness), are also present in depressed children.

In brief, depressed individuals are expected to (a) demonstrate behaviors indicative of beliefs that personal behavior is unrelated to external contingencies; (b) attribute negative outcomes to internal, stable, and global causes; (c) attributive positive outcomes to external, unstable, and specific causes; and/or (d) demonstrate negative expectations for the future. A previous review of the childhood research literature supported these assumptions (Frame, Cuddy, & Robinson, 1989), which have also been bolstered by further research (Bodiford, Eisenstadt, Johnson, & Bradlyn, 1988; Kashani, Reid, & Rosenberg, 1989; Kaslow, Rehm, Pollack, & Siegel, 1988; McCauley, Burke, Mitchell, & Moss, 1988; Meyer, Dyck, & Petrinack, 1989; Weisz et al., 1989). However, at least one recent study failed to find the expected cognitive correlates in hospitalized depressed children, as compared to hospitalized child psychiatric controls (Benfield, Palmer, Pfefferbaum, & Stowe, 1988). At this point, it is not clear that the cognitions of depressed youth are always more distorted than those of nondepressed youngsters, but they may often be.

The reasons for selecting one or more specific symptoms as the primary target for intervention can vary. In some cases, selection will result from practical decisions based on the therapist's clinical judgment of which symptoms of a particular child are most severe, most detrimental, or apparently playing a causal role in the development or maintenance of other symptoms. In other situations, treatment may be determined by adherence to a particular theoretical model of childhood depression. The types of interventions associated with the various theoretical models, and the existing evidence for the efficacy of each, will be explored below, following a short consideration of assessment methods and issues.

ASSESSMENT

There are two types of assessment of depression in children: diagnostic assessment, and assessment of individual depressive features that will be targets for intervention. The goal of the former is to determine the *type* of the disorder, a qualitative measure; the purpose of the latter is to establish the *extent* of one or more features of the disorder, a quantitative measure that will permit analysis of the degree of change resulting from therapy.

Therapists endorsing the behavioral approach tend to conduct a diagnostic assessment first, followed by a baseline assessment of selected target symptoms. These target symptoms are then reassessed frequently to determine change; when the target symptom reaches a level deemed as normal, or at least no longer dysfunctional, the treatment is considered successful. Unfortunately, the diagnostic assessment is not always repeated after intervention, to ascertain whether the entire disorder has remitted or whether treatment gains are limited to those targeted symptoms. Obviously, it is essential that diagnostic assessment be completed posttreatment, to determine the extent of the intervention's efficacy.

A detailed description of the assessment methods and instruments utilized with childhood depression is beyond the scope of this chapter, but an overview is provided here. For more specific information, the reader is referred to excellent reviews of the topic in chapters by Kazdin (1988) and Rehm and his colleagues (Rehm, Gordon-Leventon, & Ivens, 1987).

Diagnostic assessment is most often conducted by means of clinical interview, structured clinical interview, and/or standardized questionnaires. Respondents typically include parents, teachers, caregivers, and, of course, the child. Because agreement between reporters and methods is often low, the therapist is advised to use a multimethod, multisource assessment battery.

The clinical interview generally consists of establishing rapport with the child by engaging in activities such as drawing or talking about child-centered topics (favorite activities, school, pets), and then inquiring about depressive symptomatology and related features through a variety of questions geared to the child at the moment. One child might be asked: "Have you been feeling sad a lot since Christmastime?" Another might be queried: "Tell me about the last time your stomach felt bad."

The clinical interview has the advantage of flexibility; in the hands of an evaluator who is knowledgeable about the cognitive and social development of children and the symptoms of depression, it can often be more helpful with younger children than the structured interview. Professionals whose background knowledge of developmental norms and psychiatric symptomatology is limited should probably depend more on the structured interview to guide their evaluation.

A number of structured interviews are available for diagnosing childhood psychopathology, of which the Diagnostic Interview Schedule for Children (DISC; Costello, Edelbrock, & Costello, 1985) is a prime example. The interview may be conducted with the child as the reporter and/or with the parent reporting about the child. The interviewer reads aloud questions about psychiatric symptoms from a preprinted booklet, and indicates in writing whether each item was endorsed. This scoring is then used to determine whether a child qualifies for each of a number of DSM diagnoses. In this way, all questions are delivered to all patients with identical wording and in the same order, and no areas of inquiry are overlooked. In addition to its advantage of reducing interviewer bias and error, the structured interview is especially valuable for increasing interevaluator agreement and thus permitting greater validity of resulting diagnoses. The primary weakness of the approach also lies in its structure, however: there are times when children, and even adults, simply do not comprehend the standardized questions.

Evaluators frequently supplement the interview with standardized questionnaires before assigning a clinical diagnosis. Commonly used instruments include the Children's Depression Inventory (CDI; Kovacs, 1981), which is administered to the child, and the Child Behavior Checklist (CBCL; Achenbach & Edelbrock, 1983), which is completed by a parent. For each instrument, normative data are available to determine cutoff scores that are indicative of depression. Unfortunately, however, interview and questionnaire results often show little agreement with child and adult reports. When this happens, the evaluator must use clinical judgment in determining whether to assign a diagnosis.

Baseline assessment of the extent of particular depressive features can be conducted in a number of ways and may depend on the symptom being assessed. For example, the symptom of depressed affect may be defined in terms of frequency of occurrence, duration, intensity, or pervasiveness. Such symptoms may be assessed via behavioral observation by the therapist or others, or via self-monitoring by the child. For other symptoms, such as low self-esteem or the cognitive distortions of control, attribution, and expectation, standardized questionnaires are available that yield quantitative scores for each dimension of interest. At initial assessment, the evaluator should assess as many features of the depressive condition as possible, to determine the extent of dysfunction in each area. After this information is available, the therapist may then rely on either practical considerations or theory to guide in the selection of symptoms for intervention with each child and to determine the treatment of choice.

BEHAVIORAL APPROACHES TO INTERVENTION

Most of the behavioral treatment strategies that are employed with depressed children have been modeled after treatments for adult depression, and are derived from theoretical models of adult depression. The models, the types of depressive features targeted for treatment, and the nature of the treatment techniques will be presented before turning to the research studies of their efficacy.

Lewinsohn (1974) proposed that depression is caused, in part, by reduced levels of positive reinforcement in an individual's life. The initial reason for the reduction in positive reinforcement may range from loss of contact with a significant other to some change in the environment, such as the closing of a movie theater or park, or even the naturally occurring termination of a pleasant activity—the end of snow skiing at the start of warm weather, for example. If such a reduction in reinforcement is not reversed in some way, the person becomes passive and ceases to interact socially. The lack of social interaction further reduces the level of positive reinforcement received by the individual, and other symptoms of depression develop and are maintained. According to this theory, the level of pleasant events in the person's life must be increased to relieve the depression. This may be accomplished by contingency management procedures, or by requesting that the person monitor and increase his or her level of pleasant activities. It is assumed that the other symptoms of depression will dissipate when the level of positive reinforcement is sufficiently high.

An example of the application of this model can be seen in the case of a 10-year-old girl, Debra, who was referred by her mother for "moping" of 4 weeks' duration, accompanied by social withdrawal, increased sleeping, poor appetite, and frequent headaches. The mother described the child as previously healthy and well-adjusted, with frequent social interactions, and could identify no causal factor for the depressive syndrome. Careful questioning of Debra eventually revealed that a video game cartridge at which she was quite skilled had broken approximately 5 weeks earlier, and she had been told that she would need to save her own money to buy another. She saw this as a nearly insurmountable task that would require a year's savings. In the meantime, she believed she had lost status in her peer group because she could no longer demonstrate her unique skills at the game. As a result, she began to stay at home, at which time her other symptoms developed. Treatment consisted of identifying other activities at which Debra excelled (applying makeup and drawing portraits), and rewarding her via praise from her mother for engaging in those pleasant activities and for sharing them with her friends, another pleasant event. Within 3 weeks, all depressive symptoms had disappeared.

Rehm (1977) also proposed that lack of positive reinforcement is related to depression. However, he implicated a deficit in an individual's ability to evaluate his or her own performance and gain reward for accomplishments. Rehm termed this a lack of "self control," and suggested that teaching clients to monitor, recognize, and value (reward) their own positive behaviors is the key to successful intervention for depression.

In Debra's case, the therapist would have focused on Debra's contention that she had nothing to offer her friends beyond video game expertise. Debra would have been taught to keep records of her behaviors, identify those that were positive, and reward herself through self-praise or stickers for each one. This system would have served to increase both the frequency of positive social interactions and Debra's self-efficacy.

A third behavioral model of depression posits poor or unpleasant personal interactions as playing a causal role in the disorder. In some cases, aversive interpersonal interactions and subsequent social withdrawal are assumed to be the result of poor social skills. Here, the treatment of choice is social skills training, consisting of instruction, modeling, behavioral rehearsal, feedback, and training for generalization to the natural environment. In other cases, the aversive interactions may be due to factors beyond the depressed person's control, such as parental inconsistency in discipline or parental marital conflict. In such instances, training the parents in parenting skills, such as contingency management for children and negotiative problem solving for adolescents, or providing family or marital therapy may be indicated.

From the social interaction perspective, it would be necessary to assess Debra's social skills for interacting with her peers and to improve them if necessary. It would also be important for the therapist to investigate the possibilities that Debra's mother's parenting skills were lacking, leading her inadvertently to punish adaptive behaviors and reward depressive ones; or that excessive amounts of conflict and turmoil were present in the home environment.

There are several cognitive-behavioral models of depression. (a) In the revised learned helplessness model of depression (Abramson, Seligman, & Teasdale, 1978), the individual feels helpless, and thus depressed, because of faulty cognitive attributions about causal events. Specifically, the depressed person attributes negative events to causes that are personal, stable, and global, and positive events to causes that are external, unstable, and specific. These cognitions reflect the individual's beliefs that he or she is somehow responsible for, and deserving of, aversive events, but is not at all responsible for the occurrence of positive events. (b) According to Beck's (1976) cognitive theory of depression, individuals engage in a number of cognitive distortions that reflect errors in logic in interpreting the world. (c) A third model suggests that deficient interpersonal problem solving is related to depression (D'Zurilla & Nezu, 1982). This model proposes that depressed individuals may exhibit dysfunctions in the identification of problems, or the generation, evaluation, or enactment of solutions. Treatment indicated by the first two models involves cognitive restructuring, in which the client learns to identify depressive thoughts and self-statements and to replace them with appropriate, positive ones. Problem-solving training teaches the client to analyze problems and to solve them more efficiently through the consideration of various alternative solutions.

If Debra's therapist were to follow one of these cognitive models, assessment and treatment would probably involve helping her to identify her self-defeating thoughts and self-statements about the loss of her game, such as: "It broke because I'm a terrible person" or "My friends won't like me any more because I'm no good at anything." These self-statements would then be replaced with statements such as: "It's too bad that it broke, but it was an accident. There's no such thing as a 'sign' you're a bad person" or "My friends will miss watching me play this game, but I can do lots of other things with them." The problem-solving approach would be used to teach Debra a general method for handling interpersonal difficulties. In the case of the broken game, she might identify the problem as needing something that engenders admiration from friends. She would then generate some possible solutions, such as stealing a new game, getting new friends, staying at home, practicing on another game, demonstrating a different skill, or admitting the problem and seeing what her friends suggest. Evaluating the solutions would lead her to rule out stealing, getting new friends, and staying home as least appealing or adaptive, and to choose demonstrating a different skill as the most feasible solution. Finally, Debra would practice enacting her solution of demonstrating the new skill for her friends.

At present, there is little empirical evidence of relative efficacy to guide the therapist in the choice of treatment methods. The therapist must attend to the apparent deficits in the child's behavioral repertoire. With some children, it will be clear that social skills need to be improved or that attributions are dysfunctional. With other children, however, as with Debra, several or all of the behavioral deficits may exist. In such situations, Winnett, Bornstein, Cogswell, and Paris (1987) have proposed a levels-of-treatment approach to therapy. Treatments are categorized into four levels, with higher levels being characterized by greater complexity of treatment, greater degree of voluntary participation by the child, requirement of more advanced child cognitive functioning, and a greater amount of training for generalization to other situations. Thus, the school psychologist working with a reticent kindergartener might opt for a Level I treatment, while the private practitioner treating a compliant, verbal 12-year-old would probably choose Level IV. Level I treatment consists of contingency management procedures: direct reinforcement of appropriate behaviors and selective ignoring of depressive behaviors. Level II treatments are those that utilize direct reinforcement by social agents for the use of positive and accurate cognitive appraisals. Level III treatments include social skills training, problem-solving training, and simple goal setting with self-reinforcement for success. The primary Level IV intervention consists of Rehm's self-control training.

Having provided the reader a framework for the types of behavioral intervention that have been suggested by current theory, as well as some consideration of their implementation, a brief review of the scant treatment literature is now presented.

REVIEW OF TREATMENT STUDIES

As Kazdin (1989) noted, the largest knowledge base about the treatment of childhood depression involves the effects of antidepressant medications, rather than psychological interventions. This state of affairs is most unfortunate, given (a) the lack of conclusive evidence for the efficacy of medication over placebo in depressed children; (b) the possible side effects of medication; (c) the unknown long-term effects of antidepressants on the developing child; (d) the failure of medication to remedy the interpersonal deficits of depressed children; and (e) the established effectiveness of psychological interventions with depressed adults. It is encouraging, however, that even a few studies of behavioral interventions with depressed children have been conducted and are showing some evidence of effectiveness.

About half of the existing research has utilized single-subject designs, often multiple baseline. All but one of these studies have been based on the social skills model of depression and have produced promising results. For example, Calpin and his colleagues (Calpin & Cincirpini, 1978; Calpin & Kornblith, 1977, both cited in Kaslow & Rehm, 1983) successfully used this approach to modify nonassertive behaviors in hospitalized, depressed children, with improvements being maintained over a 3-month period. Petti, Bornstein, Delameter, and Conners (1980) used a multimodal treatment, including social skills training and antidepressant medication, to treat depression in a 10-year-old female inpatient. Social skills training resulted in increases in eye contact, number of smiles, speech duration, and assertive requests, and these gains were maintained at 3- and 6-week follow-ups. Specific depressive behaviors decreased, but, given the concurrent administration of imipramine, the role of social skills training in effecting these reductions could not be isolated. Schloss, Schloss, and Harris (1984) successfully employed social skills training to improve the interpersonal skills of three adolescents hospitalized with the diagnosis of schizoaffective disorder. Again, however, because these youths were also receiving antipsychotic medication, the extent of the effectiveness of the social skills training alone could not be determined.

Frame, Matson, Sonis, Fialkov, and Kazdin (1982) also successfully utilized a social skills intervention to reduce the depressive behaviors of a 10-year-old inpatient boy with a DSM-III diagnosis of depression. Specifically, inappropriate body position (slouching, hand over face), lack of eye contact, poor speech quality (low volume, mumbling, failure to answer questions), and bland effect (expressionless face and voice) were each targeted for change, in a multiple baseline design across behaviors. Treatment consisted of instruction, modeling, behavioral rehearsal, and performance feedback provided in daily individual therapy sessions over a 5-week period.

After an 8-session baseline period, appropriate body position and eye contact were taught first. Marked improvement in these behaviors was noted over 6 sessions, but speech quality and affect remained essentially unchanged. Next, training was provided to improve speech quality, in addition to body position and eye contact. Dramatic improvement in speech quality was seen over the next 5 training sessions, and body position and eye contact remained appropriate; affect was unimproved. When training for affect was instituted, improvement in that behavior was shown quickly, and the other three behaviors remained at an appropriate level. Treatment gains were maintained at a 3-month follow-up. These results are especially notable in that they were obtained in the absence of psychiatric medication and that they endured after the child's return to his home environment.

The results of these single-case studies suggest that the social skills of depressed children are amenable to behavioral intervention, and that treatment gains can be maintained at least 3 months posttreatment. However, there are limitations to these studies. First, none evaluated the children's impression of improvement nor their self-reports of depression following treatment, rendering it unclear whether behavioral improvement was accompanied by a reduction in subjective distress and remission of the depressive disorder. Second, with the exception of the Petti et al. (1980) study, assessment for the transfer of training of skills to the natural environment was not conducted.

A recent case report by Asarnow and Carlson (1988) extended the treatment of childhood depression to include a multimodal cognitive-behavioral intervention with a psychotically depressed 10-year-old female inpatient. Ten weeks of inpatient treatment and 3 months of outpatient therapy involved self-control training, cognitive restructuring, and problem-solving training. Periodic reassessment of depressive disorder showed a drop in symptomatology to the subclinical range by the time of hospital discharge and complete remission of symptoms, without recurrence, at 5-year follow-up. Unfortunately for interpretive purposes, however, the child was also treated with antidepressant medication for 2 months during the hospital stay, obscuring the exact role of the behavioral intervention in the clinical improvement.

In addition to the single-case treatment studies, three group-outcome intervention studies with depressed children have been reported. Butler, Miezitis, Friedman, and Cole (1980) compared the effects of two active treatments—role play dealing with aversive situations/emotions, and cognitive restructuring—to two control conditions—attention-placebo and regular classroom activities. The subjects were 56 fifth and sixth grade students with self-reported depression scores above the 90th percentile for their school on a battery of questionnaires (including the CDI) and measures of self-esteem, locus of control, and cognitive distortion. Children were randomly assigned to one of the four treatment conditions, and intervention was conducted in weekly 1-hour group sessions for 10 weeks. Results indicated that both active treatments were associated with reduction in self-reported depressive symptoms. However, results of unstructured interviews with teachers indicated the superiority of the role-play treatment over the cognitive restructuring for improvement in classroom behaviors and demeanor. The authors note that the cognitive restructuring approach, relying heavily on discussion and self-reflection, did not appear to be as engaging for some of the youths as was the more active role-play treatment.

Self-control training and relaxation training were compared to a wait-list control condition for the treatment of high school students' self-reported depression in a study by Reynolds and Coats (1986). Thirty subjects, selected for participation from a pool of approximately 800 high school students after a two-stage screening process, were randomly assigned to one of the three treatment conditions. Training was provided in a group format for 10 hourly sessions over a 5-week period. Results indicated that both active treatments were superior to the control condition, but not significantly different from each other, in reducing self-reported levels of depressive symptomatology by the end of treatment and at 5-week follow-up. In fact, all treatment subjects demonstrated posttreatment depression scores in the nonclinical range, while only 44% of the controls showed such change.

In a somewhat similar study, Stark, Reynolds, and Kaslow (1987) compared the use of self-control training, behavioral problem-solving therapy, and a wait-list control condition for the treatment of self-reported depression in 29 9- to 12-year-old schoolchildren. The behavioral problem-solving therapy included both problem-solving skills and a focus on increasing pleasant activities. Treatment was delivered in a group format of 12 sessions over a 5-week period. Posttreatment and 2-month follow-up assessments revealed that children in both treatment groups had improved significantly in self-reported depression, compared to pretreatment scores, with the two treatments appearing equally effective.

Although promising, the group treatment results are characterized by a number of problems. First, the procedures were conducted with a school, rather than a clinical, population who were not assessed for a diagnosis of major depression. Whether results are generalizable to a more seriously disturbed population is unclear. Second, the number of subjects receiving each type of treatment was very small (30 at most across the three studies), and results have not yet been replicated. Thus, any enthusiasm about the results must remain tempered by caution. Technically, the group studies reflect single-case results, with each group being a case. That is, because treatment was not provided individually to subjects, error cannot be assumed to have been random across subjects. This means that the number of cases used to determine the degrees of freedom in statistical tests should be based on the number of groups treated with each method, rather than the number of children. Had this standard been applied, there would not have been a sufficient number of cases for analysis. Finally, we have yet to demonstrate that these treatments are specific to depression, as opposed to other psychiatric disorders, in their efficacy.

SUMMARY

The published reports of behavioral interventions for childhood depression are encouraging. They show some evidence that behavioral treatment is related to improvement in depressive symptomatology and that such improvement is not due solely to spontaneous remission or placebo effects. In addition, our knowledge of the correlates of childhood depression is increasing rapidly.

However, much work remains to be conducted to permit the development of more sophisticated approaches to treatment. Previous work must be replicated and extended to inpatient populations. The range of interventions based on the various behavioral models of depression must be tested more thoroughly for efficacy, and such treatments must be compared to each other. We must seek information concerning the critical factors related to treatment success and the best ways to match treatments to patients.

For example, given recent findings that many children demonstrate comorbidity of depression with other psychiatric disorders (Kovacs, 1989), especially salient is the question of whether children who are demonstrating both internalizing and externalizing symptoms should be treated with interventions developed for depression and anxiety or for conduct disorder; with both types; or with some third, unique approach. In addition, as evidence accumulates that childhood suicidal behavior is much more frequent than previously assumed, with children exhibiting both internalizing and externalizing symptoms at increased risk (Asarnow & Guthrie, 1989; Velez & Cohen, 1988), it is essential that we apply our growing knowledge base about suicide risk factors (Brent et al., 1988; Cole, 1989; Hoberman & Garfinkel, 1988; Pfeffer, Newcorn, Kaplan, Mizruchi, & Plutchik, 1988) to the development of effective prevention and intervention strategies for this life-threatening behavior.

Based on the rapidity with which research in the field of childhood depression has developed over the past 15 years, perhaps we will make significant strides in all of these directions relatively soon. The quality of life of somewhere between 2% and 10% of our youth depends on it.

REFERENCES

Abramson, L. Y., Seligman, M. E. P., & Teasdale, J. D. (1978). Learned helplessness in humans: Critique and reformulation. *Journal of Abnormal Psychology, 87,* 49–74.

Achenbach, T. M., & Edelbrock, C. S. (1983). *Manual for the Child Behavior Checklist and Revised Child Behavior Profile.* Burlington: University of Vermont, Department of Psychiatry.

American Psychiatric Association. (1980). *Diagnostic and statistical manual of mental disorders* (3rd ed.). Washington, DC: Author.

American Psychiatric Association. (1987). *Diagnostic and statistical manual of mental disorders* (3rd ed. rev.). Washington, DC: Author.

Anderson, J. C., Williams, S., McGee, R., & Silva, P. A. (1987). DSM-III disorders in preadolescent children. Prevalence in a large sample from the general population. *Archives of General Psychiatry, 44,* 69–76.

Asarnow, J. R., & Carlson, G. A. (1988). Childhood depression: Five-year outcome following combined cognitive-behavior therapy and pharmacotherapy. *American Journal of Psychotherapy, 42,* 456–464.

Asarnow, J. R., & Guthrie, D. (1989). Suicidal behavior depression, and hopelessness in child psychiatric inpatients: A replication and extension. *Journal of Clinical Child Psychology, 18,* 129–136.

Beck, A. T. (1976). *Cognitive therapy and the emotional disorders.* New York: International Universities Press.

Benfield, C. Y., Palmer, D. J., Pfefferbaum, B., & Stowe, M. L. (1988). A comparison of depressed and nondepressed disturbed children on measures of attributional style, hopelessness, life stress, and temperament. *Journal of Abnormal Child Psychology, 16,* 397–410.

Bodiford, C. A., Eisenstadt, T. H., Johnson, J. H., & Bradlyn, A. S. (1988). Comparison of learned helplessness cognitions and behavior in children with high and low scores on the Children's Depression Inventory. *Journal of Clinical Child Psychology, 17,* 152–158.

Brent, D. A., Perper, J. A., Goldstein, C. E., Kolko, D. J., Allan, M. J., Allman, C. J., & Zelenak, J. P. (1988). Risk factors for adolescent suicide: A comparison of adolescent suicide victims with suicidal inpatients. *Archives of General Psychiatry, 45,* 581–588.

Butler, L., Miezitis, S., Friedman, R., & Cole, E. (1980). The effect of two school-based intervention programs on depressive symptoms in preadolescents. *American Educational Research Journal, 17,* 111–119.

Cantwell, D. P. (1990). Depression across the early lifespan. In M. Lewis & S. M. Miller (Eds.), *Handbook of developmental psychopathology* (pp. 293–309). New York: Plenum.

Carlson, G. A., & Cantwell, D. P. (1980). Unmasking masked depression in children and adolescents. *American Journal of Psychiatry, 137,* 445–449.

Cole, D. A. (1989). Psychopathology of adolescent suicide: Hopelessness, coping beliefs, and depression. *Journal of Abnormal Psychology, 98,* 248–255.

Costello, E. J., Edelbrock, C. A., & Costello, A. J. (1985). Validity of the NIMH Diagnostic Interview Schedule for Children: A comparison between psychiatric and pediatric referrals. *Journal of Abnormal Child Psychology, 13,* 579–595.

Cytryn, L., & McKnew, D. H. (1974). Factors influencing the changing clinical expression of the depressive process in children. *American Journal of Psychiatry, 131,* 879–881.

D'Zurilla, T. J., & Nezu, A. (1982). Social problem solving in adults. In P. C. Kendall (Ed.), *Advances in cognitive-behavioral research and therapy, Vol. 1* (pp. 202–274). New York: Academic Press.

Frame, C. L., Cuddy, M. E., & Robinson, S. L. (1989). Affective disorders. In M. Hersen (Ed.), *Innovations in child behavior therapy* (pp. 228–253). New York: Springer.

Frame, C. L., Matson, J. L., Sonis, W. A., Fialkov, M. J., & Kazdin, A. E. (1982). Behavioral treatment of depression in a prepubertal child. *Journal of Behavior Therapy and Experimental Psychiatry, 13,* 239–243.

Hoberman, H. M., & Garfinkel, B. D. (1988). Completed suicide in youth. *Canadian Journal of Psychiatry, 33,* 494–502.

Kashani, J. H., Carlson, G. A., Beck, N. C., Hoeper, E. W., Corcoran, C. M., McAllister, J. A., Fallahi, C., Rosenberg, T. K., &

Reid, J. C. (1987). Depression, depressive symptoms, and depressed mood among a community sample of adolescents. *American Journal of Psychiatry, 144*, 931–934.

Kashani, J. H., McGee, R. O., Clarkson, S. E., Anderson, J. C., Walton, L. A., Williams, S., Silva, P. A., Robbins, A. J., Cytryn, L. A., & McKnew, D. H. (1983). Depression in a sample of 9-year-old children. *Archives of General Psychiatry, 40*, 1217–1223.

Kashani, J. H., Reid, J. C., & Rosenberg, T. K. (1989). Levels of hopelessness in children and adolescents: A developmental perspective. *Journal of Consulting and Clinical Psychology, 57*, 496–499.

Kaslow, N. J., & Rehm, L. P. (1983). Childhood depression. In R. J. Morris & T. R. Kratochwill (Eds.), *The practice of child therapy* (pp. 27–51). New York: Pergamon.

Kaslow, N. J., Rehm, L. P., Pollack, S. L., & Siegel, A. W. (1988). Attributional style and self-control behavior in depressed and nondepressed children and their parents. *Journal of Abnormal Child Psychology, 16*, 163–175.

Kazdin, A. E. (1988). Childhood depression. In E. J. Mash & L. G. Terdal (Eds.), *Behavioral assessment of childhood disorders* (2nd ed.; pp. 157–195). New York: Guilford.

Kazdin, A. E. (1989). Childhood depression. In E. J. Mash & R. A. Barkley (Eds.), *The treatment of childhood disorders* (pp. 135–166). New York: Guilford.

Kovacs, M. (1981). Rating scales to assess depression in school aged children. *Acta Paedopsychiatrica, 46*, 305–315.

Kovacs, M. (1989). Affective disorders in children and adolescents. *American Psychologist, 44*, 209–215.

Lefkowitz, M. M., & Burton, N. (1978). Childhood depression: A critique of the concept. *Psychological Bulletin, 85*, 716–726.

Lewinsohn, P. M. (1974). A behavioral approach to depression. In R. J. Friedman & M. M. Katz (Eds.), *The psychology of depression: Contemporary theory and research* (pp. 157–184). New York: Wiley.

McCauley, E., Burke, P., Mitchell, J. R., & Moss, S. (1988). Cognitive attributes of depression in children and adolescents. *Journal of Consulting and Clinical Psychology, 56*, 903–908.

McConville, B. J., Boag, L. C., & Purohit, A. P. (1973). Three types of childhood depression. *Canadian Journal of Psychiatry, 18*, 133–138.

McGee, R., & Williams, S. (1988). A longitudinal study of depression in nine-year-old children. *Journal of the American Academy of Child and Adolescent Psychiatry, 27*, 342–348.

Meyer, N. E., Dyck, D. G., & Petrinack, R. J. (1989). Cognitive appraisal and attributional correlates of depressive symptoms in children. *Journal of Abnormal Child Psychology, 17*, 325–336.

Mezzich, A. C., & Mezzich, J. E. (1979). Symptomatology of depression in adolescence. *Journal of Personality Assessment, 43*, 267–275.

Petti, T. A., Bornstein, M., Delameter, A., & Conners, K. (1980). Evaluation and multimodal treatment of a depressed prepubertal girl. *Journal of the American Academy of Child and Adolescent Psychiatry, 19*, 690–702.

Pfeffer, C. R., Newcorn, J., Kaplan, G., Mizruchi, M. S., & Plutchik, R. (1988). Suicidal behavior in adolescent psychiatric inpatients. *Journal of the American Academy of Child and Adolescent Psychiatry, 27*, 357–361.

Puig-Antich, J. (1982). Major depression and conduct disorder in prepuberty. *Journal of the American Academy of Child and Adolescent Psychiatry, 21*, 118–128.

Rehm, L. P. (1977). A self-control model of depression. *Behavior Therapy, 8*, 787–804.

Rehm, L. P., Gordon-Leventon, B., & Ivens, C. (1987). Depression. In C. L. Frame & J. L. Matson (Eds.), *Handbook of assessment in childhood psychopathology* (pp. 341–372). New York: Plenum.

Reynolds, W. M., & Coats, K. I. (1986). A comparison of cognitive-behavioral therapy and relaxation training for treatment of depression in adolescents. *Journal of Consulting and Clinical Psychology, 54*, 653–660.

Rie, H. E. (1966). Depression in childhood: A survey of some pertinent contributors.

Journal of the American Academy of Child and Adolescent Psychiatry, 5, 653–685.

Rutter, M. (1986a). Depressive feelings, cognitions and disorders: A research postscript. In M. Rutter, C. E. Izard, & P. B. Read (Eds.), *Depression in young people* (pp. 491–519). New York: Guilford.

Rutter, M. (1986b). The developmental psychopathology of depression: Issues and perspectives. In M. Rutter, C. E. Izard, & P. B. Read (Eds.), *Depression in young people* (pp. 3–30). New York: Guilford.

Schloss, P. J., Schloss, C. N., & Harris, L. (1984). A multiple baseline analysis of an interpersonal skills training program for depressed youth. *Behavioral Disorders, 9,* 182–188.

Stark, K. D., Reynolds, W. M., & Kaslow, N. J. (1987). A comparison of the relative efficacy of self-control therapy and a behavioral problem-solving therapy for depression. *Journal of Abnormal Child Psychology, 15,* 91–113.

Ushakov, G. K., & Girich, Y. P. (1971). Special features of psychogenic depression in children and adolescents. In A. L. Annell (Ed.), *Depressive states in childhood and adolescence* (pp. 510–516). Stockholm: Almqvist & Wiksell.

Velez, C. M., & Cohen, P. (1988). Suicidal behavior and ideation in a community sample of children: Maternal and youth reports. *Journal of the American Academy of Child and Adolescent Psychiatry, 27,* 349–356.

Weisz, J. R., Stevens, J. S., Curry, J. F., Cohen, R., Craighead, W. E., Burlingame, W. V., Smith, A., Weiss, B., & Parmalee, D. X. (1989). Control-related cognitions and depression among inpatient children and adolescents. *Journal of the American Academy of Child and Adolescent Psychiatry, 28,* 358–363.

Winnett, R. L., Bornstein, P. H., Cogswell, K. A., & Paris, A. E. (1987). Cognitive-behavioral therapy for childhood depression: A levels-of-treatment approach. *Journal of Child and Adolescent Psychotherapy, 4,* 283–286.

CHAPTER 14

Behavioral Intervention for Attention Deficit-Hyperactivity Disorder

WILLIAM E. PELHAM and STEPHEN P. HINSHAW

Attention deficit-hyperactivity disorder (ADHD) is listed in DSM-III-R as one of the disruptive behavior disorders of childhood, along with oppositional-defiant disorder and conduct disorder (American Psychiatric Association, 1987). Inclusionary criteria for ADHD include developmentally inappropriate levels of inattention, impulsivity, and motoric overactivity that have been present for at least 6 months and since before the age of 7 years, and that are not accounted for by extremely unstructured or chaotic home environments, mental retardation, or pervasive developmental disorders. Current estimates place the prevalence of ADHD at 3 to 5% of the school-age population in the United States and Canada. Although boys are more likely than girls to manifest this symptom cluster, the overall clinical picture is similar for the two sexes. Importantly, among all childhood disorders, ADHD contributes one of the highest rates of referrals to child mental health services.

Conceptions about this child syndrome have been in flux over the past several decades. The overly broad definitions and presumed neurologic etiology of such labels as minimal brain dysfunction (MBD) have been replaced with more behaviorally specific and etiology-free conceptions, such as ADHD. Also, despite (a) the multifaceted nature of the construct of attention and (b) the many cognitive, behavioral, motoric, motivational, and interpersonal problems of youngsters with ADHD (Douglas, 1983; Whalen, 1989), attentional difficulties and impulsivity have superseded hyperactive behavior as the presumed core areas of dysfunction. Furthermore, ADHD does not dissipate at puberty, as was once believed; rather, it is a chronic condition in many cases, with antisocial outcomes, substance abuse, and continued attentional and interpersonal difficulties often prevalent in late adolescence and early adulthood (Weiss & Hechtman, 1986). Given the intransigence of such outcomes, initiation of treatment procedures early in the course of the disorder is a priority. In all, the core features of ADHD comprise a validated dimension of child psychopathology, and these distressingly persistent features mandate powerful intervention during childhood.

In this chapter, we will summarize the evidence regarding the efficacy of behavioral interventions for this disorder. The typical goals for behavioral procedures for ADHD are the reduction of behavioral excesses and the shaping and reinforcement of incompatible alternatives, such as academic or interpersonal skills (Hinshaw & Erhardt, in press-a). We will focus both on specific contingency management procedures, involving positive and negative consequences applied in classrooms or experimental settings, and on "standard" clinical behavior therapy, which typically involves parent training and teacher consultation. Also covered will be cognitive-behavioral interventions, which have not lived up to their initial promise for these youngsters. We shall particularly emphasize the potential for combinations of behavioral and pharmacologic treatments to effect meaningful and long-lasting change. Among our conclusions are (a) that behavioral procedures constitute an important, but often clinically insufficient, intervention for many (if not most) children with ADHD, and (b) that future investigations must emphasize integrations of behavioral and pharmacologic treatments that are performed for extended periods of time in multiple settings.

ADHD: BACKGROUND ISSUES

Associated Features and Comorbidity

Youngsters with ADHD display a host of difficulties in addition to their core symptomatology. An inattentive cognitive style, for example, can promote or exacerbate difficulty with schoolwork, and poor impulse control may lead to problematic interactions with adults and peers. Furthermore, the accumulated difficulties experienced by the child with ADHD may well take their toll on self-image. As a result, associated problems of functioning include academic failure, peer difficulties, low self-esteem, labile mood, and aggressive behavior (Campbell & Werry, 1986). Children with ADHD vary markedly with respect to the presence of such problems, leading to large individual differences within this diagnostic category. Because of the strong predictive power of several of these features—most notably, peer rejection, underachievement, and aggression—for negative outcomes in later life, our examination of the effects of behavioral intervention procedures will include these domains as key outcomes.

Not only are many cognitive, peer-related, and behavioral features often associated with ADHD, but there is substantial comorbidity of ADHD with other behavioral and emotional disorders, particularly oppositional-defiant and conduct disorders, mood disorders, and specific learning disabilities. Although the developmental, causal relationships among ADHD and these ancillary disorders remain indeterminate, such comorbidity further complicates the intervention picture for children with ADHD, requiring that multiple target areas be prioritized and that multiple modalities be employed.

With respect to both associated features and comorbidity, we should make special note of the frequent overlap of ADHD with (a) aggression or conduct disorder and (b) peer difficulties. As noted above, both of these domains are strongly associated with poor prognosis. With regard to aggression, it has been established that inattention/overactivity and aggression/conduct problems are partially independent dimensions of externalizing behavior and that relatively pure subgroups of "hyperactive" and "aggressive" children exist (Hinshaw, 1987; Loney, 1987). Although such findings lend credence to the diagnostic validity of ADHD, a large plurality or even a majority of children with ADHD have co-existing problems of aggression. Consensus is emerging that the achievement-related, classroom, social cognitive, and interpersonal difficulties of the ADHD-aggressive subgroup are significantly worse than those of children with either disorder alone (Hinshaw, 1987). The variegated deficits of this subgroup require powerful, multimodal intervention.

As for the peer domain, clear evidence exists that ADHD children are overwhelmingly rejected by agemates (Milich & Landau, 1982). Such social ostracism doubtless exacerbates the existing interpersonal difficulties that these youngsters display, leading to a vicious cycle of further rejection, followed by subsequent reductions in the opportunity for enhancement of social skill. Whereas peer rejection is often related to aggressive behavior, other features of the inattentive, impulsive style of ADHD children also contribute to social stigmatization (Atkins, Pelham, & Licht, 1989). A relevant point for intervention is that treatment procedures for children with ADHD must emphasize the enhancement of socially competent performance as well as the reduction of aggressive, conflict-laden behavior.

Etiology

Although space limitations permit only a cursory summary of current etiologic hypotheses regarding ADHD, a brief review of key issues and trends may foster an appreciation of the complex interplay of biological and psychosocial factors in the development of this disorder (see also Taylor, 1986). Unfortunately, investigations of causal factors have typically failed to separate out aggressive from nonaggressive ADHD children, rendering much of the research on etiological factors relatively nonspecific for ADHD per se.

It should perhaps not be surprising that no single, primary cause has been identified for ADHD. In all likelihood, the syndrome is as heterogeneous with respect to causes as it is to presenting symptoms and associated features. Biological risk factors that have been studied include inherited or congenital predispositions and neurotransmission dysregulation. Regarding heritable factors, whereas genetic contributions to attentional deficits and overactivity are clearly implicated, no viable twin or adoption studies have been performed with diagnosed ADHD children. Studies of the neurochemistry of ADHD have been inconclusive (Zametkin & Rapoport, 1986). Yet, certain constitutional, temperamental variables—particularly high activity and difficulty in regulation—may interact with such socialization experiences as family interactional style to create the onset of formally hyperactive behavior (Whalen, 1989). The specificity of such an interactive hypothesis for ADHD as opposed to other behavioral disorders is, however, unknown. Most prenatal and/or perinatal risk factors seem to play a small and nonspecific role in the genesis of ADHD. However, maternal alcohol and/or tobacco consumption may be associated with cognitive and behavioral problems that range from mild to quite severe, with ADHD symptomatology included at some point in the continuum (Nichols & Chen, 1981). In contrast, sugars and artificial food additives have not been found to yield a meaningful contribution to hyperactivity except, if at all, in a very small percentage of cases (Milich, Wolraich, & Lindgren, 1986).

Despite popular misconception, no hard evidence links specific child-rearing practices or socialization experiences with ADHD (Paternite & Loney, 1980). From a perspective of bidirectional causation, families with hyperactive children experience more stress and have more negative interactions than do comparison families (Johnston, 1988). For example, at least one laboratory study that manipulated child behavior has shown that ADHD behaviors cause distress in adults given charge over the children, and that this distress leads to increased alcohol consumption when the adults anticipate imminent interaction with the child (Lang, Pelham, Johnston, & Gelernter, 1989). Furthermore, coercive family interactions and family disharmony seem preferentially linked with aggressive outcomes in children (Patterson, 1982). Given the high stress within ADHD families and the common co-occurrence of aggression with ADHD, interventions directed toward improving parent–child interactions are clearly indicated for this population, even if faulty family exchanges are not the primary causal factors.

The search for specific biological versus psychosocial causal factors in ADHD too often ignores the actual confounding of such variables. Constitutional vulnerabilities, for example, are shaped by family and school environments; problematic behaviors may be both causes and consequences of deficiencies or excesses in neurotransmission; and exposure to lead is associated with lower social class. In short, increasingly complex interactional and transactional models will need to be incorporated in etiological hypotheses of this disorder.

Diagnosis

Although there is general agreement regarding the core characteristics of inattention, impulsivity, and overactivity in ADHD, there remains debate regarding how they should be operationalized. The DSMs have listed behavioral descriptors, a minimum number of which a child must exhibit, in their definitions of ADD (DSM-III; American Psychiatric Association, 1980) and ADHD (DSM-III-R; American Psychiatric Association, 1987). The descriptors were listed separately for each of the three core symptom areas in DSM-III but are listed together in DSM-III-R. Despite the attempt at operational criteria, many of the DSM-III descriptors are subjective and ambiguous, and they are not empirically determined (Quay, 1986). As a result, there has been a great deal of debate and too little research regarding precisely how to define ADHD.

The most common procedures for operationalizing the definition of ADHD in both clinical and research settings have been standardized parent and teacher rating scales, which have typically been empirically derived and on which item clusters labeled "hyperactivity" or "inattention" have been consistently identified in factor analyses (Hinshaw, 1987). In addition to the empirically derived rating scales, additional rating scales, as well as structured parent interviews, have been developed to operationalize the DSM definitions.

There are a number of limitations in the use of rating scales and interviews with parents in diagnosis of ADHD. The data obtained reflect the adult's perception of the child's behavior rather than the behavior itself. In addition, ADHD children's behavior is highly variable across situations and raters. As a result, interrater agreement between teachers and/or parents rating the same child is relatively low. Furthermore, although validity studies reveal that rating scale factors and parent interviews are correlated with direct observations and other measures of the behaviors that they are intended to reflect, these correlations are not nearly as high as desired (Atkins, Pelham, & Licht, 1989). Finally, it should be noted that rating scale *factors* rather than *items* form the basis for diagnostic decisions in many settings. Because factor scores are typically computed by adding the scores for all items loading on that factor, children can receive the same score with different combinations of symptom presence and severity, yielding heterogeneous diagnostic groups. Given these limitations, rating scales and structured interviews should obviously not be used as the sole or definitive criteria in the diagnosis of ADHD. Extreme scores on appropriate instruments, particularly teacher rating scales, are viewed as necessary but not sufficient criteria for diagnosis. Symptom onset and duration, as well as certain exclusionary criteria, must also be taken into account, and there is as yet no substitute for good clinical judgment to resolve discrepancies between different raters of the same child and between ratings and other sources of information.

A great deal of research has focused on the nature of ADHD children's behavior and performance on measures other than rating scales for diagnostic purposes, including laboratory measures and direct observations in the natural environment. To date, however, no laboratory task, psychological test, or behavioral observational scheme has reached the stage of development at which it provides sensitive and specific information in diagnosis.

Although the issues involved in diagnosing ADHD are complex, as they are in the rest of child psychopathology (Quay, 1986), it is important to note that most of these issues are of primary concern for the researcher rather than the clinician. The clinician's primary issue with an individual case should be an accurate and comprehensive *clinical* assessment rather than a diagnosis that would meet research criteria. Knowing whether a child meets diagnostic criteria for ADHD does not provide information relevant for that child's treatment—either pharmacological or psychosocial. Instead, the degree to which the child is experiencing dysfunction in daily living, the nature and frequency of the child's target symptoms, the decisions regarding the child's educational placement, and the family situation—all information gathered during a good behavioral assessment—are more pertinent to the question of appropriate treatment.

As in most other areas of psychopathology, clinicians who need to make a diagnosis for administrative or clinical reasons should follow the procedures and recommendations made in the DSMs. To provide a comprehensive basis for diagnosis, information should be gathered from both parents and teachers, with greater weight given to teacher information. As DSM-III-R notes, the diagnosis must be based on the child's behavior in the natural environment and can be ruled neither in nor out based on behavior in the clinician's office.

PHARMACOLOGIC INTERVENTION

Although the focus of this chapter is behavior therapy, treatment for ADHD cannot be adequately addressed without a discussion of pharmacotherapy. Pharmacological intervention with one of the central nervous system (CNS) stimulant drugs has been the most common mode of treatment for ADHD for the past 25 years, with more than 90% of diagnosed children being treated with a stimulant at some point and with approximately 6% of elementary school-age students receiving medication at some point (Safer & Krager, 1988). Not only do the stimulant drugs play a ubiquitous role in treatment of ADHD, but they also have been shown to be quite effective in the short-term management of the disorder. These medications should usually be a component of the comprehensive treatment of most ADHD children, and the behavioral clinician should have a major voice in the evaluation and determination of medication's role in a referred child's treatment.

Although other classes of drugs (e.g., antidepressants) have been evaluated for ADHD, they have not been widely used, and they are best considered secondary treatments (Gittelman & Kanner, 1986). The three psychostimulants that are commonly employed with ADHD children are methylphenidate (MPH; ritalin), dextroamphetamine (dexedrine), and pemoline (cylert), with many more children receiving MPH than dextroamphetamine or pemaline. The precise neural mechanisms of the stimulants' effects in humans are as yet unknown. The drugs are presumed to enhance broadly the effects of dopamine and norepinephrine by increasing their availability at the synapse

(Zametkin & Rapoport, 1986). Although at one time stimulant effects on ADHD children were thought to be different from those that would be obtained with normal children (hence, the outdated notion of the paradoxical effect), it is now clear that stimulants affect normal children and adults in the same manner that they affect ADHD children (Gittelman & Kanner, 1986). Specifically, on a variety of measures, the drugs increase activity or arousal in the CNS and improve performance on various laboratory tasks of cognitive functioning. These changes appear to be nonspecific, occurring for numerous measures of CNS function.

Cognitive and Behavioral Effects of Stimulants

On laboratory measures of attention, impulsivity, and learning, stimulants have routinely been found to improve ADHD children's performance on the order of 25%, compared to placebo levels of performance (Pelham, 1986; Swanson & Kinsbourne, 1979). For example, on a typical sustained attention or vigilance task, children on medication (compared with placebo) make fewer impulsive responses to nontarget stimuli and maintain better attention, missing fewer target stimuli. Similar average improvement in performance has been consistently reported on paired-associate learning tasks, nonsense-word spelling tasks, and other measures of learning and cognitive performance.

Given the results from laboratory cognitive tasks, it should not be surprising that beneficial stimulant effects have been observed in ADHD children's classroom behavior and performance. These effects have been reported in a very large number of studies and are among the most well-documented treatment effects in child psychopathology. Improvement is shown most clearly as a reduction in classroom disruptiveness and an increase in on-task behavior. Relative to unmedicated ADHD children, those receiving stimulants *decrease* the extent to which they (a) talk out inappropriately in class, (b) bother peers who are working, (c) violate classroom rules or engage in other behaviors (e.g., noncompliance) that require teacher attention, and (d) interact aggressively and otherwise inappropriately with peers. Furthermore, they *increase* their time on task and complete more of their assigned academic work, often with enhanced accuracy (Pelham, Bender, Caddell, Booth, & Moorer, 1985). These effects are clearly evident whether children are observed directly or rated by their teachers.

There has been considerable debate regarding whether these salutary stimulant effects on classroom behavior and performance translate into long-term gains in academic achievement—as noted above, an area in which many ADHD children suffer. Early reviews concluding that stimulants did not affect academic achievement have been severely criticized on methodological grounds (Pelham, 1986), and, because academic productivity and accuracy are among the best predictors of long-term achievement, it can be reasonably argued that ADHD children who show stimulant-facilitated improvements in daily academic performance will make long-term gains in achievement.

Studies in laboratory analogue settings have shown that stimulant drugs positively affect ADHD children's behavior during structured parent–child interactions in the same way that the drugs affect the children's behavior at school. Medicated children are less disruptive and more compliant than nonmedicated children (Barkley, Karlsson, Strzelecki, & Murphy, 1984). Similarly, recent studies have shown that, for many ADHD children, moderate doses of methylphenidate both decrease aggression and often increase prosocial interactions with peers in play settings (Hinshaw, Henker, & Whalen, 1984a; Hinshaw, Buhrmester, & Heller,

1989; Pelham & Hoza, 1987). However, several qualifications of these effects are in order:

1. The beneficial effects of medication are much more evident when the medicated children are in groups of peers rather than in dyads (cf. Cunningham, Siegel, & Offord, 1985);
2. Reductions in aggression are clearest for those children who were most aggressive prior to medication (Hinshaw, Buhrmester, & Heller, 1989);
3. These medication effects may depend on the presence of concurrent interventions, being most evident in settings in which concurrent behavioral interventions are in effect;
4. Whether stimulants improve prosocial peer interactions has not been entirely resolved.

We have been discussing stimulant effects as if an average effect were characteristic of all ADHD children. Unfortunately, not all ADHD children show positive responses to stimulant drugs, and there are considerable individual differences in the size of the drug effect for those who do respond. Approximately 70 to 80% of ADHD children respond positively to a stimulant regimen, but the remaining quarter show either an adverse response or no response. Of those who do respond, only a minority show sufficient improvement for their behavior to fall entirely within the normal range; the rest are improved but their behavior is not normalized. One variable on which the degree of a child's response to a stimulant drug depends is the administered dose. There is considerable controversy regarding what dose of stimulant is best for ADHD children. Generally, MPH is administered twice daily in doses that range from 0.25 to 0.75 mg/kg of body weight, with dextroamphetamine doses half this amount, and pemoline doses 4 to 6 times those of a single dose of MPH. Doses on the lower end of the MPH range described above are much more common than doses in the higher end of that range. Generally, the larger the dose, the larger the drug effect, and the dose–response relationship is usually linear up to 0.6 mg/kg or slightly higher (Pelham et al., 1985).

However, there are large individual differences in the size and topography of the drug response among the three-fourths of ADHD children who respond to stimulants. Although this fact has been known for some time, its profound implications for research and treatment have not been appreciated. Response to stimulants varies both across and within children and depends on dose, dependent measure, and the child's target symptoms. On many dependent measures, the group data for drug response do not accurately reflect dose effects for the individuals who made up the group. Unfortunately, no measures reliably predict drug response in individuals. Although some reviewers have argued that deficits on measures of attention predict drug response, and although a diagnosis of ADHD is generally considered a prerequisite for a stimulant trial, neither of these common beliefs is supported by data (Conners & Wells, 1986).

In addition to the salutary main effects of stimulant drugs, other side effects or treatment emergent symptoms (TES) are sometimes associated with stimulant treatment. For example, long-term stimulant treatment (2 to 4 years) with average doses of 40 mg of MPH per day results in a slight reduction in the rate of weight gain and (to a lesser extent) height gain in treated children. This effect is dependent on the total cumulative dose that the child takes, however, and can be minimized by keeping the dose low, medicating during school hours only, and discontinuing medication on weekends and holidays. Furthermore, the effects are usually small, and if children discontinue stimulant treatment, a compensatory growth rebound occurs. Stimulants can also induce socially withdrawn behavior in some treated children (Pelham & Hoza, 1987), and cognitive impairment occurs in some children at some doses (Swanson & Kinsbourne, 1979). Finally, stimulants have been reported to exacerbate motor tics when present in treated children, and they may speed the emergence of underlying Tourette's syndrome. Although many of the most serious TES are rare, and although irreversible side effects are extremely rare, medicated children nonetheless should be carefully monitored to ensure that these adverse side effects are not caused or exacerbated by stimulant therapy.

Behavioral Assessment of Pharmacotherapy

The questions facing the therapist are how to decide whether a stimulant should be used with an ADHD child and what the correct dose should be. Decisions about whether to medicate are rarely made systematically in practice. Most often, parents contact their child's physician at the insistence of the school, and the physician prescribes medication (or does not) based on his or her knowledge and beliefs regarding the role of stimulants in the treatment of ADHD. Neither drug response nor TES is measured systematically, and only rarely does the physician obtain systematic information about the child from the setting that initiated the referral—the school (Copeland, Wolraich, Lindgren, Milich, & Woolson, 1987). This process obviously has numerous shortcomings.

Alternative, data-based, behavioral procedures for determining the utility of stimulant therapy for a child and for selecting the proper dose have been advocated in recent years (Barkley, Fischer, Newby, & Breen, 1988; Pelham & Hoza, 1987; Swanson & Kinsbourne, 1979). Because of their short half-lives and quick onsets of action, stimulants can be alternated frequently with placebo for brief periods of time (days or weeks) in a short-term, clinical trial. The assessment may take a total of 2 to 5 weeks, depending on the number of drugs or doses evaluated. Thus, what is essentially a single-subject study using an alternating treatments design can be used to evaluate an individual child's response to medication and to yield data-based recommendations concerning the utility of stimulant medication in a referred child's treatment. A variety of medication assessments has been described, using different dependent measures and conducted in settings ranging from inpatient to outpatient. Most employ some type of laboratory- or office-based cognitive testing (e.g., a paired-associates learning task or a vigilance task) and teacher and parent ratings of main effects and TES. Those conducted in settings that lend themselves to gathering objective data often include behavioral observations. As noted above, because drug response in the natural environment cannot be reliably predicted from a single laboratory task, an assessment of medication effects should focus on the target symptoms on which change is desired in the settings in which the symptoms occur.

Because pediatricians and psychiatrists usually do not have the skills needed to conduct a comprehensive evaluation of this nature, behaviorally oriented psychologists and educational personnel need to work collaboratively with prescribing physicians. Some time may need to be invested initially to persuade a child's physician that a comprehensive medication evaluation is necessary. A pediatrician who is used to writing a prescription for MPH without follow-up may find unnecessarily cumbersome the prospect of referring the patient for an assessment that may take 5 weeks and incur a considerable cost. However, given that the child may take medication for years and given the complex nature of response to stimulants, such an initial evaluation is critical.

Insufficiencies of Psychostimulant Therapy

Despite their widely validated salutary effects on ADHD children, the stimulants have limitations in their clinical efficacy. We have discussed some of the limitations inherent in stimulant pharmacotherapy, and they can be briefly summarized. First, stimulants do not work for all children, and, even with drug responders, stimulant therapy is rarely sufficient to bring children into a normal range of academic and social functioning. In short, there is clearly room for improvement with additional interventions for most stimulant-treated ADHD children. Second, psychostimulant effects are limited to the time period in which the drugs are physiologically active. Stimulants typically do not provide adequate control of the child's behavior throughout the entire day, and because of potential side effects, the medications are typically not administered in the late afternoons and evenings. Therefore, interventions during the time when the medication is not active—particularly in the evenings when the child is home—are necessary. A final limitation of psychostimulant therapy is that, without exception, studies that have followed children treated with psychostimulant medication for periods up to 15 years have failed to provide any evidence that the drugs improve ADHD children's long-term prognosis (Weiss & Hechtman, 1986). Although methodological inadequacies require that these studies be interpreted cautiously, an overriding suggestion is that stimulant medication as typically administered is an insufficient long-term treatment. These limitations highlight the need for other modes of intervention for ADHD. Of additional treatments that have been investigated, behavioral interventions have shown most promise as alternatives and adjuncts to pharmacotherapy for ADHD.

BEHAVIORAL INTERVENTION STRATEGIES

Since the 1970s, a number a studies have been conducted to evaluate the efficacy of behavior modification/therapy with ADHD children, with most of these studies appearing since the previous edition of this text (Lahey, Delameter, & Kupfer, 1981). As a group, the studies have shown that behavioral interventions effect short-term amelioration of ADHD symptomatology, and that these acute effects are comparable in some domains to those obtained with low doses of stimulant medication. Behavioral interventions with ADHD children have generally fit into one of three categories (Pelham & Murphy, 1986): clinical behavior therapy, direct contingency management, and cognitive-behavioral interventions. Because these categories differ in the nature of the interventions and in their efficacies, we shall discuss them separately.

Clinical Behavior Therapy

Applications of clinical behavior therapy have typically involved training parents to implement contingency-management programs with their children and consulting with the children's teachers with the same goal (Gittelman et al., 1980; O'Leary & Pelham, 1978; Pelham et al., 1988; Pelham, Schnedler, Bologna, & Contreras, 1980). In these studies, all of which can be traced to the O'Learys' laboratory at the State University of New York at Stony Brook, the format of therapy consisted of weekly sessions with parents in the clinic and weekly visits to teachers. During these sessions and visits, basic behavior management skills were taught by the children's therapists. Parents were given assigned readings and were taught standard behavioral techniques such as time out, point systems, and contingent attention. Therapists worked with teachers to develop (a) classroom management strategies (e.g., Premack contingencies) that could be used with the target children, and (b) daily report cards that could provide feedback to parents on the children's school performance and that parents would consequate with a reward at home. The studies lasted from 8 to 20 weeks, and change was measured from pre- to posttreatment with ratings and direct observations.

In the typical outcome of this form of clinical behavior therapy with ADHD children, the treated children show considerable improvement in both classroom and home settings. For example, children in the O'Leary and Pelham (1978) study showed improvement in classroom on-task behavior that was comparable to preintervention response to stimulant medication. In Pelham et al. (1980), such comparability was found with a low (0.25 mg/kg) but not a high (0.75 mg/kg) dose of MPH, suggesting that behavior therapy's benefits match those of a lower but not a higher dose of stimulants. All of the studies revealed significant improvement in parent and teacher ratings for treated children. At the same time, however, the ADHD children rarely reached a normal level of functioning on critical dependent measures, and there were considerable individual differences in response to the behavioral interventions in the studies that reported individual data. Consider, for example, the Pelham et al. (1988) study. Here, children were classified as improved, unchanged, or worse, with a 20% change in either direction from pretreatment levels as the criterion. Using this guide, 45% of the subjects were improved on parent ratings, 80% on teacher ratings (though none of the 80% fell within the range of their normal classmates), 55% on negative peer nominations, and 60% on classroom observations of disruptive behavior. However, only 20% of the children improved in all four of these domains; more important, only 10% of the subjects were within a normal range of functioning at posttreatment in all four domains. Indeed, on treatment outcome measures such as parent and teacher rating scales, behaviorally treated ADHD children, although clinically improved, rarely fall within a normal range of functioning (Gittelman et al., 1980; O'Leary & Pelham, 1978; Pelham et al., 1980, 1988).

A number of studies have shown that standard clinical behavior therapy of the type that is likely to be implemented by therapists in community mental health, primary care, and private practice settings (e.g., weekly sessions, 8- to 20-week course) results in significant improvement on multiple measures in home and school settings for the majority of treated ADHD children. It is worth noting that these studies followed closely the formats and goals of earlier studies that examined behavioral treatment effects on conduct disordered children, with similar results (e.g., Patterson, 1974). At the same time, the data show clearly that this clinical approach is typically not a sufficient treatment. The lack of normalization of treatment effects may result from the fact that the treatment is indirect—that is, the professional trains the parents and teachers, who then implement the treatment with the child. As noted below, parents and teachers may not faithfully administer the desired procedures, thus resulting in the only partial effectiveness of the program. Attempts to deal with this problem have often involved a move to contingency management procedures directly implemented by the therapist.

Contingency Management

In contrast to standard clinical behavior therapy, contingency management approaches (as defined here) are characterized by relatively more intensive interventions, implemented directly in the setting of interest and typically by a professional. The majority of the studies have been conducted in specialized treatment facilities or in demonstrational classroom settings. As a result, the studies typically have had greater control over the independent variables than have the therapy outcome studies described above. The techniques employed in the studies have ranged from relatively more potent components such as point/token economy reward systems, time out, and response-cost programs (Robinson, Newby, & Ganzell, 1981) to manipulations of teacher attention and removal of privileges. As noted above regarding clinical behavior therapy, many of the techniques that have been employed with ADHD children have been investigated with populations of undiagnosed "behavior problem" children in the past (O'Leary & O'Leary, 1977). The purpose of these studies has been to determine whether the same kinds of techniques work with ADHD children. Because the number of studies is relatively large and because of our space limitations, we shall mention only a portion of this literature (see also Pfiffner & O'Leary, in press).

A major question of interest in the contingency management studies has been whether negative procedures such as punishment are necessary components of contingency management programs. Behavioral clinicians who have worked with conduct disorder (CD) children have long argued that the effective use of punishment is the key to parent management of CD children (Patterson, 1982). The same conclusion appears to apply to ADHD children. A recent series of studies by S. G. O'Leary and her colleagues, comprehensively reviewed in Pfiffner and O'Leary (in press), illustrates this point.

These studies have been conducted in a university laboratory school for ADHD children. The first study of the series (Rosen, O'Leary, Joyce, Conway, & Pfiffner, 1984) compared conditions in which positive consequences (teacher attention and praise), negative consequences (verbal reprimands backed up with time out and loss of privileges), and their combination were used. The children's behavior deteriorated whenever negative consequences were removed but did not depend on the presence of positive consequences. Further, "prudent negative consequences" (calmly delivered, immediate reprimands with contingent backups) were more effective than loud, delayed, lengthy, inconsistent, and emotional reprimands. Subsequent studies showed that this finding was robust even when enhanced positive procedures (e.g., special privileges, individual rewards) were included (Pfiffner & O'Leary, in press). Interestingly, when negative consequences were used consistently from the outset in the special classroom, they were more effective than when they were slowly introduced, validating the commonly believed but heretofore undocumented notion that teachers of problem children should start off strictly and ease up later.

The latest study in O'Leary's series is particularly provocative (Sullivan & O'Leary, 1989). This study showed that the *maintenance* of appropriate behavior following withdrawal of the contingencies was better for a negative consequence (loss of recess time) response cost procedure than for a reward procedure. This differential maintenance was especially true for the ADHD children with the highest baseline ratings on the conduct and the hyperactivity factors of the Conners Teacher Rating Scale. The authors concluded that these findings clearly indicate the suitability of response cost, as opposed to solely reward-based programs, for ADHD children, particularly those with the highest levels of concurrent aggression.

This series of studies, then, shows that direct contingency management procedures that include systematic negative consequences are efficacious with ADHD children. Although these studies do not include normal comparison children, the rates of behavior reported suggest that the manipulation resulted in greater normalization of functioning than do standard clinical behavioral interventions (see, e.g., Atkins, Pelham, & White, 1989).

Cognitive-Behavioral Interventions

Because of space limitations and because of the existence of Abikoff's (1987) extensive and authoritative review, we cannot provide detailed coverage of the many investigations of cognitive-behavioral treatment procedures for hyperactive children that have been performed in the past 15 years. Rather, borrowing from Hinshaw and Erhardt (in press-b), we will provide a succinct overview. There are many different types of "cognitive" intervention strategies for children; these include verbal self-instructions, problem-solving strategies, cognitive modeling, self-evaluation, self-reinforcement, and anger management training, to name a few. The underlying theme of all such procedures is the promotion of self-controlled behavior via enhancement of mediational and problem-solving strategies.

The chief conclusion from controlled outcome studies is that cognitive treatments have not lived up to their promise of providing generalized and clinically robust changes in the behavior and academic performance of hyperactive youngsters. Indeed, despite the notion that cognitive self-instructional training would provide an excellent match for the inattentive and impulsive features of the behavior of children with ADHD, there is little evidence that cognitive programs focusing primarily on self-instructional methods produce significant gains in academic achievement or reductions in problematic social behavior, or that they yield durable or generalized gains. The findings of a major, controlled investigation conducted by Abikoff and Gittelman (1985) were particularly bleak but are representative. For ADHD children who were receiving stimulant medication, essentially no positive effects of 16 weeks of intensive cognitive training were found in comparison with attention control and no-training groups, across multiple academic, cognitive, and behavioral measures. Also, although a large number of studies have examined the efficacy of training in interpersonal social skills and social problem-solving skills with ADHD children, these approaches, which have a broad scope, have usually not provided benefit for the specific social situations that pose difficulty for ADHD children (Krehbiel & Milich, 1986).

There is at least preliminary evidence that some cognitive-behavioral procedures may be worth pursuing. Focusing specifically on enhancing anger control in provocative social situations, Hinshaw, Henker, and Whalen (1984b) developed a small-group, cognitive-behavioral treatment program based on stress inoculation procedures. After receiving several weeks of general cognitive problem-solving training, hyperactive boys were taught specific skills to cope with verbal taunting and teasing. The children learned to (a) identify cognitive and behavioral signs of incipient anger, (b) develop specific strategies of their own choosing, to control inappropriately aggressive reactions, and (c) rehearse their specific strategies under increasingly realistic provocation from adult trainers and from peers. During provocation assessments that involved strident teasing from the child's training group, this strategy-based intervention was found to be superior to a control intervention emphasizing cue recognition and cognitive problem solving alone. In a recent report, Hinshaw, Buhrmester, and Heller (1989) demonstrated that similar anger-management training procedures were enhanced when participants received a moderate dosage of stimulant medication during the posttraining provocation assessment, suggesting beneficial effects of combined psychosocial and pharmacologic intervention for anger control.

Hinshaw, Henker, and Whalen (1984a) showed that when ADHD boys who received specific training in self-evaluation also received token reinforcement and stimulant medication, they showed more appropriate behavior interacting with peers compared to boys who did not receive medication or token reinforcement. We should note that, in all three of these reports, benefits occurred only when cognitive self-control procedures were paired with behavioral rehearsal or behavioral reinforcement, suggesting the need for integrative cognitive-behavioral treatments. Yet, the evaluations were quite brief and staged in these studies, and they followed the completion of training procedures by only a few days.

Given the early promise but eventual failure of most other cognitive procedures, more extensive intervention applied over longer time periods is required before self-evaluation or anger-management training can claim clinically meaningful benefits for hyperactive children. At the same time, despite discouraging outcomes for large-scale, self-instructional treatment programs, creative combinations of cognitive and behavioral treatment strategies may still be helpful for altering the interpersonal difficulties of children with ADHD. Cognitive-behavioral interventions are far from a panacea for the difficult problems of these youngsters, however. Considerable work remains to be done (a) to task-analyze the sorts of cognitive deficiencies and social problem-solving deficits displayed by hyperactive children that might be productively ameliorated via cognitive treatment procedures (Whalen, Henker, & Hinshaw, 1985) and (b) to demonstrate the incremental value of cognitive interventions beyond the effects afforded by more powerful behavioral interventions and medication. Furthermore, even though the ultimate benefits of self-control strategies may result from their application during and after extended behavioral treatments—in order to promote the generalization and maintenance that are often lacking with behavioral interventions—such an application has not yet been put to empirical test.

Insufficiencies of Behavioral Interventions

The shortcomings of behavioral interventions with ADHD children are similar to those of psychostimulant medication. First, although the studies we reviewed showed that standard clinical behavior therapy and direct contingency management are effective in improving parent and teacher ratings on standardized rating scales of ADHD, posttreatment ratings are usually one standard deviation (SD) above normative means, and direct observations of classroom behavior and classmate sociometric ratings usually reveal that children often continue to function well outside the normal range even after treatment (O'Leary & Pelham, 1978; Pelham et al., 1988). Also, as with psychostimulant medication, the short-term effects of behavioral interventions are limited to the period when the programs are actually in effect; that is, no studies have yet shown maintenance of treatment gains after therapy is terminated.

Furthermore, a substantial minority of children in these studies (comparable to the proportion cited for stimulant medication) fail to show improvement. In many cases, such failure may be attributable to the unwillingness or inability of parents and teachers to implement the behavioral programs as directed. A major problem is that a large number of teachers, who are not obligated to cooperate with outside consultants, will not implement a behavioral intervention (Witt, 1986). In addition, many parents—up to half of those beginning treatment—discontinue parent training against therapeutic advice (Firestone, Kelly, Goodman, & Davey, 1981). Even when parents and teachers apparently comply with treatment, therapist contact in standard, clinical behavior therapy is typically limited to once per week, and manipulation checks of whether parents and teachers actually follow through with treatment are almost never conducted. Indeed, parents and teachers of children who fail to show maximum improvement in intervention studies may not have implemented the treatment programs appropriately, if at all (Atkins, Pelham, & White, 1989). For example, single mothers with relatively lower levels of education, income, and contact with other adults have great difficulty implementing and maintaining behavioral treatment, with meager treatment outcomes (Wahler, 1980).

Just as some of the limitations of medication can be removed by increasing the dosage, the effects of behavior therapy can be maximized by increasing the power and comprehensiveness of the intervention. The standard clinical behavior therapy approach involving weekly contact with parents and teachers is less potent than are highly structured, closely monitored, contingency-management programs (Pfiffner & O'Leary, in press). Because it is quite time-consuming and difficult to conduct such systems unassisted, however, regular classroom teachers are typically much less willing to implement complex contingency-management programs, particularly those that involve negative consequences. In summary, the efficacy of behavior therapy depends on the motivation and capabilities of the significant adults in the child's life and on the skills of the interveners in overcoming such obstacles. If key adults are unwilling or unable to implement the interventions, and if the objections or obstacles to intervention cannot be overcome, then behavior therapy will not be effective.

A final possible limitation of behavior therapy with ADHD children is the lack of evidence for long-term effects, adequate studies of which have not been conducted. A number of studies with behavior problem children (in all likelihood a mixture of ADHD, CD, and oppositional disorder diagnostic categories) have shown that a substantial number of treated children fail to maintain treatment gains for periods of time as short as one year following intervention (Alexander & Malouf, 1983). Demonstration of generalization over time is one of the major concerns of those employing behavioral interventions with children. Unfortunately, at our current stage of knowledge, the best guess regarding the long-term effects of behavior therapy with ADHD and CD children is that short-term effects will often fail to maintain. As with psychostimulant medication, then, the absence of evidence for long-term effects is perhaps the major limitation of behavior therapy with ADHD children.

COMBINED PHARMACOLOGIC AND BEHAVIORAL INTERVENTIONS

During the past few years, it has become clear that the most effective short-term treatment for the majority of ADHD children is an intervention that combines pharmacologic and behavioral treatment (see Pelham & Murphy, 1986, for a review). This combined treatment approach is rapidly becoming the treatment of choice for ADHD. Both behavioral and pharmacologic interventions have limitations, but, as noted above, these can often be reduced by combining the two modalities. Theoretically, the effects of a combined pharmacologic and behavioral intervention can differ from the effects of the component treatments in several different ways. The two treatments can interact to potentiate one another, yielding a combined effect greater than the total of the two component effects, or they can interact to inhibit one another, yielding an effect that is less than the effects of either component. Alternatively, the combined effect can simply be additive, equaling the total of the components, or reciprocation can occur when the combined outcome is the same as that from one or the other component. Finally, the two interventions can have complementary effects; that is, each treatment can affect different symptoms such that the combined intervention affects a greater range of symptomatology than does either treatment alone. Combining behavioral and pharmacologic approaches would ideally result in additivity, complementary effects, and potentiation, thus minimizing the shortcomings of each treatment alone.

A review of 19 studies in which a combination of behavioral and stimulant treatments was used with ADHD children drew several conclusions (Pelham & Murphy, 1986). First, 13 of the 19 independent studies (68%) showed superiority for a combined treatment on at least one classroom-based task, motor, or social measure. For those studies in which a behavioral or pharmacologic effect was found, only very rarely was either of these treatments alone superior to their combination. In fact, if order of condition means, rather than statistical significance, was used to interpret results, the combination treatment was superior to component treatments in virtually every study reviewed. For the *average* ADHD child treated in these studies, a combined intervention resulted in greater improvement than did either treatment alone.

Consider, for example, the study reported by Gittelman et al. (1980). In an 8-week investigation, they compared (a) a clinical behavioral intervention (mainly teacher rather than parent training), (b) stimulant medication, and (c) both treatments combined. On a variety of measures, the combined treatment group came closer to normalization of functioning than did either treatment alone (stimulant treatment alone was next in efficacy and behavioral treatment a distant third), despite the significant within-subject gains for this clinical behavior therapy intervention alone. In another treatment outcome study, Pelham et al. (1988) examined the incremental effects of adding 0.3 mg/kg MPH b.i.d. to a 20-week behavioral intervention conducted with ADHD children in classroom and home settings. On one key measure, the Abbreviated Conners Teacher Rating Scale (ACTRS), children who received methylphenidate in addition to the behavioral intervention were rated at midtreatment by teachers as considerably better (M = 6.5, SD = 2.9) than children who received behavior therapy plus placebo (M = 12.7, SD = 6.8), both reductions from mean ratings of 19 before treatment. Eighty percent of the combined intervention children were "normalized" on this measure, compared to 30% of the behavior therapy plus placebo group. Of note is that this positive level of functioning was reached with a dose of MPH that was half that used by Gittelman et al. (1980). Other treatment studies have also shown that treated children are more likely to reach a "normalization" of functioning with a combined intervention than with the separate modalities (Hinshaw et al., 1984a; Pelham et al., 1980). However, it is important to note that, in all of these studies, the incremental beneficial effects of the combined treatments did not last after either component was withdrawn, at which point effects reduced immediately to those produced by the remaining component. In the Pelham et al. (1988) study, this pattern held true for every domain of functioning assessed. It is thus a false assumption that medication can be used for a short time to prime the child for psychosocial and educational interventions. Whether a systematic withdrawal and maintenance program could maintain the obviously beneficial effects of the combined treatment has yet to be investigated. No controlled, long-term outcome studies of combined interventions have yet been conducted.

Many combined treatment effects are additive. A graphic example of the additive effects of MPH and reinforcement is illustrated in a recent single-subject study (Schell et al., 1986). A multiply handicapped child (ADHD, mentally retarded, dysphasic) was evaluated who had been referred by his pediatric neurologist for assessment of whether psychostimulant medication, behavior modification, or the combination of the two was most effective in improving his learning and behavior. Over a period of weeks, the child learned lists of reading sight vocabulary words under different behavioral and drug conditions in an alternative treatments design (e.g., with and without reward; with placebo versus 0.3 mg/kg MPH). The initial assessment revealed that the child improved both with medication and with a behavioral program, but the combined intervention was most effective, as shown in Figure 14.1. A combined treatment regimen was therefore recommended for the child, and as of this writing he has been maintained on that treatment for the past 6 years. Five annual reassessments demonstrated the continued incremental value of the combined pharmacologic and behavioral treatment for him. It is interesting to note that this child showed additive, potentiated, and complementary effects of the combined treatment, depending on the dependent measure that was examined, highlighting the importance of multiple measures in evaluating combined treatment response.

In the Pelham et al. (1980) report, potentiation was observed for some measures. This interaction occurred with

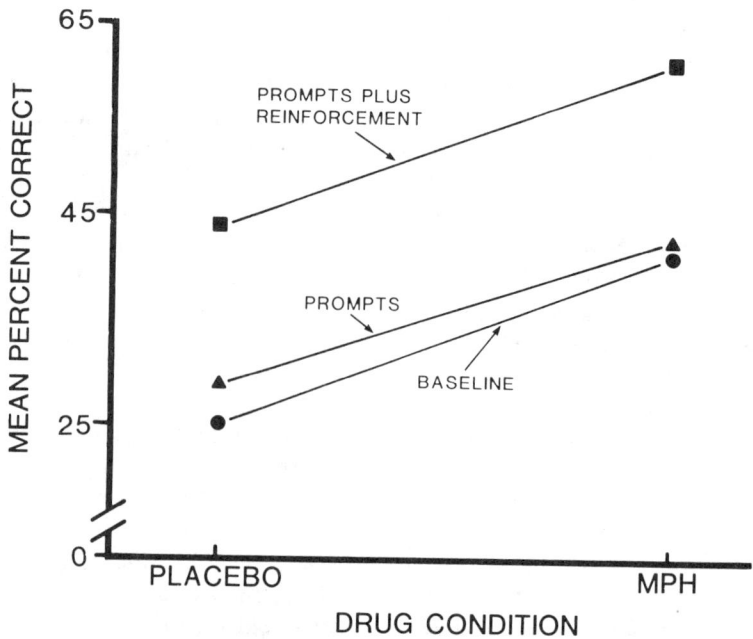

Figure 14.1. Mean percent correct as a function of medication condition and level of behavior modification. MPH = methylphenidate.

dose, such that the effects of a low dose of MPH were considerably enhanced by the behavioral intervention. Thus, an important result of combined treatments may be that maximal improvement in behavior may be reached without resorting to high dosages of psychostimulant medication, to which some of the adverse effects discussed earlier may accrue.

In a recent report, Carlson, Pelham, Milich, and Dixon (1990) conducted a within-subject evaluation of the concurrent effects of a behavioral intervention and 0.3 and 0.6 mg/kg MPH with 26 ADHD boys in a summer day treatment program classroom. Compared to a no-behavior modification ("regular classroom") condition, the full behavioral intervention included a reward and cost point system, a daily report card, and time out. Dependent measures included observations of on-task, disruptive, and rule-following behavior in the classroom, as well as numerous measures of academic productivity and accuracy. As in the Pelham et al. (1988) and Gittelman et al. (1980) papers, both the behavioral intervention and MPH had salutary effects on on-task, disruptive, and rule-following behavior. As Figure 14.2 illustrates for disruptive behavior, the effects of the behavioral intervention and 0.3 mg/kg were equivalent and additive, such that the combination of the two resulted in behavioral improvement equal to the 0.6 mg/kg dose of MPH. In other words, the effective dose of MPH could be cut in half when the behavioral program was in effect in the classroom, and there was no incremental value of the higher dose, given the behavioral intervention. Interestingly, complementary effects were also observed in this study. The drug effect was significant for all six measures of academic productivity and accuracy, while the behavioral intervention had no effect

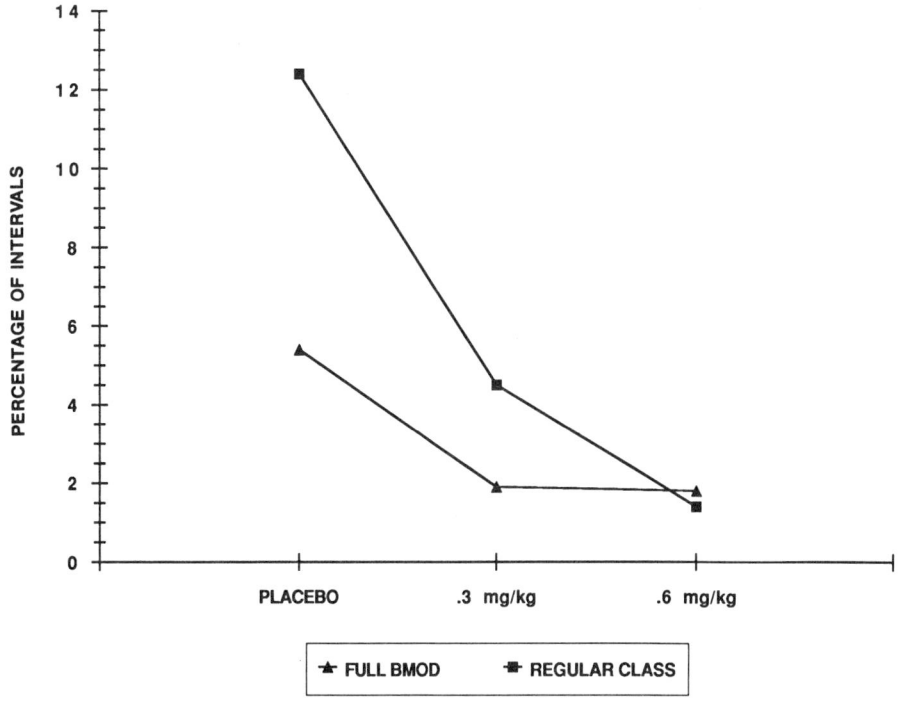

Figure 14.2. Percentage of intervals with disruptive behavior as a function of medication condition and level of behavior modification.

on any of these measures. Although behavior modification was efficacious in changing social behavior, the pharmacologic intervention was a necessary adjunct to produce academic changes in these ADHD boys.

In a single-case study that also addressed the efficacy of combined treatments, Atkins, Pelham, and White (1989) demonstrated that a low dose of psychostimulant combined with a simple behavioral program was as effective as a complex, response-cost behavioral intervention. The clinical significance of this report is enhanced by the realization that the child's teacher eventually refused to implement the behavioral program because of its time requirement. That is, despite the documented effectiveness of the response-cost program, three consecutive mainstream classroom teachers refused to implement the more complex behavioral program with this child. Thus, the combination of the pharmacological and simple behavioral interventions became his long-term treatment.

These investigations all illustrate that, because lower dosages and less restrictive behavioral interventions can be used, the risk/benefit ratio involved in combined treatments is decreased, and greater effects can be obtained with intervention levels—both pharmacologic and behavioral—that carry fewer potential hazards. We must reiterate, however, that there are large individual differences in response to medication, behavior therapy, and their combination. We have previously noted that if the children who respond to behavioral interventions and those who respond to medication are not the same children, then a combined treatment group study would yield evidence of combined treatment efficacy even though not a single individual had responded more positively to the combination than to the individual treatments (Pelham & Murphy, 1986). Although many ADHD children respond best to a combined intervention, some children respond best to one or the other component treatment. Group studies that present only averaged data can be misleading, and the combined treatment must thus be examined for individuals. The only way to know which children will respond to a combined intervention is to directly measure the child's response in a short-term treatment trial, highlighting the importance of using comprehensive behavioral assessments in evaluating treatment effectiveness in combined behavioral and psychopharmacologic interventions with ADHD children.

Because most studies of a combined approach to treating ADHD have employed between-subject designs, beyond a few case studies, limited data are available regarding what percentage of children actually respond best to a combined regimen. Initial data relevant to this question were yielded when we evaluated response to medication among a sample of ADHD children attending a summer day treatment program (Pelham & Hoza, 1987). Forty-four percent of those children were thought definitely to need medication beyond the highly structured behavioral day treatment program. An additional 25% showed an incremental response to medication beyond that shown to the behavioral treatment, but medication was recommended only if a behavioral intervention in the natural environment was insufficient.

One of the major advantages of a combined behavioral/pharmacologic treatment for ADHD is that the behavioral component of treatment can usually be reduced in scope and complexity if combined with low dosages of medication. Because less complex treatments are also less expensive, the cost-effectiveness of treatment is improved with a combined intervention. For example, a powerful, maximally effective, contingency management intervention in a referred child's classroom might require daily therapist trips to the school compared to the single weekly trip characteristic of standard clinical behavior therapy. At $75 per visit, the more powerful behavioral intervention would cost an additional $300 per week. In contrast, the addition of a low dose of psychostimulant medication to a typical clinical behavioral intervention might also maximize improvement (Atkins, Pelham, & White, 1989), but would cost less than $5 per week. Although such concerns are unimportant in research settings where costs are not borne by a child's parents, in actual practice they are often one of the primary determinants of whether parents will seek out and follow through with treatment.

In addition to potential interactive or additive effects, behavioral therapy and psychostimulant medication each have areas of deficit and effectiveness that the other intervention can complement, as Carlson et al. (1990) reported (see discussion above). For example, parent training is a standard component of a behavioral intervention for ADHD, thus ensuring that a treatment is available for the times of the day that are typically not addressed by medication. Similarly, psychostimulant medication can reduce problematic behaviors that are very difficult to treat with practical behavioral programs, such as low-rate, peer-directed aggression that occurs in the absence of adult authority (e.g., on the school playground; see Hinshaw, Henker, Whalen, Erhardt, & Dunnington, 1989). An untested but intriguing possibility is that medication might facilitate behavioral treatment of other low-rate behaviors, such as stealing, that have been relatively unresponsive to behavioral interventions alone. As we noted earlier, medication effects on prosocial and antisocial behaviors appear to be facilitated when behavioral contingencies supporting social behavior are in effect. In several ways, then, a combined intervention is more comprehensive in coverage than either treatment alone.

Finally, there are several reasons to speculate that long-term maintenance of treatment effects might be improved with a combined intervention. First, it is clear that ADHD children suffer from a lack of cognitive and behavioral skills that are necessary for academic and social adjustment (Douglas, 1983). To the extent that these skills must be acquired for successful long-term outcome, medication alone, which does not teach a child alternative behaviors for coping with problematic situations, would not be expected to be a sufficient treatment. The addition of a behavioral intervention that focused in part on teaching such skills might improve the long-term outcome that would be achieved with medication alone. Similarly, to facilitate maintenance of behavioral treatment effects, the intervention should be able to be continued by the child's parents or teachers for a protracted time and/or maintained by naturally occurring contingencies following therapy termination. Because the addition of a low dose of psychostimulant medication enables relatively greater effects to be achieved with less restrictive and more natural behavioral programs, a combined intervention may be more likely to be maintained following termination of therapeutic contact.

Although combined behavioral and stimulant interventions appear to be the emerging treatment of choice for ADHD, several qualifications are in order. One of them is that, compared to the large numbers of subjects who have been studied over considerably longer time periods with separate behavioral and pharmacologic interventions, the combined intervention is relatively unstudied. Only 167 children were treated in the 19 studies reviewed by Pelham and Murphy (1986), and the median duration of treatment was less than 3 weeks. Much more evidence is required before we have adequate knowledge regarding the procedures and effects of combined behavioral and pharmacologic treatments for ADHD, but the research conducted to date suggests that the combined approach shows more promise than any other form of intervention with ADHD children.

SUMMARY AND CONCLUSIONS

It is clear that behavioral interventions are effective for ADHD children. Results from investigations of both clinical behavior therapy and direct contingency-management approaches show unequivocal evidence for significant improvement in a majority of treated children. Given the limitations of stimulant medication, particularly its apparent lack of effect on long-term outcome, behavioral approaches are recommended in the treatment of children with ADHD. Yet, as we have discussed, behavioral therapies have their own limitations, including inferiority to relatively high dosages of stimulant medications in "head to head" comparison studies and a lack of sufficiency for the many difficult problems presented by these youngsters. Although we have discussed elsewhere, in some detail, our views on future directions for research on behavioral intervention approaches for this population (Hinshaw & Erhardt, in press-a, in press-b; Pelham & Murphy, 1986), we present several key recommendations here.

Additional investigations regarding the effects of behavioral and combined behavioral/pharmacologic treatments on peer relationships are sorely needed. In this critical domain, traditional behavioral and social skills interventions have had relatively weak effects with ADHD children (Krehbiel & Milich, 1986). The recent evidence that stimulants may promote improvements in peer acceptance (Whalen et al., 1989) highlights the need for additional research with behavioral and combined treatment approaches. We recommend that such research be conducted in settings that are as natural as possible, and that investigators focus on sports and recreation skills as well as on social skills per se (Pelham et al., 1990).

There has been a great deal of discussion regarding the potential for pharmacologic treatments to produce maladaptive attributions for ADHD children (Whalen, 1989). Although this discussion has been plagued by a lack of hard evidence, it is indeed true that treatment-related attributions that minimize the importance of personal effort and that diminish self-esteem would be counterproductive (Pelham et al., 1991). We speculate that the addition of behavioral treatments—particularly those that emphasize the child's active role in intervention procedures—to medication regimens might promote more salutary attributions. This area clearly warrants additional research.

Given the substantial, but not total, overlap between ADHD and aggression, we recommend that research on the efficacy of behavioral and combined intervention strategies be conducted with analyses of separate subgroups—those ADHD children with and without concurrent oppositional and conduct problems. None of the behavioral intervention studies to date have divided subjects on the aggression dimension, but such research would be illuminating from both theoretical and practical perspectives. It is also quite plausible that the particularly intractable problems of children with combinations of ADHD and aggressive symptomatology may require special education placement, intensive summer treatment programs, or other powerful and concentrated treatments. Alternatively, combinations of pharmacologic and behavioral interventions may enable many children to be mainstreamed in a regular classroom placement to a larger extent than might otherwise be possible. Because both legal guidelines and current educational philosophy favor integration into regular settings to the fullest extent possible, this area would appear to be another point in favor of combining medications with behavioral approaches. Yet, comparative outcome studies of special-class-placed versus combined-treatment-mainstreamed children have not been conducted.

Because the problems of ADHD children have great implications for the functioning of family systems (Lang et al., 1989), and because family discord and hostility seem directly implicated in the genesis of aggression and conduct problems, we advocate investigations of the broadening of traditional behavioral parent-training approaches to family systems domains. At the level of the parents, communications skills, stress management, and anger control may all be important areas for direct intervention; at the level of the family system, considerations of boundaries, alliances, and communication patterns may need to be addressed.

Nearly all of the investigations of behavioral treatment approaches have focused on ADHD children of elementary school age. Studies of systematic behavioral treatment for preschoolers are needed to ascertain whether the negative course often associated with ADHD can be prevented with sufficient early intervention. In addition, we advocate that studies of ADHD adolescents who continue to exhibit both school- and home-based difficulties be undertaken.

Continued research into the efficacy of self-instructionally based cognitive interventions for ADHD does *not* appear to be warranted. Well-conducted investigations have failed to provide any evidence that typical cognitive interventions increment the efficacy of stimulant medication (Abikoff & Gittelman, 1985; Brown, Wynne, & Medenis, 1985), presumably because the cognitive interventions are themselves ineffective (Abikoff, 1987). Yet, as discussed earlier, cognitive-behavioral strategies designed to promote anger control and self-evaluation have produced short-term gains; these strategies may have a role in integrated, multimodal treatments. We should also point out that, in our view, individual, insight-oriented therapies are not important candidates for addition to combination interventions, given the absence of any indication for their effectiveness with ADHD.

Finally, as should be clear from our emphasis on the need for integration of behavioral and pharmacologic treatments, research on the long-term effects of behavioral and combined interventions is mandatory. Because ADHD and other externalizing disorders are best viewed as chronic in nature (see Kazdin, 1987), professionals, educators, and parents should begin to conceptualize interventions as being delivered over periods of years, rather than weeks or months. As a result, consideration needs to be given to the means for keeping families and schools actively involved in long-term treatments. Little is known about the factors that influence whether a parent will attend management classes and continue programming for the years that may be necessary and what variables determine the length of time a child will receive concurrent medication. Research into novel ideas for chronic interventions with ADHD children is needed; this area is likely to be a major direction for the future. In sum, for all of the reasons that we have discussed, we believe firmly that combined behavioral and pharmacologic interventions are required for ADHD. Research demonstrating the effectiveness of such integrated treatment is required to validate that belief.

REFERENCES

Abikoff, H. (1987). An evaluation of cognitive behavior therapy for hyperactive children. In B. B. Lahey & A. E. Kazdin (Eds.), *Advances in clinical child psychology* (pp. 171–216). New York: Plenum.

Abikoff, H., & Gittelman, R. (1985). The normalizing effects of methylphenidate on the classroom behavior of ADDH children. *Journal of Abnormal Child Psychology, 13,* 33–44.

Alexander, J. F., & Malouf, R. E. (1983). Intervention with children experiencing problems in personality and social development. In P. H. Mussen (Ed.), *Handbook of child psychology* (pp. 913–981). New York: Wiley.

American Psychiatric Association. (1980). *Diagnostic and statistical manual of mental disorders.* (3rd ed.). Washington, DC: Author.

American Psychiatric Association. (1987). *Diagnostic and statistical manual of mental disorders* (3rd ed. rev.). Washington, DC: Author.

Atkins, M. S., Pelham, W. E., & Licht, M. H. (1989). The differential validity of teacher ratings of inattention/overactivity and aggression. *Journal of Abnormal Child Psychology, 17,* 423–435.

Atkins, M. S., Pelham, W. E., & White, K. J. (1989). Hyperactivity and Attention Deficit Disorders. In M. Hersen (Ed.), *Psychological aspects of developmental and physical disabilities: A casebook* (pp. 137–156). California: Sage.

Barkley, R. A., Fischer, M., Newby, R. F., & Breen, M. J. (1988). Development of a multi-method clinical protocol for assessing stimulant drug response in ADD children. *Journal of Clinical Child Psychology, 17,* 14–24.

Barkley, R. A., Karlsson, J., Strzelecki, E., & Murphy, J. V. (1984). Effects of age and Ritalin dosage on the mother–child interactions of hyperactive children. *Journal of Consulting and Clinical Psychology, 52,* 739–749.

Brown, R. T., Wynne, M. E., & Medenis, R. (1985). Methylphenidate and cognitive therapy: A comparison of treatment approaches with hyperactive boys. *Journal of Abnormal Child Psychology, 13,* 69–88.

Campbell, S. B., & Werry, J. S. (1986). Attention deficit disorder (hyperactivity). In H. Quay & J. Werry (Eds.), *Psychopathological disorders of childhood* (3rd ed.; pp. 111–155). New York: Wiley.

Carlson, C. L., Pelham, W. E., Milich, R., & Dixon, M. J. (1990, January). *Single and combination effects of methylphenidate and behavior therapy on the classroom behavior, academic performance and self-evaluations of children with ADHD.* Paper presented at the annual meeting of the Society for Research in Child and Adolescent Psychiatry, Costa Mesa, CA.

Conners, C. K., & Wells, K. C. (1986). *Hyperkinetic children: A neuropsychosocial approach.* Beverly Hills: Sage.

Copeland, L., Wolraich, M., Lindgren, S., Milich, R., & Woolson, R. (1987). Pediatricians' reported practices in the assessment and treatment of attention deficit disorders. *Journal of Developmental and Behavioral Pediatrics, 8,* 191–197.

Cunningham, C. E., Siegel, L. S., & Offord, D. R. (1985). A developmental dose-response analysis of the effects of methylphenidate on the peer interactions of attention deficit disordered boys. *Journal of Child Psychology and Psychiatry, 26,* 955–972.

Douglas, V. I. (1983). Attentional and cognitive problems. In M. Rutter (Ed.), *Developmental neuropsychiatry* (pp. 280–329). New York: Guilford.

Firestone, P., Kelly, M. J., Goodman, J. T., & Davey, J. (1981). Differential effects of parent training and stimulant medication with hyperactives. *Journal of the American Academy of Child Psychiatry, 20,* 135–147.

Gittelman, R., Abikoff, H., Pollack, E., Klein, D. F., Katz, S., & Mattes, J. (1980). A controlled trial of behavior modification and methylphenidate in hyperactive children. In C. K. Whalen & B. Henker (Eds.), *Hyperactive children: The social ecology of identification and treatment* (pp. 221–243). New York: Academic Press.

Gittelman, R., & Kanner, A. (1986). Psychopharmacotherapy. In H. Quay & J. Werry (Eds.), *Psychopathological disorders of childhood 3rd edition* (pp. 455–495). New York: Wiley.

Hinshaw, S. P. (1987). On the distinction between attentional deficits/hyperactivity and conduct problems/aggression in child psychopathology. *Psychological Bulletin, 101,* 443–463.

Hinshaw, S. P., Buhrmester, D., & Heller, T. (1989). Anger control in response to verbal provocation: Effect of stimulant medication for boys with ADHD. *Journal of Abnormal Child Psychology, 17,* 393–407.

Hinshaw, S. P., & Erhardt, D. (in press-a). Behavioral treatment of attention deficit-hyperactivity disorder. In V. B. Van Hasselt & M. Hersen (Eds.), *Handbook of behavior therapy and pharmacotherapy with children: A comparative analysis.* New York: Grune & Stratton.

Hinshaw, S. P., & Erhardt, D. (in press-b). Attention deficit-hyperactivity disorder. In P. C. Kendall (Ed.), *Child and adolescent therapy: Cognitive-behavioral procedures.* New York: Guilford.

Hinshaw, S. P., Henker, B., & Whalen, C. K. (1984a). Cognitive-behavioral and pharmacologic interventions for hyperactive boys: Comparative and combined effects. *Journal of Consulting and Clinical Psychology, 52,* 739–749.

Hinshaw, S. P., Henker, B., & Whalen, C. K. (1984b). Self-control in hyperactive boys in anger-inducing situations: Effects of cognitive-behavioral training and of methylphenidate. *Journal of Abnormal Child Psychology, 12,* 55–77.

Hinshaw, S. P., Henker, B., Whalen, C. K., Erhardt, D., & Dunnington, R. E. (1989). Aggressive, prosocial, and nonsocial behavior in hyperactive boys: Dose effects of methylphenidate in naturalistic settings. *Journal of Consulting and Clinical Psychology, 57,* 636–643.

Johnston, C. (1988). A behavioral-family systems approach to assessment: Maternal characteristics associated with externalizing behavior in children. In R. J. Prinz (Ed.), *Advances in behavioral assessment of children and families, Vol. 4* (pp. 161–187). Greenwich, CT: JAI Press.

Kazdin, A. E. (1987). Treatment of antisocial behavior in children: Current status and future directions. *Psychological Bulletin, 102,* 187–203.

Krehbiel, G., & Milich, R. (1986). Issues in the assessment and treatment of socially rejected children. In R. Prinz (Ed.), *Advances in behavioral assessment of children and families, Vol. 2* (pp. 249–270). Greenwich, CT: JAI Press.

Lahey, B. B., Delameter, A., & Kupfer, D. (1981). Intervention strategies with hyperactive and learning-disabled children. In S. M. Turner, K. S. Calhoun, & H. E. Adams (Eds.), *Handbook of clinical behavior therapy* (pp. 607–634). New York: Wiley.

Lang, A. R., Pelham, W. E., Johnston, C., & Gelernter, S. (1989). Levels of adult alcohol consumption induced by interactions with child confederates exhibiting normal versus externalizing behaviors. *Journal of Abnormal Psychology, 98,* 294–299.

Loney, J. (1987). Hyperactivity and aggression in the diagnosis of attention deficit disorder. In B. B. Lahey & A. E. Kazdin (Eds.), *Advances in clinical child psychology, Vol. 10* (pp. 99–135). New York: Plenum.

Milich, R., & Landau, S. (1982). Socialization and peer relations in the hyperactive child. In K. Gadow & I. Bialer (Eds.), *Advances in learning and behavioral disabilities, Vol. 1* (pp. 283–339). Greenwich, CT: JAI Press.

Milich, R., Wolraich, M., & Lindgren, S. (1986). Sugar and hyperactivity: Critical review of empirical findings. *Clinical Psychology Review, 6,* 473–513.

Nichols, P. L., & Chen, T. (1981). *Minimal brain dysfunction: A prospective study.* Hillsdale, NJ: Erlbaum.

O'Leary, K. D., & O'Leary, S. G. (1977). *Classroom management: The successful use of behavior modification* (2nd ed.). New York: Pergamon.

O'Leary, S. G., & Pelham, W. E. (1978). Behavior therapy and withdrawal of stimulant medication with hyperactive children. *Pediatrics, 61,* 211–217.

Paternite, C. E., & Loney, J. (1980). Childhood hyperkinesis: Relationships between symptomatology and home environment. In C. K. Whalen & B. Henker (Eds.), *Hyperactive children: The social ecology of identification and treatment* (pp. 105–141). Orlando: Academic Press.

Patterson, G. (1974). Intervention for boys with conduct problems: Multiple settings, treatment and criteria. *Journal of Consulting and Clinical Psychology, 42,* 471–481.

Patterson, G. (1982). *Coercive family process.* Eugene, OR: Castalia.

Pelham, W. E. (1986). The effects of stimulant drugs on learning and achievement in hyperactive and learning-disabled children. In J. K. Torgesen & B. Wong (Eds.), *Psychological and educational perspectives on learning disabilities* (pp. 259–295). Orlando: Academic Press.

Pelham, W. E., Bender, M. E., Caddell, J., Booth, S., & Moorer, S. (1985). The dose-response effects of methylphenidate on classroom academic and social behavior in children with attention deficit disorder. *Archives of General Psychiatry, 42,* 948–952.

Pelham, W. E., & Hoza, J. (1987). Behavioral assessment of psychostimulant effects on ADD children in a summer day treatment program. In R. Prinz (Ed.), *Advances in behavioral assessment of children and families, Vol. 3* (pp. 3–33). Greenwich, CT: JAI Press.

Pelham, W. E., McBurnett, K., Harper, G. W., Murphy, D. A., Milich, R., Clinton, J., & Thiele, C. (1990). Methylphenidate and baseball playing in ADD children: Who's on first? *Journal of Consulting and Clinical Psychology, 58,* 130–133.

Pelham, W. E., & Murphy, H. A. (1986). Behavioral and pharmacological treatment of attention deficit and conduct disorders. In M. Hersen (Ed.), *Pharmacological and behavioral treatment: An integrative approach* (pp. 108–148). New York: Wiley.

Pelham, W. E., Murphy, D. A., Vannatta, K., Milich, R., Licht, B. G., Gnagy, E. M., Greenslade, K. E., Greiner, A. R., & Vodde-Hamilton, M. (1991). Methylphenidate and attributions in boys with attention deficit-hyperactivity disorder. *Journal of Consulting and Clinical Psychology,* accepted pending revision.

Pelham, W. E., Schnedler, R. W., Bender, M. E., Miller, J., Nilsson, D., Budrow, M., Ronnei, M., Paluchowski, C., & Marks, D. (1988). The combination of behavior therapy and methylphenidate in the treatment of hyperactivity: A therapy outcome study. In L. Bloomingdale & R. Klorman (Eds.), *Attention deficit disorders, Vol. III.* London: Pergamon.

Pelham, W. E., Schnedler, R. W., Bologna, N., & Contreras, A. (1980). Behavioral and stimulant treatment of hyperactive children: A therapy study with methylphenidate probes in a within-subject design. *Journal of Applied Behavior Analysis, 13,* 221–236.

Pfiffner, L. J., & O'Leary, S. G. (in press). Educational placement and classroom management. In R. A. Barkley (Ed.), *Attention deficit hyperactivity disorders: A handbook for diagnosis and treatment.* New York: Guilford.

Quay, H. C. (1986). A critical analysis of DSM-III as a taxonomy of psychopathology in childhood and adolescence. In T. Millon & G. L. Klerman (Eds.), *Contemporary directions in psychopathology: Toward the DSM-IV* (pp. 151–166). New York: Guilford.

Robinson, P. W., Newby, T. J., & Ganzell, S. L. (1981). A token system for a class of underachieving hyperactive children. *Journal of Applied Behavior Analysis, 14,* 307–315.

Rosen, L. A., O'Leary, S. G., Joyce, S. A., Conway, G., & Pfiffner, L. J. (1984). The importance of prudent negative consequences for maintaining the appropriate behavior of hyperactive students. *Journal of Abnormal Child Psychology, 12,* 581–604.

Safer, D. J., & Krager, J. M. (1988). A survey of medication treatment for hyperactive/inattentive students. *Journal of the American Medical Association, 260,* 2256–2258.

Schell, R. M., Pelham, W. E., Bender, M. E., Andree, J., Law, T., & Robbins, F. (1986). The concurrent assessment of behavioral and psychostimulant interventions: A controlled case study. *Behavioral Assessment, 8,* 373–384.

Sullivan, M. A., & O'Leary, S. G. (1989). Differential maintenance following reward and cost token programs with children. *Behavior Therapy, 21,* 139–151.

Swanson, J., & Kinsbourne, M. (1979). The cognitive effects of stimulant drugs on hyperactive (inattentive) children. In G. Hale & M. Lewis (Eds.), *Attention and the development of cognitive skills.* New York: Plenum.

Taylor, E. A. (1986). The causes and development of hyperactive behaviour. In E. A. Taylor (Ed.), *The overactive child* (pp. 118–160). Oxford, England: Blackwell.

Wahler, R. G. (1980). The insular mother: Her problems in parent–child treatment.

Journal of Applied Behavior Analysis, 13, 207–219.

Weiss, G., & Hechtman, L. (1986). *Hyperactive children grown up.* New York: Guilford.

Whalen, C. K. (1989). Attention deficit and hyperactivity disorders. In T. H. Ollendick & M. Hersen (Eds.), *Handbook of child psychopathology* (2nd ed.; pp. 131–169). New York: Plenum.

Whalen, C. K., Henker, B., Buhrmester, D., Hinshaw, S. P., Huber, A., & Laski, K. (1989). Does stimulant medication improve the peer status of hyperactive children? *Journal of Consulting and Clinical Psychology, 57,* 545–549.

Whalen, C. K., Henker, B., & Hinshaw, S. P. (1985). Cognitive-behavior therapies for hyperactive children: Premises, problems, and prospects. *Journal of Abnormal Child Psychology, 13,* 391–410.

Witt, J. C. (1986). Teachers' resistance to the use of school-based interventions. *Journal of School Psychology, 24,* 37–44.

Zametkin, A. J., & Rapoport, J. L. (1986). The pathophysiology of attention deficit disorder with hyperactivity: A review. In B. Lahey & A. Kazdin (Eds.), *Advances in clinical child psychology, Vol. 9* (pp. 177–216). New York: Plenum.

CHAPTER 15

Conduct Disorder

JEAN E. DUMAS

What do you do with a disobedient, rude, destructive, uncooperative, and restless child, a child who seeks attention and dominates others, and who regularly fights, lies, or steals? Many parents and teachers ask this question every day, as they attempt to deal with the disruptions or rule violations of conduct disorder children. Not surprisingly, many clinicians are asked this question also.

Conduct disorder was one of the first childhood disorders to be clearly described in the clinical literature and one of the first ones for which specific treatment approaches were recommended (e.g., Aichorn, 1935; Symonds, 1939). In spite of the considerable clinical and research attention it has been receiving for decades, however, conduct disorder represents a growing challenge, not only for clinicians and researchers but for society as a whole. This challenge is illustrated in a recent review (Loeber, 1990) which reports that, since the 1960s, American society has seen major increases in juvenile crime, incarceration, recidivism, drug use, suicide, and overall mortality rate.

Although the past two decades have seen major advances in the assessment and treatment of aggressive, antisocial children and their families (e.g., Dumas, 1989; Kazdin, 1987; McMahon & Forehand, 1988), the task remains formidable in view of the scope of the problem. Available evidence indicates that many forms of therapy may help such children and are clearly preferable to no intervention at all (Feldman, Caplinger, & Wodarski, 1983; Kazdin, 1990; Tuma, 1989). However, the same evidence suggests that, when differences among approaches are found, these tend to favor behavioral over nonbehavioral interventions. This is not to say that nonbehavioral approaches are ineffective with aggressive, antisocial children, but more simply that there is generally more empirical evidence for the overall effectiveness of behavioral approaches than there is for other forms of intervention.

This chapter offers a survey of the current state of knowledge in the description and in the clinical management of conduct disorder from a behavioral perspective. The chapter is divided into three major sections. The first section describes the syndrome, outlines the developmental trajectories that are believed to lead to onset, and reviews the clinical and social dimensions of the disorder. In so doing, it highlights the considerable diversity of behaviors that are generally subsumed under the broad label of conduct disorder. The second section presents the three major behavioral interventions that have been used in the management of the disorder: parent training, social skills training, and cognitive skills training. Each intervention is described, as are the theoretical assumptions on which it is based and the research findings that support it. The strengths and limitations of these approaches are discussed, with particular emphasis on the factors that are known to influence the suitability of behavior therapy for aggressive, antisocial children and their families. In the last section, some of the enhancements that have been proposed to increase the effectiveness of these behavioral interventions are reviewed. They point to important innovations in the field and are indicative of the trends that future interventions are likely to follow.

THE PARAMETERS OF CONDUCT DISORDER

Defining Conduct Disorder

Traditional classification systems of childhood disorders, of which DSM-III and DSM-III-R (American Psychiatric Association, 1980, 1987) are the best known, commonly describe a class of disorders characterized by repeated conflicts between the child and his or her parents, siblings, peers, or authority figures. The most recent version of the DSM to have been submitted to empirical evaluations, DSM-III-R (American Psychiatric Association, 1987), describes aggressive, antisocial behavior in children and adolescents under the broad diagnostic class of Disruptive Behavior Disorders, a class that includes Attention Deficit Hyperactivity Disorder (ADHD), Oppositional Defiant Disorder (ODD), and Conduct Disorder (CD). The last two disorders are of relevance here. ODD refers to a behavior pattern characterized by repeated disobedience, negativism, provocation, and opposition to authority. CD, which often includes important features of ODD, is characterized by repeated violations of the basic rights of others and/or of major social rules. It is not only a more severe disorder than ODD, but one in which most symptoms can have major legal repercussions. DSM-III-R identifies three subtypes of CD: solitary aggressive, group, and undifferentiated. Although it describes this last subtype as a remainder category, DSM-III-R notes that it may comprise more children than the other two subtypes.*

Like many other psychiatric diagnoses, the DSM-III-R diagnoses of ODD and CD are inherently limited by the fact that they are essentially social in nature. When applied to a particular child or adolescent, these diagnoses reflect not only the individual's specific behavior pattern, but also the social norms and expectations of the person who is expressing concerns about that individual and/or those of the person who is making the diagnosis. Some studies indicate, in fact, that a parent's perception of a child's maladjustment may discriminate better than directly observed child behavior between children referred for psychological services and normative controls (e.g., Delfini, Bernal, & Rosen, 1976; Griest, Forehand, Wells, & McMahon, 1980). In other words, the diagnoses of ODD and CD necessarily reflect in part the social context in which they are made and the perceptions of those who make them. The typical behaviors exhibited by aggressive, antisocial children and adolescents are probably

---

*Throughout this chapter, the abbreviations ODD and CD are used to refer to the DSM-III-R diagnostic categories. The label "conduct disorder" is used in a broader sense to refer to aggressive and nonaggressive antisocial behavior that typically includes a variety of symptoms of ODD and CD.

Preparation of this manuscript was supported in part by grants from the Social Sciences and Humanities Research Council of Canada and the Medical Research Council of Canada.

frowned upon by a majority of members in most if not all societies, but they may be welcomed by some, and even adaptive in specific contexts (Fordham & Ogbu, 1986; Prinz & Miller, in press).

Despite this limitation, there is consistent evidence to support the validity of the DSM-III-R diagnoses of ODD and CD. For example, in a recent multisite study of 177 boys aged 7 to 12 years referred to outpatient clinics, Lahey et al. (1990) found that a DSM-III-R diagnosis of CD was significantly associated with a history of police contacts, school suspensions, antisocial personality disorder in biological fathers, and criminal convictions in biological relatives. More generally, empirical support for the validity of the ODD and CD diagnoses comes from the large number of taxonomic studies of child and adolescent psychopathology now available. Backed by a long research tradition (e.g., Jenkins & Glickman, 1946), the taxonomic approach provides a statistical basis on which to isolate and define distinctive behavior disorders. As reviews (Achenbach & Edelbrock, 1978; Achenbach & McConaughy, 1987; Quay, Routh, & Shapiro, 1987) and large-scale, multisite studies of children and adolescents (Achenbach, Conners, Quay, Verhulst, & Howell, 1989; Achenbach, Verhulst, Baron, & Althaus, 1987) have shown, this empirical approach has consistently isolated two core syndromes whose symptoms closely overlap with the DSM-III-R symptoms of ODD and CD. These two syndromes, which are commonly labeled "Aggressive" and "Delinquent," have been found to apply to boys and girls aged 6 to 16 years, although they appear to be especially reliable for boys. Table 15.1 compares the DSM-III-R symptoms of ODD and CD with those of the aggressive and delinquent syndromes, illustrating the clear commonalities between the findings of the diagnostic and taxonomic approaches.

Developmental Trajectories to Conduct Disorder

Early vs. Late Starters

Growing evidence suggests that there are at least two distinct trajectories to adolescent CD, characterized by a history of early or late onset of behavior problems (for excellent reviews and discussions, see Loeber, 1988a, 1990). Briefly stated, there is strong empirical support to state that: (a) the early onset of behavior problems is one of the best predictors of high frequency, severity, and duration of aggressive, antisocial behavior in later childhood (White, Moffitt, Earls, Robins, & Silva, 1990), adolescence (LeBlanc & Frechette, 1989; Tolan, 1987; Tremblay et al., in press) and adulthood (Chaiken & Chaiken, 1984; Farrington, 1983; Wolfgang, Thornberry, & Figlio, 1987); and (b) children may follow different trajectories to conduct disorder, delinquency, and criminality, with some starting their "career" early, usually in the family, and others starting it later, through their association with a deviant peer group (Blumstein, Cohen, Roth, & Visher, 1986).

Early starters initially acquire most of their dysfunctional behavior patterns at home during the preschool years (see below) and generally exhibit some symptoms of ODD (especially defiance and aggressiveness) before those of CD. Their early symptoms are likely to become associated with interactional difficulties with teachers and peers when they enter school and are predictive of chronic aggressive, antisocial conduct and poor overall social and academic adjustment. Typically, the career of early starters is characterized by high innovation and low remission rates. They tend to engage in novel (and generally more serious) antisocial acts as time passes and are slow to desist from their deviant path, often becoming juvenile recidivists and, in many cases, adult offenders. In contrast, late starters do not begin

TABLE 15.1 Comparison of the DSM-III-R Symptoms of ODD and CD with the Symptoms of Aggression and Delinquency Commonly Described in Taxonomic Studies

DSM-III-R Disorders[1]	
Oppositional Defiant Disorder (ODD)	*Aggression (continued)*
loses temper	bullies
argues with adults	demands attention
defies/refuses adult requests/rules	disobedient at home
deliberately annoys others	doesn't feel angry
blames others for own mistakes	easily jealous
is touchy or easily annoyed	impulsive
is angry and resentful	loud
is spiteful or vindictive	screams
swears or uses obscene language	shows off
	starts fights
Conduct Disorder (CD)	stubborn, irritable
steals (without confrontation)	sudden mood changes
runs away from home	sulks
lies	swearing, obscenity
sets fires	talks too much
truancy	teases
breaks into someone else's property	temper tantrums
destroys others' things	*Delinquency*
cruel to animals	alcohol, drugs
sexually coercive	ban companions
uses weapons in fights	cheats, lies
initiates physical fights	destroys others' things
steals (with confrontation)	disobedient at school
physically cruel to people	runs away from home
	sets fires
Taxonomic Syndromes[2]	steals at home
Aggression	steals outside home
argues	truancy
brags, boasts	vandalism

[1]From *Diagnostic and Statistical Manual of Mental Disorders* (3rd ed. rev.; pp. 55, 57) by American Psychiatric Association, 1987, Washington, DC: Author. Copyright 1987 by American Psychiatric association. Reprinted by permission. Symptoms listed as they are in DSM-III-R.

[2]From "Replication of Empirically Derived Syndromes as a Basis for Taxonomy of Child/Adolescent Psychopathology" by T. M. Achenbach, C. K. Conners, H. C. Quay, F.C. Verhulst, and C. T. Howell, 1989. *Journal of Abnormal Child Psychology, 17*, p. 312. Copyright © 1989 by Journal of Abnormal Child Psychology. Reprinted by permission. Symptoms listed in alphabetical order.

their disruptive career before late childhood or early adolescence. Generally, they have a somewhat better overall adjustment but are strongly influenced by antisocial peers, with their family playing only a secondary role in their developmental progression. In most cases, they have at least minimal social and academic skills and tend to limit their antisocial conduct to nonaggressive acts such as theft, truancy, and substance abuse. In addition, they have lower innovation and higher remission rates than early starters and thus tend to present problems that are more transient in nature and somewhat less severe than their more precocious counterparts (Elliott, Huizinga, & Ageton, 1985; Loeber, 1988a; Patterson, Capaldi, & Bank, 1991; Tolan, 1987).

The Developmental Trajectory of Early Starters

We consider further the developmental trajectory of early starters, because they are generally the focus of the majority of behavioral intervention programs. Although there are differences in the specific learning mechanisms that are assumed to be responsible for the acquisition and maintenance of aggressive, antisocial child behavior in early starters, there is widespread agreement that such behavior can be traced back to early dysfunctional parent–child interactions (Forehand & Long, 1988; Patterson, 1986; Wahler & Dumas, 1986a, 1989).

The role that genetic factors may play in the development of antisocial behavior remains a topic of considerable debate (DiLalla & Gottesman, 1991; Vandenberg & Crowe, 1989; Widom, 1991). However, irrespective of the extent to which a propensity to behavior problems may or may not be inherited, it would appear that many if not most early starters have an almost life-long history of behavioral difficulties. From birth, or soon thereafter, they are often described as irregular or irritable babies who do not respond well to comfort, care, or limits (Bates, Maslin, & Frankel, 1985; Thomas & Chess, 1982). In many families, especially those in which parents have minimal child-rearing skills and are exposed to multiple sources of stress (e.g., parental psychopathology, marital discord, socioeconomic disadvantage, social isolation), these adverse temperamental features are likely to become associated with parent–child conflict, discipline problems, and inattentiveness/impulsivity by age 2 or 3; with aggressive-oppositional conduct before age 5; and with the maintenance of such conduct in later childhood (Bates & Bayles, 1984; Berger, 1985; Campbell, Breaux, Ewing, & Szumowski, 1986; Richman, Stevenson, & Graham, 1982) and adolescence (Maziade et al., 1990). Developmental studies are surprisingly rare in this area. However, recent developmental evidence (Campbell & Ewing, 1990; Dishion, 1990; Dodge, 1986) suggests that an early dysfunctional parent–child relationship is commonly accompanied by later deficits in the areas of affect regulation, social and cognitive skills, and academic readiness, and that these deficits are predictive of poor school and peer adjustment in the elementary school years. If these deficits are accompanied by chronic family stress, limited parental support for the child's social, cognitive, and academic development, and limited community support for such development (e.g., if the family lives in a disintegrated neighborhood and the child attends a school with a high proportion of deviant peers), the stage appears set for the maintenance and further refinement of an aggressive, antisocial behavior pattern that reaches beyond the family, persists throughout childhood, and often extends into adolescence and even adulthood (Kolvin, Miller, Fleeting, & Kolvin, 1988; Rutter & Giller, 1983).

Clinical and Social Dimensions of Conduct Disorder

There is widespread agreement that CD and, to a lesser degree, ODD are very serious behavior disorders, with adverse consequences not only for individual children and their families, but for society as a whole. This seriousness is highlighted by well-established findings, which provide the clinical and social context within which any intervention invariably takes place.

Extent of the Problem

ODD and CD together have a prevalence rate ranging from 8% to 12% in the general population, according to the most recent epidemiological evidence available (Costello, 1990; Tuma, 1989). These estimates are based on large-scale studies conducted in different Western countries. In addition, although aggressive, antisocial conduct has traditionally been much more prevalent in boys than girls, it would seem that CD has dramatically increased in prevalence over the past decades in both genders, reducing the traditional difference in this area (Robins, 1986).

Stability, Chronicity

As has already been stated, unlike some other childhood disorders, aggressive, antisocial conduct in general, and CD in particular, show little or no spontaneous recovery but rather remain stable or worsen over time (Loeber, 1982; Olweus, 1979), generally showing increased resistance to change with age (Kazdin, 1985). Although the majority of individuals who qualify for a diagnosis of CD do not become high-rate offenders in adolescence or adulthood, children—and particularly boys—who exhibit behavior problems from an early age and in a variety of settings are most likely to continue to manifest such problems over time (Kelso & Stewart, 1986; Loeber & Dishion, 1983; Loeber, Tremblay, Gagnon, & Charlebois, 1989; Moskowitz, Schwartzman, & Ledingham, 1985; Roff & Wirt, 1984; Stattin & Magnusson, 1989; Tolan, 1987). In other words, the younger and the more deviant a child is, the less likely he or she is to revert spontaneously to a pattern of nondeviant conduct. In addition, there is now considerable evidence to show that this stability can extend beyond the individual, because patterns of antisocial behavior often cross generations (Huesmann, Eron, Lefkowitz, & Walder, 1984; Kazdin, 1987; Wahler & Dumas, 1986b).

Additional Problems

Not surprisingly, CD tends to be as pervasive as it is stable. In younger children, aggressive, antisocial behavior is commonly associated with limited intelligence, limited academic achievement, and poor school adjustment. For example, early starters have been found to score lower on standardized measures of intellectual functioning (verbal IQ in particular) than their nondeviant peers (Richman et al., 1982), to present major academic difficulties, especially in reading (Ledingham & Schwartzman, 1984; Sturge, 1982), and to have to repeat grades very often (Safer, 1984). Measures of intellectual and academic performance are predictive of later conduct problems (Stanton, Feehan, McGee, & Silva, 1990), as are overall measures of social adjustment in school, such as teacher ratings of disruptiveness, defiance, and impulsivity (Farnworth, Schweinhart, & Berrueta-Clement, 1985; Spivack, Marcus, & Swift, 1986). Although an association between poor academic achievement and conduct disorder has been clearly established, the extent to which the link may be causal is unclear, because recent longitudinal evidence suggests that low achievement in the early grades predicts antisocial attitudes and values in adolescence, rather than delinquent conduct per se (Tremblay et al., in press).

Comorbidity studies have found that many conduct disorder children also present additional dysfunctions such as attention-deficit hyperactivity (ADHD) and depression. A large number of studies have noted that a considerable overlap exists between conduct disorder and ADHD (Moffitt, 1990; Prinz, Connor, & Wilson, 1981; Szatmari, Boyle, & Offord, 1989). Working with a sample of 7- to 13-year-olds and relying on careful diagnostic procedures, Shapiro and Garfinkel (1986) found that 45% of children who qualified for a diagnosis of ODD or CD qualified also for a diagnosis of ADHD. Similarly, in a large epidemiological study conducted in Canada, Offord and his colleagues (Szatmari et al., 1989) found a comparable degree of diagnostic overlap: 59% for boys and 56% for girls, aged 4 to 11; and 30% for boys and 37% for girls, aged 12 to 16. It would appear that

ADHD is a diagnostic cofeature of both concurrent and predictive importance. For example, Walker, Lahey, Hynd, and Frame (1987) found that children who received a dual diagnosis of CD and ADHD (on the basis of DSM-III, rather than DSM-III-R criteria) presented more numerous and severe antisocial behaviors and displayed more physical aggression than children who received a diagnosis of CD only, even though they were generally younger than CD-only children. Interestingly, the same research team (Lahey et al., 1988) reported that the fathers of dual diagnosis children were much more likely to have a history of aggression, illegal activity, and incarceration than the fathers of children with a single diagnosis. The importance of ADHD is also supported by longitudinal studies, which have shown that children who qualify for a dual diagnosis present aggressive, antisocial problems of greater variety and severity over time (Loeber, 1988b; McGee, Williams, & Silva, 1984) than children without ADHD features.

Although depressive comorbidity has not been investigated to the same extent, evidence indicates that boys (but not necessarily girls) who present conduct problems in childhood (Stewart, de Blois, Meardon, & Cummings, 1980) or adolescence (Chiles, Miller, & Cox, 1980) often qualify for a diagnosis of depressive disorder. Similarly, a substantial number of depressed children have also been found to qualify for a diagnosis of CD (Kovacs, Paulauskas, Gatsonis, & Richards, 1988; Marriage, Fine, Moretti, & Haley, 1986; Puig-Antich, 1982). It would appear that depressive comorbidity in children and adolescents ranges from 15% to 33%, depending on the reference population, the level of depressive symptomatology required to establish a dual diagnosis, and whether comorbidity is established on the basis of a codiagnosis of major depressive disorder or dysthymic disorder, or of major depressive disorder only.

Taken together, the evidence just reviewed shows that conduct disorder children commonly exhibit additional difficulties of considerable importance. Most of these difficulties remain evident in older children and adolescents, but they are then compounded by additional problems, such as school dropout, delinquency, drug abuse, and teenage parenthood (Cairns, Cairns, & Neckerman, 1989; Dishion & Loeber, 1985; Elliott et al., 1985; Robins, 1981).

Costs

Finally, it should be obvious that, with its many ramifications, CD is associated with enormous psychological, social, and economic costs. For example, aggressive, antisocial children and adolescents represent approximately half of all youth referrals for mental health services (Robins, 1981). Costs extend far beyond those of psychological and psychiatric services, however, and include remedial education, law enforcement, and harm to self, others, and property (Prinz & Miller, in press). Costs increase even further when antisocial behavior continues into adulthood, as it does for about half of the most antisocial adolescents (Robins & Ratcliff, 1980).

Core Features of Conduct Disorder

Most if not all aggressive, antisocial children present a variety of deficits that have an adverse impact on their daily functioning, as well as on that of others. In the case of early starters, these deficits typically fall into three major areas: overt and covert aggression, social skills, and cognitive skills.

Overt and Covert Aggression

It has been known for a long time that dysfunctional interactional patterns are characteristic of families of aggressive, antisocial children (Patterson, 1982; Wahler & Dumas, 1987) and are usually the most prominent feature that distinguishes clinic-referred families from normative ones (Patterson, 1976a). Although researchers have assessed family functioning on a variety of dimensions, the parents of conduct disorder children have repeatedly been described as power-assertive and lax in their discipline. Specifically, the two variables of aversiveness and inconsistency have emerged as major dimensions of interest here (Dishion, 1990; Patterson, 1982; Wahler & Dumas, 1987). Antisocial children and their families commonly attempt to control each other's behavior by engaging in coercive interactions. Comparative studies have shown that aggressive, antisocial children are less likely to comply immediately to parental requests or commands, and that their parents often issue vague, unclear instructions that cannot readily be complied with (Dumas & Lechowicz, 1989; Griest et al., 1980). Parental vagueness and child noncompliance are regular antecedents of aversive interactions that are more frequent, last longer, and are more intense than those of normative families and, over time, provide repeated opportunities for deviant children to refine their coercive skills. In addition, parents have often been observed to respond to their children's disruptive acts in an inconsistent manner, by giving them both positive and negative attention. Exposure to parental inconsistency only serves to maintain rather than control antisocial behavior, because most children respond to it with increases rather than decreases in such behavior (Dumas, 1986a; Dumas & Wahler, 1985; Patterson, 1976a; Snyder, 1977).

A behavioral cluster characterized by child noncompliance and parental aversiveness and inconsistency may be the core feature of the interactional profile of early starters, at least at the beginning of their "career," but many parents of clinic-referred children express concerns about other deviant behaviors that do not lend themselves as easily to observation and measurement. These behaviors are covert-antisocial acts such as stealing, lying, cheating, and fire setting. Although covert-antisocial problems have not received much research attention to date, they have long been recognized as diagnostic features of CD (Kazdin & Esveldt-Dawson, 1986; Quay et al., 1987). Patterson (1982) and Loeber and Schmaling (1985a) have shown that children who present both overt- and covert-antisocial problems are characterized by more aversive family interactions than children who present one type of problem only. Loeber and Schmaling (1985b), Moore, Chamberlain, and Mukai (1979), and Stouthamer-Loeber, Loeber, and Green (1989) found that covert problems in childhood were predictive of delinquent offenses in adolescence.

Social Skills Deficits

When they enter school, early starters have been observed to exhibit, in their interactions with teachers and peers, behavior problems similar to the ones they manifest in their family. Broadly speaking, their behavior reflects major social skills deficits, as evidenced by their tendency to ignore or defy adult authority (Gaffney & McFall, 1981) and to lack effective, socially acceptable means of interacting with peers (Carlson, Lahey, & Neeper, 1984). Considerable evidence from both observational and sociometric studies indicates that aggression toward peers often leads quickly to peer rejection and that, once established, peer rejection tends to be maintained across the school years (Coie, Belding, & Underwood, 1988; Hymel, Wagner, & Butler, 1990; Ladd, Price, & Hart, 1990). As is the case for parental aversiveness and inconsistency, far from teaching disruptive children to moderate their aggression, rejection tends to invite further escalations in aggression on the part of ODD and CD children (Dodge & Coie, 1987), thereby only reinforcing their already deviant mode of interaction.

This is not to say that aggressive children are always rejected by their peers or that all rejected children are necessarily aggressive, but more simply that aggression is one of the best predictors (if not the best) of peer rejection, especially after the preschool years (Coie et al., 1988), and of long-term problems, such as delinquency, school dropout, and police contacts (Kupersmidt & Coie, 1990).

Cognitive Skills Deficits

To the behavioral excesses and social skills deficits of early starters, one must add important cognitive skills deficits. Briefly stated, aggressive, antisocial children and adolescents tend to misperceive the actions of others (Dodge, 1985). Specifically, they have been found to extract a limited amount of information from social situations and to attend to aggressive cues at the expense of other cues in their environment (Dodge & Newman, 1981; Gouze, 1987). In keeping with this cognitive bias, they often attribute hostile intent to others, especially in socially ambiguous situations, and tend to minimize their own aggression while perceiving their peers as more aggressive than themselves (Dodge, 1980; Dodge & Frame, 1982; Lochman, 1987). Not surprisingly, they find it difficult to offer prosocial solutions to interpersonal conflicts (Hogan & Quay, 1984), to take a different perspective from their own (Kennedy, 1982; Spivack, Platt, & Shure, 1976), to show empathy (Ellis, 1982) or, more generally, to engage in effective social problem solving (Joffe, Dobson, Fine, Marriage, & Haley, 1990; Richard & Dodge, 1982; Spivack & Shure, 1982). This problem-solving deficit is illustrated by the tendency of conduct disorder children to deal with conflictual situations by resorting to physical actions that are aggressive in nature, rather than by relying on verbal assertiveness; to evaluate aggressive solutions to interpersonal more positively, and prosocial solutions more negatively; and to respond to anger-provoking situations by exhibiting greater arousal and aggression than normative controls (Asarnow & Callan, 1985; Deluty, 1983; Klaczynski & Cummings, 1989).

BEHAVIORAL INTERVENTIONS FOR CONDUCT DISORDER

Behavioral interventions for conduct disorder children and adolescents have a history as long as that of the child behavior therapy movement itself (for reviews of early developments in this field, see Davidson & Seidman, 1974; Gelfand & Hartman, 1968; Graziano, 1975). From the beginning of the movement, behaviorally oriented clinicians and researchers have attempted to use operant and social-learning methods to address some of the most prominent features of the disorder, applying these methods in clinical (Patterson, 1974), residential (Philips, 1968), and community (Fo & O'Donnell, 1974; Stumphauzer, 1973) settings. Reviews of clinical studies, which are of interest here, have shown that, although the available evidence is limited by major substantive and methodological issues (Dumas, 1989; Gordon & Arbuthnot, 1987; Kazdin, 1987), several behavioral interventions have achieved significant successes. This is particularly true of interventions that have sought to address the behavioral excesses, or the social or cognitive deficits, of conduct disorder children and adolescents. These interventions represent the three major clinical approaches to the management of the disorder from a behavioral perspective: parent training, social skills training, and cognitive skills training.

Parent Training

Parent training (PT) makes the fundamental assumption that, whether normal or dysfunctional, a child's behavior cannot be understood apart from the social system in which he or she interacts (Dumas, 1989). In keeping with evidence that the family plays a major role in the development and/or maintenance of aggression and antisocial conduct, PT seeks to control a child's disruptive behavior by modifying the manner in which parents interact with the child (Dumas, 1989).

Although a large number of PT programs have been implemented and evaluated (Blechman, 1985; Eyberg & Boggs, 1989; Forehand & McMahon, 1981; Patterson, 1976b), most of them are of relevance to children, rather than adolescents, and generally address the symptoms of ODD rather than CD. Despite important differences in program parameters, PT approaches share the goals of teaching parents to: (a) describe their child's positive and aversive behavior in observable terms; (b) observe and record instances of such behavior; and (c) respond contingently and consistently to the behaviors they observe. The overall goal is obviously to increase prosocial behaviors (e.g., compliance, completing chores, positive sibling interactions), decrease antisocial behaviors (e.g., defiance, temper tantrums, aggression), and, in some cases, deal effectively with additional difficulties (e.g., impulsivity, bedwetting, language delays). Teaching takes place individually or in groups, in the family's home or in an institutional setting, and relies on a variety of clinical skills, such as interviewing, problem solving, modeling, role playing, guided practice with the child, and homework assignments. Throughout training, parents are taught to use specific operant or social learning techniques, including positive reinforcement (e.g., praise, tokens, tangible rewards), ignoring and distraction, punishment (e.g., time out, loss of privileges, logical consequences, mild spanking), contingency contracting, and family communication skills (e.g., information exchange, behavior management, problem solving).

In carefully designed and implemented programs, a family's progress is monitored throughout treatment with the help of multiple measures and the family is followed-up for several months, if not years, after termination to ensure that therapeutic change is maintained over time.

Reviews of the literature have shown that PT provides a clearly effective means of changing aggressive, antisocial behavior, at least in younger children (Kazdin, 1985; Sanders & James, 1983). This conclusion appears particularly reliable in view of the fact that most studies have been conducted by independent research teams and have documented positive results on the basis of multiple outcome measures, such as behavioral records collected by parents at home, direct home and school observations, and standardized questionnaires completed by parents and teachers.

In one of the first systematic evaluations of PT, Patterson (1974) worked with the parents of 27 boys (ages unspecified) who presented a variety of oppositional-defiant behaviors at home and provided consultation to the teachers of 14 of them for similar school problems. Direct observations of the children's behavior in both settings showed that the average frequency of home problems had decreased to within the normal range at the end of treatment and remained within that range during a 1-year follow-up, and that comparable improvements had been observed in school. This study had important methodological shortcomings (e.g., lack of control group, significant attrition in follow-up), but its results were replicated later in more carefully controlled evaluations (Fleischman, 1981; Fleischman & Szykula, 1981; Patterson, Chamberlain, & Reid, 1982; Patterson & Fleischman, 1979). For example, Patterson et al. (1982) randomly assigned 19 children (aged 3 to 12 years) who presented aggressive behavior of clinical intensity at home either to a structured PT program or to a variety of clinical services available in their community. Comparisons of direct observation and parental report measures available for both groups at the beginning and end of treatment showed that PT families made significantly greater improvements on both types of measures than did the families who received community services.

Long-term positive outcome data have also been obtained by Forehand and his colleagues (Baum & Forehand, 1981; Forehand et al., 1979; Forehand & Long, 1988). In what may be the longest follow-up to date, Forehand and Long attempted to contact 43 families who had participated in a structured PT program 4.5 to 10.5 years earlier. Twenty-one families were contacted and accepted to participate in a comprehensive follow-up evaluation when the target child was between 11 and 14 years of age. Results indicated that these families were functioning similarly to a sample of control families on a variety of outcome measures. It should be noted, however, that a comparison of the families who took part in this follow-up with those who did not showed that when all these families were initially referred for treatment, the nonparticipants reported less marital satisfaction and their children were observed to be less compliant at the end of treatment. This suggests that the families who participated in this long-term follow-up may have been somewhat less stressed and their children less disruptive at the time they received PT and could, therefore, have benefited more from intervention.

Building on these earlier successes, Webster-Stratton and her colleagues (Webster-Stratton, Hollinsworth, & Kolpacoff, 1989; Webster-Stratton, Kolpacoff, & Hollinsworth, 1988) developed and evaluated the long-term effectiveness of three cost-effective PT programs for conduct disorder children (aged 3 to 8 years). These studies compared an individually self-administered videotape modeling treatment, a group discussion and videotape modeling treatment, and a group discussion only treatment, with a waiting-list control group. Ninety-four mothers and 60 fathers, approximately equally divided among the three treatments, completed both a posttreatment and a 1-year follow-up assessment, which included parent and teacher reports and home observations. Although the results favored somewhat the group discussion and videotape modeling approach, they showed that significant improvements were obtained immediately after intervention and were maintained at follow-up in all three treatments. Most important, improvements judged to be "clinically significant" were obtained with approximately two-thirds of the sample, on multiple measures of parental perception of child adjustment, maternal telephone reports of target negative child behaviors, and direct observations of parent–child interactions. These results are impressive, because they do not simply confirm the effectiveness of PT, but indicate that this form of intervention can be very cost-effective for a large proportion of families, a finding that should encourage its broad dissemination.

Social Skills Training

Social skills training (SST) shares many common features with PT but focuses on the direct modification of children's or adolescents' dysfunctional behaviors. In most SST programs, participants are asked to practice prosocial skills (e.g., to learn to engage in effective communication, to deal with anger or rejection, to interact with authority figures) in the presence and with the help of adults and peers. Complex skills are broken down into discrete behavioral components and taught through techniques such as direct instruction, coaching, modeling, reinforcement and, in some cases, mild punishment (e.g., privilege or point loss).

The majority of SST studies have not been conducted with conduct disorder subjects (for reviews, see Michelson & Wood, 1980; Tisdelle & St. Lawrence, 1986; Van Hasselt, Hersen, Whitehill, & Bellack, 1979). However, there is evidence that this approach may contribute to the reduction of aggressive, antisocial behavior, although it may only have a limited impact on direct measures of delinquency (rate of offending, recidivism, etc.) (Hollin, 1990). In one of the first SST studies, Sarason and Ganzer (1973) randomly assigned 192 institutionalized male first offenders (aged 15 to 18) to one of three groups: modeling with role play, discussion (without role play), or control. The first two groups met for 16 1-hour sessions during which they were taught how to deal with common social situations, such as resisting peer pressure and applying for a job. Both groups made significant improvements on a variety of relevant outcome measures. In particular, the two intervention groups had a significantly lower proportion of recidivists at a 3-year follow-up than did the control group or the population as a whole. These results are positive, but the lack of differences between the intervention groups makes it impossible to attribute the changes to SST directly.

In another study of male offenders, Spence and Marzillier (1981) randomly assigned 76 adolescents in residential care to SST, attention placebo, or no-treatment control groups, after having obtained independent evidence that all participants significantly lacked in social skills. Treatment was administered in small groups of four and lasted for 12 1-hour sessions. Initial results favored the SST group on several outcome measures, but most gains disappeared at 3- and 6-month follow-ups and no long-term group differences were obtained on independent measures of delinquency. Comparable results have been reported in other studies of delinquent adolescents (Ollendick & Hersen, 1979; Thelen, Fry, Dolinger, & Paul, 1976) and younger disruptive children (Bornstein, Bellack, & Hersen, 1980; Michelson, Sugai, Wood, & Kazdin, 1983). In this last study, 61 boys (aged 8 to 12 years) with a variety of social adjustment problems were randomly assigned to SST, cognitive skills training (see below), or nondirective therapy groups. Treatment, which was administered in small groups for 12 1-hour sessions, resulted in significant improvements in both behavioral interventions at termination. However, these improvements were only maintained by the SST group at a 1-year follow-up, a finding that supports the efficacy of SST but is difficult to interpret, because the sample did not include clearly antisocial children and no significant changes were obtained on behavioral measures at completion or follow-up. More recently, Hansen, St. Lawrence, and Christoff (1989) taught conversational skills to inpatient older children and adolescents with ODD or CD. The impact of treatment generalized to conversations with unfamiliar persons observed outside the training setting and was maintained at 1- and 3-month follow-ups. Unfortunately, no evidence was provided that these increases in prosocial skills were accompanied by reductions in conduct disorder symptoms.

Finally, mention must be made of Bierman's school-based work with rejected preadolescents (Bierman, 1986; Bierman & Furman, 1984; Bierman, Miller, & Stabb, 1987). Bierman and Furman (1984) provided training in communication skills that are necessary to positive peer relationships (such as expressing oneself, asking questions, and making leadership bids) to groups of fifth and sixth graders who had initially been identified as lacking these skills and being low in peer acceptance.

Training promoted skill acquisition and increased skillful social interaction and self-perception of social competence at posttreatment and at a 6-week follow-up. Similar results have been reported by Bierman et al. (1987) in a study that followed-up subjects for 1 year. Although they indicate that SST can improve peer interactions, both studies are limited by the fact that they did not target clearly aggressive, antisocial children and that the positive behavioral changes they obtained were not associated with corresponding increases in peer acceptance. This last limitation suggests that the reputation of rejected children may not change, despite the fact that their behavior may have improved as a function of intervention.

Cognitive Skills Training

Focusing on the manner in which children construct reality, rather than on their more immediate, overt behavior, cognitive skills training (CST) makes the fundamental assumption that human behavior is governed to a considerable extent by the manner in which individuals attend to and interpret environmental, and especially social, events (Dumas, 1989). Based on considerable evidence that aggressive, antisocial children tend to interpret their social reality in distorted ways, CST seeks to modify systematically these children's thought processes and, more specifically, their self-statements, i.e., what they say to themselves. They make use of training techniques similar to those of SST, such as direct instruction, coaching, modeling, guided practice, and direct and vicarious reinforcement.

Several CST programs have been developed and evaluated (Camp & Bash, 1985; Kendall & Braswell, 1985; Meichenbaum, 1977; Spivack et al., 1976). Many of them rely on self-instructional training procedures initially developed by Meichenbaum and Goodman (1971) to teach children to generate self-statements (or talk to themselves) in a structured manner. Training usually proceeds in a stepwise manner for children:

1. They observe the therapist perform a relevant task (e.g., approach a peer to request help) talking aloud;
2. They perform the same task under direct instruction from the therapist;
3. They perform the task again while instructing themselves aloud;
4. They perform the task while whispering to themselves only;
5. They perform the task while engaging in covert self-statements only.

More generally, CST programs teach children to engage in practical problem solving. Effective self-statements enable the child to identify the problem that needs to be solved, review and evaluate possible solutions, choose a solution, assess the outcome (and correct his or her performance, if necessary), and provide self-reinforcement (Kendall, Reber, McLeer, Epps, & Ronan, 1990).

Reviews of the CST literature indicate that this approach has been successful in modifying targeted cognitive processes and related task performance with both impulsive, hyperactive and aggressive, antisocial children (Gresham, 1985; Hobbs, Moguin, Tyroler, & Lahey, 1980; Meador & Ollendick, 1984; Urbain & Kendall, 1980). In a classic study, Meichenbaum and Goodman (1971) assigned 15 impulsive children (aged 7 to 9 years) to self-instructional training, attention-control, or no-treatment-control groups, and provided subjects in the two intervention groups with 4 half-hour training sessions over a 2-week period. CST had a significant impact on measures of intellectual functioning and impulsiveness at the end of treatment and at a 1-month follow-up, but no effect was obtained on direct measures and teacher ratings of classroom behavior.

In one of the first CST studies with conduct disorder children, Chandler (1973) randomly assigned 45 delinquent boys (aged 11 to 13 years) to one of three types of groups: experimental groups, which received training in perspective-taking skills (through role playing and videotaped feedback); attention placebo groups, which made documentary films about their neighborhood; or control groups. The intervention groups met in groups of five for a half-day each week for 10 weeks. Results showed that the CST subjects made significant improvements in their perspective-taking skills, compared to the other subjects, and that these improvements were associated with significant reductions in delinquent behavior 1½ years later. These results have not been replicated, although additional evidence of success has been obtained in more recent studies (Arbuthnot & Gordon, 1986; Kazdin, Bass, Siegel, & Thomas, 1989; Kazdin, Esveldt-Dawson, French, & Unis, 1987a; Lochman, Burch, Curry, & Lampron, 1984; Tisdelle & St. Lawrence, 1988).

The work conducted by Kazdin and his colleagues (Kazdin et al., 1987a, 1989) will be briefly summarized here because its methodological rigor is impressive. In the first study, they worked with 56 inpatient children (aged 7 to 13 years), 70% of whom qualified for a primary or secondary DSM-III diagnosis of CD. They randomly assigned these children to individually administered problem-solving training, nondirective relationship therapy, or a contact control condition. Each intervention consisted of 20 45-minute sessions. Results showed that CST was associated with significantly greater reductions in disruptive behavior at home and school and with increases in prosocial behavior and overall adjustment as compared to the other two conditions, at the end of treatment and at a 1-year follow-up. In 1989, Kazdin et al. reported a replication and extension of this study in which they offered problem-solving skills training, problem-solving skills training with in vivo practice, or nondirective relationship therapy to 112 children of the same age, 75% of whom had received a primary or secondary diagnosis of CD. Again, results showed that, at completion of treatment and 1 year later, both forms of CST significantly reduced disruptive behavior and increased prosocial behavior at home and school. However, an analysis of the clinical significance of the results of both studies indicated that, despite these improvements, the level of deviant behavior of the majority of children in all three conditions remained outside the normative range.

Finally, a meta-analytical review of 48 outcome studies of CST published or completed between 1971 and early 1987 (Dush, Hirt, & Schroeder, 1989) provides an excellent overview of the current status of this form of intervention. Over 80% of the studies reviewed focused on the treatment of aggressive, delinquent or impulsive, hyperactive youths. Results showed that CST surpassed placebo or control interventions in overall effectiveness by approximately half a standard deviation. This suggests that the average child who receives CST is better adjusted at the end of treatment than approximately 70% of children who receive a placebo or no intervention at all. However, the authors carefully qualified this broad conclusion by showing that:

1. The superiority of CST was most pronounced immediately after treatment and generally disappeared at follow-up;
2. The efficacy of CST was generally lower with aggressive or disruptive behavior problems than with other conditions, although delinquent children seemed to benefit from CST, an apparently inconsistent finding;

3. CST appeared to be more effective with preadolescents and adolescents than with younger children, an observation that could account in part for the inconsistency just noted;
4. The efficacy of CST was also related to variables such as therapist training, intervention setting, and type of outcome measures used.

Strengths of Behavioral Interventions

As the preceding review indicates, the major strength of the behavioral interventions that have been used to modify aggressive, antisocial conduct is undoubtedly that they are able to bring about significant changes in socially relevant behaviors. In many cases, these changes appear to be directly attributable to the interventions, are superior to the changes brought about by other treatments or the passage of time, and can be maintained over time and generalize to untreated contexts. Although positive, this broad conclusion must be qualified, because PT, SST, and CST have not been found to be equally effective.

There is considerable agreement that, to date, PT is the most effective behavioral treatment approach for conduct disorder, at least in preadolescence (Dumas, 1989; Kazdin, 1987). Because there is some evidence that CST may be more effective with adolescents than with children (Dush et al., 1989), these two approaches may be the treatments of choice, depending in part on the child's age. It does indeed seem reasonable to suggest that, during childhood, the focus of one's intervention may best be placed on the family, with parents as the main targets of intervention, and that, during adolescence, intervention may be most profitable if conducted directly with the person whose behavior one wants to modify. Even though clear demonstrations that SST can have lasting effects on aggressive, antisocial conduct are still lacking, this approach should also be considered in any comprehensive treatment approach, because SST has shown promise in modifying dysfunctional peer relationships, which are not directly targeted by PT or CST but are known to play a major role in the development and maintenance of conduct disorder.

A second strength of behavioral interventions for conduct disorder is that several well-researched programs are now available in manual form for individual, group, and—in the case of PT—self-administration. Some of these manuals include Barkley (1987), Blechman (1985), Dangel and Polster (1988), Fleischman, Horne, and Arthur (1987), and Forehand and McMahon (1981) for PT; Goldstein and Glick (1987), Lochman, Lampron, Gemmer, and Harris (1987), and Michelson et al. (1983) for SST; and Camp and Bash (1985), Kendall and Braswell (1985), and Spivack et al. (1976) for CST. Most of these manuals provide clinicians with clear rationales and detailed assessment and intervention procedures, ensuring that, if followed properly, the treatment is implemented and evaluated appropriately. This is not to say that anyone can become an effective behavioral therapist by simply turning to a published manual. Indeed, most clinicians and researchers who are familiar with these approaches would agree that a thorough knowledge of behavioral principles and prior experience in behavior therapy are necessary prerequisites (e.g., Forehand & Long, 1988), because therapist experience may discriminate between studies that obtained long-term positive results and studies that did not (Kazdin, 1985; Lutzker, McGimsey, McRae, & Campbell, 1983).

Another strength of behavioral interventions is that considerable data attest to their social validity. They are time-limited, goal-directed interventions, which are likely to be shorter and not as costly as more traditional psychotherapeutic approaches or residential treatment and are generally very well received by parents and teachers (Forehand & Long, 1988; Kazdin, 1985; McMahon & Forehand, 1983).

A final advantage of behavioral interventions, PT in particular, is that their benefits may not only be maintained over time but may generalize across settings (Forehand et al., 1979) or from target child to untreated sibling (Arnold, Levine, & Patterson, 1975). This issue has unfortunately not received the attention it deserves but, as it is clear that aggressive, antisocial problems often generalize rapidly, any possibility of positive generalization of treatment effects may counteract this negative trend.

Limitations of Behavioral Interventions

The behavioral interventions reviewed here are obviously not without limitations. The majority of studies that highlight these limitations have been conducted as part of ongoing research on PT. However, it is likely that many of the limitations this research has highlighted also apply to other behavioral approaches.

Broadly speaking, the limitations to be considered here reflect both child and contextual characteristics. At the child level, there is some evidence that children who present more severe problems at time of referral are generally less likely to benefit from intervention (Dush et al., 1989; Patterson, 1982) and that available treatments may generally be more effective in developing specific skills in children or parents than in modifying the adverse outcomes associated with aggressive, antisocial conduct (Hollin, 1990). For example, Patterson indicated that stealers may benefit less from PT than children whose conduct disorder is limited to overt behavioral symptoms. The author is unaware of studies that have evaluated the effectiveness of PT, SST, or CST with children who present conduct disorder features only and children who have additional symptoms of ADHD or depression, but has suggested (Dumas, 1989) that studies that have reported outcome results of marginal significance may reflect differential effectiveness in samples that contained children with diverse patterns of conduct disorder.

There is also considerable evidence that the effectiveness of behavior therapy is limited by the contextual characteristics of the child's environment, although this evidence comes almost exclusively from PT studies. For example, many families may be unwilling or unable to participate in PT (Dumas, 1989; Kazdin, 1985). Some parents may be very limited in their own functioning, may have rejected the child, or may be unwilling to take part in a form of intervention that invariably requires them to change as much as their child. Put simply, PT may be the most effective intervention one has to offer, but it requires at least one parent who is open to change, and many conduct disorder children do not have such a parent.

Not surprisingly, several studies have shown that, even when they engage in therapy, many families may drop out before completing training (Forehand, Middlebrook, Rogers, & Steffe, 1983) or may be unable to benefit from intervention or to maintain treatment gains at follow-up (Bernal, Klinnert, & Schultz, 1980; Wahler, 1980). Failure to remain in treatment or benefit from it has been found to be associated with adverse circumstances, such as maternal depressive symptomatology, marital discord, social isolation, and socioeconomic disadvantage.

Maternal Depression

The existence of an association between a child's aggressive, antisocial conduct and maternal self-supports of depressive symptomatology or general emotional distress has often been reported (Christensen, Phillips, Glasgow, & Johnson, 1983; Forehand, Wells, McMahon, Griest, & Rogers, 1982). Maternal depressive symptoms discriminate between referred and nonreferred families and predict maternal perception of their children (Forehand et al., 1982; Griest et al., 1980), dropout from PT (McMahon, Forehand, Griest, & Wells, 1981), and child behavior toward the mother and other family members (Dumas & Gibson, 1990; Dumas, Gibson, & Albin, 1989; Forehand, Lautenschlager, Faust, & Graziano, 1986; Hops et al., 1987). Not surprisingly, maternal depressive symptomatology has also been found to be associated with the effectiveness of interventions for aggressive, antisocial child behavior (e.g., Forehand, Wells, & Griest, 1980; Patterson, 1980).

Marital Adjustment

It has been known for a long time that conduct disorder children often come from maritally discordant or separated/divorced families (Johnson & Lobitz, 1974; Oltmanns, Broderick, & O'Leary, 1977; Porter & O'Leary, 1980; Rutter et al., 1974). This association has been confirmed in a recent meta-analysis, which has shown that there is a reliable, though small, relation between marital discord and child behavior problems in boys (but not girls) (Reid & Crisafulli, 1990), and in a review, which reports that boys tend to have greater difficulty adjusting to divorce than girls and may respond to family discord by exhibiting conduct problems (Zaslow, 1989). Rutter et al. (1974) showed that child deviance was particularly associated with open discord, tension, and hostility, rather than with parental apathy and indifference toward each other. Similarly, Emery (1982) and Hetherington, Cox, and Cox (1976) reported that children of divorced parents who are no longer exposed to parental conflict may be better adjusted than children who remain in intact but conflicted families. The association between marital adjustment and child conduct problems has been confirmed in a recent study based on data from a large, nationwide sample, although it would appear to be stronger in families of clinic-referred children than in families of nonreferred children, and in families of lower socioeconomic status than in families of higher status (Jouriles, Bourg, & Farris, 1991).

In keeping with this evidence, studies that have explored the nature of the association between marital adjustment and conduct disorder have highlighted the adverse role played by interspousal and, more generally, intrafamily aggression (Fantuzzo et al., 1991; Jouriles, Barling, & O'Leary, 1987; Jouriles, Murphy, & O'Leary, 1989; Kratcoski, 1985; Wolfe, Jaffe, Wilson, & Zak, 1985). Wolfe et al. (1985) reported that sons of physically abused women presented more behavior problems and less social and academic competence than boys from a community sample of nonviolent matched families. Jouriles et al. (1989) found that interspousal aggression was a significant predictor of conduct disorder in 5- to 8-year-old children, after controlling for overall levels of marital adjustment and intrafamily aggression. Kratcoski (1985) showed that aggression between parents, parents and children, or siblings was related to the aggression that delinquent youth directed at individuals outside the family. Not surprisingly, some studies suggest that marital discord may undermine behavior therapy with children and families (Brody & Forehand, 1986; Kent & O'Leary, 1976; Reisinger, Frangia, & Hoffman, 1976).

Social Isolation and Socioeconomic Disadvantage

Finally, there is also considerable evidence that aggressive, antisocial child behavior is related to the social context in which the child and family function (Dumas & Wahler, 1985; Griest & Wells, 1983; Wahler, 1980; Wahler & Graves, 1983). For example, Dumas (1986a) studied 14 mothers who experienced severe management problems with their children and reported high levels of aversive interactions with adults in their environment. The study compared mother–child interactions on "good" and "bad" days—days on which home observations were preceded by maternal self-reports of positive community contacts or of aversive community contacts. Mothers were found to be more likely to act in an aversive and indiscriminate manner toward their children when they had experienced a large proportion of aversive contacts with adults prior to an observation than when they had not, even though their children's behavior did not differ under the two contact conditions. This suggests that daily changes in mother–child interactions in families of conduct disorder children may reflect changes in the socioemotional context in which mothers function when they are not with their children. This conclusion is supported by findings that the long-term effectiveness of PT is related to the socioemotional and socioeconomic conditions in which families function (Dumas, 1984; Dumas & Wahler, 1983; Wahler, 1980; Wahler & Dumas, 1987). At a 1-year follow-up, Dumas and Wahler (1983) found that the effectiveness of a standardized PT program was related to pretreatment measures of socioeconomic disadvantage and social isolation. Results showed that the probability that families would not benefit from the program was closely related to the presence of disadvantage, isolation, or both.

ENHANCEMENTS OF BEHAVIORAL INTERVENTIONS FOR CONDUCT DISORDER

Aware that behavioral interventions can be effective in helping conduct disorder children and their families, but that this effectiveness is often limited, many clinicians and researchers have sought to enhance their methods of intervention in several ways. In a recent review of the PT literature, Miller and Prinz (1990) described three major approaches to enhancement. Briefly stated, different approaches aim to: (a) improve or supplement an existing therapeutic intervention; (b) broaden an existing intervention to address known correlates of conduct disorder; or (c) offer more than one intervention to address several features of conduct disorder at the same time. An overview of these approaches is presented here, because ongoing work in this area points to important innovations in the management of conduct disorder from a behavioral perspective and is likely to be indicative of future clinical and research trends.

Supplementing Existing Programs

Some enhancement efforts have sought to supplement existing PT programs by providing parents with knowledge or skills in addition to specific child management techniques, or by investigating the role that the therapeutic relationship plays in bringing about behavioral change. For example, McMahon, Forehand, and Griest (1981) supplemented their standard program by teaching parents basic social learning principles and found that this had a positive impact on parental perception of their children, satisfaction with the intervention, and child adjustment at follow-up. Comparable results have been reported by Glogower and Sloop (1976) and it is now common practice in many PT programs to provide parents with an understanding of the theoretical rationale on which the program is based.

PT programs have also been supplemented by teaching parents self-control (Sanders & Glynn, 1981; Wells, Griest, & Forehand, 1980) or conflict resolution (Martin, 1977) skills. Although there is some evidence that these enhancements can have beneficial effects, it is unclear whether these effects can be maintained at follow-up or whether they can be clearly attributed to the additional skills being taught.

As intervention programs have become more complex and sophisticated, some clinicians have turned their attention to client and therapist characteristics that may adversely affect outcome and that could be addressed directly to enhance effectiveness. Recent work by Chamberlain, Patterson, and their colleagues illustrates two major issues that have traditionally been ignored in clinical behavior therapy with children: client resistance and therapist training (Chamberlain & Baldwin, 1988; Chamberlain, Patterson, Reid, Kavanagh, & Forgatch, 1984). Although resistance can include a variety of behaviors (e.g., missed appointments, tardiness, lack of cooperation with assignments, argumentativeness in therapy), this work shows that the concept can be operationally defined and predicts dropout from PT (Chamberlain et al., 1984) or limited treatment gains for aggressive children and their families (Chamberlain & Baldwin, 1988). Not surprisingly, this work has shown also that specific therapist behaviors (e.g., direct teaching, confronting) are associated with client resistance (Patterson & Forgatch, 1985), suggesting that therapists may need to be trained to deal with resistance in order to maximize their effectiveness (Chamberlain & Ray, 1988). Although the field is still waiting for empirical demonstrations that careful consideration of these issues can enhance effectiveness, the evidence available already points to the importance of addressing issues that have traditionally been considered as "soft" by behavioral clinicians and researchers. In so doing, it is in keeping with earlier discussions, which have noted that the extent of therapist training and skills, as much as client resistance to change, may discriminate to some extent between interventions that obtain long-term positive results and interventions that do not (Dumas, 1989; Kazdin, 1987; Patterson et al., 1982).

Broadening Existing Programs

Important enhancement efforts have attempted to broaden existing programs by addressing known correlates of child conduct disorder. As most of these efforts, if not all, have sought to enhance PT effectiveness, they have generally focused on parental adjustment variables. Griest et al. (1982) developed a broad enhancement package that, in addition to training in child-management skills, offered mothers of oppositional, defiant children treatment in four areas: perception of child behavior, personal adjustment, marital adjustment, and extrafamilial relationships. This enhanced program was more effective than PT alone in reducing child referral problems at posttreatment and at a 2-month follow-up. In another study that focused on parental concerns in addition to the child's referral problems, Prinz and Miller (1988) developed another enhancement package that offered parents regular opportunities to use therapy time to discuss concerns in areas such as personal, marital, work, and social adjustment. Working with families of preadolescent boys with severe cross-situational aggressive, antisocial problems, they matched these families on a number of pretreatment variables (severity of child aggression, child IQ, marital discord, parental psychopathology, parental social support, family income, family history of alcohol or drug abuse and criminality) and randomly assigned matched families to a standardized PT program or to the same program plus the enhancement package. Results showed that families who received the enhanced intervention were less likely to drop out, more likely to complete assignments, and more likely to benefit from treatment than families who received PT only. Dadds, Schwartz, and

Sanders (1987) evaluated the effectiveness of a marital intervention aimed at conflict resolution, communication, and problem solving as an enhancement to PT for families with ODD or CD children (diagnosis based on DSM-III criteria). Two groups of families (with or without marital discord) were randomly assigned to PT only or PT plus marital intervention. Results showed that families in both conditions improved significantly on several measures of child deviance and parenting behavior at posttreatment, irrespective of their initial levels of marital discord. However, maritally discordant families who participated in the enhanced program were better able to maintain their treatment gains at a 6-month follow-up than discordant families who received PT only.

Taken together, these studies provide promising evidence that broad enhancement procedures may significantly improve the effectiveness of behavioral interventions for conduct disorder and highlight the importance of considering additional family problems and concerns besides the child's referral complaints when planning intervention (Wahler & Dumas, 1989).

Developing Multifaceted Interventions

Some clinicians and researchers have sought to improve the effectiveness of their programs by offering, at the same time, two or more interventions that are known to be beneficial in their own right. Multifaceted interventions vary considerably in scope, ranging from programs that attempt to bring about change in two developmental contexts, such as home and school (Blechman, Kotanchik, & Taylor, 1981), to very comprehensive programs that seek to modify child and family functioning at several levels (Henggeler & Borduin, 1990). Because of their inherent complexity, few of these programs have been systematically evaluated. However, there is some preliminary evidence suggesting that they may hold promise. Henggeler and his colleagues have shown that their multisystemic program may have beneficial effects on several measures of functioning in abusive or neglectful families, as well as on observational measures of family interactions and child deviant behavior (Brunk, Henggeler, & Whelan, 1987), and that the same program may lead to significant reductions in adolescent antisocial conduct (Henggeler et al., 1986).

In what may be the only published study combining PT and CST to date, Kazdin, Esveldt-Dawson, French, & Unis (1987b), worked with 40 inpatient children (aged 7 to 12 years), 78% of whom qualified for a primary or secondary DSM-III diagnosis of CD. They randomly assigned these children and their parents to the combined condition (in which parents received PT and children, CST) or to a contact-control condition. Results clearly favored the first condition on a variety of outcome measures taken at posttreatment and at a 1-year follow-up. These findings obviously fail to show that combining PT and CST enhances the effect that each intervention would have if administered separately, but they are in keeping with a growing awareness that significant changes in conduct disorder may, in many cases, require long-term, multifaceted interventions that address several of the problems presented by aggressive, antisocial children and their families (Dumas, 1986b).

CONCLUSION: TREATMENT OR PREVENTION?

Anyone who has worked with conduct disorder children or adolescents is well aware of the considerable challenge that they present. This challenge is clearly illustrated by the alarming nature of the clinical and social dimensions of this disorder, and by the fact that the clinical approaches available today are often inadequate to bring about significant and lasting behavioral change. Faced with this disturbing state of affairs, several authors have expressed pessimism about our society's ability to address the needs of aggressive, antisocial children through clinical means (Gordon & Arbuthnot, 1987; Leitenberg, 1987). Others have suggested that, in more extreme cases, conduct disorder may be a chronic condition likely to have adverse effects for an individual well into adulthood (Kazdin, 1987), or may serve an important survival function in some subcultures characterized by socioeconomic deprivation and social disintegration (Prinz & Miller, 1991). In different ways, these arguments point to the limitations of exclusively clinical approaches to conduct disorder. Put simply, a behavioral intervention may not work because the child's behavior pattern may be too severe or chronic in nature, or an intervention may be inappropriate because this pattern may be quite adapted to the behavioral norms of the child's reference group.

In line with such arguments, the behavioral field has seen a recent movement toward the development, implementation, and evaluation of large-scale, multisite projects aimed at the early detection of children at risk for conduct disorder and at the provision of multifaceted services aimed at the long-term prevention of the disorder (Glezos, 1991). Such ambitious projects may represent the next phase in the development of comprehensive services for aggressive, antisocial children and their families. If successful, they will integrate a variety of behavioral intervention methods that address the child's social relationships at home, at school, and with peers, in order to prevent, or at least postpone, the development of severe and chronic conduct disorder.

REFERENCES

Achenbach, T. M., Conners, C. K., Quay, H. C., Verhulst, F. C., & Howell, C. T. (1989). Replication of empirically derived syndromes as a basis for taxonomy of child/adolescent psychopathology. *Journal of Abnormal Child Psychology, 17,* 299–323.

Achenbach, T. M., & Edelbrock, C. (1978). The classification of child psychopathology: A review and analysis of empirical efforts. *Psychological Bulletin, 85,* 1275–1301.

Achenbach, T. M., McConaughy, S. H. (1987). *Empirically-based assessment of child and adolescent psychopathology: Practical applications.* Newbury Park, CA: Sage.

Achenbach, T. M., Verhulst, F. C., Baron, G. D., & Althaus, M. (1987). A comparison of syndromes derived from the Child Behavior Checklist for American and Dutch boys aged 6–11 and 12–16. *Journal of Child Psychology and Psychiatry, 28,* 437–453.

Aichorn, A. (1935). *Wayward youth.* New York: Viking.

American Psychiatric Association. (1980). *Diagnostic and statistical manual of mental disorders* (3rd ed.). Washington, DC: Author.

American Psychiatric Association. (1987). *Diagnostic and statistical manual of mental disorders* (3rd ed. rev.). Washington, DC: Author.

Arbuthnot, J., & Gordon, D. A. (1986). Behavioral and cognitive effects of a moral reasoning development intervention for high-risk behavior-disordered adolescents. *Journal of Consulting and Clinical Psychology, 54,* 208–216.

Arnold, J., Levine, A., & Patterson, G. R. (1975). Changes in sibling behavior following family intervention. *Journal of Consulting and Clinical Psychology, 43,* 683–688.

Asarnow, J. R., & Callan, J. W. (1985). Boys with peer adjustment problems: Social cognitive processes. *Journal of Consulting and Clinical Psychology, 53,* 80–87.

Barkley, R. A. (1987). *Defiant children: A clinician's manual for parent training.* New York: Guilford.

Bates, J. E., & Bayles, K. (1984). Objective and subjective components in mothers' perceptions of their children from age 6 months to 3 years. *Merrill-Palmer Quarterly, 30,* 111–130.

Bates, J., Maslin, C., & Frankel, K. (1985). Attachment security, mother–child interaction, and temperament as predictors of behavior problem ratings at age three years. *Monographs of the Society for Research in Child Development, 50,* (1-2, Serial No. 209), 167–193.

Baum, C. G., & Forehand, R. (1981). Long-term follow-up assessment of parent training by use of multiple outcome measures. *Behavior Therapy, 12,* 643–652.

Berger, M. (1985). Temperament and individual differences. In M. Rutter & L. Hersov (Eds.), *Child and adolescent psychiatry: Modern approaches* (2nd ed.; pp. 3–16). Oxford: Blackwell.

Bernal, M. E., Klinnert, M. D., & Schultz, L. A. (1980). Outcome evaluations of behavioral parent training and client centered parent counseling for children with conduct problems. *Journal of Applied Behavior Analysis, 13,* 677–691.

Bierman, K. L. (1986). Process of change during social skills training with preadolescents and its relation to treatment outcome. *Child Development, 57,* 230–240.

Bierman, K. L., & Furman, W. (1984). The effects of social skills training and peer involvement on the social adjustment of preadolescents. *Child Development, 55,* 151–162.

Bierman, K. L., Miller, C. L., & Stabb, S. D. (1987). Improving the social behavior and peer acceptance of rejected boys: Effects of social skills training with instructions and prohibitions. *Journal of Consulting and Clinical Psychology, 55,* 194–200.

Blechman, E. A. (1985). *Solving child behavior problems at home and at school.* Champaign, IL: Research Press.

Blechman, E. A., Kotanchik, N. L., & Taylor, C. J. (1981). Families and schools together: Early behavioral intervention with high risk children. *Behavior Therapy, 132,* 308–319.

Blumstein, A., Cohen, J. M., Roth, J. A., & Visher, C. A. (Eds.). (1986). *Criminal careers and "career criminals."* Washington, DC: National Academy of Sciences.

Bornstein, M., Bellack, A. S., & Hersen, M. (1980). Social skills training for highly aggressive children. Treatment in an inpatient psychiatric setting. *Behavior Modification, 4,* 173–186.

Brody, G. H., & Forehand, R. (1986). Maternal perceptions of child maladjustment as a function of the combined influence of child behavior and maternal depression. *Journal of Consulting and Clinical Psychology, 54,* 237–240.

Brunk, M., Henggeler, S. W., & Whelan, J. P. (1987). A comparison of multisystemic therapy and parent training in the brief treatment of child abuse and neglect. *Journal of Consulting and Clinical Psychology, 55,* 171–178.

Cairns, R. B., Cairns, B. D., & Neckerman, H. J. (1989). Early school dropout: Configurations and determinants. *Child Development, 60,* 1437–1452.

Camp, B. W., & Bash, M. A. S. (1985). *"Think aloud": Increasing social and cognitive skills. A problem solving program for children.* Champaign, IL: Research Press.

Campbell, S. B., Breaux, A. M., Ewing, L. J., & Szumowski, E. K. (1986). Correlates and predictors of hyperactivity and aggression: A longitudinal study of parent-referred problem preschoolers. *Journal of Abnormal Child Psychology, 14,* 217–234.

Campbell, S. B., & Ewing, L. J. (1990). Follow-up of hard-to-manage preschoolers: Adjustment at age 8 and predictors of continuing symptoms. *Journal of Child Psychology and Psychiatry, 31,* 871–889.

Carlson, C. L., Lahey, B. B., & Neeper, R. (1984). Peer assessment of the social behavior of accepted, rejected, and neglected children. *Journal of Abnormal Child Psychology, 12,* 189–198.

Chaiken, M. R., & Chaiken, J. M. (1984). Offender types and public policy. *Crime and Delinquency, 30,* 195–226.

Chamberlain, P., & Baldwin, D. V. (1988). Client resistance to parent training: Its therapeutic management. In T. R. Kratochwill (Ed.), *Advances in school psychology, Vol. 6* (pp. 131–171). Hillsdale, NJ: Erlbaum.

Chamberlain, P., Patterson, G. R., Reid, J., Kavanagh, K., & Forgatch, M. (1984).

Observation of client resistance. *Behavior Therapy, 15,* 144–155.

Chamberlain, P., & Ray, J. (1988). The Therapy Process Code: A multidimensional system for observing therapist and client interactions in family treatment. In R. J. Prinz (Ed.), *Advances in behavioral assessment of children and families, Vol. 4* (pp. 189–217). Greenwich, CT: JAI Press.

Chandler, M. J. (1973). Egocentrism and antisocial behavior: The assessment and training of social perspective-taking skills. *Developmental Psychology, 9,* 326–332.

Chiles, A., Miller, M. L., & Cox, G. B. (1980). Depression in an adolescent delinquent population. *Archives of General Psychiatry, 37,* 1179–1184.

Christensen, A., Phillips, S., Glasgow, R. E., & Johnson, S. M. (1983). Parental characteristics and interactional dysfunction in families with child behavior problems: A preliminary investigation. *Journal of Abnormal Child Psychology, 11,* 153–166.

Coie, J. D., Belding, M., & Underwood, M. (1988). Aggression and peer rejection in childhood. In B. B. Lahey & A. E. Kazdin (Eds.), *Advances in clinical child psychology, Vol. 11* (pp. 125–158). New York: Plenum.

Costello, E. J. (1990). Child psychiatric epidemiology: Implications for clinical research and practice. In B. B. Lahey & A. E. Kazdin (Eds.), *Advances in clinical child psychology, Vol. 13* (pp. 53–90). New York: Plenum.

Dadds, M. R., Schwartz, S., & Sanders, M. R. (1987). Marital discord and treatment outcome in behavioral treatment of child conduct disorders. *Journal of Consulting and Clinical Psychology, 55,* 396–403.

Dangel, R. F., & Polster, R. A. (1988). *Teaching child management skills.* New York: Pergamon.

Davidson, W. S., & Seidman, E. (1974). Studies of behavior modification and juvenile delinquency: A review, methodological critique, and social perspective. *Psychological Bulletin, 81,* 998–1011.

Delfini, L. F., Bernal, M. E., & Rosen, P. M. (1976). Comparison of deviant and normal boys in home settings. In E. J. Mash, L. A. Hamerlynck, & L. C. Handy (Eds.), *Behavior modification and families* (pp. 228–248). New York: Brunner/Mazel.

Deluty, R. H. (1983). Children's evaluations of aggressive, assertive, and submissive responses. *Journal of Clinical Child Psychology, 12,* 124–129.

DiLalla, L. F., & Gottesman, I. I. (1991). Biological and genetic contributors to violence—Widom's untold tale. *Psychological Bulletin, 109,* 125–129.

Dishion, T. J. (1990). The family ecology of boys' peer relations in middle childhood. *Child Development, 61,* 874–892.

Dishion, T. J., & Loeber, R. (1985). Adolescent marijuana and alcohol use: The role of parents and peers revisited. *American Journal of Drug and Alcohol Abuse, 11,* 11–26.

Dodge, K. A. (1980). Social cognition and children's aggressive behavior. *Child Development, 51,* 162–170.

Dodge, K. A. (1985). Attributional bias in aggressive children. In P. C. Kendall (Ed.), *Advances in cognitive-behavioral research and therapy, Vol. 4* (pp. 73–110). Orlando, FL: Academic Press.

Dodge, K. (1986). A social information processing model of social competence in children. In M. Perlmutter (Ed.), *Minnesota symposium on child psychology, Vol. 18* (pp. 77–125). Hillsdale, NJ: Erlbaum.

Dodge, K., & Coie, J. D. (1987). Social-information-processing factors in reactive and proactive aggression in children's peer groups. *Journal of Personality and Social Psychology, 53,* 1146–1157.

Dodge, K. A., & Frame, C. L. (1982). Social cognitive biases and deficits in aggressive boys. *Child Development, 53,* 620–635.

Dodge, K. A., & Newman, J. P. (1981). Biased decision-making processes in aggressive boys. *Journal of Abnormal Psychology, 90,* 375–379.

Dumas, J. E. (1984). Child, adult-interactional, and socioeconomic setting events as predictors of parent training outcome. *Education and Treatment of Children, 7,* 351–364.

Dumas, J. E. (1986a). Indirect influence of maternal social contacts on mother-child interactions: A setting event analysis.

Journal of Abnormal Child Psychology, 14, 205–216.

Dumas, J. E. (1986b). Parental perception and treatment outcome in families of aggressive children: A causal model. *Behavior Therapy, 17,* 420–432.

Dumas, J. E. (1989). Treating antisocial behavior in children: Child and family approaches. *Clinical Psychology Review, 9,* 197–222.

Dumas, J. E., & Gibson, J. A. (1990). Behavioral correlates of maternal depressive symptomatology in conduct-disorder children: II. Systemic effects involving fathers and siblings. *Journal of Consulting and Clinical Psychology, 58,* 877–881.

Dumas, J. E., Gibson, J. A., & Albin, J. B. (1989). Behavioral correlates of maternal depressive symptomatology in conduct-disorder children. *Journal of Consulting and Clinical Psychology, 57,* 516–521.

Dumas, J. E., & Lechowicz, J. G. (1989). When do noncompliant children comply? Implications for family behavior therapy. *Child & Family Behavior Therapy, 11,* 23–37.

Dumas, J. E., & Wahler, R. G. (1983). Predictors of treatment outcome in parent training: Mother insularity and socioeconomic disadvantage. *Behavioral Assessment, 5,* 301–313.

Dumas, J. E., & Wahler, R. G. (1985). Indiscriminate mothering as a contextual factor in aggressive-oppositional child behavior: "Damned if you do, damned if you don't." *Journal of Abnormal Child Psychology, 13,* 1–17.

Dush, D. M., Hirt, M. L., & Schroeder, H. E. (1989). Self-statement modification in the treatment of child behavior disorders: A meta-analysis. *Psychological Bulletin, 106,* 97–106.

Elliott, D. S., Huizinga, D., & Ageton, S. S. (1985). *Explaining delinquency and drug use.* Beverly Hills, CA: Sage.

Ellis, P. L. (1982). Empathy: A factor in antisocial behavior. *Journal of Abnormal Child Psychology, 10,* 123–134.

Emery, R. E. (1982). Interparental conflict and the children of discord and divorce. *Psychological Bulletin, 92,* 310–330.

Eyberg, S., & Boggs, S. R. (1989). Parent training for oppositional-defiant preschoolers. In C. E. Schaefer & J. M. Briesmeister (Eds.), *Handbook of parent training: Parents as cotherapists for children's behavior problems* (pp. 105–132). New York: Wiley.

Fantuzzo, J. W., DePaola, L. M., Lambert, L., Martino, T., Anderson, G., & Sutton, S. (1991). Effects of interparental violence on the psychological adjustment and competencies of young children. *Journal of Consulting and Clinical Psychology, 59,* 258–265.

Farnworth, M., Schweinhart, L. J., & Berrueta-Clement, J. R. (1985). Preschool intervention, school success and delinquency in a high-risk sample of youth. *American Educational Research Journal, 22,* 445–464.

Farrington, D. P. (1983). Offending from 10 to 25 years of age. In K. T. Van Dusen & S. A. Mednick (Eds.), *Antisocial and prosocial behavior* (pp. 17–38). Boston: Kluwer-Nijhoff.

Feldman, R. A., Caplinger, T. E., & Wodarski, J. S. (1983). *The St. Louis conundrum: The effective treatment of antisocial youths.* Englewood Cliffs, NJ: Prentice-Hall.

Fleischman, M. J. (1981). A replication of Patterson's "Intervention for boys with conduct problems." *Journal of Consulting and Clinical Psychology, 49,* 342–351.

Fleischman, M. J., Horne, A. M., & Arthur, J. L. (1987). *Troubled families: A treatment program.* Champaign, IL: Research Press.

Fleischman, M. J., & Szykula, S. A. (1981). A community setting replication of a social learning treatment for aggressive children. *Behavior Therapy, 12,* 115–122.

Fo, W. S., & O'Donnell, C. R. (1974). The buddy system: Relationship and contingency conditions in a community intervention program for youth with non-professionals as behavior agents. *Journal of Consulting and Clinical Psychology, 42,* 163–169.

Fordham, S., & Ogbu, J. U. (1986). Black students' school success: Coping with the "burden of 'acting white.'" *The Urban Review, 18,* 176–206.

Forehand, R., Lautenschlager, G. J., Faust, J., & Graziano, W. G. (1986). Parent perceptions and parent-child interactions in clinic-referred children: A preliminary investigation of the effects of maternal depressive moods. *Behaviour Research and Therapy, 24,* 73–75.

Forehand, R., & Long, N. (1988). Outpatient treatment of the acting out child: Procedures, long term follow-up data, and clinical problems. *Advances in Behaviour Research and Therapy, 10,* 129–177.

Forehand, R., & McMahon, R. J. (1981). *Helping the noncompliant child: A clinician's guide to parent training.* New York: Guilford.

Forehand, R., Middlebrook, J., Rogers, T., & Steffe, M. (1983). Dropping out of parent training. *Behaviour Research and Therapy, 21,* 663–668.

Forehand, R., Sturgis, E. T., McMahon, R. J., Aguar, D., Green, K., Wells, K., & Breiner, J. (1979). Parent behavioral training to modify child noncompliance: Treatment generalization across time and from home to school. *Behavior Modification, 3,* 3–25.

Forehand, R., Wells, K. C., & Griest, D. L. (1980). An examination of the social validity of a parent training program. *Behavior Therapy, 11,* 488–502.

Forehand, R., Wells, K. C., McMahon, R. J., Griest, D., & Rogers, T. (1982). Maternal perception of maladjustment in clinic-referred children: An extension of earlier research. *Journal of Behavioral Assessment, 4,* 145–151.

Gaffney, L. R., & McFall, R. M. (1981). A comparison of social skills in delinquent and nondelinquent adolescent girls using a behavioral role-playing inventory. *Journal of Consulting and Clinical Psychology, 49,* 959–967.

Gelfand, D. M., & Hartman, D. P. (1968). Behavior therapy with children: A review and evaluation of research methodology. *Psychological Bulletin, 79,* 204–215.

Glezos, S. P. (1991, January–February). NIMH demonstrations to test prevention of youth suicide and conduct problems. *ADAMHA News,* p. 15.

Glogower, F., & Sloop, E. W. (1976). Two strategies of group training of parents as effective behavior modifiers. *Behavior Therapy, 7,* 177–184.

Goldstein, A. P., & Glick, B. (1987). *Aggression replacement training: A comprehensive intervention for aggressive youth.* Champaign, IL: Research Press.

Gordon, D. A., & Arbuthnot, J. (1987). Individual, group, and family interventions. In H. C. Quay (Ed.), *Handbook of juvenile delinquency* (pp. 290–324). New York: Wiley.

Gouze, K. R. (1987). Attention and social problem solving as correlates of aggression in preschool males. *Journal of Abnormal Child Psychology, 15,* 181–197.

Graziano, A. M. (1975). *Behavior therapy with children.* Elmsford, NY: Aldine.

Gresham, F. M. (1985). Utility of cognitive-behavioral procedures for social skills training with children: A critical review. *Journal of Abnormal Child Psychology, 13,* 411–423.

Griest, D. L., Forehand, R., Rogers, T., Breiner, J., Furey, W., & Williams, C. A. (1982). Effects of parent enhancement therapy on the treatment outcome and generalization of a parent training program. *Behaviour Research and Therapy, 20,* 429–436.

Griest, D. L., Forehand, R., Wells, K. C., & McMahon, R. J. (1980). An examination of differences between nonclinic and behavior-problem clinic-referred children and their mothers. *Journal of Abnormal Psychology, 89,* 497–500.

Griest, D. L., & Wells, K. D. (1983). Behavior family therapy with conduct disorders in children. *Behavior Therapy, 14,* 37–53.

Hansen, D. J., St. Lawrence, J. S., & Christoff, K. A. (1989). Group conversational-skills training with inpatient children and adolescents. *Behavior Modification, 13,* 4–31.

Henggeler, S. W., & Borduin, C. M. (1990). *Family therapy and beyond: A multisystemic approach to treating behavior problems of children and adolescents.* Pacific Grove, CA: Brooks/Cole.

Henggeler, S. W., Rodick, J. D., Borduin, C. M., Hanson, C. L., Watson, S. M., & Urey, J. R. (1986). Multisystemic treatment of juvenile offenders: Effects on adolescent behavior and family interaction. *Developmental Psychology, 22,* 132–141.

Hetherington, E. M., Cox, M., & Cox, R. (1976). Divorced fathers. *Family Coordinator, 25,* 417–428.

Hobbs, S. A., Moguin, L. E., Tyroler, M., & Lahey, B. B. (1980). Cognitive behavior therapy with children: Has clinical utility been demonstrated? *Psychological Bulletin, 87,* 147–165.

Hogan, A. E., & Quay, H. C. (1984). Cognition in child and adolescent behavior disorders. In B. B. Lahey & A. E. Kazdin (Eds.), *Advances in clinical child psychology.* New York: Plenum.

Hollin, C. R. (1990). Social skills training with delinquents: A look at the evidence and some recommendations for practice. *British Journal of Social Work, 20,* 483–493.

Hops, M., Biglan, A., Sherman, L., Arthur, J., Friedman, L., & Osteen, V. (1987). Home observations of family interactions of depressed women. *Journal of Consulting and Clinical Psychology, 55,* 341–346.

Huesmann, L. R., Eron, L. D., Lefkowitz, M. M., & Walder, L. O. (1984). Stability of aggression over time and generations. *Developmental Psychology, 20,* 1120–1134.

Hymel, S., Wagner, E., & Butler, L. J. (1990). Reputational bias: View from the peer group. In S. R. Asher & J. D. Coie (Eds.), *Peer rejection in childhood* (pp. 156–186). Cambridge: Cambridge University Press.

Jenkins, R. L., & Glickman, S. (1946). Common syndromes in child psychiatry: I. Deviant behavior traits. II. The schizoid child. *American Journal of Orthopsychiatry, 16,* 244–261.

Joffe, R. D., Dobson, K. S., Fine, S., Marriage, K., & Haley, G. (1990). Social problem-solving in depressed, conduct-disordered, and normal adolescents. *Journal of Abnormal Child Psychology, 18,* 565–575.

Johnson, S. M., & Lobitz, G. K. (1974). The personal and marital adjustment of parents as related to observed child deviance and parenting behaviors. *Journal of Abnormal Child Psychology, 2,* 193–207.

Jouriles, E. N., Barling, J., & O'Leary, K. D. (1987). Predicting child behavior problems in maritally violent families. *Journal of Abnormal Child Psychology, 15,* 165–173.

Jouriles, E. N., Bourg, W. J., & Farris, A. M. (1991). Marital adjustment and child conduct problems: A comparison of the correlation across subsamples. *Journal of Consulting and Clinical Psychology, 59,* 354–357.

Jouriles, E. N., Murphy, C. M., & O'Leary, K. D. (1989). Interspousal aggression, marital discord, and child problems. *Journal of Consulting and Clinical Psychology, 57,* 453–455.

Kazdin, A. E. (1985). *Treatment of antisocial behavior in children and adolescents.* Homewood, IL: Dorsey.

Kazdin, A. E. (1987). Treatment of antisocial behavior in children: Current status and future directions. *Psychological Bulletin, 102,* 187–203.

Kazdin, A. E. (1990). Psychotherapy for children and adolescents. *Annual Review of Psychology, 41,* 21–54.

Kazdin, A. E., Bass, D., Siegel, T., & Thomas, C. (1989). Cognitive-behavioral therapy and relationship therapy in the treatment of children referred for antisocial behavior. *Journal of Consulting and Clinical Psychology, 57,* 522–535.

Kazdin, A. E., & Esveldt-Dawson, K. (1986). The interview for antisocial behavior: Psychometric characteristics and concurrent validity with child psychiatric inpatients. *Journal of Psychopathology and Behavioral Assessment, 8,* 289–303.

Kazdin, A. E., Esveldt-Dawson, K., French, N. H., & Unis, A. S. (1987a). Problem-solving skills training and relationship therapy in the treatment of antisocial child behavior. *Journal of Consulting and Clinical Psychology, 55,* 76–85.

Kazdin, A. E., Esveldt-Dawson, K., French, N. H., & Unis, A. S. (1987b). Effects of parent management training and problem-solving skills training combined in the treatment of antisocial child behavior. *Journal of American Academy of Child and Adolescent Psychiatry, 26,* 416–424.

Kelso, J., & Stewart, M. A. (1986). Factors which predict the persistence of aggressive conduct disorder. *Journal of Child Psychology and Psychiatry, 27,* 77–86.

Kendall, P. C., & Braswell, L. (1985). *Cognitive-behavioral therapy for impulsive children.* New York: Guilford.

Kendall, P. C., Reber, M., McLeer, S., Epps, J., & Ronan, K. R. (1990). Cognitive-behavioral treatment of conduct-disordered children. *Cognitive Therapy and Research, 14,* 279-297.

Kennedy, R. E. (1982). Cognitive-behavioral approaches to the modification of aggressive behavior in children. *School Psychology Review, 11,* 47-55.

Kent, R. N., & O'Leary, K. D. (1976). A controlled evaluation of behavior modification with conduct problem children. *Journal of Consulting and Clinical Psychology, 44,* 586-596.

Klaczynski, P. A., & Cummings, E. M. (1989). Responding to anger in aggressive and nonaggressive boys: A research note. *Journal of Child Psychology and Psychiatry, 30,* 309-314.

Kolvin, I., Miller, F. J. W., Fleeting, M., & Kolvin, P. A. (1988). Social and parenting factors affecting criminal-offense rates: Findings from the Newcastle thousand family study (1947-1980). *British Journal of Psychiatry, 152,* 80-90.

Kovacs, M., Paulauskas, S., Gatsonis, C., & Richards, C. (1988). Depressive disorders in childhood: III. A longitudinal study of comorbidity with and risk for conduct disorders. *Journal of Affective Disorders, 15,* 205-217.

Kratcoski, P. C. (1985). Youth violence directed toward significant others. *Journal of Adolescence, 8,* 145-157.

Kupersmidt, J. B., & Coie, J. D. (1990). Preadolescent peer status, aggression, and school adjustment as predictors of externalizing problems in adolescence. *Child Development, 61,* 1350-1362.

Ladd, G. S., Price, J. M., & Hart, C. H. (1990). Preschooler's behavioral orientations and patterns of peer control: Predictive of peer status? In S. R. Asher & J. D. Coie (Eds.), *Peer rejection childhood* (pp. 90-115). Cambridge: Cambridge University Press.

Lahey, B. B., Loeber, R., Stouthamer-Loeber, M., Christ, M. A. G., Green, S., Russo, M. F., Frick, P. J., & Dulcan, M. (1990). Comparison of DSM-III and DSM-III-R diagnoses for prepubertal children: Changes in prevalence and validity. *Journal of American Academy of Child and Adolescent Psychiatry, 29,* 620-625.

Lahey, B. B., Piancentini, J. C., McBurnett, K., Stone, P., Hartdagen, M. A., & Hynd, G. (1988). Psychopathology in the parents of children with conduct disorder and hyperactivity. *Journal of the American Academy of Child and Adolescent Psychiatry, 27,* 163-170.

LeBlanc, M., & Frechette, M. (1989). *Male criminal activity from childhood through youth.* New York: Springer-Verlag.

Ledingham, J. E., & Schwartzman, A. E. (1984). A 3-year follow-up of aggressive and withdrawn behavior in childhood: Preliminary findings. *Journal of Abnormal Child Psychology, 12,* 157-168.

Leitenberg, H. (1987). Primary prevention of delinquency. In J. D. Burchard & S. N. Burchard (Eds.), *Prevention of delinquent behavior* (pp. 312-330). Newbury Park, CA: Sage.

Lochman, J. E. (1987). Self and peer perceptions and attributional biases of aggressive boys. *Journal of Consulting and Clinical Psychology, 55,* 404-410.

Lochman, J. E., Burch, P. R., Curry, J. F., & Lampron, L. B. (1984). Treatment and generalization effects of cognitive-behavioral and goal-setting interventions with aggressive boys. *Journal of Consulting and Clinical Psychology, 52,* 915-916.

Lochman, J. E., Lampron, L. B., Gemmer, T. C., & Harris, S. R. (1987). Anger coping intervention for aggressive children: Guide to implementation in school settings. In P. A. Keller & S. Heyman (Eds.), *Innovations in clinical practice: A source book, Vol. 6.* Sarasota, FL: Professional Resources Exchange.

Loeber, R. (1982). The stability of antisocial and delinquent child behavior: A review. *Child Development, 53,* 1431-1446.

Loeber, R. (1988a). The natural histories of juvenile conduct problems, substance use, and delinquency: Evidence for developmental progressions. In B. B. Lahey & A. E. Kazdin (Eds.), *Advances in clinical child psychology, Vol. 11* (pp. 73-124). New York: Plenum.

Loeber, R. (1988b). Behavioral precursors and accelerators of delinquency. In W.

Buikhuisen & S. A. Mednick (Eds.), *Explaining crime* (pp. 51–67). Leiden: Brill.

Loeber, R. (1990). Development and risk factors of juvenile antisocial behavior and delinquency. *Clinical Psychology Review, 10,* 1–41.

Loeber, R., & Dishion, T. (1983). Early predictors of male delinquency: A review. *Psychological Bulletin, 94,* 68–94.

Loeber, R., & Schmaling, K. B. (1985a). Empirical evidence for overt and covert patterns of antisocial conduct problems: A meta-analysis. *Journal of Abnormal Child Psychology, 13,* 337–352.

Loeber, R., & Schmaling, K. B. (1985b). The utility of differentiating between mixed and pure forms of antisocial child behavior. *Journal of Abnormal Child Behavior, 13,* 315–336.

Loeber, R., Tremblay, R. E., Gagnon, C., & Charlebois, P. (1989). Continuity and desistance in disruptive boys' early fighting at school. *Development and Psychopathology, 1,* 39–50.

Lutzker, J. R., McGimsey, J. F., McRae, S., & Campbell, R. V. (1983). Behavioral parent training: There's so much more to do. *The Behavior Therapist, 6,* 110–112.

Marriage, K., Fine, S., Moretti, M., & Haley, G. (1986). Relationship between depression and conduct disorder in children and adolescents. *Journal of the American Academy of Child Psychiatry, 25,* 687–691.

Martin, B. (1977). Brief family intervention: Effectiveness and the importance of including the father. *Journal of Consulting and Clinical Psychology, 45,* 1002–1010.

Maziade, M., Caron, C., Côte, R., Mérette, C., Bernier, H., Laplante, B., Boutin, P., & Thivierge, J. (1990). Psychiatric status of adolescents who had extreme temperaments at age 7. *American Journal of Psychiatry, 147,* 1531–1536.

McGee, R., Williams, S., & Silva, P. A. (1984). Background characteristics of aggressive, hyperactive, and aggressive-hyperactive boys. *Journal of the American Academy of Child Psychiatry, 23,* 280–284.

McMahon, R. J., & Forehand, R. (1983). Consumer satisfaction in behavioral treatment of children: Types, issues, and recommendations. *Behavior Therapy, 14,* 209–225.

McMahon, R. J., & Forehand, R. (1988). Conduct disorders. In E. J. Mash & L. G. Terdal (Eds.), *Behavioral assessment of childhood disorders* (2nd ed.; pp. 105–153). New York: Guilford.

McMahon, R. J., Forehand, R., & Griest, D. L. (1981). Effects of knowledge of social learning principles on enhancing treatment outcome and generalization in a parent training program. *Journal of Consulting and Clinical Psychology, 49,* 526–532.

McMahon, R. J., Forehand, R., Griest, D. L., & Wells, K. C. (1981). Who drops out of therapy during parent behavioral training? *Behavioral Counseling Quarterly, 1,* 79–85.

Meador, A. E., & Ollendick, T. H. (1984). Cognitive behavior therapy with children: An evaluation of its efficacy and clinical utility. *Child and Family Behavior Therapy, 6,* 25–44.

Meichenbaum, D. (1977). *Cognitive-behavior modification: An integrative approach.* New York: Plenum.

Meichenbaum, D. H., & Goodman, J. (1971). Training impulsive children to talk to themselves: A means of developing self-control. *Journal of Abnormal Psychology, 77,* 115–126.

Michelson, L., Sugai, D., Wood, R., & Kazdin, A. E. (1983). *Social skills assessment and training with children: An empirically-based handbook.* New York: Plenum.

Michelson, L., & Wood, R. (1980). Behavioral assessment and training of children's social skills. In M. Hersen, R. M. Eisler, & P. Miller (Eds.), *Progress in behavior modification, Vol. 9* (pp. 241–292). Orlando, FL: Academic Press.

Miller, G. E., & Prinz, R. J. (1990). Enhancement of social learning family interventions for childhood conduct disorder. *Psychological Bulletin, 108,* 291–307.

Moffitt, T. E. (1990). Juvenile delinquency and attention deficit disorder: Developmental trajectories from age 3 to age 15. *Child Development, 61,* 893–910.

Moore, D. R., Chamberlain, P., & Mukai, L. H. (1979). Children at risk for delinquency: A follow-up comparison of aggressive children and children who steal. *Journal of Abnormal Child Psychology, 7,* 345–355.

Moskowitz, D. S., Schwartzman, A. E., & Ledingham, J. E. (1985). Stability of change in aggression and withdrawal in middle childhood and early adolescence. *Journal of Abnormal Psychology, 94,* 30–41.

Ollendick, T. H., & Hersen, M. (1979). Social skills training for juvenile delinquents. *Behaviour Research and Therapy, 17,* 547–554.

Oltmanns, T. F., Broderick, J. E., & O'Leary, K. D. (1977). Marital adjustment and the efficacy of behavior therapy with children. *Journal of Consulting and Clinical Psychology, 45,* 724–729.

Olweus, D. (1979). Stability of aggressive reaction patterns in males: A review. *Psychological Bulletin, 86,* 852–875.

Patterson, G. R. (1974). Interventions for boys with conduct problems: Multiple settings, treatments, and criteria. *Journal of Consulting and Clinical Psychology, 42,* 471–781.

Patterson, G. R. (1976a). The aggressive child: Victim and architect of a coercive system. In L. A. Hamerlynck, L. C. Handy, & E. J. Mash (Eds.), *Behavior modification with families: Theory and research, Vol. 1* (pp. 276–316). New York: Brunner/Mazel.

Patterson, G. R. (1976b). *Living with children: New methods for parents and teachers* (rev. ed.). Champaign, IL: Research Press.

Patterson, G. R. (1980). Mothers: The unacknowledged victims. *Monographs of the Society for Research in Child Development, 45* (5, Serial No. 186).

Patterson, G. R. (1982). *Coercive family processes.* Eugene, OR: Castalia.

Patterson, G. R. (1986). Performance models for antisocial boys. *American Psychologist, 41,* 432–444.

Patterson, G. R., Capaldi, D., & Bank, L. (1991). An early starter model for predicting delinquency. In D. J. Pepler & K. H. Rubin (Eds.), *The development and treatment of childhood aggression* (pp. 139–168). Hillsdale, NJ: Erlbaum.

Patterson, G. R., Chamberlain, P., & Reid, J. B. (1982). A comparative evaluation of a parent-training program. *Behavior Therapy, 13,* 638–650.

Patterson, G. R., & Fleischman, M. J. (1979). Maintenance of treatment effects? Some considerations concerning family systems and follow-up data. *Behavior Therapy, 10,* 168–185.

Patterson, G. R., & Forgatch, M. S. (1985). Therapist behavior as a determinant for client noncompliance: A paradox for the behavior modifier. *Journal of Consulting and Clinical Psychology, 53,* 846–851.

Philips, E. L. (1968). Achievement place: Token reinforcement procedures in a home-style rehabilitation setting for pre-delinquent boys. *Journal of Applied Behavior Analysis, 1,* 213–233.

Porter, S., & O'Leary, K. D. (1980). Types of marital discord and child behavior problems. *Journal of Abnormal Child Psychology, 8,* 287–295.

Prinz, R., Connor, P., & Wilson, C. (1981). Hyperactive and aggressive behaviors in childhood: Intertwined dimensions. *Journal of Abnormal Child Psychology, 9,* 191–202.

Prinz, R. J., & Miller, G. E. (1988, November). Behavioral family treatment of conduct disorder: Learning from the dropouts. In R. J. Prinz (Chair), *Advances in behavioral family therapy.* Symposium conducted at the meeting of the Association for Advancement of Behavior Therapy, New York.

Prinz, R. J., & Miller, G. E. (1991). Issues in understanding and treating childhood conduct problems in disadvantaged populations. *Journal of Clinical Child Psychology, 20,* 379–385.

Puig-Antich, J. (1982). Major depression and conduct disorder in prepuberty. *Journal of the American Academy of Child Psychiatry, 21,* 118–128.

Quay, H. C., Routh, D. K., & Shapiro, S. K. (1987). Psychopathology of childhood: From description to validation. *Annual Review of Psychology, 38,* 491–532.

Reid, W. J., & Crisafulli, A. (1990). Marital discord and child behavior problems: A meta-analysis. *Journal of Abnormal Child Psychology, 18,* 105–117.

Reisinger, J. J., Frangia, G. W., & Hoffman, E. H. (1976). Toddler management training: Generalization and marital status. *Journal* of Behavior Therapy and Experimental Psychiatry, 7, 335–340.

Richard, B. A., & Dodge, K. A. (1982). Social maladjustment and problem solving in school-aged children. *Journal of Consulting and Clinical Psychology, 50,* 226–233.

Richman, N., Stevenson, J. S., & Graham, P. J. (1982). *Preschool to school. A behavioral study.* London: Academic Press.

Robins, L. N. (1981). Epidemiological approaches to natural history research: Antisocial disorders in children. *Journal of the American Academy of Child Psychiatry, 20,* 566–580.

Robins, L. N. (1986). Changes in conduct disorder over time. In D. C. Farran & J. D. McKinney (Eds.), *Risk in intellectual and psychosocial development.* Orlando, FL: Academic Press.

Robins, L. N., & Ratcliff, K. S. (1980). Childhood conduct disorders and later arrest. In L. N. Robins, P. Clayton, & J. Wing (Eds.), *Social consequences of psychiatric illness.* New York: Brunner/Mazel.

Roff, J. D., & Wirt, R. D. (1984). Childhood aggression and social adjustment as antecedents of delinquency. *Journal of Abnormal Child Psychology, 12,* 111–126.

Rutter, M., & Giller, H. (1983). *Juvenile delinquency: Trends and perspectives.* New York: Penguin Books.

Rutter, M., Yule, B., Quinton, D., Rowlands, O., Yule, W., & Berger, M. (1974). Attainment and adjustment in two geographical areas: III. Some factors accounting for area differences. *British Journal of Psychiatry, 125,* 520–533.

Safer, D. J. (1984). Subgrouping conduct disordered adolescents by early risk factors. *American Journal of Orthopsychiatry, 54,* 603–612.

Sanders, M. R., & Glynn, T. (1981). Training parents in behavioral self-management: An analysis of generalization and maintenance. *Journal of Applied Behavior Analysis, 14,* 223–237.

Sanders, M. R., & James, J. E. (1983). The modification of parent behavior: A review of generalization and maintenance. *Behavior Modification, 7,* 3–27.

Sarason, I. G., & Ganzer, V. J. (1973). Modeling and group discussion in the rehabilitation of juvenile delinquents. *Journal of Counseling Psychology, 20,* 442–449.

Shapiro, S. K., & Garfinkel, B. D. (1986). The occurrence of behavior disorders in children: The interdependence of attention deficit disorder and conduct disorder. *Journal of the American Academy of Child Psychiatry, 25,* 809–819.

Snyder, J. J. (1977). A reinforcement analysis of interaction in problem and non-problem families. *Journal of Abnormal Psychology, 86,* 528–535.

Spence, S. H., & Marzillier, J. S. (1981). Social skills training with adolescent male offenders II. Short-term, long-term and generalized effects. *Behaviour Research and Therapy, 19,* 349–368.

Spivack, G., Marcus, J., & Swift, M. (1986). Early classroom behaviors and later misconduct. *Developmental Psychology, 22,* 124–131.

Spivack, G., Platt, J., & Shure, M. B. (1976). *The problem solving approach to adjustment.* San Francisco: Jossey-Bass.

Spivack, G., & Shure, M. B. (1982). *Social adjustment of young children: A cognitive approach to solving real-life problems.* San Francisco: Jossey-Bass.

Stanton, W. R., Feehan, M., McGee, R., & Silva, P. A. (1990). The relative value of reading ability and IQ as predictors of teacher-reported behavior problems. *Journal of Learning Disabilities, 23,* 514–517.

Stattin, H., & Magnusson, D. (1989). The role of early aggressive behavior in the frequency, seriousness, and types of later crime. *Journal of Consulting and Clinical Psychology, 57,* 710–718.

Stewart, M. A., de Blois, S., Meardon, J., & Cummings, C. (1980). Aggressive conduct disorder of children: The clinical picture. *Journal of Nervous and Mental Disease, 168,* 604–610.

Stouthamer-Loeber, M., Loeber, R., & Green, S. M. (1989, February). *Dishonesty and covert problem behavior in adolescence and early adulthood.* Paper presented at the meeting of the Society for Research in

Child and Adolescent Psychopathology, Miami, FL.

Stumphauzer, J. S. (1973). *Behavior therapy with delinquents.* Springfield, IL: Thomas.

Sturge, C. (1982). Reading retardation and antisocial behaviour. *Journal of Child Psychology and Psychiatry, 23,* 21–31.

Symonds, P. M. (1939). *The psychology of parent–child relations.* New York: D. Appleton-Century Co.

Szatmari, P., Boyle, M., & Offord, D. R. (1989). ADDH and conduct disorder: Degree of diagnostic overlap and differences among correlates. *Journal of American Academy of Child and Adolescent Psychiatry, 28,* 865–872.

Thelen, M. H., Fry, R. A., Dollinger, S. J., & Paul, S. C. (1976). Use of videotaped models to improve the interpersonal adjustment of delinquents. *Journal of Consulting and Clinical Psychology, 44,* 492.

Thomas, A., & Chess, S. (1982). Temperament and follow-up to adulthood. In R. Porter & G. M. Collins (Eds.), *Temperamental differences in infants and young children* (pp. 168–172). London: Pitman.

Tisdelle, D. A., & St. Lawrence, J. S. (1986). Interpersonal problem-solving competency: Review and critique of the literature. *Clinical Psychology Review, 6,* 337–356.

Tisdelle, D. A., & St. Lawrence, J. S. (1988). Adolescent interpersonal problem-solving skill training: Social validation and generalization. *Behavior Therapy, 19,* 171–182.

Tolan, P. H. (1987). Implications of age on onset for delinquency risk. *Journal of Abnormal Child Psychology, 15,* 47–65.

Tremblay, R. E., Masse, B., Perron, D., & LeBlanc, M., Schwartzman, A. E., & Ledingham, J. E. (in press). Early disruptive behavior, poor school achievement, delinquent behavior and delinquent personality: Longitudinal data from male and female samples. *Journal of Consulting and Clinical Psychology.*

Tuma, J. M. (1989). Mental health services for children: The state of the art. *American Psychologist, 44,* 188–199.

Urbain, E. S., & Kendall, P. C. (1980). Review of social-cognitive problem-solving interventions with children. *Psychological Bulletin, 88,* 109–143.

Vandenberg, S. G., & Crowe, L. (1989). Genetic factors in childhood psychopathology: Implications for clinical practice. In B. B. Lahey & A. E. Kazdin (Eds.), *Advances in clinical child psychology, Vol. 12* (pp. 139–177). New York: Plenum.

Van Hasselt, V. B., Hersen, M., Whitehill, M. B., & Bellack, A. S. (1979). Social skill assessment and training for children: An evaluative review. *Behaviour Research and Therapy, 17,* 413–437.

Wahler, R. G. (1980). The insular mother: Her problems in parent–child treatment. *Journal of Applied Behavior Analysis, 13,* 207–219.

Wahler, R. G., & Dumas, J. E. (1986a). Maintenance factors in coercive mother–child interactions: The compliance and predictability hypotheses. *Journal of Applied Behavior Analysis, 19,* 13–22.

Wahler, R. G., & Dumas, J. E. (1986b). "A chip off the old block": Some interpersonal characteristics for coercive children across generations. In P. S. Strain, M. J. Guralnick, & H. M. Walker (Eds.), *Children's social behavior: Development, assessment, and modification* (pp. 49–91). Orlando, FL: Academic Press.

Wahler, R. G., & Dumas, J. E. (1987). Family factors in childhood psychopathology: A coercion-neglect model. In T. Jacob (Ed.), *Family interaction and psychopathology: Theories, methods, and findings* (pp. 581–627). New York: Plenum.

Wahler, R. G., & Dumas, J. E. (1989). Attentional problems in dysfunctional mother–child interactions: An interbehavioral model. *Psychological Bulletin, 105,* 116–130.

Wahler, R. G., & Graves, M. G. (1983). Setting events in social networks: Ally or enemy in child behavior therapy? *Behavior Therapy, 14,* 19–36.

Walker, J. L., Lahey, B. B., Hynd, G. W., & Frame, C. L. (1987). Comparison of specific patterns of antisocial behavior in children with conduct disorder with or without coexisting hyperactivity. *Journal of Consulting and Clinical Psychology, 55,* 910–913.

Webster-Stratton, C., Hollinsworth, T., & Kolpacoff, M. (1989). The long-term effectiveness and clinical significance of three cost-effective training programs for families with conduct-problem children. *Journal of Consulting and Clinical Psychology, 57,* 550–553.

Webster-Stratton, C., Kolpacoff, M., & Hollinsworth, T. (1988). Self-administered videotape therapy for families with conduct problem children: Comparison with two cost-effective treatments and a control group. *Journal of Consulting and Clinical Psychology, 56,* 558–566.

Wells, K. C., Griest, D. L., & Forehand, R. (1980). The use of a self-control package to enhance temporal generality of parent training. *Behaviour Research and Therapy, 18,* 347–358.

White, J. L., Moffitt, T. E., Earls, F., Robins, L., & Silva, P. A. (1990). How early can we tell?: Predictors of childhood conduct disorder and adolescent delinquency. *Criminology, 28,* 507–533.

Widom, C. S. (1991). A tail on an untold tale: Response to "Biological and genetic contributors to violence—Widom's untold tale." *Psychological Bulletin, 109,* 130–132.

Wolfe, D. A., Jaffe, P., Wilson, S. K., & Zak, L. (1985). Children of battered women: The relation of child behavior to family violence and maternal stress. *Journal of Consulting and Clinical Psychology, 53,* 657–665.

Wolfgang, M. E., Thornberry, T. P., & Figlio, R. M. (1987). *From boy to man, from delinquency to crime.* Chicago: University of Chicago Press.

Zaslow, M. J. (1989). Sex differences in children's response to parental divorce: 2. Samples, variables, ages, and sources. *American Journal of Orthopsychiatry, 59,* 118–140.

CHAPTER 16

Mental Retardation

MARTHA HAMILTON and JOHNNY L. MATSON

Mentally retarded individuals have been the focal point of many seminal behavior therapy studies over the years. Thus, perhaps more behavioral techniques and procedures have been used with this group than with any other population (Matson, 1990). Also, because of the substantial cognitive deficits evident in this group, the types of behavioral methods employed differ to some degree from those used with other populations. The majority of the studies have been with operant techniques, although some handicapped persons have been treated effectively with social learning and self-control procedures. Further, the number of problems investigated and types of procedures used to treat these persons is expanding rapidly.

The purpose of this chapter is to present an overview of some of the more current and innovative treatments being used to eliminate problem behavior and develop adaptive behavior in the lives of mentally retarded persons. This presentation is by no means a comprehensive review of the current literature, because such an endeavor is beyond the scope of this chapter. Readers interested in such an in-depth view should refer to Matson (1990).

In this chapter, we outline the definition and classification of mentally retarded persons. Behavioral interventions shown to be effective in ameliorating behavioral excesses and deficits in members of this population are discussed, as are critical factors that impact the clinical management of mentally retarded individuals.

Mental retardation is distinct from many other disorders addressed in this volume in that its diagnosis is statistically derived on the basis of cultural deviance, rather than clinically derived on the basis of a constellation of specific behaviors and symptoms. This distinction is important because the portion of the population requiring intervention remains relatively high and constant and therefore demands significant attention and community resources. In addition, such a statistically derived taxonomy results in a group with an extremely diverse range of behavior. Individuals demonstrate varying degrees of cognitive deficits, adaptive delays, and maladaptive behaviors. As such, this topic is at once complex and broad in scope.

DEFINITION AND CLASSIFICATION

Definitions of mental retardation have changed and been controversial through the years (Deitz & Repp, 1989), but the most widely accepted definition today comes from the American Association of Mental Retardation (AAMR):

> Mental retardation refers to significantly subaverage general intellectual functioning existing concurrently with deficits in adaptive behavior, and manifested during the developmental period. (Grossman, 1983, p. 11)

The three-part definition includes the fact that diagnosis needs to take place prior to the individual's 18th birthday. This definition also emphasizes the need for relying on careful assessment of both intellectual functioning and adaptive behavior. Assessment of intelligence is typically handled using one of the current standardized measurement tools (e.g., Stanford-Binet Intelligence Scales, Wechsler Intelligence Scales).

Adaptive behavior tends to be the overlooked portion of this definition, yet it is equally important in formulating a diagnosis and often more important than intelligence testing in developing a treatment plan. Wallander, Hubert, and Schroeder (1983) noted that assessment of adaptive functioning is often conducted as an afterthought. In part, what we consider to be a diminished regard for adaptive behavior in clinical practice may be caused by the relative infancy of the measurement instruments compared to intellectual tests. The very strong tradition behind intelligence testing in the field of developmental disabilities seems to contribute strongly to the maintenance of this trend, and the gap between assessment for classification and assessment for treatment is not adequately bridged by adaptive behavior instruments (Wallander et al., 1983). Even the specific domains that constitute adaptive behavior are still subject to controversy (Leland, 1983). However, there are a number of measurement tools that have established adequate reliability and validity and provide the practitioner with general guidance for treatment planning. Two such measures are the Vineland Adaptive Behavior Scales and the AAMR Adaptive Behavior Scales.

Adaptive behavior seems to take a secondary role in diagnosis because, in most school systems and institutions, classification of mentally retarded persons is based solely on intelligence, contrary to DSM-III-R and AAMR definitions. Persons who score between two and three standard deviations below the mean on a standardized intelligence test are considered mildly mentally retarded. Those scoring between three and four standard deviations below the mean are classified as moderately mentally retarded; those between four and five are severely mentally retarded. Scores below five standard deviations indicate profound mental retardation. These scores must be accompanied by deficits in adaptive behavior, but the guidelines are less clear concerning the degrees of adaptive deficit at various levels of mental retardation, which further compounds this problem.

TREATMENT

Having noted these practical problems in diagnosis and classification of mentally retarded persons, we should add that this condition is still one of the more reliably defined disorders, and considerable research has been done in treatment development with individuals from all classification groups. The focus of this book is, of course, on treatment. This chapter is designed to examine the most current advances in behavior therapy with mentally retarded persons. The chapter is sectioned according to those behavioral deficits and behavioral excesses discussed most frequently in the literature on treatment for mentally retarded persons. These include self-help, toileting, social skills, and language acquisition for behavioral deficits. We will then examine these behavioral excesses: stereotyped behavior, aggression, and self-injurious behavior. Each treatment area will provide a very brief historical overview followed by the more innovative and recent approaches.

Behavioral deficits and excesses are the focus of treatments for developmentally delayed individuals because of the movement known as normalization. The principle of normalization relates to culturally valued norms for behavior, appearances, experiences, and social status (Wolfensberger, 1980). Normalization refers to the goals for individuals' behavior, their environments, and the treatment they receive from others. Over the past 20 years, behavior analysts and researchers have aimed at normalizing life to the full extent that it is possible for developmentally disabled individuals. The concept of normalization spread further with the passage of Public Law 94-142, the Education for All Handicapped Children Act of 1975, because of its emphasis on placing children in the "least restrictive environment." The thrust of this movement has meant that professionals have been increasingly concerned with the interface between mentally retarded persons and the so-called normal environment. To ensure supportive and enhancing responses from those in the normal environment, training for mentally retarded persons has focused on increasing culturally expected behaviors and decreasing those that deviate from cultural norms.

TREATING BEHAVIORAL DEFICITS

Among the areas of research most frequently focused on are treatments of behavioral deficits in mentally retarded persons, such as: self-help, toileting, and language and social skills.

Self-Help Skills

The typical subcategories that comprise self-help skills include: toileting, self-feeding, dressing, and grooming. Self-help skills comprise a group of behaviors that are important if one is to live successfully in noninstitutionalized settings. These are rudimentary skills for independent functioning. Taras and Matise (1990) described how a caregiver may become trapped between the frustration of trying to train the behaviors and the frustration of having to perform them oneself. Often, providers will stick to the drudgery of performing the behavior for the child, which consumes a great deal of time, fosters greater dependence in the child, and may limit future opportunities in less restrictive settings.

Self-help skills represent one of the first behavioral domains where the efficacy of specific behavioral training techniques was demonstrated (Reid, 1983). Dating back to the early 1960s, the operant techniques that dominated the literature included: forward sequencing, backward chaining, and graduated guidance (Watson & Uzzell, 1981). Some researchers have begun to incorporate behaviorally oriented self-control procedures into self-help skills training with promising results (Matson, 1990). The overall trend in this body of research began with general verification that mentally retarded persons could be taught self-help skills and has moved toward increasing sophistication in measurement, methodology, target behaviors, and techniques (Matson, 1990). Primarily, research over the past 10 years has aimed at advancing the effectiveness and efficiency of techniques used to train self-help skills.

The relative advantages and disadvantages of forward sequencing, backward chaining, and whole-task training have formed one area of interest in recent research (see Taras & Matise, 1990; Watson & Uzzell, 1981, for detailed descriptions of these procedures). In a recent review, Spooner and Spooner (1984) analyzed eight studies that examined the comparative effects of forward sequencing, backward chaining, and whole-task training. The results of these studies were mixed: some supported chaining methods or a particular chaining method (backward) and others supported a total-task method. The authors pointed to a need for research to systematically manipulate one variable at a time in order to determine various parameters of the chaining procedures in relation to the dependent variables, subject variables, apparatus variables, and design.

Both backward chaining and forward sequencing have been criticized for the constraints on staff time while implementing these procedures, which allow for only one additional step per trial. One modification useful in promoting efficiency in backward chaining is called backward chaining the leap-aheads (Matson, 1990). The skill is task-analyzed but then taught in chunks beginning with the last behavior in the chain. After that initial step is performed to criterion, the trainer leaps ahead (skips back) several steps and trains the intermediary steps in a whole-task fashion. This method holds promise for more rapid learning (Spooner & Spooner, 1984).

Graduated guidance is a form of whole-task training (each step is practiced with every trial) that was developed by Azrin and his associates (Azrin & Armstrong, 1973; Azrin, Schaeffer, & Wesolowski, 1976). These programs were designed as highly intensive training for institutionally mentally retarded persons deficient in mealtime and dressing behaviors. They involve aversive and positive reinforcement procedures during increased training trials per day (e.g., nine "mini-meals"). Although Azrin and his colleagues have demonstrated rapid acquisition and maintenance of appropriate skills, some concerns about this method have been articulated. First, attempts to replicate the results have not been successful in terms of subjects being able to reach criterion, even with many additional training hours (Diorio & Konarski, 1984; Stimbert, Minor, & McCoy, 1977). Second, these programs have proven to be taxing on staff resources because they require a 2:1 staff-to-patient ratio and a large chunk of training time per day. A number of authors (Matson, 1990) have questioned the relative effects on staff and the effectiveness of treatments that use large amounts of training time over short versus extended calendar time (e.g., 15 hours over 3 days versus 15 hours over 10 days) but no studies to date have specifically addressed this issue.

Independence training represents a recent alternative comprehensive training program that has been implemented with mentally retarded persons for mealtime (Matson, Ollendick, & Adkins, 1980) and grooming behaviors (Matson, Marchetti, & Adkins, 1980). This method involves whole-task training that includes the operant techniques associated with more traditional approaches (e.g., verbal prompting, manual guidance, social reinforcement, shaping, chaining, and fading of prompts) with the addition of various behaviorally oriented self-control techniques (e.g., modeling, self-evaluation, self-monitoring, and peer monitoring). For a detailed review of self-control techniques with developmentally delayed clients, the reader may refer to Shapiro (1981). The research with independence training has demonstrated the superiority of this treatment package over operant whole-task training alone and no-treatment control groups (Matson, Marchetti, & Adkins, 1980).

A number of advantages of independence training approaches have been noted. These procedures are efficient in that clients are trained in groups and implementation does not appreciably increase staff time and is thus feasible for institutional settings. Also, treatment involves naturalistic social reinforcers rather than presentation of tangibles, and staff acceptability and effectiveness measures have both been favorable. From the client's perspective, this approach promotes positive social interactions with staff regarding client performance and progress, allows clients input and awareness of their own programming, and employs no aversive techniques. The authors of these studies have cautioned that the samples used were neither aggressive nor oppositional and that modifications might be needed for such client groups.

The foregoing discussion has focused on current trends and issues in self-help skills research. Initially, treatments were focused on simply demonstrating that feeding, dressing, and grooming skills could be taught to mentally retarded persons using behavioral techniques. The primary operant approaches used have been forward sequencing, backward chaining, and gradual guidance. During the past 10 years, research has focused on increasing the effectiveness of the procedures and improving the efficiency of their implementation so that caregivers are more likely to promote learning of self-help skills. Independence training was presented as a comprehensive approach that incorporates behaviorally oriented self-control procedures along with standard operant techniques. The next section examines those procedures and advances in the area of toilet training.

TOILET TRAINING

Toileting is often cited as an important adaptive skill for the mentally retarded individual (McCartney, 1990; Taras & Matise, 1990). Toileting skills represent a large and growing portion of the literature on self-help training (Matson, 1990). There are a number of reasons for the strong emphasis on toileting skills in the literature. First, toileting deficits are a common problem among mentally retarded persons. Second, bladder and bowel incontinence may seriously limit the individual's opportunities to function in increasingly normalized environments (Smith, Britton, Johnson, & Thomas, 1975). Third, this problem requires considerable caregiver resources for cleaning clients and the environment. In addition to taking staff time and energy away from training positive behaviors, the noxious nature of this cleanup task has provided strong impetus for developing methods to train toileting skills (Levine & Elliot, 1970; Reid, Wilson, & Faw, 1983; Whitman & Schibak, 1979). Finally, incontinence can have a degrading impact on the client (Azrin, Bugel, & O'Brien, 1971) and negative social consequences, such as exclusion from activities and even more general social ostracism (Bender & Valletutti, 1985).

Ellis (1963) is credited with having developed the first program for toilet training administered to institutionalized mentally retarded persons. This approach, which consisted of placing clients on the toilet at designated times and reinforcing voiding in the toilet, has been labeled the "potting procedure" (Van Wagenen, Meyerson, Kerr, & Mahoney, 1969). Ellis's work initiated the exploration of toileting deficits as resulting primarily from faulty learning. Some authors have noted that this hypothesis has only been partially supported by data (Bettison, 1986; McCartney, 1990). Bettison proposed an interaction between neurological and physiological maturation and learning as an explanation for failures and individual differences in toileting acquisition.

Reid et al. (1983) noted four focal areas in toileting research throughout the 1970s. These areas included training independent toileting (complete and sequential sets of toileting behaviors, including approaching the toilet, undressing, voiding and dressing skills, etc.), and the development and use of automated toileting devices, nighttime training methods, and rapid, intensive programs that require a large number of staff hours over short periods of calendar time.

In particular, two training programs received a great deal of research focus in toilet training during the 1970s: Van Wagenen's "forward-moving" approach (Mahoney, Van Wagenen, & Meyerson, 1971; Van Wagenen et al., 1969) and Azrin and Foxx's (1971) "rapid training" approach. A full explanation of these methods may be found in McCartney (1990). Both programs are rapid and intensive and are aimed at fully independent toileting. Both involve automatic training devices (pants alarm), consuming extra fluids to increase training trials, and graduated guidance procedures for the undressing/dressing portions of the skill sequence.

The Van Wagenen approach takes advantage of the subject's reflex voiding and uses this event as the cue to initiate a learning trial. The trainer classically conditions the interruption of this reflex by yelling "No!" and moves the client to the toileting area; thus the client begins to practice inhibition of voiding, which is a crucial skill in toileting (McCartney, 1990). The Azrin and Foxx (1971) plan includes the addition of a toilet alarm. The client is seated on the toilet at frequent intervals and reinforcers are administered for "dry pants" (also at frequent intervals) and appropriate toileting, whereas accidents are treated with an overcorrection method known as "full cleanliness training."

Smith (1979) conducted a study that compared versions of these two methods with traditional institutional procedures. Both of the intensive programs were superior to the traditional group in terms of self-initiated toileting behavior. The outcome differences between the intensive procedures were minor, however. The author stated that implementation issues and staff preference led to the Azrin and Foxx procedure as the method of choice. McCartney (1990) added that the Van Wagenen program appears to require less training time and minimal punishment.

The most innovative investigations of toileting in the 1980s came from Bettison (1986). In this review, she conceptualized toileting as a complex sequence of skills that must be performed in the proper order and, at times, in an overlapping manner (e.g., inhibition of voiding while approaching the toilet, pulling down pants, and positioning properly). In addition, some of the skills are overt, others covert. Thus, toileting presents formidable challenges to the trainer and client alike, and requires careful selection of terminal behavior that is likely to be supported by the environment during training and maintenance phases.

Bettison (1986) forged important future directions in toileting technology by examining measures of all phases of the total skill sequence including: ratings of pants-down and toilet-approach responses; accident size; time taken to void in the toilet; and the number of voiding accidents, toilet voiding, and self-initiated toileting, each as a percentage of total daily voiding. This thoroughness has allowed Bettison to explore the significance of various components in the intensive programs utilized and the influence of nontraining variables (see Bettison, 1986, for details). These data provided guidance for the development of a backward chaining procedure that eliminated some apparently superfluous procedures (overcorrection) and refined and enhanced others that trained the client to inhibit reflex voiding, attend to appropriate cues, and sequence skills properly. Bettison's (1986) research suggested that shaping procedures are most important when establishing nonvoiding skills, classical conditioning is most useful when training the inhibition of reflex voiding, and reinforcement is most important for maintenance and generalization of the established sequence.

These are some of the current trends in toileting research. Because toileting is such a pivotal behavior and the technology is so specialized for this skill, the topic has been treated separately from other self-help behaviors.

Case Example

Karen was a 5-year-old, severely mentally retarded girl who was toilet trained in her home, with her mother as the trainer. The child was nonverbal and responsive to simple commands only part of the time. She was ambulatory and demonstrated awareness of bladder function by reaching for diapers following an incident of voiding. At baseline, she would stay on the toilet for only 5 seconds. Karen was able to raise and lower her clothing but had not connected these behaviors to any environmental cues. Karen demonstrated no ability to inhibit voiding. She had accidents in 100% of the trials prior to training, and the size of her accidents indicated that she was emptying her bladder quite fully once voiding had started.

Karen's mother collected baseline for two weeks and found that her child's voiding was routinely timed. During this period, she moved the clean diaper supply from the bedroom into the bathroom so that Karen might begin to make an association between voiding and the bathroom. One hour prior to routine voiding, activities were scheduled close to the bathroom area. The goal of this phase of training was for the child to sit on the toilet appropriately. Karen was seated on the toilet with the top down at 5-minute intervals, to extend the time she was able to sit on the toilet. Once she was up to 2-minute periods of sitting on top of the toilet, the seat was raised and her mother began to shape Karen to sit on the toilet with the top up and her pants down for increasing periods of time, up to 3 minutes. Praise and edibles were used as reinforcers for shaping Karen to sit on the toilet appropriately. These training sessions lasted for 1-hour periods three times daily. Karen reached the criterion of sitting for 3 minutes with pants down and seat up within 4 days, and this behavior was maintained throughout training.

During the second phase of training, the goal was to train Karen to inhibit reflex voiding and void in the toilet. In addition, Karen was trained in the nonvoiding skill components of the toileting chain, using a backward chaining method (Bettison, 1986). The trainer would move the child through approaching the toilet, pulling down her pants, seating herself on the toilet, and standing from the toilet, and then used a gradual guidance approach to prompt pulling up her pants. This step signified the beginning of the trial. As Karen learned to exhibit a step to criterion, the training progressed back through the chain. Karen received praise and edibles for completing the training step.

Karen was given three training trials per hour during training hours. After Karen began to void in the toilet, a pants alarm was added to signal the onset of voiding, and this discriminative cue became the stimulus to begin the toileting sequence. As soon as she heard the alarm, the mother produced a very loud and firm "No!" and quickly brought Karen to the toilet area and moved her through the steps preceding the response that was currently targeted as the start of the training trial. After Karen was successful in demonstrating the entire chain, reinforcement was offered for fully independent toileting only.

Language Acquisition

Language deficiencies are a common problem among mentally retarded persons. The exact proportions of the population affected and the degree to which they are impaired remain somewhat unclear (Shapiro & Barrett, 1983). What is clear is that language dysfunction or delay is extensive within this group and that it can greatly impact a wide variety of adaptive skill areas. Communication deficits can limit a person's ability to manipulate his or her environment to meet basic needs and desires for attention, information, materials, and activities (McCoy & Buckhalt, 1990). A number of authors have noted that insufficient communication skills may serve as precursors to the development of maladaptive behavior (Lovaas, 1977; Matson, 1990; Sundberg, 1983). For example, a child may demonstrate an aggressive response to indicate displeasure with an activity. Finally, promoting normalization for mentally retarded persons would dictate an effort to train a language system most consistent with that of nonhandicapped peers, in order to promote social development as well as instructional efficacy in other training arenas.

The early research in language training was a response to the classic theoretical debate between Skinner (1957) and Chomsky (1959). Behaviorists regard language as a complex form of behavior, and the early studies focused on demonstrating that language acquisition was amenable to the principles and techniques of learning. Subjects required remediation in language skills and the focus was on training methods. Psycholinguists and cognitive psychologists viewed language deficits as a function of defective cognitive processes (Sundberg, 1983). These studies examined the development of language in normal children and their focus was on the sequence and structure of language acquisition. McCoy and Buckhalt (1990) gave a detailed account of this history, and implied that current innovations in the field of language training have resulted in a mixing of these two schools. However, Lovaas (1977) reminded readers that organic/cognitive damage approaches produce prognoses that "are so pessimistic that one would be unlikely even to start a language program if one attended to them" (p. 33). Thus, current trends are by nature applied behavioral programs that utilize psycholinguistic data to aid in determining curriculum content.

The early behavioral studies showed that rudimentary language could be trained in mentally retarded persons using basic behavioral methods (Guess, Sailor, & Baer, 1974, 1978; Hollis & Carrier, 1978). A major problem arose in that these studies failed to demonstrate adequate generalization of acquired language from the training to the natural environment. Warren and Rogers-Warren (1985) discussed nine variables that affect such treatment outcomes:

1. What is taught,
2. Who teaches,
3. How skills are taught,
4. How the student is reinforced,
5. Where teaching occurs,
6. How the content of training is organized,
7. What criteria for learning are applied,
8. How the effects of training are measured,
9. How responsive and supportive the student's environments are to new learning. (p. 8)

Changes in each of these variables can facilitate or inhibit the generalization and spontaneous production of expressive language.

Three areas of research are of particular interest in recent years: mand-model procedures, incidental teaching, and time-delay procedures. Each of these procedures will be discussed briefly.

The mand-model procedure represents a systematization of a naturally occurring interaction (Matson, 1990). Originally described by Bruner (1978), there are four steps to this interactional sequence (Rogers-Warren & Warren, 1980). First, the trainer provides stimulating materials. When the child approaches an object, the trainer asks the child to "Tell me what you want." If the child responds with a less than optimal response, the trainer either prompts or models the appropriate response/imitation and provides the child with the desired material. The advantages of this model over more traditional didactic training are that it includes training in the natural environment and uses teachers and parents as trainers. Empirical testing of this approach showed significant increases in rates of verbalization, vocabulary, and complexity of vocalizations (Rogers-Warren & Warren, 1980). Warren, McQuarter, and Rogers-Warren (1984) further investigated this model and found that effects did generalize from the training environment to another classroom. These studies were primarily concerned with training rudimentary language skills.

Incidental teaching is another training method that capitalizes on naturally occurring interactions. Hart and Risley (1982) described a procedure that is somewhat similar to those of the mand-model method. As in the previous design, the trainer either models or prompts language production following the child's demonstration of interest in some material in the environment. If the child does not respond, the trainer instructs the child to imitate the response. Finally, the trainer confirms the correct response verbally and allows the child access to the desired object. The major difference between these two programs is that incidental teaching is dependent on the child's initiation of the interaction within the natural environment; in mand-model, the opportunity for training is created by the trainer. Incidental teaching is one of the most promising areas of research in language acquisition. For further elaboration, readers may refer to a recent review of incidental teaching procedures by Warren and Kaiser (1986).

Delayed prompting is a third area of research that has received a great deal of attention in recent years. This method is designed to promote the transfer of stimulus control of language from the trainer's prompt or instruction to the naturally occurring appropriate stimulus. This procedure was first developed by Touchette (1971) in a visual discrimination learning task. It involves simultaneous presentation of the prompt and the target stimulus. Gradually, the prompt is delayed (often in increasing increments of time) so that the subject is granted the opportunity to respond to the target stimulus without the prompt. This procedure has been successfully used with training tasks other than language production.

Halle, Marshall, and Spradlin (1979) trained six mentally retarded patients to request meals when their food tray was presented, using an increasing delay procedure. Halle, Baer, and Spradlin (1981) again demonstrated the effectiveness of this technique with six mentally retarded children in a special education class. The study employed a variety of stimuli and a fixed, 5-second delay between the presentation of the stimulus and the model requesting access to the object. These data were especially important because of the generalization results. The children began to request objects not trained during the research and to ask for assistance with other tasks.

This section has reviewed only some of the more salient training procedures that are currently being investigated and utilized in language acquisition programs for mentally retarded individuals. Many other important concerns are pertinent to the effectiveness of language development with this population. Assessment of the appropriate entry level for subjects to succeed is essential (Shapiro & Barrett, 1983; Sundberg, 1983). Involving parents, teachers, and peers in training is another area of interest, because these individuals spend the most time with the person and are most familiar with his or her preferences and communication repertoires (Campbell, Stremel-Campbell, & Rogers-Warren, 1985; McCoy & Buckhalt, 1990;

Paul, 1985). All of the methods discussed share the underlying assumption that deficiencies in language development in mentally retarded persons are based on deficits in the motivational structure of the environment.

Case Example

Ned was a 5-year-old boy with spastic cerebral palsy who was confined to a wheelchair. He was functioning in the severe to profound range of mental retardation. Ned had developed a vocabulary of approximately 50 words by the age of 3½ years, at which point he experienced a sudden regression to only three or four distinguishable words. Assessment data revealed that efforts to increase Ned's expressive language were inconsistent in various environments. For example, a speech therapist hired by the family was using a communication board to augment verbalization, the classroom staff were attempting to develop some basic sign language, and the parents had not been trying to elicit language of any kind in the home for some months.

The speech therapist and the behavior analyst developed a collaborative treatment design aimed at increasing expressive speech, to be implemented in all settings. Training sessions were initiated by the trainer by presenting an array of appealing materials. Because Ned showed no interest in the items at first, the trainer was instructed to select two items and present them to Ned using large demonstrative gestures (moving one item to the left and the other to the right) and asking, for example: "Ned, do you want to play with bubbles or with the puzzle?" At first, looking at one item was used as the selection criterion; later, Ned would gesture his preference and, finally, he gestured and vocalized his choice.

This activity was then used to further develop his skills using a similar shaping process. For example, if Ned chose bubbles, the trainer would blow a few bubbles and then prompt Ned to say "bubble." Initially, any attempt at vocalization was reinforced with praise and the stimulus presentation. Once Ned was consistently producing the "b" sound, trainers began to require "bub" prior to blowing more bubbles. A time delay between stimulus presentation and prompt was implemented after a consistent responding pattern had been established. Each training session was designed to last for 20 minutes or three activities, whichever came first. This procedure was implemented three or four times daily between home and school. Ned made significant gains in vocabulary and generalization to nontraining requests for vocalization, and he began to generate verbal requests for desired training and nontraining stimuli.

SELF-INJURY AND STEREOTYPES

Among the problems that have received the most attention in the mental retardation literature are self-injury and stereotyped behavior. Twenty-three percent of the entire mentally retarded population (Maurice & Trudel, 1982), 44 percent of the residential population, and 21 percent of the community-based mental retardation population reviewed had stereotypes. These behaviors, which are rhythmical, repetitive, and typically occur in the same topography (hand to face, face to wall, etc.) have been among the most perplexing to conceptualize from an etiological standpoint and to treat (Matson, 1990). Various causes for the condition have been proposed. For example, organic causes are likely for some cases. One rare but very serious form of self-injury is Lesch-Nyhan syndrome (Lesch & Nyhan, 1964; Nyhan, 1967). The disorder, which is sex linked, is a condition caused by abnormalities in purine metabolism with the child demonstrating spasticity, choreoathetosis, mental retardation (in most cases), elevated urine uric acid, self-mutilation, and, in some cases, aggression. Similarly, self-injury may arise in Cornelia de Lange syndrome, which is characterized by low birth weight, retarded growth, hirsutism, and distinctive face and digital abnormalities (Bryson, Sakati, Nyhan, & Fish, 1971; Marie, Royer, & Rappaport, 1967).

A second class of physiologically related conditions involves homeostatic balance and is emphasized to the greatest degree with stereotypes, although it may also apply to self-injury. The assumption is that the person strives to maintain a balance of central nervous system activation. Given that the person who is mentally retarded by definition has a damaged nervous system, it is believed that this person engages in stereotypes to increase needed CNS arousal (Rojahn & Sisson, 1990). Iwata (1990) compared sensory integration (another form of external stimulation) to behavior modification methods. Sensory integration consisted of the noncontingent presentation of music, visual, and tactile stimulation. Then a behavioral program consisting of contingent reinforcement and punishment was presented. The behavioral program resulted in marked improvements but sensory integration did not. Thus, although the sensory integration theory may be appealing at present, it lacks substantial confirmatory data.

Most medications have proven ineffective, but Naloxone and Naltrexone, opiate antagonists, show some promise as effective treatments, although positive effects have not always been the result (Beckwith, Couk, & Schumacher, 1986; Szymanski, Kedesdy, Sulkes, Cutler, & Stevens-Our, 1987). Thus, at present, behavior modification appears to be the treatment of choice even where the self-injury or stereotypy may appear to be grounded in biological causes.

The operant-respondent model most likely accounts for most cases of self-injury and stereotypy—if not totally, then at least in part. One cause is positive reinforcement: the person obtains a great deal of attention by performing stereotypes or self-injury. The second cause is escape or avoidance of an oversize consequence (negative reinforcement; Schroeder, Rojahn, Mulick, & Schroeder, 1990). Numerous interventions have been developed to deal directly with the contingencies, although biological factors are also likely to be present. This cause also responds best to operant interventions.

Traditionally, interventions have relied heavily on the reinforcement-punishment paradigm. For example, Mason and Newsom (1990) treated stereotyped behaviors of three mentally retarded adolescents (profound) using sensory reinforcers, a type of reinforcement used in the past few years quite frequently for very low functioning people. The idea is to mask the reinforcement properties of various sounds, or visual or auditory sensations. In this case, hand and finger stereotypes were decreased by placing rings on the patients' fingers, thus changing the sensory input to the patients. In only one of the three cases did a patient incorporate the rings into a stereotypy, and effects were rapid. More efforts to develop alternatives to conventional operant techniques have been described.

In another unique study, reinforcement density was evaluated for three profoundly mentally retarded adults living in an institutional setting (Wieseler, Hanson, Chamberlin, & Thompson, 1988). A reinforcement schedule with fixed intervals of 15 to 90 and 180 seconds was based on the performance of an adaptive task: putting blocks in a box. There proved to be a direct correlation between rates of reinforcement and stereotypic behavior. Higher rates of reinforcement resulted in lower rates of stereotypic behavior. Thus, general reinforcement density in an environment may affect behaviors not being directly treated, as stereotypes were in this case.

Another recent development in the treatment literature on self-injury and stereotyped behavior is antecedent control. In the standard operant paradigm, it is hypothesized that behaviors are regulated and maintained by antecedents and consequences of a behavior. Functional and structural analysis, which is received as a less oversize/intrusive alternative to many behavioral interventions, consists of the identification and manipulation of antecedents (Axelrod, 1987). Thus, following the identification of a problem behavior and the determination of an appropriate measurement procedure, various issues are to be addressed. Carr (1987) suggested that the clinician identify when the behavior is attended to; when the client no longer receives reinforcement for other behaviors; and when the child is in the company of adults. Bailey (1986) more recently suggested that, in addition, the clinician should look at the following: Are there circumstances in which the behavior always occurs or never occurs? Could the client be signaling physiological deprivation such as thirst or hunger? Could the behavior be a side effect of medication? Does the client perform the behavior to escape the toughening situation or to compete with boredom or loneliness? Does the behavior only occur with certain people? Others have found such information useful and thus, to further systematize treatment efforts, scales have been developed and are termed antecedent checklists. These measures have many more questions but address similar issues. Similarly, more sensitive graphs to identify antecedents have been developed. Touchette, MacDonald, and Longer (1985) developed such a method, which they refer to as a scatterplot. This type of graph can be used to estimate the rate of a behavior at different time periods each day, with time intervals along one axis and several specific target behaviors along the other. Visual interpretation is used to establish patterns of responding. These patterns can be used to determine whether a particular cause of self-injury or stereotypy might be due to environmental factors such as those noted by Carr (1987) or Bailey (1986). Most behavior analysis studies have dealt with the delivery of consequences external to the individual, such as reprimands, DRO schedules, overcorrection, and token economies. However, the idea here is to put more emphasis on antecedent versus consequent events.

One study that supports the antecedent hypothesis was conducted by Weeks and Gaylord-Ross (1981). Working with two children who were severely mentally retarded, they found higher rates of self-injury when there were more demands placed on the patients by staff. Further, more difficult tasks escalated the rates of self-injury. Using a more efficient, less demanding treatment (errorless learning) resulted in less aberrant behavior.

Another argument is that a considerable amount of stereotyped and self-injurious behavior is a form of communication (Carr & Durand, 1985). These authors found more inappropriate behavior during academic tasks when children were receiving little attention. Teaching the patients how to ask for assistance resulted in decreases in inappropriate behavior.

Despite the various positive developments with respect to less intrusive behavioral interventions such as those noted above, combinations of reinforcement and punishment still appear to be the most effective interventions for most stereotyped and self-injurious behavior. These findings are particularly clear with the most extreme and recalcitrant forms of these behaviors. As a result, effective interventions still include overcorrection, contingent restraint, taste aversives, and similar punishers in combination with contingent reinforcement in various forms (Matson & Taras, 1989). These procedures have been described in great detail for many years. The general notion is to train and reinforce behaviors incompatible with the aberrant behavior. Thus, clients would be taught words or leisure skills with their hands, versus hand flapping or hitting themselves in the face with a hand. The problem with teaching incompatible behaviors and using DRO intervals to reinforce nonoccurrence of self-injury and stereotypy is that this approach often is not sufficient. Without consequating the aberrant behaviors, reinforcement and alternative behaviors alone are often insufficient to decrease inappropriate behavior. Furthermore, the inappropriate behaviors may occur so often that there is not an interval to reinforce or a time to teach alternative behaviors. Combined punishment and reinforcement is often a very powerful technique. For example, one follow-up study showed that effects of such a program for self-injury were maintained for 10 years (Foxx, 1990).

The topic of self-injury and stereotypy is among the most frequently discussed in the mental retardation field. Researchers are concerned about generating more effective interventions, although the number of effective interventions developed to this point is impressive. There is a great deal of research activity on this topic. Some research activity on language acquisition has occurred but there has been precious little research on self-help skills. Another very active research area is social skills, the final topic to be covered in this chapter.

Social Skills

Social skills are a defining characteristic of mental retardation; they permeate almost every aspect of the mentally retarded person's life. This statement is confirmed by a substantial amount of research suggesting that this problem covers the spectrum of mentally retarded people's behavior (Affleck, 1977; Marchetti & Campbell, 1990; Zigler, Balla, & Hoddap, 1984). Similarly, the current definition of mental retardation requires that a person display impairments in adaptive/social behavior in addition to intellectual deficiencies (Grossman, 1983). Social behavior appears to be a significant treatment area to enhance community integration and assist handicapped persons in their adjustment to various emotional problems.

Because professionals in the mental retardation field have accepted the above arguments, it should be no surprise to learn that a great deal of treatment research has appeared. Social skills technology has been used to treat aggression, depression, obsessive-compulsive disorders, community adjustment, making friends, and many other adjustment problems.

Social skills are typically trained via a social learning or operant approach. A fine-grain analysis of a skill is made and the behavior is broken into subcomponents such as eye contact, appropriate verbal content, tone of voice, and voice volume. Social skills training using the social learning theory approach involves role playing, modeling, instructions, performance feedback, and social and tangible reinforcers. Operant methods conversely involve the reinforcement and shaping of prosocial behaviors. The former method is used with mild to severely mentally retarded adolescents and adults, and the latter method is preferred for small children and profoundly mentally retarded persons.

A topic to be addressed later is the concern that many have had regarding the use of aversive/intrusive treatments. The positive nature of social skills and its general acceptance as a skill acquisition procedure have resulted in even further increases in its popularity. Numerous problems have therefore been effectively treated.

Matson and Stephens (1978), for example, targeted negative social behaviors such as arguing and fighting as forerunners of intervention for both severely mentally retarded and psychotic persons. The frequency of fighting and arguing decreased and the appropriate use of target behaviors such as posture, speech content, and affect improved markedly. Results were viewed as highly significant. Operant techniques such as reinforcement, shaping, and chaining have also been used. Whitman, Mercurio, and Caponigri (1970) combined these methods with instructions and feedback to increase ball play of two mentally retarded boys. They noted marked improvements.

Several research papers have also employed video technology to provide feedback to mentally retarded persons (King, Marcattilio, & Hanson, 1981; Meredith, Saxon, Doleys, & Kyzer, 1980). Further, table games have been suggested as a means of providing structure in social skills acquisition (Foxx, McMorrow, & Mennemier, 1984). More of these adaptations are likely to enhance social skills acquisition with mentally retarded persons.

Ralph and Birnbrauer (1986) trained three men who were mildly or moderately mentally retarded. Reinforcement, modeling, and feedbacks were used to train behaviors to acquisition. However, these clients did not evince appropriate behaviors in naturalistic settings until they had been traveled to accurate rate what had actually occurred. The correspondence training was seen as a prompt to perform correct behavior.

This social skills approach to skill acquisition has proven to be very powerful. Matson et al. (1988) were able to use feedback, modeling, and reinforcement to train three severely and profoundly mentally retarded multiple handicapped adolescents. Two of these children, in addition to mental retardation, exhibited symptoms of autism; the third was profoundly deaf. Picture prompts and tangible reinforcers were adaptations of the treatment package that were important in teaching eye contact and in-seat and on-task behaviors.

Social skills training, in these few examples and other studies, has proven to be highly effective in teaching many social behaviors to mentally retarded individuals with a variety of handicaps. These procedures are gaining rapidly in popularity and should be a standard component of educational and habilitative programs for all mentally retarded individuals.

CRITICAL FACTORS THAT IMPACT CLINICAL MANAGEMENT

Two areas of controversy that often affect treatment planning require discussion: punishment and dual diagnosis. These areas have been selected because of their central nature in the debate on the roles and types of various interventions used. Also, subsumed under these topics are mentally retarded persons with the most critical behavior problems.

Limits on Punishment

Perhaps the most significant factors affecting the clinical management of mentally retarded people are political in nature. Beginning in the 1980s, the most influential factor in clinical behavior therapy with mentally retarded persons has been the rise of advocacy organizations. These groups are more active in the area of developmental disabilities than in any other mental health domain. Among them are the Association for Retarded Citizens (ARC) and the Association for the Severely Handicapped (TASH). The emphasis of these groups has sprung from an earlier development in the mental retardation area: normalization. This concept derives from the notion that efforts should be made to change the behavior of handicapped persons so that these individuals appear as normal as possible. Some advocates have argued that procedures such as data collection should not be allowed, because of its artificial nature. Others accept data collection and some behavior modification procedures but do not endorse punishment. Procedures placed on the most onerous list are contingent electrical stimulation, taste aversion, restraint, and time out. Advocacy groups and their allies have proven to be a very potent force, and laws and regulations against behavioral procedures have been passed in various states.

Exemplifying the trend and perhaps the focal point of these debates has been the Behavior Research Institute case in Massachusetts, in which the Institute was opposed by the state office of child protection and advocacy. TASH and ARC were among those who supported the ban on all aversive strategies, with the exclusion of saying no and token fines. The debate over this case was exacerbated by the serious nature of the clients' (mean age 27 years) behavior problems. For example, one client who was 6 ft. 6 in. tall bit the nose off of a staff person during the period when restraints and aversive techniques were disallowed, in the midst of the legal debate. Similarly, another client injured 57 staff in a period of 1 year. This level of severity of aggression is commonly found in large inpatient facilities for mentally retarded persons and represents a formidable task, which may be unmanageable using reinforcement strategies alone, based on the most current research.

Behavior analysts have focused a great deal of attention on responding to the accusations of misuse of aversive techniques and the public outcry concerning this issue. Primarily, this response has come in two forms. First, there have been a number of strategies for controlled self-regulation in the administration of aversive procedures. Second, behavior analysts have sought with new rigor to systematically uncover the least intrusive methods available for suppression of injurious behavior (see the discussion of self-injurious behavior).

In 1980, the Association for the Advancement of Behavior Therapy (AABT) appointed a task force to investigate the treatment of self-injurious behavior (Favell, McGinsey, & Shell, 1982). The result of this endeavor was a set of guidelines for implementation of aversive techniques as well as suggested regulatory procedures to monitor service delivery. This model allows for a shared community and expert responsibility in determining the appropriateness of a given technique on a case-by-case basis, using objective data for decision making. Unfortunately, the legislative bodies of many states have passed laws forbidding consideration of such individualized approaches. Thus, the controversy is very much alive.

Dual Diagnosis

Dual diagnosis refers to the coexistence of mental retardation and a psychiatric disorder that cannot be attributed to the primary diagnosis. It is widely agreed, on the basis of extensive albeit varied survey data, that mentally retarded persons are more susceptible to emotional disorders than are nonretarded individuals (Benson, 1990; Ollendick & Ollendick, 1982). Matson and Frame (1986) reported rates up to five to six times greater than those for nonretarded children, and the rate increases proportionally to the degree of impairment. In spite of this consistent finding, there has been a tendency for professionals to overlook the emotional problems of developmentally delayed individuals (Matson & Frame, 1986).

Reiss, Levitan, and Szyszko (1982) empirically demonstrated this tendency to disregard psychopathology in mentally retarded persons by asking professionals to evaluate case scenarios that differed only in the presence or absence of mental retardation. These authors found that mental retardation decreased the diagnostic importance of abnormal behavior, a phenomenon that was labeled diagnostic overshadowing. Benson (1990) suggested that emotional disorders are less troublesome to caretakers and thus receive less treatment attention than noncompliance or aggression. It also has been proposed that professionals sometimes regard mental retardation as psychopathology and thus fail to recognize a developmentally delayed person's susceptibility to additional psychopathologies (Benson, 1990; Matson & Frame, 1986; Menolascino & Stark, 1984). The coexistence of mental illness with developmental delays creates unique clinical challenges to the professional. It means that the professional must be vigilant about these additional problems and tailor assessment of the individual to expose rather than circumvent problems that tend to be obscured by traditional methods.

Because issues surrounding the use of punishment and the management of dual diagnosis in the mentally retarded are currently being researched with new rigor and enthusiasm, the professional is challenged to remain up-to-date in reviewing the literature.

SUMMARY

This chapter has presented a review of some of the current issues on behavior therapy as they pertain to mentally retarded persons. Behavior modifiers have traditionally used intervention with this population and it continues to be one of the most heavily studied, if not the most heavily studied population with learning based interventions. Further, behavioral interventions appear to be the treatment of choice for many problem behaviors in this population.

The amount of research done on this population is substantial, relative to most mental health problems. It is not possible to cover adequately the numerous advances that have been made, although we have attempted to give examples of some major developments while providing references where more extensive information can be obtained. Perhaps the greatest result, however, is the transition of the field of developmental disabilities from one where handicapped people were largely viewed as untreatable 25 years ago to the point where great expectations and optimism for handicapped people now exist. These changes are largely due to behavioral methods. Furthermore, an impressive array of new interventions, particularly for self-injurious and stereotyped behaviors, has emerged in the past 5 to 10 years. Many of these developments have occurred as a result of recent concerns over the potential intrusiveness of many punishment procedures used with highly disruptive problem behaviors. Other major areas appear to be dual diagnosis and social skills, where very substantial numbers of treatment studies have been published in recent years. It is likely that this trend will continue through the next decade. Self-help skills and language conversely are seen as extremely important topics where researchers have paid far too little attention in recent years. It will be interesting to see what emerges in the next few years. Undoubtedly, however, behavioral treatments will remain the cornerstone of treatment for mentally retarded persons.

REFERENCES

Affleck, G. G. (1977). Interpersonal competencies of the mentally retarded. In P. Mittler (Ed.), *Research to practice in mental retardation. Vol. II: Education and training* (pp. 85–91). Baltimore: University Park Press.

Axelrod, S. (1987). Functional and structural analysis of behavior: Approaches leading to reduced use of punishment procedures? *Research in Developmental Disabilities, 8,* 165–178.

Azrin, N. H., & Armstrong, P. M. (1973). The "mini-meal": A method for teaching eating skills to the profoundly retarded. *Mental Retardation, 11,* 9–11.

Azrin, N. H., Bugel, C., & O'Brien, F. (1971). Behavioral engineering: Two apparatus for toilet training retarded children. *Journal of Applied Behavior Analysis, 4,* 249-253.

Azrin, N. H., & Foxx, R. M. (1971). A rapid method of toilet training the institutionalized retarded. *Journal of Applied Behavior Analysis, 4,* 89-99.

Azrin, N. H., Schaeffer, R. M., & Wesolowski, M. D. (1976). A rapid method of teaching profoundly retarded persons to dress by a reinforcement-guidance method. *Mental Retardation, 14,* 29-33.

Bailey, J. (1986). *Please don't do behavior modification on me.* Paper presented at the meeting of the Association for Behavior Analysis, Milwaukee, WI.

Beckwith, B. E., Couk, D. I., & Schumacher, K. (1986). Failure of naloxone to reduce self-injurious behavior in two developmentally disabled females. *Applied Research in Mental Retardation, 7,* 183-188.

Bender, M., & Valletutti, P. J. (1985). *Teaching the moderately and severely handicapped: A functional curriculum for self-care, motor skills, and household management, Vol. 1* (2nd ed.). Austin, TX: Pro-Ed.

Benson, B. A. (1990). Emotional problems I: Anxiety disorders and depression. In J. L. Matson (Ed.), *Handbook of behavior modification with the mentally retarded* (2nd ed.; pp. 391-420). New York: Plenum.

Bettison, S. (1986). Behavioral approaches to toilet training for retarded persons. In N. R. Ellis & N. W. Bray (Eds.), *International review of research in mental retardation, Vol. 14* (pp. 319-350). Orlando, FL: Academic Press.

Bruner, J. (1978). Prelinguistic prerequisites of speech. In R. N. Campbell & P. T. Smith (Eds.), *Recent advances in the psychology of language: Language development and mother-child interaction.* New York: Plenum.

Bryson, Y., Sakati, N., Nyhan, W. S., & Fish, C. (1971). Self-mutilative behavior in the Cornelia de Lange syndrome. *American Journal of Mental Deficiency, 76,* 319-324.

Campbell, C. R., Stremel-Campbell, K., & Rogers-Warren, A. K. (1985). Programming teacher support for functional language. In S. F. Warren & A. K. Rogers-Warren (Eds.), *Teaching functional language* (pp. 390-340). Baltimore: University Park Press.

Carr, E. G. (1987). The motivation of self-injurious behavior: A review of some hypotheses. *Psychological Bulletin, 84,* 800-816.

Carr, E. G., & Durand, M. (1985). Reducing behavior problems through functional communication training. *Journal of Applied Behavior Analysis, 8,* 11-126.

Chomsky, N. (1959). Review of B. F. Skinner, Verbal behavior. *Language, 35,* 26-58.

Dietz, D. E. D., & Repp, A. C. (1989). *Mental retardation.* In T. H. Ollendick & M. Hersen (Eds.), *Handbook of psychopathology*, 2nd ed. (pp. 75-91). New York: Plenum.

Diorio, M. S., & Konarski, E. A., Jr. (1984). Evaluation of a method for teaching dressing skills to profoundly mentally retarded persons. *American Journal of Mental Deficiency, 89,* 307-309.

Ellis, N. R. (1963). Toilet training the severely defective patient: An S-R reinforcement analysis. *American Journal of Mental Deficiency, 68,* 98-103.

Favell, J. E., McGinsey, J. F., & Shell, R. M. (1982). Treatment of self-injury by providing alternate sensory activities. *Analysis and Intervention in Developmental Disabilities, 2,* 83-104.

Foxx, R. M. (1990). "Harry"; A ten-year follow-up of the successful treatment of a self-injurious man. *Research in Developmental Disabilities, 11,* 67-76.

Foxx, R. M., McMorrow, M., & Mennemeir, M. (1984). Teaching social vocational skills to retarded adults with a modified table game: An analysis of generalization. *Journal of Applied Behavior Analysis, 17,* 343-352.

Grossman, H. J. (Ed.). (1983). *Manual on terminology and classification in mental retardation.* Washington, DC: American Association of Mental Retardation.

Guess, D., Sailor, W., & Baer, D. M. (1974). To teach language to retarded children. In R. L. Schiefelbusch & L. L. Lloyd (Eds.), *Language perspectives: Acquisition, retardation, and intervention* (pp. 529-563). Baltimore: University Park Press.

Guess, D., Sailor, W., & Baer, D. M. (1978). Children with limited language. In R. L. Schiefelbusch (Ed.), *Language intervention strategies* (pp. 101–143). Baltimore: University Park Press.

Halle, J., Marshall, A., & Spradlin, J. (1979). Time delay: A technique to increase language use and facilitate generalization in retarded children. *Journal of Applied Behavior Analysis, 12,* 431–439.

Halle, J., Baer, D. M., & Spradlin, J. E. (1981). Teacher's generalized use of delay as a stimulus control procedure to increase language use in handicapped children. *Journal of Applied Behavior Analysis, 14,* 389–409.

Hart, B., & Risley, T. (1982). *How to use incidental teaching for elaborating language.* Lawrence, KS: H & H Enterprises.

Hollis, J. H., & Carrier, J. K., Jr. (1978). Intervention strategies for nonspeech children. In R. L. Schiefelbusch (Ed.), *Language intervention strategies.* Baltimore: University Park Press.

King, R., Marcattilio, A. J., & Hanson, R. (1981). Some functions of videotape equipment in training social skills to institutionalized mentally retarded adults. *Behavioral Engineering, 6,* 159–157.

Leland, H. (1983). Adaptive and behavior scales. In J. Matson & J. A. Mulick (Eds.), *Handbook of mental retardation* (pp. 215–226).

Lesch, M., & Nyhan, W. L. (1964). A familiar disorder of uric acid metabolism and central nervous system function. *American Journal of Medicine, 36,* 561–570.

Levine, M. N., Elliot, C. B. (1970). Toilet training for profoundly retarded with a limited staff. *Mental Retardation, 8,* 48–50.

Lovaas, O. I. (1977). *The autistic child: Language development through behavior modification.* New York: Halsted.

Mahoney, K., Van Wagenen, R., & Meyerson, L. (1971). Toilet training of normal and retarded children. *Journal of Applied Behavioral Analysis, 4,* 173–181.

Marchetti, A. G., & Campbell, V. A. (1990). Social skills. In J. L. Matson (Ed.), *Handbook of behavior modification with the mentally retarded* (2nd ed.; pp. 333–350). New York: Plenum.

Marie, C., Royer, P., & Rappaport, R. (1967). Congenital hyperuricemia with neurological renal and hematologic problems. *Archives Françaises de Pediatric, 24,* 501–510.

Mason, S. A., & Newsom, C. D. (1990). The application of sensory change to reduce stereotyped behavior. *Research in Developmental Disabilities, 11,* 257–272.

Matson, J. L. (Ed.). (1990). *Handbook of behavior modification with the mentally retarded* (2nd ed.). New York: Plenum.

Matson, J. L., & Frame, C. L. (1986). *Psychopathology among mentally retarded children and adolescents.* Beverly Hills, CA: Sage.

Matson, J. L., Manikam, R., Coe, D., Raymond, K., Toras, M., & Long, N. (1988). Training social skills to severely mentally retarded multiple handicapped adolescents. *Research in Developmental Disabilities, 9,* 195–208.

Matson, J. L., Marchetti, A., & Adkins, J. A. (1980). Comparison of operant- and independence-training procedures for mentally retarded adults. *American Journal of Mental Deficiency, 84,* 487–494.

Matson, J. L., Ollendick, T. H., & Adkins, J. A. (1980). A comprehensive dining program for mentally retarded adults. *Behaviour Research and Therapy, 18,* 107–112.

Matson, J. L., & Stephens, R. M. (1978). Increasing appropriate behavior of explosive chronic psychiatric patients with a social skills training package. *Behavior Modification, 2,* 61–76.

Matson, J. L., & Taras, M. E. (1989). A 20 year review of punishment and alternative methods to treat problem behavior in developmentally delayed persons. *Research in Developmental Disabilities, 10,* 85–104.

Maurice, P., & Trudel, G. (1982). Self-injurious behavior prevalence and relationships to environmental events. In J. H. Hollis and C. E. Meyers (Eds.), *Life-threatening behavior:* Analysis and intervention. Washington, D.C.: American Association of Mental Deficiency.

McCartney, J. R. (1990). Toilet training. In J. L. Matson (Ed.), *Handbook of behavior modification with the mentally retarded* (2nd ed.; pp. 255–272). New York: Plenum.

McCoy, J. F., & Buckhalt, J. A. (1990). Language acquisition. In J. L. Matson (Ed.),

Handbook of behavior modification with the mentally retarded (2nd ed.; pp. 445–466). New York: Plenum.

Menolascino, F., & Stark, J. (Eds.). (1984). *Handbook of mental illness in the mentally retarded* (pp. 3–44). New York: Plenum.

Meredith, R., Saxon, S., Doleys, D., & Kyzer, B. (1980). Social skills training with mildly retarded young adults. *Journal of Clinical Psychology, 36,* 1000–1009.

Nyhan, W. L. (1967). The Lesch-Nyhan Syndrome: Self-destructive biting, mental retardation, neurological disorder and hyperuricemia. *Developmental Medicine and Child Neurology, 9,* 563–572.

Ollendick, T. H., & Ollendick, D. G. (1982). Anxiety disorders. In J. L. Matson & R. P. Barrett (Eds.), *Psychopathology in the mentally retarded* (pp. 77–119). New York: Grune & Stratton.

Paul, L. (1985). Programming peer support for functional language. In S. F. Warren & A. K. Rogers-Warren (Eds.), *Teaching functional language* (pp. 289–308). Baltimore: University Park Press.

Ralph, A., & Birnbrauer, J. S. (1986). The potential of correspondence training for facilitating generalization of social skills. *Applied Research in Mental Retardation, 7,* 415–430.

Reid, D. H. (1983). Trends and issues in behavioral research on training feeding and dressing skills. In J. L. Matson & F. Andrasik (Eds.), *Treatment issues and innovations in mental retardation* (pp. 213–240). New York: Plenum.

Reid, D. H., Wilson, P. G., & Faw, G. D. (1983). Teaching self-help skills. In J. L. Matson & J. A. Mulick (Eds.), *Handbook of mental retardation* (pp. 429–442). New York: Pergamon.

Reiss, S., Levitan, G. W., & Szyszko, J. (1982). Emotional disturbance and mental retardation: Diagnostic overshadowing. *American Journal of Mental Deficiency, 86,* 567–574.

Rogers-Warren, A., & Warren, S. F. (1980). Mands for verbalization: Facilitating the display of newly trained language in children. *Behavior Modification, 4,* 361–382.

Rojahn, J., & Sisson, L. A. (1990). Stereotyped behavior. In J. L. Matson (Ed.), *Handbook of behavior modification with the mentally retarded* (2nd ed.). New York: Plenum.

Schroeder, S. R., Rojahn, J., Mulick, J. A., & Schroeder, C. S. (1990). Self-injurious behavior. In J. L. Matson (Ed.), *Handbook of behavior modification with the mentally retarded* (2nd ed.). New York: Plenum.

Shapiro, E. S. (1981). Self-control procedures with the mentally retarded student. In M. Hersen, R. M. Eisler, & P. M. Miller (Eds.), *Progress in behavior modification, Vol. 12* (pp. 265–297). Orlando, FL: Academic Press.

Shapiro, E. S., & Barrett, R. P. (1983). Behavior assessment of the mentally retarded. In J. L. Matson & F. Andrasik (Eds.), *Treatment issues and innovations in mental retardation* (pp. 159–212). New York: Plenum.

Skinner, B. F. (1957). *Verbal behavior.* New York: Appleton-Century-Crofts.

Smith, P. (1979). A comparison of different methods of toilet training the mentally handicapped. *Behaviour Research and Therapy, 17,* 33–43.

Smith, R., Britton, P., Johnson, M., & Thomas, D. (1975). Problems involved in toilet training of institutionalized mentally retarded individuals. *Behaviour Research and Therapy, 3,* 301–302.

Spooner, F., & Spooner, D. (1984). A review of chaining effects: Implications for future research and practice. *Education and Training of the Mentally Retarded, 10,* 114–124.

Stimbert, V. E., Minor, J. W., & McCoy, J. F. (1977). Intensive feeding training with retarded children. *Behavior Modification, 1,* 517, 529.

Sundberg, M. L. (1983). Language. In J. L. Matson & S. E. Breuning (Eds.), *Assessing the mentally retarded* (pp. 285–310). New York: Grune & Stratton.

Szymanski, L., Kedesdy, J., Sulkes, S., Cutler, A., & Stevens-Our, P. (1987). Naltrexone in treatment of self-injurious behavior: A clinical study. *Research in Developmental Disabilities, 8,* 179–190.

Taras, M. E., & Matise, M. (1990). Acquisition of self-help skills. In J. L. Matson (Ed.), *Handbook of behavior modification with the mentally retarded*, 2nd ed. (pp. 273–304). New York: Plenum.

Touchette, P. E. (1971). Transfer of stimulus control: Measuring the moment of transfer.

Journal of the Experimental Analysis of Behavior, 15, 347, 354.

Van Wagenen, K., Meyerson, L., Kerr, N. J., & Mahoney, K. (1969). Field trials of a new procedure for toilet training. *Journal of Experimental Child Psychology, 8,* 147–159.

Wallander, J., Hubert, N., & Schroeder, C. (1983). Self-care skills. In J. L. Matson & S. E. Breuning (Eds.), *Assessing the mentally retarded* (pp. 209–246). New York: Grune & Stratton.

Warren, S. F., & Kaiser, A. P. (1986). Incidental language teaching: A critical review. *Journal of Speech and Hearing Disorders, 51,* 291–299.

Warren, S. F., McQuarter, R. J., & Rogers-Warren, A. K. (1984). The effects of mands and models on the speech of unresponsive socially isolate children. *Journal of Speech and Hearing Disorders, 47,* 42–52.

Warren, S. F., & Rogers-Warren, A. K. (Eds.). (1985). *Teaching functional language.* Austin, TX: Pro-Ed.

Watson, L. S., & Uzzell, R. (1981). Teaching self-help skills to the mentally retarded. In J. L. Matson & J. R. McCartney (Eds.), *Handbook of behavior modification with the mentally retarded* (pp. 151–176). New York: Plenum.

Weeks, M., & Gaylord-Ross, R. (1981). Task difficulty and aberrant behavior in severely handicapped students. *Journal of Applied Behavior Analysis, 14,* 449–463.

Whitman, T. L., Mercurio, J. R., & Caponigri, V. (1970). Development of social responses in two severely retarded children. *Journal of Applied Behavior Analysis, 3,* 133–138.

Whitman, T. L., & Schibak, J. W. (1979). Behavior modification research with the severely and profoundly retarded. In N. R. Ellis (Ed.), *Handbook of mental deficiency, psychological theory of research.* Hillsdale, NJ: Erlbaum.

Wieseler, N. A., Hanson, R. H., Chamberlin, T. P., & Thompson, T. (1988). Stereotypic behavior of mentally retarded adults adjunctive to a positive reinforcement schedule. *Research in Development Disabilities, 9,* 393–404.

Wolfensberger, W. (1980). A brief overview of the principle of normalization. In R. J. Flynn & K. E. Nitch (Eds.), *Normalization, social integration, and community services.* Baltimore: University Park Press.

Zigler, E., Balla, D., & Hoddap, R. (1984). On the definition and classification of mental retardation. *American Journal of Mental Deficiency, 89,* 215–230.

CHAPTER 17

Behavioral Treatment for Children with Autism

LAURA SCHREIBMAN, MARJORIE H. CHARLOP, and PATRICIA F. KURTZ

Autism was first identified as a distinct clinical syndrome by Leo Kanner (1943), who noted that a group of children displayed symptoms characterized by extreme withdrawal, bizarre repetitive behaviors, and pervasive deficits in language and social behavior. Following is a description of the behaviors characteristic of autism.

Deficits in social behavior are typically seen. The children are withdrawn and aloof, do not establish eye contact, and prefer to be alone. They generally fail to develop social relationships and avoid interactions with people. As infants, they do not bond to their parents and may resist holding or cuddling. When older, they seldom seek attention or comfort from others and do not play with peers.

Approximately 50% of autistic children *fail to acquire communicative language.* Those who do acquire speech commonly display echolalia. Immediate echolalia is the repetition of an utterance just heard, such as a child's repeating "Do you want a drink?" when asked by his mother. Delayed echolalia is the contextually inappropriate repetition of an utterance heard sometime in the past (e.g., hours, days), such as a jingle from a television commercial. These children also commonly display pronominal reversal, saying, for example, "*You* want a cookie" rather than "*I* want a cookie." Generally, autistic children's speech is rote and mechanical sounding, and is often used in a self-stimulatory rather than communicative manner.

Autistic children frequently display *ritualistic behavior and insistence on sameness* in their environment. They may be quite compulsive, lining up toys or sorting objects by color or size. They also may develop intense attachments to particular objects, such as vacuum cleaners, credit cards, or pieces of string, or preoccupations with concepts such as colors or numbers. Many children also establish rigid routines, such as wearing only certain items of clothing, eating only specific foods, or traveling the same route to school. The children manifest a marked resistance to change in their environment; any disruption (e.g., rearranging the furniture) may be quite upsetting.

Autistic children also display characteristic *abnormalities in response to the physical environment.* They may seem oblivious to a sudden loud noise or the departure of a parent, yet may scream at the turning of a newspaper page. As such, they are said to display an "apparent sensory deficit." Unusual responsiveness is

---

Preparation of this chapter was facilitated by U.S.P.H.S. Research Grants MH 39434 and MH 28210 from the National Institute of Mental Health.

also evident in learning situations, where autistic children typically respond to only a limited amount of the available, relevant information. This failure to respond to simultaneous multiple cues, or stimulus overselectivity, interferes with learning and generalization of new behaviors (Schreibman, 1988).

Self-stimulatory behavior is frequently displayed by many autistic children. Their bizarre, repetitive, stereotyped movements may involve gross motor behavior (e.g., hand flapping, body rocking) or subtler activities (e.g., rubbing textures, sniffing objects), and seem to serve no other function than to provide sensory feedback. If permitted, autistic children may engage in self-stimulation for prolonged periods, thus interfering with treatment, learning, and other appropriate activities.

The most dangerous and dramatic behavior displayed by many autistic children is *self-injurious behavior* (SIB), which occurs when the child inflicts physical damage to his or her own body. Head banging and self-biting are most common, but a variety of topographies are seen, including face scratching, hair pulling, and elbow or leg banging. SIB may range in intensity from relatively mild (e.g., lightly slapping the face) to severe or life-threatening (e.g., banging the head on a wall).

Displays of *inappropriate affect* are also characteristic of autistic children. Many children exhibit inappropriate reactions, such as laughing when frightened or hurt, or crying or tantrumming for no apparent reason. Some children also display flattened affect or mood swings. Often, they are fearless in dangerous situations (e.g., crossing busy streets), yet they may display intense, irrational fears of harmless objects such as, for example, sesame seeds, rubber balls, or ferns.

The intellectual functioning of children with autism was previously thought to be normal. Unfortunately, it is now known that most autistic children are *functionally mentally retarded*. Approximately 80% of these children score below 70 on IQ tests. However, many children do display islets of superior abilities in such areas as math, music, and mechanics.

Autistic children are generally physically healthy and attractive. They are often described as having an excellent memory, and as being clever and manipulative. Also, they commonly display behavior problems such as tantrums, aggression, noncompliance, pica, bed wetting, and feeding problems.

At this time, the exact cause of autism is unknown but is believed to be organic and present from birth. Early theories suggesting autism was caused by the parents and the home environment have not been supported by experimental research (see Schreibman, 1988 for a review).

THE BEHAVIORAL APPROACH TO AUTISM

The behavioral model views the syndrome of autism as a cluster of specific behaviors and seeks to promote measurable and observable changes in these behaviors. In general, *behavioral deficits* are increased by teaching and systematically reinforcing occurrences; *behavioral excesses* are the targets of reduction and elimination. Through the use of behavioral assessment, a functional definition of the syndrome specific to an individual child is made. Individual behaviors are operationally defined, variables controlling such behaviors are identified, and appropriate treatment procedures are applied.

In contrast to the traditional conceptualization of the syndrome as a "disease," a behavioral definition of autism specific to each child permits reliable observation and measurement and suggests an effective treatment and a prognosis. This is particularly important in view of the tremendous heterogeneity that exists within the autistic population. The behavioral model is the only treatment approach empirically demonstrated to be effective with autistic children (Egel, Koegel, & Schreibman, 1980). This chapter describes recent advances in research on behavioral treatment of autistic children.

BEHAVIORAL EXCESSES

The three general categories of behavioral excesses are self-injurious behavior (e.g., head banging, face slapping, eye gouging), self-stimulatory behavior (e.g., body rocking, arm flapping, spinning), and disruptive behavior (e.g., aggression, tantrums, property destruction). Because these behaviors often interfere with learning and hinder the child's progress, their reduction and elimination are critical aspects of successful treatment.

A wide array of procedures has been devised to reduce behavioral excesses. *Extinction* is the removal of the environmental event that maintains the inappropriate behavior. For example, if a child's tantrums were maintained by social attention, extinction would be implemented when the tantrums were ignored. *Punishment* is the application of an unpleasant stimulus contingent upon the occurrence of an inappropriate behavior. Stimuli that have been effective in reducing behavioral excesses include a loud "No," contingent spank, water mist spray, and electric shock. Because the use of electric shock and other physical aversives is understandably unpopular and does hold the potential for misuse, the development of effective and less intrusive procedures has been a focus of ongoing research efforts (e.g., Horner et al., 1989). *Time out* is a mild punishment technique in which the occurrence of an inappropriate behavior is followed by a period of time during which a variety of reinforcers are no longer available (White, Nielsen, & Johnson, 1972).

For example, following an aggressive act, a child would be required to sit in a chair in the corner for 2 minutes. *Overcorrection* is another mild but effective form of punishment during which the child engages in related effortful behavior contingent on the occurrence of inappropriate behavior (Foxx & Azrin, 1973). To illustrate, a child who engaged in self-stimulatory head weaving would be forced to practice appropriate head movements.

It is generally recommended that the least intrusive punishment procedures be used first, but such punishers may not be effective because of previous inconsistent or incorrect use. Furthermore, less intrusive punishers may not achieve rapid results, which is unacceptable when the behavior problem is severe. However, the use of more intrusive procedures raises serious ethical concerns, and their use is prohibited in many settings. In a recent study, Charlop, Burgio, Iwata, and Ivancic (1988) developed a procedure to enhance the effects of less intrusive or "mild" punishers. Three developmentally delayed children who displayed severe behavior problems (e.g., aggression, SIB, destructive behavior) were presented with treatment sessions to compare the differential effects of constant versus varied punishers. During the single presentation condition, a single punisher (time out, "No," or overcorrection) was presented contingent on inappropriate behavior throughout the session. During sessions of the varied punisher condition, all three punishers were available; thus, contingent on an inappropriate behavior, one of the three punishers was administered. Results indicated that the varied punisher format was associated with larger decreases in these behaviors than was the presentation of single punishers. Importantly, these results suggest that severe behavior problems may be reduced using relatively "weak" punishers, without the use of more intrusive punishment procedures.

Another recent advance in the treatment of problem behavior has been the development of the functional analysis methodology (Iwata, Dorsey, Slifer, Bauman, & Richman, 1982). This procedure consists of observing occurrences of problem behavior during various analogue conditions (e.g., high versus low task demands; absent versus noncontingent versus contingent social attention). In many cases, it is possible to identify variables that are associated with, and may serve to maintain, the occurrence of self-injury, tantrums, or aggression. In their seminal article, Iwata et al. (1982) determined that the motivation of self-injury differed for each child, but tended to fall into one of three categories (essentially those identified by Carr, 1977). Several of the subjects engaged in self-injury for *attention,* and these children would show high frequencies of self-injury during conditions of the functional analysis in which attention was provided as a consequence. However, self-injury was seen at zero or low frequencies in all other conditions. Another motivation for self-injury was *escape* from demands or work situations, and the third category consisted of those children who engaged in self-injury regardless of the condition, more as a *stereotypic* or self-stimulatory type of behavior. The information obtained from a functional analysis leads to the selection of an appropriate treatment specific to the motivation or function of the self-injury. For example, an attention-motivated child would have all attention contingent on self-injury removed, with attention provided for periods when self-injury did not occur.

Along these lines, Carr and Durand (1985) demonstrated that a functional analysis may yield information suggestive of the use of inappropriate behavior as a means of communication. Stimuli that were discriminative for problem behavior (i.e., difficult demands, low adult attention, or both) were identified for each child. Then, to replace the inappropriate behavior, each child was taught a communicative phrase that was functionally equivalent to that behavior. Thus, a student who engaged in SIB for attention was taught to ask "Am I doing good work today?" to appropriately solicit adult praise. Similarly, a student who displayed aggression during difficult tasks was taught to verbally request assistance by saying "I don't understand" to the adult. Results indicated that disruptive behavior was greatly reduced or eliminated following treatment, supporting the hypothesis that some behavior problems may serve a communicative function.

Another important line of research in nonaversive treatments of severe behavior is the stimulus control approach (Touchette, MacDonald, & Langer, 1985). Touchette and his colleagues noted that the usual method of plotting average frequency in line graphs obscures major changes in rate of problem behavior, thus making identification of controlling stimuli quite difficult. They suggested that a scatter plot assessment of *patterns* of problem behavior may provide important and useful information about controlling stimuli. The scatter diagram is a grid on which time of day is segmented (e.g., half-hours, hours) on the vertical axis and successive days are represented on the horizontal axis. To plot data, cells on the grid are filled if problem behavior occurred in the time interval, and left blank if none occurred. After several days of observation, relationships among problem behavior and time of day, physical environment, class of activities, and/or other variables may be identified. The controlling variable(s) may then be removed, to reduce or eliminate the problem behavior. In spite of the general difficulty in eliminating autistic children's inappropriate behaviors, the recent studies described above suggest that less intrusive treatment procedures may indeed be quite effective.

BEHAVIORAL DEFICITS

The behaviors in this category include speech and language, social behavior and play, attention, and motivation. Each of these areas will be addressed in turn.

Speech and Language

One of the most debilitating aspects of autism is the children's failure to acquire communicative speech and language. Those children who are echolalic need to acquire meaning to their words, and the 50% of autistic children who are functionally mute need very intensive therapy to merely occasion sounds. The reader is referred to Lovaas, Berberich, Perloff, and Schaeffer (1966) for the verbal imitation training paradigm that has often been successful in teaching functionally mute autistic children to speak.

A more recent and quite promising speech and language intervention program that has been demonstrated to both establish speech in functionally mute children as well as facilitate communicative speech for echolalic children is the Natural Language Paradigm (NLP) (Koegel, O'Dell, & Koegel, 1987). NLP is generally conducted during short play sessions in which the therapist and child play together with a variety of toys and activities. During a session, the therapist models a variety of appropriate responses for the child to imitate. All attempts to verbally communicate are reinforced with access to a toy and with praise. Thus, this program incorporates specific variables that closely approximate normal language interactions (e.g., turn taking, sharing, natural consequences). It also includes variables that facilitate motivation to respond (e.g., reinforcement of attempts to respond, novel stimuli, task variation, direct reinforcers). NLP also incorporates facilitators of generalization to extra-therapy settings. As a means to further enhance generalization, Laski, Charlop, and Schreibman (1988) trained parents of echolalic and nonverbal autistic children to use NLP during play sessions at home. The results indicated that, following NLP training, both nonverbal and echolalic children increased the frequency of their verbalizations.

As mentioned earlier, many autistic children do speak. However, their speech is predominantly echolalic. Because of the presence of some speech and/or echolalia, the procedures for teaching speech to these children may differ from those described for teaching mute children. Many earlier procedures have been designed to decrease echolalic speech (e.g., Lovaas, 1977; Risley & Wolf, 1967; Schreibman & Carr, 1978), but there has been a recent emphasis on using echolalia to advantage to teach appropriate speech. Instead of eliminating echolalia, Charlop (1983) designed a procedure that utilized echolalia to teach receptive labeling. In this procedure, the therapist verbally labeled one of two objects. The child was then allowed the opportunity to echo this verbalization. The experimenter then placed the objects before the child and labeled the object again, and the child handed the experimenter an object. For example, the therapist would say, "Boat," wait for the child to echo "Boat," then present a toy boat and car and again say "Boat" and allow the child to select the correct object. Charlop (1983) suggested that by echoing the word "boat," the children may have provided their own discriminative stimulus before manually responding, thus facilitating acquisition and generalization of object labels. These findings suggest that echolalia may be a useful tool in the treatment of autistic children.

Although many techniques have been quite successful, speech remains an extremely difficult and complex behavior to teach, and language use often fails to occur outside of the training environment. Therefore, recent research has focused on teaching language under more natural conditions, to promote spontaneous, generalized language use. Importantly, because these procedures are designed to refine and naturalize the children's speech, these procedures focus not only on the natural environment per se, but on the use of the natural environment to facilitate more sophisticated and generalized use of speech.

One such procedure, time delay, has been very effective in teaching spontaneous speech (Charlop, Schreibman, & Thibodeau, 1985). This procedure consists of transferring stimulus control of an appropriate response from the therapist's prompt (e.g., saying "Cookie") to the presentation of a stimulus (i.e., a cookie). Generally, this is accomplished by presenting the stimulus and modeling the correct verbal response; gradually, the presentation of the prompt is delayed (e.g., in 2 sec increments), until the child anticipates the prompt and speaks spontaneously. The effectiveness of this procedure was demonstrated in a series of studies. Charlop et al. (1985) taught seven autistic children to spontaneously request desired items (e.g., "I want cookie") without any verbal cues, but in the mere presence of these objects. The transfer of stimulus control to less obvious cues such as certain actions, settings, or temporal cues has also been studied. In one such study, the time delay procedure was successfully employed to teach autistic children to spontaneously provide verbal expressions of affection (e.g., "I love you") in the presence of an action (a hug) (Charlop & Walsh, 1986).

This procedure has also been effective in promoting setting-cued speech. For example, autistic children were successfully taught to make spontaneous requests in appropriate environments, such as "I want to swing" at the playground, or requesting a cookie in the kitchen (Schreibman, Charlop, & Tryon, 1981). More recently, Charlop and Bieber (1988) taught parents of autistic children to implement the time delay procedure at home, to increase their children's spontaneous speech. In this study, autistic children were taught to speak spontaneously in response to temporal cues. That is, parents implemented the time delay procedure at specific times throughout the day to teach contextually appropriate speech. For example, the children were taught to say "Good morning, Mom" upon waking, "May I have a snack, please?" when returning from their day at school, and "Good night, Mom" at bedtime. Results indicated that parents effectively employed the procedure to increase their children's spontaneous speech. Importantly, the children's spontaneous speech occurred at the appropriate times of day but in a variety of settings, suggesting that the children's behavior was not dependent on a specific location but more on a temporal variable within their day.

Another promising line of research has investigated the effects of modeling in facilitating autistic children's speech and language. Conflicting findings regarding the efficacy of modeling have been reported (Charlop & Walsh, 1986; Varni, Lovaas, Koegel, & Everett, 1979), but a few studies (e.g., Charlop, Schreibman, & Tryon, 1983) have demonstrated that autistic children can benefit from observation of models. In one study, four low-functioning autistic children learned to receptively label objects through observation of an autistic peer model (Charlop et al., 1983). Results indicated that peer modeling was an effective procedure. Additionally, as compared to a traditional discrete trial approach, generalization and maintenance of correct responding were superior in the peer modeling condition. This line of research has been extended recently by Charlop and Milstein (1989), who assessed the efficacy of using video modeling to increase autistic children's conversational speech. In this study, verbal autistic children observed a videotape of two adult models engaging in conversations about specific toys. Results indicated that the children learned appropriate conversations through video modeling, and generalized these skills to other topics of conversation than those that were modeled. In general, the results of these studies suggest that modeling may be an effective procedure for improving autistic children's speech.

Much progress has been made in increasing autistic children's severe deficits in speech and language. This, in addition to future research, will shed a more promising light on autistic children's communicative abilities.

Social Behavior and Play

Remediating autistic children's deviant social behavior and play is one of the most challenging areas of treatment. Early research demonstrated the difficulty entailed in establishing social stimuli (e.g., hugs, praise) as reinforcers (e.g., Lovaas et al., 1966), and in teaching autistic children appropriate toy play (Koegel, Firestone, Kramme, & Dunlap, 1974). The procedures used were not easily adapted to natural settings and did not yield durable or generalized gains. Recent studies have focused on structuring the natural environment to teach the children behaviors that may lead to increased social responsiveness and potential establishment of social reinforcers.

One promising line of research involves training of nonhandicapped peers to increase autistic children's social interactions in natural settings. Strain and his colleagues (e.g., Odom, Hoyson, Jamieson, & Strain, 1985) demonstrated that teaching socially competent preschoolers to initiate interactions (e.g., by saying "Let's go play" and giving the autistic child a toy) resulted in large increases in autistic children's social behavior. Training teachers to prompt autistic children to initiate peer interactions resulted in additional positive changes.

Oke and Schreibman (1990) found that training nonhandicapped peers to initiate social/play interactions with an autistic child had limited effects. While the nonhandicapped peers were receiving reinforcement (small toys, stickers) for initiating and interacting, they did so. However, when reinforcement was no longer available, the children ceased to initiate or interact. These investigators found significant, and durable, effects when the autistic child was trained (via videotape feedback and modeling) to initiate interactions. In addition, these effects generalized to unfamiliar nonhandicapped peers and resulted in a concomitant decrease in the autistic child's disruptive behavior.

Another line of research has focused on teaching autistic children cooperative play (Charlop, Milstein, & Moore, 1989). Through the use of video modeling, pairs of autistic children learned initiation, turn taking, and termination skills involved in cooperative play. Importantly, cooperative play skills generalized to a variety of untrained games, to play with a nonhandicapped peer, and to natural settings. Increases in independent play were also observed during free-play activities. In summary, the results of the above studies are quite encouraging in that effective techniques are being developed and refined to treat one of the most pervasive deficits displayed by autistic children.

Attention

As previously mentioned, many autistic children display unique attentional deficits such as "stimulus overselectivity." Stimulus overselectivity has been defined as the failure to respond to the simultaneous presentation of multiple cues in the environment. Because overselective responding has been shown to interfere with discrimination learning, language acquisition, social behavior, and generalization of learned behaviors (Lovaas, Koegel, & Schreibman, 1979), the development of treatment procedures to rectify this problem has been an important area of research.

One approach has been to develop techniques that allow autistic children to learn despite their overselective responding. For example, "prompts," such as pointing to or underlining the correct answer, are common teaching techniques used to guide the child in learning new discriminations. An added cue or "extra-stimulus" prompt is gradually faded out until the child responds correctly without the prompt. However, the use of such an extra-stimulus prompting procedure is actually providing an additional cue and may defeat its own purpose. That is, overselective autistic children often respond only to the prompt and, upon total removal of the prompt, fail to attend to the training stimulus. Schreibman (1975) devised a "within stimulus" prompt in which, rather than adding a cue, a relevant feature inherent in the training stimulus is used as a prompt when teaching discriminations. The relevant feature of the training stimulus—the one necessary to make the discrimination—is initially exaggerated (made bigger, darker). Once responding occurs to the exaggerated version of the relevant cue, it is gradually faded out until the child is responding correctly to the stimuli in their original form.

The above method takes advantage of autistic children's overselective responding but is not feasible to use with many types of tasks. A second approach has been developed to directly remediate overselectivity by teaching the children to respond to multiple cues (Koegel & Schreibman, 1977). Schreibman, Charlop, and Koegel (1982) demonstrated that autistic children who failed to learn difficult discrimination tasks when provided with an extra-stimulus pointing prompt could learn to respond to multiple cues after training on several successive conditional discriminations. First, the children were pretested to demonstrate that they did not respond to multiple cues and failed to use a pointing prompt to learn a visual discrimination. Then, a series of conditional discriminations was presented. During training, three stimuli (e.g., geometric shapes) were presented, with the correct stimulus consisting of a shape plus an extra-stimulus prompt (e.g., circle with a line drawn below it). After the child reached the criterion of touching the correct stimulus, the testing phase of the conditional discrimination program was introduced. Note that, as of this point, the child might still have been responding to the correct stimulus on the basis of one cue (e.g., the circle *or* the line). However, during the testing phase, the stimuli were presented in such a manner that the child needed to respond to both cues (the circle *and* the line) in order to make a correct response, because the other distractor stimulus also featured components of the correct stimulus (e.g., a circle without a line and a square with a line). Once the criterion was met, a new stimulus set was presented and the process was repeated. After the child demonstrated no overselective responding on two consecutive stimulus sets, the child was again tested to determine whether he or she would now respond to multiple cues and use the pointing prompt with the pretest stimuli. Results indicated that, while the children had previously "overselected" to the pointing prompt and failed to attend to the training materials, following multiple cue training, they were able to learn from such a prompt. Importantly, these findings suggested that autistic children could learn from a more traditional teaching technique and may be generally able to respond to their environment in a manner more similar to that of nonhandicapped children.

Motivation

Autistic children's extreme lack of motivation to learn is a serious problem confronted by teachers, therapists, and parents. Unlike normal children, autistic children do not appear interested in achievement, praise, success, or other social reinforcers. When presented with difficult tasks, these children frequently engage in inappropriate behaviors (e.g., tantrums, SIB) to escape the learning environment, or may cease responding altogether. Thus, increasing motivation is crucial to the child's continued improvement and to overall treatment success.

A number of techniques have been developed to enhance autistic children's motivation to learn new tasks. Because of the children's unresponsiveness to social reinforcers, researchers and clinicians initially focused on the contingent presentation of primary reinforcers, such as food, to motivate the children to respond. Several strategies have been developed to increase the effectiveness of food reinforcers; among them are providing a variety of food reinforcers rather than just one (Egel, 1981) and pairing a specific food reinforcer with a specific response (Litt & Schreibman, 1981). Despite these efforts, the fact remains that food reinforcers may be problematic. Specifically, they are artificial reinforcers, particularly for older children; they are not likely to be available in the nontreatment environment (thus limiting generalization); and they are subject to satiation effects.

One line of research has focused on interspersing trials of previously learned "maintenance" tasks with trials of a new "acquisition" task. Dunlap and Koegel (1980) demonstrated superior motivation using this procedure. Few correct responses are typically made during initial learning of a task, but task interspersal procedures ensure that the child receives a high frequency of reinforcement during the learning session for correct maintenance task responding. Attention and responsiveness are thus maintained, resulting in increased task acquisition. In an extension of this work, Charlop, Kurtz, and Milstein (1986) assessed the effects of reinforcement contingencies, in conjunction with task interspersal, on the acquisition of new tasks. These authors reported that learning of new tasks occurred more rapidly when only praise or no reinforcers were presented for interspersed maintenance tasks, and food reinforcers were presented solely for correct acquisition task response. Thus, schedules of reinforcement that favored the acquisition task enhanced learning.

Other manipulations of reinforcer delivery have increased motivation in these children. For example, Koegel, Dyer, and Bell (1987) demonstrated that social responsiveness may be improved greatly by giving the child the opportunity to choose the nature of the learning task and the reinforcer. Such increases in motivation have also been demonstrated when autistic children receive reinforcement for attempts at correct responses, instead of only for specific correct responses (Koegel, O'Dell, & Dunlap, 1988).

Other researchers have approached the motivation problem by identifying new reinforcers. In one study, Charlop, Kurtz, and Casey (in press) assessed the effectiveness of using autistic children's aberrant behaviors as reinforcers to increase correct task responding. In three experiments, reinforcer conditions of self-stimulation, delayed echolalia, and obsessive behavior were compared to food reinforcer and varied (food/aberrant behavior) reinforcer conditions. For example, during sessions of the delayed echolalia condition, each child was permitted to utter a delayed echo after each correct task response; similarly, the child was allowed 3 to 5 seconds to engage in self-stimulation as a reinforcer during the self-stimulation condition. Results indicated that task performance was highest when brief opportunities to engage in an aberrant behavior were provided as reinforcers. Varied reinforcers were also effective in improving performance. Importantly, no negative side effects were observed as a result of allowing the children brief periods to engage in such behaviors.

Research into the nature of reinforcers, variables relating to their method of delivery, and other aspects of the learning environment have allowed behavior therapists to increase the repertoire of effective reinforcers for this population. Importantly, a good deal of recent research has focused on developing more natural reinforcers. Koegel and Williams (1980) showed that, when a reinforcer was obtained as a natural part of the task, it was more effective than when presented in a task-independent manner. Thus, in teaching the preposition "in," it was more effective to have the edible reinforcer placed inside the task stimulus (direct reinforcer) as opposed to merely handing the edible to the child (indirect reinforcement). One important reason for normalizing reinforcers is that such reinforcers are more likely to be encountered in the natural environment and might thus be expected to enhance the generalization of treatment effects.

Generalization

The procedures described in this chapter have greatly increased our ability to effect powerful treatment effects and have been encouraging in terms of facilitating generalization of treatment gains. However, the fact remains that the generality of treatment effects may not be satisfactory. Treatment gains do not always generalize to nontreatment environments (stimulus generalization), across untreated behaviors (response generalization), or over time (maintenance). Treatment is of little value if generalization does not occur, and this has led researchers to place an increasing emphasis on the occurrence and assessment of generalization effects.

Stokes and Baer (1977) described strategies to promote generalization of behavior change, several of which have been added to the treatment of children with autism. One approach to facilitating generalization is to make the treatment environment more similar to the natural environment.

This can be done in several ways. For example, the use of *intermittent schedules of reinforcement* during treatment provides an atmosphere that approximates the natural environment wherein behaviors are rarely reinforced on a continuous schedule. Several studies (e.g., Koegel & Rincover, 1977) have suggested that intermittent schedules increase the durability of treatment gains by reducing the discriminability of the reinforcement schedules used in the treatment and nontreatment settings.

Another strategy is to use *naturally maintaining contingencies* (natural reinforcers) during training, which will make the treatment and nontreatment environments similar (Stokes & Baer, 1977). Thus, reinforcers should be like those found in the individual's natural environment, and the behaviors taught should be those that will lead to access of these reinforcers. To illustrate, Carr, Binkoff, Kologinsky, and Eddy (1978) taught autistic children to use sign language to request items that would be found in the natural environment. The children were taught to spontaneously request (via signing) their favorite toys as opposed to common objects (e.g., pictures of farm animals). When the children signed for their preferred items in the natural environment, they were likely to receive the item. This constitutes reinforcement for generalization and would likely enhance the generality of the spontaneous behavior of the children. In addition, this procedure incorporates another of the generalization strategies identified by Stokes and Baer (1977): *use of common stimuli* (those found in treatment and nontreatment settings).

Another way to ensure the generalization of treatment effects is to use procedures that directly train generalization. *Sequential modification* occurs when generalization is programmed in every nongeneralized condition (e.g., across people, settings, behaviors). To illustrate, if a child was taught appropriate eating skills but used these skills only at home and not at school, the child would be taught to use the skills at school. However, it may be quite difficult and impractical to train a behavior in every situation in which it did not occur. In such cases, an alternative approach is to *train sufficient exemplars* (Stokes & Baer, 1977). For example, Schreibman and Carr (1978) taught echolalic children to say "I don't know" (rather than echo) when presented with a verbal stimulus for which they had no response (e.g., "Who's the President?"). The investigators trained individual examples of these stimuli (e.g., "What is a zebra?", "Where is Cincinnati?") until the children would respond with "I don't know" to additional examples without training.

Both sequential modification and training sufficient exemplars may be quite tedious, and it is usually impossible to determine beforehand how many situations or exemplars will be required for training before generalization is achieved. To reduce this problem, Stokes and Baer (1977) suggested using *mediated generalization*. In this procedure, behaviors that occasion the target response and that are likely to occur in both the treatment and nontreatment situations are used.

The most common mediator is language. Children giving self-instructions in different environments are using this generalization strategy. Few studies have utilized mediated generalization with the autistic population but, as noted earlier, Charlop (1983) demonstrated that such children might be able to use the echolalia as a verbal mediator. The results of this study revealed that the children learned faster when allowed to echo the label of an object before handing it to the experimenter. Importantly, generalized treatment gains were seen for echolalic children with this procedure but not for nonverbal children. Charlop (1983) suggested that mediated generalization occurred for echolalic children because, unlike the nonverbal children, they provided their own self-imposed discriminative stimulus (echo for the object's label) before handing over the requested object in the generalization setting.

In recent years, there has also been a change of emphasis in the development of generalization strategies: investigators are turning more and more to the natural environment to enhance generalization. This makes intuitive sense because our treatment goal is to achieve generalized gains in the natural environment where the child lives. As a result of this recent focus, several promising techniques have emerged. These include incidental teaching, training pivotal target behaviors, and self-management.

Incidental teaching enhances generalization by embedding teaching trials within the child's daily activities. Using this strategy, the therapist or teacher is vigilant for teaching opportunities signaled by the child and can thus use natural stimuli and reinforcers during the trial. For example, a child reaching for an apple might be required to say "apple" (or some approximation) before receiving the apple. The child is obviously motivated for the fruit and the teacher can take advantage of the naturally occurring stimulus and subsequent reinforcer (i.e., apple). McGee, Krantz, Mason, and McClannahan (1983) taught autistic children to receptively learn labels of objects used in meal preparation (e.g., knife, sandwich). The training occurred in the kitchen during the daily lunch preparation. This "loose structure" in the teaching situation (wherein the child can sample a range of correct responses and reinforcers) helps promote generalization (Stokes & Baer, 1977).

A second procedure for enhancing generalization involves teaching *pivotal target behaviors* as opposed to a large number of individual target behaviors. Pivotal behaviors are those that, if changed, may influence many other behaviors and result in widespread changes in the children's functioning. Two pivotal behaviors so far identified as having the potential for effecting widespread behavioral changes are motivation and responsivity to multiple cues (Koegel et al., 1989). Increasing the pivotal behavior of motivation involves incorporating the specific procedures shown to enhance motivation (see above). These include, for example, interspersal of maintenance tasks, task variation, child choice, and reinforcement for attempts. In addition, the procedures include strategies for promoting generalization, such as using loose structure, common stimuli, and the natural environment. These motivation- and generalization-enhancing procedures have been combined in a language training program called the Natural Language Paradigm (Koegel et al., 1987), which was described earlier. Similarly, because we know how to increase the responsiveness of autistic children to simultaneous multiple cues (see "Attention" above), these procedures are also included. Thus, the children receive training on successive conditional discriminations, which leads to increased responsivity to multiple cues and associated behavioral improvements (Schreibman, 1988).

Self-management procedures typically involve self-monitoring and self-reinforcement and can be taught as a part of an intervention strategy to promote generalization. Most of the research in child self-management has involved disruptive children, but recently researchers have successfully employed these techniques with autistic children (e.g., Koegel & Koegel, 1986; Stahmer & Schreibman, in press). Using this procedure, the investigators first prepare for the training of self-monitoring by carefully defining both appropriate and inappropriate target behaviors. Functional reinforcers, chosen by the child, are identified and an appropriate period of time, or unit of behavior small enough to ensure success on the child's part, is determined. Next, the child learns to self-monitor. During this stage of the training, the child is taught to discriminate between correct and incorrect behavior. This may be accomplished via modeling, or, if the child is more severely handicapped, the child may be prompted to engage in the appropriate behavior. Following this, the child is taught to self-observe, self-evaluate, and then record the fact that a unit of behavior has occurred. After the child has demonstrated the ability to perform the self-management in the training setting, he or she is prompted to perform the activity under appropriate natural stimulus conditions. Once this performance is established, fading of the formal self-management activities is implemented.

It should be apparent that research into achieving generalization of treatment effects has become a top priority with people providing treatment to autistic children. In addition to these specific strategies, generalization has been enhanced by extending the treatment environment. Specifically, parent training programs, classroom training programs, and teaching homes (small community-based residential settings) have all been designed by behavioral strategists and have proven to be extremely useful in the broad-based treatment of children with autism.

CONCLUSION

The discussion in this chapter is intended not only to acquaint the reader with the behavioral approach to the treatment of a complex and challenging disorder, but also to provide a description of how the field has evolved over the past 25 years. There is little argument about the utility of the behavioral treatment of children with autism, and it is a tribute to its emphasis on ongoing evaluation and experimental methodology that the treatment has been in a constant state of refinement.

Earlier practitioners of the methodology focused on individual behaviors and the identification of specific environmental manipulations that would lead to desired behavior change. Indeed, the first reports of the success of procedures such as positive reinforcement for speech, time-out, and/or extinction as treatments for severely disruptive behaviors provided the earliest effective treatments for some of the behaviors so characteristic of autism. However, as exciting as these earlier successes were, it eventually became apparent that our treatments and resultant behavioral improvements were too narrow and limited in terms of broader and more durable treatment effects. Analysis of these limitations led to the development of more complex and comprehensive treatment perspectives and procedures. For example, the more recent emphasis on functional analyses, stimulus control, pivotal target behaviors, and self-management represents the behavioral approach's recognition of the need to (a) address behavior change from many angles and (b) affect wider response repertoires, within the natural/social contexts of the child's life. The result is that we are able to be much more efficient and effective treatment providers for these children. The future will undoubtedly see further exciting developments.

REFERENCES

Carr, E. G. (1977). The motivation of self-injurious behavior: A review of some hypotheses. *Psychological Bulletin, 84,* 800–816.

Carr, E. G., Binkoff, J. A., Kologinsky, E., & Eddy, M. (1978). Acquisition of sign language by autistic children. I. Expressive labeling. *Journal of Applied Behavior Analysis, 11,* 489–501.

Carr, E. G., & Durand, V. M. (1985). Reducing behavior problems through functional communication training. *Journal of Applied Behavior Analysis, 18,* 111–126.

Charlop, M. H. (1983). The effects of echolalia on acquisition and generalization of receptive labeling in autistic children. *Journal of Applied Behavior Analysis, 16,* 111–126.

Charlop, M. H., & Bieber, J. (1988). *Teaching parents to increase their autistic children's speech using a time delay procedure.* Paper presented at the meeting of the Association for Behavior Analysis, Philadelphia.

Charlop, M. H., Burgio, L. D., Iwata, B. A., & Ivancic, M. T. (1988). Stimulus variation as a means of enhancing punishment effects. *Journal of Applied Behavior Analysis, 21,* 89–95.

Charlop, M. H., Kurtz, P. F., & Casey, F. G. (in press). Using aberrant behaviors as reinforcers for autistic children. *Journal of Applied Behavior Analysis.*

Charlop, M. H., Kurtz, P. F., & Milstein, J. P. (1986). *Too much reinforcement, too little behavior: An analysis of reinforcement contingencies with autistic children.* Paper presented at the meeting of the Association for Behavior Analysis, Milwaukee, WI.

Charlop, M. H., & Milstein, J. P. (1989). Teaching autistic children conversational speech using video modeling. *Journal of Applied Behavior Analysis, 22,* 275–286.

Charlop, M. H., Milstein, J. P., & Moore, M. E. (1989). *Teaching autistic children cooperative play.* Paper presented at the meeting of the Association for Behavior Analysis, Milwaukee, WI.

Charlop, M. H., Schreibman, L., & Thibodeau, M. G. (1985). Increasing spontaneous verbal responding in autistic children using a time delay procedure. *Journal of Applied Behavior Analysis, 18,* 155–166.

Charlop, M. H., Schreibman, L., & Tryon, A. S. (1983). Learning through observation: The effects of peer modeling on acquisition and generalization in autistic children. *Journal of Abnormal Child Psychology, 11,* 355–366.

Charlop, M. H., & Walsh, M. E. (1986). Increasing autistic children's spontaneous verbalizations of affection: An assessment of time delay and peer modeling procedures. *Journal of Applied Behavior Analysis, 19,* 307–314.

Dunlap, G., & Koegel, R. L. (1980). Motivating autistic children through stimulus variation. *Journal of Applied Behavior Analysis, 13,* 619–627.

Egel, A. L. (1981). Reinforcer variation: Implications for motivating developmentally disabled children. *Journal of Applied Behavior Analysis, 14,* 345–350.

Egel, A. L., Koegel, R. L., & Schreibman, L. (1980). A review of educational treatment procedures for autistic children. In L. Mann & D. Sabatino (Eds.), *Fourth review of special education* (pp. 109–149). New York: Grune & Stratton.

Foxx, R. M., & Azrin, N. H. (1973). The elimination of autistic self-stimulatory behavior by overcorrection. *Journal of Applied Behavior Analysis, 6,* 1–14.

Horner, R., Dunlap, G., Koegel, R. L., Carr, E. G., Sailor, W., Anderson, J., & O'Neill, R. E. (1989). *Toward a technology of "nonaversive" behavioral support.* Manuscript submitted for publication.

Iwata, B. A., Dorsey, M. F., Slifer, K. J., Bauman, K. E., & Richman, G. S. (1982). Toward a functional analysis of self-injury. *Analysis and Intervention in Developmental Disabilities, 2,* 3–20.

Kanner, L. (1943). Autistic disturbances of affective contact. *Nervous Child, 2,* 217–250.

Koegel, R. L., Dyer, K., & Bell, L. K. (1987). The influence of child preferred activities on autistic children's social behavior. *Journal of Applied Behavior Analysis, 20,* 243–252.

Koegel, R. L., Firestone, P. B., Kramme, K. W., & Dunlap, G. (1974). Increasing spontaneous play by suppressing self-stimulation in autistic children. *Journal of Applied Behavior Analysis, 7,* 521–528.

Koegel, R. L., & Koegel, L. K. (1986). Generalization issues in the treatment of autism. *Seminars in Speech and Language, 8,* 241–256.

Koegel, R. L., O'Dell, M. C., & Dunlap, G. (1988). Motivating speech use in nonverbal autistic children by reinforcing attempts. *Journal of Autism and Developmental Disorders, 18,* 525–538.

Koegel, R. K., O'Dell, M. C., & Koegel, L. K. (1987). A natural language teaching paradigm for nonverbal autistic children. *Journal of Autism and Developmental Disorders, 17,* 187–200.

Koegel, R. L., & Rincover, A. (1977). Research on the difference between generalization and maintenance in extra-therapy responding. *Journal of Applied Behavior Analysis, 10,* 1–12.

Koegel, R. L., & Schreibman, L. (1977). Teaching autistic children to respond to simultaneous multiple cues. *Journal of Experimental Child Psychology, 24,* 299–311.

Koegel, R. L., Schreibman, L., Good, A., Cerniglia, L., Murphy, C., & Koegel, L. K. (1989). *How to teach pivotal behaviors to children with autism: A training manual.* University of California, Santa Barbara.

Koegel, R. L., & Williams, J. (1980). Direct vs. indirect response–reinforcer relationships in teaching autistic children. *Journal of Abnormal Child Psychology, 4,* 536–547.

Laski, K. E., Charlop, M. H., & Schreibman, L. (1988). Training parents to use the natural language paradigm to increase their autistic children's speech. *Journal of Applied Behavior Analysis, 21,* 391–400.

Litt, M. D., & Schreibman, L. (1981). Stimulus specific reinforcement in the acquisition of receptive labels by autistic children. *Analysis and Intervention in Developmental Disabilities, 1,* 171–186.

Lovaas, O. I. (1977). *The autistic child.* New York: Irvington.

Lovaas, O. I., Berberich, J. P., Perloff, B. F., & Schaeffer, B. (1966). Acquisition of imitative speech in schizophrenic children. *Science, 151,* 705–707.

Lovaas, O. I., Koegel, R. L., & Schreibman, L. (1979). Stimulus overselectivity in autism: A review of research. *Psychological Bulletin, 86,* 1236–1254.

McGee, G. G., Krantz, P. J., Mason, D., & McClannahan, L. E. (1983). A modified incidental-teaching procedure for autistic youth: Acquisition and generalization of receptive object labels. *Journal of Applied Behavior Analysis, 16,* 329–338.

Odom, S. L., Hoyson, M., Jamieson, B., & Strain, P. S. (1985). Increasing handicapped preschoolers' peer social interactions:

Cross-setting and component analysis. *Journal of Applied Behavior Analysis, 18,* 3–16.

Oke, N. J., & Schreibman, L. (1990). *Training social initiations to a high-functioning autistic child: Assessment of collateral behavior change and generalization in a case study. Journal of Autism and Developmental Disorders, 20,* 479–497.

Risley, R. T., & Wolf, M. M. (1967). Establishing functional speech in echolalic children. *Behaviour Research and Therapy, 5,* 73–88.

Schreibman, L. (1975). Effects of within-stimulus and extra-stimulus prompting on discrimination learning in autistic children. *Journal of Applied Behavior Analysis, 8,* 91–112.

Schreibman, L. (1988). *Autism.* Newbury Park, CA: Sage.

Schreibman, L., & Carr, E. G. (1978). Elimination of echolalic responding to questions through the training of a generalized verbal response. *Journal of Applied Behavior Analysis, 11,* 453–463.

Schreibman, L., Charlop, M. H., & Koegel, R. L. (1982). Teaching autistic children to use extra-stimulus prompts. *Journal of Experimental Child Psychology, 33,* 475–491.

Schreibman, L., Charlop, M. H., & Tryon, A. S. (1981). *The acquisition and generalization of appropriate spontaneous speech in autistic children.* Paper presented at the American Psychological Association Annual Convention, Los Angeles.

Stahmer, A. C., & Schreibman, L. (in press). Teaching children with autism appropriate play in unsupervised environments using a self-management treatment package. *Journal of Applied Behavior Analysis.*

Stokes, T. F., & Baer, D. M. (1977). An implicit technology of generalization. *Journal of Applied Behavior Analysis, 10,* 349–368.

Touchette, P. E., MacDonald, R. F., & Langer, S. N. (1985). A scatterplot for identifying stimulus control of problem behavior. *Journal of Applied Behavior Analysis, 18,* 343–351.

Varni, J., Lovaas, O. I., Koegel, R. L., & Everett, N. L. (1979). An analysis of observational learning in autistic and normal children. *Journal of Abnormal Child Psychology, 7,* 31–43.

White, G. D., Nielsen, G., & Johnson, S. M. (1972). Time-out duration and the suppression of deviant behavior in children. *Journal of Applied Behavior Analysis, 5,* 111–120.

PART THREE
Behavioral Medicine

CHAPTER 18

Eating Disorders

DONALD A. WILLIAMSON, BARBARA A. CUBIC, and RICHARD D. FULLER

Behavioral treatment of eating disorders has been intensively studied over the past 15 years, yielding a well-developed clinical research literature. This chapter will review the literature pertaining to behavioral treatment of obesity, bulimia nervosa, and anorexia nervosa. The emphasis of the chapter will be on clinical techniques that have been developed for the treatment of these disorders. For each disorder, a behavioral formulation will be described and research pertaining to the effectiveness of behavioral approaches will be reviewed.

OBESITY

Clinical Description and Conceptualization

Obesity is generally defined as an excess of fat tissue. For purposes of a simple operational definition, a weight criterion of greater than 20% above ideal weight has often been utilized in the clinical research literature. Using this criterion, estimates of the prevalence of obesity in Western societies have ranged from 6% in children to over 20% in adults (Bellack & Williamson, 1982; Williamson, Prather, Heffer, & Kelley, 1988).

There is general consensus that most cases of obesity can best be conceptualized within the framework of the energy balance model. This model proposes that obesity is the end result of stored energy caused by consuming more energy than has been expended. In this conceptualization, obesity is viewed as a normal adaptive response of the body to store excess energy for periods of starvation, low food supply, and so on. From this perspective, obesity is not necessarily the result of *disordered* eating. Nevertheless, cognitive-behavioral factors are known to strongly influence eating, which in some cases results in behavior patterns that cause the development of obesity—for example, binge eating, excessive snacking, and inactivity. Williamson, Davis, Duchmann, McKenzie, and Watkins (1990) have recently elaborated this energy balance model to more explicitly specify behavioral influences upon energy intake and expenditure. This theoretical model, which is illustrated in Figure 18.1, proposes that excessive eating is maintained by short-term positive reinforcement. Avoidance of an active lifestyle is maintained by short-term negative consequences (e.g., fatigue). The net result of this positive energy balance (consuming more energy than is expended) is storage of energy in the form of increased adiposity. The "normal" response to weight gain is dieting, which is usually reinforced by immediate weight loss. This long-term effect of dieting is lowered

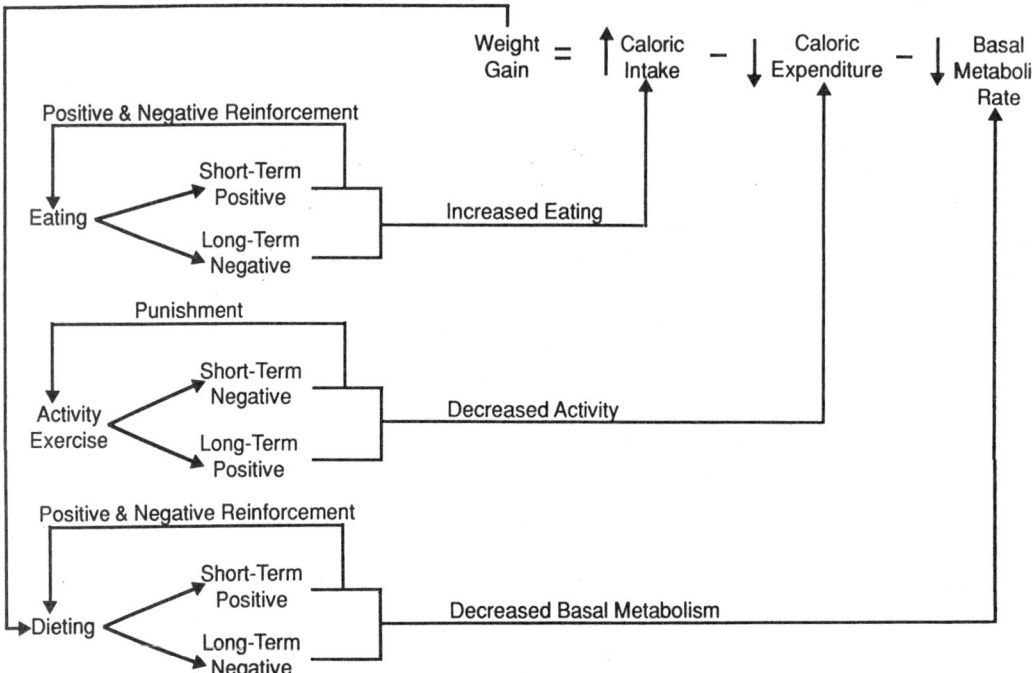

Figure 18.1. Energy balance model of obesity. *Note.* Reprinted with permission from *Assessment of Eating Disorders: Obesity, Anorexia, and Bulimia Nervosa*, (p. 00) by D. A. Williamson, C. J. Davis, E. G. Duchmann, S. J. McKenzie, & P. C. Watkins, 1990. Copyright 1990 by Pergamon Press PLC.

basal metabolic rate, which increases the likelihood of further weight gain. A more complete description of this conceptualization and further discussion of assessment methods for obesity can be found in Williamson et al. (1990).

Treatment

Basic Methods

Most behavioral treatment methods for obesity are based on the energy balance model in that they are designed to modify excessive eating and sedentary life-styles. The basic treatment methods used for both adults and children are summarized below.

1. *Stimulus control* procedures are commonly used to modify the antecedents of eating so that a more restricted set of environmental circumstances comes to function as discriminative stimuli for eating. These procedures generally involve instructions to eat three meals (and sometimes one snack) at the same times and places each day. The rationale is that, by following this procedure, a person will associate only a few situations with eating and all other situations will gradually be extinguished as conditioned stimuli for predigestive responses (e.g., salivation, gastric motility, insulin secretion) and no longer set the occasion for eating.

2. *Direct modification of eating behavior* is generally prescribed to modify faulty eating habits that result in excessive caloric intake. These procedures usually involve training the obese patient to slow down the pace of eating and to break the "clean plate habit." Shopping habits may require modification, to control the availability of binge foods or those high in calories.

3. *Establishment of life-style exercise programs* is often utilized to increase

caloric expenditure, which directly facilitates weight loss. Consistent aerobic exercise has been shown to reverse the adverse effects of dieting upon basal metabolism. Most studies have found that the most effective exercise programs are those that promote increased activity as a part of the person's life-style.

4. *Self-monitoring* of eating, exercise, and behavior change is commonly used to increase the person's awareness of relevant behaviors and to assess behavior change over time.

With children and adolescents, parents are usually involved in the treatment program by losing weight together or through parental monitoring and/or contingency contracting. Several studies (Brownell, Heckerman, Westlake, Hayes, & Monti, 1978; Murphy et al., 1982) have found that involvement of spouses in the treatment of adults is useful for long-term weight maintenance. In recent years, the primary emphasis of clinical research has been to evaluate other methods for promoting better weight loss and improved maintenance of weight loss. Methods that have been evaluated include: longer treatment periods, very low-calorie diets, relapse prevention, and booster sessions (Foreyt, 1987). The following section reviews the research findings related to both basic behavioral methods and the more recent approaches for improving short-term weight loss and long-term weight maintenance. For more details related to behavioral treatment methods for obesity, the interested reader may refer to Agras (1987).

Research Findings

Most recent studies of obesity in children and adults have utilized treatment protocols involving about 15 to 20 weekly sessions, usually in small groups of 5 to 10 people. These studies have yielded average weight losses of about 15 lbs (Foreyt, 1987; Williamson et al., 1988). Over 100 controlled studies have established that behavioral methods are superior to no treatment, placebo, and traditional diets for producing initial weight loss (Epstein & Wing, 1987; Foreyt, 1987). The primary deficiency of behavioral (and other) approaches is a failure to produce consistent long-term weight maintenance. There is an emerging consensus that the regaining of weight may be caused in part by homeostatic mechanisms involved in energy regulation.

Studies investigating the relative effects of the different components of comprehensive behavioral treatment programs have consistently found exercise to be associated with greater weight loss and weight maintenance (Bennett, 1986; Epstein & Wing, 1987). Involvement of parents, spouses, and family members has been found to be associated with satisfactory maintenance of weight loss over about 2 years of follow-up (Epstein & Wing, 1987; Murphy et al., 1982). After 4 years, however, these beneficial effects of family support appear to attenuate to some degree (Murphy, Bruce, & Williamson, 1985). Similarly, combining behavior therapy with very low-calorie diets (400 to 500 kcal/day) was found to produce very large (average of over 19 kg) initial weight losses (Wadden & Stunkard, 1986), but follow-up at 3 years found that most subjects had regained the weight they had lost (Wadden, Stunkard, & Liebschutz, 1988).

Recent investigations have studied variables that were associated with long-term weight maintenance. These studies found that longer treatment periods (Bennett, 1986; Perri, Nezu, Patti, & McCann, 1989) and more intensive weight maintenance programs (Perri et al., 1988) were beneficial over follow-up periods of about 18 months. Also, Marcus, Wing, and Hopkins (1988) found that compulsive binge eaters had an unusually poor response to traditional behavioral treatment methods. Further progress may be forthcoming if future studies are able to identify subject characteristics associated with positive or negative response to treatment and program components that maximize weight loss and maintenance.

Case Example

David was 20 years old at the time of referral. He weighed 340 lbs at a height of 6 ft 3 in. He had been overweight since early adolescence. He had attended college for 1 year, but had failed out due to poor attendance at classes and a failure to study adequately. He was a bright young man from an affluent family, but was generally "failing in life." At the time of referral, he was employed delivering pizzas. He reported that his friends were amazed at the amounts of food he consumed. For example, if a pizza was not delivered, he could easily consume one or more in an evening. He acknowledged binging on a daily basis. Unlike most persons who secretively binge, David ate large quantities of food in public. Analysis of this behavior pattern suggested that he received considerable attention from others for his eating habits.

David's treatment spanned a 3-year period. Behavioral and nutritional treatment programs were established to promote the consumption of 1,600 kcal/day in 3 meals. Stimulus control procedures were used to establish environmental control of eating habits. Binging was inhibited by reducing the availability of binge foods and establishing behavioral contracts to gradually reduce the frequency and size of binges. After losing about 50 lbs, he began a lifestyle exercise program that initially involved regular play of racquetball and later added weight lifting.

Over the first 18 months of treatment, he lost about 120 lbs, bringing his weight to about 220 lbs. He has now maintained this weight for almost 4 years. Throughout his treatment, self-management procedures were applied to other problematic habits. He returned to college on a probationary status and recently graduated with a grade point average of about 3.0. At last contact, he was pursuing a career in the Air Force.

This case represents long-term behavioral treatment of obesity complicated by frequent binge eating. As is common in these cases, David's psychological problems went beyond eating and weight. Though successes of this magnitude are not common, we have had several other cases (both male and female) who have lost over 100 lbs and maintained the weight loss over several years of follow-up. In all of these cases, treatment was long-term with a broad scope. Weight loss goals were always steady, moderate losses of about 6 to 8 lbs each month.

Summary

Behavioral treatment procedures for obesity have been found to be effective for weight loss purposes. Long-term weight maintenance remains problematic, however. Recent investigations have focused on variables that may improve long-term success rates. At present, it is premature to evaluate whether these new approaches will yield more promising long-term results.

BULIMIA NERVOSA

Clinical Description and Conceptualization

Bulimia nervosa is an eating disorder in which episodes of binge eating are followed by purgative behavior. According to the diagnostic criteria established by the American Psychiatric Association (1987), the patient must average at least two binges weekly for 3 months to be diagnosed bulimia nervosa. Also, purgative methods must be utilized to avoid weight gain. Binges and purges typically occur in secret. The amounts and types of food consumed during bulimic binges vary considerably. Average caloric content of binges has been estimated to be over 1,000 kcal. Common binge foods include sweets, starches, and snack foods. Self-induced vomiting is used more frequently as a purgative method. However, the use of laxatives or diuretics, intense exercise, enemas, and restrictive dieting are also common. Awareness that the eating pattern is abnormal, a fear of not being able to voluntarily control the eating, and preoccupation with body shape and weight also must be present for a diagnosis of bulimia nervosa.

Medical complications resulting from bulimia include, but are not limited to, dental erosion, electrolyte imbalances, dehydration, esophageal tears, edema, kidney malfunction, gastric ruptures, cardiac arrhythmias, and occasionally death. Studies evaluating the secondary problems associated with bulimia nervosa have consistently reported depression, anxiety, and neuroticism to accompany the eating disorder (Williamson et al., 1990). We have found secondary diagnoses of dependent, passive-aggressive, and borderline personality disorders to be common among bulimics seen in our clinic.

Williamson et al. (1990) have proposed that body image disturbances, fear of weight gain, and overconcern with body size are central underlying determinants of bulimia nervosa. Figure 18.2 displays this model. Factors directly affecting the binge-purge cycle are enclosed in the dotted ellipse. Most bulimics maintain a high degree of dietary restraint in order to avoid weight gain and maintain thinness. The dieter develops rigid rules regarding food intake, leaving the bulimic physiologically deprived of energy and constantly hungry. These cognitions are often manifested in an all-or-none attitude

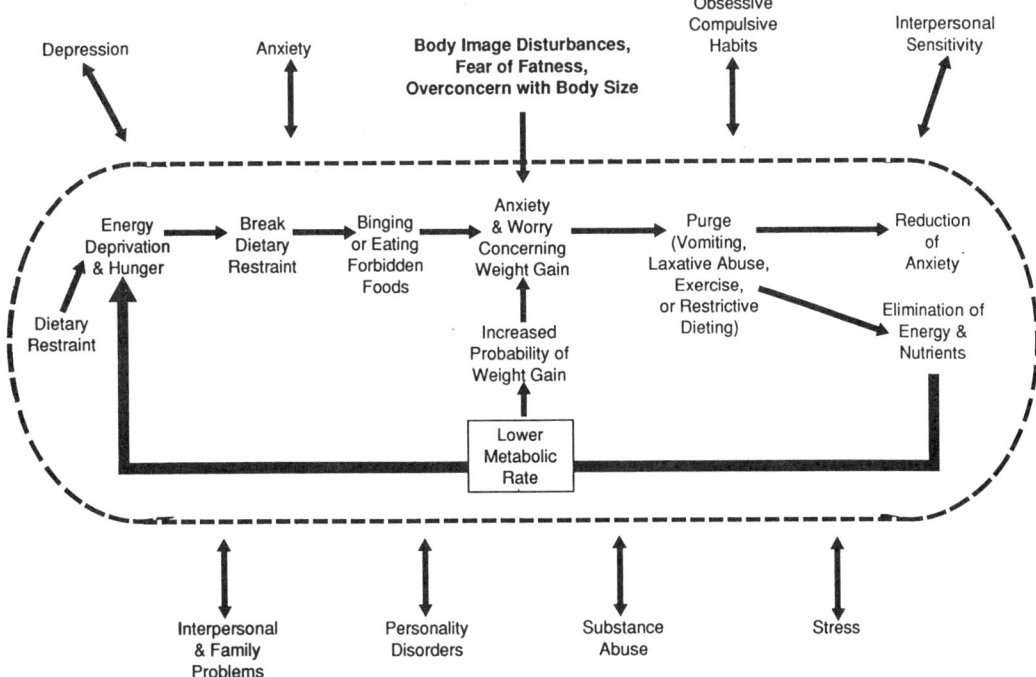

Figure 18.2. Behavioral model for bulimia nervosa. *Note.* Reprinted with permission from *Assessment of Eating Disorders: Obesity, Anorexia, and Bulimia Nervosa,* (p. 00) by D. A. Williamson, C. J. Davis, E. G. Duchmann, S. J. McKenzie, & P. C. Watkins, 1990. Copyright 1990 by Pergamon Press PLC.

about the diet. Violation of dietary restraint has been found to result in binging. Binge eating then creates anxiety and obsessional cognitions regarding potential weight gain. Purging functions to reduce this anxiety while also maintaining energy deprivation and hunger, which sets the occasion for reoccurrence of binging. Ironically, the binge–purge cycle may actually increase the individual's potential for weight gain by lowering basal metabolic rate (Bennett, Williamson, & Powers, 1989). Because the bulimic has a morbid fear of weight gain, the binge–purge behavior is likely to increase if weight increases. Bidirectional arrows to the variables outside the ellipse represent the reciprocal nature between bulimia and common secondary psychological problems. For a more complete discussion of behavioral assessment procedures for the primary and secondary psychopathology of bulimia nervosa, the reader may refer to Williamson et al. (1990).

Treatment

Most bulimics do not present for treatment until they have experienced the disorder for several years. When these patients do request treatment, typical goals are to discontinue binging and purging without gaining weight. Recognition of irrational ideas pertaining to body shape and weight is generally lacking. Patients are often adamant that weight gain during treatment will not be tolerated.

Basic Methods

The initial goal of treatment in bulimia nervosa is directed at disrupting the binge–purge cycle (Fairburn, 1981). The patient's dietary cycle must be altered and the irrational cognitive attributes and ineffective coping skills must be modified. Long-term goals are acceptance of a weight maintenance program through healthy nutritional habits and development of realistic attitudes related to body size.

Following a thorough assessment, the first step in treatment is to have the patient disclose the problems with eating, weight, and so on, to significant others (Agras, 1987). Throughout treatment, the patient should self-monitor relevant eating habits (e.g., binges, purges, situations that set the occasion for binging and purging, and mood states before eating and after purging). The basic behavioral treatment methods that have been developed for bulimia nervosa are summarized below.

1. *Exposure* (to eating) *with response prevention* (of purging) is based on the anxiety model of bulimia illustrated in Figure 18.2. This model proposes that purging has the function of reducing anxiety much like compulsive rituals reduce anxiety associated with obsessional thinking in Obsessive-Compulsive Disorder. This treatment method involves having the patient eat foods that produce anxiety while preventing the opportunity to purge (Rosen, 1987). Initially, this type of exposure treatment is conducted in a therapeutic environment. Foods chosen for exposure are presented in a hierarchical fashion, depending on the patient's perception of the amount of anxiety associated with eating each type of food. This approach is conceptually similar to systematic desensitization and differs somewhat from the flooding approach initially described by Rosen and Leitenberg (1982). Following ingestion of the food, the patient is encouraged to relax, discuss the emotional reaction to eating the food, and dispute irrational cognitions such as "This one cookie will make me fat." Both the anxiety and the urge to vomit typically diminish within 2 hours, and the patient is able to use this experience to reconceptualize the causes of the anxiety, for example, attributing the anxiety to irrational cognitions as opposed to eating the foods per se. Later in treatment, homework assignments are usually prescribed whereby

the same process is conducted in the absence of therapeutic supervision.

2. *Temptation exposure with response prevention* involves exposure to environmental cues that typically set the occasion for binging followed by prevention of the opportunity to binge. This procedure is based on an extinction model. To implement this method, a thorough list of the antecedents of binging must be developed and presented during in vivo exposure sessions. For instance, if a patient typically binges on cookies, the therapist might place cookies on the table and the patient would handle the cookies, smell the, and so on, but not be allowed to eat them. Successes at self-control should be reinforced by the therapist.

Initially, temptation exposure with response prevention should be conducted during therapy sessions. Later in therapy, the procedure can be implemented in the patient's natural environment through structured homework assignments. To assist the patient in resisting urges to binge, a list of incompatible behaviors (e.g., calling a friend, going for a walk, going to a movie) can be developed and practiced in therapy sessions.

3. *Cognitive restructuring* involves teaching the patient to challenge irrational attitudes and beliefs about food, diet, and weight. The patient is taught, through self-monitoring, to recognize thought patterns that are maladaptive and to develop alternative thoughts that could be viewed as more rational. At first, the patient is often unable to identify distorted cognitions and the therapist must not only point out faulty thinking but also provide evidence for why these thoughts are irrational. As the patient progresses, alternative thought patterns can be shaped. The patient should be encouraged to seek experiential evidence for the irrationality of his or her own thoughts via "behavioral experiments," which directly test irrational beliefs. For example, the patient could eat three meals a day without purging and observe weight changes, to learn that fears of weight gain are unfounded.

4. *Body image therapy* is often required because most bulimics view themselves as being overweight and desire an extremely thin body size and shape (Williamson, Davis, Goreczny, & Blouin, 1989). Williamson et al. (1990) have proposed that the body image disturbances found in bulimia nervosa are a dynamic process: environmental challenges that activate the fear of weight gain (e.g., bloatedness after binging, tight clothes, minor weight gain) magnify the discrepancy between the patient's perceived body size and ideal body size, leading to even greater dissatisfaction with body size. Based on this formulation, two types of body image disturbances must be addressed in therapy: (a) stable perceptual and attitudinal distortions related to body size and (b) cognitive/emotional reactions to challenges of fears related to weight gain.

Relaxation, systematic desensitization, and cognitive therapy have been used to modify body image disturbances. The patient is taught to concentrate on different body parts and, as anxiety occurs, relaxation is used to reduce anxiety. This exposure to body cues can initially be accomplished via imagery and later by in vivo exposure such as mirror confrontation or wearing tight clothing in therapy sessions. During body image therapy, the patient is instructed to self-monitor irrational cognitions about eating and body size and to challenge them by substituting rational thoughts and observing contrary evidence. Through this process, disturbances of body image can be modified by pointing out misperceptions so that sensations perceived as fatness are interpreted more rationally.

5. *Energy balance training* is based on the energy balance model discussed in the preceding section on obesity. The rationale for this set of procedures is that most bulimics are deficient in normal weight

control methods. Thus, energy balance training relies on the same behavioral techniques used for weight control. The patient is taught to maintain a healthy diet and exercise program, which helps to eliminate binging and purging. Discussions about proper nutrition should stress eating three balanced meals per day and the physiological needs of the body. The patient can be taught to plan meals using dietary exchange methodology. We have found that this approach avoids the development of further obsessions about the caloric content in the meal plan. Deviations from the scheduled meal plan are explored and the patient is taught to identify problems in advance and to work toward acquiring skills that will prevent these problems in the future. Behavioral contracts are often used to achieve designated behavioral goals (e.g., one purge-free day or consumption of a forbidden food).

Pharmacological Treatment

The use of psychotropic medications has been based on the theory that bulimia is a variant of affective disorders. This affective variant hypothesis has not been strongly supported by empirical research. Most reviews of this literature have concluded that bulimia and depression often covary but are distinctly unique psychiatric syndromes (e.g., Hinz & Williamson, 1987). The efficacy of antidepressants in the treatment of bulimia cannot be denied, however. In a recent review of the literature, Agras (1987) noted that, following a trial of antidepressants, binges and purges were often reduced by more than 50%. Thus, severe cases of bulimia or patients who do not respond to cognitive behavioral interventions may warrant a trial of antidepressant medication. At present, there is no empirical basis for the prediction of a positive response to antidepressants. Current research suggests that potential for relapse is also high when the medication is withdrawn, suggesting that treatment with antidepressants should be integrated with behavioral treatments.

Research Findings

Empirical support for cognitive-behavioral treatment of bulimia nervosa is quite extensive. At present, nine controlled outcome studies have been conducted and all have shown cognitive-behavioral therapy to be superior to a variety of control conditions (Agras, 1987).

In a comprehensive review of cognitive behavioral treatment of bulimia, Rosen (1987) concluded that behavioral techniques generally lead to about 70% reduction in self-induced vomiting. A combination of behavioral and cognitive techniques has generally been found to be more effective than either alone.

Williamson, Prather, et al. (1989) found both inpatient and outpatient cognitive behavioral programs to be effective. In contrast to anorexia nervosa, bulimia nervosa is most commonly treated in the outpatient setting. Outpatient treatment produced a more gradual process of recovery and longer maintenance of treatment gains. Inpatient treatment led to more rapid improvement, which was followed by partial relapse. Based on these data, we have begun prescribing partial hospitalization as an intermediate step between inpatient and outpatient treatment. A partial hospitalization program can provide extensive day treatment with overnight and weekend stays at home. This protocol eases re-entry into the natural environment, producing greater generalization of treatment effects and reducing the potential for relapse.

Long-term follow-up studies of cognitive behavioral treatment have been reported only recently. Mitchell et al. (1989) published the first study of a large group with follow-up longer than 6 months. Their study suggested that a majority of patients maintain improvement at 2-year follow-up, but most patients continue to report at least mild symptoms of bulimia nervosa. Subjects displaying the most severe eating disorder problems at follow-up were those with the most severe eating problems at baseline. This finding is consistent with that reported by Williamson, Prather, et al. (1989).

Case Example

Susan was an 18-year-old freshman attending a major university at the time of referral. She was resistant to being evaluated for an eating disorder and came to the initial session at the insistence of her parents. They had discovered that she was purging via self-induced vomiting, though she denied it. The evaluation was conducted on an outpatient basis and she eventually acknowledged frequent binging and purging as well as excessive concern about weight gain. She weighed 110 lbs at a height of 5 ft 2 in. She continued to be resistant to treatment and generally minimized the significance of her eating problems. She acknowledged depression and suicidal ideation. Given her resistance and depression, we recommended that she be hospitalized in a structured program for eating disorders.

Shortly after admission, Susan became more honest about the severity of her bulimic behavior. She reported purging most meals and binging several times per day on junk food and food from restaurants. She always purged after binging. She knew that she could not control her eating, but feared "disappointing her family and friends" by admitting these problems.

Initial treatment focused on control of binging and purging and reduction of fears related to weight gain. Exposure with response prevention was conducted at every meal. At first, she experienced considerable anxiety after eating moderate sized meals, but this anxiety decreased over the course of treatment. During the third week of hospitalization, we introduced the consumption of "forbidden" foods (i.e., foods which she would eat only if she intended to purge). Cognitive therapy to challenge irrational beliefs regarding weight gain was utilized in group and individual therapy throughout the hospitalization. She was discharged to outpatient therapy after 4 weeks. Her weight was 108 lbs at the time of discharge. She was incredulous that she had lost weight while eating normally (about 1,600 kcal/day).

Susan was followed in individual and group therapy for about 14 months following hospitalization. Over the period, group therapy was faded from 4 sessions per week to once every 2 weeks. She had several partial relapses over the course of outpatient treatment, but regained control over binging and purging in each case. At long-term follow-up, 4 years after discharge, she was nearing completion of her undergraduate degree and planning to attend graduate school or law school. Her weight was stable at about 110 lbs. She had not purged or severely restricted her eating for over 2 years.

This case is typical of most severe bulimics. Relatively brief hospitalization is often required to gain control over binging and purging. Hospitalization must be followed with intensive outpatient therapy over a period ranging from 6 to 18 months.

Summary

Existing research suggests that cognitive and behavioral techniques are quite effective for reducing the frequency of binging and purging. Most behavioral programs for bulimia nervosa include a diversity of treatment components—most commonly, self-monitoring, meal planning, exposure with response prevention, and cognitive restructuring. Recent studies with long-term follow-up suggest that most bulimics continue to express some problems with eating and body image and some have significant relapses. Future studies must begin to investigate these problems so that better relapse prevention strategies can be developed.

ANOREXIA NERVOSA

Clinical Description and Conceptualization

Anorexia nervosa is characterized by an overwhelming drive for thinness and a morbid fear of being fat, resulting in the practice of extreme weight reduction methods. Such methods include compulsive exercising, very restrictive eating to the point of starvation, and, in some cases, self-induced vomiting or use of laxatives following the consumption of even small amounts of food. Weight loss can be rapid when these strategies are employed, and often requires immediate hospitalization to prevent further weight loss.

The American Psychiatric Association (1987) has specified four diagnostic criteria for anorexia nervosa:

1. Refusal to maintain normal body weight or failure to gain weight during adolescence;
2. Intense fear of gaining weight;
3. Presence of body image disturbance (e.g., feeling fat when emaciated);
4. Absence of three consecutive menstrual cycles.

Williamson et al. (1990) have proposed that the extreme weight reduction methods used by the anorexic patient are motivated by the desire to reduce anxiety produced by distorted thoughts concerning body shape and weight. This model is consistent with earlier behavioral theories of anorexia nervosa (e.g., Slade, 1982). This model, which is illustrated in Figure 18.3, proposes that central characteristics of anorexia nervosa are disturbance of body image, fear of weight gain, and overconcern with body size. These central concerns interact with the core psychopathology of anorexia nervosa (enclosed in the dashed lines that form an ellipse) to produce anxiety about weight gain. To avoid anxiety, the anorexic utilizes starvation, exercise, or purgative methods. Rapid weight loss can occur when these methods are employed, which reinforces extreme behavioral efforts to lose weight. The model also proposes that starvation has the effect of suppressing appetite, making it easier to maintain dietary restraint. One side effect of starvation is lowered basal metabolic rate (Keesey & Powley, 1986), which exacerbates the fear of fatness by increasing the probability of weight gain.

Treatment

Basic Methods

Effective treatment of anorexia nervosa usually requires hospitalization because of the medical complications caused by emaciation. It has been our experience that anorexics rarely gain weight with outpatient treatment. Inpatient treatment using behavioral methods involves interventions aimed at improved eating habits and weight restoration, and cognitive techniques to modify faulty beliefs regarding weight gain and body size. During the initial phase of treatment, an extensive behavioral assessment should be undertaken with the patient and family. For a more complete discussion of these methods, readers can refer to Williamson et al. (1990). Treatment methods and treatment goals must be agreed on by the patient and, if warranted, the patient's parents or family, prior to admission (Agras, 1987). Because the hospital setting is an aversive environment, which most anorexics prefer to avoid, the duration of hospitalization should not be contingent on weight gain, so as to eliminate the incentive of binging or other methods to rapidly gain weight to obtain release from the hospital. Following

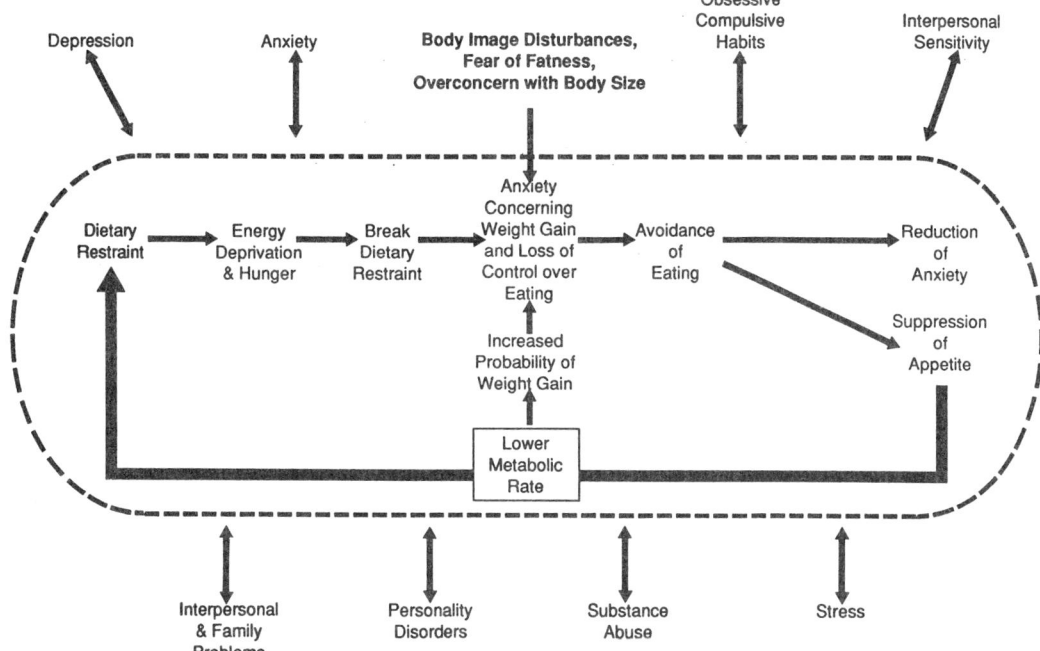

Figure 18.3. Behavioral model for anorexia nervosa. *Note.* Reprinted with permission from *Assessment of Eating Disorders: Obesity, Anorexia, and Bulimia Nervosa,* (p. 23) by D. A. Williamson, C. J. Davis, E. G. Duchmann, S. J. McKenzie, & P. C. Watkins, 1990. Copyright 1990 by Pergamon Press PLC.

the initial evaluation period, treatment goals should be explicitly formulated, including the amount of weight gain expected, the amount of food to be eaten each day, and reinforcers for compliance with treatment. The consequences for not achieving these goals must also be delineated. The following sections describe behavioral approaches that have been developed for achieving these goals.

1. *Operant conditioning* techniques have been utilized for the purpose of producing rapid weight gain. Because of the low weight of most anorexic patients and the adverse physical and psychological effects of a nutritionally deprived state (Keys, Brozek, Henschel, Mickelson, & Taylor, 1950), the first goal of treatment must be weight restoration. Positive reinforcement has been used to increase caloric intake and to produce weight gain. Common reinforcers include unit privileges, physical activities, and social activities. Research findings suggest that contingencies placed on weight gain over the course of a week are more effective, because of daily weight fluctuations, and are more easily implemented than those that focus on eating behavior (Bemis, 1987; Touyz, Beumont, & Dunn, 1987). Positive reinforcers are delivered if weight gain equals or exceeds the previously determined amount; failure to gain the prescribed weight results in negative consequences such as bed rest, seclusion, loss of ward privileges, and, if necessary, tube feeding (Bemis, 1987).

Agras, Barlow, Chapin, Abel, and Leitenberg (1974) reported that feedback concerning the amount of calories consumed and weight gain facilitated weight restoration by presumably reducing the anorexics' fear of rapid, uncontrolled weight gain. However, we have found that such information only serves to increase the anorexics' existing preoccupation with caloric intake and weight gain. For this reason, anorexics are provided meal plans of unspecified caloric values.

2. *Meal planning* is required in order to modify anorexics' unhealthy attitudes regarding the body's nutritional needs. Education concerning the energy requirements of the human body can help the anorexic patient understand the necessity for the consumption of three well-balanced meals. Beumont, O'Connor, Touyz, and Williams (1987) recommend that initially a dietician should prescribe meal plans to ensure that caloric intake is adequate for weight gain and that a variety of foods are eaten. Later, the patient may be allowed to select the menu but each meal must continue to be approved by the dietician.

3. *Cognitive restructuring* is required to modify anorexics' dysfunctional beliefs about eating and body size. The first step in cognitive therapy is the identification of these dysfunctional cognitions. Self-monitoring of these thoughts is then prescribed, to heighten awareness of their occurrence. Having identified the dysfunctional thoughts, patients are taught to dispute their validity by generating supportive or contradictory evidence for each thought. This process is identical to that described for bulimia, though anorexics are often more recalcitrant in their efforts to modify these cognitions.

4. *Body image therapy* used in the treatment of anorexia nervosa is very similar to that described for bulimia. We have found that, when anorexics are at a "preferred" weight level (i.e., very thin), they often do not report significant concern about body size. It is only after they begin to gain weight that body image concerns are manifested. Therefore, it is essential that cognitive-behavioral methods are integrated into inpatient treatment so that these body image disturbances can be addressed as weight increases.

5. *Family therapy* is often required because of the intense family conflict over eating and weight loss that normally occurs in families with an anorexic (Russell, Symukler, Dare, & Eisler, 1987). We have found that family therapy should focus on improved communication and reduction of parental control over the anorexic's eating habits.

Research Findings

Because of the medical complications associated with most cases of anorexia nervosa, it is very difficult to conduct controlled evaluations of treatment procedures. For example, using control conditions such as waiting-list control groups or minimal therapy would be very risky, if not unethical, because death or severe health problems result when anorexia is untreated. For these reasons, studies of behavioral treatment for anorexia have utilized either single-case or single-group experimental designs to evaluate their efficacy. Operant conditioning approaches have been found to be very effective for purposes of weight restoration (Agras & Kraemer, 1984; Bemis, 1987). Efficient and effective implementation of these operant approaches generally requires hospitalization. In some cases, patients who are less emaciated and are not vomiting or purging may be treated on an outpatient basis, provided that they maintain a prescribed weight and weight gain is accomplished over several months (Hsu, 1986).

Long-term follow-up studies concerning the effectiveness of cognitive-behavioral treatment approaches for anorexia nervosa have only recently been reported. Kennedy and Garfinkel (1989) reported "intermediate" to "good" treatment outcome for 83% of their anorexic sample 1 to 5 years following discharge. Fifty percent weighed above 85% of recommended body weight, 54% had regular menses, and 96% were in part-time education or occupation. These data are similar to findings reported over longer periods of follow-up. Studies that have reported favorable results frequently employ other concurrent treatment modalities (e.g., insight oriented therapy, group therapy, pharmacotherapy, family therapy, and body-image therapy). To more fully understand the efficacy of cognitive-behavioral therapy alone, future research must control for the influence of these other treatment modalities.

Case Example

Frances was a 19-year-old college student referred for treatment of anorexia nervosa by her psychiatrist. She had been treated in a general psychiatric hospital 1 year prior to referral and had made little progress. Frances was 5 ft 3. in tall and weighed 83 lbs upon admission. She reported eating very little food each day (estimated to be less than 500 kcal). She exercised for at least 3 hours each day by attending aerobics classes and running. When she did consume a normal meal, she purged it via self-induced vomiting. She occasionally used laxatives when she felt that she was "eating too much." She never binged (i.e., ate large quantities of food). She was obsessed with fears of weight gain, believing that if she began eating normally, she would rapidly gain weight and become "repulsively obese." She weighed herself constantly and each time she gained even 1 pound she felt very fat.

Frances came from an upper-class family; her father was a physician in a small city about 100 miles away. She was currently enrolled in a local university and was about to fail out of school because of poor grades. She reported that she could hardly study because she was so busy exercising and worrying about her weight. She also felt lethargic and depressed, and could no longer find the motivation required by a college curriculum. She had a limited social life because "everyone wanted to drink and eat" when they were socializing.

She reported a 6-year history of problems related to eating and body size. At age 13, she was about 20 lbs overweight. She was teased by peers and chastised by her mother, who was preoccupied with appearance and social standing. Her father helped her begin a diet and, when she began to lose weight, he and her mother heaped praise on her. She lost 20 lbs in about 3 months and continued her diet, losing an additional 10 lbs. She weighed about 105 lbs at that time. Further weight loss was quite difficult. At first, she tried intensive dieting. Then she began jogging. Next, she began to purge meals that she consumed. These more extreme weight-loss methods resulted in further weight loss and eventually her parents became concerned. By this time, she was 14 years old. When her parents began to insist that she eat, she began to purge more often. Her weight fluctuated between 95 and 105 lbs for the next few years. At age 16, she was referred to a psychiatrist who treated her for about 6 months without significant effects upon the eating disorder. After she entered college and moved out of her home, at age 18, she was able to eat more restrictively and exercise more vigorously. These habits led to rather rapid weight loss, which precipitated her first hospitalization. During this hospitalization she gained weight, to about 95 lbs, and was discharged to the care of the psychiatrist. Over the next year, she lost 12 lbs and was referred for intensive treatment of anorexia nervosa. At the time of referral, she had not menstruated for at least nine months.

Frances was diagnosed anorexia nervosa with primary problem areas of: (a) extreme fear of weight gain, (b) irrational beliefs and attitudes regarding body size and weight regulation, (c) extreme dietary restraint, (d) use of purgative methods, and (e) body image disturbances of body image distortion and extreme preference for thinness. It was anticipated that she would express strong dissatisfaction with body size when weight gain was initiated. In addition to the core symptoms of anorexia nervosa, initial evaluation suggested a clinical level of depression, avoidant personality features, and significant obsessional characteristics related to perfectionism and social evaluation. Assessment of the family environment suggested that her parents had modeled and reinforced habits related to achievement and making the "proper social impression." During early adolescence, Frances had been modestly overweight and her parents established reinforcement contingencies to promote weight loss. Over the course of the next few years, she was reinforced for weight loss and thinness. Eventually, negative consequences, including lethargy and depression, were manifested. By this time, the maintenance factors of anorexia nervosa illustrated in Figure 18.3 were operative, resulting in loss of control over eating, exercise, and other weight control activities.

Frances was admitted to a comprehensive inpatient treatment program for eating disorders. The treatment staff included psychiatrists, psychologists, clinical social workers, nurses, and clinical dieticians. The first goal of treatment was improvement of nutritional intake to stop weight loss and to prepare for weight gain. A meal plan of 1,000 kcal/day was initially prescribed and was gradually increased to 2,000 kcal/day over the first 10 days of treatment. She was observed for at least 2 hours after each meal, to prevent purging and to help her learn to cope with feelings of anxiety and bloatedness. All meals were eaten with other eating disorder patients under therapeutic supervision. All foods consumed were carefully recorded so that caloric and nutritional estimates could be made. Unit activities and privileges were made contingent on weight maintenance and achievement of caloric goals.

Frances was compliant with the treatment program until caloric goals exceeded 2,000 kcal/day. She began to eat less than 100% of her meal plan with complaints of bloatedness and anxiety concerning weight gain. She was participating in group and individual therapy for reduction of fears related to weight gain. These therapy programs directly addressed irrational cognitions related to weight gain. Despite such cognitive intervention, she continued to resist efforts to increase caloric intake beyond 2,000 kcal/day. Removal of unit privileges and orders for bed rest had little impact on her behavior. The next step in her treatment plan was a medical order to augment her meal plan with nutritional supplements. This program involved supplementing calories that were not consumed with an equivalent amount of liquid glucose. For example, if the meal plan established a caloric goal of 2,500 kcal/day and she only consumed 2,000 kcal, then 500 kcal of nutritional supplement was prescribed. Several days of consuming about 300 to 700 kcal of liquid glucose resulted in compliance with the meal plan during the third week of hospitalization. By the end of that week, she was consuming 3,000 kcal/day and began to gain weight. By the fourth week, she was eating 3,500 kcal/day and gaining 2 to 3 lbs per week. Minimal goals of 1.5 lbs per week in addition to eating 100% of her meal plan were established for granting weekend passes and unit privileges.

During this first month of hospitalization, Frances became more actively involved in cognitive-behavior therapy to modify faulty thinking related to weight and body size. By the end of the first month, she weighed 87 lbs and was eating without experiencing extreme anxiety. She was not allowed to exercise during this entire period.

During the second month of hospitalization, she continued to modify eating habits and fears related to weight gain. She gained an additional 10 lbs and was able to set a goal weight of 100 to 105 lbs. During this second month of hospitalization, family therapy was introduced with weekly family therapy sessions and participation in a family therapy group once per week. The goals for these sessions were: (a) establishment of open and honest communication, (b) reduction of parental control, and (c) improvement of assertiveness related to expression of emotions and requests for behavior change.

After 10 weeks of inpatient treatment, Frances achieved a weight of 101.5 lbs and was discharged to a partial hospitalization program. In this program, she attended therapy sessions from 7:00 A.M. to 9:00 P.M. Monday through Friday, including eating all three meals with staff of the eating disorders program. At night and on weekends, she lived in an apartment with her roommates. During inpatient treatment, they were invited to participate in group therapy to help significant others assist in the treatment of eating disorders. After 3 weeks of partial hospitalization, she was discharged to outpatient therapy, which initially involved four groups per week and one individual/family therapy session. Over the next 14 months, this schedule was faded to weekly group therapy and biweekly individual/family therapy sessions.

Over this period, which spanned almost 1.5 years, Frances was able to attain a weight level between 100 and 105 lbs and her fears related to eating and weight gain were much reduced. At the time of termination, 12 months later, she was planning to graduate from college and had developed a satisfactory social life. She dated on a regular basis and had many friends.

This case illustrates the complexity of treating severe eating disorders such as anorexia nervosa. The case was chosen as representative of anorexics whom we have treated. Such cases must be viewed as long-term and as requiring a diversity of treatment approaches throughout various phases of therapy.

Summary

Behavior therapy for anorexia nervosa has generally favored inpatient treatment using operant reinforcement contingencies for modification of eating habits and restoration of body weight. More recent studies have incorporated cognitive interventions to modify irrational thinking about weight, dieting, and eating. Recent follow-up studies have found that these more comprehensive treatment programs are effective over follow-up of 5 years.

We have found that anorexics often require 4 to 8 weeks of inpatient treatment followed by 2 to 6 weeks of partial hospitalization. Outpatient follow-up of 6 months to 2 years is often required to prevent relapse and to ultimately reduce the irrational fears of weight gain that motivate the anorexic.

CONCLUSION

Behavior therapy for obesity, bulimia, and anorexia nervosa has been extensively studied over the past 15 years. During this period, behavioral methods have moved from experimental methods to being adopted by the general health-care profession. Empirical tests of the efficacy of these methods have consistently shown behavioral approaches to be very effective, especially for short-term behavior change. The primary deficiency of behavioral approaches has been the finding that a substantial number of patients relapse following short-term treatment. These findings should not be particularly surprising, given the recalcitrant nature of chronic obesity, bulimia, and anorexia nervosa. For these reasons, it is probable that future research in this area will recognized the need for comprehensive long-term treatment programs for the eating disorders.

REFERENCES

Agras, W. S. (1987). *Eating disorders: Management of obesity, bulimia, and anorexia nervosa.* New York: Pergamon.

Agras, W. S., Barlow, D. H., Chapin, H. N., Abel, G. G., & Leitenberg, H. (1974). Behavior modification of anorexia nervosa. *Archives of General Psychiatry, 30,* 279–286.

Agras, W. S., & Kraemer, H. C. (1984). The treatment of anorexia nervosa: Do different treatments have different outcomes? In A. J. Stunkard & E. Stellar (Eds.), *Eating and its disorders* (pp. 193–207). New York: Raven Press.

American Psychiatric Association. (1987). *Diagnostic and statistical manual of mental disorders* (3rd ed. rev.). Washington, DC: Author.

Bellack, A. S., & Williamson, D. A. (1982). Obesity and anorexia nervosa. In D. Doleys, R. Meredity, & A. Ciminero (Eds.), *Behavioral medicine: Treatment and assessment strategies* (pp. 295–316). New York: Plenum.

Bemis, K. M. (1987). The present status of operant conditioning for treatment of anorexia nervosa. *Behavior Modification, 11,* 432–463.

Bennett, G. A. (1986). Behavior therapy for obesity: A quantitative review of the effects of selected treatment characteristics on outcome. *Behavior Therapy, 17,* 554–562.

Bennett, S. M., Williamson, D. A., & Powers, S. K. (1989). Bulimia nervosa and resting metabolic rate. *International Journal of Eating Disorders, 8,* 417–424.

Beumont, P. J. V., O'Connor, M., Touyz, S. W., & Williams, H. (1987). Nutritional counseling in the treatment of anorexia and bulimia nervosa. In P. J. V. Beumont, G. D. Burrows, & R. C. Casper (Eds.), *Handbook of eating disorders Part 1: Anorexia and bulimia nervosa* (pp. 349–359). Amsterdam: Elsevier.

Brownell, K., Heckerman, C., Westlake, R., Hayes, S., & Monti, P. (1978). The effects of couples training and partner co-operativeness in the behavioral treatment of obesity. *Behaviour Research and Therapy, 16,* 323–333.

Epstein, L. H., & Wing, R. R. (1987). Behavioral treatment of childhood obesity. *Psychological Bulletin, 101,* 331–342.

Fairburn, C. G. (1981). A cognitive behavioral approach to the treatment of bulimia. *Psychological Medicine, 11,* 707–711.

Foreyt, J. O. (1987). Issues in the assessment and treatment of obesity. *Journal of Consulting and Clinical Psychology, 55,* 677–684.

Hinz, L. D., & Williamson, D. A. (1987). Bulimia and depression: A review of the affective variant hypothesis. *Psychological Bulletin, 102,* 150–158.

Hsu, L. K. G. (1986). The treatment of anorexia nervosa. *American Journal of Psychiatry, 143,* 573–581.

Keesey, R. E., & Powley, T. L. (1986). The regulation of body weight. *Annual Review of Psychology, 37,* 109–133.

Kennedy, S. H., & Garfinkel, P. E. (1989). Patients admitted to a hospital with anorexia nervosa and bulimia nervosa: Psychopathology, weight gain, and attitudes toward treatment. *International Journal of Eating Disorders, 8,* 181–190.

Keys, A., Brozek, J., Henschel, A., Mickelson, O., & Taylor, H. L. (1950). *The biology of human starvation.* Minneapolis: University of Minnesota Press.

Marcus, M. D., Wing, R. R., & Hopkins, J. (1988). Obese binge eaters: Affect, cognitions, and response to behavioral weight control. *Journal of Consulting and Clinical Psychology, 56,* 433–439.

Mitchell, J. E., Pyle, R. L., Hatsukami, D., Goff, G., Glotter, D., & Harper, J. (1989). A 2–5 year follow-up study of patients treated for bulimia. *International Journal of Eating Disorders, 8,* 157–165.

Murphy, J. K., Bruce, B. K., & Williamson, D. A. (1985). A comparison of measured and self-reported weights in a 4-year follow-up of spouse involvement in obesity treatment. *Behavior Therapy, 16,* 524–530.

Murphy, J. K., Williamson, D. A., Buxton, A. E., Moody, S. C., Absher, N., & Warner, M. (1982). The long-term effects of spouse involvement upon weight loss and maintenance. *Behavior Therapy, 13,* 621–693.

Perri, M. G., McAllister, D. A., Gange, J. J., Jordan, R. C., McAdoo, W. G., & Nezu, A. M. (1988). Effects of four maintenance programs on the long-term management of obesity. *Journal of Consulting and Clinical Psychology, 56,* 529–534.

Perri, M. G., Nezu, A. M., Patti, E. T., & McCann, K. L. (1989). Effect of length of treatment on weight loss. *Journal of Consulting and Clinical Psychology, 57,* 450–452.

Rosen, J. C. (1987). A review of behavioral treatment for bulimia nervosa. *Behavior Modification, 11,* 464–486.

Rosen, J. C., & Leitenberg, H. (1982). Bulimia nervosa: Treatment with exposure and response prevention. *Behavior Therapy, 13,* 117–124.

Russell, G. F. M., Symukler, G. I., Dare, C., & Eisler, I. (1987). The evaluation of family therapy in anorexia nervosa and bulimia nervosa. *Archives of General Psychology, 44,* 1047–1056.

Slade, P. (1982). Toward a functional analysis of anorexia nervosa and bulimia nervosa. *British Journal of Clinical Psychology, 21,* 167–179.

Touyz, S. W., Beumont, P. J. V., & Dunn, S. W. (1987). Behavior therapy in the management of patients with anorexia nervosa. *Psychotherapy and Psychosomatics, 48,* 151–156.

Wadden, T. A., & Stunkard, A. J. (1986). Controlled trial of very low calorie diet, behavior therapy, and their combination in the treatment of obesity. *Journal of Consulting and Clinical Psychology, 54,* 482–488.

Wadden, T. A., Stunkard, A. J., & Liebschutz, J. (1988). Three-year follow-up of the treatment of obesity by very low calorie diet, behavior therapy, and their combination. *Journal of Consulting and Clinical Psychology, 56,* 925–928.

Williamson, D. A., Davis, C. J., Duchmann, E. G., McKenzie, S. J., & Watkins, P. C. (1990). *Assessment of eating disorders: Obesity, anorexia, and bulimia nervosa.* New York: Pergamon.

Williamson, D. A., Davis, C. J., Goreczny, A. J., & Blouin, D. C. (1989). Body image disturbances in bulimia nervosa: Influences of actual body size. *Journal of Abnormal Psychology, 98,* 97–99.

Williamson, D. A., Prather, R. C., Bennett, S. M., Davis, C. J., Watkins, P. C., & Grenier, C. (1989). Uncontrolled evaluation of inpatient and outpatient cognitive-behavior therapy for bulimia nervosa. *Behavior Modification, 13,* 340–360.

Williamson, D. A., Prather, R. C., Heffer, R. W., & Kelley, M. L. (1988). Eating disorders. In J. L. Matson (Ed.), *Treating childhood and adolescent psychopathology: A handbook* (pp. 367–396). New York: Plen

CHAPTER 19

Chronic Pain: Behavioral Conceptualizations and Interventions

DENNIS C. TURK, THOMAS E. RUDY, and BRUCE A. SORKIN

Humans have experienced pain from earliest recorded time, yet, despite this long history and significant advances in biomedical knowledge and practice during the past century, methods to permanently and consistently ameliorate pain continue to elude health care providers. Millions of individuals suffer intractable pain associated with a wide diversity of syndromes. The pain that these individuals experience can be divided into four general types:

1. Acute pain (e.g., postsurgery, broken bone);
2. Pain related to malignancy and other ongoing disease processes (e.g., tumor infiltration of bone, end-stage renal disease);
3. Acute recurrent pain (e.g., migraine headaches, trigeminal neuralgia);
4. Chronic intractable pain unrelated to malignancies (e.g., low back pain, diabetic neuropathy).

In this chapter, we will focus on the two latter categories of pain, chronic intractable and recurrent acute, because they have received the greatest amount of attention by psychologists. First, however, it is important to note that there is substantial evidence that psychological factors are relevant to acute pain as well (Peck, 1986). Additionally, the application of psychologically based models and treatment interventions has largely been ignored in the cancer pain literature. Turk and Fernandez (1990) argued that cancer and pain associated with cancer appear to hold a unique position among both the lay public and health care providers. These authors suggested that many of the behavioral principles and variables that we will discuss below are readily applicable to patients who have been diagnosed with cancer.

The failure to find satisfactory pain control strategies has resulted to some extent from the adherence to a unidimensional, sensory-physiological conceptualization of pain that can be attributed to the philosopher Descartes dating back to the mid-17th century. This model is based on a specificity conceptualization that postulates the amount of pain experienced is directly proportional to the

---

Preparation of this chapter was supported in part by Grant ARNS38698 from the National Institute of Arthritis and Musculoskeletal and Skin Diseases and Grant DE07514 from the National Institute of Dental Research and a contract from the Baltimore Therapeutic Equipment Company.

amount of peripheral nociceptive input associated with identifiable tissue damage. This model is predicated on the assumption that some form of tissue damage excites receptors that respond exclusively to nociceptive stimuli that in turn initiate pain-specific nerve impulses that are transmitted along specific pain pathways to a "pain center" located in the brain, where the experience of pain will motivate actions to avoid further harm. This sensory view of pain has been retained despite the fact that pharmacological, medical, and surgical procedures designed to cut or block the transmission of nociceptive stimuli (i.e., sensory information that may be interpreted as pain) along various pathways in the nervous system have generally proven to be unsuccessful.

A variety of diverse clinical findings is not handled well by a simple sensory-physiological model. For example, this model cannot explain why individuals: (a) with the same extent of tissue pathology vary widely in their report of pain intensity; (b) with objective radiographic evidence of degenerative changes do not report any pain; (c) with minimal objective physical pathology complain of severe pain; and (d) with the same physical diagnosis and identified tissue pathology treated with the same intervention respond in distinctly different ways. It is also perplexing to note that rarely do patients who are eventually diagnosed with cancer indicate that pain contributed to their decision to seek medical attention; yet, after the diagnosis is made, there is a marked increase in reports of pain. Such paradoxes have instigated attempts to reformulate models of pain, including an increased emphasis on the importance of psychological variables.

Three discrete areas have served as primary facilitators of interest in the role that psychological factors play in pain perception. These areas are: (a) Fordyce, Fowler, and DeLateur's (1968) application of operant conditioning principles to chronic pain; (b) the demonstration of the voluntary control of the autonomic nervous system (originally viewed as involuntary) and the control of inappropriate and overlearned voluntary muscle responses using biofeedback (Basmajian, 1963); and (c) Melzack and his colleagues' (Melzack & Casey, 1968; Melzack & Wall, 1965) formulation of the gate control model of pain. These areas underscored the contributions of cognitive and affective factors in symptom interpretation and physical as well as psychological responses to nociception, and the role of contingencies of reinforcement on overt behavioral manifestations of pain and suffering. Each of these areas not only influenced how pain has been conceptualized but also has served as an impetus for the development of new assessment methods and innovative treatment modalities.

In this chapter, we will review the conceptual basis of operant and respondent conditioning and the cognitive-behavioral perspective as they have been applied to chronic and recurrent acute pain. We also will discuss the therapeutic interventions that follow from these behavioral conceptualizations. Throughout our discussion, we will consider the empirical data for each model and the evidence for the efficacy of the various treatment modalities predicated on these behavioral models. It will become evident that, although we discuss the operant, respondent, and cognitive models separately, they have many areas of overlap and, indeed, can be viewed as complementary.

OPERANT CONDITIONING IN CHRONIC PAIN

Central to the operant conditioning perspective of chronic pain is the important distinction between pain as a private experience and observable and quantifiable "pain behaviors." Pain behaviors include observable communications of pain, distress, and suffering (e.g., moaning, grimacing, limping, and seeking analgesic medication). From this perspective, pain behaviors *and not pain per se* are the targets of assessment and treatment. Only the former are assumed to be directly amenable to behavioral assessment and treatment.

The operant model proposes that acute pain behaviors may come under control of external contingencies of reinforcement and thus lead to the development of a chronic problem. The rate of emitting pain behaviors (e.g., complaining, distorted ambulation) may be increased through positive reinforcement, for example, by immediate attention from a spouse after a complaint of pain. Behavioral displays may also be increased by negative reinforcement, for example, by removing demands to complete a boring or strenuous task at work made contingent on the display of pain behaviors. Moreover, behaviors incompatible with pain, "well behaviors" (e.g., activity), may be directly punished (e.g., when a well-meaning spouse admonishes the patient for engaging in what he or she considers to be harmful exercises). Finally, response costs can operate to decrease "well behaviors" when, for example, individuals are told by lawyers or employers that they will lose their pending litigation case if they are observed doing the very activities they most need to do to recondition themselves.

The basic principles underlying the operant model have been summarized succinctly by Fowler, Fordyce, and Berni (1969, p. 1226):

1. Behavior is largely a function of its consequences.
2. Behavior which is followed by positive or rewarding consequences will tend to be maintained or to increase in rate.
3. Behavior which is followed by neutral [or negative] consequences will tend to diminish or drop out altogether.

These principles suggest that if behaviors signaling pain result in positive consequences, the frequency of these pain behaviors will increase. The patient may receive attention (often sympathy) and frequently is relieved of responsibilities when such behaviors are displayed. Attention and legitimized abdication of responsibility are all presumably rewarding experiences. Thus, pain behaviors originally elicited reflexively or emitted as random operants may come to occur, totally or in part, in response to reinforcing environmental events. Elimination of positive reinforcement for pain behaviors in conjunction with positive reinforcement of well behaviors should, according to the "law of effect," lead to extinction of maladaptive pain behaviors and increased activity.

Health care providers have long considered pain as being synonymous with nociception *and* as a symptom of pathology. It is important, however, to make a tripartite distinction among nociception, pain, and suffering. Pain, because it involves conscious awareness, selective abstraction, appraisal, ascribed meaning, and learning is best viewed as a *perceptual process.* Suffering, which includes interpersonal disruption, economic distress, occupational problems, and myriad other factors associated with pain's impact on life functioning, is largely a response to the perception of pain. Nociception precedes and directly relates to unconditioned responses (e.g., reflexively withdrawing one's hand from a hot stove).

Nociception is also associated with sensory stimuli that are capable of being perceived as painful. In sharp contrast to the nociceptive model, operant pain behaviors can occur in the absence of and thus may be independent of nociception. Specifically, Fordyce (1976) suggests that the maintenance of pain behaviors may occur through a process of reinforcement. The operant conditioning model does not concern itself directly with pain but rather with overt manifestations of pain and suffering. Because of the consequences of specific behavioral responses, it is proposed that pain behaviors may persist after the initial cause is resolved or greatly reduced (e.g., tissue inflammation).

It is also probable that the deconditioning resulting from reinforced inactivity can result directly in increased nociception. That is, reduction of activity invariably leads to decreased muscle strength, tone, and flexibility. Muscles that were involved in the original injury generally heal rapidly but, because of underuse of these muscles, they become weakened and subject to nociception when pressed into service. Another example is when a person is reinforced for displaying an abnormal gait pattern (e.g., limping). Eventually, the maladaptive muscle response patterns that develop may lead to nociception arising from myofascial syndromes that are a consequence of distorted gait.

Further, the reinforcement contingencies surrounding the chronic pain patient will have an effect on suffering or on how well the patient copes with his or her situation, the experience of pain notwithstanding. For example, it is clear that aspects of the patient's life, such as medication usage and social, religious, occupational, and sexual activity levels, will all be affected by environmental contingencies in addition to the amount of pain experienced. A comprehensive pain management program must make these aspects of a patient's life important, if not the most important, targets of treatment rather than focusing on experienced pain per se. Thus, the operant model can legitimately be seen as addressing quality-of-life issues, as well as issues of pain reduction.

Several studies provide evidence that supports the underlying assumptions of the operant conditioning model. Cairns and Pasino (1977) and Doleys, Crocker, and Patton (1982) demonstrated that pain behaviors can be decreased by verbal reinforcement and the setting of exercise quotas. Block, Kremer, and Gaylor (1980) demonstrated that pain patients reported differential levels of pain in an experimental situation, depending on whether they were observed by their spouses or ward clerks. Pain patients with nonsolicitous spouses reported more pain when neutral observers were present than when spouses were. When solicitous spouses were present, pain patients reported more pain than in the neutral observer condition. Flor, Kerns, and Turk (1987) noted that chronic pain patients reported more intense pain and less activity if they indicated their spouses were solicitous. The latter two studies suggest that spouses, at least solicitous ones, can serve as discriminative stimuli for the display of pain behaviors by chronic pain patients, including reports of pain intensity.

TREATMENT BASED ON THE OPERANT CONDITIONING MODEL

Treatments based on the operant model include:

1. Positive reinforcement for activity and inattention to extinguish learned maladaptive behaviors;
2. Use of medication on a time-contingent rather than on an as-needed basis, with gradual reductions in the quantity of analgesic medications;
3. Physical activity to increase strength, endurance, and flexibility, which should also lead to corrective neuromuscular feedback;
4. Assertiveness and social skills training to provide patients with more appropriate means to secure rewards or avoid punishment in situations where they have become accustomed to displaying pain behaviors.

Operant treatments are usually conducted on an inpatient basis because this permits far better control of the external reinforcement contingencies. Spouse participation is strongly encouraged because the spouse is probably the most important reinforcing agent and he or she can facilitate transfer of new behavioral patterns to the home environment. The methods of achieving these goals include withdrawal of attention for pain behaviors, and attention and reinforcement of well behaviors. Increased activity levels are promoted by establishing exercise quotas, reinforcing activity using time-contingent or task completion-contingent rest rather than pain-contingent rest, and giving praise and attention for effort and goal accomplishments. Rewards for requesting medications are eliminated by altering administration of medication from the usual *prn* (take as needed; pain-contingent) to a fixed interval (time-contingent) schedule. The quantity of medication is usually tapered according to a predetermined schedule (usually 10 to 20%/day).

Treatments based on the operant model have targeted patients with chronic pain that is not associated with malignancies. Several reports of the efficacy of operant treatment have appeared in the literature (e.g., Anderson, Cole, Gulickson, Hudgens, & Roberts, 1977; Fordyce et al., 1973; for recent reviews see Linton, 1986, and Turner & Romano, 1984). However, despite the apparent success of the operant approach, several substantial limitations exist, including its predominant focus on pain behaviors. For example, Cairns and Pasino (1977) demonstrated that removal of positive reinforcement resulted in return to baseline levels of inactivity, and the data reported by Doleys et al. (1982) and Dolce, Crocker, Moletteire, and Doleys (1986) suggest that generalization and maintenance may be particularly problematic. These results raise some concerns about the long-term efficacy of operant treatment programs conducted in a controlled inpatient setting. Furthermore, inpatient treatment can be prohibitively expensive. Several studies (e.g., Linton & Gotestam, 1984) have demonstrated that outpatient relaxation programs can be as effective as the results reported for inpatient operant programs. Finally, the relatively large number of selection criteria for acceptance into operant treatment programs (Turk & Flor, 1987) may limit the general utility of the operant model. There are also problems with the number of patients who are willing to enter inpatient treatment programs (Turk & Rudy, 1989) and with the level of patient satisfaction with the treatments received in programs based on the operant model (Kotarba, 1983).

Early reviews of operant treatment for chronic pain frequently indicated that the results were limited by a lack of controls, inadequate measurement of behavioral factors, and numerous other methodological concerns. However, these reviews usually concluded that the results were "promising." Unfortunately, it is now two decades since the original formulation of the operant model by Fordyce and his colleagues (Fowler et al., 1969) and we are still left with the frequently reiterated conclusion that "the results are promising but more and better controlled research is needed before any definitive statement can be made as to the long-term efficacy and mechanism by which operant approaches have their effect" (p. 1228).

SELF-REGULATION OF MALADAPTIVE PHYSIOLOGICAL RESPONSES

A primary assumption of a number of theories of acute recurrent and chronic pain syndromes, notably musculoskeletal pain syndromes (e.g., tension headaches, myofascial pain) and vascular pain syndromes (migraine headaches, Raynaud's disease), is that maladaptive autonomic functioning (e.g., constriction of peripheral vascular blood flow in response to stress), overlearned voluntary muscular patterns (e.g., bracing, limping, or jaw clenching), or both, can cause pain.

Basmajian (1963) demonstrated that motor units in the muscle could be voluntarily controlled and changes in function could be obtained through learning techniques. Several years later, Miller (1969) and others demonstrated that autonomic visceral and glandular functioning could also be altered through learning.

These studies served as impetuses for treatments designed to modify maladaptive neuromuscular and vascular responses postulated to have an etiological role in several pain syndromes. Specifically, relaxation and electromyographic (EMG) biofeedback were proposed for syndromes believed to have a myogenic basis, and autogenic training and vascular biofeedback (peripheral temperature, cephalic artery) were proposed for treatment of syndromes with a hypothesized vascular origin.

The earliest conceptualizations of relaxation and biofeedback treatments were predicated on three assumptions: (a) specific physiological factors caused pain, (b) voluntary control over these factors would alleviate the symptoms, and (c) providing feedback leading to conscious control regarding the putative maladaptive physiological activity could be generalized beyond the clinic (Budzynski, 1973). This amounted to a sensory-physiological model not unlike that of the conventional medical perspective. That is, there is a physical cause of symptoms (excessive levels of muscular tension of vascular activity) and reduction of the physical causes would result in the elimination of pain. Thus, the original views of relaxation, autogenic training, and biofeedback might be considered as psychological analogs of analgesic medication.

When individuals learn to regulate physiological parameters such as muscle tension or skin temperature using biofeedback, the learning mechanism is most likely to be operant conditioning of autonomic responses and overlearned maladaptive muscular patterns. Individuals emit a response and are reinforced or punished by the feedback stimulus itself. That is, success at the task is deemed reinforcing. The change in physiological functioning is usually subtle, and shaping of the response occurs over repeated trials. Further, patients may not be fully aware of the methods by which they are affecting control. One can distinguish this learning process from a classical conditioning paradigm insofar as the desired response (relaxation) is not elicited and paired with a neutral stimulus, but rather is emitted and reinforced. The change in the feedback stimulus thus follows rather than anticipates the desired behavior.

The operant model is demonstrated in vivo when relaxation is used as an active coping skill (Goldfried, 1977). An example of an in vivo avoidance learning paradigm would be when a patient goes through a stressful period without experiencing a headache when he or she uses relaxation during the stressful period. Similarly, if an individual has neck spasms and relaxes and the pain diminishes, this is a case of negative reinforcement. Relaxation, in this case, leads to the cessation of an unconditioned punisher (pain).

Efficacy of Biofeedback and Relaxation

A vast literature exists reporting on the efficacy of biofeedback and relaxation for tension headaches and migraine headaches (Blanchard, Andrasik, Ahles, Teders, & O'Keefe, 1980; Blanchard et al., 1982), temporomandibular pain disorders (Scott & Gregg, 1980), and Raynaud's disease (Freedman, Ianni, & Wenig, 1983). The literature of the efficacy of biofeedback in the treatment of back pain is somewhat less clear (Dolce & Raczynski, 1985). Moreover, Holroyd and Penzien (1986) recently demonstrated that the efficacy of biofeedback for headaches appears to have declined over time, with earlier studies consistently demonstrating more potent effects. In early studies of biofeedback applied to headache patients, college student volunteers were the most likely subjects; more recently, clinical samples have served as the subjects. Holroyd and Penzien noted that the effects tend to be greatly influenced by age, with the results being better for younger and nonclinical subject samples.

The relationship between physiological self-control and pain reduction, however, remains unclear. Changes in pain-specific parameters are not reliably associated with the physiological changes postulated to mediate the pain syndrome. Many studies have demonstrated no baseline differences in electrophysiological responses between patients with specific medical diagnoses and normal control subjects, and little relationship between control of physiological function and reduction of symptoms (see Flor & Turk, 1989a, for a review).

To illustrate these issues, we can examine the Andrasik and Holroyd (1980) study. In this study, the authors compared EMG biofeedback for decreasing, increasing, or stabilizing frontalis muscle tension with a no-treatment control group. The three treatment groups all showed significant reductions in the frequency and intensity of headaches compared to the control groups. There were no significant differences in reduction of headache activity among the three treatment groups, despite the fact that each group learned to control the frontalis muscles in the specified direction. That is, subjects who learned to *increase* frontalis muscle tension, purportedly the cause of tension headache and the usual target of biofeedback training for tension headaches, reported *equivalent* declines in headaches compared to those subjects who decreased frontalis tension.

Analogous studies with migraine headache patients (Kewman & Roberts, 1980) and chronic back pain patients (Bush, Ditto, & Feuerstein, 1985) demonstrated virtually identical results regarding the specificity of biofeedback. Kewman and Roberts reported no differences in migraine symptoms, regardless of whether subjects were trained to raise *or* lower peripheral skin temperature, and Bush et al. demonstrated similar reductions in reported pain regardless of whether the back pain patients were taught to raise or lower paraspinal EMG levels. Thus, the mechanisms by which biofeedback produces its beneficial effects remain an open question. The failure to find an association between specific psychophysiological parameters and reported symptoms is especially interesting because the original rationale for using biofeedback was that it would reduce physiological reactivity believed to cause the pain symptoms. Moreover, biofeedback and relaxation are usually targeted at reducing baseline levels of muscle tension. If there are no demonstrations of abnormalities at baseline between patients and normals and if symptoms are unrelated to psychophysiological parameters, then we have to ask, why teach patients to reduce specific psychophysiological parameters?

Several investigators have suggested that biofeedback does not have a direct effect on maladaptive autonomic or sympathetic nervous system activity but rather serves to increase patients' perceptions of self-efficacy and self-control (Biedermann, McGhie, Monga, & Shanks, 1987; Fydrich, Rudy, & Turk, 1988; Holroyd et al., 1984). These models imply the central role of cognitive processes in biofeedback. This interpretation may explain why relaxation treatment often produces results similar to those of biofeedback, even though no specific muscles are targeted in many relaxation treatments (Jessup, 1989). Similarly, it would explain why patients with muscle spasms in their backs could report decreases in symptoms when feedback is provided from a distal site such as the frontalis muscles. We must be cautious in our interpretation of these data and should not use them as a basis for not using biofeedback with pain patients, because these data are based on group averages. There may be important individual differences in physiological responses that are masked when the data are aggregated within groups.

It is possible that there are subgroups of patients who do demonstrate site-specific maladaptive neurophysiological responses and for whom biofeedback has a direct effect on symptoms (Blanchard et al., 1983). It is also important to reiterate the point that biofeedback should not merely teach patients to relax in the nonthreatening confines of the treatment setting. This procedure is unlikely to yield generalization, the overlearning necessary for treatment success, or the presumed goal of counterconditioning to anxiety or tension-provoking situations. It is important, then, to examine biofeedback studies that have trained subjects to relax when exposed to high levels of environmentally relevant stressors. Finally, it is worth noting that successful control of physiological activity made evident by biofeedback may serve to enhance patients' self-efficacy regarding their ability to relax. If patients believe that specific physiological parameters are related to their symptoms, then the feedback serves as a direct, face valid, and objective measure of success that the patients can accept as support for their own control over the putative cause of their symptoms.

CLASSICAL CONDITIONING AND PAIN

Gentry and Bernal (1977) were the first to suggest that classical conditioning of pain and tension may occur in an acute pain state caused by some form of physical damage leading to a pain–tension–pain cycle. This model views pain both as a response to and an antecedent of specific autonomic activity. Lentham, Slade, Troup, and Bentley (1983) postulated that once an acute pain problem exists, conditioned fear of movement may develop and motivate avoidance of activity, and thereby lead to immobilization. Individuals who suffer from acute pain, regardless of the cause, may adopt specific protective and adaptive behaviors (e.g., limping, reclining) in order to avoid pain and, therefore, may never obtain "corrective feedback" because they fail to perform more natural movements (Philips, 1987a; Rachman & Lopatka, 1988). Reduction in physical activity may subsequently result in muscle atrophy, increased impairment, and increased disability. In this manner, the physical abnormalities may actually be secondary to changes in behavior initiated through a learning process.

When the pain symptoms persist, more and more situations may elicit anxiety and pain. Dependence on medication and depression may follow, further intensifying the pain–tension cycle. Thus, psychological expectations may lead to modified behavior that, in turn, may produce physical changes leading to still further physical deconditioning. With chronic pain, the anticipation of suffering or prevention of pain may be sufficient for the long-term maintenance of the maladaptive avoidance behaviors.

The respondent and operant models need not be seen as mutually exclusive. Although the patient may develop a conditioned pattern of bracing, gait and postural disturbances, and anxiety through respondent means, it is important to note that these disturbances may then be maintained through operant conditioning. In this sense, the formulation is analogous to the two-factor theory of the development of phobias (Eysenck & Rachman, 1965; Mowrer, 1960). The two-factor theory states that a neutral situation, such as being in a market, is contingently paired with fear caused by an aversive unconditioned stimulus (UCS), such as fainting due to influenza (an unconditioned response, UCR), and, subsequently, the neutral situation serves as a conditioned stimulus (CS) eliciting fear. This classically conditioned fear elicited in the previously neutral situation does not extinguish, however, because the phobic individual is negatively reinforced with anxiety reduction for avoiding the situation and thereby effectively minimizing contact and acquisition of corrective feedback.

Consistent with the two-factor model, Goldstein and Chambless (1978) and Chambless and Goldstein (1980) described the complex agoraphobic who has not merely suffered one intense aversive conditioning event, but rather, is receiving reinforcement from others for his or her passive avoidant behaviors. The two-factor theory, although consistent with data concerning treatment of phobias, has been criticized as being an inadequate explanation for the development and maintenance of them (e.g., Thorpe & Burns, 1983).

To illustrate the proposed process more explicitly from a respondent conditioning perspective, the patient may have learned to associate increases in anxiety and muscle tension with numerous stimuli that were originally associated with nociceptive stimulation. Thoughts about movement and certain sitting or standing positions originally are neutral stimuli because they do not elicit muscle spasm, pain, or anxiety. Nevertheless, after repeated pairing with nociceptive stimuli (an unconditioned stimulus) that leads to the unconditioned response of bracing, muscle spasm, and anxiety; thoughts about movement; and the originally neutral sitting positions become conditioned stimuli. They can thereafter elicit spasm, anxiety, and muscle tightness (conditioned responses). Unfortunately, the very nature of the conditioned response is painful. Thus, although the original association between injury and pain results in anxiety regarding movement, with time the anxiety may lead to increased muscle tension and pain even if the original nociceptive stimuli are no longer present. Nonoccurrence of pain is a powerful reinforcer of inactivity.

Treatment Based on Respondent Conditioning

The respondent model described above gives priority for the maintenance of pain to the psychological principles of classical conditioning. In contrast to the operant view of physical causation, the respondent model emphasizes the learned contingency of movement and nociception. Treatment from this model would focus on extinguishing the connection by exposure and disconfirmation. Specifically, the respondent model would explain part of the efficacy of physical therapy, for example, on the basis of exposure to the feared activities and the breaking of the association between hurt and harm (Fordyce, 1988).

From the respondent model, classical conditioning factors can contribute to exacerbations of pain in two ways. First, because of the avoidance of activity due to the anticipation of pain (classically conditioned muscle spasm), the patient becomes deconditioned, which in turn makes it even more likely that future physical activities will instigate nociception. Second, and more important from a respondent perspective, because patients do not expose themselves to physical activities believed to be painful, there is no chance for the conditioned response to be extinguished. Additionally, stimulus generalization can occur in which activities similar to the feared activity are also avoided.

The theoretical basis for biofeedback and relaxation training based on the respondent conditioning model assumes that the bracing and muscle spasm seen in many pain patients represents a conditioned response either to external stimuli or to internal nociceptive stimuli (interoceptive conditioning). From this perspective, the mechanism by which biofeedback or relaxation would have a clinical effect is by reducing the presumed maladaptive physiological response and subsequent experiencing of pain through counterconditioning.

Despite the fact that the role of avoidance has been hypothesized in the maintenance of pain behaviors, few systematic investigations of this mechanism have been reported. Fordyce, Shelton, and Dundore (1982) presented a case study that investigated the avoidance of aversive consequences as a mechanism for maintaining pain behavior. For this patient, guarding pain behavior (limping, protective movement) appeared to be maintained by anticipated nociceptive stimuli and, consequently, pain. The authors hypothesized that avoidance behavior does not necessarily require intermittent nociception from the site of physical pathology, in that environmental reinforcement or successful avoidance of aversive activity also can account for the maintenance of guarding behavior. These behaviors can be maintained by anticipation of aversive consequences as well (Schmidt, 1985).

GATE CONTROL MODEL

Early theories of pain hypothesized a direct periphery to brain transmission with the analogy of pain to a telephone transmission line (Melzack, 1973). This specificity theory postulated that pain was a sensation with specific receptors, nerve tracts, and reception sites localized in the brain. A second, related theory, intensity theory, suggested that there were no specific receptors; rather, when there was a level of stimulation in any sensory channel that was above a certain threshold, pain would be experienced. On the basis of these theories, therapeutic modalities were developed that were designed to cut or block the pain pathways or to raise the threshold for pain.

In the 1960s, there was a resurgence of interest among investigators in pain and its treatment. Based on available research and clinical observations, Melzack, Wall and their colleagues (i.e., Melzack & Casey, 1968; Melzack & Wall, 1965) detailed the inadequacy of simple specificity and intensity models of pain. They proposed a new conceptual model of pain, the gate control model, designed to incorporate available physiological data and clinical experience. According to this model, pain is not merely an automatic sensory phenomenon, but rather "a highly personal, variable experience influenced by cultural learning, the meaning of the situation, attention and other cognitive activities" (Melzack & Dennis, 1978, p. 1). The gate control model proposed that, in addition to the traditionally recognized dimension of nociception (the sensory-discriminative component), there also existed motivational-affective and cognitive-evaluative components. The gate control model postulated that there were important physiological pathways that are capable of augmenting or diminishing the subjective experience of pain. Importantly, some of the proposed pathways involved "top down" processing, which is to say that emotions and cognitive phenomena presumably traveling down the spinal cord from the brain could modulate sensory information traveling up the spinal cord toward the brain.

The gate control model has undergone several revisions since its original description. The current formulation stresses both electrical and neurochemical transmission. There are three types of afferent neurons converging on the dorsal horn of the spinal cord. Two of these, designated A-delta and c fibers, are small-diameter, unmyelinated fibers. According to the gate control model, these fibers directly excite transmission cells sending pain signals to the brain as well as excite cells within the substantia gelatinosa that potentiates the action of the transmission cells. A group of large-diameter fibers also impinges on the dorsal horn but these fibers inhibit the action of the transmission cells through their action on cells in the substantia gelatinosa. These large-diameter fibers are believed to convey information about temperature and light touch (Krishnan, France, Erikkson, & Ellinwood, 1988). In most cases, these modalities are postulated to inhibit perception of pain. The revised model also suggests that the large-diameter fibers can excite transmission cells leading to an actual augmentation of pain perception. Clinically, this is observed when light touch is perceived as painful, such as when one uses a towel to dry oneself off when one has a sunburn.

The gate control model also addresses the role of descending or efferent pathways. The cortex, which is largely responsible for higher cognitive functions such as thinking, planning, and evaluating, can interfere with the flow of information from the transmission cells to the brain. Thus, pain signals can be disrupted even before they reach the level of conscious awareness. Finally, the brain stem receives signals from the transmission cells but then acts as a feedback gain control, essentially modulating further input from the transmission cells.

One of the most innovative aspects of the modified gate control model was proposed as an answer to the paradox of why organisms would develop unmyelinated fibers, inherently incapable of quickly transmitting information, when they could develop myelinated fibers (Melzack & Wall, 1982). Melzack and Wall proposed that the slow and fast transmitting portions of the gate control mechanism serve different functions. The slowly conducting fibers essentially serve as a background setting against which sensory information is compared. Some of the messages conveyed by the unmyelinated neurons occur electrically; basic changes in neurons themselves occur as a result of slowly changing neurochemical conditions within the cells. Melzack and Wall note that the unmyelinated cells are rich in peptides, including enkephalins that are chemically similar to morphine and that have been recognized as important neurochemicals involved in pain perception.

A final note about the gate control model of pain is that the "gate" is not an all-or-none block to sensory stimuli. Indeed, it is an extremely complex mechanism capable of blocking or augmenting the perception of pain either globally or for only selective parts of the body (Melzack & Dennis, 1978). Further, it can account for the complex within which the sensory information is received. For example, the body senses light touch on a wound caused by grooming differently from the same light touch caused by an external prod (Melzack, 1973).

The gate control model has not been without its critics, especially regarding the physical basis of the proposed gating mechanism (Nathan, 1976; Whitehorn & Burgess, 1973). Nevertheless, it has been hailed as a resilient theory with reasonable explanatory and heuristic value (Turk, Meichenbaum, & Genest, 1983; Weisenberg, 1977).

Because it attributes the perception of pain to more than simply sensory stimulation, the gate control model explains why the surgical, electrical, or neurolytic ablation of pain pathways has not always been effective in eliminating pain. The gate control model provides a basis for treatments as diverse as nerve stimulation produced through transcutaneous electrical devices (Long & Hagfors, 1975; Wall & Sweet, 1967) or deep brain stimulation, anesthetic nerve blocks, heat, ice, vibration, massage, acupuncture (Gaupp, Flinn, & Weddige, 1989), and even psychological therapies (Melzack & Wall, 1982). Regardless of the initial cause of nociception, the gate control model postulates that multiple modalities may bring about relief, and to this end simultaneous modalities are encouraged.

In the final analysis, it must be stated that the greatest strength of the gate control model—namely, its breadth and flexibility—is also its greatest weakness. Although the model has generated a huge body of research and clinical applications and has been able to explain many diverse and seemingly contradictory data in a parsimonious and elegant fashion, it has not, at least as far as psychological techniques are concerned, provided any predictions as to which techniques will be superior. In fact, not a single therapeutic modality can be said to be derived directly from the gate control model.

COGNITIVE-BEHAVIORAL PERSPECTIVE

Multidimensional views of pain make an important distinction between nociception, that is, processing of stimuli that are defined as related to the stimulation of nociceptors and capable of being experienced as pain, and pain per se. Pain is viewed as a perceptual phenomenon comprised of the integration and modulation of a number of afferent and efferent processes. The complex interplay of the action of receptors, afferent and efferent neurons, and spinal as well as supraspinal processes contributes to the experience of pain, which need not be equated with peripheral stimulation.

The role of cognitive factors has been emphasized in perception and behavioral response to nociception (Turk et al., 1983). From the cognitive-behavioral perspective, people who experience chronic or recurrent nociception are viewed as having negative expectations about their own ability to control certain motor skills without pain (Schmidt, 1985). They adopt a negative set about pain and how pain will affect their lives, and appraise their situation as one in which there is little they can do to cope with the nociception experienced. Such negative, maladaptive appraisals about the situation and personal efficacy may reinforce the experience of demoralization and dysphoric mood, symptom preoccupation, inactivity, and overreaction to nociceptive stimulation. These cognitive appraisals and expectations are postulated as having an effect on behavior, leading to reduced effort and activity that may contribute to increased psychological distress (helplessness) and, subsequently, physical limitations.

From the cognitive-behavioral perspective, patients' interpretations of nociception and their resources can have both direct and indirect effects on physiological processes that may maintain and exacerbate pain. Cognitive interpretations may have a direct effect on physiology by increasing autonomic and sympathetic nervous system arousal and, potentially, muscle spasm, and an indirect effect by reducing physical activity and, consequently, reduced muscle flexibility, strength, and tone. Equally pernicious is the case where the patient's belief system leads him or her to expect that he or she "should" be able to do tasks at preinjury levels or that he or she "must" try to engage in a strenuous task either out of bravado, guilt, or desperation, or because of a belief that he or she is "cured." In these cases, the patient will engage in a cycle of overactivity and flare-up followed by pain and inactivity.

Moreover, cognitive interpretations will affect how patients present symptoms to significant others, including health care providers. Overt communications of pain, suffering, and distress will enlist responses that may reinforce the pain behaviors and the view of the seriousness, severity, and uncontrollability of pain. That is, complaints of pain may lead physicians to prescribe more potent medications, order additional diagnostic tests, and in some cases perform surgery. Family members may express sympathy, excuse the patient from usual responsibilities, and encourage passivity. It should be obvious that the cognitive-behavioral perspective integrates the operant conditioning emphasis on external reinforcement contingencies and the respondent view of learned fear and avoidance within the framework of an information processing perspective.

Research Supporting the Cognitive-Behavioral Formulation

A number of studies have been conducted to examine the contribution of the cognitive components of the pain experience (see Turk & Rudy, 1986, for an overview). For example, Flor and Turk (1989b) examined the relationship between general and situation-specific pain-related thoughts, convictions of personal control, pain severity, and disability levels in chronic low back pain patients and rheumatoid arthritics. The general and situation-specific cognitive variables were more highly related to reports of pain and disability than were disease-related variables for both samples. The combination of situation-specific and general cognitive variables explained 32% and 60% of the variance in pain and disability, respectively. The addition of disease-related variables improved the predictions only marginally. Flor, Turk, and Birbaumer (1985) demonstrated that psychological stress produced significant increases in site-specific muscular activity in chronic low back pain patients. These effects were independent of demographic or disease-status variables such as diagnosis, duration of pain, and number of surgeries.

Self-Efficacy

A central construct in the cognitive-behavioral model of chronic pain is self-efficacy (Bandura, 1977). A self-efficacy expectation is defined as a personal conviction that one can successfully perform certain required behaviors is a given situation. It has been suggested that given sufficient motivation to engage in a behavior, it is an individual's self-efficacy beliefs that determine whether a given behavior will be initiated, how much effort will be expended, and how long effort will be sustained in the face of obstacles and aversive experiences. From this perspective, the occurrence of coping behaviors is conceptualized as being mediated by the individual's beliefs that situational demands do not exceed coping resources. Individuals with weak efficacy expectancies are viewed as less likely than individuals with strong expectancies to emit coping responses and less likely to persist in the presence of obstacles and aversive consequences.

Mastery experiences gained through performance accomplishments are hypothesized to have the greatest impact on establishing and strengthening expectancies, because they provide the most information about actual capabilities. Successful versus unsuccessful physical therapy may be distinguished by the presence versus the absence of changes in perceived self-efficacy in conjunction with physical improvements in tolerance, strength, and endurance. Patients need to learn to make a distinction between hurt and harm. One group of pain patients may stop an activity when it hurts, often for fear of exacerbating the physical injury (they also stop because they wish to avoid the noxious sensations per se).

There is a second group of patients, less frequently considered, who continue to be unrealistically active because they have unrealistic self-efficacy beliefs. These patients may continue to overdo their activities and "crash and burn." They may continue to engage in this pattern, believing that when their pain levels decrease, they will be cured and can go back to their activities in an unmodified form. Unfortunately, this is a consequence of being exposed to and accepting an acute formulation of pain. Eventually, patients come to believe that all activity is dangerous and that they cannot do any activity without experiencing what they erroneously label "reinjury," and they thus enter the ranks of the underactive patients. These patients are exemplified by refusal to engage in physical therapy because "it makes them worse." Physical therapy and psychological counseling that emphasizes "working through" the pain and breaking the hurt–harm link will provide corrective feedback of capabilities and reinforce the patient's perceived self-efficacy and, subsequently, increased efforts.

Additionally, physical therapy and psychological approaches can help patients learn to pace activities better, understand that increased pain is not reinjury necessitating total incapacitation, and help them label and change thoughts that would make them susceptible to engaging in unrealistic behaviors (e.g., "If I don't go hunting, my friends will never respect me"). Thus, techniques that enhance mastery experiences (e.g., graded task accomplishments with both physical and verbal feedback) will, according to Bandura (1977), be powerful tools for bringing about behavior change. Moreover, the patient's self-attribution of task accomplishment should enhance maintenance of improvements (Kopel & Arkowitz, 1975). In this way, cognitive variables are the primary determinants of behavior, but these variables are altered most effectively by performance-based accomplishments.

Support for the Role of Self-Efficacy in Pain

We will review the literature on pain and self-efficacy in some detail, for we believe that it is an important construct that may unify operant, respondent, and cognitive-behavioral models. Support for the importance of self-efficacy as specifically related to pain has been demonstrated in laboratory studies (e.g., Bandura, O'Leary, Taylor, Gauthier, & Gossard, 1987; Dolce, Doleys, et al., 1986; Litt, 1988; Neufeld & Thomas, 1977), with headache patients (e.g., Gauthier, Cote, & Drolet, 1985; Holroyd et al., 1984), temporomandibular pain disorders (Fydrich et al., 1988), back pain (Council, Ahern, Follick, & Kline, 1988; Dolce, Crocker, Moletteire, & Doleys, 1986), arthritis (Lorig, Chastain, Ung, Shoor, & Holmon, 1989), and heterogeneous clinical populations (e.g., Dolce, Crocker, & Doleys, 1986; Kores, Murphy, Rosenthal, Elias, & Rosenthal, 1985).

Neufeld and Thomas (1977) examined the effects of providing false efficacy feedback for subjects using relaxation to cope with laboratory-induced nociception. Subjects were provided with prearranged feedback indicating that they were either successful or unsuccessful at achieving relaxation. Subjects who had received relaxation training plus positive efficacy feedback tolerated the nociception significantly longer and had higher pain thresholds than subjects given low efficacy feedback, despite the fact that there were no actual differences between the groups in their subjective ratings of the level of relaxation achieved. Dolce et al. (1986) reported that self-efficacy expectancies were significantly correlated with pain tolerance times and were better predictors of tolerance than ratings of pain intensity. Moreover, self-efficacy expectancies and pain tolerance times following treatment were both found to predict follow-up performance one week later. Also using a laboratory approach, Litt (1988, study 1) demonstrated that changes in self-efficacy predicted changes in actual tolerance for nociceptive stimulation. Staub, Tursky, and Schwartz (1971) demonstrated that subjects become less upset when they perceived themselves as able to control a stressful or painful event.

These data suggest that self-efficacy expectations may have a causal role in behavioral responses to nociceptive stimulation.

Holroyd et al. (1984) and Gauthier et al. (1985) have both reported that self-efficacy expectancies are predictive of headache patients' responses to biofeedback. In the Holroyd et al. (1984) study, 43 cases of recurrent tension headache patients were randomly assigned to four EMG biofeedback conditions. Half of those patients received feedback for reducing frontalis EMG levels and half received feedback for increasing EMG levels. All subjects, however, were told they were learning to decrease muscle tension. In addition, half of the subjects in each of these groups received bogus feedback indicating high levels of success and half received feedback reflecting only mild success. Despite the direction of the EMG feedback that patients received, patients who received high success feedback displayed significantly greater reductions in headache activity and significantly higher self-efficacy ratings than did those who received mild success feedback. Furthermore, higher self-efficacy ratings were observed to significantly correlate with larger reductions in headache activity scores while actual EMG levels failed to be associated with headache activity.

Gauthier et al. (1985) examined the effects of vascular biofeedback in 30 female migraine patients. Patients were assigned to a biofeedback condition with performance goals, a biofeedback condition with no performance goals, or a waiting-list control condition. Both biofeedback conditions were found to be effective in alleviating migraine headaches. Self-efficacy expectancies were again found to be significant predictions of outcome at the end of treatment.

Dolce, Crocker, Moletteire, and Doleys (1986) focused on the role of setting exercise quotas on performance of exercise, concern about engaging in exercise, and self-efficacy expectancies pertaining to each exercise in two studies. The first study utilized a multiple baseline design across behaviors. Exercise quotas were shown to increase levels of previously avoided exercise. In addition, when quotas were implemented, self-efficacy ratings were observed to increase while concern ratings decreased. Self-efficacy expectancies were found to closely parallel increases in actual exercise levels during treatment ($r = .69$, $p < .001$). These results were then replicated with 14 consecutively treated chronic pain patients in a second study, which used a repeated measures design.

Dolce, Crocker, Moletteire, and Doleys (1986) concluded that exercise quota systems were effective for reversing patterns of inactivity, as well as for increasing efficacy beliefs and for reducing concern over engaging in strenuous activities. The high degree of association between self-efficacy ratings and actual exercise levels was also seen as providing support for the postulation in self-efficacy theory that success experiences are effective means of increasing self-efficacy expectancies.

In another study, Dolce, Crocker, and Doleys (1986) observed that chronic pain patients' posttreatment self-efficacy ratings were significantly correlated with exercise levels, medication use, and work status at follow-up periods ranging from 6 to 12 months. Dolce and his colleagues have suggested that, if self-efficacy expectancies are related to maintenance, then those patients who do not increase their perceptions of self-efficacy following treatment, despite any other posttreatment improvements, are likely to be good candidates for relapse. Empirical support for this relationship has been found for other areas of self-management, such as smoking (Condiotte & Lichtenstein, 1981) and alcoholism (Rist & Watzl, 1983). Stevens, Peterson, and Maruta

(1988) also emphasized the importance of individuals' perceptions of their illness and suggested that individual differences in perceptions associated with posttreatment improvements may be useful predictors of patients prone to relapse.

The interrelated role of fear avoidance and self-efficacy was illustrated in a study reported by Council et al. (1988). They found that actual physical performance of back pain patients was best predicted by self-efficacy ratings, which appeared to be determined by pain response expectancies. The authors interpreted these results as suggesting that daily pain experience determines pain response expectancies for specific movements. Pain response expectancies appear to influence performance and associated pain behavior through their effects on efficacy expectancies. These findings also indicate that pain response expectancies associated with specific movements are based on generalized expectancies drawn from daily experiences and suggest that chronic pain patients have well-established ideas of how much pain they will experience in different situations. These beliefs about the results of activity may cause patients to avoid certain activities for fear of the consequences, including the belief that they may become more functionally impaired (Philips, 1987a).

The persistence of such avoidance will reduce the opportunities for experiencing disconfirmations that are followed by corrected predictions. The prediction of pain promotes pain-avoidance behavior, and overpredictions of pain promote excessive avoidance. Insofar as the pain-avoidance behavior succeeds in preserving the overpredictions from repeated diconfirmation, they will continue unchanged (Rachman & Lopatka, 1988). By contrast, repeatedly engaging in behavior that produces significantly less pain than was predicted will be followed by adjustments in subsequent prediction, which also will become more accurate. These increasingly accurate predictions of pain will be followed by increasingly appropriate avoidance behavior, up to and including the elimination of all avoidance, if that is medically appropriate.

Philips (1987b) found a significant correlation ($r = .81$) between patients' self-efficacy and self-rating of the magnitude of pain problem at the 12-month follow-up. In this study, treatment produced a 25% increase in self-efficacy and, as self-efficacy increased, avoidance behavior was diminished. The dramatic change in the relationship between self-efficacy and the magnitude or size of the perceived problem suggests the possibility that an important effect of treatment is the development of a sense of control over pain. The increasing exercise and reduced avoidance achieved by these patients may be the crucial therapeutic effect.

Finally, in a study conducted by Kores et al. (1985), pain patients in an inpatient pain management program recorded self-efficacy ratings for a number of activities as well as for general improvement. Subjects were divided into high and low self-efficacy groups on the basis of these ratings. By the end of treatment, high self-efficacy subjects spent significantly more time sitting and standing than low self-efficacy subjects and rated themselves as generally more improved. Although it was not statistically significant, high self-efficacy patients scored substantially better than did low self-efficacy patients at walking distance, reduction of pain, and down time. In some studies (see Bandura, 1989), self-efficacy beliefs actually lagged behind subjects' behavior. That is, subjects did better than they believed. If in treatment patients do well but are not aware of their improvements, they may be more prone to relapse. Thus, it is important to encourage patients to monitor their behavior and accomplishments so as to focus attention on achievements and thereby reinforce their perceptions of greater capacity and self-efficacy.

Cognitive-Behavioral Treatment

The application of cognitive-behavioral treatment approaches to pain evolved from research on a number of psychological problems (i.e., anxiety disorders and depression). In general, the cognitive-behavioral approach is concerned with using environmental manipulations, as are adherents of the operant approach, and gives attention to the potential stress-induced muscular reactivity as well as fear-induced avoidance of activity of the respondent models. Many behavioral (reinforcement, exposure) as well as cognitive techniques (e.g., cognitive restructuring, problem-solving training, coping skills training) are used. However, in the cognitive-behavioral approach, strategies based on these models (e.g., biofeedback, extinction of pain behaviors, reinforcement of activity) represent feedback trials that provide an opportunity for the patient to question, reappraise, and acquire self-control over maladaptive thoughts, feelings, behaviors (including avoidant behaviors), and physiological responses.

Turk and Rudy (1987) suggested that this general perspective is more important than the specific techniques used to bring about the desired change. Turk and Rudy further suggested that the cognitive behavioral perspective is based on five central assumptions:

1. Individuals are active processors of information and not passive reactors;
2. Thoughts (appraisals, expectancies) can elicit or modulate mood, affect physiological processes, influence the environment, and serve as impetuses for behavior; conversely, mood, physiology, environmental factors, and behavior can influence thought processes;
3. Behavior is reciprocally determined by the individual and environmental factors;
4. Individuals can learn more adaptive ways of thinking, feeling, and behaving;
5. Individuals are capable of and should be involved as active agents in charge of maladaptive thoughts, feelings, and behaviors.

Cognitive-behavioral therapy is designed to help patients identify, reality-test, and correct maladaptive conceptualizations and dysfunctional beliefs about themselves and their plight. Patients are encouraged to become aware of and to monitor the impact that negative pain-engendering thoughts and feelings play in the maintenance of maladaptive behaviors. Additionally, patients are taught to recognize the connections linking cognition, affect, and behavior along with their joint consequences. Finally, patients are encouraged to test the effects of these cognitions and beliefs with selected homework assignments. The cognitive-behavioral therapist is concerned not only with the role that patients' thoughts play in contributing to disability and to the maintenance and exacerbations of nociception (directly and indirectly), but is also concerned about the nature and adequacy of the patient's behavioral repertoire. Detailed description of cognitive-behavioral treatment is beyond the scope of this chapter. The interested reader is encouraged to see one of the many publications that describe this approach in depth (Turk et al., 1983; Turk & Rudy, 1989).

The efficacy of a variety of cognitive-behavioral techniques has been evaluated in a number of laboratory analogue and clinical pain studies. Laboratory studies have demonstrated the effectiveness of these techniques in the enhancement of tolerance for a variety of nociceptive stimuli (Fernandez & Turk, 1989). The clinical effectiveness of cognitive-behavioral interventions has been demonstrated with a wide range of acute, acute recurrent, and chronic non-cancer-related pain syndromes, including headaches (e.g., Bakal, Demjen, & Kaganov, 1981; Holroyd, Andrasik, & Westbrook, 1977), arthritis (Bradley et al., 1987; O'Leary, Shoor, Lorig, & Holman, 1988; Parker et al., 1988), low back pain (Turner & Clancy, 1988), and heterogeneous samples of chronic non-cancer pain patients (Corey, Etlin, & Miller, 1987; Hazard et al., 1989; Moore & Chaney, 1985).

COMMONALITIES ACROSS BEHAVIORAL INTERVENTIONS

There have been numerous review papers reporting on the efficacy of treatment interventions based on the operant, respondent, and cognitive-behavioral models (Jessup, 1989; Keefe, Gil, & Rose, 1986; Linton, 1986; Turner & Romano, 1984). These reviews all tend to conclude that the various treatments have proven to be successful but that there are a number of factors (e.g., methodological, statistical) that temper the generally positive outcomes. An interesting question that can be raised is how such diverse approaches can all have positive effects.

Turk and Holzman (1986) were struck with the similarity of conclusions among the diversity of treatment interventions and suggested that there might be some commonalities across the approaches. They examined the components of the treatments and identified the following set of features that seem to be common, more or less, for each:

1. Reconceptualize the cause of patients' pain so that it is consistent with the rationale underlying the treatment.
2. Foster a sense of optimism.
3. Individualize the treatment to match the needs of each patient.
4. Emphasize active patient participation and responsibility.
5. Provide skills acquisition.
6. Orchestrate perceptions of self-efficacy throughout treatment.
7. Emphasize that the patient should attribute goal accomplishments to himself or herself.

CONCLUSIONS

What we have attempted to do in this chapter is to present a description of the most prominent behavioral models of pain and the interventions that have evolved from these models. We provided a brief overview of the research that supports these models as well as the efficacy of the treatments aligned with the models. What should be apparent is that, although we have discussed the operant, respondent, and cognitive-behavioral models separately, they have much in common and they complement each other, creating a "metamodel" of chronic pain that is based on a wide range of behavioral principles. We noted commonalities that appear to underlie the different treatment strategies and emphasized the potential for self-efficacy to serve as a unifying construct (see also Jessup, 1989).

Matching of Patients to Treatments

Perhaps the more important and appropriate question for treatment studies is not whether the treatment is successful but how successful the treatment is for which patients with what characteristics (Turk & Rudy, 1989). The most appropriate strategy might be to maximize the commonalities (nonspecifics) for all patients but simultaneously individualize treatments to specific physiological, psychosocial, and behavioral characteristics. The exclusive reliance on group effects may mask important subject-by-treatment interactions. For example, Flor et al. (1985) reported that a subset of back pain patients demonstrated site-specific muscular response to psychological stress. Medical status variables did not predict which patients demonstrated the abnormal muscular response; however, depression did predict responders. Thus, not all back pain patients would be expected to respond to paraspinal EMG biofeedback designed to modify stress reactivity. If these results were replicated, it might be suggested that depressed back pain patients who demonstrated the specific response would be the most appropriate candidates for a biofeedback treatment component. It would seem to make little sense to offer site-specific biofeedback to the subset of patients who reveal no baseline elevations in paraspinal EMG or stress-induced reactivity, except perhaps to increase self-efficacy expectations.

When biofeedback proves effective, it is possible that there is more than one mechanism at work. For some patients—those with demonstrated maladaptive neuromuscular reactivity—the biofeedback might have a direct effect on modification of physiological functioning along with increased perceptions of self-efficacy. For the subset of patients who do not demonstrate site-specific maladaptive responding, biofeedback might be effective not by changing the physiological activity, but by altering perceptions of self-efficacy and subsequently altering perceptions of helplessness and more adaptive behaviors that had previously been avoided (Lazarus, 1975; Meichenbaum, 1976).

Another example of the importance of matching specific components of treatment to patient characteristics is revealed by examining the treatment outcome study reported by Moore and Chaney (1985). The authors examined the additive contribution of spouse inclusion in a group cognitive-behavioral intervention. Both treatment groups benefited significantly from the treatment; however, there were no between-group differences. The authors concluded from these results that spouses did not contribute to treatment. However, no effort was made to determine the quality of the marriage. Recently, Flor, Turk, and Rudy (1989) demonstrated that quality of the marital relationship mediated the effects of spouse reinforcement of pain behaviors. Turk and Rudy (1987) found that one subgroup of chronic pain patients was characterized by the perception of lack of support from significant others in the patient's environment. It is possible that this subgroup of patients might benefit to the greatest extent from spouse involvement. In the Moore and Chaney study, differences between patients regarding perceptions of significant others were not considered. All patients were collapsed within groups. The outcome might have been quite different had treatment been matched to specific subgroups of pain patients.

Collapsing both responders and nonresponders together in between-group designs might account for the confusion in the literature. Identifying the characteristics of responders and nonresponders to the diverse behaviorally based treatments may contribute to alternative ways to classify pain patients rather than relying exclusively on traditional medical diagnosis (Turk, 1990; Turk & Rudy, 1987).

Caveats

A number of factors limit the generalizations that can be drawn from the treatment outcome studies of psychological modalities used with chronic pain patients. Turk and Rudy (1989, 1990) and Turk, Rudy, and Sorkin (1991) have drawn attention to the uniqueness of the sample of patients referred to pain clinics. They also note that a substantial number of patients who are evaluated at such clinics never enter treatment either because of exclusion criteria used or because patients chose not to enter treatment (e.g., no third-party coverage, inconvenient, unmotivated). Moreover, a subset of patients drops out of treatment or is dropped from treatment.

The levels of adherence with treatment recommendations are particularly low and it is no wonder that relapse rates are quite high. It is unrealistic to expect brief treatments ranging from several hours to a few weeks to produce lasting changes (e.g., Cairns & Pasino, 1977) without teaching patients how to generalize what they have learned to their natural environment, increasing self-attributions of success, enhancing self-efficacy, and making significant changes in the patient's environment. Perhaps one of the most problematic aspects of bringing about enduring change is the difficult task of integrating significant people in the patient's life into the treatment process. Much greater effort is needed to involve significant others in treatment and to alter environmental factors that can undermine therapeutic gains.

Turk and Rudy (1990) noted that the number of patients available at follow-up can be as low as 20%. When each of these factors is considered, it becomes evident that the treatment outcome results reported are based on very small and possibly unrepresentative samples of people who have chronic pain. Much more research is needed to understand the differences between those chronic pain patients who are treated and available for follow-up in pain treatment outcome studies and the large majority of people with chronic pain who are not represented in these studies.

Despite these limitations, psychological interventions based on the operant, respondent, and cognitive-behavioral conceptualizations have proven to be effective with samples of patients with recalcitrant chronic pain. Matching patients to treatments, focusing on alterations of self-efficacy, and involvement of significant others should augment these outcomes and foster maintenance of posttreatment gains.

REFERENCES

Anderson, T. P., Cole, T. M., Gulickson, G., Hudgens, A., & Roberts, A. H. (1977). Behavior modification of chronic pain: A treatment program by a multidisciplinary team. *Clinical Orthopaedics and Related Research, 129,* 96-100.

Andrasik, F., & Holroyd, K. A. (1980). A test of specific and nonspecific effects in the biofeedback treatment of tension headache patients. *Journal of Consulting and Clinical Psychology, 48,* 575-586.

Bakal, D. A., Demjen, S., & Kaganov, J. A. (1981). Cognitive-behavioral treatment of chronic headache. *Headache, 21,* 81-86.

Bandura, A. (1977). Self-efficacy: Toward a unifying theory of behavioral change. *Psychological Bulletin, 84,* 191-215.

Bandura, A. (1989). Human agency in social cognitive theory. *American Psychologist, 44,* 1175-1184.

Bandura, A., O'Leary, A., Taylor, C. B., Gauthier, J., & Gossard, D. (1987). Perceived self-efficacy and pain control—opioid and nonopioid mechanisms. *Journal of Personality and Social Psychology, 53,* 563-571.

Basmajian, J. V. (1963). Control and training of individual motor units. *Science, 141,* 440-441.

Biedermann, H. J., McGhie, A., Monga, T. N., & Shanks, G. L. (1987). Perceived and actual control in EMG treatment of back pain. *Behaviour Research and Therapy, 25,* 137-147.

Blanchard, E. B., Andrasik, F., Ahles, T. A., Teders, S. J., & O'Keefe, D. (1980). Migraine and tension headache: A meta-analytic review. *Behavior Therapy, 11,* 613-631.

Blanchard, E. B., Andrasik, F., Arena, J. G., Saunders, N. L., Jurish, S. E., Teders, S. J., & Rodichok, L. D. (1983). Psychophysiological response to behavioral treatment of chronic headache. *Behavior Therapy, 14,* 357-374.

Blanchard, E. B., Andrasik, F., Neff, D. F., Teders, S. J., Pallmeyer, T. P., Arena, J. G.,

Jurish, S. E., Saunders, N. L., Ahles, T. A., & Rodichok, L. D. (1982). Sequential comparison of relaxation training and biofeedback in the treatment of three kinds of chronic headache or, the machines may be necessary some of the time. *Behaviour Research and Therapy, 20,* 569–581.

Block, A. R., Kremer, E. F., & Gaylor, M. (1980). Behavioral treatment of chronic pain: The spouse as a discriminative cue for pain behaviors. *Pain, 9,* 243–252.

Bradley, L. A., Young, L. D., Anderson, K. O., Turner, R. A., Agudelo, C. A., McDaniel, L. K., Pisko, E. J., Semble, E. L., & Morgan, T. (1987). Effects of psychological therapy on pain behavior of rheumatoid arthritis patients. Treatment outcome and six-month follow-up. *Arthritis and Rheumatism, 30,* 1105–1114.

Budzynski, T. (1973). Biofeedback procedures in the clinic. *Seminars in Psychiatry, 5,* 537–547.

Bush, C., Ditto, B., & Feuerstein, M. (1985). A controlled valuation of paraspinal EMG biofeedback in the treatment of chronic low back pain. *Health Psychology, 4,* 307–321.

Cairns, D., & Pasino, J. A. (1977). Comparison of verbal reinforcement and feedback in operant treatment of disability due to low back pain. *Behavior Therapy, 8,* 621–630.

Chambless, D. L., & Goldstein, A. (1980). The treatment of agoraphobia. In A. Goldstein and E. B. Foa (Eds.), *Handbook of behavioral interventions* (pp. 322–415). New York: Wiley.

Condiotte, M. M., & Lichtenstein, E. (1981). Self-efficacy and relapse in smoking cessation programs. *Journal of Consulting and Clinical Psychology, 49,* 648–658.

Corey, D. T., Etlin, D., & Miller, P. C. (1987). A home-based pain management and rehabilitation program: An evaluation. *Pain, 29,* 219–230.

Council, J. R., Ahern, D. K., Follick, M. J., & Kline, C. L. (1988). Expectancies and functional impairment in chronic low back pain. *Pain, 33,* 323–340.

Dolce, J. J., Crocker, M. F., & Doleys, D. M. (1986). Prediction of outcome among chronic pain patients. *Behaviour Research and Therapy, 24,* 313–319.

Dolce, J. J., Crocker, M. F., Moletteire, C., & Doleys, D. M. (1986). Exercise quotas, anticipatory concern and self-efficacy expectations in chronic pain: A preliminary report. *Pain, 24,* 365–372.

Dolce, J. J., Doleys, D. M., Raczynski, J. M., Lossie, J., Poole, L., & Smith, M. (1986). The role of self-efficacy expectancies in the prediction of pain tolerance. *Pain, 27,* 261–272.

Dolce, J. J., & Raczynski, J. M. (1985). Neuromuscular activity and electromyography in painful backs: Psychological and biomechanical models in assessment and treatment. *Psychological Bulletin, 97,* 502–520.

Doleys, D. M., Crocker, M., & Patton, D. (1982). Response of patients with chronic pain to exercise quotas. *Physical Therapy, 62,* 1111–1114.

Eysenck, H. J., & Rachman, S. (1965). *The causes and cures of neurosis.* London: Rutledge and Kegan Paul.

Fernandez, E., & Turk, D. C. (1989). The utility of cognitive coping strategies for altering perception of pain: A meta-analysis. *Pain, 38,* 123–125.

Flor, H., Kerns, R. D., & Turk, D. C. (1987). The role of the spouse in the maintenance of chronic pain. *Journal of Psychosomatic Research, 31,* 251–260.

Flor, H., & Turk, D. C. (1989a). The psychophysiology of chronic pain: Do chronic pain patients exhibit symptom-specific psychophysiological responses? *Psychological Bulletin, 105,* 215–259.

Flor, H., & Turk, D. C. (1989b). Rheumatoid arthritis and back pain: Predicting pain and disability from cognitive variables. *Journal of Behavioral Medicine, 11,* 251–265.

Flor, H., Turk, D. C., & Birbaumer, N. (1985). Assessment of stress-related psychophysiological reactions in chronic back pain patients. *Journal of Consulting and Clinical Psychology, 53,* 354–364.

Flor, H., Turk, D. C., & Rudy, T. E. (1989). Relationship of pain impact and significant other reinforcement of pain behaviors: The mediating role of gender, marital status, and marital satisfaction. *Pain, 38,* 45–50.

Fordyce, W. E. (1976). *Behavioral methods for chronic pain and illness.* St. Louis: Mosby.

Fordyce, W. E. (1988). Pain and suffering: A reappraisal. *American Psychologist, 43,* 276–282.

Fordyce, W. E., Fowler, R. S., & DeLateur, B. J. (1968). An application of behavior modification techniques to a problem of chronic pain. *Behaviour Research and Therapy, 6,* 105–109.

Fordyce, W. E., Fowler, R. S., Lehmann, J. F., DeLateur, B. J., Sand, P. L., & Trieschmann, R. B. (1973). Operant conditioning in the treatment of chronic pain. *Archives of Physical Medicine and Rehabilitation, 54,* 399–408.

Fordyce, W. E., Shelton, J., & Dundore, D. (1982). The modification of avoidance learning pain behaviors. *Journal of Behavioral Medicine, 4,* 405–414.

Fowler, R. S., Fordyce, W. E., & Berni, R. (1969). Operant conditioning in chronic illness. *American Journal of Nursing, 69,* 1226–1228.

Freedman, R. R., Ianni, P., & Wenig, P. (1983). Behavioral treatment of Raynaud's disease. *Journal of Consulting and Clinical Psychology, 51,* 539–549.

Fydrich, T., Rudy, T. E., & Turk, D. C. (1988, November). *Efficacy of biofeedback in patients with chronic TMJ pain.* Paper presented at the Joint Meeting of the Canadian and American Pain Societies, Toronto, Canada.

Gaupp, L. A., Flinn, D. W., & Weddige, R. L. (1989). Adjunctive treatment techniques. In C. D. Tollison (Ed.), *Handbook of chronic pain management* (pp. 174–196). Baltimore: Williams & Wilkins.

Gauthier, J., Cote, L., & Drolet, M. (1985). Migraine and blood volume pulse biofeedback: How does clinical improvement relate to perceived self-efficacy? *Canadian Psychology, 26,* abstract #167.

Gentry, W. D., & Bernal, G. (1977). Chronic pain. In R. Williams and W. D. Gentry (Eds.), *Behavioral approaches to medical treatment* (pp. 173–182). Cambridge, MA: Ballinger.

Goldfried, M. R. (1977). The use of relaxation and cognitive relabeling as coping skills. In R. B. Stuart (Ed.), *Behavioral self-management: Strategies, techniques, and outcomes* (pp. 103–126). New York: Brunner/Mazel.

Goldstein, A. J., & Chambless, D. L. (1978). A reanalysis of agoraphobia. *Behavior Therapy, 9,* 47–59.

Hazard, R. G., Fenwick, J. W., Kalisch, S. M., Redmond, J., Reeves, V., Reid, S., & Frymoyer, J. M. (1989). Functional restoration with behavioral support—A one-year prospective study of patients with chronic low-back pain. *Spine, 14,* 157–161.

Holroyd, K. A., Andrasik, F., & Westbrook, T. (1977). Cognitive control of tension headache. *Cognitive Therapy and Research, 1,* 121–134.

Holroyd, K. A., & Penzien, D. B. (1986). Client variables and the behavioral treatment of recurrent tension headache: A meta-analytic review. *Journal of Behavioral Medicine, 9,* 515–536.

Holroyd, K. A., Penzien, D. B., Hursey, K. G., Tobin, D. L., Rogers, L., Holm, J. E., Marcille, P. J., Hall, J. R., & Chila, A. G. (1984). Change mechanisms in EMG biofeedback training. Cognitive changes underlying improvements in tension headaches. *Journal of Consulting and Clinical Psychology, 52,* 1039–1053.

Jessup, B. A. (1989). Relaxation and biofeedback. In P. D. Wall & R. Melzack (Eds.), *Textbook of pain* (2nd ed.; pp. 989–1000). New York: Churchill Livingstone.

Keefe, F. J., Gil, K. M., & Rose, S. C. (1986). Behavioral approaches in the multidisciplinary management of chronic pain: Programs and issues. *Clinical Psychology Review, 6,* 87–113.

Kewman, D. G., & Roberts, A. H. (1980). Skin temperature biofeedback and migraine headaches: A double-blind study. *Biofeedback and Self-Regulation, 5,* 327–345.

Kopel, S., & Arkowitz, H. (1975). The role of attribution and self-perception in behavior change. *Genetic Psychology Monographs, 92,* 175–212.

Kores, R., Murphy, W. D., Rosenthal, T., Elias, D., & Rosenthal, R. (1985). *A self-efficacy scale to predict outcome in chronic pain treatment: Preliminary results.* Paper presented at the Sixth Annual Meeting of the Society of Behavioral Medicine, New Orleans.

Kotarba, J. A. (1963). *Chronic pain: Its social dimensions*. Beverly Hills, CA: Sage.

Krishnan, K. R. R., France, R. D., Erikkson, L., & Ellinwood, E. H. (1988). Neuroanatomy and neurophysiology of chronic pain. In R. D. France and K. R. R. Krishnan (Eds.), *Chronic pain* (pp. 30–41). Washington, DC: American Psychiatric Press.

Lazarus, R. S. (1975). A cognitively oriented psychologist looks at biofeedback. *American Psychologist, 30,* 553–561.

Lentham, J., Slade, P. D., Troup, J. D. G., & Bentley, G. (1983). Outline of a fear-avoidance model of exaggerated pain perception. *Behaviour Research and Therapy, 21,* 401–408.

Linton, S. J. (1986). Behavioral remediation of chronic pain: A status report. *Pain, 24,* 125–141.

Linton, S. J., & Gotestam, K. G. (1984). A controlled study of the effects of applied relaxation and applied relaxation plus operant procedures in the regulation of chronic pain. *British Journal of Clinical Psychology, 23,* 291–299.

Litt, M. D. (1988). Self-efficacy and perceived control: Cognitive mediators of pain tolerance. *Journal of Personality and Social Psychology, 54,* 149–160.

Long, D., & Hagfors, N. (1975). Electric stimulation in the nervous system: The current status of electrical stimulation of the nervous system for relief of pain. *Pain, 1,* 109–123.

Lorig, K., Chastain, R. L., Ung, E., Shoor, S., & Holman, H. R. (1989). Development and evolution of a scale to measure perceived self-efficacy in people with arthritis. *Arthritis and Rheumatism, 32,* 37–44.

Meichenbaum, D. (1976). Cognitive factors in biofeedback therapy *Biofeedback and Self-Regulation, 1,* 201–216.

Melzack, R. (1973). *The puzzle of pain.* Harmonsworth, England: Penguin

Melzack, R., & Casey, K. L. (1968). Sensory, motivational and central control determinants of pain: A new conceptual model. In D. Kenshalo (Ed.), *The skin senses* (pp. 423–443). Springfield, IL: Thomas.

Melzack, R., & Dennis, S. G. (1978). Neurophysiological foundations of pain. In R. A. Sternbach (Ed.), *The psychology of pain* (pp. 1–26). New York: Raven Press.

Melzack, R., & Wall, P. D. (1965). Pain mechanisms: A new theory. *Science, 150,* 971–980.

Melzack, R., & Wall, P. D. (1982). *The challenge of pain.* New York: Basic Books.

Miller, N. E. (1969). Learning of visceral and glandular responses. *Science, 16,* 434–445.

Moore, J. E., & Chaney, E. F. (1985). Outpatient group treatment of chronic pain: Effects of spouse involvement. *Journal of Consulting and Clinical Psychology, 53,* 326–334.

Mowrer, O. H. (1960). *Learning theory and behavior.* New York: Wiley.

Nathan, P. W. (1976). The gate control theory of pain: A critical review. *Brain, 99,* 123–158.

Neufeld, R. W. J., & Thomas, P. (1977). Effects of perceived efficacy of a prophylactic controlling mechanism of self-control under painful stimulation. *Canadian Journal of Behavioral Science, 9,* 224–232.

O'Leary, A., Shoor, S., Lorig, K., & Holman, H. R. (1988). A cognitive-behavioral treatment for rheumatoid arthritis. *Health Psychology, 7,* 527–544.

Parker, J. C., Frank, R. G., Beck, N. C., Smarr, K. L., Buescher, K., Phillips, L. R., Smith, E. I., Anderson, S. K., & Walker, S. E. (1988). Pain management in rheumatoid arthritis patients—A cognitive-behavioral approach. *Arthritis and Rheumatism, 31,* 593–601.

Peck, C. (1986). Psychological factors in acute pain management. In M. J. Cousins & G. D. Phillips (Eds.), *Acute pain management* (pp. 251–274). Edinburgh: Churchill Livingstone.

Philips, H. C. (1987a). Avoidance behavior and its role in sustaining chronic pain. *Behaviour Research and Therapy, 25,* 373–379.

Philips, H. C. (1987b). The effects of behavioral treatment on chronic pain. *Behaviour Research and Therapy, 25,* 365–377.

Rachman, S., & Lopatka, C. (1988). Accurate and inaccurate predictions of pain. *Behaviour Research and Therapy, 26,* 291–296.

Rist, F., & Watzl, H. (1983). Self-assessment of relapse risk and assertiveness in relation to treatment outcome of female alcoholics. *Addictive Behaviors, 8,* 121–127.

Schmidt, A. J. M. (1985). Cognitive factors in the performance level of chronic low back pain patients. *Journal of Psychosomatic Research, 29,* 183-189.

Scott, D. S., & Gregg, J. M. (1980). Myofascial pain of the temporomandibular joint: A review of the behavioral-relaxation therapies. *Pain, 9,* 231-241.

Staub, E., Tursky, B., & Schwartz, G. E. (1971). Self-control and predictability: Their effects on reactions to aversive stimulation. *Journal of Personality and Social Psychology, 18,* 157-162.

Stevens, V. W., Peterson, R. A., & Maruta, T. (1988). Change in perceptions of illness and psychosocial adjustment. Findings of a pain management program. *Clinical Journal of Pain, 4,* 249-256.

Thorpe, G. L., & Burns, L. E. (1983). *The agoraphobic syndrome.* New York: Wiley.

Turk, D. C. (1990). Strategies for classifying chronic orofacial pain patients. *Anesthesia Progress, 37,* 155-160.

Turk, D. C., & Fernandez, E. (1990). On the putative uniqueness of cancer pain: Do psychological principles apply? *Behaviour Research and Therapy, 28,* 1-13.

Turk, D. C., & Flor, H. (1987). Pain > pain behaviors: Utility and limitations of the pain behavior construct. *Pain, 31,* 277-295.

Turk, D. C., & Holzman, A. D. (1986). Commonalities among psychological approaches in the treatment of chronic pain: specifying the meta-constructs. In A. D. Holzman and D. C. Turk (Eds.), *Pain management: A handbook of psychological treatment approaches* (pp. 257-268). Elmsford, NY: Pergamon.

Turk, D. C., Meichenbaum, D., & Genest, M. (1983). *Pain and behavioral medicine: A cognitive-behavioral perspective.* New York: Guilford.

Turk, D. C., & Rudy, T. E. (1986). Assessment of cognitive factors in chronic pain: A worthwhile enterprise? *Journal of Consulting and Clinical Psychology, 54,* 760-768.

Turk, D. C., & Rudy, T. E. (1987). Toward the comprehensive assessment of chronic pain patients. *Behaviour Research and Therapy, 25,* 237-249.

Turk, D. C., & Rudy, T. E. (1989). An integrated approach to pain treatment: Beyond the scalpel and syringe. In C. D. Tollison (Ed.), *Handbook of chronic pain management* (pp. 222-237). Baltimore, MD: Williams & Wilkins.

Turk, D. C., & Rudy, T. E. (1990). Neglected factors in chronic pain treatment outcome studies—referral patterns, failure to enter, and attrition, *Pain, 43,* 7-25.

Turk, D. C., Rudy, T. E., & Sorkin, B. A. (1991). *Neglected topics in chronic pain treatment outcome studies—determination of success.* Manuscript submitted for publication.

Turner, J. A., & Clancy, S. (1988). Comparison of operant behavioral and cognitive-behavioral group treatment for chronic low back pain, *Journal of Consulting and Clinical Psychology, 56,* 261-266.

Turner, J. A., & Romano, J. (1984). Evaluating psychologic interventions for chronic pain: Issues and recent developments. In C. Benedetti, C. R. Chapman, & G. Maricca (Eds.), *Recent advances in the management of pain, Vol. 6* (pp. 168-193). New York: Raven Press.

Wall, P. D., & Sweet, W. H. (1967). Temporary abolition of pain in man. *Science, 155,* 108-109.

Weisenberg, M. (1977). Pain and pain control. *Psychological Bulletin, 84,* 1008-1044.

Whitehorn, C., & Burgess, P. R. (1973). Changes in polarization of central branches of myelinated mechanoreceptor and nociceptor fibers during noxious and innocuous stimulation of the skin. *Journal of Neurophysiology, 36,* 226-237.

CHAPTER 20

Behavioral Strategies in the Prevention of Disease

OLIVER OYAMA and FRANK ANDRASIK

As one looks back at the previous edition of this text, and in particular the chapter entitled "Behavioral Perspectives in Preventive Medicine" (Masek, Epstein, & Russo, 1981), one is struck by the changes that have occurred since that publication as well as by what has stayed the same. The business of health care has remained stable, with the health care industry still the third largest industry in the United States. Health care expenditures, however, have realized a marked increase in the total percent of the gross national product represented by such expenditures, from 9.4% in 1981 to 10.9% in 1986 (U.S. Bureau of the Census, 1988). If present trends continue, these statistics will likely increase in future years.

The leading causes of death among Americans also remain relatively stable, with cardiovascular disease, cancer, and accidents remaining the major causes of premature deaths in the United States (Johns, Hovell, Ganiats, Peddecord, & Agras, 1987). One disturbing statistic that has not remained stable is the growing number of individuals affected by these life-threatening conditions. An example is the 17.5% increase in the number of cases of chronic heart disease in the United States over the 5-year period from 1980 to 1985 (U.S. Bureau of the Census, 1988). Furthermore, other life-threatening conditions such as diabetes mellitus, pulmonary disease, chronic liver disease, and acquired immune deficiency syndrome (AIDS) are also on the upswing (Jonas, 1988; Kelley, St. Lawrence, Hood, & Brasfield, 1989) and contribute to a large number of deaths each year. The health care community has traditionally focused its attention on developing cures for such conditions. However, nearly all of the above-mentioned conditions are in part preventable. Everly and Feldman (1985) shared the following analogy in the form of a story that illustrates well the development of the growing interest in prevention strategies by the health care community:

> The story is of a little village by a river in which one day were heard the cries of a drowning man floating down the river. Through heroic effort, the villagers managed to save him. The next day the villagers spotted two more people floating along in similar straits. They too were rescued. Gradually more and more people were discovered floating down the river. The villagers began to devise increasingly innovative means of rescuing them. Specially fitted boats, trained observers, and safety nets were organized—the villagers became increasingly adept at rescuing potential drownees. The numbers continued to increase, however, threatening to overwhelm the resources of the village. Although very proud of their rescue capabilities, the villagers realized they could not continue to

cope with the problem with their present systems. Then, and only then, did someone propose, "Why don't we walk upriver to find out who or what is throwing all these people into the river in the first place? (p. xi)

Since 1981, there has emerged a growing clinical and empirical interest by the health care community in prevention strategies to address high-risk behaviors. This movement to be proactive in the intervention of disease has opened the door to the application of existing behavioral strategies to the prevention of a number of medical conditions. Table 20.1 presents a list of the more common areas that are open to behavioral modification (Johns et al., 1987).

Behavioral interventions in the area of mental health often utilize a model focusing on the antecedent(s), the target behavior(s), and/or the consequence(s) of behavior. A similar model can be applied to the prevention of disease (see Figure 20.1). This model is related to one proposed by Russell (1986) but goes further to address the full dynamics of this feedback loop. By conceptualizing prevention as intervening with antecedents, target behaviors, and/or consequences, behavioral techniques can be targeted to any of the three aspects of the model to effect a decline of health-compromising behaviors and an increase in positive health care behaviors.

Six common health care behavior changes seem to be the target for clinicians and researchers alike. Table 20.2 lists these frequently recommended health behavior changes for common chronic diseases (Russell, 1986).

Behavioral strategies used in prevention have not been limited to any one approach. By applying biofeedback, relaxation training, systematic desensitization, reinforcement procedures, observational learning, and behavioral rehearsal, to name a few, clinicians have been successful in enhancing health care behaviors and preventing a variety of medical conditions.

TABLE 20.1. Areas for Health Risk Behavior Modification

Smoking
Hyperlipidemia
High blood pressure
Dietary habits related to disease
High sodium; low calcium, magnesium, potassium—high blood pressure
High fat—cardiovascular disease and cancer of the prostate, breast, colon, and pancreas
High simple carbohydrates—diabetes mellitus
Low fiber—diabetes mellitus, digestive diseases, cardiovascular disease, colon cancer
Low intake of Vitamins A and C—cancer
Sedentary life-style
Obesity
Substance abuse (alcohol and drug)
Nonuse of seatbelts
High-risk sexual behavior
Nonadherence to recommended immunization and screening procedures
High stress levels and Type A personality
High-risk situations for childhood accidents, neglect, and abuse
Poor dental hygiene/infrequent care
Sun exposure
Poor-quality relationships/supports
Occupational risks

From "Primary Care and Health Promotion: A Model for Preventive Medicine," by M.B. Johns et al., 1987, *American Journal of Preventive Medicine, 3* (6), p. 351. Copyright © 1987, American Journal of Preventive Medicine. Used with permission.

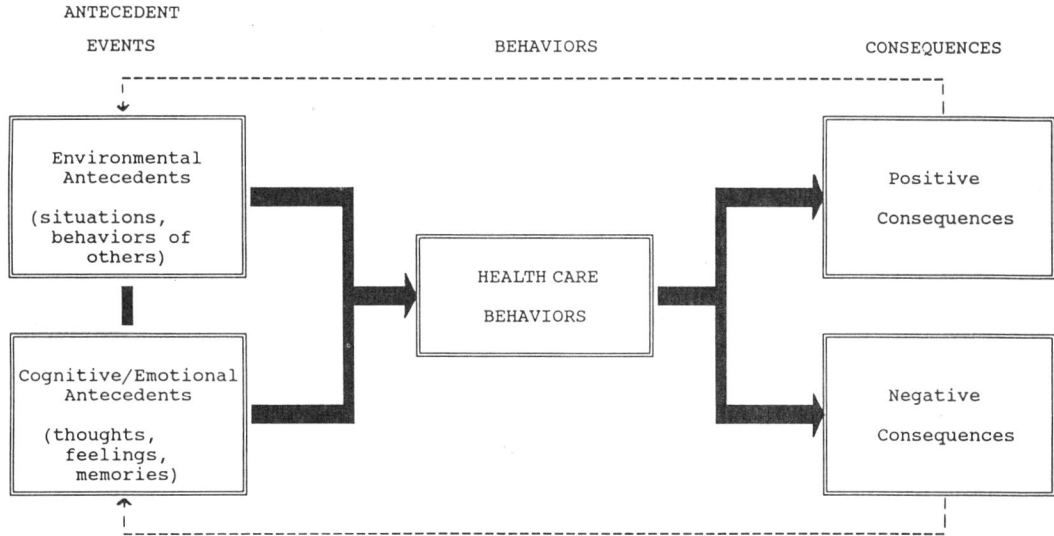

Figure 20.1. Model of health care behavior: antecedent events, behaviors, and consequences.

A good example of the implementation of behavioral strategies in the prevention of disease comes from the large community clinical trials of cardiovascular risk reduction efforts. Two such studies include the Stanford Three Community Study (Farquhar et al., 1977; Stern, Farquhar, Maccoby, & Russell, 1976) and the World Health Organization's large-scale heart disease prevention trials in Belgium, Italy, Spain, Poland, and the United Kingdom (Kornitzer, De Bocker, Dramair, & Thilly, 1980; Puska et al., 1976). In both studies, massive health screenings and health education were provided to residents in different towns or countries. Health education involved media campaigns aimed at smoking cessation, increase in exercise, dietary changes, and pharmacological control of hypertension. Additionally, some participants received individual and group counseling addressing these health behavior changes. The results of these large community studies suggested that the risks of cardiovascular disease could be influenced by community-wide prevention efforts.

This chapter is devoted to a discussion of the three types of prevention strategies; primary, secondary, and tertiary (Cowen, 1973). In each of the next three sections, prevention will be defined using this typology: examples of behavior therapy techniques for each strategy will be provided with case examples and review of empirical support, followed by a discussion of future development of the particular prevention approach. The reader is reminded that, although a distinction is made in prevention strategies, similar behavior therapy techniques can be applied any time during the traditional course of a disease or illness by only slightly modifying the focus of therapy. A brief discussion of compliance and adherence issues in prevention programs will follow the section on prevention strategies. The chapter ends with thoughts on future directions for clinical and research applications of prevention efforts.

PRIMARY PREVENTION

At the turn of the century, infectious diseases or *external pathogens* (influenza, pneumonia, tuberculosis, and so on) were the main causes of morbidity and

TABLE 20.2. Matrix of Health Care Behaviors Frequently Recommended for Chronic Diseases

Disease or Condition	Health Behaviors Frequently Recommended					
	Drug Adherence	Weight Loss	Diet Adherence	Physical Activity	Smoking Cessation	Stress Reduction
Cardiovascular						
Hypertension	X	X	X	X	X	X
Postmyocardial infarction	X	X	X	X	X	X
Coronary heart disease	X	X	X	X	X	X
Endocrine						
Diabetes	X	X	X	X		X
Gastrointestinal						
Constipaton			X	X		
Dyspepsia			X			
Irritable bowel syndrome	X		X			
Peptic ulcer	X		X		X	X
Ulcerative clolitis	X		X			
Genito uniary						
Sexual dysfunction						X
Immunological						
Asthma	X				X	X
Rheumatoid arthritis	X	X				X
Rhinitis	X			X		
Systemic lupus erythematosis	X					X
Neurological						
Epilepsy	X					
Oncological						
Color	X		X			
Lung	X				X	
Mouth	X				X	
Pain						
Low back	X	X				X
Tension headache	X					X
Pulmonary						
Chronic bronchitis	X	X		X	X	
Emphysema	X	X		X	X	
Renal						
Chronic renal disease	X		X			
Surgery	X	X	X	X		X

Note. Behavioral Counseling in Medicine: Strategies for Modifying At-Risk Behavior (p. 5) by M. L. Russell, 1986, New York: Oxford University Press. Copyright © 1986 by Oxford University Press. Used with permission.

mortality in humans. Modern medicine has been highly effective in bringing these disease states under control. Present-day diseases, however, have more to do with *behavioral pathogens,* or the ways in which people choose to live their lives. Examination of the leading causes of death today (see Table 20.3) reveals that personal habits and life-style behaviors are intricately linked to morbidity and mortality, prompting Sexton (1979) to conclude that today "the way of life determines the way of death." Primary prevention focuses on the behavioral antecedents of disease, with the goal of preventing illness onset. Primary prevention activities focus on individuals or groups of individuals who currently show no evidence of the disease or condition of interest.

Preventing illness is a formidable task, even when risk factors are clear. Take the example of smoking, which is the behavioral antecedent associated most frequently with the health problems listed in Table 20.3. Tobacco is the only product that, when used as instructed, results in

TABLE 20.3. Behavior Associated with Leading Causes of Death

Underlying Cause	Behaviors
Diseases of the heart	Excessive consumption of calories/animal fats
	Smoking
	Inadequate physical activity
	Engaging in Type A behavior
Malignant neoplasms	Smoking
	Inadequate consumption of dietary fiber
	Sexual behaviors
Cerebrovascular diseases	Smoking
	Excessive consumption of sodium/calories
Accidents	Excessive consumption of alcohol
	Nonuse of safety restraints
Influenza and pneumonia	Smoking
Diabetes	Excessive consumption of calories/dietary sugar
Arteriosclerosis	Smoking
Cirrhosis of the liver	Excessive consumption of alcohol
Bronchitis, emphysema, and asthma	Smoking
	Inadequate response to stress

Adapted from "Behavioral Epidemiology," by M. M. Sexton, 1979, in *Behavioral Medicine: Theory and Practice* (p. 5), edited by O. F. Pomerleau and J. P. Brady, Baltimore: Williams & Wilkins. Copyright © 1979 by The Williams & Wilkins Co.

death and morbidity. Despite this, every day numerous children and adolescents initiate the habit and a significant number of adults continue to smoke or return to smoking after failed attempts to stop. Multiple psychosocial and physiological factors exert control over smoking at various stages to varying degree, which provides insights into why this behavior is so prevalent and resilient to treatment (Lichtenstein, 1982). Psychosocial factors (availability, curiosity, rebelliousness, social pressure, modeling, and so on) are chiefly responsible for initiating smoking. Once smoking becomes more regular, the reinforcing effects of nicotine, in conjunction with ongoing psychosocial influences, promote continuation of the behavior. Decisions to attempt to stop are influenced primarily by psychosocial variables (health, expense, social support, and aesthetics, for example), whereas relapses are influenced by psychosocial and physiological variables (withdrawal symptoms, stress and frustration, social pressure, and the abstinence violation effect, among others). In addition to these powerful psychosocial and physiological influences, the interventionist must contend with cultural norms, economic factors, and political agenda (Mechanic, 1985). Such is true for all health behaviors. Treatments for asymptomatic smokers, for example, target the various controlling factors through antismoking information, which stresses the dangers of smoking and benefits of nonsmoking; antecedent stimulus control techniques, to aid subjects in modifying or avoiding smoking cues; aversive conditioning procedures, designed to counteract the reinforcing effects of smoking; contingency contracting, including a commitment to quit and specification of reinforcements and penalties to motivate performance; skill training, to cope more effectively with urges/thoughts to smoke; nicotine fading, to shape gradual decreases in nicotine intake; and nicotine gum, to serve as a temporary substitute behavior and minimize withdrawal symptoms (Lichtenstein, 1982; Owen, Halford, & Gilbert, 1986).

Achieving and maintaining abstinence are difficult with chronic smokers, suggesting that prevention of smoking onset may be the wisest course. Epidemiological data indicate that regular smoking in childhood is highly likely to lead to a lifetime of adult smoking, that the critical period for smoking onset is between the ages of 10 and 18, and that the more delayed the onset of smoking the less the risk of subsequent morbidity and mortality. Hence, primary prevention programs typically target preteens and teenagers. Evans (1985) and Flay, d'Avernas, Best, Kersell, and Ryan (1983) described what have become model programs for prevention of smoking among adolescents. The model of Flay et al. (1983), termed the Waterloo Smoking Prevention Project, will be reviewed in brief for purposes of illustration.

School-Based Case Example

The integrative model of Flay et al. (1983), illustrated in Figure 20.2, draws from diverse literatures (information-processing, value-expectancy formulations, personality theory, self-efficacy theory, attribution theory, and consistency theory). The

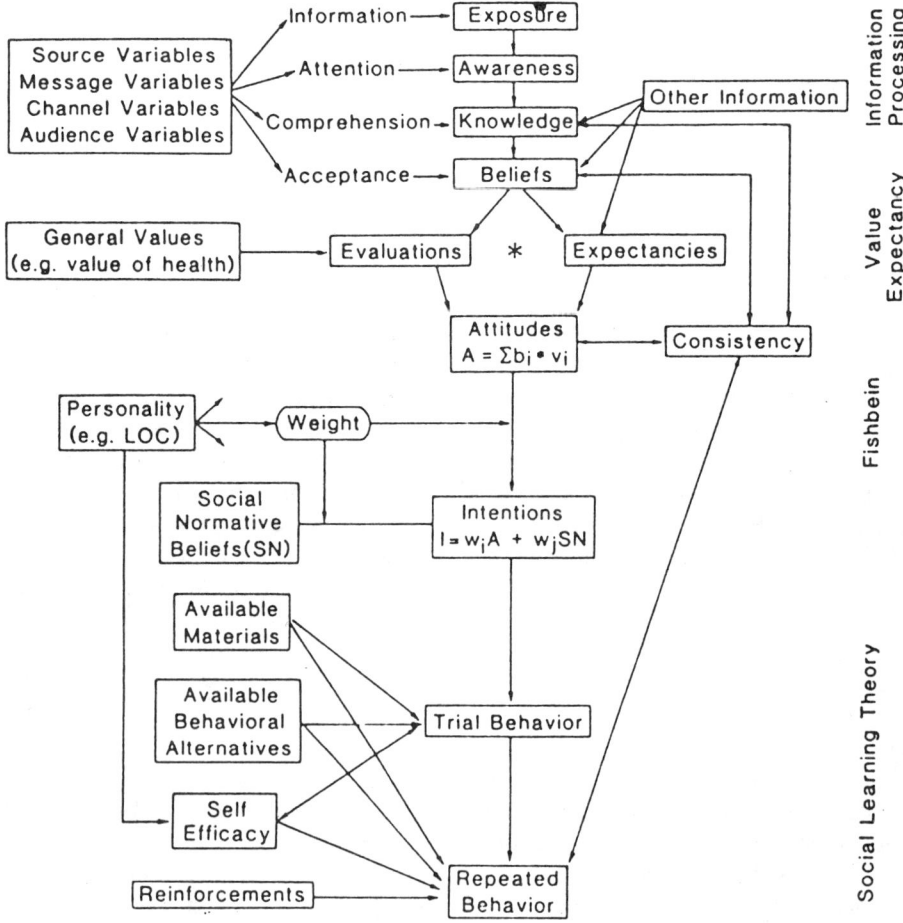

Figure 20.2. Integrative model of health attitude and behavior change. From B. R. Flay, J. R. d'Avernas, A. Best, M. W. Kersell, & B. A. Ryan, "Cigarette Smoking: Why Young People Do It and Ways of Preventing It," in *Pediatric and Adolescent Behavioral Medicine: Issues in Treatment, 10* (p. 154) edited by P. J. McGrath & P. Firestone, 1983. Springer Publishing Company, Inc., New York 10012; used by permission.

model postulates the following sequence for primary prevention. Information needs to be presented in a manner that is easily attended, comprehended, and accepted. This information may change beliefs, attitudes, and intentions to act, provided values, expectancies, and social influences are considered and the individual has been provided the necessary control and coping skills. This model helps explain why many primary prevention programs fail; they focus most of their effort at the top of the model and do not give enough attention to elements closer to behavior.

The core program of Flay et al. has three major components that are delivered in six 1-hour weekly sessions to sixth graders during the first three months of the school year. The first component (sessions 1 and 2) provides information about the reasons for and harmful effects of smoking. Information is elicited from, rather than provided to, the children, in order to foster development of future attitudinal and behavioral changes and social skills acquisition. This approach makes information more credible and salient, forces children to examine their beliefs, and ensures more comprehensive coverage. Information is transmitted in multiple ways (video tapes, posters, role plays, and class discussions) to facilitate attention, comprehension, and retention. The second component (sessions 3 and 4) explicates social influences that encourage smoking (peers, family, and media) and teaches children ways to resist such pressures. The final component (sessions 5 and 6) targets decision making and public commitment by asking children to integrate what has been learned, to complete a decisional balance sheet about smoking (listing harms and benefits to self and others "if I smoke," and who will approve and disapprove "if I smoke"), to make a decision about starting to smoke, and to announce this decision publicly to classmates. Two maintenance sessions are provided in grade six to ensure that issues, skills, and decisions remain salient and relevant. Two booster sessions are provided in grade seven (wherein students are asked to develop their own smoking prevention program and present portions of it to classmates) and one in grade eight (wherein students discuss the social benefits and consequences of smoking and the pressures/influences to smoke and complete additional decision-making assignments) to counteract expected increased peer pressure to smoke.

Evaluation

The Waterloo program was evaluated in 22 schools, randomly assigned to experimental or control groups, matched according to urban/rural classification and socioeconomic status (Flay et al., 1985). Questionnaires and a biochemical measure (salivary thiocyanate) to validate smoking exposure were collected five times over a 2-year study period. Students were classified into one of five categories at the start of the project (never smoked, tried once, quitter, experimenter, and regular smoker). The experimental groups were found to be superior to the control groups on all measures, with effects being most clear for those having some experience with smoking before the program began and for those with smoking peer and family models.

Evans (1985) believed school is a nearly ideal setting in which to carry out prevention programs of various types, although administrative requirements can constrain certain plans. Well-reasoned, empirically grounded prevention programs are sorely needed for significant health problems. Flay et al. (1985) pointed out the methodological problems that have plagued prevention research of this type. These include: small sample sizes and resultant weak statistical power; nonrandom assignment to conditions, which often leads to pretreatment incomparability; design/ program breakdowns during execution;

incomplete and unreliable measures; failure to consider effects due to attrition; inadequate tracking of subjects over time; and failures to stratify samples on relevant risk dimensions. Future interventions need to consider the above and to: include more complete attention to behavioral antecedents to illness; tailor programs to individuals at different behavioral stages; incorporate process analyses to support the integrity of intervention and identify active components; consider broader socioeconomic issues; and incorporate "anticipatory guidance" into standard office visits (anticipation of common problems and provision of information and advice).

SECONDARY PREVENTION

Secondary prevention is the process of early detection of an illness followed by treatment or the modification of unhealthy behaviors, with the goal of returning the individual to a healthy life-style. Early detection may take various forms, including: routine blood glucose monitoring for patients with a family history of diabetes; breast self-examination and/or mammograms for women; blood pressure monitoring; and cholesterol screening—to name a few. Once the initial stages of an illness are identified, the health care professional uses secondary prevention strategies to control the illness, preventing its further development. Common medical strategies used in secondary prevention may include: beginning insulin therapy for the newly detected diabetic; antihypertensive therapy and dietary sodium restrictions for the newly detected hypertensive; surgical removal of a breast tumor in the patient with a newly detected cancerous breast lump; or dietary modification in the newly detected hypercholesterolemic. Behavior therapy techniques also are being applied to assist in these cases. Behavioral rehearsal and reinforcement procedures are used to aid the new insulin user in learning how to self-inject insulin. Problem-solving and stimulus-control strategies are applied to dietary modifications for patients with hypertension or hypercholesterolemia, and relaxation training and cognitive relabeling are used to aid women in recovering from radical mastectomy. In each of these applications, stress management is considered one of the goals of the prevention strategy. A similar application (discussed at length below) is the use of behavior therapy techniques in the preparation of patients for stressful medical procedures.

The behavioral sciences have, over the past decade, come to understand stress in the medical setting as an interplay between the individual and the environment (Ludwick-Rosenthal & Neufeld, 1988). The patient preparing for a stressful medical procedure brings to that situation a unique set of expectations, fears, and other cognitions that interact with situational variables leading to differential responding to the procedure. Therefore, some patients are more emotionally "prepared" for the procedure and others less so. The empirical literature suggests that those less prepared for these procedures, those with high levels of fear and anxiety, require longer hospital stays and greater amounts of anesthetics during and analgesics following the procedure; have poorer psychological recovery from the procedure; and report higher levels of pain and psychological distress (Bodley, Jones, & Mather, 1974; Johnson, Leventhal, & Dabbs, 1971; Ludwick-Rosenthal & Neufeld, 1988). By reducing the stress or emotional trauma of the situation through preparation with behavioral strategies, these outcomes can be successfully modified.

An example of behavior therapy at work in the secondary prevention strategy of preparation for stressful medical procedures is the preparation patients receive for coronary artery bypass graft (CABG) surgery. These patients have been diagnosed as having occluding arterial vessels and, without a CABG, these patients run the risk of a lethal heart attack. A CABG involves the actual "bypassing" of the occluded portion of the coronary artery(ies) with vessels harvested from other parts of the body. Although becoming relatively routine, the procedure is not without risks and requires an optimal surgical candidate and good participation from the patient following the procedure, to ensure a successful outcome (Razin, 1984). In some hospitals, routine psychological preparation is given to all pre-CABG patients. This preparation may consist of:

1. Providing the patient with information regarding the procedure and recovery,
2. Providing information regarding the sensations that might be expected throughout the various stages of the procedure,
3. Training in relaxation prior to the procedure,
4. Providing information about pain management options available during recovery,
5. Instructing the patient in the techniques for coughing and turning in bed during recovery.

These strategies assist the patient in cognitively and behaviorally preparing for the upcoming stressful procedure, reduce fear and anxiety, and thereby maximize successful outcome.

Case Example

Mr. Weston is a 56-year-old male hospitalized following a minor heart attack. It is determined that one of his coronary arteries is 85% occluded, requiring CABG because he is at risk for a future lethal heart attack. Upon notification of the necessity for the surgery, Mr. Weston becomes visibly anxious and verbalizes fear of undergoing the procedure. The behavioral medicine clinician (psychologist, psychiatrist, mental health trained nurse) is consulted and provides Mr. Weston with supportive counseling. The clinician uses a videotape describing the procedure that depicts a patient being prepared for the procedure, being wheeled to the operating room, undergoing the procedure, and recovering. The patient is encouraged to voice concerns or ask questions that might help him feel more prepared for the procedure. Additionally, one of the physical therapists in the hospital visits Mr. Weston and instructs him in how to cough and turn in bed following the procedure so as not to tear his sutures or cause additional pain. Mr. Weston, feeling more at ease with the procedure and what is expected of him, agrees to the CABG. He rehearses the above skills prior to the procedure. The day after the surgery, both the behavioral medicine clinician and physical therapist visit him in the coronary care unit recovery room to assess his mental status and coping strategies, remind him of his role in recovery, and respond to any questions. During the week of recovery, each professional periodically assesses Mr. Weston's coping and provides appropriate feedback to him, his family, and his health care team.

Evaluation

This case provides a typical scenario involving behavioral strategies used in preparing a patient for a CABG. Empirical studies suggest that such strategies are effective (Marshall, Penckofer, & Llewellyn, 1986; Owens, McCann, & Hutelmyer, 1978).

Such formal preparation of patients for stressful medical procedures has become an acceptable and routine standard of practice in most major medical centers. In an excellent review of outcome studies in this area, Ludwick-Rosenthal and Neufeld (1988) discussed several issues to guide future application and research in psychological preparation for invasive medical procedures. These authors recommend that future empirical study consider:

1. Inclusion of attention control groups,
2. Incorporation of manipulation checks,
3. Elimination of differential treatment of comparison groups involving variables other than those being manipulated,
4. Use of dependent variables with established validity,
5. Control for subject differences and, in particular, prior experience with the procedure.

Furthermore, interventions must be evaluated based on clinical effectiveness and not strictly on statistically significant treatment effects. The meaningfulness of reductions in certain outcome measures without parallel reductions in self-report anxiety or fear measures, for example, is questionable.

The cost-effectiveness of different preparatory procedures also is of significance in today's cost-conscious health insurance environment. The use of the most effective strategies with preselected patients, provided by the least costly health care professional, is considered optimal. Comprehensive preparatory interventions cannot be provided to all patients who undergo stressful procedures. Future work in this area must focus not only on the preselection of patients but also on the development of a variety of preparatory strategies such that strategies can be matched to patient needs. The "smorgasbord" approach to preparatory intervention, although widely utilized, is being replaced with interventions that better meet the needs of the individual patient and the health care environment.

TERTIARY PREVENTION

Tertiary prevention aims to limit and contain the damage caused by an established disease process. Here, the goal of intervention is improved management of or coping with the chronic illness condition. Treatment is difficult and often complicated by various factors. Intervention is typically aimed at modifying cognitive-perceptual processes, social learning factors, emotional factors, and psychosocial factors intricately linked to the development and maintenance of illness behavior (Feuerstein, Labbe, & Kuczmierczyk, 1986; Tobin, Reynolds, Holroyd, & Creer, 1986). Education, the first step in intervening, stresses the importance of the individual's taking an active role in treatment and begins with a nontechnical discussion of the individual's condition which emphasizes those determinants potentially under the individual's control. This education often helps to combat feelings of helplessness and to encourage the individual to become actively involved in treatment.

Cognitive-perceptual processes (heightened perceptual sensitivity to bodily sensations, irrational or self-defeating cognitions about symptom cause and the significance of symptoms, and so on) are dealt with by cognitive-behavioral therapy and attention-shifting techniques. For example, a burn patient may be taught to evoke imagery that is incompatible with pain, to construe the pain as arising from another problem (virus), or to view the pain in a detached manner.

External contingencies often come into play and complicate intervention further by promoting illness behavior. Illness behavior (symptom complaints, doctor shopping, bodily posturing, passivity) develops as a result of observational learning; positive reinforcement of illness behavior or insufficient reinforcement or punishment of well behavior by family, friends, and physicians; and/or avoidance learning (as a result of a social skill deficit or social anxiety). Social learning approaches seek to alter inappropriate reinforcement contingencies and to teach improved coping skills via instructions, modeling, and role play.

Depression is a common accompaniment of chronic illness, with many patients experiencing a major depressive syndrome (American Psychiatric Association, 1987). Medication and various psychotherapies (Beck's cognitive therapy, Lewinsohn's social learning approach, interpersonal therapy) are often helpful. Anxiety and tension states, which can be both accompaniments and contributors, are typically dealt with by progressive muscle relaxation training, biofeedback, systematic desensitization, meditation, and hypnosis. Finally, the patient with chronic illness is often faced with adapting to numerous changes in his or her social and physical functioning (diminished work capacity, impaired family/marital relations, arduous litigation, iatrogenic complications due to intervention and long-term medication use). Successful intervention often requires expertise from various professionals (physician, psychologist, physical therapist, occupational therapist, social worker), as discussed by Turk, Rudy, and Sorkin in Chapter 19.

Every year, approximately 500,000 individuals are subject to closed head injuries. About 50,000 of these result in serious injury. In the early 1970s, only about 10% of this latter category survived. Air evacuation, paramedical services, and advances in medical technology have improved survivability greatly, such that nearly all (90%) survive now. Advances in acute care have far outstripped innovations in long-term rehabilitation. We now have a large population of head-injured patients requiring extensive, comprehensive long-term care, with few guidelines for appropriate care. The following example illustrates a supportive group approach, which has applicability to other chronic conditions.

TABLE 20.4. Areas of Problems Following Head Injury

Intrapersonal			Interpersonal		
Physical	Emotional	Mental	Family/Spouse	Acquaintances	Employment
Gross and fine motor movements (hemiparesis, slowing of dexterity) Vision (diplopia, reduced visual field) Smell/taste Fatigue	Mood swings (lability) Loss of impulse control (irritability) Depression (suicidal thought) Identity crisis Denial Lack of motivation (apathy)	Recent memory disturbance Attentional disorder Word finding difficulties Problems in abstract thinking (locking into an idea without properly considering alternatives)	Financial changes (loss of income, applying for social security, litigation) Accepting caretaker role Dependency issues Altered relationship (loss of spouse and sexual partner)	Initial support (separate between curious and supportive friends) Lack of understanding Isolation Risk of making new friends	Loss of prestige Insecurity False hope Reduced to nonproductive level, now what Lack of resources for retraining

From *Applications in Behavioral Medicine and Health Psychology: A Clinician's Source Book* (p. 275), edited by R. M. Ruff, R. W. Evans, and R. Green, 1987, Sarasota, FL: Professional Resource Exchange, Inc. Copyright © 1987 by Professional Resource Exchange, Inc.

Example of Group Treatment for Head Trauma

The program developed by Ruff, Evans, and Green (1987) has four specific aims:

1. To develop a specialized service for a growing patient population whose adjustment problems have been woefully neglected,
2. To provide support and information to family members who have unexpectedly been forced into caretaker roles,
3. To compile a comprehensive program capitalizing on expertise from various disciplines,
4. To extend service beyond acute recovery to long-term recovery.

Presenting problems of patients are widespread and include various intrapersonal and interpersonal aspects, as listed in Table 20.4.

Group meetings, for patients and families, are held weekly for 12 consecutive months. Treatment is structured into three phases. In Phase I (lasting about 8 to 10 weeks), clinicians from various disciplines present information about the effects of head injury (see Table 20.5). Lecturers are encouraged to incorporate audiovisual aids, handouts, mnemonic devices, repetition, cues, and frequent review to ensure important points are processed and retained. In Phase II (lasting about 4 months), patients and family members occasionally meet in subgroups. The aim of this phase is to stimulate participants to recognize changes that have occurred as a result of the trauma. In the patient subgroups, topics center on various problems, such as those listed in Table 20.6. Discussions in family subgroups are less structured and focus generally on recounts of past experiences, sharing of resources, and updates on recent developments. In Phase III (lasting about 6 months), work in subgroups is intensified, with subgroup meetings taking place 3 out of 4 weeks. The format of these sessions is less structured; therapists encourage patients and families to talk about their own needs and problems.

TABLE 20.5. Lecture Series—Phase I

Presenter	Topic
Driving Specialist	Defensive Driving Skills Learning to Drive Again with Handicaps
Neuropsychologist	Brain-Behavior Relationships Cognitive Rehabilitation
Nutritionist	Diet Planning—Positive Effects on Recovery
Occupational Therapist	Vocational Skills Training Vocational Counseling
Physical Therapist	Physical Rehabilitation Daily Exercising Skills
Psychologist	Systematic Desensitization Relaxation Training Problem-Solving Skills
Social Worker	Family Therapy Referrals and Placement Opportunities
Speech Therapist	Language and the Brain Speech Therapy
Recreational Therapist	Creative Relaxation Planning Leisure Time Alternatives Community Resources for the Handicapped

From *Applications in Behavioral Medicine and Health Psychology: A Clinician's Source Book* (p. 276), edited by R. M. Ruff, R. W. Evans, and R. Green, 1987, Sarasota, FL: Professional Resource Exchange, Inc. Copyright © 1987 by Professional Resource Exchange, Inc.

Evaluation

Data collected from 24 head-injured patients and their family members document important changes in several dimensions (improved interactions, enhanced family relations, return to the workforce but at a lower occupational level, and so on). These authors/therapists believe group treatment to be superior to individual treatment in accomplishing behavior change and reducing dropouts. It is felt that the presence of other profoundly impaired

TABLE 20.6 Group Therapy Discussion Topics—Phase II

Topic	Sample Inquiry by Therapists
Memory Functioning	Have you noticed if you've been forgetful since the injury? Are you having unusual difficulties remembering faces, names, dates?
Physiological Changes	Have your sleeping patterns or eating habits changed since the injury?
Self-disclosure	Have you noticed any changes in the way you talk to others about personal matters?
Sexuality	Has your desire for sexual activity changed at all since the injury? Have your sexual habits changed?
Socialization	Do you visit with your friends or go out as much as you used to prior to the injury?
Body Image	Have you noticed any changes in the way you view yourself physically since the injury?
Motivation	Have you noticed any changes in your ability in starting to do a job or task?
Alcohol	Have your drinking habits changed since the injury? Has your tolerance for alcohol changed since the injury?
Employment	Has the injury affected your job performance? If so, how?
Suicide/Depression	Have you had thoughts of harming yourself since the injury? Have you noticed any changes in your mood since the injury?
Role Changes	Has your wife/husband/father/mother had to take over any of your duties?

From *Applications in Behavioral Medicine and Health Psychology: A Clinician's Source Book* (p. 278), edited by R. M. Ruff, R. W. Evans, and R. Green, 1987, Sarasota, FL: Professional Resource Exchange, Inc. Copyright © 1987 by Professional Resource Exchange, Inc.

individuals helps to break down denial, a major contributor to discontinuing treatment, and also affords patients opportunities to help themselves by helping others, removing patients from the role of passive recipients of treatment. Finally, group treatment presents an economical means for incorporating various disciplines. Not all problems can be managed successfully in the group setting; referrals are made for sexual adjustment difficulties and psychotropic consultations for various psychiatric symptoms (for example, depression, suspiciousness, and impulsivity). Approaches such as this will likely become more prominent in the future, to promote life-long adjustment and enhanced coping for chronic illness conditions.

COMPLIANCE AND ADHERENCE

"If true tragedy lies in the failure to achieve that which can be achieved, then noncompliance is a tragic flaw in our efforts to reap the benefits of treatments that work when they are taken" (Haynes, Wang, & Gomes, 1987, p. 156). This quote applies to prevention as defined in the previous sections. The issue of compliance and adherence (hereafter used interchangeably) in prevention programs is likely the single most crucial issue in the effectiveness of prevention strategies. Noncompliance is an even more salient concern for behavioral specialists interested in prevention strategies because those behaviors of greatest noncompliance tend to be those requiring major lifestyle changes (e.g., smoking cessation, weight loss), those behaviors that are preventive in nature, and those behaviors that are targeted for change in the asymptomatic patient (German, 1988).

Promoting adherence in prevention programs is essential and can be handled in multiple ways. The reader is directed to Meichenbaum & Turk (1987), Marlatt & Gordon (1985), and Cameron & Best (1987) for excellent discussions of strategies to maximize adherence. As a general model for consideration in maximizing compliance in disease prevention behavioral change programs, the current authors offer the following suggestions. As the health care professional:

1. Attempt to understand the patient's *individual needs and expectations* and tailor the intervention strategy to these needs and expectations;
2. Ensure the patient's *understanding* of the behavioral change being recommended;
3. Ensure that the patient is provided with and accepts the *justification* for the behavioral change request;
4. Maximize the patient's perceived *ownership* or responsibility for the behavioral change;
5. Maximize the assistance by the patient's *support network* in initiating and maintaining the behavior change;
6. Give *reinforcement/verification* of the above suggestions at subsequent meetings with the patient.

FUTURE DIRECTIONS

The future of behavioral strategies in the prevention of disease appears bright. As the interest in health education and promotion continues to grow, so does the involvement of the behavioral sciences in prevention. Necessary in this growth is a greater emphasis on the development of theories that justify the application of behavioral strategies to the prevention of disease. Cameron and Best (1987) discussed this issue of atheoretical interventions as applied to clinical-compliance research. In order for coherence and direction to be achieved in this line of clinical and empirical study, theoretical grounding is required. Without such grounding, the area becomes inundated with reports lacking conceptual structure, a condition that leads to fragmented interventions and stagnation of the research. By relying on established behavioral principles in the designing of research and the provision of service, these concerns can be effectively managed.

In line with the above recommendation, future work in the prevention field must continue to document the efficacy of existing behavioral prevention strategies and develop a greater specificity of these approaches. A number of questions have arisen regarding specificity in behavioral prevention strategies. One such question comes from the cardiovascular risk reduction studies and has to do with whether prevention strategies should target personal behaviors individually, in small groups, or on a larger environmental scale. Similarly, does the health care worker interested in prevention target one behavior or multiple health-compromising behaviors? Best (1989) elucidated four questions that might offer appropriate direction for the study of the specificity of behavioral prevention strategies. These include the questions of: when should the intervention occur (primary, secondary, tertiary); for how long should the intervention occur; what mediates the intervention (motivation, skills, attitudes); and what are the targets for intervention (the individual, the environment, behaviors, knowledge)? Added to Best's list might be questions regarding which interventions are appropriate for which illness/condition; how to provide the intervention (videotape, audiotape, live); where to intervene (hospital, home, work site); who provides the intervention (psychologist, physician, nurse, or other professional), and who receives the intervention (patient selection). Addressing these questions in future empirical study will lead to the provision of more efficient and effective behavioral prevention strategies.

A discussion of prevention strategies, particularly as related to physical health and well being, without addressing cost-benefit issues would be remiss. In 1983, the concept of diagnosis related groups

(DRGs) passed into law. This allowed for federal reimbursement of medical expenses based not on length of inpatient stay but on the specific diagnosis. Needless to say, this has led to a greater emphasis on abbreviated inpatient stays, a shift from inpatient to outpatient procedures, and, to some degree, an emphasis on primary care and disease prevention approaches. The challenge for those interested in administering prevention strategies in the health care setting, clinicians and empiricists alike, is to convince the reimbursing agents that money is well spent in prevention strategies and can lead to a reduction in the total cost of health care. It will be imperative that future empirical study of prevention approaches answer the questions posed above and develop prevention strategies that provide maximum benefit at the lowest possible cost.

With a growing number of identifiable medical conditions, it is worth considering those illnesses or conditions that warrant extra clinical or empirical attention because of their salience or historical lack of attention. The Society of Public Health Education recently published a statement on national health promotion disease prevention objectives for the year 2000 (Schwartz & Eriksen, 1989). This statement addresses those areas and populations that warrant prevention emphasis. They include minority health issues such as: cancer prevention in minorities and in the blue-collar and female population; control of HIV infection in all minority groups; smoking prevention in minorities, women, and teenagers; reduction of stroke and cardiovascular disease in blacks, particularly in the southern "stroke belt"; and additional data on Hispanic health issues. Emphasis is placed on smoking cessation across the board, adolescent health issues, prevention of illness in the homeless, depression recognition and suicide prevention in the teen population, and development of prevention/education programs for the aging population. Prevention focus in these areas is needed and behavior therapy is positioned to play a primary role in the development of such prevention strategies.

Finally, as these national health goals suggest, there is much work to accomplish in prevention. To assist in this national directive, training programs in the behavioral sciences, medicine, nursing, and the other health care professions must incorporate prevention and health promotion education as part of their curriculum.

REFERENCES

American Psychiatric Association. (1987). *Diagnostic and statistical manual of mental disorders (3rd ed. rev.).* Washington, DC: Author.

Best, J. A. (1989). Intervention perspectives on school health promotion research. *Health Education Quarterly, 16,* 299–305.

Bodley, P. O., Jones, H. V., & Mather, M. D. (1974). Preoperative anxiety: A qualitative analysis. *Journal of Neurology, Neurosurgery, and Psychiatry, 37,* 230–239.

Cameron, R., & Best, J. A. (1987). Promoting adherence to health behavior change interventions: Recent findings from behavioral research. *Patient Education and Counseling, 10,* 139–154.

Cowen, E. L. (1973). Social and community interventions. *Annual Review of Psychology, 24,* 423–472.

Evans, R. I. (1985). Psychologists in health promotion research: General concerns and adolescent smoking prevention. In J. C. Rosen & L. J. Solomon (Eds.), *Prevention in health psychology* (pp. 18–33). Hanover, NH: University Press of New England.

Everly, G. S., Jr., & Feldman, R. H. L. (Eds.). (1985). *Occupational health promotion: Health behavior in the workplace.* New York: Wiley.

Farquhar, J. W., Maccoby, N., Wood, P. D., Breitrose, H., Haskell, W. L., Meyer, A. J., Alexander, J. K., Brown, B. W., McAlister, A. L., Nash, J. D., & Stern, M. (1977).

Community education for cardiovascular health. *Lancet, 1,* 1192–1195.

Feuerstein, M., Labbe, E. E., & Kuczmierczyk, A. R. (1986). *Health psychology: A psychobiological perspective.* New York: Plenum.

Flay, B. R., d'Avernas, J. R., Best, A., Kersell, M. W., & Ryan, B. A. (1983). Cigarette smoking: Why young people do it and ways of preventing it. In P. J. McGrath & P. Firestone (Eds.), *Pediatric and adolescent behavioral medicine: Issues in treatment, Vol. 10* (pp. 132–183). New York: Springer.

Flay, B. R., Ryan, K. B., Best, J. A., Brown, K. S., Kersell, M. W., d'Avernas, J. R., & Zanna, M. P. (1985). Are social-psychological smoking prevention programs effective: The Waterloo study. *Journal of Behavioral Medicine, 8,* 37–59.

German, P. S. (1988). Compliance and chronic disease. *Antihypertensive Drug Effects, 11* (Suppl. II), 56–60.

Haynes, R. B., Wang, E., & Gomes, M. D. M. (1987). A critical review of interventions to improve compliance with prescribed medications. *Patient Education and Counseling, 10,* 155–166.

Johns, M. B., Hovell, M. F., Ganiats, T., Peddecord, M., & Agras, W. S. (1987). Primary care and health promotion: A model for preventive medicine. *American Journal of Preventive Medicine, 3,* 346–357.

Johnson, J. E., Leventhal, H., & Dabbs, J. M. (1971). Contributions of emotional and instrumental processes in adaptations to surgery. *Journal of Personality and Social Psychology, 20,* 55–64.

Jonas, S. (1988). Health promotion in medical education. *American Journal of Health Promotion, 3,* 37–42.

Kelley, J. A., St. Lawrence, J. S., Hood, H. V., & Brasfield, T. L. (1989). Behavioral intervention to reduce AIDS risk activities. *Journal of Consulting and Clinical Psychology, 57,* 60–67.

Kornitzer, M., De Bocker, G., Dramair, M., & Thilly, G. (1980). The Belgian heart disease prevention project: Modification of the coronary risk profile of an industrial population. *Circulation, 61,* 18–25.

Lichtenstein, E. (1982). The smoking problem: A behavioral perspective. *Journal of Consulting and Clinical Psychology, 50,* 804–819.

Ludwick-Rosenthal, R., & Neufeld, R. W. J. (1988). Stress management during noxious medical procedures: An evaluative review of outcome studies. *Psychological Bulletin, 104,* 326–342.

Marlatt, G. A., & Gordon, J. R. (Eds.). (1985). *Relapse prevention.* New York: Guilford.

Marshall, J., Penckofer, S., & Llewellyn, J. (1986). Structured postoperative teaching and knowledge and compliance of patients who had coronary artery bypass surgery. *Heart and Lung, 15,* 76–82.

Masek, B. J., Epstein, L. H., & Russo, D. C. (1981). Behavioral perspectives in preventive medicine. In S. M. Turner, K. S. Calhoun, & H. E. Adams (Eds.), *Handbook of clinical behavior therapy* (pp. 475–499). New York: Wiley.

Mechanic, D. (1985). Health and behavior: Perspectives on risk prevention. In J. C. Rosen & L. J. Solomon (Eds.), *Prevention in health psychology* (pp. 6–17). Hanover, NH: University Press of New England.

Meichenbaum, D., & Turk, D. C. (1987). *Facilitating treatment adherence.* New York: Plenum.

Owen, N., Halford, K., & Gilbert, A. (1986). Smoking. In N. J. King & A. Remenyi (Eds.), *Health care: A behavioral approach* (pp. 41–50). New York: Grune & Stratton.

Owens, J. F., McCann, C. S., & Hutelmyer, C. M. (1978). Cardiac rehabilitation: A patient education program. *Nursing Research, 27,* 148–150.

Puska, P., Koskela, K., Pakarinen, H., Puumalainen, P., Soininen, V., & Tuomilehto, J. (1976). The North Karelia Project: A programme for community control of cardiovascular diseases. *Journal of the Scandinavian Society of Medicine, 4,* 57–60.

Razin, A. M. (1984). Psychotherapeutic intervention in angina: I. A critical review. *General Hospital Psychiatry, 6,* 250–257.

Ruff, R. M., Evans, R. W., & Green, R. (1987). Long-term remediation of head injured patients. In J. A. Blumenthal & D. C. McKee (Eds.), *Applications in behavioral medicine and health psychology: A clinician's source book* (pp. 271–298). Sarasota, FL: Professional Resource Exchange, Inc.

Russell, M. L. (1986). *Behavioral counseling in medicine: Strategies for modifying at-risk behavior.* New York: Oxford University Press.

Schwartz, R., & Eriksen, M. (1989). Statement of the Society for Public Health Education on the national health promotion disease prevention objectives for the year 2000. *Health Education Quarterly, 16,* 3–7.

Sexton, M. M. (1979). Behavioral epidemiology. In O. F. Pomerleau & J. P. Brady (Eds.), *Behavioral medicine: Theory and practice* (pp. 3–21). Baltimore: Williams & Wilkins.

Stern, M. P., Farquhar, J. W., Maccoby, N., & Russell, S. H. (1976). Results of a two-year education campaign on dietary behavior: The Stanford three community study. *Circulation, 54,* 826–833.

Tobin, D. L., Reynolds, R. V. C., Holroyd, K. A., & Creer, T. L. (1986). Self-management and social learning theory. In K. A. Holroyd & T. L. Creer (Eds.), *Self-management of chronic disease: Handbook of clinical interventions and research* (pp. 29–55). Orlando: Academic Press.

U.S. Bureau of the Census. (1988). *Statistical abstract of the United States* (108th ed.). Washington, DC: U.S. Government Printing Office.

PART FOUR

Special Populations

CHAPTER 21

Family Violence

JOHN R. LUTZKER and VINCENT B. VAN HASSELT

INCIDENCE

It now seems almost inconceivable that, as late as the 1960s, the horror of child abuse and neglect had failed to reach public or professional attention to any significant degree. This changed in 1962 when Kempe, Silverman, Steele, Droegemueller, and Silver published their article, "The Battered Child Syndrome," in the *Journal of the American Medical Association.* Only in recent years has the magnitude of the problem and its long-term side effects for the individual and society come into focus. Data from nationwide surveys suggest that between 10 and 16 children out of every 1,000 in the United States are abused and/or neglected annually (National Center on Child Abuse and Neglect, 1988). Reports of incidents have risen dramatically across most states, and most incidents of child neglect are reported than of child abuse (Lutzker, 1990).

Family violence, however, is not limited to child maltreatment. Violent episodes between husbands and wives also have been estimated to occur at an alarmingly high rate. For example, there are indications that spouse abuse occurs at least once in 20% to 30% of families in the United States (Stark & Flitcraft, 1988). Further, 30% of American wives are victims of some act of physical aggression by their partner (Straus, Gelles, & Steinmetz, 1980). In addition, approximately 10% to 15% of the women in this country are victims of serious and repeated physical aggression from their partners (Straus et al., 1980). In fact, according to data provided by the Federal Bureau of Investigation (1982), nearly 30% of all female homicide victims are killed by their husbands or boyfriends. It is increasingly apparent that spousal violence has become a problem of epidemic proportions.

DEFINITIONS AND THEORIES

There are several difficulties in formulating definitions of child abuse and neglect, although these terms are clearly distinct. Physical abuse becomes problematic as to when it is distinguishable from socially acceptable forms of punishment and discipline. Even religious beliefs can complicate definitions of neglect when related to certain health care practices. There is now a consensus, however, that abuse and neglect are different from each other in that abuse involves acts of *commission* against a child, whereas neglect refers to acts of *omission* that threaten a child's health and well-being. Essentially, abuse

---

We are grateful to Tracey K. Eck and Roberta Solomon for their assistance in the preparation of this manuscript.

consists of causing or allowing nonaccidental physical injuries to occur that are physically apparent or permanent. Neglect has been defined as the failure to provide for a child's welfare, support, education, and medical care (including, but not limited to, failure to provide adequate food, clothing, and shelter).

Etiologic theories of family violence historically have been constructed by sociologists and psychiatrists. Gelles (1980) suggested that most theories have been presented as intraindividual, social, psychological, or sociocultural. Gelles (1983) further argued that an exchange or social control theory would seem most relevant. This theory emphasizes that child abuse and neglect occur in a disturbed social climate and that adults actually assess the "costs" of their aggression toward children, usually concluding that there is a low probability of facing consequences for their abusive acts.

Lutzker (1984) proposed that abuse and neglect should be viewed as an "ecobehavioral" problem. That is, the difficulties in families that precipitate abuse and neglect involve *multifaceted* issues such as poverty, anger and stress control deficits, poor parenting practices, skill deficiencies in children, inadequate home safety and cleanliness, inadequate nutrition, and health risk factors. Consequently, successful treatment requires a concurrent focus on several of these disparate issues. As a part of an ecobehavioral perspective, Lutzker and Newman (1986) further articulated that child abuse and neglect is a *community* problem in need of community solutions. Specifically, in addition to being multifaceted, treatment needs to be community-based, provided directly in homes, schools, and foster care settings (i.e., wherever the problems occur).

Numerous definitions of spouse abuse have been offered over the past several years (Roy, 1977; Straus et al., 1980; Walker, 1979, 1984), but the description of this problem offered by Geffner and Pagelow (1990) reflects most current perspectives in the area:

> [S]pouse abuse refers to a pattern of behavior in a relationship by which one person victimizes the other. Abuse can take many forms: physical, sexual, verbal, and/or phychological. It can also refer to intense and continuous degradation or intimidation for the purpose of controlling the actions or behavior of the other person, or placing that other person in fear of serious bodily injury to self or another. (p.113)

This definition raises a number of issues that have received increased attention from clinicians and researchers in the field. First, spouse abuse may involve violence by husbands toward wives, wives toward husbands, or, in some cases, both. However, most remedial efforts have been directed toward violence against women, primarily because of the potential for more serious injury in these episodes. Second, contrary to early psychodynamic perspectives, Geffner and Pagelow (1990) underscored that the battered party is "victimized" and is not a psychologically impaired or "masochistic" individual who is responsible for, or who has elicited, aggression. Fortunately, "victim blaming" has diminished as a result of the consistent lack of empirical support for this viewpoint and the growing awareness of deleterious effects of such a perspective on victims. Third, unlike earlier definitions, current conceptualizations strongly embrace the notion that spouse abuse does not only refer to acts of physical violence and aggression. Rather, sexual, verbal, and psychological forms of abuse are all included under the rubric of spousal violence.

One of the most clearly articulated models of spouse abuse is provided by O'Leary and his colleagues (O'Leary, 1987; O'Leary & Arias, 1987a,b; O'Leary, Malone, & Tyree, 1989). This social learning paradigm implicates five major etiological factors in spouse abuse. These include: (a) violence in the family of origin (observation of parental aggression; being beaten as a child), (b) aggression as a personality style, (c) stress, (d) alcohol use and abuse, and (e) relationship dissatisfaction (O'Leary, 1987). According to this theory, spouse abuse is a multiply determined phenomenon with the aforementioned variables interacting in a manner that leads to abusive behavior. This model is currently under investigation through extensive longitudinal research conducted by O'Leary and his associates.

To summarize, child abuse is an act of harmful commission toward a child. Child neglect is an act of omission endangering a child's health and well-being. Spouse abuse is an act of violence that may be physical, sexual, verbal, and/or psychological in nature. Contemporary theorists recognize that family violence is not explainable from a unidimensional theory. Rather, there is a convergence of support for the view that multiple family, child, and broader environmental (ecological) issues impinge on this problem.

ASSESSMENT

Child Abuse and Neglect

Assessing child abuse and neglect is not possible through standardized devices such as intelligence testing or personality assessment and diagnosis. However, there are certain environmental variables (e.g., poverty) and adult and child characteristics that predict these problems. Also, direct observation of parent–child interactions, conditions of safety and cleanliness, and the amount of parental community/social support all warrant attention (Lutzker, 1984; Wahler, 1980; Walker, Bonner, & Kaufman, 1988). Further, substance abuse by parents, a personal history of being a victim of abuse, single-parent status, and unemployment are additional factors that predict abuse by adults. Several characteristics of children also appear to predict child abuse and neglect. Some of these are: multiply handicapping conditions, whiny or "colicy" behavior, hyperactivity, noncompliance, and prematurity (see Ammerman, Cassisi, Hersen, & Van Hasselt, 1986; Ammerman, Van Hasselt, & Hersen, 1988). It has been observed that two behavioral extremes often suggest that a child has been maltreated: (a) extreme social withdrawal, or (b) extreme attachment and dependence on nonfamilial adults.

To obtain relevant information concerning maltreatment, interviewing and self-report methods have been commonly employed strategies. To obtain reliable parental reports regarding child maltreatment, Ammerman, Hersen, and Van Hasselt (1988) designed the Child Abuse and Neglect Interview Schedule (CANIS). The CANIS is a semi-structured interview used to evaluate presence of maltreatment behaviors (e.g., corporal punishment) and factors associated with abuse, such as history of maltreatment. Although originally developed for families with children with disabilities, this 45-minute interview can be utilized with families of nondisabled children as well.

The Child Abuse Potential Inventory (CAPI; Milner, 1986) was devised to detect at-risk status. In addition to an Abuse Potential Scale, the CAPI includes three validity scales (Inconsistency, Lie, Random Responding). Although this measure has been used primarily as a screening device, psychometric characteristics (e.g., temporal stability, convergent and predictive validity) appear to be adequate (Kaufman & Walker, 1986; Milner, 1986). Because of the possibility of misclassification, it has been recommended that the CAPI be employed in conjunction with other indexes of abuse (Kaufman & Walker, 1986).

Hally, Polansky, and Polansky (1980) developed the Childhood Level of Living

Scale (CLLS) as a method of scaling essential components of child care and neglect. This instrument targets parents of children ages 4 through 7 years and consists of 99 items that encompass nine factors; four of these factors are descriptive of emotional/cognitive (psychological) care, and five are descriptive of physical care.

Self-reports of anger and arousal also have been included in recent child abuse research. For example, the Novaco Anger Control Scale (NACS; Novaco, 1975) has been used to evaluate anger and arousal control problems that parents may be having. The NACS consists of brief descriptions of situations involving provocation in which the respondent endorses the degree of anger he or she would experience if that event should occur. Sample items include "You are talking to someone and they do not answer you," and "Noise and disorder at the dinner table." A 5-point scale of arousal level is used for scoring of each of the items comprising this scale. The MacMillan-Olson-Hansen Anger Control Scale was specifically designed to assess anger experienced by abusing parents in response to difficult child behaviors. This measure requires parents to rate 50 child-related situations as problematic or nonproblematic. Further, respondents are asked to rate the degree of anger elicited by each scenario using a 5-point scale.

Another target of behavioral assessment in recent child abuse investigations is family problem-solving skills. One approach used for this purpose is the Parent Problem-Solving Instrument (PPSI; Azar et al., 1984). The PPSI includes 10 "child-bearing problem situations" and adheres to a means–end problem-solving approach. All responses on this device are scored on the following dimensions: number of items on which relevant solutions are provided, total number of means given, number of items on which multiple means are given, number of means on which elaboration occurred, and total number of content categories that were employed. Azar et al. (1984) found that the PPSI discriminated between groups of abusive/neglectful mothers and nonmaltreatment control mothers.

Hansen et al. (1989) examined the utility of a problem-solving measure that evaluates these abilities in both child- and non-child-related domains. The Parental Problem-Solving Measure (PPSM) classifies problematic situations into five areas: (a) child behavior and management, (b) anger and stress control, (c) interpersonal problems, (d) financial, and (e) child-care resources. Responses to this 25-item instrument are rated for number and effectiveness of solutions generated. The advantage of the PPSM is in determining whether problem-solving deficits in maltreatment parents are specific to child-management difficulties, or whether they are generalizable across areas.

Spouse Abuse

Assessment of spouse abuse typically has consisted of clinical interviews with the battered spouse to ascertain: (a) whether abuse is currently occurring; (b) the medical condition of the abused spouse and the needs (medical, nutritional, psychological) of any children in the household; (c) the potential for abuse and level of endangerment in homes where abusive behavior is not presently being exhibited, but has been emitted in the past; (d) the psychological and psychiatric status (e.g., depression, anxiety, suicidal ideation) of the abused individual (see Geffner & Pagelow, 1990; Margolin, 1987). In addition, an effort is made to obtain evidence of major risk factors that have been associated with spouse abuse. For example, the assessor will attempt to obtain knowledge of: the client's experience with abuse and violence (i.e., history of marital violence in the family of origin), vulnerability factors (e.g., unemployment, high stress levels) that increase the probability of subsequent violence, and available sources of social and financial support.

Several self-report methods also have been utilized in spouse abuse research. Most notably, assaultive behavior has been evaluated in numerous investigations with the Conflict Tactics Scale (CTS) developed by Straus (1979). The CTS evaluates the types of behaviors that couples employ in resolving conflicts or differences. Behaviors range from the use of discussion, debate, and reasoning in resolving conflicts (Reasoning Scale) to the application of verbal behaviors that harm or threaten the spouse (Verbal Aggression Scale). The CTS also includes behaviors that attempt to physically injure the partner. These "tactics" are rated on a 7-point scale (0 = never; 6 = more than 20 times). In their investigations of the efficacy of behavioral treatment with spouse abusers, Saunders and Hanusa (1986) and Hamberger and Hastings (1988) employed the CTS for purposes of screening and treatment outcome measurement, respectively.

Typically, less formal and systematic approaches to assessment have been noted. In some studies, frequency of abusive episodes, as reported by violent males receiving treatment, have been the primary outcome measure (e.g., Edleson, Miller, Stone, & Chapman, 1985). In others, an attempt has been made to corroborate the males' reports by obtaining spouses' input as well (Edleson & Grusznski, 1989). Other investigators have administered multiple self-report measures for purposes of assessment and to determine treatment outcome. For example, in an evaluation of the effectiveness of cognitive-behavioral skills training with spouse abusers, Hamberger and Hastings (1988) employed the Millon Clinical Multiaxial Inventory (Millon, 1983), the Novaco Anger Scale, the Conflict Tactics Scale, and the Beck Depression Inventory (Beck, Ward, Mendelson, Moch, & Erbaugh, 1961). The latter measure also has been commonly employed in evaluating depressive symptomatology in victims of marital violence (Meyers-Abell & Jansen, 1980).

As with child maltreatment, assessment of problem-solving skills in marital violence also has been a focus of clinical and investigative endeavors. Launius and Jensen (1987) used six interpersonal problem situations (three abusive and three general) to assess "alternative generation and response evaluation components of the overall problem-solving process" in battered women. An example of a problem situation is as follows: "You and a friend are standing in a long line outside of a theater hoping that you will be able to get tickets. Two people walk up to their friend standing in line and ask if they could cut in. Their friend says yes. You don't appreciate this. What can you do?" (p.156). After reading each of the situations, subjects were asked to "list all the possible things they could do in that situation to help solve the problem." Responses were scored on the basis of total number of alternatives generated, total number of effective alternatives generated, and the type of alternative chosen for use in the situations. These indexes were shown to differentiate battered women from controls.

In an effort to provide more direct measurement of problem-solving skills in maritally violent couples, Morrison, Van Hasselt, and Bellack (1987) had abusive–maritally discordant–nonabusive, and normal couples participate in two 12-minute dyadic problem-solving interactions. These discussions were videotaped and retrospectively rated on several verbal behaviors: response duration, praise/appreciation, open-ended questions, interruptions, agreements, disagreements, and compromise/suggestion. Although interesting from a procedural and methodological standpoint, this strategy failed to discriminate between groups.

Another area that has been examined is assertion in abusive couples. Early case descriptions portrayed abusive males as pathologically passive and dependent (Faulk, 1974; Shainess, 1977), submissive, and less verbally fluent than their wives (Snell, Rosenwald, & Robey, 1964). Victims of abuse have been described as aggressive and socially immature (Scott, 1974) as well as unassertive with their spouses (Davidson, 1978; Rosenbaum & O'Leary, 1981). More empirically based efforts, however, have shown that abusive couples are not significantly different from nonabusive–maritally discordant couples on indexes of assertion (see O'Leary & Curley, 1986). Moreover, there are indications that when assertion deficits are observed, it is the abusive male who is in need of skills remediation (Rosenbaum & O'Leary, 1981).

To measure assertion in abusive partners, O'Leary and Curley (1986) developed a spouse-specific measure of assertive and aggressive behaviors within the marital context. This 29-item instrument consists of two parts: one evaluates assertive behaviors directed specifically toward one's spouse; the other measures aggressive responses directed toward one's spouse. An example of an item on the assertive subscale is: "I can express a differing point of view to my mate without much difficulty." Other assertion measures that have been employed in behavioral research on spouse abuse include the Wolpe-Lazarus Assertiveness Scale (Wolpe & Lazarus, 1966) and the Adult Self Expression Scale (Gay, Hollandsworth, & Galassi, 1975).

The assessment of spouse abuse is a complex process. As Geffner and Pagelow (1990) cogently pointed out, "[since] both victims and their abusers are likely to minimize or deny the occurrence of spousal violence, professionals need to draw upon their training, experience, and their observational skills to make accurate assessments" (pp. 121–122). Further complicating evaluative efforts are data confirming that abusers and victims provide different reports, even when both admit to the violence (O'Leary & Arias, 1988). In most cases, the wife is likely to be a more reliable informant since she is on the receiving end of the violent behavior. Moreover, impaired memory of behaviors during rage episodes, excessive concern about others' perceptions of their social undesirability, and psychological defensiveness all point to the potentially suspect veridicality of the perpetrators' reports (Elliot, 1976; Rosenbaum & Maiuro, 1990). It is apparent that multiple and varied assessment methods are called for in evaluations of spouse abuse.

TREATMENT

Child Abuse and Neglect

The two predominant therapeutic strategies directed toward child abuse and neglect can be broadly characterized as social work, with emphasis on providing families a number of services (Bryce & Lloyd, 1981), and behavioral intervention, with emphasis on the direct treatment of mitigating problems (e.g., parenting, stress control). Although social work programs may have some value in ameliorating certain difficulties related to child maltreatment, the lack of individual case material and program evaluation data usually does not permit clear evaluation and replication of these programs (Lutzker & Newman, 1986).

A variety of behavioral treatment strategies has been applied. Some of these include teaching parents to praise their children (Gilbert, 1976), behavior management (Wolfe, Kaufman, Aragona, & Sandler, 1981), stress reduction (Jacobson, 1938; Schilling & Poppen, 1983), and what Wahler and Dumas (1986) call "mand review," in which mothers are taught to review the manner in which they present commands and other antecedent cues to their children.

Illustrative of behavior management approaches to child maltreatment is the programmatic research that has been conducted over the past decade by Wolfe and his colleagues (e.g., Wolfe, 1987; Wolfe et al., 1982; Wolfe & Sandler, 1981; Wolfe, Sandler, & Kaufman, 1981). For example, Wolfe et al. (1982) reported a case study on the use of parent training to diminish "abuse-related" responses with a mother who emitted high rates of aversive behaviors toward her three children. Treatment incorporated the "bug-in-the-ear" device to provide feedback to the parent during interactions with her children. Through this procedure, prompts were provided to decrease rates of hostile physical and verbal statements. Training also involved instructions, prompting, and feedback to increase positive parent behaviors (praise, hugs, pats). A multiple baseline design across targeted behaviors indicated a reduction in hostile parent responses and increased positive behaviors as a function of the behavioral intervention. Further, gains were maintained in both the clinic and home settings at a 2-month follow-up.

In a second study (Wolfe & Sandler, 1981), three abusive mothers and their families received training in parenting effectiveness strategies and contingency contracting. Parent training consisted of readings in child management and problem-solving instruction to more effectively deal with challenging behaviors exhibited by children. In contingency contracting, parents were delivered a previously selected reinforcer contingent on their use of certain child management techniques (e.g., token reinforcement procedures). Results of a two-variable withdrawal design indicated that the combined treatment strategy led to a substantial decrease in maladaptive interactions. Further, improvement was still observed at 3-, 8-, and 12-month follow-up assessments.

Wolfe et al. (1981) examined the efficacy of group sessions that included: (a) child management training—problem solving and modeling of appropriate child management approaches; (b) stress management and anger control—deep muscle relaxation, reinforcing self-statements; (c) developmental education—films and readings in human development and child management. This approach also included training and behavior rehearsal in the home setting. Improvements in parenting skills showed up in home observations, as well as parental and caseworker reports. A 1-year follow-up revealed that no episodes of child abuse occurred among treated parents.

One of the first efforts directed toward early intervention and prevention of child maltreatment was recently conducted by Wolfe, Edwards, Manion, and Koverola (1988). Here, 30 mother–child dyads at risk for child abuse were randomly assigned to either an information/personal growth group provided by a child protection agency, or a behavior parent-training-plus-information group. Parent training included instruction in "fundamental child management skills" via modeling, instructions, and therapist and videotape feedback. In addition, activities (prompting, behavior rehearsal) to improve children's adaptive abilities (e.g., language and social skills) were employed. Further, *in vivo* desensitization was provided to parents in the behavioral prevention group. Information/personal growth group controls participated in social activities (arts and crafts) and discussions of health- and family-related topics (e.g., nutrition). There were significant improvements in parenting skills and child problems following treatment and at a 3-month follow-up for mothers who received the behavioral treatment. Also, caseworker ratings of participants' maltreatment risk and child management skills were significantly greater for the behavioral condition.

In an examination of the potential differential treatment effects of the types of components applied by Wolfe et al. (1981), Egan (1983) compared stress management, child management training, and a waiting-list control condition of abusive parents. Although child management training led to improvements in parenting skills, stress management produced changes in parental feelings.

Azar (1984) compared the following treatment conditions: (a) cognitive-behavioral treatment that included child management training, stress management training, communication work, and cognitive restructuring; (b) insight-oriented treatment; (c) a waiting-list control condition. A group treatment approach was used that included home visits between sessions. Azar (1984) found improvements in the home and in caseworker reports for both treatment conditions relative to waiting-list controls; no differences between interventions were observed at the end of treatment. However, a 1-year follow-up indicated that only the cognitive-behavioral group showed no recidivism at a 1-year follow-up.

There are estimates that between 22% and 50% of abuse cases involve adolescents (Pagelow, 1989). Yet, investigations concerning treatment of abusive families with children in this age group are virtually nonexistent. One exception is a report by Schellenbach and Guerney (1987), which described a multiple component behavioral approach that included training in: empathic communication and negotiation skills, problem solving, goal setting, reinforcement, and constructing behavioral contracts. Incentives (lottery prizes) also were utilized to increase attendance and compliance. Training was provided over seven group sessions and produced positive consumer satisfaction ratings. Unfortunately, no outcome data were reported.

Each of these behavioral interventions seems logical in that poor parenting techniques, inability to control stress, and other deficiencies have been identified as parental characteristics that contribute to child maltreatment (see Lutzker, 1990). However, there are two limitations with these strategies. First, most reports of these techniques have been limited to a small number of families. Thus, issues of external validity are pertinent. Second, previous theories would conclude that, although teaching parents new behavior management techniques might improve parent–child relationships, future incidents of child abuse and neglect are not likely to be prevented without examining and treating other problems in the family "ecosystem."

ECOBEHAVIORAL APPROACHES

With multiple etiologic factors in child maltreatment, it seems only logical that to be effective and durable, treatment must address as many of these variables as possible. This is the essence of the ecobehavioral approach. From an ecobehavioral perspective, child abuse is viewed as a multifaceted problem requiring multifaceted and comprehensive assessment and treatment. "Eco" is derived from ecology, a view of the family not unlike other ecosystems in nature. For example, it is well known how interdependent animals and plant life are in a tidepool. Any change in the animal or plant life necessarily affects all other life in the tidepool. An ecobehavioral perspective views the family in a similar manner.

The "behavioral" aspect of ecobehavioral refers to the direct methodologies of behavior analysis and therapy. This focus involves behavioral assessment utilizing primarily direct observation of behavior and the use of single-case experimental designs. This *methodology* is not necessarily tied to a given set of *procedures*. For example, although many traditional behavior modification techniques might be employed (e.g., positive reinforcement for teaching parents child management, progressive muscle relaxation for reducing stress in a parent), humanistic counseling procedures might also be used. However, any strategies that are implemented are nonetheless examined within the *methodology* of behavior analysis.

Another hallmark of ecobehavioral intervention is *in situ* treatment. Specifically, all services are provided in homes, in schools, or in day-care or foster-care sites—that is, wherever problem behavior occurs. *In situ* treatment is based on the premise that behavior change is more likely to be durable and generalize when treatment is provided in the actual setting in which the problems are occurring. Further support of *in situ* treatment is that many families would find it very difficult to attend treatment at clinics outside of their homes.

Thus, ecobehavioral treatment resembles social work services in that multiple, often community-oriented, interventions are provided. Yet, the directive and empirical nature of ecobehavioral strategies distinguishes them from other social services.

Project 12-Ways is an ecobehavioral approach to child abuse and neglect. Lutzker, Frame, and Rice (1982) first described the multiple treatment services offered by Project 12-Ways. These included: parent training, stress reduction for parents, assertiveness training, self-control training for parents, basic skill training for children, reciprocity marital counseling, job finding, money management, health maintenance and nutrition, home safety, and a single-parent prevention program. Operational since 1979, Project 12-Ways periodically augments, reduces, or modifies these original services.

Lutzker, Wesch, and Rice (1984) identified four ways to assess the impact of a model such as Project 12-Ways. These are: clinical; single-case experimental designs; controlled multiple research with families; and program evaluation. Clinical refers to the methodology of a behavioral approach that focuses on data collection. Most data obtained from the 75 to 100 families seen annually by Project 12-Ways are not publishable because: (a) reliability observations often cannot be conducted, (b) the data might be exclusively self-report, or (c) adequate experimental design was not employed. These "clinical" data are not, however, without value. They can be used to demonstrate treatment progress (or lack thereof) to parents. In addition, they can be employed in counselor supervision (Rice & Lutzker, 1983) and in the treatment process. For example, a mother might criticize her child less frequently after being asked to self-record daily criticisms.

Several illustrations of single-case designs have been reported by Project 12-Ways investigators. Rosenfield-Schlichter, Sarber, Bueno, Greene, and Lutzker (1983) used a variation of a withdrawal design to examine the separate and combined roles of a contingent allowance, state-provided homemaker services, and follow-up visits by counselors. Each condition produced improved hygiene in the young boy and young girl who were victims of neglect in their home.

In another single-case experiment, Campbell, O'Brien, Bickett, and Lutzker (1983) initiated in-home relaxation procedures to reduce migraine headaches in a self-referred mother. This client was concerned that she might kill her noncompliant 4-year-old daughter if she did not obtain professional assistance. Once the frequency of headaches was greatly reduced, systematic parent training was provided. This produced large increases in child compliance. Then, marital counseling was provided to both parents. This procedure increased marital satisfaction. Through counseling, the husband acquiesced to the wife's returning to her previous nursing position. The resultant improved family income allowed the child to spend some time in day-care, instead of being home with her mother all day. Overall, relationships in this family ecosystem changed considerably as a function of the ecobehavioral services that were provided.

A third single-case design was described by Sarber, Halasz, Messmer, Bickett, and Lutzker (1983). This study involved a 4-year-old child who had been removed from her home because of maternal neglect (lack of adequate nutrition). The mother in this case was illiterate and had moderate mental retardation. Using match-to-sample procedures involving imitation and social reinforcement, the mother was taught to plan a week of nutritious meals. This was accomplished by placing pictures of foods representing the four major food groups in envelopes on a large planning board. Each food group was color-coded such that the pictures were placed on cards that represented a particular food group. Four different colored cards ran along the bottom of the planning board. In order to "plan," the mother matched a picture of a food (the color of its card) with a card on the board. After planning meals, she once again used a match-to-sample procedure by finding a matched picture of the food picture that she had placed on the planning board. These pictures were placed individually in pages of clear plastic in a two-ring binder which thus served as a "shopping list." The mother then took the list to the store where she again matched pictures, this time from the shopping list to actual store products. A pre–posttest design demonstrated the effects of training on meal planning. Further, a multiple baseline design across food groups showed the success of the training procedures on shopping. With additional support in the way of parent training and other counseling, the child was successfully returned to her natural home. Lengthy follow-up showed that the mother was able to maintain her nutritious meal planning and shopping skills.

Finally, a single-case study documented generalization of parenting skills with a neglectful mother of a 4-year-old boy (Dachman, Halasz, Bickett, & Lutzker, 1984). The mother was trained to use descriptive praise and discrete, simple commands during structured, unstructured, and academic sessions with her son. In addition to measuring child compliance and maternal commands and praise, observers surreptitiously recorded how often the mother criticized her son during these sessions. As praise and appropriate commands by the mother increased, and child compliance increased, maternal criticisms of the child, which were quite evident during baseline, nearly disappeared. Counselors also utilized problem-solving strategies to assist this mother in finding day-care for her son, employment, and improved housing.

The above-mentioned single-case experiments are characterized by reliable data and employment of adequate research designs. However, the external validity of the findings remains open to question. Until replicated, the procedures in these studies are not known to be effective with families other than the particular ones with which they have been implemented. Yet, the empirical nature of these efforts provides evidence of the utility of specific behavioral procedures in the treatment of factors that contribute to child maltreatment.

Research using single-case designs with multiple families or investigations including group designs extend the generality of treatment strategies. For example, Tertinger, Greene, and Lutzker (1984) developed an assessment device to quantify safety hazards accessible to children in the homes of families referred for child abuse and neglect. The Home Accident Prevention Inventory (HAPI) (Tertinger, Greene, & Lutzker, 1988) was employed to assess hazardous categories such as fire and electrical, solid and liquid poison, and suffocation items. Additionally, individual items within these categories were tallied. After the homes of six families were assessed with the HAPI to collect baseline data, a counselor-education program was provided to each family on methods for improving the safety conditions in their homes. A multiple baseline design across hazardous categories showed the positive impact of the counselor-education program as determined by the HAPI in unannounced follow-up visits.

Although effective, the counselor-education program provided by Tertinger et al. (1984) was "labor-intensive" and may have been dependent on the unique skills of the counselor who delivered it. Therefore, in a systematic replication, Barone, Greene, and Lutzker (1986) developed a slide–tape program, along with a manual that presented safety information similar to that which was provided by the counselor in the previous study. The program was delivered in three showings to each of three participating families; no other counselor interventions regarding home safety were provided. Considerable reductions in hazards in the homes across families were found on the HAPI in several long-term unannounced follow-up visits.

An assessment device similar to the HAPI, the Checklist for Living Environments to Assess Neglect (CLEAN), was designed to assess filth and clutter in homes of families referred for severe neglect due to extraordinary lack of normal hygiene (Watson-Perczel, Lutzker, Greene, & McGimpsey, 1988). Individual motivation systems were then developed to assist families in reducing filth and clutter in their homes. Multiple baseline designs across rooms in each home showed that whenever motivation programs were put into effect in a particular room, CLEAN scores improved considerably. These motivation programs included feedback, such as a "pie-chart" showing the degree to which improvements had been made, or posted instant-camera photos. Feedback was often "backed up" by positive reinforcers (e.g., activities with counselors, extended visits of children who had been temporarily removed from the home).

Affective adult–child interactions were examined in two families referred for abuse (Lutzker, Megson, Webb, & Dachman, 1985). Parents were taught a number of previously validated adult–child interaction skills in order to improve their affect with their children, which had been shown lacking during baseline observations. Some of these skills included behaviors such as leveling (i.e., interacting with children at their eye level), voice intonation, and passive touch. A multiple baseline design across families revealed improvement not only in the skills parents were taught with the "target" children, but with those children's siblings, with whom the parents had not been trained. Also, affect training for parents increased positive child behaviors and compliance at rates usually observed only with structured behavior management training that focuses on positive reinforcement and time-out procedures. It might be argued that affect training is more natural, and perhaps more effective in the long run, than more traditional behavior management strategies (Lutzker, Touchette, & Campbell, 1988).

Prompting procedures were used to teach young single mothers who were at high risk for child abuse to engage in stimulation activities with their babies (Lutzker, Lutzker, Braunling-McMorrow, & Eddleman, 1987). Multiple baseline designs across responses (use of affectionate words and guided play) showed considerable increases in mother–baby stimulation in several single-parent families. Delgado and Lutzker (1988) taught young single parents to identify and report their babies' illnesses. Multiple baseline designs across pairs of parents demonstrated the utility of a structured education program in teaching a number of important medically related skills.

Program evaluation attempts to ascertain the effectiveness of services provided. In the case of child abuse and neglect, this means examining recurring episodes during treatment and following termination of formal intervention. In three program evaluations (Lutzker & Rice, 1984, 1987; Lutzker, Wesch, & Rice, 1984), Project 12-Ways data have consistently shown: (a) dramatic decreases in child maltreatment and (b) lower rates of recidivism among Project 12-Ways families relative to comparison families in the same region who received services elsewhere. Lutzker and Newman (1986) have suggested that all large-scale projects undergo systematic and ongoing program evaluation.

Spouse Abuse

Victims

There is surprising lack of research concerning intervention strategies for victims of spouse abuse. Most treatment efforts directed toward victims have been carried out in the context of women's shelters that have emerged over the past several years to deal with the deleterious effects of marital violence. With regard to treatment goals, Geffner and Pagelow (1990) pointed out that "individual treatment of battered women in a shelter or similar setting has primarily focused on empowering the victim, reducing social isolation, providing social advocacy, reducing dependence, increasing assertiveness, and improving self-esteem . . . the main concern is to remove the victim from the violent home and eliminate contact with the abuser in order to maintain her safety" (pp. 126–127).

Most shelters typically offer supportive and therapeutic process groups for residents who have been abused. However, in recent years, an increasing proportion of programs have utilized a variety of behavioral interventions to improve social and emotional adjustment and to increase decision making, interpersonal effectiveness (e.g., assertiveness), and problem-solving skills in victims of abuse. Some of the specific techniques that have been used include: systematic desensitization to reduce levels of stress and anxiety; anger management to deal with feelings of anger and outrage associated with being a victim of violence; cognitive restructuring and rational-emotive strategies (Ellis & Harper, 1975) to diminish feelings of self-blame, hopelessness, and depression; problem-solving and conflict resolution skills training to enable the individual to identify options, carry out adaptive responses, and resolve current difficulties; assertion training to increase independence and the ability to stand up for one's rights and deny unreasonable requests.

Considerable investigative attention has focused on assertiveness in abused women (Martin, 1976), although the utility of assertion training with this population has been questioned on at least two accounts (see discussion by O'Leary, Curley, Rosenbaum, & Clarke, 1985). First, although there are indications that many abusive males demonstrate deficiencies in assertion, there is a lack of data attesting to assertion deficits in battered women (e.g., Rosenbaum & O'Leary, 1981). Second, and more important, there is evidence that a wife's assertive response to a violent male may further elevate levels of danger and aggression (Ball & Wyman, 1978). However, in abusive couples who choose to remain together, O'Leary et al. (1985) contend that "assertion training for battered women in the context of broad spectrum therapy may be appropriate if general issues, that is, ones outside the marital unit, are addressed. Gaining confidence in handling situations in an assertive way outside the home may increase self-esteem, and may help a battered woman feel less intimidated, more in control of her situation, and less fearful of leaving an intolerable situation" (p. 321).

Meyers-Abell and Jansen (1980) provided a case illustration of assertion training with a battered woman. In this report, the client was an 18-year-old woman with three young children. She had been abused for nearly 4 years and received 10 sessions of group assertion training during a 1-month stay at a shelter for battered women. Some of the topics that were covered in the group included: distinctions among passive, aggressive, and appropriately assertive behavior; verbal and nonverbal components of assertion; personal rights; and dealing with feelings of depression, anxiety, guilt, and hostility. Results indicated improved scores on measures of depression and assertiveness following assertion training. Further, the client continued to have difficulties with her husband after leaving the shelter, and she eventually filed for divorce.

Perpetrators

Individual and group treatment programs for abusive males have been conducted for at least a decade (e.g., Eddy & Myers, 1984; Frank & Houghton, 1982). Illustrative is the work of Edleson and his colleagues (Edleson, 1984; Edleson & Grusznski, 1988; Edleson, Miller, Stone, & Chapman, 1985), who designed a multielement group behavioral strategy for abusive men. Treatment ingredients consist of:

1. Self-monitoring of behavioral antecedents to angry feelings and outbursts;
2. Cognitive restructuring to remediate faulty thinking styles and irrational belief systems;
3. Interpersonal problem-solving skills training to adaptively resolve conflicts in the home;
4. Relaxation training to develop a response incompatible with irritation or anger.

Edleson et al. (1985) examined the effects of the above-mentioned intervention in a multiple baseline design across three groups, each composed of three males (age range, 21 to 40 years) with a history of physical aggression toward their spouses. Groups were conducted over a 12-week period with a 2- to 2½-hour meeting each week. Participants were asked to self-report any episodes of violence that occurred over the course of treatment. Diminished rates of physical battering were noted as a function of treatment. Further, gains were maintained in seven of the nine participants in follow-ups ranging up to 21 weeks. These findings are encouraging, but the veridicality of males' self-reports, the only basis of measurement in this study, is suspect.

In one of the few large-scale efforts to quantify treatment outcomes, Edleson and Grusznski (1989) analyzed 4 years' evaluation data obtained from treatment programs for batterers. A group of 156 males who completed treatment were compared with 67 males who failed to complete the program. Treatment involved orientation meetings (reviews of cues and alternatives to violence), supportive self-help groups, and structured therapy groups (relaxation training, monitoring of antecedents, altering self-statements). Edleson and Grusznski (1989) found that approximately two-thirds of the completers were not violent at follow-up (average interval of 9.5 months). In addition, almost half of the noncompleters were reported to be nonviolent as well.

With violent males Saunders and Hanusa (1986) implemented a cognitive-behavioral intervention that involved assertion training, relaxation training, cognitive restructuring, and consciousness raising that dealt with violence. The goals of this program were to "impart skills which are incompatible with aggression" and to develop "attitudes which are associated with nonviolent marriages, attitudes which support sex-role equality, and egalitarian decision-making" (p. 359). Evaluation of pre–post treatment differences for the 92 male participants, who received 20 sessions of treatment, revealed significant improvements on measures of depression, anger, jealousy, and attitudes concerning women's roles. Although these results are encouraging, the lack of a comparison group and follow-up data suggest that the results must be interpreted with caution.

Another cognitive-behavioral approach for wife batterers was presented by Hamberger and Hastings (1988). These investigators applied cognitive restructuring, communication/assertion training, and active-coping relaxation training to 32 abusive males over 12 2½-hour weekly group meetings. Thirty-six program dropouts comprised the comparison group. There was a significant decrease in violence following treatment and up to a 1-year follow-up for completers. However, evidence of continued psychological abuse, associated with unchanged personality disturbances in these men, was observed after termination of the intervention.

Couples Therapy

Several reports have described the application of couples therapy to relationships that are characterized by marital violence. This has been an area of some controversy due to the potential for physical and/or psychological harm in women who remain with a violent spouse (Margolin, Sibner, & Gleberman, 1988). However, it is estimated that nearly 50% of battered women return to their abusive environments; and many of them are battered again (Gondolf & Fisher, 1988). Rosenbaum and O'Leary (1981) made several recommendations that are relevant to the consideration of conjoint therapy for abusive couples. Of paramount importance is determining whether the wife is safe in her current situation. Also, the wife's knowledge and awareness of alternative interventions must be evaluated. Yet, as Margolin (1979) underscored, "Proposing conjoint marital therapy as one alternative in working with abusive couples does not imply that preservation of the marriage is appropriate for all abusing couples. In the case where one partner is in danger of physical harm that cannot be contained through stopgap measures directed toward the couple, the most therapeutic course is for the couple to terminate rather than work on the relationship" (p. 14).

For cases where the wife is not in danger of physical harm and the couple expresses the desire to improve their marital relationship, Margolin (1979) proposed a multiple-component behavioral treatment program. Based on a social learning conceptualization of family violence, this intervention combines the following elements:

1. Identification of anger cues,
2. Establishment of ground rules,
3. Development of an action plan,
4. De-cueing the victim (i.e., eliminating behaviors that serve as antecedents for verbal or physical assaults),
5. Modification of faulty cognitions regarding the marital relationship,
6. Initiation of problem-solving skills training,
7. Improving the general tone of the relationship.

Margolin (1979) presented a case illustration of the successful implementation of her approach. This strategy has become a model for current clinical efforts with abusive couples.

Linquist, Telch, and Taylor (1983) also employed a broad-spectrum behavioral intervention for abusing couples. Here, a combination of communication skills, anger control, stress management, and problem-solving skills training was applied. Couples were more assertive and satisfied with their marriages following treatment. In addition, they reported less anger, aggression, and jealousy. Although no episodes of violence occurred at the end of therapy, improvement was not consistently maintained across all participants at a 6-week follow-up assessment.

Many community-based service providers now offer a combination of cognitive-behavioral and psychoeducational approaches with abusive couples. For example, anger and stress management techniques, along with assertion and problem-solving skills training, are increasingly being used. Often, "nonviolence contracts" are developed and appear to be most effective during initial treatment phases (Rosenbaum & O'Leary, 1986). The purpose of these contracts is to eliminate abusive episodes while attempting to enhance the overall quality of family life in couples who have sought to remain together and improve their relationship.

SUMMARY AND FUTURE DIRECTIONS

Recent surveys and epidemiological data indicate that child maltreatment and spouse abuse have grown to epidemic proportions in this country. Behavioral clinicians and researchers have responded to these increasing problems and their deleterious effects with a proliferation of assessment and treatment efforts in recent years. Behavioral models of both child and spousal violence have been articulated and are undergoing continuous empirical study. In light of the urgent need for treatment of victims as well as perpetrators of family violence, there has been a burgeoning number of behavioral intervention studies with these populations over the past decade. Significant gains in application of behavioral methods have been made, particularly in the area of child maltreatment. However, behavioral approaches with these problems clearly are at the nascent stage. Continued investigation is needed to expand the behavioral assessment and treatment strategies developed to date in the categories reviewed in this chapter. In particular, there is a need for more comprehensive and broad-spectrum evaluation of family characteristics, risk factors, and treatment outcome for all forms of family violence. As Ammerman (1990) pointed out with regard to child maltreatment, "The etiology of child abuse and neglect is multifactorial and complex. There are multiple pathways to maltreatment that combine and interact in nonlinear ways. No single causative factor has emerged" (p. 249). These statements are equally relevant for the problem of spouse abuse. However, the techniques of behavioral assessment, with their emphasis on objective measurement of clearly specified behaviors (Wolfe & Bordeau, 1987) are particularly well-suited to the tasks of: (a) determining factors of etiologic significance, (b) identifying problem areas, and (c) evaluating treatment outcome.

Another area requiring increased attention from behavioral researchers in the future is education and prevention. With rare exceptions in the field of child maltreatment (Wolfe et al., 1988; Wolfe & Manion, 1984), few inroads have been made in either family violence education or prevention. Yet, in considering strategies for wide-scale reduction of family violence, Margolin (1987) pointed out that "the goal of reducing the overall incidence of wife battering can be achieved only through community-based prevention programs" (p. 112). The same goal has been discussed elsewhere concerning the primary and secondary prevention of child abuse and neglect (Ammerman, 1990; Rosenberg & Reppucci, 1985). Indeed, the ever increasing prevalence of family violence, the recalcitrance of associated forms of family dysfunction, the severely debilitating effects of child and spouse abuse, and the alarmingly high recidivism rates of these disorders all dictate that such efforts must be a priority in future investigative endeavors.

REFERENCES

Ammerman, R. T. (1990). Etiological models of child maltreatment. *Behavior Modification, 14,* 230-254.

Ammerman, R. T., Cassisi, J. E., Hersen, M., & Van Hasselt, V. B. (1986). Consequences of physical abuse and neglect in children. *Clinical Psychology Review, 6,* 291-310.

Ammerman, R. T., Van Hasselt, V. B., & Hersen, M. (1988). Maltreatment of handicapped children: A critical review. *Journal of Family Violence, 3,* 53-73.

Azar, S. T. (1984). *An evaluation of the effectiveness of cognitive-behavioral versus insight-oriented mothers groups with child maltreaters.* Unpublished doctoral dissertation, University of Rochester.

Ball, P. G., & Wyman, E. (1978). Battered wives and powerlessness: What can counselors do? *Victimology: An International Journal, 2,* 545-552.

Barone, V. J., Greene, B. F., & Lutzker, J. R. (1986). Home safety with families being treated for child abuse and neglect. *Behavior Modification, 10,* 93-114.

Beck, A., Ward, C., Mendelson, M., Moch, J., & Erbaugh, J. (1961). An inventory for measuring depression. *Archives of General Psychiatry, 4,* 561-571.

Bryce, M., & Lloyd, J. C. (Eds.). (1981). *Treating families in theme.* Beverly Hills, CA: Sage.

Campbell, R. V., O'Brien, S., Bickett, A., & Lutzker, J. R. (1983). In-home parent-training, treatment of migraine headaches, and marital counseling as an ecobehavioral approach to prevent child abuse. *Journal of Behavior Therapy and Experimental Psychiatry, 14,* 147-154. (Indexed in the *Inventory of Marriage and Family Literature, Vol. X,* Family Resource Center, 1984.)

Dachman, R. S., Halasz, M. M., Bickett, A. D. & Lutzker, J. R. (1984). A home-based ecobehavioral parent-training and generalization package with a neglectful mother. *Education and Treatment of Children, 7,* 183-202.

Davidson, T. (1978). *Conjugal crime.* New York: Hawthorne Books.

Delgado, L. E., & Lutzker, J. R. (1988). Training young parents to identify and report their children's illnesses. *Journal of Applied Behavior Analysis, 21,* 311-319.

Eddy, M. J., & Myers, T. (1984). *Helping men who batter: A profile of programs in the U.S.* Arlington, TX: Texas Council on Family Violence.

Edleson, J. L. (1989). Working with men who batter. *Social Work,* 237-242.

Edleson, J. L., & Grusznski, R. J. (1988). Treating men who batter: Four years of outcome data from the domestic abuse project. *Journal of Social Service Research, 12,* 3-22.

Edleson, J. L., Miller, D. M., Stone, G. W., & Chapman, D. G. (1985). Group treatment for men who batter. *Social Work Research & Abstracts, 21,* 18-21.

Egan, K. (1983). Stress management and child management with abusive parents. *Journal of Clinical Child Psychology, 12,* 292-299.

Elliot, F. A. (1976). The neurology of explosive rage: The dyscontrol syndrome. *The Practitioner, 217,* 51-60.

Ellis, A., & Harper, R. A. (1975). *A new guide to rational living.* North Hollywood, CA: Wilshire Book Co.

Faulk, M. (1974). Men who assault their wives. *Medical Science Law, 14,* 180-183.

Frank, P. B., & Houghton, B. D. (1982). *Confronting the batterer: A guide to creating the spouse abuse workshop.* New York: Volunteer Counseling Service of Rockland County.

Gay, M. L., Hollandsworth, J. G., & Galassi, J. P. (1975). An assertiveness inventory for adults. *Journal of Counseling Psychology, 22,* 340-344.

Geffner, R., & Pagelow, M. D. (1990). Victims of spouse abuse. In R. T. Ammerman & M. Hersen (Eds.), *Treatment of family violence: A sourcebook.* New York: Wiley.

Gelles, R. J. (1980). Violence in the family: A review of research in the seventies. *Journal of Marriage and the Family, 42,* 873-885.

Gelles, R. J. (1983). An exchange/social control theory. In J. D. Finkelhor, R. J. Gelles, G. T. Hotaling, & M. A. Straus (Eds.), *The dark side of families,* (pp. 151–165). Beverly Hills, CA: Sage.

Gilbert, M. T. (1976). Behavioral approach to the treatment of child abuse. *Nursing Times, 72,* 140–143.

Gondolf, E. W., & Fisher, E. R. (1988). *Battered women as survivors.* Lexington, MA: Lexington Books.

Hally, C., Polansky, N. F., & Polansky, N. A. (1980). *Child neglect: Mobilizing services* (DHHS Publication No. OHDS 80-30257). Washington, DC: U.S. Government Printing Office.

Hamberger, L. K., & Hastings, J. E. (1988). Skills training for treatment of spouse abusers: An outcome study. *Journal of Family Violence, 3,* 121–130.

Hansen, D. J., Pallotta, G. M., Tishelman, A. C., Conaway, L. P., & MacMillan, V. M. (1989). Parental problem-solving skills and child behavior problems: A comparison of physically abusive, neglectful, clinic, and community families. *Journal of Family Violence, 4,* 353–368.

Jacobson, E. (1938). *Progressive relaxation.* Chicago: University of Chicago Press.

Kaufman, K. L., & Walker, C. E. (1986). Review of the Child Abuse Potential Inventory. In J. D. Keyser & R. C. Sweetland (Eds.), *Test critiques, Vol. 6* (pp. 55–64). Kansas City, MO: Westport.

Kempe, C. H., Silverman, E. N., Steele, B. E., Droegemueller, W., & Silver, H. K. (1962). The battered-child syndrome. *Journal of the American Medical Association, 181,* 105–112.

Launius, M. H., & Jensen, B. L. (1987). Interpersonal problem-solving skills in battered, counseling, and control women. *Journal of Family Violence, 2,* 151–162.

Linquist, C. U., Telch, C. F., & Taylor, J. (1983). Evaluation of a conjugal violence treatment program: A pilot study. *Behavioral Counseling and Community Interventions, 3,* 76–90.

Lutzker, J. R. (1984). Project 12-Ways: Treating child abuse and neglect from an ecobehavioral perspective. In R. F. Dangel and R. A. Polster (Eds.), *Parent training: Foundations of research and practice* (pp. 260–291), New York: Guilford.

Lutzker, J. R. (1990). Behavioral treatment of child neglect. *Behavior Modification, 14,* 301–315.

Lutzker, J. R., Frame, R. E., & Rice, J. M. (1982). Project 12-Ways: An ecobehavioral approach to the treatment and prevention of child abuse and neglect. *Education and Treatment of Children, 5,* 141–155.

Lutzker, S. Z., Lutzker, J. R., Braunling-McMorrow, D., & Eddleman, J. (1987). Prompting to increase mother–baby stimulation with single mothers. *Journal of Child and Adolescent Psychotherapy, 4,* 3–12.

Lutzker, J. R., & Newman, M. (1986). Child abuse and neglect: Community problem, community solutions. *Education and Treatment of Children, 9,* 344–354.

Lutzker, J. R., Megson, D. A., Webb, M. E., & Dachman, R. S. (1985). Validating and training adult–child interaction skills to professionals and to parents indicated for child abuse and neglect. *Journal of Child and Adolescent Psychotherapy, 2,* 91–104.

Lutzker, J. R., & Rice, J. M. (1984). Project 12-Ways: Measuring outcome of a large-scale in-home service for the treatment and prevention of child abuse and neglect. *Child Abuse and Neglect: The International Journal, 8,* 519–524.

Lutzker, J. R., & Rice, J. M. (1987). Using recidivism data to evaluate Project 12-Ways: An ecobehavioral approach to the treatment and prevention of child abuse and neglect. *Journal of Family Violence, 2,* 283–290.

Lutzker, J. R., Touchette, P. E., & Campbell, R. V. (1988). Parental positive reinforcement might make a difference: A rejoinder to Forehand. *Child and Family Behavior Therapy, 10,* 25–33.

Lutzker, J. R., Wesch, D., & Rice, J. M. (1984). A review of Project 12-Ways: An ecobehavioral approach to the treatment and prevention of child abuse and neglect. *Advances in Behaviour Research and Therapy, 6,* 63–73.

Margolin, G. (1979). Conjoint marital therapy to enhance anger management and reduce spouse abuse. *American Journal of Family Therapy, 7,* 13–23.

Margolin, G., Sibner, L. G., & Gleberman, L. (1988). Wife battering. In V. B. Van Hasselt, R. L. Morrison, A. S. Bellack, & M. Hersen (Eds.), *Handbook of family violence.* New York: Plenum.

Meyers-Abell, J. E., & Jansen, M. A. (1980). Assertive therapy for battered women: A case illustration. *Journal of Behavior Therapy & Experimental Psychiatry, 11,* 301–305.

Millon, T. (1983). *Millon Clinical Multiaxial Inventory Manual.* Minneapolis, MN: Interpretive Scoring Systems.

Milner, J. S. (1986). The Child Abuse Potential Inventory: Manual, (2nd ed.). Webster, NC: Psytec.

Morrison, R. L., Van Hasselt, V. B., & Bellack, A. S. (1987). Assessment of assertion and problem-solving skills in wife abusers and their spouses. *Journal of Family Violence, 2,* 227–238.

National Center on Child Abuse and Neglect (1984). *Study of national incidence and prevalence of child abuse and neglect: 1988* (DHHS Contract No. 105-85-1701). Washington, DC: U.S. Government Printing Office.

Novaco, R. W. (1975). *Anger control: The development and evaluation of an experimental treatment.* Lexington, MA: Lexington Books.

O'Leary, K. D., & Arias, I. (1987a). Marital assessment in clinical practice. In K. D. O'Leary (Ed.), *Assessment of marital discord.* Hillsdale, NJ: Erlbaum.

O'Leary, K. D., & Arias, I. (1988). Assessing agreement of reports of spouse abuse. In G. T. Hotaling, D. Finkelhor, J. T. Kirkpatrick, & M. A. Straus (Eds.), *Family abuse and its consequences: New directions in research* (pp. 218–227). Beverly Hills, CA: Sage.

O'Leary, K. D., & Curley, A. D. (1986). Assertion and family violence: Correlates of spouse abuse. *Journal of Marital and Family Therapy, 12,* 281–289.

O'Leary, K. D., Curley, A., Rosenbaum, A., & Clarke, C. (1985). Assertion training for abused wives: A potentially hazardous treatment. *Journal of Marital and Family Therapy, 11,* 319–322.

Pagelow, M. (1989). The incidence and prevalence of criminal abuse of other family members. In L. Ohlin & M. Tonry (Eds.), *Family violence* (pp. 263–314). Chicago: University of Chicago Press.

Rice, J. M., & Lutzker, J. R. (1983). Group and individual feedback, public posting, and prompting to increase counselor supervision. *The Clinical Supervisor, 1,* 77–90.

Rosenbaum, A., & O'Leary, K. D. (1981). Marital violence: Characteristics of abusive couples. *Journal of Consulting and Clinical Psychology, 49,* 63–71.

Rosenbaum, A., & O'Leary, K. D. (1986). Treatment of marital violence. In N. Jacobson & A. Gurman (Eds.), *Clinical handbook of marital therapy* (pp. 385–405). New York: Guilford.

Rosenbaum, A., & Maiuro, R. D. (1990). Perpetrators of spouse abuse. In R. T. Ammerman & M. Hersen (Eds.), *Treatment of family violence: A sourcebook* (pp. 280–309). New York: Wiley.

Rosenberg, M. S., & Reppucci, N. D. (1985). Primary prevention of child abuse. *Journal of Consulting and Clinical Psychology, 51,* 674–682.

Rosenfeld-Schlichter, M. D., Sarber, R. E., Bueno, G., Greene, B. F., & Lutzker, J. R. (1983). Maintaining accountability for an ecobehavioral treatment of one aspect of child neglect: Personal cleanliness. *Education and Treatment of Children, 6,* 153–164.

Roy, M. (1977). *Battered women.* New York: Van Nostrand Reinhold.

Sarber, R. E., Halasz, M. M., Messmer, M. C., Bickett, A. D., & Lutzker, J. R., (1983). Teaching menu planning and grocery shopping skills to a mentally retarded mother. *Mental Retardation, 21,* 101–106.

Saunders, D. G., & Hanusa, D. (1986). Cognitive-behavioral treatment of men who batter. The short-term effects of group therapy. *Journal of Family Violence, 1,* 357–372.

Schellenbach, C. J., & Guerney, L. F. (1987). Identification of adolescent abuse and future intervention. *Journal of Adolescence, 10,* 1–12.

Schilling, D. J., & Poppen, R. (1983). Behavioral relaxation training and assessment.

Journal of Behavior Therapy and Experimental Psychiatry, 14, 99–107.

Scott, P. D. (1974). Battered wives. *British Journal of Psychiatry, 125,* 433–441.

Shainess, N. (1977). Psychological aspects of wife battering. In M. Roy (Ed.), *Battered women: A psychosociological study of domestic violence.* New York: Van Nostrand Reinhold.

Snell, J. E., Rosenwald, R. J., & Robey, A. (1964). The wife-beater's wife: A study of family interaction. *Archives of General Psychiatry, 11,* 107–112.

Stark, E., & Flitcraft, A. (1988). Violence among intimates: An epidemiological review. In V. B. Van Hasselt, R. L. Morrison, A. S. Bellack, & M. Hersen (Eds.), *Handbook of family violence* (pp. 293–317). New York: Plenum.

Straus, M. A. (1979). Measuring intrafamily conflict and violence: The Conflict Tactic (CT) Scales. *Journal of Marriage and the Family, 41,* 75–86.

Straus, M. A. (in press). The Conflict Tactics Scale and its critics: An evaluation and new data on validity and reliability. In M. A. Straus & R. J. Gelles (Eds.), *Physical violence in American families: Risk factors and adaptations in 8.145 families.* New Brunswick, NJ: Transaction Books.

Straus, M. A., Gelles, R. J., & Steinmetz, S. (1980). *Behind closed doors: Violence in the American family.* New York: Doubleday/Anchor.

Tertinger, D. A., Greene, B. F., & Lutzker, J. R. (1984). Home safety: Development and validation of one component of an ecobehavioral treatment program for abused and neglected children. *Journal of Applied Behavior Analysis, 17,* 159–174.

Tertinger, D. A., Greene, B. F., & Lutzker, J. R. (1988). Home accident prevention inventory. In M. Hersen & A. S. Bellack (Eds.), *Dictionary of Behavioral Assessment Techniques.* (pp. 246–298) New York: Pergamon.

Wahler, R. G. (1980). The insular mother: Her problems in parent-child treatment. *Journal of Applied Behavior Analysis, 13,* 207–219.

Wahler, R. G., & Dumas, J. E. (1986). Maintenance factors in coercive mother-child interactions: The compliance and predictability hypothesis, *19,* 13–22.

Walker, C. E., Bonner, B. L., & Kaufman, K. L. (1988). *The physically and sexually abused child: Evaluation and treatment.* New York: Pergamon.

Walker, L. E. (1979). *The battered woman.* New York: Harper & Row.

Walker, L. E. (1984). *The battered woman syndrome.* New York: Springer.

Watson-Perzcel, M., Lutzker, J. R., Greene, B. F., & McGimpsey, B. J. (1988). Assessment and modification of home cleanliness among families adjudicated for child neglect. *Behavior Modification, 12,* 57–81.

Wolfe, D. (1987). Child abuse. In R. T. Ammerman & M. Hersen (Eds.), *Treatment of family violence.* New York: Wiley.

Wolfe, D., Kaufman, K., Aragona, J., & Sandler, J. (1981). *The child management program for abused parents: Procedures for developing a child abuse intervention program.* Winter Park, FL: Anna Publishing.

Wolfe, D., & Sandler, J. (1981). Training abusive parents in effective child management. *Behavior Modification, 5,* 320–335.

Wolfe, D., Sandler, J., & Kaufman, K. (1981). A competency-based parent training program for child abusers. *Journal of Consulting and Clinical Psychology, 49,* 633–640.

Wolfe, D., St. Lawrence, J., Graves, K., Brehony, K., Bradlyn, D., & Kelly, J. A. (1982). Intensive behavioral parent training for a child abusive mother. *Behavior Therapy, 13,* 438–451.

Wolfe, D., & Manion, I. G. (1984). Impediments to child abuse prevention: Issues and directions. *Advances in Behaviour Research and Therapy, 6,* 47–62.

Wolfe, D., & Bordeau, P. A. (1987). Current issues in the assessment of abusive and neglectful parent-child relationships. *Behavioral Assessment, 9,* 271–290.

Wolfe, D., Edwards, B., Manion, I., & Koverola, C. (1988). Early intervention for parents at risk of child abuse and neglect: A preliminary investigation. *Journal of Consulting and Clinical Psychology, 56,* 40–47.

Wolpe, J., & Lazarus, A. A. (1966). *Behavior therapy techniques: A guide to the treatment of neuroses.* New York: Pergamon.

CHAPTER 22

Behavioral Marital Therapy

ILEANA ARIAS

A national survey conducted by the Institute for Social Research (1974) demonstrated that "marriage and family life are the most satisfying parts of most people's lives and being married is one of the most important determinants of being satisfied with life" (p. 4). Indeed, married American adults have lower age-standardized death rates, especially from heart disorders, while unmarried individuals have death rates higher than average from cirrhosis of the liver, pneumonia, motor vehicle accidents, suicide, and homicide (Glick, 1988). All but approximately 3% to 4% of American adults will marry at least once during their lifetime (Carter & Glick, 1976). Marriage is clearly normative behavior in our society.

Although marriage is desirable for many and has been shown to be related to men's and women's physical and psychological health, marital satisfaction and marital stability are elusive for a sizable segment of adult men and women. Marital difficulties are the problems most commonly presented by individuals seeking services at mental health facilities (Veroff, Kulka, & Douvan, 1981); approximately 42% of individuals seeking psychotherapeutic services view their marriage as the primary problem they experience (Gurin, Veroff, & Feld, 1960). Although the rate of marriages had been stable for more than 100 years (National Center for Health Statistics, 1973), the rate of marital dissolution by divorce had been increasing, such that, by 1974, more marriages were ended by divorce than by death (Glick, 1980). At its peak, Norton and Mooreman (1987) estimated, the rate of divorce of first marriages among women between the ages of 35 and 39 was 56%. Further, although approximately 75% of divorced individuals remarry, 61% of divorced men and 54% of divorced women end their second marriages in divorce as well (Glick, 1984). Currently, the divorce rate in the United States seems to have stabilized at slightly under 50% of first marriages.

Marital disruption, especially divorce, has been shown to have widespread destructive effects on the physical and psychological well-being of adults (Bloom, Asher, & White, 1978; Holmes & Rahe, 1967; Somers, 1979) and children (Emery, 1988; Hetherington, Cox, & Cox, 1986; Wallerstein, 1985), presenting costs to both the individuals involved and society at large. Similarly, marital discord can produce or exacerbate a wide range of individual physical and psychological problems (Beach & Nelson, 1990; Markman, Duncan, Storaasli, & Howes, 1987). Appropriate professional response to such a state of affairs calls for research and applied efforts to understand and limit, or prevent, the detrimental impact of marital dissatisfaction and divorce on adults and children. Marital interventions are conceptualized herein as direct attempts to alleviate marital discord and, in appropriate cases, as divorce prevention measures.

BEHAVIORAL MODEL OF MARRIAGE

Social Exchange Theory

The theoretical underpinnings of current behavioral or cognitive-behavioral models of marriage can be traced to social exchange theory (Stuart, 1980). The hallmark of social exchange theory is the conceptualization of interpersonal relationships as consisting primarily of bargaining processes (Thibaut & Kelley, 1959). Social behavior is defined as the exchange among parties of both material and nonmaterial goods. Consistent with stimulus–response (S–R) theory, social behavior is considered a function of consequent rewards and costs. Relationship satisfaction is high for a particular individual as long as his or her rewards equal or exceed the costs resulting from the exchange process. However, an increased probability of dissolution results when costs of continuing the relationship outweigh the rewards available from the relationship, and other options appear potentially more satisfying. That is, individuals evaluate the reward:cost ratio, or satisfaction, associated with a particular relationship relative to the ratios attributed to other potential relationships (Kelley & Thibaut, 1978). A relationship is maintained if positive reciprocity or exchange in that relationship is maximized relative to other potential relationships.

Marital Satisfaction and Stability

According to Weiss (1978), marital interactions occur in 12 areas, which can be divided into three major categories: (a) appetitive or affectional interactions, (b) instrumental interactions, and (c) by-products of the marriage. The affectional category includes areas of interaction such as sex, companionship, and communication. These areas of interaction establish and maintain intimacy, representing gains that are expected from marriage. The instrumental category includes areas of interaction such as child care, financial decision making, and household management. Instrumental areas of interaction represent obligations and commitments associated with marriage, and potentially major sources of relationship costs. Areas of interaction included in the "by-product" category—personal habits and appearance, and self and spouse independence—represent individual characteristics that can be either positively or negatively related to the marriage but are not expected nor required as "gains" from the spouse or the relationship.

From a social learning theory perspective, marital satisfaction is maintained by high levels of personal gains relative to costs resulting from marital interactions, and by high reciprocity or equity between the spouses. When marital satisfaction decreases as a result of a change in the reward:cost ratio or in reciprocity in any area(s) of interaction, it can be restored to former levels by changing the pattern of exchange. In order to successfully change patterns of interaction, spouses must possess and apply skills in each of four competency categories: (a) objectification, (b) support–understanding, (c) problem solving, and (d) behavior change (Weiss, 1978). Objectification refers to the individual's ability to specify sources of rewards and costs for each spouse and identify determinants of successful and unsuccessful exchange. Support–understanding refers to the individual's ability to establish intimacy through empathy for the spouse and expression of warmth and understanding. Problem solving refers to the ability to generate, agree on, and implement solutions to conflict, and behavior change refers to the ability to use positive, rather than aversive, control strategies (Jacobson & Margolin, 1979). Application of competency skills to conflict in the area of interaction increases the reward:cost ratio and restores equity.

Marital Dissatisfaction and Instability

In the absence of the requisite skills outlined above, or their application to conflict, dysfunctional patterns of marital interaction cannot be changed. Inability or unwillingness to delineate exact sources of dissatisfaction, to express understanding in the context of requesting change, and to negotiate conflict through the use of positive control strategies (i.e., compromise) maintains the reward:cost imbalance and the experienced inequity. The perception of continued inequity and continued losses in the relationship facilitates focus on maximizing personal gains without regard for the partner or the future reciprocity level of the marriage. The probability of dissolution (i.e., separation or divorce) increases over time as a function of the couple's failure to restore equity and the perception or anticipation of greater rewards and equity associated with relationship alternatives.

Empirical Support of the Model

Research generally has supported social exchange and social learning theory perspectives of marriage and marital satisfaction. Maritally dissatisfied couples relative to satisfied couples exhibit higher rates of occurrence of negative behavior and lower rates of positive behavior (Barnett & Nietzel, 1979; Birchler, Weiss, & Vincent, 1975; Margolin, 1981). Thus, as the model specifies, dissatisfied couples derive greater relationship costs relative to rewards. Dissatisfied couples are more reactive than nondistressed partners to their spouses' negative behaviors (Levenson & Gottman, 1983). Further, distressed spouses, relative to nondistressed spouses, attempt to change interaction or exchange patterns by employing aversive rather than positive behavior control strategies (Patterson & Reid, 1970), and, hence, exchange negative behaviors at a higher rate than positive behaviors (Billings, 1979; Gottman, 1979; Revenstorf, Hahlweg, Schindler, & Vogel, 1984; Vivian, Smith, & O'Leary, 1988). Importantly, nondistressed couples appear to evaluate relationship reciprocity over time; distressed couples track reciprocity over the short run (Jacobson & Margolin, 1979).

These and related findings have encouraged the development of techniques based on social exchange and social learning principles. Interventions aimed at increasing positive exchange and improving the reward:cost ratio in the marriage will be presented and discussed below as standard components of behavioral marital therapy.

BEHAVIORAL MARITAL INTERVENTION

The primary goals of behavioral marital therapy are to increase the occurrence of positive marital events and decrease the occurrence of negative marital events. Behavioral marital therapists attempt to achieve these goals by providing distressed couples with the interactional skills deemed necessary to resolve conflict and increase intimacy in a direct, structured, and time-limited manner. As with other behavioral approaches to dysfunctional behavior, skills are taught by employing a variety of techniques including instruction, modeling, behavior rehearsal, and corrective feedback. Therapy sessions are conjoint. Exceptions to the conjoint format are made at the initial assessment and during the course of therapy in order to assess individual concerns such as the evaluation of therapy's effectiveness or partner noncompliance.

ASSESSMENT

The goals of assessment in behavioral marital therapy are:

1. To establish a "therapeutic" atmosphere;
2. To evaluate the appropriateness of conjoint, marital therapy for the couple;
3. To specify the areas of interaction that are problematic for the couple;
4. To specify the skills or competencies the couple needs to develop and apply, in order to resolve the conflict.

Establishing a Therapeutic Atmosphere

Application and subsequent success of a rational approach, such as behavioral marital therapy, to resolving interpersonal conflict depends on the spouses' level of trust toward each other and the therapist. The spouses' ability and willingness to self-disclose greatly influence the accuracy or appropriateness of interventions and, subsequently, their therapeutic impact. Lack of trust in the partner frequently may characterize couples presenting with long-standing conflict and may be identified as a target for treatment subsequent to the assessment phase. Lack of trust in the therapist or in therapy can be minimized and prevented by conveying understanding and appreciation for the current experience and desires of both spouses. Reflection and related empathy techniques are ideally suited for accomplishing these goals. Further, the therapist must convey impartiality in her or his communications and conceptualizations. Each spouse should be given "equal time" in identifying sources of dissatisfaction. Conflicts and complaints of either spouse can be redefined as "couple" problems. The contribution of each spouse, intentional or not, to the existing dysfunctional situation must be identified. Although the therapist cannot and should not guarantee success, he or she can increase hope and trust by stating a strong commitment to carefully examining the couple's difficulties and helping them to explore potential solutions.

Evaluating the Appropriateness of Marital Therapy

Engaging couples in marital therapy presumes the potential beneficial impact of conjoint therapy on each spouse's level of adjustment and satisfaction. The spouses' distress must be conceptualized as the result of dysfunction in one or more areas of interaction. Some distress may be a consequence, entirely or partly, of some individual dysfunction such as chronic depression (Beach, Arias, & O'Leary, 1990). However, to the extent that the marital interactions are disrupted, marital therapy may provide relief beyond that provided by resolution of the individual problem (Beach, Sandeen, & O'Leary, 1990). Most significant in evaluating the appropriateness of marital therapy are the spouses' goals and expectations. Congruence between the couple's goals and expectations and the stated goals and objectives of behavioral marital therapy increase chances of success. Additionally, similarity in the husband's and wife's goals is essential. Spouses presenting divergent, nonnegotiable goals will not be able to engage in the collaborative, problem-solving endeavor that epitomizes behavioral marital therapy.

Specifying Areas of Conflict and Required Skills

Behavioral marital therapists rely on self-report and observational information obtained via clinical interviews and paper-and-pencil measures. There are a variety of well-researched paper-and-pencil measures of global marital adjustment and functioning, such as the Marital Adjustment Test (MAT; Locke & Wallace, 1959), the Dyadic Adjustment Scale (DAS; Spanier, 1976), and the Marital Satisfaction Inventory (MSI; Snyder, 1981). Behavioral marital researchers have developed self-report (Areas of Change Questionnaire (ACQ); Weiss & Birchler, 1975) and spouse observation measures (Spouse Observation Checklist (SOC); Wills, Weiss, & Patterson, 1974) that facilitate clear and precise specification of behavioral characteristics of distressed couples. Specifically, these measures assess the occurrence of, and satisfaction with, rewards and costs in the areas of interaction identified by Weiss (1978). Measures such as the ACQ and DAS can be used to assess therapeutic progress and therapy success at termination as well. Consistent with the ideographic approach to treatment, however, behavioral marital therapists rely heavily on the clinical interview (O'Leary & Arias, 1987).

STRUCTURE OF THERAPY

Initial Interview

The initial interview with distressed couples is an exception to the conjoint format employed by behavioral marital therapists. The spouses are seen together for the initial 15 to 20 minutes of the interview. The process, assumptions, and goals of behavioral marital therapy are presented. In each other's presence, the spouses provide a brief description of the problems they are experiencing, the issues central to their dissatisfaction, and their reasons for seeking professional help at the current time. The therapist is attentive to the level of agreement on the issues discussed. Based on each spouse's perceptions of the problems, attributed sources of the problems, and expressed levels of comfort and satisfaction with the decision to seek outside intervention, the therapist decides which spouse is less committed to therapy. The less committed spouse can be expected to be the more noncompliant partner and, potentially, the greater obstacle to therapeutic progress and success.

After the brief conjoint meeting, spouses are interviewed individually. The primary goal of the individual interview is to obtain a candid, uninhibited appraisal of the marriage and the conflict from each spouse. Topics that may not be appropriate or wise to introduce in the presence of the partner, such as extramarital affairs and liking for the spouse, can be examined closely during individual interviews. Each spouse is able to present personal versions of the situation during the individual interview, which facilitates establishing rapport with each spouse. The spouse deemed less committed is interviewed first, while the partner completes paper-and-pencil measures. O'Leary and Arias (1987) suggest completion of an assessment package that evaluates individual personality functioning as well as global and specific marital dimensions. Results of the personality or psychological assessment of each individual spouse provides a context that can facilitate the conceptualization of the marital dysfunction and enhance the probability of effective intervention.

At the closing of the individual interviews, the information presented by each spouse is summarized, focusing on the positive and constructive aspects of the material presented. For example, careful note can be made that, although marital interactions have deteriorated over time, the couple has expressed commitment to the marriage and each other by seeking therapy.

Developmental Marital History

After getting a commitment from the couple to continue therapy if appropriate, a developmental history will be obtained before initiating any relationship changes. Marital developmental histories typically are obtained during the second session, employing a conjoint format.

The historical information obtained will help the therapist understand the development of the dysfunction and suggest appropriate potential solutions. Further, by covering material and situations that preceded the marital discord, couples are reoriented toward actual or potential positive aspects of their relationships (Jacobson & Margolin, 1979).

Spouses are asked to trace the development of their relationship beginning with their initial meeting. In the process, each spouse states what was attractive about the other when they met, what activities the couple engaged in during courtship and early marriage, what contributed to their decision to marry, and their expectations for marriage and the partner when they decided to marry. In addition to covering the more positive aspects of their past, couples discuss the extent to which their expectations were met. Antecedents or circumstances surrounding the emergence of dysfunctional interactions are specified. In summarizing the development of dysfunction, a behavioral conceptualization of the couple's discord is presented. Implications for treatment of the behavioral conceptualization are outlined and offered to the couple as a potential strategy for resolving their conflict. If the couple agrees to proceed, the spouses are instructed to generate self- and partner changes that would increase marital functioning and their satisfaction. The changes specified by each spouse will be used as the starting point for therapeutic intervention.

Initial Positive Change

The timely increase of positive marital events is central to maintaining commitment to therapy and the marriage. Experiencing prompt positive change increases spouses' motivation to compromise when they address problematic areas (Weiss, Hops, & Patterson, 1973). Thus, in addition to alleviating some of the presenting marital distress, early positive change provides a more constructive base from which couple negotiations are conducted. Generating initial positive change targets provides an early opportunity for developing objectification skills. Spouses are required to clearly specify desired changes. Specification of desired changes requires attending to dimensions in marital interaction that influence global and daily marital functioning and satisfaction.

Noncontingent Behavior Change Agreements

Initial behavior change among discordant couples can be accomplished through the use of noncontingent change agreements. The omission of explicit contingencies produces decreased perceptions of coercion and fewer external attributions for self- and partner behavior change. The best articulated form of noncontingent change agreements is the "caring days" procedure developed by Stuart (1980). The caring days technique attempts to increase the occurrence of caring behaviors. Spouses are instructed to be specific and prescriptive in generating behaviors that would show caring for each other. Caring days items should be "small," potentially doable on a daily basis, and *not* central to the couple's major concerns. Spouses may include items such as "Ask me how my day was" or "Hold my hand when walking to and from the car," but not items such as "Let me decide the type of family car to buy" or "Discipline the children."

Spouses generate 20 to 30 caring items applicable to either or both spouses. The list of caring behaviors generated must not favor one spouse over the other. A comparable number of behaviors that would be pleasing to the wife and the husband should be included. The list is an open one, allowing the couple to add caring behaviors in the future. Each spouse is responsible for engaging in at least five of the caring behaviors on the list. Spouses keep a written record of which items they engaged in, and when. The written record aids the therapist in monitoring actual change, and helps the spouses become more aware of their own behavior toward their partner. Successful self-monitoring can be replaced with partner-monitoring. Each spouse is still responsible for engaging in five behaviors daily; however, they are to keep track of the behaviors that the partner engages in. Partner-monitoring ensures that spouses will attend to positive behavioral change in their partners.

There are no positive or negative consequences specified for compliance or noncompliance with the caring days technique. The necessity for increasing positive behaviors for alleviating marital distress, that is, a behavioral conceptualization of marital satisfaction, is emphasized to the couple and a personal commitment to change is solicited. The success of the caring days procedure, in part, rests on reassurance that the procedure is not designed to "cure" the marital distress and the significant, problematic issues faced by the couple. Rather, the procedure is presented as a technique for building a foundation from which the couple can employ other measures to resolve more fundamental difficulties. By avoiding the use of external sources of reinforcement for change, coercive or aversive control strategies are deemphasized. Rather, the caring days technique emphasizes routine, internally motivated positive control strategies that may be associated consequently with marital satisfaction, generalizability, and maintenance of therapeutic gains.

Communication Skills Training

The predominant mode for establishing intimacy and for interpersonal negotiation is verbal and nonverbal communication. The process of communication entails the encoding and transmission of a message, in the context of "noise," which is decoded and interpreted by another (cf. Stuart, 1980). This process of communication serves to provide a response to another's verbally or nonverbally transmitted message, thereby reinforcing the other's past behavior and providing a stimulus for the other's next behavioral response. The probability for committing errors during the complex activities of encoding, transmitting, and decoding verbal and nonverbal messages is high. The implications of the high probability rate are that the message intended by one individual does not necessarily correspond to the impact of the communication on another. Research strongly indicates that errors in communication—low correspondence between communication intent and impact—are significantly more frequent among distressed than nondistressed married couples (Gottman, 1979). Communication skills training is a central component of behavioral marital therapy because of the pivotal role of communication in problem solving and in support–understanding areas of marital competency.

Goals of Communication Skills Training

Communication skills training attempts to increase the spouses' accurate understanding of each other's self-expression, in order to establish a symmetrical pattern of interaction (Stuart, 1980). In symmetrical as opposed to complementary patterns of communication, both negotiating parties have similar options and comparable decision-making power. That is, the behavior of one party does not limit the options of the other. For example, in a relationship characterized by symmetry in communication, and consequently symmetry in power, the husband may *ask* the wife when would it be best for him to work out at his health spa. On the other hand, in a relationship characterized by complementarity, the husband may *tell* his wife that he will be working out after work, and so, she has to pick up the kids at day-care and make dinner. Discordant couples' communication patterns have been found to be characterized by complementarity, whereas happily married couples exhibit more symmetrical patterns of communication (Gottman, 1979).

Listening Skills

Errors in the transmission, decoding, and interpretation of messages are avoided by strengthening listening skills. The role of the listener and necessary skills for effective listening receive initial primary focus during training, because it is the listener at any point in time who determines whether communication occurs (Nierenberg & Calero, 1973). That is, once the process of communication is initiated by the transmission of a message, it ceases the minute the receiver of the message does not acknowledge the message. The listener can interrupt the communication process by failing to attend to the speaker or by failing to address the content of the message. Failure to address the content of the message results when the listener invalidates or dismisses the message, or simply changes the topic. The listener's failure to facilitate communication may result from intentional or unintentional violations of effective listener guidelines.

Generally, spouses can adopt one of two listener strategies: empathic listening or deliberative listening. The goal of empathic listening is the accurate understanding of the message. Deliberative listening entails the evaluation of the various components of the transmitted message. Behavioral marital therapy emphasizes the use of empathic listening. Skills that facilitate accurate understanding and can convey that understanding are the focus of listener skills training. Four major skills are targeted:

1. Establishing a physical orientation toward the speaker through eye contact and physical proximity;
2. Suspending interruptions of the speaker and allowing the speaker to signal, verbally or nonverbally, when he or she has completed the transmission;
3. Summarizing the message transmitted;
4. "Checking out" the decoded and interpreted message with the speaker (Gottman, Notarius, Gonso, & Markman, 1976).

Speaker Skills

Training spouses in speaker skills addresses errors of encoding and transmission. Communication skills training identifies the following functions of the speaker, which are listed in order of increasing complexity and difficulty: self-expression, request making, clarification, and provision of feedback. Behavioral marital therapists address and emphasize skills in each of these areas sequentially and cumulatively.

Self-expression is used to increase self-understanding and understanding of the self by the partner, by putting personal experience into words. The speaker is to focus on the present and should be brief, providing only the pertinent information. Explanations or justifications are to be avoided. The speaker is instructed to use declarative sentences and avoid questions. Specifically, the use of "I" statements (Gottman et al., 1976) are emphasized as a means of achieving self-expression and accepting responsibility for such self-expression. An example of an effective statement of self-expression may be: "I love you and think you are a good partner." In contrast, failure to express the self and not take responsibility for personal experience might be indicated by the following: "Don't you think that I love you? Would I still be married to you if I didn't think you were a good partner?"

Request making incorporates the skills central to self-expression; that is, the speaker focuses on the present, is brief, and uses "I" statements to make requests of the partner. Responsibility for the requests is emphasized further by the prescription to use words such as "want" and "would like" rather than "need" or "should." "I would like some help with the children at bath time" is to replace the almost instinctual "You should help me with the children at bath time." Additionally, spouses are reintroduced to the magic word: PLEASE.

Seeking clarification of a message received is a required component of communication in behavioral marital therapy. A listener skill emphasized in training is "checking-out" messages with the speaker. As with other functions, the speaker must take responsibility for not understanding and for seeking clarification. This is best accomplished by summarizing the message, as understood by the speaker, and then asking the partner if the summary matches the intended message. Thus, rather than accuse the partner of not making sense, the spouse can state: "I understand you to say that you want me to free up some time for you after dinner by giving the children their baths. Is this what you are asking me to do?"

Perhaps the most difficult skill to master is providing feedback, either positive or corrective, to the partner. Couples who have a history of acrimonious interactions are not highly motivated to give each other feedback, nor to provide corrective feedback in a nonaccusatory manner. Distressed spouses either will not or cannot provide positive or corrective feedback effectively, because of their history or because they never had the skills. In either case, it is important for spouses to develop these skills in order to shape and reinforce the spouse for making positive changes.

Positive feedback should be timely and clear. Spouses are instructed to begin by offering global positive feedback and then proceed to more specific positive feedback, such as: "I think you're doing a great job with the kids. It was great of you to help them with their homework tonight." When corrective feedback is offered, it should be preceded by positive feedback.

However, spouses should not invalidate the positive feedback preceding the corrective feedback. Corrective feedback should be timely, specific, descriptive, objective, and should be limited to situations that can lead to significant desirable change. That is, although the partner could floss his or her teeth in a more effective manner, the feedback should be offered only if the change in flossing is meaningful to the spouse and will have an impact on the experience of the partner and the relationship.

Problem-Solving Skills Training

Behavioral marital therapists employ problem solving as the method of choice in negotiating the removal of negative, destructive, and unpleasant behavior. Problem-solving skills training directly increases discordant couples' skills and success in the problem-solving and behavior change areas of competency.

Behavioral marital therapists define problem solving as "structured interaction between two people designed to resolve a particular dispute between them" (Jacobson & Margolin, 1979, p. 215). Problem solving represents a set of rules or a process that is taught to discordant couples so that they may resolve conflict across topics, situations, and time. Problem-solving skills training appears to be the optimal strategy for increasing positives; decreasing negatives; attributing change and increased satisfaction to internal, stable, and global causes; and, thus, increasing generalization and maintenance of therapeutic gains.

Negotiation Strategies

The application of problem solving to the negotiation of couples' difficulties can be guided by one of two general negotiation strategies: the one-winner approach and the two-winner approach (cf. Stuart, 1980). The one-winner approach is characterized by bargainers negotiating for the greatest possible level of personal gain. Accordingly, bargainers adopting a one-winner strategy begin the process with excessive demands and concede little. Situations in which the negotiating parties will not have contact with each other in the future and/or where immediate goals are more important than long-range goals—for example, divorce among young, affluent, childless couples—seem ideally suited for the use of a one-winner strategy. A two-winner strategy may be more productive and effective for each individual in situations in which parties will have future contact and, hence, long-range goals may be as important as or more important than immediate goals. The two-winner strategy is characterized by integrative bargaining. Under such conditions, bargainers recognize the outcome of the negotiation as equitable and recognize the potential, future relationship costs resulting from imbalanced or inequitable negotiation agreements. Relative to nondiscordant spouses, discordant couples, in fact, present a higher level of exchange orientation, focusing on immediate reciprocity (Broderick & O'Leary, 1986).

Distressed couples, who have been shown to be characterized by coercive control strategies that accomplish immediate gains in favor of long-term gains, are more likely to present for treatment with a history of one-winner approaches to the negotiation of relationship change. Spouses' willingness and success in the application of problem solving necessitates replacing a one-winner negotiation strategy with a two-winner strategy where compromise is the key to successful, long-range problem resolution. To this end, couples are encouraged to focus on generating equitable, working solutions to their grievances, rather than determining which spouse is "right" or "wrong" on the issues, and expecting the "wrong" spouse to change. To accomplish this goal, couples are made cognizant and reminded throughout therapy to focus on the long-term gains for each of them and for their relationship.

Phase I: Problem Definition

Although seemingly simple and straightforward, the initial phase of problem solving is a critical determinant of couples' success in learning and applying problem solving. During this phase, the spouses outline their grievances and state their requests for change. More specifically, the goals of the problem definition phase are: (a) to provide a description of the undesirable behavior; (b) to specify the circumstances under which the undesirable behavior occurs and the consequences to the distressed partner; and (c) to request an alternative behavior from the spouse. The rules, objectives, and goals of problem solving are explained during this initial phase, and precedents for spouses' conduct during subsequent phases of problem solving are set during problem definition. The therapist is most active during the problem definition phase, devoting much of his or her intervention to communication issues.

Couple Guidelines. Both spouses are responsible for making sure that only one problem or grievance is negotiated during a particular application of problem solving. Additional problems that may be related or raised during problem-solving discussions are to be noted but discussed at another time during a separate, unrelated problem-solving application. Discussion of any problem must be limited to the present, excluding past instances or anticipated future behavior. In stating grievances and requesting change, spouses must be clear, direct, and honest about their needs, and must state such requests with the expectation that compromise will be required. Attending to these guidelines is facilitated by setting aside a place and time that will be devoted to problem solving specifically and routinely.

Speaker Guidelines. Spouses alternate taking the role of the speaker who states a grievance and requests change. Which partner adopts the speaker role first depends on the topic chosen for problem solving. Initially, the topic chosen should be one that, although important to the couple, is not significant enough or central enough to trigger excessive negative affect. Highly volatile topics or issues will impede the application of problem-solving procedures. The speaker is to avoid overgeneralizations. Instead, he or she is to provide a brief, specific, and descriptive statement of the partner's behavior that is problematic, in the form of "I feel _____ when you do _____." The use of "I" statements increases the amount of responsibility that the speaker assumes for the problem under discussion and, hence, minimizes the partner's defensiveness to the request for change.

Listener Guidelines. The listener's objectives are to understand and validate the speaker's concerns and desired alternatives. Validation does not mean agreement; validation refers to the listener's acknowledgment of the speaker's right to find objection with the partner's behavior and to request change. The listener is to remain nonjudgmental. For the moment—that is, during problem definition—the issue is not whether the speaker is accurate, rational, or justified; rather, the issue is appreciating the speaker's experience of the partner's behavior and the relationship. Validation of the speaker is accomplished by paraphrasing, summarizing, and reflecting the speaker's message.

Therapist Guidelines. The therapist is primarily responsible for enforcing the rules of problem solving and ensuring that the couple follows the guidelines specified above. The amount of therapist involvement is a function of the couple's presenting skill level and ability to comply with the rules and guidelines of problem-solving procedures. Resistance to problem solving may result from the spouses' unassertiveness or inability to take risk and trust the partner. Lack of trust may not only interfere with the implementation of problem solving, but may also lead spouses to identify "safe" problems for resolution. At the conclusion of the problem definition phase, the therapist must determine that the "correct" problem has been identified and defined by assessing the anticipated impact of the solution to the problem. For example, if the problem has been defined by the spouse as the other's lack of time spent with the children, the therapist may ask the spouse how satisfied he or she would be if the partner took the children and spent all day Saturday with only them at the park. If the issue is spending time with the children, the spouse would anticipate feeling positively. However, if the issue is spending time with the spouse, and focusing on time spent with the children was a safe way of asking for personal time, the spouse would not anticipate the problem's being resolved. In the latter situation, the spouse may complain that spending time at the park rather than at home was not as desirable, that time should be spent as a family, and so on.

Phase II: Generation of Solutions

Once the problem has been defined and agreed on, a solution has to be generated and negotiated. The generation of solutions is accomplished best by brainstorming. Spouses keep a written record of potential solutions they offer, without regard to their feasibility or consequences on implementation initially. This uncensored approach maximizes the number of possible solutions generated and, hence, the probability that the problem will be resolved. Generating multiple possible solutions increases disinhibition in problem solving, increases options, and instills hope in the couple regarding their differences. When couples do not seem to be able to generate solutions to their stated problems, the therapist may prompt them by offering solutions. Unless the couple's skills are very deficient, the solutions offered by the therapist should not be the optimal solutions. The therapist can offer solutions that will probably not be implemented but will serve to initiate some brainstorming by the clients. For example, if the problem is lack of time together, the therapist may suggest that the spouses quit their jobs in order to have more time together. The couple is unlikely to agree to quitting their jobs, but such a suggestion may prompt them to suggest changing their job schedules, rearranging their free time at home, and so on.

Evaluation of the solutions proposed takes place once the couple, not the therapist, can generate additional solutions. Spouses delete solutions that seem totally unfeasible or undesirable, such as quitting jobs, and specify the advantages and disadvantages of the remaining solutions. Additionally, spouses determine the extent to which the remaining solutions will resolve the problem with regard to both immediate and long-term concerns. Again, the therapist's role during this phase is to provide the couple with feedback and alert them to potential immediate and long-range disadvantages of the solutions that they may not see.

Phase III: *Change Agreement*

With the aid of the therapist, the couple chooses the solution with the fewest costs and greatest rewards for implementation. The implementation of solutions is experimental. Couples negotiate the implementation of a solution knowing that the problem may not be resolved and a new solution may have to be generated and/or implemented in the future. In essence, the product of the change agreement phase of problem solving is a self-specified homework assignment. Each spouse specifies what he or she agrees to do in order to alleviate the discord. The therapist must ensure the equity of the change agreement; each spouse should be engaging in comparable change, and benefits of the change should be comparable as well.

Contingency Contracting. The change agreements resulting from problem solving may be informal or constructed into more formalized contingency contracts. Contingency contracts essentially are written agreements made by the couple with the assistance and mediation of the therapist. Such agreements specify the behaviors desired of the marital partners *and* the consequences to each spouse for compliance and noncompliance. Two major types of contingency contracting are employed by behavioral marital therapists: quid pro quo contracts and parallel or "good faith" contracts (Weiss, Birchler, & Vincent, 1974).

Quid pro quo and parallel contracts are structured to clearly specify changes in behavior desired of each spouse by the other. Positive consequences are specified for compliance and negative consequences are specified for noncompliance in both types of contract. When employing quid pro quo contracts, each individual's behavior change is rewarded by the partner's behavior change. Parallel contracts, on the other hand, employ independent change agreements, whereby compliance or change in one spouse is not contingent on the other spouse's compliance. For example, a quid pro quo contract might specify that if Paul does the laundry on Monday night, Laura will take care of the bills on Wednesday and vice versa; however, if Paul does not do the laundry on Monday night, Laura will not take care of the family bills on Wednesday night and vice versa. Alternatively, a parallel contract might specify that Paul can attend his union's weekly meetings on Thursday night, if, and only if, he does the laundry on Monday night; Laura can attend town council meetings on Tuesday nights, if, and only if, she takes care of the bills the preceding Wednesday night.

The likelihood of success of both quid pro quo and parallel contracts is related to meeting certain basic requirements. The terms of the contract, that is, the prescriptions for behavior change, should be stated clearly and specifically. Behavioral targets should be overt and stated in a positive and prescriptive, rather than proscriptive, manner. That is, contracts should state what each spouse is supposed to do rather than what each is supposed to *not* do. Hence, contracts are ideally suited for increasing positives but not decreasing negatives directly. Behavioral change requested of an individual by definition is often demanding and undesirable. However, changes demanded of each spouse by the contract should not be personally offensive or aversive to the individual. For example, although Paul (in the example above) may not like doing the laundry and finds the request inconvenient, this activity is not fundamentally aversive to him. On the other hand, specifying increased sexual or affectionate activity with Laura subsequent to her recent admission of her extramarital affair with Paul's best friend may be genuinely aversive and to be avoided by the contract. In general, affectional behaviors are invalidated when they are seen as coerced and, hence, should not be incorporated into quid pro quo or parallel contracts. Although rewards for compliance are built into and specified clearly by both types of contracts, punishers for noncompliance are to be avoided, in order to decrease reactivity and feelings of coercion. Finally, equity between the spouses should be maximized. The amount of time and effort, objectively and subjectively determined, required by the contract should be comparable for both spouses.

Change agreements generated during problem solving, whether structured in the form of a contingency contract or less formalized, are implemented for the week in between therapy sessions. The success of the implementation of the change agreement and the effectiveness of the change agreement are evaluated during the subsequent session. If the solution proved ineffective, sources for lack of success are identified and a new problem-solving session is conducted.

Problem solving offers the advantage of simultaneously addressing the content, or outcome, and the process of behavior change. By focusing on content, problem solving allows couples to directly increase positive and decrease negative behaviors and events while addressing topics or issues of personal relevance. The focus on the process of negotiating behavior change provides the couple with a set of skills whose application can be generalized across situations and time. The skills taught increase the probability of engaging in positive control strategies to effect change in an equitable fashion.

EMPIRICAL EVALUATION OF BEHAVIORAL MARITAL THERAPY

Behavioral Marital Therapy vs. Wait-List Controls

Behavioral approaches to the treatment of marital distress have received some empirical scrutiny. The available outcome studies primarily focus on the impact of behavioral marital therapy packages and their various components on spouses' global marital satisfaction, as measured by the MAT or DAS, at the end of therapy and at follow-up. Both narrative (Beach & O'Leary, 1985) and meta-analytic (Hahlweg & Markman, 1988) reviews of the controlled outcome research have been conducted. Hahlweg and Markman (1988) concluded that overall behavioral marital therapy packages have produced significantly greater positive changes on global satisfaction than either wait-list or nonspecific treatment controls. The superior efficacy of behavioral marital therapy remained evident at 1-year follow-up.

Similarly, analysis of individual components of behavioral marital therapy suggests that communication skills training (Baucom, 1982; Hahlweg, Revenstorf, & Schindler, 1982; Turkewitz & O'Leary, 1981), problem solving (Hahlweg et al., 1982; Jacobson, 1978; Turkewitz & O'Leary, 1981), and behavioral contingency contracting (Baucom, 1982; Boelens, Emmelkamp, MacGillavry, & Markvoort, 1980; Crowe, 1978) are more effective than a wait-list control in producing global marital satisfaction changes. Initial comparison of individual behavioral marital therapy components (Jacobson et al., 1985) indicated that discordant couples treated with behavior exchange procedures (i.e., contracting) exclusively showed more deterioration from posttreatment levels of global satisfaction at 6 months posttreatment than couples treated with communication/problem-solving procedures or a combination of contracting and communication/problem solving. However, the advantages of communication/problem solving presented alone or in combination with contracting were no longer evident 1 year after termination of therapy. Hence, the individual components of behavioral marital therapy programs appear to be comparably effective in alleviating marital distress relative to no treatment either alone or in combination.

Behavioral Marital Therapy vs. Theoretically Alternative Treatment Packages

Cognitive Marital Therapy

Increasing attention has been devoted to cognitive-behavioral processes in marital functioning and satisfaction (Epstein & Baucom, 1989). Notably, (a) spouses' attributions of causality and responsibility for each other's behavior and (b) the effects of attribution processes on marital satisfaction have received considerable attention. In response to the growing body of literature documenting the significant association between attributional processes and marital satisfaction and functioning, Baucom and Lester (1986) compared the use of cognitive-behavioral techniques to traditional behavioral marital therapy. The cognitive intervention employed in their study primarily entailed the specification and modification of spouses' causal attributions for marital events. The results indicated that, indeed, the cognitive intervention had a significant, positive effect on cognitive variables assessed; the behavioral intervention did not. Both treatments were significantly effective in creating positive changes in global marital satisfaction. However, neither treatment proved to be superior to the other either at the end of therapy or at a 6-month follow-up. Thus, although attributional variables distinguish distressed from nondistressed couples, and cognitive interventions were shown to produce significant changes in attributional activity and global satisfaction, cognitive interventions do not appear to be superior to traditional behavioral marital therapy at this time.

Emotionally Focused Marital Therapy

Basic social psychological principles have been extended and applied in order to further understand individuals' marital experiences (cf. Bradbury & Fincham, 1987). There is a growing body of empirical evidence that not only do emotional processes distinguish distressed from nondistressed married couples, but affect and affective processes significantly predict marital functioning and satisfaction over time (Levenson & Gottman, 1983, 1985). Behavioral marital therapists have not designed therapeutic interventions to modify affect or affective processes directly. Rather, to date, traditional marital therapy conceptualizes affect as a product of behavior and cognitions, and its modification is achieved indirectly by altering patterns of behavior and thought. Nonbehavioral treatment packages directly assessing and modifying affect have been proposed, however. Greenberg and Johnson's (1988) emotionally focused marital therapy includes components common to cognitive and behavioral marital therapies. However, employing techniques from gestalt and systems approaches to psychotherapy, emotionally focused marital therapy emphasizes unexpressed and/or unacknowledged feelings of the spouses, and helps the distressed couple come to a new understanding of their relationship based on the exploration of these feelings. Johnson and Greenberg (1985a) compared emotionally focused marital therapy with a problem-solving intervention and a wait-list control. Emotionally focused marital therapy was associated with significantly greater gains at both posttreatment and a 2-month follow-up, relative to both the problem-solving intervention and the wait-list control. The superior efficacy of emotionally focused marital therapy documented by Johnson and Greenberg must be interpreted with caution. A complete package of emotionally focused therapy was compared to only one component of traditional behavioral marital therapy. The emotionally focused therapy in the outcome study was conducted by the study's first author (Johnson), who codesigned and was highly experienced in the use of emotionally focused therapy. The problem-solving intervention was delivered by less experienced therapists with little experience or knowledge in behavioral marital interventions. Moreover, Johnson and Greenberg's initial results have not been replicated in subsequent studies employing therapists of comparable experience and expertise with both behavioral and emotionally focused therapies (Goldman, 1987; Johnson & Greenberg, 1985b), and addition of emotionally focused therapy techniques to traditional marital therapy has not increased the latter's efficacy (Baucom & Sayers, 1988). Emotionally focused therapy techniques designed to directly alter affect in marriage offer alternatives to traditional behavioral marital therapy components. However, their superior or incremental effectiveness for the treatment of distressed couples remains to be documented.

Caveats

The outcome research suggests that behavioral marital therapy produces statistically significant improvements in global measures of marital satisfaction relative to no treatment and to theoretically alternative treatments such as cognitive and emotionally focused marital therapies. However, approximately only one-third of couples treated with behavioral marital therapy moved from the distressed range to the nondistressed range of scores on standard marital adjustment inventories (Jacobson et al., 1984). Hence, while the effectiveness of behavioral marital therapy has been empirically supported, it is not clear that behavioral marital therapy routinely provides fully satisfactory change in couples' marital satisfaction.

As Beach and Bauserman (1990) suggest, the available research does not address directly the potential sources of the less than optimal outcome of behavioral marital therapy. Behavioral marital therapy and its numerous components actually may be limited in their effectiveness. If so, behavioral marital therapists should increase their therapeutic armamentarium. Numerous theorists and researchers have addressed the potential increment in behavioral marital therapy's effectiveness by including components that more directly attempt to alter cognitive (Epstein & Baucom, 1989) and affective (Bradbury & Fincham, 1990; Greenberg & Johnson, 1988) marital dimensions. This represents important ongoing work in the field of behavioral marital therapy, the impact of which is yet to be satisfactorily evaluated.

Alternatively, behavioral marital therapy actually may be effective when the objectives or mediating goals of the behavioral approach to marital discord are achieved. Decreased effectiveness may be the result of ineffective implementation of behavioral techniques, or of couple noncompliance and nonparticipation in the change process. If so, Beach and Bauserman (1990) argue that future research should focus on the general process of behavioral change and delineate factors that result in couples' failing to participate fully and prevent them from achieving central mediating goals of therapy.

Behavioral marital therapy is an approach to the alleviation of marital distress that is continually challenged by its proponents in an effort to expand its current limits. It seems likely that the "face" of behavioral marital therapy will continue to change in the coming decade. It may well be that changes will be proposed in the range of techniques used by behavioral marital therapists, in the patterning of the components of intervention, or in strategies to enhance maintenance. Regardless, it seems likely that behavioral marital therapy will remain the most rigorously researched approach to the treatment of marital discord.

REFERENCES

Barnett, L. R., & Nietzel, M. T. (1979). Relationship of instrumental and affectional behaviors and self-esteem to marital satisfaction in distressed and nondistressed couples. *Journal of Consulting and Clinical Psychology, 47,* 946–957.

Baucom, D. H. (1982). A comparison of behavioral contracting and problem solving/communications training in behavioral marital therapy. *Behavior Therapy, 13,* 162–174.

Baucom, D. H., & Lester, G. W. (1986). The usefulness of cognitive restructuring as an adjunct to behavioral marital therapy. *Behavior Therapy, 17,* 385–403.

Baucom, D. H., & Sayers, S. L. (1988, November). *Expanding behavioral marital therapy.* Paper presented at the 22nd Annual Convention of the Association for Advancement of Behavior Therapy, New York.

Beach, S. R. H., Arias, I., & O'Leary, K. D. (1990). *Marriage and depressive symptomatology in wives: Longitudinal relationships.* Manuscript submitted for publication.

Beach, S. R. H., & Bauserman, S. A. K. (1990). Enhancing the effectiveness of marital therapy. In F. D. Fincham & T. N. Bradbury (Eds.), *The psychology of marriage* (pp. 349–374). New York: Guilford.

Beach, S. R. H., & Nelson, G. M. (1990). Pursuing research on major psychopathology from a contextual perspective: The example of depression and marital discord. In G. Brody & I. E. Siegel (Eds.), *Family research, Vol. II* (pp. 227–259). Hillsdale, NJ: Erlbaum.

Beach, S. R. H., & O'Leary, K. D. (1985). Current status of outcome research in marital therapy. In L. L'Abate (Ed.), *The handbook of family psychology* (pp. 1035–1072). Homewood, IL: Dorsey Press.

Beach, S. R. H., Sandeen, E. E., & O'Leary, K. D. (1990). *Depression in marriage: A model for etiology and marriage.* New York: Guilford.

Billings, A. (1979). Conflict resolution in distressed and nondistressed married couples. *Journal of Consulting and Clinical Psychology, 47,* 368–376.

Birchler, G. R., Weiss, R. L., & Vincent, J. P. (1975). A multimethod analysis of social reinforcement exchange between maritally distressed and nondistressed spouse and stranger dyads. *Journal of Personality and Social Psychology, 31,* 349–360.

Bloom, B. L., Asher, S. J., & White, S. W. (1978). Marital disruption as a stressor: A review and analysis. *Psychological Bulletin, 85,* 867–894.

Boelens, W., Emmelkamp, P., MacGillavry, D., & Markvoort, M. (1980). A clinical evaluation of marital treatment: Reciprocity and counseling versus system-theoretic counseling. *Behavioral Analysis and Modification, 4,* 85–96.

Bradbury, T. N., & Fincham, F. D. (1987). Affect and cognition in close relationships: Toward an integrative model. *Cognition and Emotion, 1,* 59–87.

Bradbury, T. N., & Fincham, F. D. (1990). Attribution in marriage: Review and critique. *Psychological Bulletin, 107,* 3–33.

Broderick, J. E., & O'Leary, K. D. (1986). Contributions of affect, attitudes, and behavior to marital satisfaction. *Journal of Consulting and Clinical Psychology, 54,* 514–517.

Carter, H., & Glick, P. C. (1976). *Marriage and divorce: A social and economic study.* Cambridge, MA: Harvard University Press.

Crowe, M. J. (1978). Conjoint marital therapy: A controlled outcome study. *Psychological Medicine, 8,* 623–636.

Emery, R. E. (1988). *Marriage, divorce, and children's adjustment.* Newbury Park, CA: Sage.

Epstein, N., & Baucom, D. H. (1989). Cognitive-behavioral marital therapy. In A. Freeman, K. M. Simon, L. E. Beutler, & H. Arkowitz (Eds.), *Comprehensive handbook of cognitive therapy* (pp. 491–513). New York: Plenum.

Glick, P. C. (1980). Remarriage: Some recent changes and variations. *Journal of Family Issues, 1,* 455–478.

Glick, P. C. (1984). Marriage, divorce, and living arrangements: Prospective changes. *Journal of Family Issues, 5,* 7–26.

Glick, P. C. (1988). Fifty years of family demography: A record of social change. *Journal of Marriage and the Family, 50,* 861–871.

Goldman, A. (1987). *Systematically and emotionally focused therapies: A comparative outcome.* Unpublished doctoral dissertation, University of British Columbia, Vancouver, BC.

Gottman, J. M. (1979). *Marital interaction: Experimental investigations.* New York: Academic Press.

Gottman, J. M., Notarius, C., Gonso, J., & Markman, H. (1976). *A couple's guide to communication.* Champaign, IL: Research Press.

Greenberg, L. S., & Johnson, S. M. (1988). *Emotionally focused therapy for couples.* New York: Guilford.

Gurin, G., Veroff, J., & Feld, S. (1960). *Americans view their health: A nationwide interview survey.* New York: Basic Books.

Hahlweg, K., & Markman, H. J. (1988). Effectiveness of behavioral marital therapy: Empirical status of behavioral techniques in preventing and alleviating marital distress. *Journal of Consulting and Clinical Psychology, 56,* 440–447.

Hahlweg, K., Revenstorf, D., & Schindler, L. (1982). Effects of behavioral marital therapy on communication and problem solving skills. *Journal of Consulting and Clinical Psychology, 52,* 553–566.

Hetherington, M. E., Cox, M., & Cox, R. (1986). Long-term effects of divorce and remarriage on the adjustment of children. *Annual Progress in Child Psychiatry and Child Development, 1986,* 407–429.

Holmes, T. H., & Rahe, R. H. (1967). The Social Readjustment Rating Scale. *Journal of Psychosomatic Research, 11,* 213–218.

Institute for Social Research. (1974). Measuring the quality of life in America. *ISR Newsletter, 2,* 1–4.

Jacobson, N. S. (1978). Specific and nonspecific factors in the effectiveness of a behavioral approach to the treatment of marital discord. *Journal of Consulting and Clinical Psychology, 46,* 442–452.

Jacobson, N. S., Follette, V. M., Follette, W. C., Holtzworth-Munroe, A., Katt, J. L., & Schmaling, K. B. (1985). A component analysis of behavioral marital therapy: 1-year follow-up. *Behavior Research and Therapy, 23,* 549–555.

Jacobson, N. S., Follette, W. C., Revenstorf, D., Baucom, D. H., Hahlweg, K., & Margolin, G. (1984). Variability in outcome and clinical significance of behavioral marital therapy: A reanalysis of outcome data. *Journal of Consulting and Clinical Psychology, 52,* 497–504.

Jacobson, N. S., & Margolin, G. (1979). *Marital therapy: Strategies based on social learning and behavior exchange principles.* New York: Brunner/Mazel.

Johnson, S. M., & Greenberg, L. S. (1985a). The differential effects of experiential and problem-solving interventions in resolving marital conflict. *Journal of Consulting and Clinical Psychology, 53,* 175–184.

Johnson, S. M., & Greenberg, L. S. (1985b). Emotionally focused marital therapy: An outcome study. *Journal of Marital and Family Therapy, 11,* 313–317.

Kelley, H. H., & Thibaut, J. W. (1978). *Interpersonal relations.* New York: Wiley.

Levenson, R. W., & Gottman, J. M. (1983). Marital interaction: Psychological linkage and affective exchange. *Journal of Personality and Social Psychology, 45,* 587–597.

Levenson, R. W., & Gottman, J. M. (1985). Physiological and affective predictors of change in relationship satisfaction. *Journal of Personality and Social Psychology, 49,* 85–94.

Locke, H. J., & Wallace, K. M. (1959). Short marital adjustment and prediction tests: Their reliability and validity. *Marriage and Family Living, 21,* 251–255.

Margolin, G. (1981). Behavior exchange in distressed and nondistressed marriages: A family life cycle perspective. *Behavior Therapy, 12,* 329–343.

Markman, H. J., Duncan, S. W., Storaasli, R. D., & Howes, P. W. (1987). The prediction and prevention of marital distress: A longitudinal investigation. In K. Hahlweg & M. J. Goldstein (Eds.), *Understanding major mental disorder: The contribution of family interaction research* (pp. 266–289). New York: Family Process Press.

National Center for Health Statistics. (1973). *100 years of marriage and divorce statistics, United States, 1867–1967.* Rockville, MD: DWEW Publication No. (HRA) 74-1902.

Nierenberg, G. I., & Calero, H. H. (1973). *Meta-talk: Guide to hidden meanings in conversations.* New York: Trident Press.

Norton, A. J., & Mooreman, J. E. (1987). Current trends in marriage and divorce among American women. *Journal of Marriage and the Family, 49,* 3–14.

O'Leary, K. D., & Arias, I. (1987). Marital assessment in clinical practice. In K. D. O'Leary (Ed.), *Assessment of marital discord: An integration for research and clinical practice* (pp. 287–312). Hillsdale, NJ: Erlbaum.

Patterson, G. R., & Reid, J. B. (1970). Reciprocity and coercion: Two facets of social systems. In C. Neuringer & J. L. Michael (Eds.), *Behavior modification in clinical psychology.* New York: Appleton-Century-Crofts.

Revenstorf, D., Hahlweg, K., Schindler, L., & Vogel, B. (1984). Interaction analysis of marital conflict. In K. Hahlweg & N. S. Jacobson (Eds.), *Marital interaction: Analysis and modification.* New York: Guilford.

Snyder, D. K. (1981). *Manual for the Marital Satisfaction Inventory.* Los Angeles, CA: Western Psychological Services.

Somers, A. R. (1979). Marital status, health, and the use of health services. *Journal of Marriage and the Family, 41,* 267–285.

Spanier, G. B. (1976). Measuring dyadic adjustment: New scales for assessing the quality of marriage and similar dyads. *Journal of Marriage and the Family, 38,* 15–28.

Stuart, R. B. (1980). *Helping couples change: A social learning approach to marital therapy.* New York: Guilford.

Thibaut, J. W., & Kelley, H. H. (1959). *The social psychology of groups.* New York: Wiley.

Turkewitz, H., & O'Leary, K. D. (1981). A comparative outcome study of behavioral marital therapy and communication therapy. *Journal of Marital and Family Therapy, 7,* 159–169.

Veroff, J., Kulka, R. A., & Douvan, E. (1981). *Marital health in America: Patterns of help seeking from 1957 to 1976.* New York: Basic Books.

Vivian, D., Smith, D. A., & O'Leary, K. D. (1988, November). *Emotional expression at premarriage as a predictor of discord at 18 and 30 months post-marriage.* Paper presented at the 22nd Annual Convention of the Association for Advancement of Behavior Therapy, New York.

Wallerstein, J. S. (1985). Children of divorce: Preliminary report of a ten-year follow-up of older children and adolescents. *Journal of the American Academy of Child Psychiatry, 24,* 545–553.

Weiss, R. L. (1978). The conceptualization of marriage from a behavioral perspective. In T. S. Paolino & B. S. McCrady (Eds.), *Marriage and marital therapy: Psychoanalytic, behavioral and systems perspectives* (pp. 165–239). New York: Brunner/Mazel.

Weiss, R. L., & Birchler, G. R. (1975). *Areas of change*. Unpublished manuscript, University of Oregon.

Weiss, R. L., Birchler, G. R., & Vincent, J. P. (1974). Contractual models for negotiation training in marital dyads. *Journal of Marriage and the Family, 36,* 321–331.

Weiss, R. L., Hops, H., & Patterson, G. R. (1973). A framework for conceptualizing marital conflict: A technology for altering it, some data for evaluating it. In L. D. Handy & E. L. Marsh (Eds.), *Behavior change: Methodology, concepts, and practice* (pp. 309–342). Champaign, IL: Research Press.

Wills, T. A., Weiss, R. L., & Patterson, G. R. (1974). A behavioral analysis of the determinants of marital satisfaction. *Journal of Consulting and Clinical Psychology, 42,* 802–811.

Author Index

Abe, K., 231
Abel, G. G., 175, 176, 177, 178, 179, 182, 191, 365
Abikoff, H., 267, 268, 270, 273, 275, 279
Abraham, K., 100
Abrams, D. B., 207, 208, 212, 213
Abramson, L. Y., 100, 104, 251
Absher, N., 357
Achenbach, T. M., 247, 249, 287
Adams, H. E., 139, 176, 177
Adams, N. H., 136
Adkins, J. A., 320
Adler, C., 41
Adler, R. H., 32
Affleck, G. G., 329
Ageton, S. S., 288, 291
Agras, S., 33, 231
Agras, W. S., 3, 4, 45, 48, 74, 178, 184, 187, 188, 189, 190, 237, 357, 360, 364, 365, 366, 397, 398
Aguar, D., 295, 300
Agudelo, C. A., 390
Aher, D. K., 386, 388
Ahles, T. A. 378, 380
Aichorn, A., 285
Akhtar, S., 67, 68
Akiskal, H. S., 105

Albala, A. A., 101
Albin, J. B., 301
Alden, L., 128
Alexander, J. F., 272
Alexander, J. K., 399
Alford, G. S., 185
Allan, M. J., 255
Allain, A. N., 123
Allen, L., 231
Allen, T., 212
Allgood-Hill, B., 77
Allman, C. J., 255
Alloy, L. B., 104
Alphs, L. D., 136, 144
Althaus, M., 287
Althof, S. E., 167
American Psychiatric Association, 13, 16, 20, 32, 87, 99, 102, 103, 109, 117, 118, 119, 120, 121, 122, 123, 124, 126, 129, 130, 131, 157, 159, 175, 205, 227, 246, 259, 262, 286, 358, 364, 407
Amies, P. L., 15, 17, 19, 22, 34
Amin, M. M., 82
Ammerman, R. T., 419, 431
Ananth, J., 81
Ancis, J., 40
Anderson, B., 90
Anderson, C.M., 143, 150, 155, 170

Anderson, D. J., 53
Anderson, E. A., 105
Anderson, G., 301
Anderson J., 339
Anderson J. C., 231, 246, 247
Anderson, K. O., 390
Anderson, S. K., 390
Anderson, T. P., 377
Andrasik, F., 378, 380, 390
Andreasen, N. D., 146
Andree, J., 274
Andrew, M., 176
Andrews, G., 40, 49, 82
Angelino, H., 231
Anker, A. L., 210, 211
Annis, A. L., 215
Annis, H. M., 214
Anthony, J. C., 3
Anthony, W. A., 137
Antonuccio, D., 107
Aragona, J., 422, 423
Arbuthnot, J., 293, 298, 305
Archer, R. P., 123
Arena, J. G., 378
Arias, I., 418, 422, 440, 441
Arkowitz, H., 179, 190, 191, 198, 386
Armon, D. J., 215
Armstrong, P. M., 320
Arndt, I. O., 208
Arnold, J., 300
Arnow, B. A., 45, 48

Arthur, J. L., 299, 301
Asarnow, J. R., 254, 255, 293
Asberg, M., 103
Asher, S. J., 437
Atkeson, B., 87
Atkins, M., 185
Atkins, M. S., 262, 270, 272, 276, 277
Auerbach, R., 163
Avitzur, E., 87
Axelrod, S., 328
Ayllon, T., 232
Azar, S. T., 420, 424
Azrin, N. H., 181, 211, 212, 320, 321, 322, 339

Baer, D. M., 324, 346, 347
Baer, J. S., 214, 217
Baer, L., 75, 81, 82
Bailey, J., 328
Bakal, D. A., 390
Baker, L., 231
Baker, T. B., 206, 207, 215
Baldwin, D. V., 303
Ball, G., 49
Ball, P. G., 428
Balla, D., 329
Ballenger, J. C., 100, 101
Bamrah, J. S., 139, 142
Ban, T. A., 82
Bancroft, J., 181, 189
Bandura, A., 7, 45, 50, 73, 82, 107, 385, 386, 388
Bank, L., 288
Banks, D. S., 118, 119
Barbach, L. G., 162
Barbaree, H. E., 176, 181, 191, 194, 195, 196
Barkley, R. A., 264, 266, 299
Barling, J., 301
Barlow, D. H., 3, 4, 5, 10, 15, 16, 40, 41, 42, 43, 44, 45, 46, 47, 48, 49, 50, 51, 53, 54, 55, 56, 57, 58, 60, 68, 70, 73, 74, 82, 91, 158, 162, 175, 177, 178, 179, 181, 186, 187, 188, 189, 190, 236, 237, 365
Barnett, L. R., 439
Baron, G. D., 287
Barone, V. J., 427
Barouche, F., 115
Barrett, C. L., 232

Barrett, R. P., 323, 325
Barrowclough, C., 139, 140, 142
Bash, M. A. S., 297, 299
Basmajian, J. V., 374, 378
Bass, D., 298
Bates, J. E., 289
Baucom, D. H., 450, 451
Bauer, D. H., 231
Baum, C. G., 295
Baum, M., 6
Bauman, K. E., 340
Bauserman, S. A. K., 108, 451, 452
Bayles, K., 289
Beach, S. R. H., 108, 437, 440, 449, 451, 452
Beal, L. S., 194
Beary, J. F., 55
Beck, A., 421
Beck, A. T., 21, 23, 51, 53, 56, 100, 101, 102, 103, 104, 109, 110, 251
Beck, G., 40, 177
Beck, J. G., 155, 158, 159, 160, 161, 162, 163
Beck, N. C., 256, 390
Beck, S., 179
Becker, J., 109
Becker, J. V., 176, 178, 196
Becker, R. E., 15, 20, 25, 34
Beckwith, B. E., 327
Bedrosian, R. C., 110
Beidel, D. C., 14, 15, 16, 17, 19, 20, 21, 33, 67, 68, 69, 70, 72, 74, 75, 77, 78, 81, 82, 128, 130
Beitrose, H., 399
Belding, M., 292, 293
Bell, L. K., 345
Bellack, A. S., 107, 108, 137, 138, 139, 148, 149, 153, 179, 190, 191, 192, 193, 296, 355, 421
Belsher, G., 111, 112
Bem, S. L., 178
Bemis, K. M., 365, 366
Bender, M., 273, 321
Bender, M. E., 264, 265, 267, 268, 271, 274, 275
Benfield, C. Y., 248
Bennett, G. A., 357
Bennett, S. M., 360, 362, 363

Benson, B. A., 331, 332
Benson, H., 55
Bentall, R. P., 139
Bentley, G., 380
Berberich, J. P., 341, 343
Berchick, R. J., 53
Berg, C. J., 238
Berger, M., 289, 301
Bergersen, S. G., 181
Berkowitz, R., 143
Bernal, G., 380
Bernal, M. E., 286, 300
Bernay, T., 235
Berni, R., 375, 377
Bernier, H., 289
Bernstein, D. A., 54
Berrueta-Clement, J. R., 290
Berry, S., 100
Best, A., 402, 403
Best, C. L., 89
Best, J. A., 409, 410
Bettes, B., 144, 147
Bettison, S., 321, 322, 323
Beumont, P. J. V., 365, 366
Bhate, S. R., 235
Bichard, S., 48
Bickett, A., 425
Bickett, A. D., 426
Bidermann, H. J., 379
Bieber, J., 342
Bierman, K. L., 296, 297
Bigelow, G. E., 203, 210, 211
Biglan, A., 301
Billings, A., 439
Billings, A. G., 103, 105
Binkoff, J. A., 207, 208, 346
Biran, M., 8
Birbaumer, N., 385, 391
Birchler, G. R., 439, 441, 448
Birnbrauer, J. S., 330
Bishop, S., 110
Black, B., 236
Black, J. L., 92, 210, 211
Blackburn, I. M., 110
Blackshaw, L., 194
Blagg, N. R., 232
Blanchard, E. B., 7, 10, 40, 48, 49, 50, 52, 53, 54, 55, 175, 177, 178, 179, 189, 378, 380
Bland, K., 45
Blane, H. T., 203
Blashfield, R. K., 118, 216

Blatt, S. J., 104
Blazer, D. G., 41
Blechman, E. A., 294, 299, 304
Block, A. R.., 376
Block, P., 104, 106
Bloom, B. L., 437
Blouin, D. C., 361
Blowers, C., 55, 56
Blowers, C. M., 45
Blumstein, A., 287
Boag, L. C., 247
Boczkowski, J. A., 138
Bodiford, C. A., 248
Bodley, P. O., 404
Bodner, D., 167
Boersma, K., 73
Boggs, S. R., 294
Boice, R., 47, 48
Bolelens, W., 450
Bologna, N., 267, 268, 273, 274,
Bolton, D., 237
Bonn, J. A., 51
Bonner, B. L., 419
Boone, S. E., 137
Booth, S., 264, 265
Bordeau, P. A., 431
Borden, J. W., 16, 68, 71, 133
Borduin, C. M., 304
Borkovec, T. D., 8, 46, 54, 55, 56
Bornstein, M., 252, 253, 254, 296
Boudewyns, P. A., 90, 92
Boulougouris, J. C., 71, 74, 75, 78
Bourg, W. J., 301
Bourque, P., 8
Boutin, 289
Bowen, L., 137, 138
Boyd, H. H., 41
Boyd, J., 151
Boyd, J. H., 3, 41
Boyd, J. L., 139
Boyle, M., 290
Bradbury, T. N., 450, 451
Bradley, L. A., 390
Bradlyn, A. S., 248
Bradlyn, D., 423
Braiker, H. B., 215
Bran, T. A., 52
Brantley, P. J., 123, 126, 139

Brasfield, T. L., 397
Braswell, L., 297, 299
Braunling-McMorrow, D., 427
Breaux, A. M., 289
Breen, M. J., 266
Breen, N. J., 118
Brehony, K., 423
Breier, A., 41
Breiner, J., 295, 300, 303
Brender, W., 164
Brent, D. A., 255
Breslau, N., 52, 54
Bright, P., 40
Bristow, A. R., 179
Britton, P., 321
Broderick, J. E., 301, 446
Brody, G. H., 301
Brown, B. W., 399
Brown, G., 53
Brown, G. W., 103, 137
Brown, L. B., 105
Brown, P. T., 186
Brown, R. A., 107
Brown, R. T., 279
Brown, T. A., 40, 52
Brownell, K. D., 184, 185, 375
Brozek, J., 365
Bruce, B. K., 357
Bruggesser, H. H., 32
Bruner, J., 324
Brunk, M., 304
Bryce, M., 422
Bryson, Y., 327
Buckhalt, J. A., 324, 325
Budenz, D., 110,
Budrow, M., 267, 268, 271, 273, 275
Budzynski, T., 378
Buell, M. M., 194
Bueno, G., 425
Buescher, K., 390
Bugel, C., 321
Buhrmester, D., 264, 265, 270, 278
Burch, P. R., 298
Burgess, P. R., 383
Burgio, L. D., 339
Burke, J. D., 3
Burke, P., 248
Burlingame, W. V., 248
Burnam, A., 100
Burnman, A., 68

Burns, L. E., 42, 381
Burton, N., 246
Burton, T., 41, 45, 48
Bush, C., 379
Butler, G., 22, 34, 56, 57
Butler, L., 254
Butler, L. J., 292
Butler, R. W., 92
Buttolph, L., 82
Buxton, A. E., 357

Caddell, J., 264, 265
Caddell, J. M., 89, 90, 92
Caddy, G. R., 208
Caird, W. K., 162, 189
Cairns, B. D., 291
Cairns, D., 376, 377, 392
Cairns, R. B., 291
Calero, H. H., 444
Calhoun, J. F., 125
Calhoun, K., S., 87, 131, 176
Callahan, E. I., 181
Callahan, E. J., 214
Callan, J. W., 293
Callon, E. B., 126
Cameron, O. G., 41
Cameron, R., 409, 410
Camic, P., 169
Camp, B. W., 297, 299
Campbell, C. R., 325, 329
Campbell, R. V., 299, 425, 427
Campbell, S. B., 260, 289
Campeas, R., 32, 34
Candy, J., 32
Cannon, D. S., 206
Cantwell, D. P., 231, 246, 247, 256
Capaldi, D., 288
Caplinger, T. E., 285
Caponigri, V., 330
Cappell, H., 213
Caputo, G., 40
Carey, R. J., Jr., 75
Carlisle, J. M., 175, 183, 188
Carlson, C. L., 275, 277, 292
Carlson, C. R., 129
Carlson, G. A., 246, 247, 254
Carnevale, G., 87
Carol, M. P., 55
Caron, C., 289
Carpenter, C., 232
Carpenter, W. T., 135, 136, 144

Carr, E. G., 328, 339, 340, 341, 346, 347
Carrier, J. K., Jr., 324
Carrigan, W. F., 187
Carroll, B. J., 101
Carter, H., 437
Casey, F. G., 345
Casey, K. L., 374, 382
Cash, T. F., 40
Casriel, C., 210, 211
Cassisi, J. E., 419
Castell, D., 186
Castonguay, L. G., 183
Catalan, J., 44, 160, 168, 170
Cautela, J. R. 183, 184, 207
Cavallaro, L. A., 42
Cerniglia, L., 348
Cerny, J. A., 40, 44, 45, 50, 51
Ciminero, A. R., 176
Chaiken, J. M., 287
Chaiken, M. R., 287
Chalkley, A., 49
Chamberlain, P., 292, 294, 303
Chamberlain, T. P., 327
Chambers, A., 55, 56
Chambless, D. L., 40, 43, 72, 381
Chaney, E. F., 213, 390, 391
Chandler, M. J., 298
Chapin, H. H., 231
Chapin, H. N., 365
Chaplin, E. W., 43
Chaplin, T. C., 187
Chapman, D. G., 421, 429
Chapman, L. J., 121
Charlebois, P., 290
Charlop, M. H., 339, 341, 342, 343, 344, 345, 347
Charney, D. S., 41, 69, 106
Chastain, R. L., 386
Chaudhry, D. R., 41
Chen, T., 261
Cheslow, D. L., 238, 239
Chess, S., 289
Chila, A. G., 379, 386, 387
Childress, A. R., 207, 208
Childs-Clarke, A., 45
Chiles, A., 291
Chomsky, N., 324
Christensen, A., 179, 191, 300
Christensen, H., 82
Christoff, K. A., 296

Clancy, J., 182
Clancy, S., 390
Clark, D., 49, 51
Clark, D. B., 33
Clarke, C., 428
Clarke, J. C., 22, 26, 34, 207
Clarkson, S. E., 247
Clinton, J., 278
Clum, G. A., 90, 92
Coats, K. I., 254
Cobb, J., 55, 56, 81, 82
Cobb, J. P., 45
Coe, D., 330
Coffey, M. L., 238, 239
Cogswell, K. A., 252
Cohen, D., 48, 49
Cohen, D. J., 67
Cohen, J., 210
Cohen, J. M., 287
Cohen, P., 255
Cohen, S. D., 42
Cohen, S. L., 45
Coie, J. D., 292, 293
Cole, D. A., 255
Cole, E., 254
Cole, J. O., 136
Cole, T. M., 377
Collier, J., 163
Collins, J. F., 110
Collins, S., 237
Comfort, A., 193
Conaway, L. P., 420
Condiotte, M. M., 387
Condron, M. K., 157
Conners, C. K., 253, 254, 265, 287
Connolly, J. C., 10
Connor, P., 290
Conrad, S. R., 188
Contreras, A., 267, 268, 273, 274
Conway, G., 269
Cooney, N. L., 213
Cooper, A. A., 189
Cooper, J. E., 70, 78
Cooper, N. A., 90, 92
Copeland, L., 266
Copemann, C. D., 207
Corcoran, C. M., 246
Cordes, C., 136
Corey, D. T., 390
Corn, K. J., 41

Costello, A. J., 249
Costello, C. G., 111, 112
Costello, E. J., 249, 289
Cote, L., 386, 387
Cote, R., 289
Couk, D. I., 327
Council, J. R., 386, 388
Cowdry, R. W., 124
Cowen, E. L., 399
Cowles, K. S., 212
Cox, B. J., 40
Cox, G. B., 291
Cox, M., 301, 437
Cox, R., 301, 437
Coyne, J. C., 105
Craighead, W. E., 100, 103, 105, 108, 111, 112, 248
Craske, M. G., 40, 41, 42, 44, 45, 46, 48, 50, 51, 52, 53, 54, 60
Creer, T. L., 406
Crisafulli, A., 301
Crocker, M. F., 376, 377, 386, 387
Cromwell, R. L., 146
Cronkite, R. C., 103, 105
Croughan, J., 103
Crowe, L., 289
Crowe, M. J., 450
Crowe, R. R., 41, 53
Crowley, T. J., 210, 211
Crown, S., 163
Cuddy, M. E., 248
Cullington, A., 22, 34, 57
Cumming, G. F., 194
Cummings, C., 291
Cummings, E. M., 293
Cunningham, C. E., 265
Cunningham-Rathner, J., 176, 177
Curley, A. D., 422, 428
Curran, J. P., 191, 192, 193
Curry, J. F., 298
Curry, S. J., 214, 217, 248
Curtis, G. C., 41
Cutler, A., 327
Cutler, H. S. G., 212
Cytryn, L. A., 245, 247

Dachman, R. S., 426, 427
Dabbs, J. M., 404
Dadds, M. R., 303, 304
D'Afflitti, J. P., 104

Dancu, C. V., 14, 15, 17, 21, 46, 47, 90, 128
Dangel, R. F., 299
Daniels, M., 100
D'ardenne, P., 163
Dare, C., 366
d'Avernas, J. R., 402, 403
Davey, J., 272
Davidson, T., 422
Davidson, W. S., 293
Davies, L., 169
Davis, C. J., 355, 356, 359, 360, 361, 362, 363, 364, 365
Davis, C. S., 214, 215
Davis, J., 138
Davis, J. M., 153
Davis, K. L., 102, 105
Davison, G., 188
Davison, G. C., 125, 232
Dawson, M. E., 139
Deagle, E. A., 40
DeAmicis, L. A., 169
Dearth, N., 139
de Blois, S., 291
DeBocker, G., 399
Debush, R. F., 32
Deford, H. A., 210, 211
DeGiovanni, I. S., 231
Deitz, D. E. D., 317
Dekker, J., 73
Delameter, A., 253, 254, 267
DeLateur, B. J., 374, 377
Delfini, L. F., 286
Delgado, L. E., 427
Deluty, R. H., 293
DeMayo, R., 104
Demjen, S., 390
Demming, B., 203
Den Hengst, S., 73
Dennis, C., 32
Dennis, S. G., 382, 383
Denny, D. R., 8
DePaola, L. M., 301
Derogatis, L. R., 158
Derry, P. A., 102
DeRubeis, R. J., 110
deRuiter, C., 47, 49
DeSanto, N., 138
deSilva, P., 45
DeTejada, I. S., 157, 158, 167
DeVigne, J. P., 101
Diamond, R., 136

Dibble, E., 105
DiClemente, C. C., 216
DiLalla, L. F., 289
DiNardo, P. A., 10, 16, 40, 41, 42, 48, 49, 52, 53, 54
Diorio, M. S., 320
Dishion, T., 289, 290, 291, 292
Ditto, B., 379
Dixon, M. J., 275, 277
Djenderedjian, A., 178
D'Lugoff, B., 210
Dobbins, K., 50, 55
Dobson, K. S., 293
Docherty, J. P., 110
Dodge, C. S., 15, 20, 25, 34
Dodge, K. A., 289, 292, 293
Dohrenwend, B. D., 89
Dolan, M. P., 87, 210, 211
Dolce, J. J., 377, 378, 386, 387
Dolder, M., 32
Doleys, D. M., 330, 376, 377, 386
Dollard, J., 71
Dollinger, S. J., 296
Dollins, J., 231
Donahoe, C. P., 137
Donovan, D. M., 205, 214
Doppelt, H. G., 73, 74, 75
Dorsey, M. F., 340
Dorward, J., 40
Dougher, M. J., 207
Douglas, V. I., 259, 277
Douvan, E., 437
Dow, M. G., 100
Dramair, M., 399
Droegemueller, W., 417
Drolet, M., 386, 387
Duchmann, E. G., 355, 356, 359, 360, 361, 364, 365
Duckert, P., 210
DuFour, L., 48
Dumas, J. E., 285, 289, 290, 291, 292, 293, 294, 299, 300, 301, 302, 303, 304, 422
Duncan, S. W., 437
Dundore, D., 392
Dunlap, G., 339, 343, 345
Dunnington, R. E., 277
Durand, M., 328
Durham, R. C., 56

Dush, D. M., 298, 299, 300
Dyck, D. G., 257
Dyer, K., 345
D'Zurilla, T. J., 57, 125, 251

Earls, C. M., 183
Earls, F., 287
Ebrahimi, S., 55, 56
Eddleman, J., 427
Eddy, M., 346
Eddy, M. S., 429
Edelbrock, C., 287
Edelbrock, C. A., 249
Edelbrock, C. S., 249, 256
Edleson, J. L., 421, 429
Edwards, B., 423, 431
Edwards, N. B., 193
Egan, K., 424
Egel, A. L., 339, 345
Eggeraat, J. G.
Ehlers, A., 40
Ehrman, R., 208
Eisenstadt, T. H., 248
Eisler, R. M., 210
Elias, D., 386, 388
Elkin, I., 110
Elkins, R., 238
Elkins, R. L., 207
Ellicott, A., 104
Ellinwood, E. H., 383
Elliot, C. B., 321
Elliot, F. A., 422
Elliott, D. S., 288, 291
Ellis, A., 56, 428
Ellis, E., 87
Ellis, N. R., 321
Ellis, P. L., 293
Emery, G., 56, 103, 109
Emery, R. E., 301, 437
Emmelkamp, P. M. G., 7, 21, 24, 42, 43, 45, 47, 73, 74, 450
Endicott, J., 53, 103
Engelsmann, F., 81
Epps, J., 297
Epstein, L. H., 357, 397
Epstein, N., 450, 451
Erbaugh, J., 421
Erhardt, D., 260, 270, 277, 278
Erickson, W. D., 177
Erikson, M., 413
Erikkson, L., 383

Eron, L. D., 290
Esveldt-Dawson, K., 292, 298, 304
Etlin, D., 390
Eunson, K. M., 110
Evans, D. L., 102
Evans, D. R., 175, 188
Evans, M., 168
Evans, M. D., 114
Evans, R. I., 402, 403
Evans, R. W., 407, 408
Everett, N. L., 342
Everly, G. S., 397
Everaerd, W. T. A. M., 159, 169
Ewing, L. J., 289
Eyberg, S., 294
Eysenck, H. J., 380

Fagan, P. J., 158
Fagg, J., 168, 170
Fairbank, J. A., 90, 92
Fairburn, C. G., 360
Fallahi, C., 256
Falloon, I. R. H., 22, 139, 140, 142
Fantuzzo, J. W., 301
Farnworth, M., 290
Farquhar, J. W., 399
Farrington, D. P., 287
Farris, A. M., 301
Faulk, M., 422
Faust, J., 301
Favell, J. E., 331
Faw, G. D., 321
Federal Bureau of Investigation, 417
Feehan, M., 290
Feigenbaum, W., 43
Feinberg, M., 101
Feinberg, T. E., 144, 147
Feld, S., 437
Feldman, M. P., 181, 182, 186
Feldman, R. A., 285
Feldman, R. H. L., 397
Fenichel, O., 175
Fenwick, J. W., 390
Fernandez, E., 373, 389
Ferro, P., 136
Feuerstein, M., 379, 406
Fialkov, M. J., 253
Fichten, C. S., 164
Figlio, R. M., 287

Fincham, F. D., 450, 451
Fine, S., 291, 293
Finkelstein, R., 228
Firestone, P., 272
Firestone, P. B., 343
First, M. B., 103
Fischer, M., 266
Fischer, S. C., 74
Fish, C., 327
Fisher, E. B., 139
Fisher, E. R., 430
Fiester, S. J., 110
Fieve, R. R., 104
Fithian, M. A., 194
Flament, M. F., 238
Flannery, R. B., 131
Flay, B. R., 402, 403
Fleeting, M., 289
Fleischman, M. J., 294, 299
Fleischmann, R. L., 69
Fleming, B., 131
Flinn, D. W., 383
Flitcraft, A., 417
Flor, H., 376, 377, 379, 385, 391
Florio, L., 41
Fo, W. S., 293
Foa, E. G., 43, 45, 46, 47, 67, 71, 72, 73, 74, 75, 77, 78, 79, 82, 89, 208, 236
Follette, V. M., 450
Follette, W. C., 450, 451
Follick, M. J., 386, 388
Fordham, S., 287
Fordyce, W. E., 374, 375, 377, 381, 382
Forehand, R., 285, 286, 289, 292, 294, 295, 299, 300, 301, 302, 303
Foreyt, J. O., 357
Forgatch, M. S., 303
Fowler, R. S., 374, 375, 377
Foxx, R. M., 322, 329, 330, 331, 339
Foy, D. W., 137, 212
Fracher, J. C., 157
Frame, C. L., 248, 253, 291, 293, 331, 332
Frame, R. E., 425
France, R. D., 383
Frances, A., 49
Francis, G., 228, 230, 231, 233, 238

Frangia, G. W., 301
Frank, E., 90, 112, 155, 170
Frank, P. B., 429
Frank, R. G., 390
Frankel, K., 289
Frechette, M., 287
Freedberg, E. J., 213, 214
Freedman, R. R., 378
Freeman, H., 142, 153
French, N. H., 298, 304
Freud, S., 100
Freund, K., 178, 186
Freve, A., 48
Friedman, J., 169
Friedman, J. M., 166
Friedman, L., 301
Friedman, R., 254
Fry, R. A., 296
Frymoyer, J. M., 390
Furby, L., 194
Furey, W., 303
Furman, W., 296
Fydrich, T., 379, 386
Fyer, A. J., 17, 32, 34, 53

Gaffney, L. R., 292
Gagnon, C., 290
Gajdos, E., 7
Galassi, J. P., 422
Gallagher, R., 40
Gallops, M. S., 53
Galloway, D., 232
Ganiats, T., 397, 398
Ganzell, S. L., 269
Ganzer, V. J., 296
Garcia, K., 231
Gardner, D. L., 124
Gardos, G., 136
Garfinkel, B. D., 255, 290
Garfinkel, P. E., 366
Garside, R. F., 235
Garssen, B., 47, 49
Garvey, M. J., 110
Garvey, W. P., 232
Gatsonis, C., 291
Gaupp, L. A., 4, 383
Gauthier, J., 48, 386, 387
Gawin, F. H., 210
Gay, H. L., 422
Gaylor, M., 376
Gaylord-Ross, R., 328
Gearing, M. L., 87
Geer, J. H., 159

Geffner, R., 418, 420, 422, 428
Gelder, M. G., 13, 15, 17, 19, 22, 34, 42, 44, 57, 78, 181, 182, 190
Gelernter, S., 261, 279
Gelfand, D. M., 293
Gellers, R. J., 417, 418
Gemmer, T. C., 299
Genest, M. 383, 384, 389
Gentry, W. D., 380
George, F. S., 184, 185
Geraci, M., 41
Gerardi, R. J., 87
German, P. S., 409
Ghosh, A., 44
Gibat, C. C., 194
Gibbon, M., 103
Gibbons, X. X., 18
Gibson, J. A., 301
Gil, K. M., 390
Gilbert, A., 401
Gilbert, F. S., 142
Gilbert, M. T., 422
Gillan, P., 42
Giller, H., 289
Gingerich, S., 139
Gino, A., 206
Girelli, S. A., 90
Girich, Y. P., 247
Gitlin, B., 49
Gitlin, M., 104
Gittelman, R., 263, 264, 267, 268, 270, 273, 275, 279
Gittelman-Klein, R., 235
Gladsjo, J. A., 215, 216
Glasgow, R. E., 300
Glass, D. R., 110
Glazer, M., 214
Gleberman, L., 430
Gleser, G. C., 89
Glezos, S. P., 305
Glick, B., 299
Glick, P. C., 437
Glickman, S., 287
Glogower, F., 302
Glosser, D. S., 210
Glotter, D., 362
Glynn, T., 302
Gnagy, E. M., 278
Godley, M., 212
Goetz, D., 32, 34
Goff, G., 370

Goldberg, D. C., 169
Goldfried, M. R., 378
Goldfried, N., 125
Goldfried, N. R., 57, 125
Golding, J. M., 68
Goldman, A., 451
Goldman, H. H., 136, 139
Goldsmith, D. S., 210, 211
Goldstein, A. J., 381
Goldstein, A. P., 299
Goldstein, C. E., 255
Goldstein, G. 150
Goldstein, I., 157, 158, 167
Goldstrom, I. D., 136
Golombeck, S., 163
Gondolf, E. W., 430
Gonso, J., 444
Good, A., 348
Goodman, J., 297
Goodman, J. T., 272
Goodman, W. K., 69
Gordon, D. A., 293, 293, 305
Gordon, J., 217
Gordon, J. R., 95, 203, 206, 214, 215, 409
Gordon-Leventon, B., 249
Goreczny, A. J., 361
Gorman, J. M., 15, 17, 32, 34, 53
Gorman, L. F., 15, 32
Gossard, D., 32, 386
Gotestam, K. G., 377
Gottesman, I. I., 289
Gotlib, I. H., 105
Gottman, J. M., 439, 443, 444, 450
Gouze, K. R., 293
Grabowski, J., 208
Graham, M., 215
Graham, P. J., 231, 289, 290
Graves, K., 423
Graves, M. G., 301
Gray, J. J., 189
Grayson, J. B., 46, 72, 73, 74, 75, 77,
Graziano, A. M., 231, 234, 235, 293
Graziano, W. G., 301
Greden, J. K., 101
Greeley, J., 213
Green, B. L., 89
Green, K., 295, 300
Green, M., 146

Green, R., 407, 408
Green, S. M., 292
Greenberg, L. S., 451
Greene, B. F., 425, 426, 427
Greenfield, S., 100
Greenslade, K. E., 278
Greenstein, R., 208
Greenwald, D. P., 149, 152, 213
Greenwald, M., 46, 47
Greenwald, M. A., 213
Gregg, J. M., 378
Greiner, A. R., 278
Grenier, C., 362, 363
Gresham, F. M., 297
Griest, D. L., 286, 292, 300, 301, 302, 303
Griez, E., 51
Griffiths, R. L., 203
Grossman, H. D., 329
Grossman, H. J., 318
Grossman, L., 237
Grove, W. M., 110
Grusnzski, R. J., 421, 429
Guerney, L. F., 424
Guess, D., 324
Guild, D., 178
Gulickson, G., 377
Gurin, G., 437
Guroff, J. J., 105
Gursky, D. M., 40
Guthrie, D., 255

Hadzi-Pavlovic, D., 82
Hafner, R. J., 42, 43, 45
Hagfors, N., 383
Hahlweg, K., 439, 449, 450, 451
Hakstian, A. R., 107
Halasz, M. M., 426
Haley, G., 291, 293
Haley, S., 92
Halford, K., 401
Hall, G. M., 212
Hall, J. R., 379, 386, 387
Hall, S. M., 212, 214
Hallam, R. S., 10, 45, 237, 238
Halle, J., 325
Hally, C., 419
Hamberger, L. K., 421, 430
Hamburg, S., 209
Hamilton, M., 103

Hamilton, M. W., 139
Hampe, E., 232
Hammen, C. L., 102, 104
Hamovit, J., 105
Hamra, B. J., 41
Handley, R., 137, 139
Hansen, D. G., 148, 149
Hansen, D. J., 296, 420
Hanson, C. L. 304
Hanson, R., 330
Hanson, R. H., 327
Hanusa, D., 420, 429
Harbison, J. J, 186
Hardin, M. T., 239
Harper, G. W., 278
Harper, J., 362
Harper, R. A., 56, 425
Harpin, R. E., 22
Harris, C. V., 208, 214
Harris, E. L., 41
Harris, L., 253
Harris, S. R., 299
Harris, T. O., 103
Harrison, J., 51
Hart, B., 325
Hart, C. H., 292
Hartdagen, M. A., 291
Hartlage, S., 104
Hartman, D. P., 293
Hartman, W. A., 194
Haskell, W. L., 399
Haskitt, R. F., 101
Haslam, M. T., 51
Hastings, J. F., 421, 430
Hathaway, G. R., 177
Hatsukami, D., 362
Hawkins, J., 216
Hawthorne, J. W., 210, 211
Hawton, K., 160, 168, 170
Hayes, D., 207
Hayes, S. C., 184, 185, 357
Haynes, R. B., 409
Haynes, S. N., 180
Hays, R. D., 100
Hazard, R. G., 309
Hechtman, L., 259, 267
Heckerman, C., 357
Hedrick, K. E., 212
Heffer, R. W., 355, 357
Hegrenes, J. R., 232
Heiman, J. R., 164
Heimberg, R. G., 15, 20, 25, 34

Heinrichs, D. W. 136, 144
Heller, T., 264, 265, 270
Helzer, J. E., 88, 103
Henderson, J. G., 19
Henggeler, S. W., 304
Heninger, G. R., 41, 69, 106
Henker, B., 264, 270, 271, 273, 277, 278
Henningfield, J. E., 203
Henschel, A., 365
Herceg-Baron, R. L., 103, 108
Herman, S., 236
Herman, S. H., 188
Herron, E., 136
Hersen, M., 107, 108, 138, 149, 210, 228, 419, 296
Hester, R. K., 204, 205, 208, 209, 210, 214, 217, 218
Hetherington, E. M., 301
Hetherington, M. E., 437
Hibbert, G., 57
Higson, P. J., 139
Hill, C. L., 69
Himadi, W., 44, 45
Himle, J., 41
Himmelhoch, J., 81, 107, 108
Hinshaw, S. P., 260, 262, 264, 270, 271, 273, 277, 278
Hinz, L. D., 362
Hirt, M. L., 298, 299, 300
Hobbs, S. A., 297
Hoberman, H. M., 106, 107, 255
Hoddap, R., 329
Hodgson, R. J., 69, 71, 73, 74, 188, 208
Hoelscher, T. J., 56
Hoenig, J., 139
Hoeper, E. W., 246
Hoffman, E. H., 301
Hogan, A. E., 293
Hogan, D. R., 166
Hogarty, G. E., 136, 143, 149, 150
Holden, A. E. O., 44
Hole, V., 139
Holland, A., 81, 82
Hollander, E., 32, 34
Hollandsworth, J. G., 422
Hollin, C. R., 296, 300
Hollingsworth, C., 237
Hollinsworth, T., 295
Hollis, J. H., 324

Hollon, S. D., 104, 109, 110
Holm, J. E., 379, 386, 387
Holman, H. R., 390
Holmen, M. L., 183, 184
Holmes, M. R., 148, 149
Holmes, T. H., 437
Holmon, H. R., 386
Holroyd, K. A., 378, 379, 386, 387, 390, 406
Holt, P., 40, 49
Holtz, W. C., 181
Holtzman, P. S., 121
Holtzworth-Monroe, A., 114, 450
Holzman, A. D., 79, 390
Honzik, M. P., 231
Hood, H. V., 397
Hoogduin, C. A., 49
Hooley, J., 138, 139
Hope, D. A., 15, 20, 25, 34
Hopkins, J., 357
Hops, H., 442
Hops, M., 301
Horne, A. M., 299
Horner, R., 339
Hornsveld, R. H. J., 71
Houghton, B. D., 429
Hovell, M. F., 397, 393
Howell, C. T., 287
Howes, P. W., 437
Hoyson, M., 343
Hoza, J., 265, 266, 276
Hsu, L. K. G., 139, 366
Huber, A., 278
Huber, C., 231, 234
Hubert, N., 318
Hudgens, A., 377
Huesmann, L. R., 290
Hughes, C., 90
Huizinga, D., 288, 291
Hunt, G. M., 211, 212
Huntzinger, R. M., 229
Hursey, K. G., 386, 387
Hutelmyer, C. M., 405
Hutter, C. K., 90
Hyer, L., 90, 92
Hymel, S., 292
Hynd, G. W., 291

Ianni, P., 378
Iezzi, A., 177
Ignasiak, D., 231, 234
Imber, S. D., 110

Infantino, A., 44
Institute for Social Research, 437
Ito, J. R., 214
Ivancic, M. T., 339
Ivens, C., 249
Iwata, B. A., 339, 340
Iwata, B. M., 218, 327
Izard, C. E., 100

Jackel, L., 53, 54
Jackson, P. R., 213
Jacob, R. G., 16, 33, 79, 81, 82, 130
Jacobson, E., 54, 422
Jacobson, N. S., 105, 108, 439, 442, 445, 450, 451
Jaffe, P., 301
James, J. E., 294
James, N. M. I., 101
Jameson, J. S., 43
Jamieson, B., 343
Jamison, K. R., 104
Jannoun, L., 44
Jansen, M. A., 421, 429
Jansson, L., 15, 42, 43, 47
Jaremko, M. E., 90
Javna, C. D., 149, 152
Jeans, J., 235
Jeffrey, R. W., 7, 45
Jenike, M. A., 75, 81, 82
Jenkins, R. L., 287
Jensen, B. L., 421
Jensen, G. B., 158, 160
Jerremalm, A., 8, 9, 10, 27, 36, 42, 47
Jessup, B. A., 379, 390
Joffe, R. D., 293
Johansson, J., 9, 15, 27, 34
Johns, M. B., 397, 398
Johnsen, J., 210
Johnson, J. E., 404
Johnson, J. H., 248
Johnson, M., 321
Johnson, M. O., 18
Johnson, S. M., 300, 301, 339, 451
Johnson, V. E., 155, 156, 159, 161, 168, 194
Johnston, C., 261, 279
Johnston, D. W., 42, 43, 44
Johnston, P., 196
Johnston, W. E., 213, 214

Jonas, S., 397
Jones, H. V., 404
Jones, R., 196, 214
Jordan, C. G., 90
Josephson, S., 49
Jouriles, E. N., 108, 301
Joyce, S. A., 269
Judd, L. L., 237
Jurish, S. E., 378, 380

Kadden, R. M., 213
Kagan, J., 18
Kaiser, A. P., 325
Kalisch, S. M., 390
Kaloupek, D. G., 92
Kanfer, F. H., 177
Kanner, A., 263, 264
Kanner, L., 337
Kanno, P. H., 159
Kaplan, G., 255
Kaplan, H. S., 155, 194
Kaplan, M., 176, 191
Kappell, L., 32
Karlsson, J., 264
Karno, M., 68
Kaser, H. E., 32
Kashani, J. H., 246, 247, 248
Kashima, K. M., 194
Kaslow, N. J., 248, 253, 254
Katt, J. L., 450
Katz, M. M., 100
Katz, S., 267, 268, 273, 275
Kaufman, K. L., 419
Kaufmann, K., 422, 423, 424
Kavanagh, K., 303
Kay, B., 235
Kazdin, A. E., 7, 123, 228, 249, 252, 253, 279, 285, 290, 292, 293, 294, 296, 298, 299, 300, 303, 304, 305
Keane, T. M., 87, 89, 90, 92, 212
Kearney, C. A., 228, 233
Kedesdy, J., 327
Kee, K., 153
Keefe, F. J., 177, 390
Keesey, R. E., 364
Kegel, A., 164
Keith, G. S., 142
Kelley, H. H., 438
Kelley, J. A., 397
Kelley, M. L., 355, 357

Kelly, D. A., 32
Kelly, J. A., 423
Kelly, M. J., 272
Kelly, R. J., 181, 196
Kelso, J., 290
Kempe, C. H., 417
Kendall, P. C., 104, 297, 299
Kennedy, R. E., 293
Kennedy, S. H., 366
Kent, R. N., 301
Kerr, N. J., 321, 322
Kersell, M. W., 402, 403
Kewman, D. G., 379
Keys, D. J., 14, 15, 17, 21, 128, 365
Khatami, M., 214
Kidd, K. K., 105
Kilmann, P. R., 163
Kilpatrick, D. G., 89, 90, 123
Kilts, C., 238
King, A. R., 123
King, R., 239, 330
Kinsbourne, M., 264, 266
Kipper, D. A., 92
Kirsch, I., 48
Kirschenbaum, S., 41
Klaczynski, P. A., 293
Klass, E. T., 16
Kleber, H. D., 210
Klein, D. F., 5, 17, 40, 43, 53, 235, 267, 268, 273, 275
Klein, H. M., 40
Klimes, I., 57
Kline, C. L., 386, 388
Klingner, A., 82
Klinnert, M. D., 300
Klosko, J., 48, 49
Klosko, J. S., 50, 51
Kloss, J. D., 213
Knopf, J., 169
Koegel, L. K., 341, 348
Koegel, R. K., 341, 348
Koegel, R. L., 339, 342, 343, 344, 345, 346, 348
Koenigsberg, H. W., 137, 139
Kolko, D. J., 236, 255
Kologinsky, E., 346
Kolpacoff, M., 295
Kolvin, I., 193, 235, 289
Kolvin, P. A., 289
Konarski, E. A. Jr., 320
Kopel, S., 386
Kores, R., 386, 388

Kornblith, S. J., 152
Kornetsky, C., 146
Kornitzer, M., 399
Kotanchik, N. L., 304
Kotarba, J. A., 377
Kovacs, M., 109, 110, 246, 249, 255, 291
Kovalski, M. B., 213
Koverola, C., 423, 431
Kozak, M. J., 208
Kozak, M. S., 45, 46, 72, 82
Kraaimaat, F., 47, 49, 71
Kraft, A. R., 49
Krager, J. M., 263
Kraemer, H. C., 366
Kramer, M., 3
Kramme, K., 343
Krane, R. J., 157, 158, 167
Krantz, P. J., 347
Krantz, S., 102
Kratcoski, P. C., 301
Krehbiel, G., 270, 278
Kremer, E. F., 376
Krishnan, K. R. R., 383
Kronfol, Z., 101
Krueger, M., 40
Kuczmierczyk, A. R., 406
Kuiper, N. A., 102, 104
Kuipers, A. C. M., 47
Kuipers, L., 143
Kulka, R. A., 437
Kupersmidt, J. B., 293
Kupfer, D. J., 112, 267
Kursh, D., 167
Kurtz, P. F., 345
Kyzer, B., 330

Labbe, E. E., 406
Labenski, B. J., 139
Laberge, B., 48
Ladd, G. S., 292
Lader, M. H., 32
Ladouceur, R., 8
Lahey, B. B., 267, 291, 292, 297
Lambert, L., 301
Lampron, L. B., 298, 299
Lancashire, M., 42
Landau, S., 261
Landis, C. A., 169
Landy, F. J., 4
Lang, A. R., 261
Lang, P. J., 27, 72

Lange, A. R., 279
Langevin, R., 177, 178, 190
LaPierre, Y., 32
Laplante, B., 289
Lapouse, R., 231
Larkin, K. T., 15
Laski, K., 278
Laski, K. E., 341
Last, C. G., 44, 48, 228, 230, 231, 236
Latimer, P. R., 73, 75
Launius, M. H., 421
Lautenschlager, G. J., 301
Law, T., 274
Lawrence, C., 210
Laws, D. R., 176, 183, 184, 194, 195
Lazarus, A. A., 232, 422
Lazarus, R. S., 391
Leaf, P. J., 41
Lease, C. A., 230
Leber, W. R., 110
LeBlanc, M., 287, 290
Lechowicz, J. G., 292
Leckman, J. F., 67, 105
Ledingham, J. E., 287, 290
Leff, J., 139, 143
Lefkowitz, M. M., 246, 290
Lehmann, J. F., 377
Leiblum, S. R., 157, 158
Leitenberg, H., 178, 181, 184, 305, 360, 365
Leland, H., 318
Lelliott, P., 44
Lentham, J., 380
Lentz, R. J., 138
Leonard, H. L., 238, 239
Leonard, K. E., 203
Lesch, M., 326
Lester, G. W., 450
Levenson, R. W., 439, 450
Leventhal, H., 404
Levin, A. P., 32, 34
Levin, R. A., 118, 124, 126
Levine, A., 300
Levine, B. A., 43
Levine, J. L., 110
Levine, M. N., 321
Levine, S. B., 167
Levinson, D. F., 137
Levinson, T., 215
Levis, D. J., 182
Levitan, G. W., 331

Levitt, K., 48
Lewinsohn, P. M., 100, 105, 106, 107, 250
Liberman, R. P., 137, 138, 149, 214
Libman, E., 164
Licht, B. G., 278
Licht, M. H., 262
Lichstein, K. L., 56
Lichtenstein, E., 387, 401
Liebowitz, M. R., 17, 32, 34, 53, 118, 120, 131
Liebschutz, J., 357
Liebson, I. A., 203, 210, 211
Lief, H. I., 155
Lieterberg, H., 45
Lindahl, I. L., 8, 10
Linden, W., 5, 8
Lindgren, S., 261, 266
Linehan, M. M., 111, 112, 124
Linford-rees, W., 183
Linnoila, M., 238
Linquist, C. U., 430
Linton, S. J., 377
Lippens, K., 185
Lipton, D. N., 179
Lipton, D. S., 210, 211
Litt, M. D., 345, 386
Little, L. M., 192
Litwin, E. M., 41
Llewellyn, J., 405
Lloyd, G. G., 22
Lloyd, J. C., 422
Lobitz, G. K., 301
Lobitz, W. C., 164
Lochman, J. E., 293, 298, 299
Locke, H. J., 440
Loeb, P. C., 212
Loeber, R., 285, 287, 288, 290, 291, 292
Logan, A. C., 40
Lohr, N., 101
Loney, J., 260, 261
Long, D., 383
Long, N., 289, 295, 299, 300
Lopatka, C., 48, 380, 388
LoPiccolo, J., 159, 164, 165, 166, 169
Lorig, K., 386, 390
Lossie, J., 386
Lovaas, O. I., 324, 341, 342, 343
Lowe, C. F., 139

Luber, R. F., 149
Lucas, J. A., 40, 41
Lucas, A., 236
Luchins, D. J., 144, 147
Lucock, M. P., 23
Ludwick-Rosenthal, R., 404, 406
Lukens, E., 229
Lumry, A., 104
Lustman, P. J., 110
Lutzker, J. R., 299, 417, 418, 419, 422, 424, 425, 426, 427, 428
Lutzker, S. Z., 427
Luxenberg, M. G., 177
Lyons, J. A., 87
Lyons, J. S., 138
Lytle, R., 55, 56

Maany, I., 208
Maccoby, N., 399
MacCullough, M. J., 181, 182, 186
MacFarlane, J. N., 231
MacGillavry, D., 450
MacMillan, V. M., 420
Madonia, M. J., 149, 152
Magnusson, D., 290
Magura, S., 210, 211
Mahoney, K., 321, 322
Maisto, S. A., 119, 124, 126, 127, 128, 131, 208
Maiuro, R. D., 422
Maletzky, B. M., 183, 184
Mallams, J. H., 212
Malatesta, V., 139
Malouf, R. E., 272
Manderscheid, R. W., 136
Manikam, R., 330
Manion, I., 423, 431
Mannuzza, S., 53
Mansdorf, I. J., 229
Marcattilio, A. J., 330
Marchetti, A., 320, 329
Marchione, K., 46, 47, 48
Marcille, P. J. 379, 386, 387,
Marcus, J., 290
Marcus, M. D., 357
Margolin, G., 420, 430, 431, 439, 442, 445, 451
Margraf, J., 40, 51
Marhoeffer-Dvorak, S., 90
Marie, C., 327

Markman, H. J., 437, 444, 449
Marks, I., 22
Marks, D., 267, 268, 271, 273, 275
Marks, J. M., 3, 4, 5, 10, 13, 15, 17, 42, 43, 44, 45, 48, 73, 78, 81, 82, 181, 182, 190
Marks, T., 104
Markvoort, M., 450
Marlatt, G. A., 95, 194, 203, 205, 206, 213, 214, 215, 217, 409
Marques, J. K., 194
Marquis, J. N., 188
Marriage, K., 291, 293
Marshall, A., 325
Marshall, J., 405
Marshall, W. L., 8, 43, 45, 176, 179, 181, 185, 191, 194, 195, 196
Marston, A. R., 191
Martin, B., 302
Martin, L. Y., 53
Martin, M., 49
Martin, P., 168, 170
Martino, T., 301
Martinson, W. D., 191
Maruta, T., 387
Marzillier, J. S., 296
Masak, B. J., 397
Maslin, C., 289
Mason, D., 347
Mason, S. A., 327
Masse, B., 287, 290
Massel, H. K., 137, 138
Master, D., 46, 48
Masters, W. H., 155, 156, 157, 159, 161, 168, 194
Masui, T., 231
Mather, M. D., 404
Mathew, R. J., 50, 55
Mathews, A. M., 42, 44, 45, 55, 56
Matise, M., 319, 321
Matson, J. L., 253, 317, 319, 320, 321, 324, 326, 328, 329, 330, 331, 332
Mattes, J., 267, 268, 273, 275
Matthews, S., 142
Mattick, R. P., 22, 25, 26, 34, 82

Maurice, P., 326
Maurer, A., 231
Mavissakalian, M., 46, 47, 48, 81
Mawson, D., 81, 82
Mayol, A., 104
Maziade, M., 289
Mazure, C., 69
McAlister, A. L., 399
McAllister, H., 186
McAllister, J. A., 246
McAnulty, R. D., 176, 177
McBurnett, K., 278, 291
McCaffrey, R. J., 92
McCann, B. S., 15, 69
McCann, C. S., 405
McCann, K. L., 357
McCartney, J. R., 321, 322
McCaul, M. E., 210, 211
McCauley, E., 248
McChesney, C.M., 41
McClannahan, L. E., 347
McConaghy, N., 181
McConaughy, S. H., 287
McConville, B. J., 247
McCoy, J. F., 320, 324, 325
McCrady, B. S., 212
McCrary, J. L., 193
McDaniel, L. K., 390
McDonald, R., 81, 82
McDonel, E. C., 179
McEvoy, L., 88
McFall, R. M., 179, 292
McGee, G. G., 347
McGee, R., 231, 246, 247, 290, 291
McGhie, A., 379
McGill, C. W., 139, 142
McGimpsey, B. J., 427
McGimsey, J. F., 299
McGinsey, J. F., 331
McGuire, M., 144, 147
McGuire, R. J., 175, 183, 188
McKenzie, S. J., 355, 356, 359, 360, 361, 364, 365
McKinley, J. C., 177
McKinney, W. T., 105
McKnew, D. H., 245, 247
McLean, P. D., 107
McLeer, S., 297
McLellan, A. T., 207, 208

McMahon, R. J., 285, 286, 292, 294, 295, 299, 300, 301, 302
McMorrow, M., 330
McNally, R. J., 40
McNamee, G., 44
McQuarter, R. J., 325
McRae, S., 299
Meador, A. E., 297
Meardon, J., 291
Mech, E. V., 231
Mechanic, D., 401
Medenis, R., 279
Meehl, P. E., 121
Megson, D. A., 427
Meichenbaum, D., 56, 90, 297, 383, 384, 389, 391
Melman, A., 158, 167
Mello, N. K., 203
Mellstrom, B., 238
Melzack, R., 374, 382, 383, 384
Mendelson, J. H., 203
Mendelson, M., 421
Menlove, F. L., 189
Mennemier, M., 330
Menolascino, F., 332
Mercrio, J. R., 330
Meredith, R., 330
Merette, C., 289
Mersch, P. P., 21, 24, 47
Messmer, M. C., 426
Meyer, A. J., 399
Meyer, J., 183
Meyer, N. E., 248
Meyer, V., 73, 119, 123, 129
Meyers, R., 212
Meyers, T., 429
Meyers-Abell, J. E., 421, 429
Meyerson, L., 321, 322
Mezzich, A. C., 247
Mezzich, J. B., 15, 69
Mezzich, J. E., 247
Michelson, L., 46, 47, 48, 81, 296, 299
Mickelson, O., 365
Middlebrook, J., 300
Miezitis, S., 254
Mikkelson, E., 238
Mikulincer, M., 87
Milich, R., 261, 266, 270, 275, 277, 278
Miller, A., 232

Miller, C. L., 296, 297
Miller, D. M., 421, 429
Miller, F. J. W., 289
Miller, G. E., 287, 291, 302, 303, 305
Miller, J., 267, 268, 271, 273, 275
Miller, L. C., 232
Miller, M. L., 291
Miller, N. E., 71, 378
Miller, P., 232
Miller, P. C., 390
Miller, P. M., 210
Miller, W. R., 204, 205, 207, 208, 209, 210, 212, 214, 217, 218
Millon, T., 421
Mills, H. L., 74, 237
Mills, J. R., 74, 237
Mills, K. H., 163
Milner, J. S., 419
Milofsky, E. S., 216
Milstein, J. P., 342, 343, 345
Milton, F., 45
Mineka, S., 19
Minichiello, W. E., 75
Minkoff, K., 139
Minor, J. W., 320
Mintz, J., 214
Miranda, J., 104
Mischel, W., 118
Mitchell, J. E., 362
Mitchell, J. R., 248
Mizruchi, M. S., 255
Moch, J., 421
Moffitt, T. E., 287, 290
Moguin, L. E., 297
Moletteire, C., 377, 386, 387
Money, J., 175
Monga, T. N., 379
Monk, M. A., 231
Monroe, S. M., 103
Monteiro, W., 42
Montgomery, S. A., 103
Monti, P. M., 191, 192, 207, 208, 213, 357
Moody, S. C., 357
Mooney, K. C., 231, 234, 235
Moore, D. R., 292
Moore, J. E., 390, 391
Moore, M. E., 343
Mooreman, J. E., 437
Moorer, S., 264, 265

Moos, R. H., 103, 105
Morales, R. G., 139
Moretti, M., 291
Morgan, T., 390
Morrison, R. L., 421
Moras, K., 53
Morey, L. C., 216
Morganstern, F. S., 183
Morin, C., 185
Morokoff, P. J., 167
Morrison, R. L., 137, 139, 148, 179, 190, 191, 192, 193
Morse, E., 207, 215
Moser, A. J., 138
Moskowitz, D. S., 290
Moss, S., 248
Mott, M. E., 139
Mowrer, O. H., 6, 71, 380
Mueser, K. T., 92, 137, 138, 139, 149
Mukai, L. H., 292
Mulick, J. A., 327
Munby, J., 43
Munby, M., 22, 34, 42, 44
Mundim, F. D., 32
Munjack, D. J., 159
Munoz, R. F., 210
Murdock, R. P., 207
Murphy, C. M., 301
Murphy, D. A., 278
Murphy, D. L., 69, 81
Murphy, G. E., 110
Murphy, H. A., 267, 273, 276, 277, 278
Murphy, J. K., 357
Murphy, J. V., 264
Murphy, W. D., 177, 386, 388
Mussare, F., 136
Myers, J. K., 3
Myers, L. S., 167

Nagler, E., 178
Nardi, A. E., 32
Nash, J. D., 399
Nathan, P. E., 206
Nathan, P. W., 383
National Center for Health Statistics, 437
National Center on Child Abuse and Neglect, 417
Neckerman, H. J., 291
Neeper, R., 292

Neff, A., 378
Neftel, K. A., 32
Nelson, G. M., 437
Nelson, H. F., 212
Nelson, P., 40, 41
Nelson, R., 55, 56, 108
Nelson, R. O., 180
Nemec P. B., 137
Nemeroff, C. B., 102
Nesse, R. M., 41
Neufeld, R. W. J., 386, 404, 406
Neuchterlein, K. H., 139
Newby, R. F., 266
Newby, T. J., 269
Newcorn, J., 255
Newsom, C. D., 327
Newman, J. P., 293
Newman, M., 418, 422, 428
Nezu, A., 87, 251
Nezu, A. M., 357
Niaura, R. S., 207, 208
Nichols, P. L., 261
Nielsen, G., 339
Nierenberg, G. I., 444
Nietzel, M. T., 439
Nilsson, D., 267, 268, 271, 273, 275
Noble, H., 232
Noel, N. E., 212
Norton, A. J., 437
Norton, G. R., 40
Norwood, R. M., 19
Notarius, C., 444
Novaco, R. W., 420
Novic, J., 144, 147
Noyes, R. Jr., 41, 53
Nunn, B., 212
Nutter, D., 157
Nyhan, W. L., 326
Nyhan, W. S., 327

O'Brien, C. P, 207, 208, 214
O'Brien, F., 321
O'Brien, G. T., 44, 45, 48, 49, 236
O'Brien, S., 425
O'Connor, M., 366
O'Dell, M. C., 341, 345, 348
Odom, S. L., 343
O'Donnell, C. R., 293
O'Donohue, W. T., 159
Oei, T. P. S., 40, 42, 213

O'Farrell, T. J., 212
Offord, D. R., 265, 290
Ogbu, J. U., 287
Ohman, A., 18
Oke, N. J., 343
O'Keefe, D., 378
Olajide, D., 50
O'Leary, A., 386, 390
O'Leary, K. D., 108, 269, 301, 418, 419, 422, 428, 430, 431, 439, 440, 441, 446, 449, 450
O'Leary, M. R., 213
O'Leary, S. G., 267, 268, 269, 271, 272
Olinger, L. J., 104
Oliveau, D., 3, 4, 231
Ollendick, D. G., 331
Ollendick, T. H., 228, 229, 233, 296, 297, 320, 331
Oltmanns, T. F., 301
Olweus, D., 290
O'Neill, R. E., 339
Orvaschel, H., 3
Orzack, M. H., 146
Ost, L. G., 4, 5, 8, 9, 10, 15, 19, 27, 34, 42, 43, 47, 50
Osteen, V., 301
O'Sullivan, G., 44
Overholser, J. C., 179
Owen, N., 401
Owens, J. F., 405
Ozarow, B. J., 67, 71, 72, 73, 74, 75, 78, 79, 82

Pabst, P., 237
Pagelow, M. D., 418, 420, 422, 424, 428
Pallmeyer, T. P., 378
Pallotta, G. M., 420
Palmer, D. J., 248
Paluchowski, C., 267, 268, 271, 273, 275
Pancentini, J. C., 291
Paolino, T. J., Jr., 212
Papp, L., 32, 34
Paris, A. E., 252
Parker, G. B., 105
Parker, J. C., 390
Parloff, M. B., 110
Parmalee, D. Y., 248
Pasino, J. A., 376, 377, 392
Paternite, C. E., 261

Pato, M. T., 69, 81
Patterson, E. T., 87
Patterson, G. R., 288, 289, 291, 293, 294, 300, 301, 303, 439, 441, 442
Patti, E. T., 357
Pattison, E. M., 203
Patton, D., 376, 377
Paul, G. L., 138
Paul, L., 326
Paul S. C., 296
Paulauskas, S., 291
Pauls, D. L., 105
Payne, L. L., 43
Pearce, J. F., 183
Pechacek, T. F., 209
Peck, C., 373
Pecknold, J., 81, 82
Peddecord, M., 397, 398
Pederson, J., 142
Pedraza, M., 207, 208
Peer, D. F., 45
Pelham, W. E., 261, 262, 264, 265, 266, 267 268, 270, 271, 272, 273, 274, 275, 276, 277, 278, 279
Pellegrini, L. M., 139
Penckofer, S., 405
Penk, W. E., 87, 210, 211
Pennypacker, H. S., 217, 218
Penzien, D. B., 378, 379, 386, 387
Perel, J. M., 112
Perissaki, C., 75, 78
Perline, R., 144, 147
Perloff, B. F., 341, 343
Perper, J. A., 255
Perri, M. G., 357
Perris, C., 139
Perron, D., 287, 290
Perry, J. C., 131
Pershad, D., 67, 68
Persons, J. B., 104
Peselow, E. D., 104, 106
Peters, L., 22, 25, 26, 34
Peterson, L., 229
Peterson, R. A., 40, 387
Petrinack, R. J., 248
Petti, T. A., 253, 254
Pfeffer, C. R., 255
Pfefferbaum, B., 248
Pfiffner, L. J., 269, 272
Philips, H. C., 380, 388

Phillips, E. L., 293
Phillips, L. R., 390
Phillips, S., 300
Piasecki, J. M., 110
Pilkonis, P. A., 19, 110
Pisko, E. J., 390
Pithers, W. D., 194
Platt, J., 293, 299
Plutchick, R., 255
Polakow, R. L., 207
Polansky, N. A., 419
Polansky, N. F., 419
Polefka, D., 232
Polich, J. M., 215
Pollack, E., 267, 268, 273, 275
Pollack, S. L., 248
Pollard, C. A., 19, 41
Pollard, H. J., 41
Polster, R. A., 299
Poole, L., 386
Poppen, R., 422
Porceddu, K., 139, 142
Porter, S., 301
Powers, S. K., 360
Powley, T. L., 364
Prather, R. C., 355, 357, 362, 363
Pretzer, J., 131
Price, J. M., 292
Price, L. H., 69
Prinz, R. J., 287, 290, 291, 302, 303, 305
Prochaska, J. O., 216
Prue, D. M., 92
Prusoff, B. A., 103, 105, 115
Puig-Antich, J., 247, 291
Purohit, A. P., 247
Pyle, R. L., 362

Quay, H. C., 262, 263, 287, 292, 293
Quevillon, R. P., 159
Quinlan, D. M., 104
Quinn, J. T., 186
Quinsey, V. L., 179, 181, 187
Quinton, D., 301

Rabavilas, A. D., 74, 74, 75, 78
Rabkin, J. G., 137
Rachman, S. J., 6, 42, 45, 46, 48, 68, 69, 71, 73, 74, 181, 188, 380, 388

Raczynski, J. M., 100, 378, 386
Rahe, R. H., 437
Ralph, A., 330
Rankin, H., 208
Rapaport, S., 139
Rapee, R. M., 10, 15, 40, 41, 42, 48, 49, 53, 54, 55, 56, 57
Rapoport, J. L., 261, 264
Rappaport, J. A., 47, 238, 239
Rappaport, R., 327
Rasmussen, S. A., 69
Ratcliff, K. S., 103, 291
Rawson, R. A., 214
Ray, J., 303
Raymond, K., 330
Razin, A. M., 405
Read, P. B., 100
Reber, M., 297
Redmond, J., 390
Rees, W., 51
Reeves, V., 390
Reich, B., 119, 123
Reich, J., 18, 41, 176, 191
Reid, D. H., 319, 321
Reid, J., 303
Reid, J. B., 203, 294, 303, 439
Reid, J. C., 248, 257
Reid, S., 390
Reid, W. J., 301
Reisinger, J. J., 301
Reiss, D. J., 143, 150
Reiss, S., 331
Rehm, L. P., 100, 108, 191, 248, 249, 251, 253
Rekers, G. A., 190
Repp, A. C., 317
Reppucci, N. D., 431
Resick, P. A., 87, 89, 90
Revenstorf, D., 439, 450, 451
Reynolds, E. H., 178, 190
Reynolds, R. V. C., 406
Reynolds, W. M., 254
Reznick, J. S., 18
Ricciardi, J., 82
Rice, J. M., 428
Rice, K. M., 50, 55
Richard, B. A., 293
Richards, C., 291
Richman, G. S., 340
Richman, N., 231, 289, 290
Riddle, M. A., 239

Rie, H. E., 245
Rienzo, D., 186
Rifkin, A., 144, 147
Rijken, H., 47, 49
Riley, A. J., 164
Riley, G. J., 164
Rimmele, C. T., 207
Rincover, A., 346
Risen, C. B., 167
Riskind, J. H., 53
Risley, R. T., 341
Risley, T., 325
Rist, F., 387
Ritter, R., 7, 189
Robbins, A. J., 247
Robbins, D. R., 236
Robbins, F., 274
Roberts, A. H., 377, 379
Roberts, W. R., 87
Robey, A., 422
Robinowitz, R., 87, 210, 211
Robins, C. J., 104, 106
Robins, L. N., 88, 103, 287, 290, 291
Robinson, L. A., 105
Robinson, P., 155
Robinson, P. W., 269
Robinson, S. L., 248
Rodichok, L. D., 378, 380
Rodick, J. D., 304
Roff, J. D., 290
Rogers, L., 379, 386, 387
Rogers, M., 232
Rogers, T., 300, 301, 303
Rogers, W., 100
Rogers-Warren, A. K., 324, 325
Rohsenow, D. J., 207, 208
Rojahn, J., 327
Romano, J., 377, 390
Ronan, K. R., 297
Ronnei, M., 267, 268, 271, 273, 275
Roper, G., 73
Rose, S. C., 390
Rosen, A. J., 138
Rosen, J. C., 360, 362
Rosen, L. A., 269
Rosen, P. M., 286
Rosen, R., 177
Rosen, R. C., 155, 157, 159
Rosenbaum, A., 422, 428, 430, 431

Rosenberg, M. S., 431
Rosenberg, S. D., 214
Rosenberg, T. K., 246, 248
Rosenberg, H., 70, 71
Rosenfeld-Schlichter, M. D., 425
Rosenthal, R., 386, 388
Rosenthal, T. L., 56, 386, 388
Rosenwald, R. J., 422
Rossi, M., 32
Roth, J. A., 287
Rothbaum, B. O., 89
Rouleau, J. L., 176, 191
Rounsaville, B. J., 103, 108
Routh, D. K., 287, 292
Rowlands, O., 301
Roy, M., 418
Roy-Byrne, P. P., 41
Royer, P., 327
Rubin, H. B., 177
Rubinstein, D., 155, 170
Rudy, T. E., 377, 379, 385, 386, 389, 390, 391, 392
Ruff, R. M., 407, 408
Rugg, D., 214
Rupert, P. A., 50, 55
Rush, A. J., 109, 110, 113
Russell, G. F. M., 366
Russell, M. L., 398
Russell, S. H., 399
Russo, D. C., 397
Rust, J., 163
Rutter, M., 100, 247, 289, 301
Rutven, L., 150
Ryan, B. A., 402, 403
Rychtarik, R. G., 92, 212

Sacco, W. P., 109
Safer, D. J., 263, 290
Saigh, P. A., 239, 240
Sailor, W., 324, 339
Sakati, N., 327
Salge, R., 40
Salkovskis, P. M., 23, 49, 75, 77, 78
Sanchez-Craig, M., 216
Sand, P. L., 377
Sandberg, D., 32, 34
Sandberg, G., 159
Sandeen, E. E., 440
Sanders, M. R., 294, 302, 303, 304

Sanderson, W. C., 10, 15, 41, 53, 54, 57
Sanderson, W. S., 41
Sandler, J., 422, 423, 424
Sarason, I. G., 296
Sarber, R. E., 425, 426
Sartory, G., 46, 48, 50
Saslow, G., 177
Sata, L. S., 160
Satterberg, J., 178
Saunders, B. E., 89
Saunders, D. G., 421, 429
Saunders, N. L., 378, 380
Saxon, S., 330
Sayers, S. L., 451
Scahill, L., 239
Scarth, L., 235
Sceery, W., 238
Schachter, S., 216
Schaeffer, B., 341, 343
Schaeffer, R. M., 320
Schaffer, C., 144, 147
Schell, R. M., 274
Schellenback, C. J., 424
Schiavi, R. C., 157
Schibak, J. W., 321
Schilling, D. J., 422
Schindler, L., 439, 450
Schloss, C. N., 253
Schloss, P. J., 253
Schmaling, K. B., 292, 450
Schmidt, A. J. M., 382, 384
Schmidt, C. W., 158
Schmidt, E., 186
Schnedler, R. W., 267, 268, 271, 273, 274, 275
Schreibman, L., 338, 339, 341, 342, 343, 344, 345, 347, 348
Schoen, L., 185
Schooler, N., 136, 142
Schover, L. R., 160, 162, 166, 167
Schreiner-Engel, P., 157
Schroeder, C. S., 318, 327
Schroeder, H. E., 298, 299, 300
Schroeder, S. R., 327
Schultz, L. A., 300
Schumacher, K., 327
Schwartz, C. E., 75
Schwartz, G. E., 386
Schwartz, R., 411

Schwartz, S., 303, 304
Schwartzman, A. E., 287, 290
Schweinhart, L. J., 290
Scott, D. S., 396
Scott, P. D., 422
Seely, R. K., 177
Segal, Z. V., 179
Segraves, R. T., 158, 169
Seidman, E., 293
Seidner, A. L., 236
Seligman, M. E. P., 4, 100, 104, 251
Semble, E. L., 390
Serber, M., 185
Sevire, J., 142
Sexton, M. M., 401
Seymour, R., 81
Shainess, N., 421
Shanks, G. L., 379
Shapiro, E. S., 320, 323, 325
Shapiro, S. K., 287, 290, 292
Sharfstein, S. S., 136
Shaw, B. F., 104, 109, 113
Shea, M. T., 110
Shear, K. 49
Sheehan, D. V., 40
Sheehan, K. H., 40
Shell, R. M., 331
Shelton, J., 382
Shen, W. W., 160
Sher, K., 213
Sherman, J. E., 207, 215
Sherman, L., 301
Sherrill, J. T., 216
Shield, J. A., 100
Shoor, S., 386, 390
Shore, J., 89
Shrout, P. B., 89
Shuckit, M. A., 109
Shure, M. B., 293, 299
Sibner, L. G., 430
Sides, J. K., 55
Siegel, A. W., 248
Siegel, L. S., 265
Siegel, T., 123, 298
Siever, L. S., 102, 105, 121
Silva, P. A., 231, 246, 247, 287, 290, 291
Silver, H. K., 417
Silverman, E. N., 417
Silverman, W. K., 92, 228, 233
Simons, A. D., 110

Singh, H., 137
Sisson, L. A., 327
Sisson, R. W., 211, 212
Skinner, B. F., 324
Skinner, H. A., 216
Slade, P. D., 364, 380
Slifer, K. J., 340
Sloop, E. W., 302
Smarr, K. L., 390
Smith, A., 248
Smith, D., 232
Smith, D. A., 439
Smith, E. I., 390
Smith, M., 386
Smith, P., 322
Smith, R., 321
Snell, J. E., 422
Snidman, N., 18
Snyder, D. K., 441
Snyder, J. J., 292
Sobell, L. C., 203, 217
Sobell, M. B., 203, 217
Solomon, Z., 87
Solyom, C., 32, 45
Solyom, L., 32, 82
Somers, A. R., 437
Sonis, W. A., 253
Sookman, D., 82
Sorenson, S. B., 68
Sorkin, B. A., 391
Sotsky, S. M., 110
Southworth, S., 48
Spanier, G. B., 441
Speiss, W. F., 159
Spence, S. H., 296
Spitzer, R. L., 103
Spivack, G., 290, 293, 299
Spohn, H. E., 136
Spooner, D., 319, 320
Spooner, F., 319, 320
Spradlin, J., 325
Spring, B., 137
Stabb, S. D., 290, 297
Stahmer, A. C., 348
Stanley, L., 237
Stanley, M. A., 16, 68, 70, 81, 82, 130
Stanton, M. D., 212
Stanton, W. R., 290
Stark, E., 417
Stark, J., 332
Stark, K. D., 254
Stattin, H., 290

Staub, E., 386
Steffe, M., 300
Steele, B. E., 417
Steer, R. A., 53
Stefanis, C., 74
Steinberg, D., 237
Steiner, B., 178
Steiner, M., 101
Steinman, C. M., 181
Steinmetz, J. L., 107
Steinmetz, S., 417, 418
Steketee, G. S., 46, 67, 71, 72, 73, 74, 75, 77, 78, 79, 82, 89
Stephens, R. M., 329
Sterm, R. S., 81, 82
Stermac, L. E., 179
Stern, M., 399
Stern, R. S., 43, 48
Sternberg, D. E., 106
Sterner, V., 8, 10
Sterner, U., 10
Stetson, D., 44
Stevens, J. S., 248
Stevens, V. W., 387
Stevens-Our, P., 327
Stevenson, I., 193
Stevenson, J. E., 231
Stevenson, J. S., 289, 290
Stewart, A., 100
Stewart, B. D., 90
Stewart, M. A., 290, 291
Stickler, G., 236
Stimbert, V. E., 320
Stitzer, M. L., 210, 211
St. Lawrence, J. S., 148, 149, 296, 298, 397, 423
Stock, W., 159, 164
Stockwell, T., 208, 213
Stokes, T. F., 346, 347
Stoltzman, R., 3
Stone, G. W., 421, 429
Stone, M. H., 118, 120, 131
Stone, P., 291
Storaasli, R., 437
Stout, R. L., 212
Stouthamer-Loeber, M., 292
Stowe, M. L., 248
Strain, P. S., 343
Straus, M. A., 417, 418, 421
Strauss, C. C., 228, 230, 231, 236
Strauss, J. S., 135

Stravynski, A., 22
Street, L., 40, 46, 48
Strug, D. L., 210
Strzelecki, E., 264
Stuart, R. B., 438, 442, 443, 445
Stumphauzer, J. S., 293
Stunkard, A. J., 357
Sturge, C., 290
Sturgeon, D., 143
Sturgis, E. T., 176, 295, 300
Styron, W., 100
Sugai, D., 299
Sulkes, S., 327
Sullivan, B. J., 8
Sullivan, J. M., 107
Sullivan, M. A., 269
Summer, J. H., 153
Summergrad, P., 81
Sundberg, M. L., 324, 325
Suomi, S. J., 19
Sussman, S., 138
Sutker, P. B., 123
Sutton, S., 301
Swanson, J., 266
Swartzman, L., 158
Swedo, S. E., 238, 339
Sweet, W. H., 383
Swift, M., 290
Swinson, R. P., 41
Sylvester, D., 314
Symonds, P. M., 285
Symulker, G. I., 366
Szatmari, P., 290
Szumowski, E. K., 289
Szykula, S. A., 294
Szymanski, L., 327
Szyszko, J., 331

Tallman, K., 45
Tanguay, P., 237
Taras, M. E., 319, 321, 328
Tarika, K., 101
Tarrier, N., 139, 140, 142
Tatum, E., 89
Taube, C. A., 136
Taylor, C. A., 210
Taylor, C. B., 45, 48, 386
Taylor, C. J., 304
Taylor, G. A., 212
Taylor, E. A., 261
Taylor, H. L., 365
Taylor, J., 430

Teasdale, J., 100, 104, 181, 251
Teders, S. J., 378, 380
Teigen, J., 138
Telch, C. F., 430
Telch, M. J., 40, 41, 45, 48
Teri, L., 107
Ternes, J., 208
Terrace, H. S., 187
Terranova, M. D., 137, 138
Tertinger, D. A., 426, 427
Thase, M. E., 108
Thelen, M. H., 296
Thibaut, J. W., 438
Thibodeau, M. G., 342
Thiele, C., 278
Thilly, G., 399
Thiry, M. R., 8
Thivierge, J., 289
Thomas, A., 289
Thomas, C., 123, 298
Thomas, D., 321
Thomas, P., 386
Thompson, T., 327
Thompson, W. D., 105
Thompson-Pope, S. K., 118, 119
Thornberry, T. P., 287
Thorpe, G. L., 42, 381
Thorpe, J. G., 186
Thyer, B. A., 41
Tiefer, L., 158, 167
Tischler, C. E., III, 3
Tisdelle, D. A., 296, 298
Tishelman, A. C., 420
Tobin, D. L., 379, 386, 387, 406
Todd, T. C., 212, 213
Tolan, P. H., 287, 288, 290
Toras, M., 330
Torgersen, S., 18, 105
Touchette, P. E., 325, 328, 427
Touzy, S. W., 365, 366
Towlin, K. E., 67
Town, C., 213
Townsley, R. M., 14, 19, 20
Tremblay, R. E., 287, 290
Trieschmann, R. B., 377
Troughton, E., 41
Troup, J. D. G., 380
Trudel, G., 326
Tryon, A., 342
Tuason, V. B., 110

Tuchfield, B. S., 216
Tucker, J. A., 203, 208, 214, 215, 216
Tuma, J. M., 285, 289
Tunstall, C., 214
Turk, D. C., 373, 376, 377, 379, 383, 384, 385, 386, 389, 390, 391, 392, 409
Turkat, I. D., 118, 119, 120, 121, 122, 123, 124, 125, 126, 127, 128, 129, 131, 132, 139, 180
Turkewitz, H., 450
Turner, J. A., 377, 390
Turner, L. A., 167
Turner, R. A., 390
Turner, R. M., 43, 73, 74, 75, 124
Turner, S. M., 14, 15, 16, 17, 19, 20, 21, 33, 45, 67, 68, 69, 70, 71, 72, 74, 75, 77, 78, 79, 81, 82, 118, 128, 130, 131, 132, 138, 149
Tursky, B., 386
Turvey, A. A., 56
Twentyman, C. T., 179, 213
Tyrer, P., 32
Tyrer, P. J., 32
Tyroler, M., 297

Uhde, T. W., 41
Ulrich, R., 136
Ultee, K. A., 43
Underwood, M., 292, 293
Ung, E., 386
Unis, A. S., 298, 304
Upper, D., 70, 71
Urbain, E. S., 297
Urey, J., 304
Ushakov, G. K., 247
Uzzell, R., 319

Vaillant, G. E., 216
Valletutti, P. J., 321
van Dam-Baggen, R. M. J., 71
Vandenberg, S. G., 289
van den Hout, M. A., 51
Van Den Steen, N., 81
ven der Helm, M., 21, 24
Van Hasselt, V. B., 296, 419, 421
van Kraanen, J., 74
Van Landingham, W. P., 92

Vannatta, K., 278
Van Wagenen, K., 321, 322
Van Wagenen, R., 322
Varni, J., 342
Varni, J. W., 190
Vaughn, C., 139, 142
Velez, C. M., 255
Verhulst, F. C., 287
Verma, S. K., 67, 68
Verma, V. K., 67, 68
Vermilyea, B. B., 10, 53, 54
Vermilyea, J. A., 10, 40, 47, 48, 49, 52, 53, 54
Veroff, J., 437
Veronen, L. J., 89, 90
Versiani, M., 32
Vincent, J. P., 439, 448
Visher, C. A., 287
Vissia, E., 21, 24
Vivian, D., 439
Vodde-Hamilton, M., 278
Vogel, B., 439
Vollmer, W., 89
Von, J. M., 89
Vorkauf, H., 32
Vuchinich, R. E., 203, 208, 214, 215, 216

Waddell, M. T., 43, 48, 49
Wadden, T. A., 357
Wagner, E., 292
Wahler, R. G., 272, 289, 290, 291, 292, 300, 301, 304, 419, 422
Walbeck, N. H., 177
Walder, L. O., 290
Walker, C. E., 419
Walker, E., 144, 146, 147
Walker, J. L., 291
Walker, L. G., 418
Walker, S. E., 390
Wall, P. D., 374, 382, 383, 384
Wallace, C. J., 137, 138, 149, 150
Wallace, K. M., 440
Wallander, J., 318
Wallerstein, J. S., 437
Walsh, M. E., 342
Walton, L. A., 247
Wang, E., 409
Ward, C., 421
Ward, T., 196
Ware, J., 100

Warner, M., 357
Warren, S. F., 324, 325
Warwick, H. M. C., 49, 75, 78
Watkins, J. T., 110
Watkins, P. C., 355, 356, 359, 360, 361, 362, 363, 364, 365
Watson, L. S., 319
Watson, R., 186
Watson, S. M., 304
Watson-Perzcel, M., 427
Watt, J. G., 210
Watts, S., 139, 142
Watzl, H., 387
Webb, M. E., 427
Webster-Stratton, C., 295
Weddige, R. L., 383
Weeks, C., 44
Weeks, M., 328
Weilburg, J. B., 81
Weinrott, M. R., 194
Weisenberg, M., 383
Weiss, B., 248
Weiss, R. L., 438, 439, 441, 442, 448
Weiss, G., 259, 267
Weissman, M. M., 3, 41, 103, 105, 108
Weisz, J. R., 248
Welch, M. W., 232
Wells, K., 300
Wells, K. B., 100
Wells, K. C., 265, 286, 292, 295, 300, 301, 302
Wells, K. D., 301
Wells, K. G., 112
Wenig, P., 378
Werry, J. S., 260
Wesch, D., 425, 428
Wesolowski, M. D., 320
Wessels, D., 49
Wessels, H., 7, 43
West, D., 90
Westbrook, T., 390
Westlake, R., 357
Wetzel, R. D., 110
Whalen, C. K., 259, 261, 264, 270, 271, 273, 277, 278
Wheeler, D., 177

Whelan, J. P., 304
White, G. D., 339
White, J. L., 287
White, K. J., 270, 272, 276, 277
White, S. W., 437
Whitehill, M. B., 296
Whitehorn, C., 383
Whitman, T. L., 321, 330
Wickramasekera, I., 184, 189
Widiger, T. A., 121
Widom, C. S., 289
Wieseler, N. A., 327
Wig, N. H., 67, 68
Wilkinson, D. A., 216
Williams, C. A., 303
Williams, H., 366
Williams, J., 346
Williams, J. B. W., 103
Williams, S., 231, 246, 247, 291
Williams, S. L., 45, 46, 47
Williams, T. A., 100
Williamson, D. A., 355, 356, 357, 359, 360, 361, 362, 363, 364, 365
Wills, T. A., 441
Wilson, C., 290
Wilson, G. T., 8
Wilson, P. G., 321
Wilson, S. K., 301
Wincze, J. P., 162, 188, 189
Wing, J. K., 137
Wing, R. R., 357
Winget, C., 89
Winkler, R. C., 139
Winnett, R. L., 252
Wirt, R. D., 290
Wise, T. N., 158
Wisocki, P. A., 183, 184
Witt, J. C., 271
Woerner, M. G., 43
Wohlberg, G., 146
Wolf, M. M., 341
Wolfe, D., 301, 422, 423, 424, 431
Wolfe, J., 87
Wolfenberger, W., 319

Wolff, H. H., 42
Wolfgang, M. E., 287
Wolpe, J., 7, 10, 155, 180, 181, 189, 193, 422
Wolraich, M., 261, 266
Wong, S. E., 137, 138
Wood, P. D., 399
Wood, R., 296, 299
Woody, G. E., 208
Woolson, R., 266
Woolston, J. L., 239
Wordarski, J. S., 285
Wright, C. L., 45
Wyman, E., 428
Wynne, M. E., 279

Yadalam, K. G., 137
Yaguchi, M., 211
Yarnold, P. R., 153
Yates, W., 18
Young, B. G., 175, 183, 188
Young, E., 113
Young, J. E., 110
Young, L. D., 179, 390
Youngsen, M. A., 104
Yule, B., 301
Yule, W., 22, 232, 301

Zajac, Y., 178
Zak, L., 301
Zametkin, A. J., 261, 264
Zane, G., 45, 46
Zanna, M. D., 403
Zarete, T., 137
Zaslow, M. J., 301
Zeichner, A., 138
Zelenak, J. P., 255
Zerface, J. P., 191
Zigler, E., 329
Zilbergeld, B., 162, 168, 193
Zimbardo, P. G., 19
Zimering, R. T., 89, 90, 92
Zimmer, D., 169
Zitrin, C. M., 43
Zohar, J., 69, 81
Zohar-Kadouch, R., 69, 81
Zubin, J., 137
Zuckerman, M., 177

Subject Index

Agoraphobia:
   clinical syndrome, 39–42, 381
   cognitive-behavioral treatment of, 42–47
   see also Panic disorder, Panic attacks
Agoraphobic avoidance, 40
Alcoholism, see Substance abuse
Anger management training, 123, 270–271
Anorexia nervosa, 355, 364–369
Anorgasmia, 160
Antidepressant medications, 252, 253, 254
   see also Specific medications
Antisocial personality disorder, 122–124
Anxiety-reduction strategies, 77
   see also Specific procedures
Anxiolytic drugs, 15
Applied relaxation, 50
   see also Relaxation training
Applied tension, 10
Areas of Change Questionnaire, 441
Arthritis, 385, 386, 390
Assertive behavior, 421–422
Assertiveness training, 49, 57, 90, 131, 193, 376–377
   see also Social skills training
Assessment of heterosocial skills, 179–180
Assessment of gender behavior:
   behavior checklist, 18
   Feminine Identity Scale, 178
   Sex Role Inventory, 178
Assessment of sexual arousal, 177–178

Attention deficit-hyperactivity disorder (ADHD):
   anger management training, 270–271
   classroom management strategies, 268
   clinical behavior therapy, 260, 267
   cognitive-behavioral treatment of, 260, 270
   contingency management procedures, 260, 268, 269, 275
   diagnosis, 262
   pharmacologic treatment of, 263, 272
Autism:
   characteristics, 337
   functional analysis of, 340
   self-injurious behavior, 338
   self-stimulatory behavior, 338
Aversion relief, 186
Aversion therapy, 181–184, 206–207, 331
Avoidant disorder of childhood:
   behavioral treatment of, 231
   diagnosis, 231
Avoidant personality disorder, 119, 127–129

Backward chaining, 319–320
Basal metabolism rate, 360, 364
Beck Depression Inventory, 421
Behavioral family therapy, 139–143
Behavioral marital therapy, 108
   see also Marital therapy, Cognitive marital therapy
Behavioral self-control training, 208–210
Beta-blocking drugs, 15

Between-session habituation, 71–72, 75, 81–82
  see also Within session habituation; Extinction; Flooding, Response prevention
Binge eating, 355, 357, 359, 360, 361, 363, 366
Biofeedback, 119, 378, 379, 380, 381, 389, 391
  see also Specific type
Bioinformational theory of anxiety reduction, 72
Body image, 359, 361, 364, 366, 367
Borderline personality disorder, 124–125
Breathing retraining, 49
Bulimia nervosa, 355, 358–364, 369

Cancer, 373
Caring days in marital therapy, 442–443
Central nervous system (CNS) stimulant drugs, 263–264
Cephalic artery biofeedback, 378
Chaining, 391
  see also Backward chaining
Checklist for Living Environments to Assess Neglect, 427
Chemical and olfactory aversion, 182–183
Child Behavior Checklist, 249–250
Child abuse, 417
  assessment of, 419–420
  behavioral treatment of, 422–424
  ecobehavioral approach, 424–428
Child Abuse and Neglect Interview Schedule, 419
Child neglect, 417
  assessment of, 419–420
  behavioral treatment of, 422–424
  ecobehavioral approaches, 424–428
Childhood depression:
  assessment of, 248–250
  comorbidity, 255
  developmental approach, 246–247
  masked depression, 245
  prevalence, 246
  psychoanalytic view, 245
  suicidal behavior, 255
  symptoms of, 247
  treatment of, 250–255
Childhood Level of Living Scale, 419–420
Children's Depression Inventory, 249, 254
Classroom management, 270
Clomipramine, 81–82
Closed head injuries, 407–409
Cocaine abuse, see Substance abuse
Cognitive-behavioral therapy, 79
  see also Specific disorders, Cognitive therapy
Cognitive-behavioral treatment of depression, 254
Cognitive marital therapy, 450
  see also Behavioral marital therapy, Marital therapy
Cognitive restructuring, 50, 51, 56, 166, 252, 254, 361, 365, 366, 389, 429
Cognitive rituals, 68
  see also Compulsions
Cognitive skills training, 297–299
Cognitive theory of depression, 251–252
Cognitive therapy, 77, 78, 81, 109
  see also Cognitive-behavioral therapy
Communication skills training, 141, 443–445
Communication training, 90, 323–324, 341–343
Community reinforcement, 211
Compulsions, 67–68, 78, 82
  types of, 68
  see also Cognitive rituals
Conduct disorders:
  behavioral treatment of, 293–299
  comorbidity, 290–291
  definition of, 286
  developmental factors, 287–289
  effects of maternal depression, 300
  prevalence of, 289–290
  subtypes, 292
  taxonomic studies of, 287
Conflict Tactics Scale, 421
Contingency contracting, 448–449
Contingency management, 210, 251, 252, 260, 268–269, 275, 376–377
Coping skills training, 389
Cornelia de Lange Syndrome, 327
  see also Mental retardation
Counterconditioning, 380, 382
Couples therapy, 430–431
Covert rehearsal, 124
Covert sensitization, 183–184, 207
Cylert, see Pemoline

Deep muscle relaxation, 54
  see also Relaxation training
Dependent personality disorder, 129–130
Depression, 75, 81, 82, 99
  see also Unipolar depression, Childhood depression
Desensitization, 192
Developmental marital history, 441–442

Dexedrine, see Dextroamphetamine
Dextroamphetamine, 263-264
Diabetic neuropathy, 373
Diagnostic Interview Schedule for Children, 249
Diaphragmatic breathing training, see Breathing retraining
Differential reinforcement of other behavior, 328-329
Directed masturbation, 164
Disease prevention models:
  primary, 399-404
  secondary, 404-406
  tertiary, 406-409
Disruptive behavior disorders, see Conduct disorders, Attention deficit hyperactivity disorder
Diuretic abuse, 359
Dual diagnosis, 331-332
Dyadic Adjustment Test, 441
Dyspareunia, 159
Dysthymia, 41
  see also Depression

Eating behavior:
  inpatient treatment, 362, 365, 368-369
  modification of, 356
  outpatient treatment, 362-363, 365, 367
Echolalia, 341
Ecobehavioral approaches, 424-431
Electromyographic (EMG) biofeedback, 378, 379, 386, 387, 391
Emotional processing explanation of anxiety reduction, 72, 82
Emotionally focused marital therapy, 450-451
  see also Marital therapy
Energy balance model of obesity, 355-357, 361-362
Energy balance training, 362-363
Erectile dysfunction, 158
Estrogen deficiency, 158
Ethical issues, 176
  see also Legal issues
Exercise, 356, 357, 359, 364, 387
Exposure, 23, 43, 57, 72, 90-95, 207-208
  variations of, 43-47
  see also Interoceptive exposure
Exposure-based treatments, 5, 6, 8-10, 43, 119, 360-361
  see also Flooding, systematic desensitization, modeling, response prevention

Expressed emotion in schizophrenia, 139, 142
Extinction, 77, 339
  theories of, 72, 82
  see also Habituation
Eysenck Personality Inventory, 19

Fading, 8, 187, 320
Family therapy, 77, 79, 212-213, 251, 357, 367, 369
Family violence:
  assessment of, 419-420
  definitions of, 417
  incidence of, 417
  theories of, 418
Faradic aversion, 182
Feminine Identity Scale, 178
Flooding, 6, 7, 71, 73, 74, 75, 77-82
  imaginal, 7, 124
  in vivo, 7
  theory of, 71
  treatment variations, 74
  types of, 73-74
  see also Exposure
Fluoxetine, 81

Gate control model of pain, 382-383
Gender identity disturbances, 178-179
Generalization training, 251, 254
Generalized anxiety disorder (GAD), 16, 41, 52-57
  clinical syndrome, 52
  cognitive-behavioral treatment of, 54-57
  features of presentation, 52

Habituation, 6-7, 72, 76
  see also Extinction, Within session habituation, Between session habituation
Headache, 377, 379, 386, 387, 390
  see also Specific type
Histrionic personality disorder, 125-126
Home Accident Prevention Inventory, 427
Hypoactive sexual desire, 157-158

Imaginal exposure, 74
  see also Exposure, In-vivo exposure, Flooding
Imaginal flooding, 72
  see also Flooding, In-vivo flooding, Exposure
Impulse control training, 123, 127

Interoceptive conditioning, 381–382
Interoceptive exposure, 50, 51, 58
  see also Exposure
Interpersonal skills training, 128
  see also Social skills training
Interpersonal problem-solving skills training, 251–252, 429
In-vivo exposure, 42, 49
  see also Exposure, Imaginal exposure
In-vivo flooding, 72
  see also Flooding, Imaginal flooding, Exposure

Kegel exercises, 164

Laxative abuse, 359, 364, 367
Learned helplessness model of depression, 251–252
Legal issues, 195
  see also Ethical issues
Lesch-Nyhan syndrome, 326
  see also Mental retardation
Leyton Obsessional Inventory, 69
Low back pain, 373

Marital Adjustment Test, 440
Marital dissatisfaction and instability, 251, 439
Marital satisfaction and stability, 438–439
Marital Satisfaction Inventory, 441
Marital therapy, 7, 77, 79, 212–213, 251
  see also Behavioral marital therapy, Cognitive marital therapy
Masked depression, 245–246
Masturbatory conditioning, 188
Masturbatory satiation, 185
Maudsley Obsessional-Compulsive Inventory, 69
Meditation, 55
Mental Retardation:
  adaptive behavior, 318
  communication, 323–326
  definition of, 317–318
  diagnosis, 318
  normalization, 319
  pharmacological treatment of, 327
  self-help skills, 319–322
  treatment of, 323–326
Methylphenidate (MPH), 263
Migraine headaches, 377
Millon Clinical Multiaxial Inventory, 421
Modeling, 6, 73, 320, 342–343

Multimodal assessment, 176
National Vietnam Veterans Readjustment Study, 88
  (NVVRS), see also Post-traumatic stress disorder
Naloxone, 327
Naltrexone, 327
Narcissistic personality disorder, 126–127
Natural Language Paradigm (NLP), 341
Neuroleptics, 136
Nociception, 375, 376, 384
Nociceptive stimuli, 374, 381, 389
Nocturnal penile tumescence testing, 158
Novaco Anger Control Scale, 420

Obesity, 355–358, 369
Obsessions, 67
  nature of, 67
  see also Obsessive compulsive disorder
Obsessions without rituals, 82
Obsessive-compulsive disorder, 41, 69–71
  behavioral treatment of, 81
  issue of relapse, 81
  maintenance of treatment gains, 77
  patient management issues, 77
  use of audiotapes, 77
  use of home visits, 76
Obsessive-compulsive disorder in children:
  behavioral treatment of, 238
  diagnosis, 237
  pharmacologic treatment of, 238–239
Obsessive-compulsive personality disorder, 130
Olfactory aversion therapy, 182–183
Operant conditioning, 365–366
Opiate addiction, see Substance abuse
Opposition defiant disorder, see Conduct disorder
Orgasmic dysfunctions, 159
Orgasmic reconditioning, 188–189
Overanxious disorder:
  behavioral treatment of, 8
  diagnosis, 229
Overcorrection, 328, 339
Overvalued ideation, 68, 75, 78, 79, 81

Pain:
  classical conditioning model of, 380–382
  cognitive-behavioral model of, 384–388
  gate control model, 382–384
  self-efficacy model of, 385–389
Pain-avoidance behavior, 388

Pain behaviors, 375, 376, 377, 382, 384, 389
Pain-tension—pain cycle, 380
  pain cycle, 380
Panic attacks:
  method of induction, 51
  prevalence, 40
  typologies, 40
  see also Agoraphobia, Panic disorder
Panic disorder, 39
  clinical syndrome, 39–41
  cognitive-behavioral treatment of, 49–52
  comorbidity, 42
  in children,
    behavioral treatment of, 236–237
    diagnosis, 236
  see also Agoraphobia, Panic attacks
Papaverine, 158
Paranoid personality disorder, 119–120
Paraphilic disorders, 175–196
  assessment of, 176–180
  see also Sexual deviation
Parent Problem-Solving Instrument, 420
Parent training, 423, 251, 293–295
Passive-aggressive personality disorder, 130–131
Pause technique, 165
Peer monitoring, 320
Pemoline, 263
Penile plethysmography, 178
Penile prostheses, 167
Penile sensory threshold, 158
Peripheral temperature biofeedback, 378
  see also Biofeedback
Personality disorders:
  Cluster A disorders, 119–122
  Cluster B disorders, 122–127
  Cluster C disorders, 127–131
  diagnostic reliability, 118
  prevalence, 118
Pharmacotherapy, 67, 81
Phobias, 380
  in children, 232–233
  behavioral treatment of:
    school phobia, 232–233
    simple phobia, 234–235
    social phobia, 233–235
  diagnosis, 231
  pharmacological treatment of, 235–236
  see also Specific type
Pleasant events, 250, 254

Post-traumatic stress disorder (PTSD),
  behavioral treatment of, 89–95
  diagnosis, 87
  in children:
    behavioral treatment of, 239–240
    diagnosis, 239
  prevalence of, 88–89
Premature ejaculation, 159
Primary obsessional slowness, 68, 78, 82
Problem-solving training, 57, 90, 125, 141–142, 251–252, 254, 270, 389, 445
  see also Interpersonal problem-solving skills training
Prostaglandin E_1, 158
Punishment, 269, 330, 339
Purging, 358–362, 364, 366–368

Raynaud's Disease, 377, 378
Reinforcement Schedules, 346
Relapse prevention, 95, 176, 194, 214–215, 356, 387
Relaxation training, 42, 49, 54, 77, 79, 90, 93, 119, 128, 378–379, 381, 386, 429
Response-cost, 269
Response practice, 191–192
Response prevention, 67, 71–75, 77, 79, 81–82, 90, 207, 360–361
  characteristics which may affect treatment, 75
  implementation of, 75
  outcome research, 73
  theory of, 71
  treatment variations, 74
  see also Flooding
Retarded ejaculation, 159
Ritalin, see Methylphenidate

School phobia, see Phobia, Separation anxiety disorder
Schizophrenia:
  assessment, 140, 146–147
  behavioral treatment of, 137–150
  description of, 135
  pharmacological treatment of, 136
  stress-vulnerability model, 137
Schizoid personality disorder, 120–121
Schizotypal personality disorder, 121–122
Self-control procedures, 319, 379
Self-control training, 252, 254
Self-dialogue in the treatment of post-traumatic stress disorder, 90

Subject Index

Self-efficacy theory, 45, 379–380, 385–392
   for anxiety reduction, 73, 82
Self-help skills, 319–321
Self-injurious behavior (SIB), 338
Self-monitoring, 250, 320, 357
Self-regulation of pain, 377–378
Self-reinforcement, 191, 252
Self-stimulatory behavior, 338
Sensate focus, 162
Separation anxiety disorder, 228
Serotonergic antidepressants, 81
   see also antidepressants
Sex education, 162
Sex Role Inventory, 178
Sexual disorders:
   arousal disorders, 158–159
   aversions, 157
   desire disorders, 157–158
   response, 155
Sexual deviations:
   models of, 175
   multimodal assessment of, 176
Sexual dysfunction:
   behavioral treatment of, 160–166
   description of, 156–160
   long-term outcome, 168–169
   medical treatment of, 166–168
   primary versus secondary, 156
   situational, 156
Shame aversion, 184–185
Shaping, 186–187, 320
Simple phobia, 16, 41
   age of onset, 4
   in children, 234–235
   mode of acquisition, 4
   preparedness, 4
   prevalence, 4
Smoking behavior, 400–401
Social exchange theory, 438
Social perception skills, 146–147, 149–150
Social phobia, 41, 54
   age of onset, 17–18
   assessment of, 14
   autonomic response pattern, 15
   behavioral treatment of, 21–22
   characteristic fears, 15
   cognitive-behavioral treatment of, 20
   concurrent Axis I and II disorders, 16
   definition of, 13
   familial patterns, 18
   in children, 233–235
   influence of temperamental factors, 18
   personality factors, 18
   pharmacological treatment of 15, 32–35
   relationship to shyness, 19
   subtypes, 20
   Social skills training, 22–23, 77, 79, 107–108, 119, 143–149, 191, 213, 251–253, 295–297, 329
   see also Assertiveness training, Interpersonal skills training
Spousal abuse:
   assessment of, 420–422
   definition of, 418–419
   treatment of perpetrators, 429–431
   treatment of victims, 428–429, 430–431
Spouse Observation Checklist, 441
Starvation, 364
Stimulus control procedures, 356
Stimulus generalization, 381
Stimulus over-selectivity, 343–344
Stress inoculation training (SIT), 90
Stress management, 90–91, 213–214, 421
   see also Stress inoculation training
Stressful medical procedures, 404–405
Substance abuse:
   assessment and diagnosis, 205–206
   behavioral models, 203–204
   behavioral intervention, 204–214
   context-dependence, 204
   disease model of, 203
   environmental influences on treatment outcome, 215–218
   problem of technology transfer, 217–218
   recovery without treatment, 216
   reinforcement value, 203
   treatment matching, 216–217
Systematic desensitization, 6, 42, 78, 162, 192
   see also Desensitization

Taste aversion, 331
Temporomandibular pain disorders, 378, 386
Temptation exposure with response prevention, 361
Tension headaches, 377–378
Thought stopping, 79, 90
Time management procedures, 57
Timeout procedures, 331, 339
Token economies, 13, 328
Transvestism, 178
Trigeminal neuralgia, 373
Two factor theory of fear, 71, 380–381

Unipolar depression, 41, 54
  assessment of, 102–103
  definition of, 102
  etiology, 103–105
  symptoms of, 101–102
  treatment of, 106–111
  see also Depression, Childhood depression

Vaginal dilators, 164–165
Vaginismus, 159
Vascular biofeedback, 378, 387

Vasovagal response in blood phobia, 10
Very low calorie diets, 357

Waterloo Smoking Prevention Project, 402–404
Within-session habituation, 72, 75, 80, 82
  see also Between session habituation, Habituation, Extinction

Yale-Brown Obsessive-Compulsive Inventory, 69